WOMEN IN TIBET

JANET GYATSO
HANNA HAVNEVIK
editors

Women in Tibet

HURST & COMPANY, LONDON

First published in the United Kingdom by
C. Hurst & Co. (Publishers) Ltd,
41 Great Russell Street, London WC1B 3PL

Printed in India

A catalogue record for this book is available from the British Library.

ISBNs
1–85065–654–1 *casebound*
1–85065–653–3 *paperback*

ACKNOWLEDGEMENTS

The editors would like to express their appreciation to Michael Dwyer and Christopher Hurst for their initial impetus to produce a study on women in Tibet, and for their ongoing and generous support for this publication. We also thank all the contributors to the book, who were willing to draw on their extensive research and knowledge and to focus on the often elusive question of the history of women in Tibetan society. We are furthermore grateful to Charles Hallisey for perspicacious comments on the Introduction.

The Department of Culture Studies and Oriental Languages at the University of Oslo and the Divinity School at Harvard University are both to be thanked for various subventions that were crucial to the completion of the book. Gratitude is also due to Dominique Townsend and Warner Belanger of Harvard University for their assistance in copy-editing the manuscript, and to Jonathan Derrick for producing the index.

July 2005

JANET GYATSO
HANNA HAVNEVIK

CONTENTS

ILLUSTRATIONS

THE CONTRIBUTORS

ROBERT BARNETT is a lecturer in International and Public Affairs at Columbia University in New York and the coordinator of Columbia's Modern Tibetan Studies Program. He has a doctorate from Cambridge University. His main publications, as author or editor, include *Resistance and Reform in Tibet* (London/Bloomington, Indiana 1994), *Leaders in Tibet: A Directory* (London 1997), *A Poisoned Arrow: The Secret Petition of the 10th Panchen Lama* (London 1998) and *La Città Illegibile* (Milan 1999). He is currently working on leadership, cinema, television and other forms of contemporary culture and political history in Tibet.

HILDEGARD DIEMBERGER, a PhD in Social Anthropology (Vienna 1992), has a research and teaching post in the Mongolia and Inner Asia Studies Unit of Cambridge University, and is a research associate of the Austrian Academy of Sciences. She has published extensively on the anthropology of Tibet and the Himalayan regions and co-authored translations of the *Shel dkar chos 'byung* (Vienna 1996) and of the *dBa' bzhed* (Vienna 2000) with Pasang Wangdu.

JANET GYATSO is Hershey Professor of Buddhist Studies at the Divinity School, Harvard University. She is the author of *Apparitions of the Self: The Secret Autobiographies of a Tibetan Visionary* (Princeton 1998) and editor of *In the Mirror of Memory: Reflections on Mindfulness and Remembrance in Indian and Tibetan Buddhism* (Albany 1992). She is currently working on a study of empirical thinking in Tibetan medical writing, and on ideas of sex and gender in Tibetan medicine and monasticism.

HANNA HAVNEVIK is an associate professor at the Department of Culture Studies and Oriental Languages, University of Oslo. She is the author of *Tibetan Buddhist Nuns: History, Cultural Norms and Social Reality,* Oslo, 1989, and 'The Life of Jetsun Lochen Rinpoche (1865–1951) as Told in Her Autobiography' (PhD, Oslo University, 1999). One of her ongoing research projects, conducted with Dr Agata Bareja-Starzynska of the University of Warsaw, is the revitalization of Buddhism in Mongolia after 1990. In collaboration with Prof. Tseyang Changngopa, Prof. Janet Gyatso and Cand. Sociol. Sissel Thorsdalen she is presently engaged in building a center for research on women and gender studies in Tibetan culture at Tibet University.

ISABELLE HENRION-DOURCY completed her PhD thesis in anthropology at the University of Brussels ('Ache Lhamo. Jeux et Enjeux d'une Tradition Théâtrale Tibétaine'). Her studies focus on '*ache lhamo*', Tibetan opera, both in the People's Republic of China and in exile. She has written articles on non-monastic Tibetan music.

CHARLENE E. MAKLEY is an anthropologist and currently Luce Assistant Professor of Asian Studies in the Anthropology Department at Reed College in Portland, Oregon. She is currently engaged on a book on gender relations and monasticism in the Tibetan town of Labrang and collaborative research on Amdo Tibetan women's work and migration experiences in the midst of the massive 'Develop the West' campaign launched in China in 1999.

DAN MARTIN received a doctorate in Tibetan Studies from Indiana University. His most recent book is *Unearthing Bon Treasures* (Leiden 2001). He is also co-author and volume editor of a comprehensive catalogue of the Bon scriptures (Osaka 2003).

KURTIS R. SCHAEFFER received his PhD from Harvard University in 2000. He is currently Assistant Professor of Buddhist Studies at the University of Alabama. He is the author of *Himalayan Hermitess: The Life of a Tibetan Buddhist Nun* (Oxford 2004), and a book on the history of the Indian Buddhist saint Saraha in Tibet. He is the co-author, with Leonard W. J. van der Kuijp, of *An Early Tibetan Survey of Buddhist Literature: The Bstan pa rgyas pa rgyan gyi nyi 'od of Bcom ldan ral gri*, to be published in the Harvard Oriental Series. He is the editor of E. Gene Smith's *Among Tibetan Texts* (Boston 2000). His current research is on the history of the book and of the five arts and sciences in Tibet.

TASHI TSERING, formerly Research and Cultural Officer of the Library of Tibetan Works and Archives in Dharamsala, India, is Director of Amnye Machen Institute, Tibetan Centre for Advanced Studies, Dharamsala. He has published learned articles on Tibetan religious, political and genealogical history.

HELGA UEBACH studied Indology, Tibetology and Mongolian at the University of Munich (DPhil 1967). She is a research assistant at the Central and East Asian Studies Committee of the Bavarian Academy of Science and Humanities and is involved in preparing a reference dictionary of written Tibetan. She has published a number of articles on state organization and the historical geography of the Tibetan empire (7th to 9th centuries). In 1987 she published a book on the thirteenth-century chronicle *Me tog phreng ba* of Nel-pa Paṇḍita (Munich).

INTRODUCTION

While it would be nice to be able to say that this book will fill out our knowledge of the history and present situation of women in Tibet, that would be to assume that we can specify what it is that we don't know about them. It is more accurate to say that the book is only a step—and not much more than a preliminary step—towards building such knowledge.

Until now the field of Tibetology has produced few studies of Tibetan women. Certain notions have often been assumed, such as that Tibetan women have enjoyed more freedom than their counterparts in other Asian countries; and that models of female divinity in Indo-Tibetan religions have had a liberating effect on women's social status.[1] But such notions are far from substantiated and are likely to be misleading. Meanwhile little is known about the actual sociology and experience of Tibetan women.[2] This collection is meant to help correct that ignorance—both directly, and indirectly by calling attention to the necessity of correction.

The contributors to *Women in Tibet* look at pieces of the extant historical, literary, and ethnographical archive, first and foremost simply to do the archaeological spadework and to collect data. Such spadework goes a long way in advancing our knowledge about the situations of Tibetan women in particular socio-economic milieus, at particular moments in history, and in particular locations. But the data so collected also gives us footholds from which pertinent theoretical questions can begin to be explored. Some reflections of this sort are already ventured in several of the essays here. Still, broader issues become apparent from the vantage point of looking at the volume as a whole. It is worthwhile to consider not only what contributions to such issues the individual chapters in this

[1] Concerning the former, see Taring 1978: 186–7 and Lhamo 1985: ch. 9. On the latter, see n. 3 below.

[2] Among the few exceptions are several historical studies, including the survey of biographies of Machig Labdron in Kollmar-Paulenz 1993; the overview of female monastics in Havnevik 1989, and the general survey provided in Chayet 1993. Tsering 1985 laid out many of the extant materials for a history of Tibetan women, and Tsering 2000 followed up on some of that program. An early effort to present Tibetan biographies of women in English is Allione 1984. Pommaret 1989 is a study of women 'delog' practitioners that combines history and ethnography. A sociological study of Tibetan women in exile is provided by Seele-Nyima 2001. More focussed ethnographical work on women is exemplified by Ortner 1983; Levine 1988; Huber 1994; Gutschow 1997; Buffetrille1998; and van Ede 1999.

book can make, but also what we are doing when we isolate Tibetan women as a topic for study in the first place.

The book is exceptional in that nearly half of the chapters consider Tibetan women currently living in the People's Republic of China (PRC): in the Tibet Autonomous Region (TAR) and in several western provinces of China outside the TAR. Contemporary Tibetan culture in the PRC has been relatively ignored by social scientists and historians, although in recent years a few anthropologists have managed to conduct research there that provides accounts of how women and various other groups are faring in both modern and traditional roles. Some of the chapters also consider Tibetan women in exile in South Asia, although the expatriate community receives relatively little attention. The remaining chapters focus on discrete periods in traditional Tibet and in a few border regions outside the main polity.

There are many more questions that need to be scrutinised before one can have a fuller appreciation of women's situation in Tibetan history and society. Practical difficulties of conducting research in Tibet have resulted in the neglect of many key issues, including the sexual division of labour, the relative economic positions of women and men, the organization of gender relations within the family and the household, relations between women and men in everyday social affairs, and women's access to education and healthcare. Hence, far from providing an overview, this volume offers detailed data and reflection only on circumscribed topics.

Most of the chapters focus on the lives of individual women, constructed through texts or anthropological data. Of the authors who relied mostly on textual material, Helga Uebach and Dan Martin represent a style of research that involves systematic scouring of the relevant literature for whatever pieces of information about women are there to be discovered. In most cases that information is indeed scanty, with the exception of a major figure like the eleventh-twelfth-century century female master Machig Labdron who is the subject of several lengthy biographies. In fact Martin passed over this well-known personage quickly in order to bring to the fore his findings about other women of the period. Schaeffer, on the other hand, provides detailed information about one woman, of the seventeenth-eighteenth century, based on her very important autobiography. Although it is far from established that the particulars of this single woman's life should be deemed representative of other women in her milieu, we have no choice but to glean whatever we can from this example, given the rarity of such autobiographical writing by women throughout Tibetan history.

The other chapters, focusing on contemporary women, are based largely on fieldwork data and oral interviews, with some input from textual sources such as newspaper articles and reports, journals and contemporary histories. Like Martin and Uebach's chapters, those by Charlene Makley, Hildegard Diemberger, Isabelle Henrion-Dourcy, Tashi Tsering and Robert Barnett also survey the lives of representative and sometimes outstanding women, attempting to construct some picture of the contours of their opportunities—and limitations—and how they have negotiated their situation and achieved some fulfilment in their particular milieux and occupations.

In its emphasis on fact-finding and data collection, this volume endeavours to respond to what feminist historians like Joan Scott and others have called for, namely a review of the available sources for more information in order to correct the under-representation of women—in both the primary sources and modern academic study (Scott 1988: 28–50). But apart from this basic orientation—i.e. to focus exclusively on, for example, nuns or female singers as distinct from monks or male singers—an overt feminist agenda rarely takes centre stage in this volume. This reticence is no doubt a holdover from the longstanding tendency in Tibetan Studies to presume that the deployment of feminist issues constitutes an obfuscating projection of modern, 'Western' concerns on the object of study. In other words, if Tibetan women historically had no idea about feminism–by which we mean here the broad movement that recognizes injustices to women due to androcentric or misogynist bias, is critical of those injustices, and would foster modes of action and experience that have hitherto been discouraged by such biases–then to bring such concerns to bear on a study of Tibetan women says more about the researcher than about Tibetan women themselves. But there are others who would maintain that contemporary theories and methods do indeed facilitate the discovery of valid and useful information about another time and place that would not be readily perceptible if the researcher analysed her subject matter exclusively in an emic perspective. If it is granted that it would be a good thing to have more information about the history of Tibetan women than most Tibetan sources provide overtly, one can say that a feminist project to look for and single out that information produces accurate knowledge about Tibet which would not be available if the researcher operated only according to traditional Tibetan ideas.

In fact, that same feminist focus sometimes leads one to discover indications of attitudes that we can at least dub 'protofeminist' in traditional Tibet. One example would be an early twentieth-century collection of religious biographies exclusively of women–a rarity in Tibetan literature –which furnishes evidence of the desire of its editor (a woman) to correct the fact that women had been overlooked in traditional historiography (bDe-chen 1985, see Rossi forthcoming and Gyatso forthcoming). Also the student of women of Tibet today, as much as in any part of the world, must assume the real possibility of direct exposure to feminist ideas throughout Tibetan society, across class, level of education, and the rural-urban divide—ideas which certainly at this point cannot be characterized as fundamentally Western at all.

In any event, quite apart from any debates about the appropriateness of applying a feminist perspective to Tibetan Studies, researchers, despite their best intentions, do bring to their work theoretical concerns from their own world. Thus a feminist stance, even if not explicit, can be discerned in more than a few of the contributions here. Merely to agree to single out 'woman' as a category of research already reflects a feminist agenda, if only for its attempt to do for Tibetan women what has been done for women of many other societies in different periods of history: we notice that we have little information about half the population of Tibet, so we set out to correct that imbalance.

Yet interest in the topic of Tibetan women is not limited to the desire to fill out history. Or, more simply, it is not merely to join a trend. The way we construe the category of Tibetan women entails assumptions that are of interest in their own right, not to mention their bearing on other issues in Tibetan history, culture and literature, and the assumptions we bring to their study. What do we assume, as a start, to be the definition of 'woman' in the Tibetan context? Does the researcher impose her own idea of what a woman is, or does she realize that the category might be construed differently in different times and places, and attempt to discern its semantic range for the culture, period, or even the individual under discussion? Certainly if one attempts to do the latter one will discover a complex set of factors that adds to the category's connotations. Even a bare physical or anatomical definition of woman as a sex in Tibetan history, as contained in traditional medical descriptions, is pervaded by gender and other loaded conceptions (Gyatso 1999; 2003). Further, the knotty questions of what Tibetan women themselves have to do—or not—with such gender stereotypes permeates any study of Tibet. How do we get at the historical situation of individuals when the data at hand is so heavily loaded with, and determined by, cultural ideals and distortions? A study of actual women—in tandem with this perennially unstable, provocative, and always instructive category of 'woman'—should help us to begin to addressing methodologically such a question.

It is also productive to ask whether gender must be the only cultural ideal that mediates our analyses of Tibetan women. In other words, what other (still culturally determined) dimensions are there of both the conditions that have constricted women as a group, and the avenues by which they have evaded such constraints? Surely the question of what women experience in Tibet, beyond what pertains to 'womanness', would help us to get an even fuller picture of what kinds of lives historical female humans have led there.

Luce Irigiray suggests that the problems that arise from the study of sex and gender constitute 'the burning issue', if not the 'salvation', of our age (Irigaray 1995: 165). Without doubt these problems are various and multifaceted. One facet in particular that seems to preoccupy several of the contributors to this volume is that of feminine difference. This would indeed be a question about gender: can we identify a common feature—in female monastics, say, or female oracles, or *yoginīs*—that is attributable to the fact of being a female and which would somehow differentiate female monastics generically from male ones, and so on? Thus Diemberger wonders whether being a woman is somehow more conducive to serving as an oracle than being a man. Barnett suggests that women political protesters bring a 'female' style to bear in their mode of expressing their feelings. These speculations are about gender because they toy with stereotyping and essentialization; yet they remain intriguing and hard to resist. Can women be said, in any coherent or convincing sense, to do things differently from men? Do they have special talents or particular weaknesses that can be somehow attributed to the conditions surrounding being a woman?

This tricky set of questions will be revisited below. Note for now a methodological point: it is not necessarily true that generalizations about 'women' are essentializing. If they are descriptive rather than normative, if they describe tendencies on the part of a certain group to respond to particular conditions that indeed persist *in general* precisely because of gender stereotypes that are current in the community in question, they remain historically specific. The tendencies are seen as the products of particular socio-economic conditions rather than being innate. One can of course always ask if the generalizations are correct, or how pervasive is their relevance, but there is still a crucial distinction to be drawn between such an idea and those studies of women and gender in Tibet in recent years that have been more interested in exploring the truth of gender stereotypes *ahistorically*. The most salient example of such a propensity would be to accept Tibetan normative pronouncements as universally applicable. Such ahistoricism is often in the service (and naturally so) of an agenda to stretch Tibetan gender norms so that they might enhance the lives of modern non-Tibetan women; an example would be the claim that *all* women, everywhere, are ultimately *ḍākinīs*.[3] Such an agenda has

[3] Examples are Shaw 1994; Willis 1989b; and Simmer-Brown, 2001. Klein 1995 alternates between describing related Tibetan ideas about female principles, and recommending ways in which non-Tibetans could appropriate them. Allione 1984 also argues that western

obvious feminist roots of its own, and is not necessarily invalid or deleterious; it is just that it is not the agenda of the current volume.

Yet another kind of ahistoricism—more limited, but indeed deleterious for its inaccuracies—would be to presume uncritically that mainstream gender ideals in fact govern Tibetan women's lives, that the deified figure of the *ḍākinī*, for example, actually serves as a model of female personality formation (Simmer-Brown 2001).[4] This is not to argue that such ideals have had no purchase at all on the construction of women's identities; witness, for example, the use of the term *ḍākinī*, in Tibetan translation, in certain outstanding women's titles (Sera Khandro and Drigung Khandro are two well-known examples from the twentieth century). But this hardly demonstrates that women have been 'empowered' to think of themselves as *ḍākinīs* on a regular basis. (Nor does it necessarily follow that the *ḍākinī* role model, to the degree that it has been actually operative, has been good for Tibetan women. One can imagine a feminist critique of a gender norm that construes women as unpredictable and hard to understand.)[5] Finally, an even more limited ahistoricism, again misleading and inaccurate, is the presumption that a female gender ideal like the *ḍākinī* has remained stable over time. That would be to fail to ask how such ideals developed and changed under varying circumstances in Tibetan history.[6]

The concern of the authors of this volume is rather to be as historically and ethnographically specific as possible, to show how, under what conditions, and in what particular ways gender ideals and stereotypes are—and are not—deployed both by individual women and by the societies around them. It is precisely around the question of the extent and limits of gender categories that another issue with roots in contemporary feminism has worried several of the authors in this volume, especially those working with written sources. This is the problem of finding 'genuine' women's voices, or female perspectives, in the accounts of women's lives. Virtually all the information that we have from traditional textual sources about Tibetan women is written by men, operating in the ambit of androcentric institutions and textual traditions.

---

women can use Tibetan Buddhist feminine norms to further western feminist goals. Similar assumptions are evident in Gross 1987.

4 Herrmann-Pfandt 2001 takes largely a Jungian perspective, but widely assumes that Tibetan women were directly affected by the *ḍākinī* archetype, and that this influence was positive.

5 See Judith Butler's critique of the notion of the 'semiotic' in Julia Kristeva's view (Butler 1990: 79–93).

6 Most of the material mentioned in notes 3 and 4 disregards history in this way. The editors of this volume could be found to be guilty of this fault as well (Gyatso 1998a; Havnevik 1999).

There are various reasons why the search for the genuine or pure is going to be a dubious enterprise. First, just because a work is written by a woman does not mean that she has not assimilated androcentric or even misogynistic biases, especially given the preponderance of men as the model authors in all genres of Tibetan literature. But it is far more pertinent to ask: what is a woman's perspective anyway? Would not its recognition involve yet another set of gender essentializations? Perhaps yes, at least for some feministically-inclined Tibetologists, but even a reliable representation of the experiences of women's predicaments in Tibetan society cannot be tied to the sex of who wrote it. We can find a woman author like Orgyen Chokyi repeating misogynisms well known in Tibetan literature (Schaeffer). And on the other hand, we can note that the authors of quite sympathetic accounts of archetypal female dilemmas—forced marriage; pressures to marry and have children; harassment and rape of single women—are often Tibetan men.[7]

To attempt to go beyond that, to identify something like voice or style that tends to be typical of Tibetan women writers as distinct from male ones, would involve subtle literary analysis. And it is not determined in advance whether there are actual differences to be discerned in the first place. One could think of the characteristically elusive, suggestive, and sometimes even chaotic utterances of the (unsurprisingly) nameless female prophets in the fourteenth-century master Longchen Rapchampa's autobiographical writings, but those utterances are in fact written by a man (Germano and Gyatso 2000). Elusiveness and suggestiveness had already served as classic features of the speech of the woman muse for several centuries before Longchenpa. It is a style that fits with the figure of the *ḍākinī*,[8] but this again concerns gender ideals, not the actual speech or writing of actual women. For the latter, studies and translations of the autobiographies of a few religious Tibetan women are beginning to come out, such as the autobiographies of the eminent nineteenth–twentieth-century teacher Jetsun Lochen from central Tibet (Havnevik 1999) and of Orgyen Chokyi discussed in this volume by Schaeffer.[9] Close consideration of these and other works will provide us with a more substantial

[7] Two notable examples are the hagiographies of Yeshe Tsogyal (Gyatso forthcoming) and Machig Labdron (Kollmar-Paulenz 1993). Gyatso 1998a has pointed to an exceptional male imagination of the concerns of women in the writing of Jigme Lingpa.

[8] It might also remind us of the deliberate refusal of 'patriarchal' grammar sometimes explored by some western feminists (and, critiqued by others); the classic statement of this project is Cixous 1981. But compare Butler's position as in note 5 above.

[9] Schaeffer 2004 provides a translation of the entire text; Holly Gayley is preparing a study of the autobiography of the twentieth century teacher Tare Lhamo; and Sera Khandro's autobiography is currently being studied by Sarah Jacoby.

basis for determining if there is anything that can be singled out as distinctive in traditional Tibetan women's writings. A similar sort of consideration of modern Tibetan women's writing would yield interesting results as well, but few such women writers are active at present, either on the literary scene in the PRC or in exile. Accompanying that shortage is the lack of consideration of issues of gender or the sex of writers in scholarly analyses of modern Tibetan literature.[10]

In short, any generalizations that we wish to proffer will have to be based on historical data, and the fact of the matter is that we have little such data to work with. Besides the works just mentioned there are probably very few other women's autobiographies in the entire history of traditional Tibetan literature. Indeed women are rarely discussed in historical writing at all, except for the briefest mention of someone's mother, or consort, who not infrequently is nameless or referred to only elliptically. Martin is especially clear here about the imbalances in coverage between male and female teachers in the medieval period, as Uebach is keenly aware of the desultory nature of the data that she must piece together to get even a bare sense of the power wielded by aristocratic women during the dynastic period.

It is hoped that more scholarly attention will be directed at preserving and gathering information on contemporary Tibetan women. This scholarship can be expected from both foreign and Tibetan scholars, especially given the generally Marxist and occasionally feminist orientation in China.[11] Such winds have been felt in the Tibetan Autonomous Region as well, where a recent encouraging development is the establishment at Tibet University in Lhasa of the Institute of Women and Gender Studies with the support of the TAR's Women's Federation, under the direction of Professor Tseyang Changnogpa and in cooperation with the University of Oslo. But again, the historical situation will remain opaque without more of the kind of narrowly-defined study that has been attempted in this volume.

Our confidence about some of the baseline conditions common to Tibetan women that emerge from this volume is nonetheless sturdy, for

[10] We are grateful to Lauran Hartley for the foregoing assessment; her own doctoral thesis considers the relative dearth of women writers in modern Tibet: Hartley 2003. One study of a piece by a woman writer is Lhag pa phun tshogs 1990, but the essay does not consider broader questions relating to gender. Virtanen 2000 studies stories written by men that focus on women's situations. Hartley 1999 considers a story by a female Tibetan writer and her concern to portray women's issues.

[11] The journal *g.Yu mtsho*, published by the Amnye Machen Insititute in Dharmasala, India, is devoted to Tibetan women past and present, and promises to encourage attention to women by Tibetan scholars in exile. An informative and interesting publication, albeit largely pictoral, is Daixian 1995. More self-congratulatory is Liu 1994.

no other reason than the consistency of the findings. Across the spectrum of timeframes, geographical areas, and social classes, the authors discover women who achieve prominence in Tibetan society and make substantial contributions, both in activities normally dominated by men and in areas that perhaps are especially encouraging to women. This is testimony to the resourcefulness of Tibetan women, especially given the other reliable generalization that we can make, namely, the enduring androcentrism and misogynistic gender tropes. Most common is the damning moniker of 'low birth' *(skye-dman),* used since at least the eleventh century and in the last several hundred years the standard word in both writing and speech for 'woman', often invoked by both men and women as a way of letting etymology prove the fact of a matter (see Changopa forthcoming). The reference is to Buddhist ideology, the notion found in many Buddhist works that it is a sorrowful fate, attributable to bad karma, to take birth as a woman. This robust conception in Tibetan society is not ameliorated by the occasional (if equally Buddhist) trumping of such a pejorative association with the default assertion that all constructions, including the 'low birth woman', are 'empty' (see Martin's essay)—at least in terms of social reality. It is a truism, presumed at all levels of Tibetan society, that to be a woman is to have bad karma, low status, and poor abilities.[12]

There are other sources for Tibetan androcentrism and misogyny beyond Buddhism (that is, if we can fully separate such traditions as Tibetan medicine, with its Ayurvedic roots, from Buddhism in the first place.). Certainly the idea that women are cursed by an extra thirty-two illnesses that men do not have, evident as early as the writings of the eleventh-century disciples of Phadampa (Martin), is fundamentally a medical notion, since the details of these illnesses come from the *rGyud bzhi* and other Tibetan medical texts.[13] But just as Tibetan medicine invokes, when convenient, Buddhist misogynistic tropes, Tibetan Buddhists draw in turn on medical theories concerning the inferiority of the female body. We find paradigmatic examples already in the early biographical materials studied here by Martin, such as Kunga's pronouncement that women are generically weak and his assertion that 'Women's bodies are vessels of pain, and women's minds are vessels of suffering.'

[12] The pervasive misogyny and androcentrism of many Buddhist texts was first explored in modern scholarship by Paul 1989. For a good general overview, see also Sponberg 1992.

[13] Although we can speculate—so far without evidence—that the number 32 might be influenced by Buddhism, serving as a negative counterpart to the obviously positive 32 marks of a buddha, marks that by definition women cannot have. Throughout Buddhist literature—with the exception of a few, late tantric sources—women cannot become buddhas. This matter has been discussed by several modern feminist scholars, beginning with Paul 1989.

Whatever their source, such gender stereotypes pervade Tibetan social conceptions and operate actively to restrict women's liberty and opportunities. This point is brought home most forcefully in this volume by Schaeffer's study, where the Buddhist male master's low esteem of women is painfully manifest. He refuses Orgyen Chokyi permission to go into retreat and again to write her autobiography, in both instances on the grounds of her inferiority as a woman. But although she struggles against these injustices, Orgyen Chokyi herself accepts the basic premise that the fate of being a woman is especially poignant, and she characterizes her life as a 'mountain of suffering', a predicament she ascribes to the particular difficulty inherent in living as a woman. A very similar set of negative conceptions, discrimination and abuse was still actively in operation in the twentieth century, as the autobiography of the nun Jetsun Lochen (Havnevik 1999) displayed in detail. Apparently the same unfortunate syndrome remains at work today, certainly in the ethnography Makley presents in this volume, where we learn that the population around the monastery town of Labrang continues to see women as having inferior intelligence, excessive attachment and uncontainable desire. But even more insidious than these familiar Buddhistic misogynisms is the presumption that follows: that nuns are a lesser store of merit and thus less efficacious in performing ritual services for the laity. In this way gender stereotypes have tangible effects, severely undermining the ability of female monastic institutions to sustain themselves. Mackley holds out some hope that the negative profile of the female cleric may change, due to recent virtuosity in fasting rituals by nuns in Labrang. We can add that the well-known heroic resistance to the Chinese authorities on the part of nuns in central Tibet may possibly improve the status of nuns in general in the Tibetan world. Yet the sad but popular equation that Makley finds between women and stray dogs may be an association that is stubbornly hard to shake.

Given these demoralizing gender caricatures, the evident success that we see in this volume of at least some women, in some kinds of endeavours and in some moments and places shows either that Tibetan gender stereotypes are not hard-and-fast, or that they are not singular or powerful enough to predominate in all cases and to make all women subordinate to all men. Probably both are true. To demonstrate the first point will require close analysis of the gender norms themselves. Signs of some flexibility are evident (Gyatso 2003), but we will leave the details of such an argument aside for now, since gender *per se* is not the focus of this volume. More to the point in the present context is the second possibility, namely that we can identify other historical forces and patterns beyond those of gender which have determined the conditions of women as a group.

We would also argue that women have had recourse to such patterns, thereby evading the limiting or negative stereotypes. One can discern several ways in which this has happened from the studies in this volume.

These alternative patterns demonstrate that gender norms do not entirely determine the life of women. Clearly one such alternate—and well-travelled—path that is not particularly a function of gender is the route to power and influence taken by persons not in powerful positions themselves but who can capitalize on their association with those who are. An instance where such use of associations has worked for Tibetan women is seen in Uebach's study of noble women of the imperial period. Although the principal actors were the patriarchs of the Yarlung dynasty, there is evidence of the overt participation of their female relatives in the political struggles of the time. Especially striking are the titles of women in this period: '*trichen*,' which suggests that the person so named is a throne holder; '*mangmoje*', which Uebach translates 'sovereign lady of many'; and even '*tsenmo*,' the female form of '*tsenpo*', the principle title for the Yarlung emperors. These female relatives not only served as major patrons for the erection of Buddhist monuments and icons, but also forged political alliances and exerted their political will on behalf of their sons. Some even gained power of their own, as in the case of Empress Trimalo, who was *de facto* regent of the empire for four years.

Another setting in which association with the powerful has afforded influence for women has been that of the tantric couple. Martin's discussion here of an early case, that of Machig Ongjo, allows us to imagine the particulars of how this pattern would work in the tantric context. Consorts of male masters have continued to become teachers in their own right down to the present—an outstanding instance would be Khandro Tsering Chodron, consort of the previous Dzongsar Khyentse, still living in Bhutan at the time of this writing; another would be Tare Lhamo, the famed consort of the lama Jigme Phuntsok, who died recently in Golok.[14] But the point to be noted is that association is equally a route to eminence for persons of low status other than women. One obvious example would be the way that prominent servants have acquired influential positions in Tibetan politics.[15] But even if we limit our attention to conjugal alliance, we find that male commoners have frequently married into aristocratic families and thereby taken on the privilege of their wives (D.D. Tsarong is a well-known case in point from the twentieth century [Tsarong 2000]). In fact the hagiography of the paradigmatic Tibetan female consort Yeshe

14 Jigme Phuntsok is not the same as Khanpo Jigme Phuntsok of Serthar.

15 One of the many examples that could be cited is the case of Kumbela, personal attendant of the Thirteenth Dalai Lama (Goldstein 1989: ch.5).

Tsogyal provides a striking model of a male slave—her own consort Acarya Sale—who becomes a force in his own right only after he is taken up and trained by his female master. Such examples show that when women rely on their connections or associations in order to gain position, they are enacting cultural patterns that do not map onto gender per se, and thus cannot be said to be typical of women *per se*.

Beyond association, we can also recognize in Martin's essay another way in which women have been able to achieve power and influence, but which is not necessarily gendered or typical of women in particular. This has to do with appropriateness of setting: people who lack social status have sometimes thrived in special contexts that are not structured around such status. So we can speculate that the relatively non-standardized and open environment of yogic communities such as that surrounding Phadampa allowed more leeway than hierarchical monastic settings for recognizing the outstanding female teachers and prophets that Martin describes. Here again the same dynamic is operative for other kinds of low status persons as well. For example, men who stood outside the power orbit of the state-sponsored monastic centres due to regional or filial connections to other schools often forged a yogic community as a base for creating a different kind of religious standing. This route was frequently taken by Nyingmapa visionaries.

Still, we might be tempted to make a special point about women, arguing that a defining feature of monastic institutions, throughout Buddhist history, has been to serve as a site for rationalizing women's subordination, that being the direct result of the overt androcentrism, if not misogyny, of monastic celibate discipline. Hence one wonders if religious communities not regimented by monastic law, especially those advocating the practice of tantric consort yoga, are prone to make room for the flourishing of female talent in particular. And yet we also need to note that this potentially propitious liberality does not always result in guaranteeing an obliteration of misogyny. Even with its much-touted positive images of the divine nature of women, the world of tantra has by no means actually accorded special honour to human women generically. Indeed there are many examples in Tibetan Buddhist history of disregard if not disparagement of the consorts of high lamas.[16] Schaeffer's work in this volume provides one striking illustration of a loose yogic community where a rising star was discouraged and reviled just for being a woman.

[16] Here is an early example in writing of a striking use of an honorific for the author's son and a non-honorific for his consort for the same word ('body') in a single sentence (and note that the consort nonetheless is an emanation of Yeshe Tsogyal): '…*mTsho rgyal gyi sprul pa/ jo 'bum ma'i lus las sku bltams.*' Nyang-ral 1979/80, vol. 2: 354.

Thus, if under some conditions non-monastic or non-institutionalized communities have produced female leaders like those described by Martin, negative gender conceptions from Buddhist textual culture were often mobilized anyway to subordinate women in such communities.

The question remains intriguing: were there vocational and social settings in which the relative absence of androcentric social status made for a special fostering of women? One vocation considered in this volume in which some women have thrived, at least in the twentieth century, is traditional Tibetan medicine. Tashi Tsering's valuable survey of recent medical practitioners indicates that there are few records to enable study of the field in the premodern period, but he is able to cite at least some historical evidence of the existence of female doctors in Tibet in the past as well. However, Tibetan medicine is certainly not free of androcentric biases of its own, and as already noted, it preserves Buddhistic misogyny in its traditional literature. But it may be that in practice a relative freedom from the hierarchies that reigned in the best organized and regulated domains of Tibetan society, namely monastic institutions and government agencies, enabled some of the healing traditions to develop more flexible and unconventional ways of passing down knowledge and recognizing successors. Perhaps that left room for the training of female experts. An important factor that may also be in play is the strong interest in the empirical—as opposed to the ideal—in healing traditions, and a corresponding pragmatic urgency for virtuosity. In other words, perhaps medicine, due to the relatively swift verifiability of its efficacy (as compared to, say, the soteriological claims of Buddhism or Bon), has fostered more of a non-gendered meritocracy than did other corners of Tibetan learning and science—at least in the modern period. Here again, then, opportunities have issued from a particularly appropriate setting for women to be trained and for individual talent to be acknowledged.

There are other cases too of a greater visibility of female careers in more liberal Tibetan contexts. One good example is to be found in Henrion-Dourcy's chapter on the performing arts. Not only may this field be said to be propitious for women because of its relative freedom from institutional stricture, but there are other reasons for its appropriateness. At least in recent Tibetan history, the performing arts, whether practiced by males or females, have been looked upon generically with some disdain, for they are regarded as being secular and frivolous if not profane. But this works to the advantage of women. The generic association of dramatic artists with beggars actively facilitates and encourages the recruitment of unattached and low-status persons (both men and women) into dramatic troupes, from which opportunities for creativity and virtuosity then follow. Thus it may be no accident that one of the primary arenas for excellence of female performance is that of the low-class beer vendors and social 'greeting maids'. Similarly, the traditional wandering bards of Tibet, who also have low social status, have frequently been women. The attention that results in these contexts does not then ameliorate those artists of the low position; quite the contrary, even the virtuosic female *nangma* stars are despised, no doubt because they are related, in popular perception, to various kinds of prostitutes who also excel at singing and dancing. The point rather is pragmatic: women have found here arenas for artistic expression and recognition while setting aside or circumventing issues about status and privilege.

We might similarly connect the eminence of certain female oracles to the marginal and ambiguous status of oracles and soothsayers more generally in Tibetan religion. (Note, by the way, that the higher-level state oracles tended to be males.[17] The same is true of the performing arts: while the field generically has low status, there have been a few prestigious and state-sponsored forums for performance, such as the festival of the Shoton, where women were barred from participating.) Female village oracles have been widespread in Tibetan cultural areas, but little studied by modern scholars in the TAR before the work of Diemberger, as represented in this volume. This is a case where women have had real power, sometimes exceeding that of their male counterparts. In the areas studied by Diemberger, serious conflict in the community over the building of temples or the punishment of criminals causes advice to be sought from the deities through the mediation of the oracle. This role is usually filled by a woman, whose pronouncements trump the opinions of the lamas.

In the foregoing we have explored social patterns that worked for the betterment of women but which are not in themselves tied to gender. It still remains to be asked whether gender itself has also had some agency in this betterment. Given that women of influence or virtuosity in Tibet inevitably experience gender-based denigration, this perennial methodological (or better, historical) question recurs: can we assume that Tibetan women have recognized their situation as limiting or oppressive precisely because they are women? Another way of putting this would be to ask to how much the feminism of the contributors to this volume can be said to be shared—in some approximate form—by the women described. To what extent have those women mustered their own agency to establish gender parity, with the idea that theirs was a particular problem for women? And in particular, to what extent have they drawn on what they regard as specifically women's kinds of power or abilities? Barnett,

[17] For studies of a high Tibetan female oracle see Changngopa 2002 and Havnevik 2002.

for example, is surely right to suggest that there are many ways—most undocumented—in which Tibetan women have acted strategically for political gain, but we are far from certain that they have felt motivated to do simply because they are women.

We have already mentioned that one can safely assume some awareness of (and, as must naturally follow, some interest in) the basic aspirations of feminism on the part of modern Tibetan women, both in China and without. The situation is of course quite different in the premodern period but it was also pointed out above that some hints of what might be considered a kind of protofeminist awareness in traditional Tibetan writing can be identified.[18] The question remains: how often did the sorts of women detailed in this volume have recourse to such sentiments?

We should not be surprised to see feministic inklings among *yoginīs* and nuns in particular. There is a long history of the Buddhist monastic order (that is, despite its enduring androcentrism) and other renunciate communities serving as an alternative life-space for women, where they could escape their unhappy circumstances in society. The classic Pali collection *Therīgāthā* clearly connected the monastic life to deliverance from specifically female predicaments such as oppressive husbands and misogynistic disparagement. One finds similar aspirations among Tibetan nuns. Orgyen Chokyi suggests some of this sentiment in celebrating the independence she has achieved by taking up the life of the renunciate:

> Before, when I was tending the kitchen fire, I had to get out of bed by lamp before dawn. Now I do not have to get up at dawn if I do not want to. If I want to take soup, I am free to do so when I am hungry... I can wear clothes on the path, and I can go naked when I am in my cell practicing ... self-empowered, I have escaped people. I have attained autonomy. (Schaeffer, this volume)

As in other parts of the Buddhist world, terms for female renunciates in Tibet are employed loosely to refer to various lifestyles and levels of ordination, although there are few references to the fully ordained *bhikṣuṇī* (Tib. *dge-slong-ma*). Scholars have assumed that there were no bhikṣuṇīs in Tibet, as also came to be the case in many other Asian Buddhist countries. Therefore it is worth observing the evidence produced by Martin here of *bhikṣuṇī* ordination at various historical moments, suggesting that the lineage was not altogether absent in Tibet after all.[19] In any event, Makley's insights on gender and Tibetan nuns are not dependent on

[18] Some classic moments of feminist writing in Tibetan literature are summarized in Gyatso 1998a: ch. 6.

[19] Other evidence provided in Diemberger's contribution to this volume. See also *Mi nyag* 1987: 71–2, 96. We thank Tashi Tsering for this reference.

which level of ordination a woman takes. Rather, she finds that the mere fact of leaving householder status and shaving one's head is already enough to 'perform' most of the gender-bending that the taking of monastic vows accomplishes in public perception—a bending that has been used deliberately by individual women to escape their conventional gendered roles as wives and mothers.

Given such an example of Tibetan women's conscious manipulation of cultural norms, it is discouraging to learn how for the nuns in Labrang female gender identity nonetheless remains relatively immutable. This turns out to be so despite the 'monastic androgyny' that is otherwise associated with the renunciation of family life and traditional gender markers like hair. Makley found that nuns tend to be 'resexed' in lay conception, i.e. reassigned with the female attributes associated with the very misogynistic stereotypes that monastic status ought to have neutralized. This reassignment emerges in the sharp distinctions drawn in public gossip between monks and nuns. The latter are often characterized as suffering from the 'negative corporeality of females' and attendant uncontrollable passions—or, in other words, the standard Buddhistic misogynisms.[20] We can guess that a similar resexing attached to the image of the yoginīs in Martin's and Schaeffer's chapters, where for example Orgyen Chokyi refers to her own body as a 'broken vessel,' destined generically to suffering simply by virtue of being female. Such recalcitrance of negative gender tropes even in women's writing forces one to question the ability of women to achieve that third androgynous gender of the renunciate. That 'third gender' seems to Mackley to retain a masculinist stamp rather than being truly neutral, precisely because of its discouragement of women. We are once again pursuing a question about gender conception, but nonetheless becoming a nun in Labrang means to resist—effectively and in actuality—the 'normal' vocations with which women are linked.

So the upshot is mixed. When Makley argues that oppositionality is read quite literally in the very appearance of a nun's body, she implies that the laity perceive a non-female-specific cultural ideal in the nun. Certainly this ideal is achieved more fully by men, but it is available to women in part, even if it is then taken away from them by gossip. Monastic oppositionality itself, then, would again be a cultural stamp that is not essentially about gender, like some of the other patterns explored above. Yet that same stamp can also be mobilized for what surely are the very feministic sentiments of Orgyen Chokyi, who from the heights of her

[20] Such gossip and misogynisms are also found among Tibetans in exile communities in northern India (Havnevik 1989: 144–50).

renunciate position can ironically recount the disappointment of her parents at her own birth after learning she was not a boy (Schaeffer, this volume).[21] We can hardly deny Orgyen Chokyi the label of feminist when she angrily asks if her parents would have preferred a lazy, trouble-making boy to a religiously virtuous daughter as herself. Also impressive is the way she thinks about being female as something that teaches one about samsaric suffering. She resolves that having gained this female-based knowledge she will not waste it when she attains a male body in the future, criticizing in the same breath the many men who squander this precious opportunity.

Most of the other studies in this volume reveal little explicit attention on the part of their heroines to the female dimensions of their aspirations or their predicaments. But it still may be the case that Tibetan women sometimes do draw on specifically female resources—perhaps unself-consciously—to achieve what they want. It is possible for example that aristocratic women's status and political agency during the Yarlung dynasty,where the maternal uncles (*zhang*) of the imperial consort were given special rank, and ladies could have property of their own,was bolstered by the importance of maternal clans and traces of matriliny still resonant during the apogee of the dynasty—an idea little explored since the work of Erik Haarh (1969).[22]

One kind of special efficacy that we can sometimes attribute to women would be based in the stereotypic virtues that are considered innately female. An example in the present volume would be the gentleness—which has been a standard trait expected of women in Tibetan culture as in the modern West—that Barnett credits with creating a feminized, less violent kind of political protest by Tibetan nuns as compared to monks. But the chapters here also provide evidence of more historically-contingent powers of women. To connect women's influence to the ancient matrilineal powers surviving in the imperial period would be a case in point. Another concerns the long-held association, in certain Tibetan areas, of women with geographical features. Diemberger's work provides examples of women whose maternal forebearers are considered the 'owners' of certain holy lakes, thereby constituting a lineal relation to the perceived powers of that lake, especially the oracular knowledge of the female deities associated with it. It is these deities who in turn possess

21 Jetsun Lochen recalls how her father, too, was in despair when he discovered that the child born to him by his mistress was a girl. After scolding and beating up his woman he wanted to throw their infant daughter out of their tent. See Havnevik 1999, vol. 2: 152–3.

22 It is important to keep in mind, however, that in matrilineal societies, where descent passes from a woman's brother to her son, the major political power of the descent group is almost always in the hands of men (see, e.g., Keesing 1976: 253–9).

human female oracles and instill into them charisma, the ability to prophesy, and influence in communal negotiations.

Actually the gentleness just referred to turns out to be more forceful—and more complex—than would at first appear. We see this in the way that those same 'gentle nuns' have come to represent Tibetan cultural identity. It is easily evident to the visitor to Tibet today that there are a large number of nuns, of all ages, in both the urban centres and in nunnery retreats. While we lack the data to compare this phenomenon with the state of affairs in old Tibet, Makley's research alone shows a 100 per cent increase in the number of nuns in Labrang since 1949 (this volume). These are no doubt many reasons for such a resurgence; no doubt one factor is the age-old recourse that economically precarious families have taken sending one or more children to the monastery, which often guaranteed a minimal living situation and education. But adopting the monastic way of life in Tibet today also strongly signals resistance to PRC rule and the accompanying social shift towards modernity, and this in turn may have something to do with gender: there is something about being female that performs this symbolic message especially well. In the current volume, two chapters address the connections between the gender of female monastics and a show of Tibetanness.[23] However, whereas in Makley's research becoming a nun signals a rejection of traditional Tibetan cultural markers, the nuns that Barnett has studied have come to signify Tibetanness in a positive fashion. Above and beyond factors of regional difference, the contradiction can be resolved by noting that different kinds of national identity are operative in the two cases. In Makley's work it is traditional women's roles that are at stake, which have become metonymical of Tibetan social order as a whole; in Barnett's it is Tibetan identity as defined *vis-à-vis* the Chinese state. It is the latter case that is pertinent to our argument here: while one would expect male gender tropes to provide the quintessential roles for performing opposition, it turns out that 'femaleness'—indeed gentleness in particular—is even more suited to such a performance, especially in the case of the passive resistance that has become emblematic of clerical dissent to Chinese rule in Tibet. Again, the basic situation is gender-blind: any minority in China made weak by Han hegemony might use similar symbolic displays. But since the feminine stands for powerlessness generically, Tibetan womanhood becomes overdetermined as a quintessential icon of an oppressed minority. All the more powerful, then, is the 'passive resistance' of such a weak one: this is a power that results from a strategic reversal.

[23] The increase of nuns in central Tibet in the 1980s and resistance to PRC rule has also been pointed out by Havnevik 1994 and Havnevik 1995.

There is a whole range of ways in which Tibetan women capitalize upon such reversals, and the power that sometimes accrues, ironically, to people of low status.[24] In Tibet as elsewhere, this pattern is once again not limited to women. Tibetan social history provides numerous examples that centre upon men, the most outstanding of which would surely be the tradition, germane to both classical Indic religion and Chinese Taoism, of assigning charisma and power to the world-renouncer through a dialectical process. But for women this pattern can work in distinctive ways. Sometimes, as already seen above, it proceeds largely pragmatically; an example would be the sickness/initiation/danger period in the life of the medium. Diemberger's work suggests that this marginalized position outside societal boundaries can serve the particular function, in the case of a woman oracle, of allowing her to transcend gender boundaries, in addition to the class and vocational boundaries more usually recognized as being obviated in the oracle's career.

There are also reversals of low status that benefit women in other ways, beyond serving as instruments for evasions of cultural bias. Women's marginality and association with impurity can also be assigned a positive value in their own right. Such associations place women in a privileged position to do certain things, a prime example of which would be the oracle's channelling of the dark sides of community issues. Diemberger provides a variety of reasons why this vocation works especially well for female oracles, who seem to predominate in this role at the local village level, at least in some parts of Tibet today, and possibly also in the past. The kinds of concerns that local mediums most often address—birth, death, local conflicts—are considered inherently defiling, but these are also features closely associated with women's own imputed sources of defilement. In other words, there is a homology between feminine gender stereotypes and the demands of the job, and this spells advantage for women.

A related point can be made about contemporary Tibetan singers who convey covert and forbidden political messages in their popular songs. Henrion-Dourcy's study suggests that it is easier for women than for men to get away with such subterfuge. Not only is there less unease with women's expression of heartfelt emotions than when men attempt it (again a gender conception that is as valid for recent Tibetan society as it is in the West). Women could also be said to tend to be more at home with ambiguous wordplay and *double entendre*. These are ploys to which

[24] Classically described by Lewis 1971. The association between women, marginality and possession is, however, being challenged in a number of studies—see, e.g., Larsen 1995: 21–3.

marginal people sometimes need to resort—much more, in any event, than those with license to speak and assert their will freely. While such a tendency would be a product of historical circumstance, it is often passed as representing something inherently true about women, across time and place. Note also that again it is not a talent exclusive to women; it is just that women may have a special advantage in cultivating it.

We are hardly unfamiliar with the figuration of women as having a talent for mediation, especially when facilitating cultural contact. One need only think of archetypical female 'bridges' like Sacajewa who guided the Lewis and Clark expedition through her native American land, or La Malinche who served Cortez as translator and mediator, to find ready parallels to the special female function exemplified by the Tibetan saint Yeshe Tsogyal. In the story of Tibet's conversion to Buddhism, Yeshe Tsogyal stands as the quintessential female bridge, not only interculturally, by initiating Tibet's reception of the Indian master Padmasambhava's tantric teachings. As a woman she was the quintessential recipient of such teachings anyway. We pointed out above that women achieve eminence as consorts through their association with powerful lamas. Here we can add that the ideal gender virtues illustrated by Yeshe Tsogyal serve as an authorizing reference point for Tibetan women who would achieve virtuosity as a female consort. One of these features is her female 'receptivity', which takes on a special meaning in the context of tantric yoga, making the woman the ideal model of tantric disciple. Another is seen in the key role that the woman is thought to play in facilitating the meditative experiences of the male yogic expert. Part of the reason why the female has special talents for this role is that her putative inherent defilement makes her a means or device to transgress monastic norms. Again, then, we can note that an opportunity for eminence and virtuosity for women emerges from specifically female traits, albeit ones that in other contexts are cast as flaws.[25]

In terms of traditional Tibetan norms, consortship is among a small handful of roles in which women achieve eminence. Nonetheless, although historical works refer to many such consorts, indicating that this was a position that women often assumed, we know little about them. As scholars continue to pore over the little evidence that we do have, hopefully more will emerge about the activities these partners of religious masters engaged in, their education, and the nature of the autonomy that they could muster. There also can be no doubt that for many Tibetan women consortship was not an educational opportunity at all but rather an occasion for abuse. This too will surely emerge as our knowledge

[25] These ideas are discussed in more detail in Gyatso 1998a: ch.6.

about women consorts grows. Evidence of abuse may be most accessible in the present, especially in some Tibetan exile communities where young girls can be summoned briefly for a lama's use.

We also find in Martin's chapter a window on Tibetan women who became masters of yoga not by being consorts at all but rather on their own, as solo meditators, in both Buddhism and Bon. Judging only from the large number of female recluses in mountain caves today in the TAR, it can be assumed that there have been many such women historically, most of whom never achieved fame or had anything written about them.[26] Nonetheless these solo female masters merit as much study as the sources allow. Most likely much of what we find will fall into the same hagiographical schemas as are well known for men, but some indication of the specifically female dimensions of their careers can already be seen in the biographies of Orgyen Chokyi and Jetsun Lochen. As for yogic virtuosity in particular, if we are to ask if it can have a particularly female cast, mention might be made of what is probably the most mysterious and arcane 'special female talent' of them all. This concerns an assumption about a special female facility and 'openness' for tantric yoga that can be heard in conversation sometimes in contemporary Tibetan yogic communities. There is little in writing to support this view,[27] but there is an interestingly similar notion at work in the oracle traditions discussed here by Diemberger. Among those oracles, skill in 'opening the door of the energy channels' seems to be gendered as a quintessentially female operation, even if male oracles also regularly perform this function.

In considering the question of the self-conscious agency of Tibetan women, we find ourselves looking for the ideals that would inspire it, and female gender norms—ideas about special female virtues, special female connections, even special female handicaps—are the first things that come to mind. There can be no question that historical Tibetan women have taken lessons from such ideals. Negative caricatures are accepted as serious limitations and are sometimes the targets of irony or dissent; positive images become model templates for self-betterment. These ideals are expressed overtly in normative statements, but they can also be construed from stories and biographies, which provide a schema for female personality formation. Like the normative statements, the figuration of women in narrative has also been positive and inspiring, dismissive and demeaning, or just neutral.[28] Among the most exalted of these in the

26 One outstanding example was Ayu Khandro, whose life story is interestingly narrated by Namkhai Norbu (see Allione 1984: 235–64).

27 One brief but influential allusion on the superiority of the female body for tantric yoga is to be found in Yeshe Tsogyal's hagiography (Dowman 1984: 86).

28 One of the richest sources for female character in Tibetan literature is the fictionalized

world of religion are the hagiographies of Machig Labdron and Yeshe Tsogyal, the two most common historical (or quasi-historical) personages of whom a woman can be identified as a reincarnation or emanation. The iconography and lore of the Indo-Tibetan deities Vajrayoginī and Tārā also serve for such a function.

To have authorizing referents for women is extremely important in the context of Tibet's entrenched system of *tulku* (reincarnation) recognition, and outstanding women, both inside Tibet and in exile, still have recourse today to these and other figures in crafting their identity and position.[29] We find in Orgyen Chokyi's autobiography striking examples of an individual explicitly taking courage from ideal female models, who include Tārā, Dorje Phagmo, Nangsa Obum and Gelongma Pelmo (Schaeffer, this volume). No doubt these exemplars have served as counterweights to the other stereotypes, the negative ones of the inferior, debased female, which recur in the studies in this volume. But we are far from knowing to what degree such disparate gender models cancel each other out, or whether they simply operate simultaneously, in tandem, producing perhaps a creative tension of contradictory choices. And while the hagiographies of the likes of Machig Labdron, Yeshe Tsogyal and Mandarava (see Gyatso 1998b: 1–14) responded explicitly to the misogynist models, it is not known how effective these responses were in transforming either social conceptions at large or the particular self-conceptions of individual women.

We have tried in this introduction to highlight issues that affect women as a group—not only those that emanate from the ideals and their accompanying 'gender trouble', but also those that are not so much about gender, but rather are held in common by women and other groups. In the end we cannot say with any precision how much individual Tibetan women have thought of themselves as members of some category like 'woman,' and how much they have seen their situation in terms of other human issues. A microcosm of precisely the complex mix that exists on the ground—and surely resists the false tension of the foregoing opposition—would be the relationship between student and teacher, the quintessential locus for the transmission of Tibetan tradition, where cultural norms and individuality are inextricably intertwined. Orgyen Chokyi's autobiography provides an example of what may well have been a recurring pattern for women, namely an important association with a

---

biography of Milarepa by Tsang-nyon Heruka (Evans-Wentz 1969), which has both female heroines and villains, frequently cast specifically as being prototypically female.

[29] Several eminent Tibetan women are claimed to be emanations of Yeshe Tsogyal today, including Drigung Khandro and the sister of Khanpo Jigme Phuntsok Rinpoche in Golok.

female mentor.[30] Gendered habits and conditions have made same-sex student-teacher bonds more likely than heterosexual ones in Tibet, especially for female students—although women have also often had male masters for their major teachings, and, much more rarely, men have taken teachings from women.[31] We can only begin to imagine the complex webs of interaction between a pair like Orgyen Chokyi and the outstanding meditator Sonam Drolma, which would doubtless have revolved around not only the perpetuation of gender norms but also many other kinds of negotiations and adjustments in the course of leading their lives and making their own histories.

To bring to the foreground personal and historical contingency in an investigation of gender norms makes us realize again how valuable for learning the history of women is a literary genre like autobiography, which in Tibet is notable for managing to elude dogma and highlight individual difference.[32] But even candid autobiographical writing remains limited by textual formulae and culturally-entrenched genre conventions. Hence the great hope sometimes placed in anthropology, especially for a topic like that of women, who are mostly either dismissed in written sources or entirely absent from them. The hope is that ethnography will provide a different set of data on actual conditions, revealing information about an entire social group rather than only about those who are seen as fit as to be enshrined in texts. Of course, it is not the case that anthropology any more than the study of texts, offers a more genuine picture of what the world of Tibetan women is 'really like' than the study of texts does. Surely both are always filtered through the interpretational schema of the culture, not to mention those of the researcher.

The best we can do, in the end, is to approach this complex topic from as many angles as we can. Iconography, musicology and medicine would be among some of the other promising disciplines that would enhance our knowledge further. The present volume is largely limited to text-based history and anthropology, because these were the two disciplines in which its editors were able to find scholars who had researched the theme. But, on reflection, the range of approaches that this collection spans has the merit of inspiring a set of methodological observations of their own. Both for Tibetan studies in general, and for the particular topic of women and gender studies within Tibetology, it is useful to reflect on what kinds of particular knowledge textual study and anthropological

30 Another example of a highly influential relationship with a female mentor can be seen in Ayu Khandro's relation with her aunt (Allione 1984: 240–3).

31 One good example of the latter is seen again in the life of Ayu Khandro when Norbu entreats her for initiations.

32 This point has been argued in Gyatso 1998a.

study each facilitate, and especially how they might inform each other. The combination provides us with two different kinds of cultural norm, one textual and the other oral; it also allows some comparison of historical circumstances with contemporary situations. One might even go so far as to use the picture of the world that is found in the field to help imagine the social circumstances that produced our historical textual sources. This is not to claim an historical exactitude for such a method. The limitations on the sources for Tibetan studies make it highly unlikely that we will often be able to have anthropological data for the same world that produced a text that we are reading. Still, at least while there remain in Tibetan society discernible continuities between the present and the last few centuries, Makley's research about the lay and monastic populations around Labrang, for example, can help us to appreciate the texture of the community interactions to which historical nuns like Jetsun Lochen or Orgyen Chokyi refer. And the work of Diemberger on current female spirit mediums provides a modern-day contextualization of the mysterious women who channelled spirits for the fourteenth-century tantric master Longchenpa (Germano and Gyatso 2000). Methodological diversity stretches our ability to imagine. It encourages us to consider the evidence from many angles. It also reminds us of the many culturally specific assumptions that we bring to the way that we understand even seemingly straightforward data, and cautions us about the various ways in which our hasty conclusions can be wrong.

This volume only provides fragments of the history and diversity of women in Tibet. It spans two very vast divides–between old and new Tibet, and between the increasingly disparate worlds of Tibetans in Tibet and Tibetans in exile. A common thread running through the chapters concerns the methodological problems that attend the study of 'women of Tibet': the selectivity of what gets reported, the variety of historical positions within Tibetan society on the status of women, and the repeated examples of exceptions to the rule. The class of women is not synonymous with what (the disparate) gender norms describe. We are reminded repeatedly of the pitfalls of generalization, not only because of local and temporal differences but also because of the shifting sense of what it means to be a woman and what it means to be a person, irrespective of gender, throughout Tibetan history.

Why should we expect to be able to say anything generically about women in Tibet? The editors hope that the title of the volume alone will spark the question of what we mean by it in the first place, not to mention why we single out the topic. It might also make us think about what it would mean to write a book about 'men in Tibet', i.e. men construed not as humans but as a class distinct from women. We isolate our topics out of our own contemporary concerns, but we hope that in the present case we have also shone light on the pitfalls of assuming that such topics necessarily have an actual historical referent. Perhaps in the process we have also indicated areas of future research concerning those people of Tibet, past and present, who happen to have been women.

Part I

WOMEN IN TRADITIONAL TIBET

LADIES OF THE TIBETAN EMPIRE (7TH–9TH CENTURIES CE)

Helga Uebach

When asked about women in the period of the Tibetan empire (seventh to ninth centuries CE), many Tibetans as well as others interested in Tibetan culture would at least be able to mention two names: the Nepali and the Chinese consorts of the emperor Songtsen Gampo (d. 649). The two consorts are credited with the introduction of Buddhism to Tibet and with the foundation of the two holiest temples in Lhasa, the Jokhang and the Ramoche temples. Statues of the emperor accompanied by his wives on either side have been highly revered up to the present day in the Jokhang and in the Potala palace. So deep is the reverence that the fact that these two ladies came from foreign countries never seems to have mattered.

THE SOURCES

But what about the other Tibetan women from the imperial period? Information about them is scarce. Only very few of them are known and all of these were noble women. In many cases only their names and their titles have been transmitted. As we will see, however, sometimes names and titles can tell stories, even history.

From where can information about the Tibetan ladies during the period of the Tibetan empire be gained? Our primary sources are the so-called old Tibetan texts. Their discovery at the beginning of the twentieth century by the scholarly explorers R. A. Stein and Paul Pelliot has been sensational and has opened new dimensions in Tibetan studies. The most important texts used in the following are the *Annals*, the *Genealogy* and the *Chronicle* (Bacot *et al.* 1940: *Annals*, 13–66; *Genealogy*, 81–2, 86–9; *Chronicle*, 97–170; facsimile editions in Spanien and Imaeda 1979: pl. 579–91, 554–6, 557–77). These all were found in the cave temple of the Thousand Buddhas at Tunhuang, a site on the ancient silk-road. This region had been under the firm control of the Tibetans from the second half of the eighth century onward and this is why a great number of Tibetan texts were to be found there, among other writings. The texts had

Statues in the Jokhang of Emperor Songtsen Gampo and his Napali and Chinese wives. Behind, between Songtsen Gampo and his Chinese wife, is a statue of Padmasambhava. (Photo: Aurthur Sand 2004)

been stored in a cave walled up in the middle of the eleventh century CE and had remained there for centuries.

Then there are imperial inscriptions engraved on huge stone pillars dating from the middle of the eighth century onward, which have survived in Tibet. There are also two bells bearing inscriptions that have been preserved in temples (Richardson 1985; Li and Coblin 1987) and a few imperial edicts that have been faithfully transmitted by a Tibetan historian (dPa'-bo 1969). Beside these primary sources we will bracket a number of later historiographies and other texts, where traditional accounts, stories and legends of some of the ladies of the imperial period have been transmitted. These works were compiled by Buddhist monks who interpreted history from a clerical perspective.[1]

The *Genealogy*, which covers prehistoric times up to the end of the Tibetan empire, lists the names of the Tibetan emperors together with the full names of those of their consorts who bore future emperors. The full names include the name of the clan from which each consort descended. This enables us to begin introducing the ladies from the historical period of the reign of the emperor Songtsen Gampo.

[1] In general these works are not quoted here. For references of the ladies in these texts see Haarh 1969: 52–60.

Statue representing, according to Tibetan oral tradition, Trimonyen Dongtsen of the Mong clan, the consort of Emperor Songtsen Gampo, holding her son Gungsong Gungtsen. (Photo: Jampa L. Panglung 1983)

WOMEN DURING THE REIGN OF EMPEROR SONGTSEN GAMPO

Dringma Togo

The mother of Songtsen Gampo was named Dringma Togo of the clan of Tsepong. Her clan had played an important role in uniting the different principalities that were to form the Tibetan empire.

Trimonyen Dongteng

Songtsen Gampo was married to a lady of the Mong clan. Her name was Trimonyen Dongteng. Nothing but the name of this lady is known. It is interesting to note, however, that there is a statue which, according to tradition, is a representation of this empress. This statue can be seen in a small cave-styled temple in the uppermost part of the Potala palace, which also houses clay statues of the emperor Songtsen Gampo and his councillor Gar, among others. The clay figure of Trimonyen Dongteng shows her seated cross-legged on a throne holding a boy in her lap (Chayet and Meyer 1983: 82–5).[2] At first sight it resembles representations of the Virgin Mary. If tradition proves true, the statue of Trimonyen Dongteng, apart from the statues of the above-mentioned Chinese and Nepali consorts of Songtsen Gampo, is the only visual representation of a Tibetan empress known at present.

From 650 CE onward, we are on firm historical ground for information about Tibetan ladies, since primary sources like the *Annals* contain year-by-year entries covering the period from 650 to 747. In a few introductory lines preceding the annalistic-style entries, the *Annals* report that the Chinese consort of Songtsen Gampo had been escorted to Tibet by the councillor Gar and that her husband died after three years in her company. She is referred to as Munchang Kongcho and given the title 'tsenmo' (*btsan-mo*, 'mighty one [fem.]'). This is the female equivalent of the emperor's title 'tsenpo' (*btsan-po*, 'mighty one'). Her name is only mentioned once again on the occasion of funeral ceremonies held for her in 683.[3]

Songtsen Gampo had in rapid succession subdued the neighbouring rulers up to the Chinese borders. He then started menacing these borders too and demanded a Chinese princess in matrimonial alliance. The annals of the T'ang dynasty (Pelliot 1961: 3–5, 82–84) report that his demand was first denied, but when threatened, the Chinese emperor consented to enter negotiations with the Tibetan envoy, the councillor of the Gar clan. A seventh century Chinese painting shows Gar on the way to an audience with the Chinese emperor (Karmay 1977: 64). Tibet had for the first time entered a relationship called 'uncle and nephew' or 'father-in-law and son-in-law' with China. For Songtsen Gampo this matrimonial alliance with the big neighbour China was a triumph adding to his reputation and power.

Semarkar

Songtsen Gampo is said to have married three more wives, the Nepali princess[4] already mentioned above, a noble lady from Minyak and a princess of Zhangzhung, a country that he had subdued and which was to revolt repeatedly. His matrimonial alliance with Zhangzhung was a double arrangement including the marriage of Songtsen Gampo's sister to

[2] For a photo of the empress see Uebach 1997: 68.

[3] On a detailed description of the marriage in the *Maṇi bka' 'bum* , a later Tibetan work, see Bacot 1935: 1–60.

[4] Some scholars have doubted the historicity of the Nepali marriage. The introductory lines of the *Annals* show, however, that the Tibetans where well-aware of Nepali politics (see Petech 1967: 271, 272).

the Zhangzhung ruler. The story of Songtsen Gampo's sister, Imperial Princess Semarkar, is told in some detail in the *Chronicle*. In the *Chronicle*, in contrast to the *Annals*, a great number of historical events of the Tibetan empire have been given literary expression.

Semarkar was given in marriage to Ligmyihya, the ruler of Zhangzhung, but she was not simply sent there as a bride. Her marriage is described in the following terms: 'To be the master of Zhangzhung, the imperial princess Semarkar went to Ligmyihya to practise state power.'[5]

Soon, however, news reached Songtsen Gampo that Semarkar was not likely to have a son by Ligmyihya and therefore another revolt of Zhangzhung might arise. Songtsen Gampo therefore sent his councillor to Zhangzhung. The councillor did not meet Imperial Princess Semarkar in her new home, the castle of Khyunglung Ngulkar, but found her fishing on the shore of Lake Manasarovar. The councillor saluted her respectfully. Semarkar asked about the well-being of her brother, the emperor. The councillor replied that the emperor was fine. She asked whether he, the councillor himself, was happy. He replied that he was.

Then the councillor informed her of the message from her brother, saying that Semarkar was to send him a written report. Semarkar replied that she wanted to honour him, the councillor, by arranging a feast. On the occasion of the feast, Semarkar sang a long song. A few lines of this song may show what the songs, frequently encountered in the *Chronicle*, were like. At the same time they may give an impression of the situation of Semarkar:

> The share of land which was imparted to me
> is a Kyunglung Ngulkar [a castle of silver in Kyunglung].
>
> … others say that:
>
> 'looking from the outside, it is abyss and rock,
> looking from the inside, it is gold and gem.'
> To have it before
> my face, isn't it scorn?
> It is grey and empty.
> …
> The share of food which was imparted to me
> is fish and barley.
> To eat it by me, isn't it scorn?
> Fish and barley chewed are bitter …[6]

The song has been studied carefully by scholars along with the other three songs. Apart from being fine examples of old Tibetan poetry, the

[5] I follow the translation of Uray 1972: 36.

[6] Quoted from Uray 1972: 10, but without the italics and brackets used by Uray.

hidden message of Semarkar can be interpreted as the following. The first song is a personal complaint of Semarkar, as well as an allusion to the fact that her husband was not a vassal worth trusting, but full of hatred. It also indicates that he avoided consummating the marriage. In the second song Semarkar describes a tribal hunt of wild yak, thus inviting her brother Songtsen Gampo to wage war against Zhangzhung. She indicates in detail how to hunt the yak, alluding to how to conduct the war. The third song illustrates a fishing scene, where the fish-eating otters and owls are waiting to steal the fisherman's catch. This is a warning against the neighbouring hostile countries. In the fourth song Semarkar lyrically expresses her homesickness. She sings about her wish to return home while recounting the stages of a journey in her homeland through beautiful natural surroundings. Upon his departure the councillor asked Semarkar for a written message for her brother. Instead she handed him a sealed bonnet. In his report to the emperor Songtsen Gampo, the councillor faithfully repeated the song of Semarkar. When Songtsen Gampo opened the bonnet, he found around thirty fine old turquoises. He interpreted the coded message thus: 'If we dare fight Ligmyihya, let us wear the turquoises! If we don't dare to fight him, we are like women. Let us wear the bonnet!' Then he waged war against Ligmyihya, who was overthrown.

The fate or further life of Semarkar is not mentioned at all. It should perhaps be added here that the emphasis laid on the written message must not be mistaken to imply that ladies like Semarkar were versed in writing. Rather, the story is more fanciful than strictly historical and serves largely to augment the achievements of Songtsen Gampo. In any event, another passage of the *Chronicle* credits Songtsen Gampo with the introduction of the Tibetan script in Tibet.

Mangpang: the mother of Emperor Manglon Mangtsen

The heir of Songtsen Gampo was Gungsong Gungtsen. He died before his father, but he had left a son named Manglon Mangtsen. In the *Genealogy*, the name of his mother is Mangmoje Trikar. Instead of her clan name, her personal name is preceded by 'kongcho', the title used for the Chinese princess. It is highly improbable that the Chinese princess was the mother of Emperor Manglon Mangtsen, because of the testimony of the *Annals*. The *Annals*, as a rule, carefully differentiate forms of address. Usually the mothers of the heir to the throne are addressed by the honorific kinship term 'yum' (*yum*, 'mother') or 'chi' (*phyi*, 'grandmother') (Uebach 1997: 53–74). This is not the case with the Chinese princess. In all likelihood the mother of Manglon Mangtsen was the 'great-grandmother' Mangpang, whose death is reported in 706 CE and for whom the funeral ceremonies were held in 707.

It is not known whether the mother of Emperor Manglon Mangtsen played a role during his infancy. It seems unlikely that she did so, because councillors of the Gar clan continued to be in office and in fact were the rulers of the empire.

Imperial Princess Nyamoteng

In 671 CE another imperial princess called Nyamoteng went to the country of Zhangzhung. She was given as a bride to Nyashur Pungyegyug. She was probably a daughter of Manglon Mangtsen.

Empress Trimalo; de facto regent of the Tibetan empire

The next empress mentioned in the *Annals* was Trimalo Triteng of the clan of Dro. She was the consort of Emperor Manglon Mangtsen. The *Annals* report that she hosted a great feast in 675. We are, however, not informed what occasioned the celebration. It may even have been the celebration of her own marriage. In the next year, 676, her husband died and she gave birth to the emperor Tridusong.

Trimalo was to become an outstanding personality in the history of the Tibetan empire, though more than twenty years were to pass before her name was mentioned in the *Annals* again. The reason for this long silence becomes evident from a song of her son Tridusong contained in the *Chronicle*. The emperor Tridusong sang this song of triumph after he had overcome the councillor of the Gar clan. In his song, Tridusong accused the Gar councillor of aspiring to become emperor and compared him with a frog who aspired to fly.[7]

Actually it was only in his twenty-second year that Tridusong was in a strong enough position to free himself from the regimentation of the Gar councillor. There is good reason to assume that his mother Trimalo was involved, to say the least, in discreetly preparing the fall of the councillor of the Gar clan. To realize this, it was imperative to have strong allies and matrimonial alliances were the usual way to attain these.

Trimoteng

The *Annals* report that in 688 the imperial princess Trimoteng went to the country of Dagpo to practise state power. Trimoteng seems to have been more fortunate than Semarkar had been in Zhanzhung. The rulers of the vassal country Dagpo were loyal. They had already been matrimonially

[7] Part of this song is translated in Snellgrove and Richardson 1968: 62–3.

allied with the Tibetan emperor in former times. This is why they were addressed by the kinship term 'won' (*dbon*), 'nephew' or 'son-in-law' of the Tibetan emperor, and had hereditarily held high offices. Won Dagyal, who according to the *Annals* was in office in the years 687–8 and 690, seems to have been the husband of the imperial princess Trimoteng. The Won Dagyal, who in the *Annals* is seen to hold the highest office from 706 onward, was most probably her son.

In order to win another powerful ally, the imperial princess Triwang was sent in 689 as a bride to the ruler of the Azha country. The Tibetan emperor officially conferred the title 'won' on her son in 727.

Trimalo's political role

For the year 696 the *Annals* informs us that the empress Mangmoje summoned many men or craftsmen. 'Mangmoje' (*mang-mo rje*) is not a name, but the female form of an honorific and qualifying address meaning 'sovereign lady of many'. Here it can hardly have been applied to anyone else but to the empress Trimalo. Her summoning of many men was the last stage in the preparations to fight the Gar councillor. In 698, pretending to entertain himself by sports, her son Tridusong departed to the north where he and his followers met the great councillor on his return from a successful campaign against China. They overthrew him by surprise. The Gar councillor together with hundreds of his followers managed to escape to China where they were well-received. Tridusong thus put an end once and for all to the reign of the councillors of the Gar clan. They had held office from the time of Emperor Songtsen Gampo onward and their office had become hereditary.

After the defeat of the Gar councillor, the empress 'mother' (yum) Trimalo appeared again on the political scene. In the year 700 we are informed that Trimalo resided in Onchangdo, where she received an envoy from the Chinese emperor. While Tridusong was engaged in warfare at the frontier, his mother obviously acted as his representative. This is why, during his absence from central Tibet until 704, references to her residence, i.e. the imperial court, regularly occur in the *Annals*. In 704 a son was born to Emperor Tridusong named Gyaltsugru. His mother's name, Mother Tsenmatok, is given upon her death in 721 and again in 723, on the occasion of the funeral ceremonies held for her. It is the *Genealogy* that provides her full name, Tsenmatok Togteng from the clan of Chim. Later in the year 704 the emperor Tridusong died in a campaign in south-eastern Tibet.

From 705 onward, the empress Trimalo is addressed 'chi', 'grandmother'. Since her grandson, the future emperor, was still a minor, Trimalo was de facto the regent of the Tibetan empire. In this same year

705, an elder son or brother of Tridusong was dethroned or excluded from inheriting the throne (Petech 1967: 255–6), the empress Trimalo doubtless favouring her infant grandson. In 708 the *Annals* report the death of yet another lady who was addressed with the title tsenmo, named Gatun, which in fact is the Tibetan rendering of the Turkic title *khatun*. She seems to have been a princess from a Turkic-speaking ally of the Tibetans and she was married either to Manglon Mangtsen or to his son Tridusong.

According to the annals of the Chinese T'ang dynasty, the 'grandmother' Trimalo regularly maintained contacts with the Chinese court. For years she had negotiated another matrimonial alliance with China. Finally the negotiations were successful and the Chinese princess Kimshang Kongcho left for Tibet. The T'ang annals report that the Chinese emperor shed tears when his adopted daughter left, and that he was especially worried because she was very young (Pelliot 1961: 14, 96). On her way to Tibet, she stayed for a while at the court of the Azha ruler, whose wife was the Tibetan imperial princess Triwang already mentioned. In 710 the young princess Kimshang and the Tibetan emperor-to-be, aged six years, lived in the castle of Dragmar as husband and wife. So it is reported in the *Annals*.

Trimalo continued to reign up to the year 712. Then her grandson was formally enthroned at the age of eight and given the regal name Tride Tsugtsen. In the same year we are informed about the death of Grandmother Trimalo. The funeral ceremonies for her took place in 713.

The empress Trimalo doubtless lived an extraordinary life. In the *Annals*, the entries regarding her cover a period of no less than thirty-seven years. After the birth of Tridusong, her name is not mentioned during the next twenty years. When her son was still a minor, the power was in the hands of the councillors of the Gar clan. After their defeat, she first acted as the representative of Tridusong while he was engaged in warfare at the borders of the empire. Upon his death and the birth of his heir in 704, Trimalo repelled another pretender to the throne and took the reign of the empire in her own hands. With powerful and loyal councillors, headed by the matrimonially allied nephew or son-in-law ruler of Dagpo at her side, Trimalo was able to reign over the vast empire successfully for eight years, until her death and the enthronement of her grandson, Tride Tsugtsen. She must indeed have been an impressive personality and a very gifted and powerful ruler to be accepted in a society dominated by male warriors.

It is noteworthy that later historiographers do not at all mention the reign of the empress Trimalo. This is not surprising because from the Buddhist point of view there is nothing to report about her. There is, however, one exception. In a genealogical list dating from the thirteenth century, Trimalo is given the title 'trichen' (*khri-chen*; 'great throne'). This may reflect a faint memory of her grandeur.[8]

The Chogro lady's song to the emperor

The victorious campaign of Trimalo's son Tridusong against the great councillor of Gar must have meant a personal tragedy for the wife of Gar (or his son), a lady of the Chogro clan. Upon his return from this campaign, Tridusong met the Chogro lady in her homeland Dam, north of Lhasa. The *Chronicle* describes the meeting. First Tridusong sang a long song of triumph, already mentioned above. Then a man from his retinue sang another long song repeating the emperor's triumph over Gar and offending, perhaps even threatening the lady. There is no politeness shown. No greeting of the wife of the defeated enemy took place. The Chogro lady in her short song returned the offence in a clever way:

> Ah! On the plain of Dam
> I did not search for the face of the Divine coming!
> Had I searched for the face of the Divine coming,
> I would have bowed and saluted respectfully
>
> Standing upright and saluting respectfully
> In the circumstances is not the proper custom!

Although not all the allusions of the songs are comprehensible, there is no doubt that the Chogro lady made it perfectly clear that the emperor was unwelcome in her homeland. Using a pretext she deliberately avoided showing him due respect. Instead of bowing, she appears to have remained standing upright. From a rather fragmentary portion of the *Chronicle*, it can also be concluded that she finally joined her husband and took refuge in China.

THE IMPERIAL CONSORTS OF TRIDE TSUGTSEN AND TRISONG DETSEN

Kimshang Kongcho

It has already been mentioned above that the empress Trimalo had arranged a matrimonial alliance for her grandson Tride Tsugtsen and the Chinese princess Kimshang Kongcho. Very little is known about Kongcho's life in Tibet from Tibetan sources. According to the *Annals*, she dismissed a Tibetan councillor in 730. The text may also be interpreted in

[8] Grags-pa 1968b. See also Tucci 1971: 128–9.

another way, to indicate that a pro-Kongcho councillor was dismissed. Already the year 723 seems to have been troublesome for the princess. In this year, according to Chinese sources, she had secretly sent two Chinese envoys to the Kashmiri ruler inquiring whether he could give her asylum (Chavannes 1969: 205–6). The *Annals* record that she died in 739 and that the funeral ceremonies for her were held in 741.

Additional information about Kongcho is supplied by prophecies concerning Khotan and its religious history (Thomas 1935: 83; Cannata 1990: 64–7). It is reported that Kongcho used her influence so that a great number of Buddhist monks from the western region, who had been driven to flight by warfare, were admitted into Tibet. At that time an epidemic of smallpox broke out in Tibet and high officials held the refugee monks and Kongcho to be responsible for the death of many Tibetans. When the first signs of the epidemic showed on Kongcho's body, she is said to have asked the emperor's permission to donate all her belongings and servants to the Buddhist monks. This was granted.

Lhapang

As usual, the Chinese princess had not been the only consort of the emperor. The *Annals* informs us of another wife. She is addressed 'cham' (*lcam;* 'sister'), which in this context means co-wife. Her name was Lhapang. She is only referred to on the occasion of the funeral ceremonies following her death in 732. Lhapang may have been the mother of a son of the emperor called Lhawon in the *Annals*. The funeral ceremonies for him are reported to have taken place in 741.

It is only in the year 742, when the emperor Tride Tsugtsen was thirty-eight years old, that the *Annals* record the birth of the heir to the throne, Trisong Detsen. His mother is addressed 'mangmoje', 'sovereign lady of many'. Her full name is provided by the *Genealogy* as Mangmoje Shiteng of the Nanam clan. Mangmoje's death is announced in the same year as the birth of her son. The funeral ceremonies of yet another woman called 'jomo' (*jo-mo*; 'lady'), that is, Lady Tritsun, is reported in the year 745. She may have been another consort of Tride Tsugtsen.

There are two ladies called 'jewa' (*je-ba*) in the *Annals*. This form of address is not attested elsewhere and its meaning is still unknown. It might be assumed that it is used for daughters of a co-wife, in order to distinguish them from daughters of the emperor who were addressed as 'imperial princesses'. The first of these two ladies, whose name was Dronmalo, went as a bride to the Khagan of the Turgesh in 734. The other lady, Trimalo, who shared the name of the great empress, went as a bride to the ruler of Bruzha (Gilgit).

The consorts of Emperor Trisong Detsen

The emperor Trisong Detsen assumed power at the age of thirteen in 755. A son was born to him in 760. Neither his name, nor the name of his mother are recorded in a second fragment of the *Annals*, covering the period of 743–763, dealing particularly with military affairs. According to the *Genealogy*, Trisong Detsen was married to a lady of the Tsepong clan called Magyal Dongkar. She gave birth to two of his sons, Mu-ne Tsen and Desong Tsen. Trisong Detsen had, however, also married some other ladies. Their names are transmitted in later historiographical literature with slightly varying orthography. His other consorts were Lhamotsen from the Chim clan, Tsogyal of Kharchen, Trigyal Mangmotsen from the Dro clan and Gyalmotsun from the Phoyong clan.

Trisong Detsen ruled the empire for a period of more than forty years (r.755 - *c*.797/8). He reorganized the administration and legislation of the state. His greatest deed, however, was the adoption of Buddhism as a state religion in the 780s. The imperial edict in favour of Buddhism was sworn by 'the emperor and his son and the mother of his son' as well as by all the officials of the empire.[9] A short version of the edict was engraved on a stone pillar that still can be seen in Samye, the first Tibetan monastery (Tucci 1950: pl. 3). The sources say that its building could only be realized after the great religious master Padmasambhava had been invited from India and had suppressed the hostile local demons. Then the first Tibetans were ordained as monks.

Women's contributions at Samye Monastery

In connection with the building of the monastery of Samye, an account is transmitted which introduces ladies who, though of noble descent, had not been consorts of Emperor Trisong Detsen (Stein 1961: 31,15–32,3). It says that when the principal statues for decorating the monastery of Samye were made, the emperor ordered them to be made in Tibetan style. Therefore the most beautiful Tibetan men and women were chosen to serve as models. The most beautiful females were two ladies of the Chogro clan, called Buchung and Lhabumen. The first served as model for the statue of the goddess Mārīcī, the second for the one of the goddess Tārā. It would have been interesting to know what the ideal of female beauty in the eighth century was like. The statues of the two goddesses were probably made of clay and no longer exist.

The adoption of Buddhism had its effects also with regard to the imperial consorts. All or some of them—the later historiographies do not

[9] Transmitted by the Tibetan historian Pawo Tsuglag Trengwa (dPa'-bo 1962: 109a1). For the translation and the text see also Tucci 1950: 45, 96.

The bell in Samye believed to have been donated by Jomo Gyalmotsen and her son. (Photo: H. Havnevik 2004)

always agree—are said to have erected temples in Samye. Two of the imperial consorts donated bells for the monastery. These bells still exist. They bear inscriptions showing the names of the donors and the names to whom the merit was dedicated. The bell kept in Samye names as donor the imperial consort 'Jomo Gyalmotsen, mother and son'. It is dedicated to the 'divine emperor Trisong Detsen, "father and son, husband and wife" … who may attain supreme enlightenment'. (Richardson 1985: 34–5; Li and Coblin 1987: 334, 337). The identity of the consort named as donor is uncertain. Her name resembles that of the imperial consort of the Phoyong clan.

The other bell is presently kept in the monastery of Tramdrug in the lower Yarlung valley. Its inscription names as donor the imperial consort Jomo Changchub who dedicated it to the 'divine emperor Tride Songtsen', the younger son of Trisong Detsen (Richardson 1985: 82–3; Li and Coblin 1987: 343,345). This bell therefore seems to be slightly later than the one mentioned first.

The empress-nun Changchub

The donor of this bell is generally identified in the historiographic literature with Trisong Detsen's consort of the Dro clan, called Trigyal Mangmotsen, who had taken vows and become a nun. Changchub (*byang-chub*) is indeed a name with Buddhist significance, meaning 'supreme enlightenment', and fits well as a nun's name. A Chinese dossier of the Great Debate held at Samye between Chinese and Indian masters praises the Tibetan empress of the clan Dro who is said to have been present (on the Chinese side) during the debate. She is described as a nun '… who in the field of passions made the pearl of moral conduct shine …' (Demiéville 1952: 25–33).

The lady Changchub not only seems to have been a very pious nun, but also a woman with forethought. In an early chronicle the following story is told:

> … the monastery of Gegye at Samye, which housed a number of statues, was her legacy. She thought that because she had no children and because the homeland of her parents was so far away that they could not come to take care [of the temple] in the future, she had statues for its decoration made from bronze in the western region. While they were transported to central Tibet, two statues fell into the water [and were probably lost]. She had the walls of the temple made of burnt brick, got the junctions filled up with molten lead, and had a roof made of copper set up. For the offering of music, she donated a bell. (Stein 1961: 46.3–10)

Tradition credits this pious lady with the enactment of a 'little law' or 'additional law'. It is worth noting that this information is not found in the chapters dealing with religious foundations, but in the section about law and the state in a few historical works. The content of this law is hard to understand and it must be taken into consideration that, in the course of the transmission, textual corruption may have crept in. In any event, the first part of the law as it is transmitted says: 'She taught men to do male obeisance. She taught women to do female obeisance.' The second part concerns a different subject: 'The foundation for obtaining wealth is to mark the field with border stones and to balance … autumn and spring.'[10] Usually the term 'little law' is used in the historical works in the context of the minority of an heir to the throne. In these cases the councillors enact a 'little law' in order to reign on his behalf. The subject of Changchub's law is different.[11] Even though its intentions are not quite clear to us, it was doubtless meant for the benefit of the subjects.

[10] mKhas-pa 1987: 268. Quoted also by dPa'-bo 1962: 112b7–113a1.

[11] For other examples of a 'little law' see Uebach 1987: 96–7 n. 436.

Magyal Dongkar: 'the bloody queen'

Magyal Dongkar, Trisong Detsen's consort of the Tsepong clan, was the mother of the heir to the throne. Much attention is given to her in the later literary tradition related to Padmasambhava. In this tradition a long novel is dedicated to the story of her life.[12] She is said to have wondered where her husband the emperor Trisong Detsen spent many hours of the night. She followed him and found out that he was being instructed in Buddhist doctrine by the pious monk Vairocana. Out of jealousy she wanted to discredit Vairocana and therefore tried to seduce him. When her attempt failed, she behaved like Potiphar's wife, slandering the man who rejected her. As a result of her false accusations and after her endless efforts, the monk Vairocana was finally exiled. Vairocana in his turn took revenge, causing leprosy to strike her. Magyal Donkar suffered greatly for years. Vairocana felt pity for her and sent a goddess disguised as a soothsayer. She told Magyal Donkar that she would be cured as soon as she confessed and repented her sin. Magyal Dongkar did so in the presence of Padmasambhava. As penance he ordered her to recite a long list of names of the Buddha. After doing so, she recovered completely. Her repentance, however, was not genuine. This became evident when she left the place, because no lotuses spread from her footprints, as they did from those of the others present.

Another unflattering story about Magyal Dongkar is preserved in historiographic tradition. This story narrates that she murdered her elder son because he had married the junior wife of his father, a lady from the Phoyong clan. Magyal Donkar is said to have murdered the Phoyong lady too. According to tradition, this is why the orthography of her name Magyal has been slightly changed, so that it became a surname meaning 'bloody queen'.

Killing and murder are not infrequently reported for the period of the early Tibetan empire. A murderer empress, however, seems to be unique. In any event, one wonders what eventually happened to Magyal Dongkar. Was it possible for an empress to get away with murder? Tradition is silent about her fate. Her younger son, the emperor Tride Songtsen, briefly mentions in an edict engraved in stone that there was disagreement between his father and his elder brother and '… before I obtained the kingdom there was some confusion and contention between evil spirits' (Richardson 1985: 46–7; Li and Coblin 1987: 264, 276). I think that the 'contention between evil spirits' alludes to the murder ascribed to his mother. It is likely that Magyal Dongkar was believed to have been possessed by an evil spirit when she committed the murder.

[12] The *bTsun mo bka'i thang yig* of the *bKa' thang sde lnga* was translated into German by Laufer 1911.

The punishment of women

Little to nothing is known about the punishment of women. A few references to imperial ordinances in religious laws (*chos-khrims*), as distinct from royal laws (*rgyal-khrims*), are quoted in the historical writings. For example, we read, 'The noses of women should not be cut off!' (Stein 1961: 51,15). Cutting off the nose, or more precisely, the tip of the nose, is well-known to have been the usual punishment for wives who committed adultery in India in ancient times. It is likely that customs of that sort were adopted in Tibet along with Buddhist thought from India. Hitherto I have only come across one textual reference that attests to the punishment of women. It occurs in the following context. Three male members of the Dro clan erected a temple in order to atone for the fact that their maternal aunt had committed suicide after they cut off the ornament of her head (her hair) (Uebach 1987: 117). Cutting off hair was certainly not a joke, but rather a kind of punishment.

Yeshe Tsogyal; imperial consort and tantric partner

Mention should also be made of another woman who devoted herself to a religious life, though not as a nun. This is Yeshe Tsogyal who according to tradition was an outstanding female religious master of that period. There is uncertainty in the texts about her early life. She is said to have been married to the emperor Trisong Detsen. Later the emperor offered her as a consort to Padmasambhava. Whatever her worldly life may have been like, it soon seems to have been dominated by her extraordinary religious achievements. It was with Padmasambhava that Yeshe Tsogyal is said to have practised tantric teachings and to have reached the ultimate goal (Dowman 1984; Gross 1989; Gyatso forthcoming). Images of Yeshe Tsogyal together with Padmasambhava and his other consort Mandarava are numerous and are part of standard Tibetan iconography. Yeshe Tsogyal has been highly revered in the Nyingma school of Tibetan Buddhism up to the present day.

The three Jomo sisters

The next emperor had, according to the *Genealogy*, no offspring and his reign was short. His younger brother, Tride Songtsen, succeeded him to the throne. He married Lhagyal Mangmoje of the Dro clan. The emperor married two other ladies as well. This is known from an edict he issued in favour of Buddhism and an oath he pledged on the occasion of the building of the monastery of Karchung. The name of the consort of the Dro clan attested there is Trimoleg, which might be her official name as the principal consort. The names of the other consorts are Jomo Legmotsen of the Chim clan and Jomo Tsengyal of the Chogro clan. The three consorts are collectively referred to as 'the jomo sisters' (*jo-mo mched*), or less literally 'the co-consorts'. All three consorts, too, took the same oath to support Buddhism. Then all the vassal kings, the councillor and officials took oaths as well (dPa'-bo 1962: 129b7–130a2; Tucci 1950: 54, 103). The designation of 'the jomo sisters' is also attested in another inscription of the emperor in favour of his tutor, the monk and great councillor Nyang Tingngedzin (Richardson 1985: 58–9; Li and Coblin 1987: 272, 293).

Empress Pelkyi Ngangchul's suicide

There is no evidence from old Tibetan texts regarding the consorts of Tritsug Detsen, the son of Tride Songtsen. In later historical works only the name of one consort is transmitted. She was a lady of the Chogro clan named Pelkyi Ngangchul. The emperor is described as a fervent Buddhist and he seems to have been a capable ruler too. During his reign, the great councillor and monk Drenka Pelkyi Yonten negotiated and concluded the last great peace treaty of 821/3 CE (Richardson 1985: 106–43; Li and Coblin 1987: 34–137) with China from a position of strength. The pillar with a bilingual Tibetan-Chinese inscription of this treaty is still to be seen in front of the Jokhang temple in Lhasa. As later historical literature has it, some councillors aimed at putting an end to the pro-Buddhist politics of the emperor and his great councillor. They conspired to falsely accuse the great monk councillor and the imperial consort of having sexual intercourse. The two were condemned and the great councillor was killed. The imperial consort Pelkyi Ngangchul flung herself down an abyss. Her relatives took revenge and killed the emperor.[13] Since Pelkyi Ngangchul had not yet given birth to a son, the brother of the emperor, Uidumtsen, ascended to the throne.

Uidumtsen is described as a persecutor of Buddhism. According to tradition he was murdered by a Buddhist monk. Rumours about two consorts of Uidumtsen struggling to save the throne for their respective sons are reflected in the historical literature. The grand Tibetan empire that had reached its greatest territorial extension during the reign of his grandfather Trisong Detsen was, however, torn by internal fights between the clans and finally collapsed.

IMPERIAL LADIES' POSITION IN TIBETAN SOCIETY

Having introduced the women, or rather ladies, known from the period of the Tibetan empire we wonder what their position and role in Tibetan

[13] According to Nyang-ral: Meisezahl 1985: 309.1.5–310.2.3.

society were like. For the early period, the *Annals* give the impression that the female members of the imperial household are only interesting from the dynastic point of view and that their importance was evaluated with regard to state power. Most of the empresses are mentioned for the first time upon the birth of the heir to the throne and then again upon their death and the funeral ceremonies held. Sisters and daughters of the emperor are only named upon their marriages. Co-consorts of the emperor, except for the Chinese princess Kimshang Kongcho, are only mentioned upon their deaths.

The *Annals* at our disposal are only excerpts of a larger text, which was probably far more detailed. The excerpts were made to serve as manuals for governing and as guidelines for bureaucratic practice in regions conquered by the Tibetans (Uray 1975: 158–9). Our knowledge about these women would perhaps be more detailed if a full version of the *Annals* had been transmitted. The *Annals* have been criticized because of their sober and brief information, but at least they supply exact data. The lack of such data from around 750 CE onward is much regretted.

Ranks and titles

As I have shown elsewhere, the *Annals* demonstrate that the female members of the imperial household were of differing ranks (Uebach 1997). The form of address for the lady ranking highest was 'empress', i.e. 'tsenmo'. This title is applied to the principal consort of the emperor, to the imperial princesses, since they were daughters of the emperor, and to both Chinese consorts and a consort of Turkic origin. As a rule, the empress who had given birth to the heir of the throne was addressed by the respectful term 'yum', 'mother' or 'chi', 'grandmother'. A high-ranking empress is sometimes also addressed 'mangmoje'. This term of address is also transmitted as the qualifying part of ladies' names. Unless preceded by a kinship term or followed by a personal name, such a title may pose a problem of identification.

It can be observed that imperial princesses married to foreign rulers kept their title 'tsenmo'. There was a terminological distinction in Tibetan between an imperial princess who went as a bride to another ruler (*bag-mar gshegs / btang*) and one who went to wield state power in a vassal country (*chab-srid-la gshegs*). The latter was the case with the imperial princess Semarkar in the country of Zhangzhung and with the imperial princess Trimoteng in the country of Dagpo.

The ladies ranking lower than the empress and the imperial princess are addressed by the kinship term 'cham' (*lcam*; 'sister') or by 'jomo' ('lady'). Both are respectful terms designating co-wives and daughters of co-wives of the emperor. It is not clear what the rank of ladies addressed as 'je-wa' (*je-ba*) was. Perhaps they were daughters of co-wives.

The imperial edicts and inscriptions dating from the second half of the eighth century do not reflect the distinctions in address known from the *Annals*. The imperial consorts are addressed 'jomo'. The different consorts of an emperor are collectively called 'jomo che' (*jo-mo mched*), 'the jomo sisters', which reflects sororal polygyny.

The clan from which a lady descended was a decisive factor in old Tibetan society. This is why the personal name of a lady in general is preceded by the name of her clan. The only exception is the *Annals*, where the ladies' personal names are provided throughout, without indication of their clan. I can think of no convincing reason why this is so. Fortunately the *Genealogy* furnishes at least the clan name of the mothers of the heir to the throne. The name of the clan of a lady seems to have been even more important than her personal name. It is common practice to drop the personal name of a lady in favour of her clan name and then simply to add the word 'za' (*za'/ bza'* ; 'wife'). This may have been a simple way to distinguish between the different consorts of an emperor. There is far more to it than that, however. The struggle among the Tibetan clans for power and supremacy was a threat felt permanently by the emperor. It also endangered the Tibetan state as a whole. Therefore, the emperors had to make their choice of consorts among the most powerful clans in order to get strong allies. To overcome the rivalry of powerful clans, the emperors frequently took consorts from three to five different clans.

The lives of imperial ladies and their powerful supporters

It is well-known that in the Tibetan patrilinear, exogamous clan system, the maternal uncle (*zhang*) of a lady played an important role (Stein 1972: 94, 108). Not only was his consent to the marriage of his niece imperative, his influence and protection lasted for a lifetime. This is reflected in the old Tibetan texts, too, where the maternal uncles of imperial consorts are described as high-ranking. Moreover, from the mid-eighth century onward, maternal uncles as a rule held high offices, e.g. as 'maternal uncle-councillor' (*zhang-blon*) and this became a hereditary post (Tucci 1950: 57–61). Their influence in state affairs was great on the one hand and, on the other hand, they were able to look after the interests of their nieces. What could better attest to such a position than the word of an emperor? The emperor Tride Songtsen granted great privileges to his councillor and monk Nyang Tingngedzin, the words of which he engraved on a pillar (which still exists), where he explains his reasons for the grant:

> … from my childhood until I obtained the reign of empire he took the place of father and mother. Taking the place of an attending maternal uncle, he cared for me (Richardson 1985: 47; Li and Coblin 1987: 264, 276).

The ladies of the Tibetan empire obviously did not live a life of seclusion. Formulas in letters preserved in Central Asian areas dominated by the Tibetans show that it was customary to pray for the 'well-being of [high official] father and son, husband and wife'.[14] The imperial consorts hosted great feasts. They could follow their own ways in religious practice and even take vows and become nuns. The ladies also surely kept property of their own. This may be concluded from their generous pious donations. There is also a law transmitted dealing with theft which refers to the punishment for stealing property from an empress (*btsan-mo*), sister/co-consort (*lcam*), maternal aunt (*sru*) and a lady/co-consort (*jo-mo*) (Thomas 1936: 281, 285).

One interesting question remains. The husbands of some of the empresses, for example Trimalo and Tsenmatok, the mother of Tride Tsugtsen, died young. Trimalo outlived her husband for thirty-six years and Tsenmatok outlived hers for seventeen years. Did they re-marry or were they bound to be widows? The sources do not answer this question. They are absolutely silent on the subject. Only one case, where the son of Tride Songtsen had taken over a co-consort of his father as wife, is recorded in the historical works.

In general, there is no doubt that Tibetan societies of the empire were dominated by men and that warriors were held in high esteem. As for women, due to the genre of the sources, the only ladies who are known to us were imperial consorts.[15] They played an active role outside the confines of their palaces. They ranked high in society, in fact second in place after the emperor and higher than the rulers of the vassal countries who were followed in rank by the maternal uncle-councillors. By way of matrimonial alliances, imperial princesses were entrusted to exercise state power in vassal countries. Apart from their direct intervention at the helm of state affairs, they participated in other ways too, such as when an oath was avowed for the edict of adopting Buddhism as state religion and for other edicts as well. If the need was felt, an extraordinary imperial consort even enacted a law. Given the opportunity, the outstanding Empress Trimalo did not hesitate to take the reign of the empire into her hands.

[14] Thomas 1935: 186, B 7, 385, 6. The term *stangs-dbyal*, meaning 'husband and wife', was unknown to Thomas in his pioneer translation.

[15] It is much regretted that information about ordinary women from the imperial period has not hitherto become known. In the documents found in Tibetan dominated areas of Central Asia, there is some information on women, but these pertain to the local inhabitants. Therefore these do not permit us to draw conclusions about Tibetan women.

THE WOMAN ILLUSION?

RESEARCH INTO THE LIVES OF SPIRITUALLY ACCOMPLISHED WOMEN LEADERS OF THE 11TH AND 12TH CENTURIES*

Dan Martin

When people who have, like myself, taken [rebirth] in 'low' bodies realize the meaning of the Mother of [All] Buddhas (Prajñāpāramitā), even when they transcend, through reflexive awareness, the spheres of objectifying (or goal orientation),

they still ought to grasp on to these [Cutting] teachings which, like lamps, cast light on the supreme objective.

[Commentary:] Although the words 'low bodies' might, in line with ordinary worldly conventions, signify a discarding of self-importance, still, since the woman herself is an emanation body, she cannot be 'low'. *Vajra Tent* says, 'With the illusory form of a woman, [the Buddha] teaches the Dharma for those with desire. The woman illusion, buddhahood itself, exorcises all illusions.' *Supreme Bliss* says, 'Of all illusions, the woman illusion is particularly sublime [holy].'[1] (From *Hair-Tip*, by Machig Labdron; the commentary was possibly composed by the Third Karmapa)

* Dedicated to my sister, Kim Martin. A dictionary of Tibetan women by Tashi Tsering of Dharamsala has long been in preparation for publication. Unfortunately it is not yet available to me. Claudia Seele-Nyima, Kurtis Schaeffer and Cyrus Stearns read earlier drafts of this chapter, and some of their suggestions have been incorporated here, with thanks.

[1] See Orofino 1987: 42–3, 74 (column 531) for the Tibetan text, an Italian translation, and exact references to the scriptural passages. It is quite impossible to convey the pregnant sense of this passage. Gautama Buddha's mother had a name that means [projected] 'Illusion' (Gyudrul[ma]; Māyā or Māyādevī). Insight is primarily gained through illusion (to state it differently, illusion serves as both medium and means in the pursuit of enlightenment). Insight (the main emphasis of the Prajñāpāramitā) is the Mother of All Buddhas, the source of all enlightenment. These associations are clearly intended (Labdron even identifies herself with Māyādevī at one point, Savvas 1990: 61). The statement, 'Of all illusions, the woman illusion is particularly sublime' is also found in the *Five Stages* (*Pañcakrama*); see Snellgrove 1987: I 302.

INTRODUCTION

As an approach to the study of women in Tibetan history, it is not entirely necessary to adopt a particular theoretical line. All that is required is a basic recognition that at any given point in time women have formed slightly less or, more likely, slightly more than half the population. Any attempt to do history without taking account of what women were accomplishing and contributing will be unsatisfactory, and will fail to do justice to the period under consideration. In the following, there are no great conclusions in terms of gender theory, just some research into the literary sources that might be taken as bases for further reflection and argument. The main question is simply how much can we find out about the lives of people who were (1) Tibetan-born and (2) women, who (3) lived in the eleventh through twelfth centuries and (4) achieved public recognition for spiritual accomplishment or religious leadership? Indian and Nepali Buddhist women leaders like Niguma, Gelongma Pelmo, Bharima and Drupai Gyalmo are excluded from consideration here, regardless of their undeniable importance for the Indian and Tibetan religious lineages they initiated.

Since this essay is not about eleventh through twelfth-century Tibetan women in general, but about women who were recognized for their accomplishments in the area of Buddhist religion and spirituality, we should add one important observation. If there was—and I believe this was so—a reluctance in those and later times to recognize, and therefore record for posterity, the accomplishments of women, it becomes justifiable and even necessary to magnify what evidence we do have (and this holds regardless of their potential value as models for contemporary emulation; see Willis 1999). It will then be true that our history of the past will be different from the past's sense of its own history, but as the historian more than anyone else is acutely aware, history has a history of its own, and always has. What is arguably necessary is a 'usable past'—as that term is used by Rita Gross (1993)—that will not erase the past's usages of *its* pasts, which is in itself an important object for historical exploration and understanding.

We might further reason that canonization is a temporal phenomenon, and the criteria for sainthood in the past are not at all likely to be identical to the criteria for sainthood in the present. Saint recognition may be granted many centuries after a person's death, but that person will nevertheless be every bit as holy as if they had been canonized within their own lifetimes. We might assume, although here we feel the rising heat of potential controversies, that there were in fact many more women than those mentioned in the sources who led accomplished Buddhist lives and were influential during their times, but nevertheless were marginalized or even left out of the historical record because of a tendency to exclude them from the (over the next centuries progressively more and more) predominating male monastic institutions who reserved for themselves responsibility for the record keeping. Tibetan Buddhism, unlike Roman Catholicism, never had a formal legal mechanism for saint canonization. In Tibet, canonization (if we may call it such) was a question of record keeping, of history and biography writing, depending on the continuity of particular spiritual lineages.

It is just a fact that much less is known about accomplished women during this time than is known about accomplished men. With some effort, I could compile a list of over a hundred religious men with clear identities—including birth dates and in most cases death dates as well—born between the years 1100 and 1178. To do the same for women, I came to realize, would be much more complex since it is very difficult to establish clear identities for most of them (in many cases we are left with little more than a name), and they are rarely supplied with birth and death dates. I would estimate very roughly that the sum total of biographical information available for women leaders of the eleventh and twelfth centuries is about one or two per cent, as compared to ninety-nine or ninety-eight per cent for the men. The disparity has a distinctly blinding glare.[2]

There are a number of difficult questions regarding women during this period. For example, were there active nunneries in Tibet during this time? Were the nuns fully ordained as *bhikṣuṇīs*? Were the nuns active, influential and respected in their local communities or regions? Were there sectarian differences in the recognition of laypersons' spiritual accomplishments? Was there a tendency in the Tibetan historical tradition to obscure or confound the contributions by ordained or laywomen religious leaders? Were the circumstances of women's lives such that they were less likely to achieve prominence? In the following, we hope to beam some thin rays of light on a few of these more particular historical issues, without necessarily proposing overwhelming 'conclusions'. We will start with the most famous women, without going into much detail about their lives, since there exists already a literature about them that is easily available in English.

[2] One further refinement should be added here. Tibetan personal names do not often carry explicit gender markers. Even when they do, men's names may, rather often, contain feminine gender elements (like the endings '*-mo*' and '*-ma*' in Lhamo, 'goddess' and Drolma, Sanskrit Tārā). Unless unambiguously feminine-gendered terms like 'cham' (*lcam*) or 'jomo' (*jo-mo*) are used, or unless the context clarifies matters, we cannot be sure if a figure was a woman or not. There is also the problem that names of men like Rechungpa or Kunden Repa may be confounded with the women's names Rechungma and Kunden Rema. Women's names not supplied with feminine gender markers of some sort may be, and have been, taken for men's names. A name with an apparent feminine gender marker like Yumo or Shen Dormo (both appear later on) might be mistakenly assumed to belong to a woman.

THE THREE BEST-KNOWN WOMEN

To begin with, by far the best known of women leaders for posterity was Machig Labdron. Labdron, perhaps the most significant disciple of Phadampa Sangye, is most famous for the 'Cutting' ('Cho'; *gCod*) lineages which flowed from her into the Nyingma, Kagyu and, still later, the Gelug sects.[3] All her teachings were 'received' Buddhist teachings, conveying the esoteric sense of the Perfection of Insight,[4] but she might have been responsible for bringing these received teachings into an array centred on the metaphor of Cutting, meaning a spiritually sophisticated 'exorcism' of the outer and inner 'demons' that hinder the unfolding of full knowledge (*jñāna*) and complete enlightenment. The Tibetan sources provide widely differing dates for her. Even though modern authors may confidently state her birth and death years, they are not to be trusted.[5] She

[3] The question of the possible priority of Bon in the history of Cutting teachings is one that I will not go into here, although it is certainly worth pursuing. See Chaoul 1999. For a general analytical study of Tibetan historical and biographical sources for both Cutting and Peacemaking (*Zhi-byed*) teachings see Kollmar-Paulenz 1993.

[4] The historical emergence of Cutting is quite a difficult issue (as are its differences from Peacemaking). Some of these Buddhist teachings are believed to have been received by Labdron through direct visionary encounters with high forms of Buddha. (There is a very useful discussion of this issue in Gyatso 1985: 331–3.) A text of the Indian Cutting teachings by the Brahmin Āryadeva (who certainly is not the famous one by that name (ibid.: 326) exists in two different Tibetan translations. The Tibetan translation used by the Cutting tradition itself, accomplished by Phadampa alone, but then written down and edited by Zhama Lotsawa (brother of Machig Zhama, on whom more will be said shortly), is available in English in Edou 1996: 15–23. Although Labdron is often portrayed in more recent sources as a long time disciple of Phadampa, this is probably not historically accurate. The *Peacemaking Collection* (Kun-dga' 1979, vol. 2: 313) does say, 'He [Phadampa] had no more than one personal conversation with Majo Chonema. She was a wild woman [*mo rgod-ma*]', and this 'Chonema' has been identified as referring to Labdron (Chos-kyi 1992: 49; cf. Roerich 1976: 982). She does merit a single mention ('Zangri Machig Lamdron') in an early thirteenth century history contained in the *Peacemaking Collection* (Kun-dga' 1979, vol. 4: 346), as one who received the Cutting precepts from Phadampa during his 'middle' visit to Tibet. It is entirely possible that the true origins of Cutting are to be found in teachings given by Phadampa, during his previous visit to Tibet, to Kyo Shakya Yeshe, who then passed them on to Labdron (see the discussion in Edou 1996: 37). This line of argument might make Labdron the founder not of Cutting but rather of the more specific lineage known as Women's Cutting (*mo-gcod*).

[5] The dates that have been proposed for her birth include the years 1031, 1055, 1099, 1102 and 1103. The dates 1055 to 1154 (as in Savvas 1990: 3) or 1055 to 1149 (as in Kollmar-Paulenz 1993: xi, but note, too, on p. 70, the dates 1049–1155) seem the most likely, although they are far from being well-established. Her age at death ranges from ninety-one to ninety-nine. There are some sources on her life, so far not utilized, in *gCod tshogs* 1985, and this volume also includes several of the works she composed. The dates for Phadampa Sangye, too, are unsettled, although I believe that his period of greatest

most probably lived from about the middle of the eleventh century to about the middle of the twelfth. Since there is a considerable amount of material available in English, we will say no more about her here.[6]

Probably the second most illustrious woman of the times was Machig Zhama.[7] She was famous for a particular lineage of 'Path Including Result' ('Lamdre'; *Lam-'bras*) teachings,[8] primarily absorbed by the other Path Including Result lineages that flowed through Sakya lineages, although it also entered into various eclectic traditions of other schools in the late twelfth and thirteenth centuries. Unique among the women religions leaders of her times, her dates are quite clear and uncontroversial.

---

influence was his stay in Dingri that lasted from about 1097 until his death in 1117 (see Chos-kyi 1992: 61, 117). A large number of other dates have been given in the Tibetan sources.

[6] A brief biography is supplied in Allione 1986: 150–87, another is found in Crook and Low 1997: 297–315, and still another in Savvas 1990: 52–81. For an important discussion of the biographical sources see Kollmar-Paulenz 1998. A major monographic study, Edou 1996, contains a translation of the same biography translated by Allione, noting the critical comments in the review by Herrmann-Pfandt 2001. For remarkable studies of texts composed by Labdron, see Orofino 1987, where there are Italian translations of *bKa tshoms chen mo* and the *Insight's Hair-Tip* (*Shes rab skra rtse*, with its commentary attributed to Karmapa III Rangchung Dorje). See also Savvas 1990: 154–94, where we find a translation of Labdron's *Eight Added Chapters on the Teachings Extraordinarily* (Pertaining to Cutting) (*Thun mong ma yin pa le lag brgyad*). I am aware of many other studies on Cutting, but will not list them all here. More works by Labdron remain untranslated, although they have been available to the world now for decades in the reprinting of the *gDams ngag mdzod*. According to Chos-kyi 1992: 232 and Gang-pa 1992: 316, there was a complete set of Labdron's works (a *bka'-'bum*) which included most prominently the texts with the titles *Bka' tshom chen mo, Yang tshom chen mo, Nying tshom le'u lag, gNad them, Khong rgol, gSang ba brda' chos la bzla skor gsum, gZhi lam du slong ba* and *Khyad par gyi gdams ngag*. All of these just-mentioned titles were put in writing during her last years, and were translated into an Indian language. Most of these titles have in fact been preserved in the collection known as *Treasury of Precepts* (*gDams ngag mdzod;* for English translations of the titles, see Edou 1996: 163; see also Kollmar-Paulenz 1993: 193–4).

[7] English literature on Machig Zhama, not nearly so abundant, includes Diemberger and Hazod 1994 and Lo Bue 1994: 482. Also available in English is Roerich 1976: 210, 219–226, 229–30, 919, but be aware of the confusion in this translation of the two identities of Labdron and Zhama, first noticed in Gyatso 1985: 329. One of the most important sources, given its relatively early date, is the *Zhib mo rdo rje*, a history of Path Including Result teachings composed somewhere between 1216 and 1244 (see Stearns 2001 where more details about Zhama's life are to be found).

[8] The Path Including Result teachings originated in a vision of the divine consort of Hevajra, named Nairātmyā (Tib. *bDag-med-ma*, [f.] 'Non-self'), beheld by the Mahāsiddha Virūpa. It was first taught by a divine female form of Buddha (a 'focus of high aspirations', a *yi-dam*). The fourth member in the line of transmission, the lay master Gayadhāra (d. 1103), brought these teachings to Tibet in the year 1041, where they were (orally) translated into Tibetan by Drogmi (on whom, see below). For more details see ibid.

She lived from 1062 to 1149 CE. Various forms of her name are Zham, Zhama Chungma, Zha Chungma (Zhwa Chungma[9] and Zhang Chungma also occur, although the latter, like Zham, may be considered a mistake) and Lhajema. She had a quite well-known younger brother named Khonphuwa Chokyi Gyaltsen (1069–1144), and so she may also be referred to as 'Sister of Khonphuwa'. Her youngest brother was to become Zhama Lotsawa Senge Gyalpo, a translator responsible for many canonical translations from Indian language works still found in the Tengyur collection. She was born in southern Tibet, in Phadrug, the fourth of six (some say seven) children and the only daughter. Her father's real name was Zhama Dorje Gyaltsen (d. 1098), although he also had the curious nickname 'Mouse Quarrel' (*byi-ba hab-sha*). Her mother was called Gyagar Lhamo ('Indian Goddess'). In her fourteenth year, a marriage was arranged for her with one Aba Lhagyal, but she found married life uninspiring and turned her mind toward religion, eventually escaping her unhappy marriage by pretending to be insane.[10] From age sixteen through twenty-one, she was a *mudrā* or 'consort' (*phyag-rgya-ma*) of the Ma translator Gewe Lodro (1044–89). When she was twenty-seven, Ma was poisoned to death, and she had to go to Shab to arrange for his cremation. In her early thirties she struggled against seven difficult obstacles, including serious medical conditions, and in part in order to find a cure, she visited the widely renowned Indian teacher Phadampa Sangye. Apart from him, she studied with a long list of teachers, including Vairocana, the Oriyan translator and teacher of the radical spiritual songs of the Mahāsiddhas.[11] Most crucial for posterity was her meeting with Seton Kunrig, since it was through him that she received the Path Including Result teachings

[9] The name Zhachungma (meaning 'She of the Small Hat') is said to have been given by Drapa Ngonshe to Machig Labdron (see Kollmar-Paulenz 1993: 139). However, in Choskyi 1992: 96 and in the text on the 24 jomos (discussed below), it is clearly a name for Machig Zhama.

[10] Feigning insanity in order to escape duties or responsibilities is especially well known in the history of Chinese Daoism, but cases of it are known in Tibetan history as well. For examples, see Roerich 1976: 99, 1030. Of course, psychologically speaking, impossible social conditions, in particular an unbearable family life, may strongly contribute to genuine mental problems. It may be, too, that the perception of such psychological disturbances as 'feigned' or 'real' may also depend in some part on a process of social recognition (saints are never 'really' insane…). On the other hand, feigning insanity, since it is conscious and calculated, would seem to be quite distinct from the utterly free and spontaneous activities of the mad Buddhist saint, as depicted in Ardussi and Epstein 1978 and Silver 1987; compare the discussion of *zhig-po* and *zhig-mo* below. The first kind of insanity breaks oppressive social ties *in order* to practise religion, while the second is a *celebration* of spiritual attainment.

[11] On Vairocana (A.K.A. Vairocanarakṣita or Vairocanavajra) see Martin 1992: 254–5 and Schaeffer 2000.

which would be passed on in subsequent centuries under the name 'The Zhama System of Path Including Result' (*Lam-'bras Zha-ma-lugs*). During the later years of her life (beginning approximately at age forty), she travelled about teaching together with her brother Khonphuwa, and their fame spread far and wide.

There is an interesting story about her relationship with her nephew, the son of Khonphuwa, who would later become a significant Path Including Result teacher. His name was Lhaje Dawa Ozer (1123–82).[12] His mother died when he was two, and he was raised by his aunt Zhama, about sixty at the time, who, it is said, nourished him with milk from her finger for the first ten years of his life. Dawa Ozer spent most of his later years in Nepal, but he was able to amass a considerable fortune, and he erected the two silver reliquaries for enshrining the remains of his father and his aunt. Among the famous men who received esoteric teachings from Zhama were Khyung Tsangpa and Phagmo Drupa. Zhang Rinpoche received (and practised) her lineage indirectly, through his teachers Lingkawa and Yerpawa. Yangonpa eventually made known the titles of three of her instructions on the 'intermediate state' (*bar-do*) between death and rebirth. Unfortunately, nothing longer than a few lines of her teachings seems to survive in writing.[13] The degree of the impact her teaching activities had on Path Including Result lineages that *have* survived is one of those unfortunate historical unknowns.[14]

A third figure who will not be discussed here in detail, although she must belong to the twelfth century, is Nangsa Obum, native to the region that includes the town of Gyantse. Her story has been summarized and translated a number of times.[15] It is very difficult to judge the historicity

[12] His story is to be found in Roerich 1976: 229–32. A biography of both him and his father was written by one Joton Wangchuk Drak, but I have been unable to learn about its present existence. The account of Zhama causing a jet of milk to fall from her ring finger may be connected to the idea that saints no longer have ordinary blood, but milk instead (the story is told, for example, about her near contemporary Khyung Tsangpa).

[13] One brief passage has been identified in Stearns 2001. I have noticed two further brief samples of her teachings in 'Jig-rten 1969–71, vol. 5: 85.

[14] There are some general discussions of the Path Including Result transmissions, for example Mang-thos 1988: 133 and Kong-sprul 1985, vol 1: 522–3, which would at least indicate that the Zhama system was adopted or mixed into still other Path Including Result transmissions. Still, there is nothing in these sources about what in particular the Zhama system contributed. It is interesting that Kong-sprul 1985 names three direct disciples of Zhama herself, one of which was a woman who was evidently a locally prominent political leader, named Ponmo Shertsul, who continued one of the Zhama lineage streams. A 'ponmo' (*dpon-mo*) is a woman chieftain of a local administrative area (of a township or *rdzong*).

[15] For examples, Allione 1986: 61–140; Bacot 1936; Cunningham 1940; Ross 1995: 83–90 and Waddell 1972: 553–65. The Tibetan text has been published several times in differing versions. Because of her association with Rechungpa (1084–1161) among others

of her life, but even if it is in some part fiction, as is often the case, fiction can be made to tell cultural truths larger than any set of supposed facts. Her involuntary marriage, her thwarted desire to lead a life of religion, and the injustices she suffered at the hands of her in-laws reflect the experiences of many Tibetan women in history, which may largely explain her story's popularity. It belongs to the 'delog' (*'das-log*) genre in that it includes an account of her return from the dead. It is extremely popular as a subject for laypeople's masked dance-opera performances called 'lhamo' (*lha-mo*; 'goddess'), and might also be told at home, or by a more professional storyteller (*ma-ṇi-pa*) in the marketplace illustrating the story by pointing to a scroll painting with narrative scenes. It certainly provided Tibetan women with a model for transcendence, as well as an at least partial mirror of their social situations.

All the remaining women covered in the following pages share one characteristic besides their gender, and that is that there is relatively little literary information on them, and generally not much prospect of drawing out a complete biographical sketch. I have arbitrarily divided them into the categories of (1) prophets, (2) disciples, (3) lineage holders (which ought to include the lineage founders Labdron and Zhama), (4) leaders of popular religious movements, (5) teachers, and (6) nuns, with the recognition that these categories are based on the roles they play in the limited literary references we have located. The categorical lines are blurred, and increasingly so the more we learn about them. In particular, the women in the category of lineage holders are likely, at some point in their biographies, to have filled most or all of the other roles.

PROPHETS

Primarily known for her prophetic role is one Ngulmo Gyale Cham. She was a disciple of Dzeng Dharmabodhi (1052–1168) who was in turn a disciple of Phadampa and Labdron and many other luminaries of the day. While he followed the Cutting and other esoteric teachings, Dzeng's greatest fame was due to his spreading of the Nyingma teachings known as Vajra Bridge, and his rather unusual ascetic practices which would remind us today of 'extreme sports' (or of Japanese Shugendō). For five

(Milarepa and Phadampa are also mentioned), she must belong to the late eleventh or more likely twelfth century. I have not yet been able to locate her name in the biographies of Rechungpa. One source, which renders her name Nangsa Odebum, after telling how she was forced against her will to marry a chief after she was seen at the festival at Gyantse, quite improbably has her go on to become the famous wife of Marpa named Damema (Khyung-po 1984: 29–33; a translation of this important woman's biography is said to be forthcoming). On delog stories in general, see in particular Epstein 1982.

years he wandered about Tsang Province stark naked, taking high-dives into icy waters, leaping into abysses, striking his head with rocks and burning himself alive. His biography mentions that he gave esoteric precepts to Ngulmo, which included the *Four Statements* (*Yi ge bzhi pa*) and the Great Perfectedness.[16] She is referred to here as a 'superhuman madwoman' (*zhig-mo*). We are accustomed to seeing this word in the masculine form (*zhig-po*), which means a person who has totally dissolved (*zhig-pa*) ordinary clinging to the concept of self as well as the usual bonds of social life. 'Madmen' and 'madwomen' are people who act out their realization of Buddhist truths in unconventional, 'crazy' ways.[17]

The only other known episode of Ngulmo's life would be the prophetic statements she made to Ten-ne (a follower of Phadampa's Peacemaking [*Zhi-byed*] teachings, he lived 1127–1217), explaining how he obtained his name. There are three literary sources of this story known to me (Chos-kyi 1992: 210; Roerich 1976: 930–1; Kun-dga' 1979 vol. 4: 405). The story may be paraphrased as follows:

When Ten-ne was three years old, he asked his mother, 'Where is the region of Mal Tsondru Lama?' His mother replied, 'In the gorge of Lhodrag. Why do you want to know?' 'Because these are the region and name of my previous rebirth,' he responded.

Years later, when Ten-ne reached his twenty-fifth year, he conceived the idea to visit what had been his home country in his previous rebirth in the gorge of Lhodrag. On his way, in Yamdrok, the region surrounding the famous lake by that name, he met two lamas from Emnyal[18] and the three of them went about begging. His two new companions recommended that together they should visit the nearby La-u Monastery before going on to Lhodrag, saying that there was to be found in that monastery a group of chaplains who had dissolved worldly bonds

[16] Das 1992: 177–180 and Roerich 1976: 180–1. Mentioned here, too, is a 'nun' (*ma-jo*) who vanished without leaving any trace at a lake called Monkha Zermo. 'Majo' is a title of problematic meaning used with some frequency in genuinely twelfth century works which then became obsolete (and is not in any dictionary). It is possible that it is a contraction of *ma-gcig jo-mo*. My impression is that it means something more than simply 'nun', perhaps 'abbess' or 'nun teacher.' One way Phadampa would address Labdron was 'Majo Chonema', according to Chos-kyi 1992: 49 and Roerich 1976: 982, in which Chonema means 'woman chaplain.' For sources on the *Four Statements*, an especially esoteric Kagyu Mahāmudrā transmission based on the words of Saraha delivered to Marpa in a dream, see Martin 1984: 91–2.

[17] In Roerich 1976: 181, *zhig-mo* is translated 'one who had abandoned all worldly laws', but elsewhere in Roerich 1976: 132, *zhig-po* is translated 'mad ascetic.' Don-grub 1985: 585 defines *zhig-po* as *bdag-'dzin zhig-pa-po*, 'one who has dissolved selfish grasping (to the illusion of the self).' It seems to be more or less closely synonymous with the appelative *'khrul-zhig(-pa)*, 'one who has dissolved erroneous appearances', further interpreted as one who has realized emptiness (see Roerich 1976: 960).

[18] This refers to E and Nyal, two adjacent regions, both located to the east of Tsetang along the Brahmaputra river. Lhodrag is close to the modern northern border of Bhutan.

(*mchod-gnas zhig-po*) serving a Tulku Se Jo-se. One of the four, they said, was Majo Gyale Cham, an old beggar woman who was always laughing but possessed the powers of clairvoyance. Before telling the story, it is necessary to know that, at the time, Ten-ne had the name Jo-se Jigten Drak. When they met with Gyale Cham she didn't speak to the other two men, but grabbed Jigten Drak by the hand and exclaimed, 'Goodness! Goodness! If it isn't big brother Ten-ne! What a surprise! What a surprise! Drink from these breasts of mine! Child, don't go to Lhodrag gorge! The house of Nang went to war and was destroyed without a trace. Child, your teacher is in the northern sun, so do go to Uru and there you will meet the son of Yemo Peldren.'[19] On the basis of this prophecy, Ten-ne eventually located his teacher Patsab[20] and received the complete one-on-one transmission of the Peacemaking teachings.

Another prophet was Dremo. The very name means 'old woman', and therefore is more likely a nickname than a proper name. It is said that Ngok Do-de (1090–1166), while staying at some springs in Tsang province, was preparing to visit his consort one evening when a woman *siddhā* appeared at his doorstep and said, 'If you go tonight there may be an accident. But if you go tomorrow night an exceptional child will be born.' This prophecy came true in 1115 when his son Tsangtsa Jotsul was born (Roerich 1976: 408–9).[21]

This Dremo is almost certainly the same as a known disciple of Rechungpa (1083–1161). The story goes that Rechungpa was travelling through the gorge of Nub territory when, 'At a place called Pangchen, one of his disciples was bitten by a dog, forcing them to stay there a few

[19] The implication of this story is, according to my current understanding, that Gyale Cham had been Ten-ne's sister in his previous live as Mal Tsongdru Lama in Lhodrag. As one proof of her familiarity, she addressed him with a childhood nickname from his previous life Ten-ne, which thereafter stuck as his name in his present life. It is also possible that Gyale Cham made the nickname Ten-ne on the basis of the second syllable of the name Jigten Drak. The son of Yemo Peldren may easily be identified as Ten-ne's teacher Patsab Tsultrim Bar (1077–1158), in his turn a disciple of Phadampa's student Kunga (see Roerich 1976: 923, 925).

[20] His biography is found at Chos-kyi 1992: 205, where his name is rendered Batsab Gompa. He was born in Lower Phenyul to the father Batsab Ton Bumdrak and mother Yemo Peldren in the year 1077. He barely missed meeting Phadampa himself (when Patsab arrived at Dingri, Phadampa was on his funeral pyre), which made him quite despondent, but a beggar woman, a hidden yoginī, reassured him and made a prophecy which sent him to study with Phadampa's student Kunga. This is yet another example of a woman's prophecy helping people to find their way to their most important spiritual teacher. According to Roerich 1976: 929, Ten-ne met Patsab in 1150, and the latter died in 1158, at age eighty-two (i.e., eighty-one).

[21] A longer (and probably later) biography of Rechungpa, rGod-tshang 1992: 378–9, contains a fairly closely parallel passage, except that the 'few days' are instead 'a few months', the disciple bitten by the dog is named Rinchen Drak, and a few other small pieces of information are provided. The same story is told more briefly in rTa-tshag 1994: 55.

days. During this time, he gave initiations and precepts to one Jomo Tsunma, who was quite amazed at this, and said not to bite a still more serious bite than that dog (?). Then the woman went to her own home area, Shambu. There she meditated and turned out to be a *siddhā* known as Jomo Dremo.'[22]

There were other women by the same name (well, the same apart from minor spelling differences), and they are already confounded with each other in the sources. One Jomo Dremo of Rong Chutsen ('Hot Springs Gorge') had been a disciple of the eighth-century Indian teacher Vimalamitra (Roerich 1976: 126, 177). The *Blue Annals*' author believes that this eighth century woman was the same one who made the prophecy to Ngok Do-de, 'This Sgre-mo [Dremo] was a great *siddhā* and lived long. It is said that Vimalamitra had entrusted to her many Vajrayānic tantras. Sgre-mo's prophecy came true…' (Roerich 1976: 409). It seems just possible that, as the same author suggests, our prophet Dremo was the same nun who presented Atiśa with a gift of a model horse made of gold with a turquoise boy riding on it (Roerich 1976: 256). However, it hardly seems possible that, regardless of how 'old' her name might seem to make her, she could have been quite so long-lived as to last from the eighth century into the twelfth.

One woman known to us simply as 'The Mad Woman of Lhasa' (*lHa-sa'i sMyon-ma*) had a role in the discovery of the so-called 'Pillar Testament' (*bKa' chems ka bkol ma*). This might merit her placement among the prophets.[23]

We might also mention, although she does not fit our criteria since she was not a Tibetan but an Indian (or Nepali?), the yoginī Metok ('Flower', perhaps her real name was Puṣpā). A story of her prophetic statements

[22] Rwa lung 1975: 217. She is mentioned again later in the text in a list of Rechungpa's disciples, where she is called Jomo Dremo of Tsang (p. 222). The name, the appellative *siddhā*, the location in Tsang, as well as the period are all shared by both the prophet and the disciple. Therefore they must be identical. There was another woman disciple of Rechungpa named Rechungma (not the same as the disciple of Milarepa called Rechungma!) whose story should also be studied. She meditated at Namtso, and when she died at Semodo (an island in the lake Namtso), she did not leave a body behind (her story is alluded to in Roerich 1976: 439, and told in greater detail in the biographies of Rechungpa). Kurtis Schaeffer pointed out to me a third important woman disciple of Rechungpa named Tsun Chungma, born to the Yo family of Loro region. She must have been born in about 1102 CE, because in her sixteenth year she wanted to travel to Dingri to meet Phadampa, but on the way she learned of his death (in 1117). Her story is told in rGod-tshang 1992: 466–76, where she is credited with the supreme attainment of Mahāmudrā before dematerializing into a blaze of light in her forty-eighth year. There are other names listed among his disciples that clearly belonged to women, names like Lhachig Dembu, Denza Lhasang and Jomo Yango, although I have not located biographical information about them yet.

[23] Her story has been told in German in Eimer 1983.

made during her visit to Tibet in about 1160, may be found in English elsewhere (Roerich 1976: 135–7).[24] As an example of the many more obscure prophetic women, we might mention the unnamed woman at Tangkya, a returnee from death, who prophesied to Taglung Tangpa (founder of the Taglung lineage, he lived 1142–1210) about the future gathering of his disciples (ibid.: 611).[25]

DISCIPLES

I decided not to lay much emphasis on women who were disciples of famous religious figures, mainly because disciples, as such, are followers, not leaders. Nevertheless, it may be that many of these achieved publicly (or at the very least literarily) recognized signs of advanced spiritual attainment, or that they in fact had leadership roles or lineages that have since been obscured. Therefore they do belong here, and we will mention some of their names.

We begin with the eleventh-century women disciples of Drogmi. His full name being Drogmi Lotsawa Shakya Yeshe, he is best remembered for introducing the Path Including Result teachings into Tibet. The initiator of the Sakya tradition, Khon Konchok Gyalpo, was among his followers. He was also a translator from Indian languages. His dates are not very certain, but they might be 993 to 1050 (or 1077?). Among a group of seven disciples who achieved 'accomplishments' (*siddhis*), four were women: Tomo Dorje Tso, Sangmo Kon-ne, Shabmo Chamchig and Chemo Namkha.[26]

Among the disciples of that most famous of Tibetan yogins, Milarepa, are his sister Peta and his childhood fiancé Dze-se. According to Sangye Darpo's sixteenth-century history, five women—Peta, Dze-se, Drichamma, Sa-le O and Peldar Bum—were among Milarepa's disciples that entered the sky life without leaving physical bodies behind, a traditional 'sign of saintly death'. It lists separately a group of his disciples, 'the four sisters',

24 The story is also of some interest because it mentions the receiving of a Vajrayāna initiation by a (Tibetan) woman named Wangmo (or Wang Chungma, or Jomo Wangmo, she was the mother of the famous Nyingma teacher Zhigpo Dutsi, 1149–99).

25 Jigten Gonpo's mother gave a neighbour who had been bereaved a lesson in impermanence which Jigten Gonpo later said was the highest Mahāmudrā teaching, and his grandmother was evidently elevated to become a spiritual guardian of the Drigung school; see Das 1992: 90–1, 110–11.

26 These names are according to Roerich 1976: 208. The first three of these women achieved the accomplishments within a single human embodiment. The fourth achieved only the ordinary *siddhis* (i.e. miraculous powers). Elsewhere, their names appear in the forms Tomo Dorje Tso, Tre Goma Kon-ne, Shabamo Chamchig and Chemo Namkhamo (see Madrong 1997: 73, in turn based on Grags-pa 1968a: 174). Mang-thos 1988 lists the four names as (1) Shamo Chamchig, (2) Chemo Namkha, (3) Semo Ko-ne and (4) Tomo Dorje Tso. More details about these women, based primarily on so-far extremely rare sources, are available in Stearns 2001.

as Rechungma of Tsonga, Sa-le O of Nyanang, Peldar Bum of Chung and Chamo Beta (i.e., his sister Peta).[27] It would seem that another interesting woman disciple would be Shen Dormo, said to have entered the initial stage of the spiritual path at the moment of death.[28] However, Shen Dormo was most definitely a man.[29] Their stories will not be told here, but it is interesting to notice that most of the women disciples of Milarepa tend to be referred to with the rather unusual term *nya-ma*, an obsolete word, still remembered but difficult to define or etymologize. There are times when the word is used to cover both disciples and patrons regardless of gender.[30]

Of other early Kagyu teachers—three of Rechungpa's women disciples have been mentioned already[31]—we might mention that Gampopa

[27] Sangs-rgyas n.d.: 51. I was able to make use of a photocopy of this manuscript thanks to E. Gene Smith. Unfortunately, large portions of it are nearly or entirely illegible. (For more on this work see Martin 1997: no. 167. Kurtis Schaeffer has informed me that other copies are to be found in the Nepali National Archives.) Accounts of all these women may be found in Milarepa's famous biography and song collection, available in English in Lhalungpa 1977 and Chang 1977. Account of Peldarbum ('Bardarbom') in Chang 1977: 136–48; Sa-le O ('Sahle Aui') in Chang 1977: 408–20 and Rechungma in Chang 1977: 259–74. The chapter about Sa-le O was composed by Ngendzong Tonpa, himself a disciple of Milarepa. The history by Nyang-ral 1988: 493 mentions, unfortunately without listing the individual names, a group of nine women disciples of Milarepa who were *siddhās* (*grub-thob-ma*).

[28] On Shen Dormo (i.e., 'Shindormo'), see Chang 1977: 11–2, 23, 33, 552–7; rendered 'rDor-mo' in Roerich 1976: 434 and 'Shen Dormo' in Lhalungpa 1977: 151. In all these English-language sources he is identified as a woman.

[29] I thank Stearns for pointing this out to me. The song collection of Milarepa, in the original Tibetan, says that the patron (*yon-bdag*, not *yon-bdag-mo*) Shen Dormo had the greatest faith in Milarepa from the beginning, that he and his spouse Legse (Bum) invited Milarepa to Tsarma. Another clue that Shen Dormo was a man is that he is never listed among the women disciples of Milarepa. Like Shen Dormo, Legse Bum is said to have entered the initial stage of the path, only in her case this occurred when she was still living ('Lesebum'; see Chang 1977: 562). Although considered a very significant step, this is quite far from attaining the direct vision of the truth which signals the beginning of 'sainthood' (*'phags-pa*). However, dPa'-bo 1980: 784 mentions the disciple (*nya-ma*) Legse in a list of six women disciples who 'went to the sky life in their present incarnations' (these six names evidently are those of the 'six women *siddhās* who kept the appearance of being householders'; also mentioned, without listing, are the 'twelve cotton-clad women' [*ras-ma bcu-gnyis*]).

[30] However, in cases where both genders are intended, the expression would be *nya-ma pho-mo-rnams*, 'disciples both male and female'; it is interesting here that the inclusive term for all his disciples is formed upon the term for his women patrons/disciples. The word *nya-ma* is further discussed in Uebach 1990: 343, citing its single occurrence in the *sBa bzhed*.

[31] Although we have no other information apart from her name, there was among the four main disciples of Tsangpa Sumpa (one of the most famous of the disciples of Rechungpa) a woman named Jomo Dron-ne of Tsang. She must date to the late twelfth or early thirteenth centuries. There is reference to her in the brief fifteenth-century Kagyu history by Drugchen II (for bibliographical reference see Martin 1997: no. 126). It is possible that she could be identical to the Majo Dron-ne who was a teacher of Zhang Yudragpa (1123–93).

wrote a few of his works for the benefit of a 'woman patron of Olkha'. Since these texts include quite advanced Mahāmudrā instructions, we may assume that she was among his more spiritually advanced students.[32] Her story would seem to be just one more story of a remarkable woman unfortunately left untold.

There were three groups of Machig Labdron's disciples who are said to have held her lineage. The second group is called the 'four daughters', but we have no information about them apart from their names and localities.[33] Also in the Cutting lineage, we might mention Chamo Ladu, a.k.a. Drubchungma, born to Machig Labdron when the latter was in her thirtieth year; and Lantogma, daughter of Tonyon Samdrub.[34] We save our comments on the largest group of women disciples, totalling twenty-four, for later discussion.

Sachen Kunga Nyingpo (1092–1158) had a group of three women disciples. Their names are simply listed as (1) Jocham Phurmo, the mother of his son Kunga Bar, (2) Jomo Ba-u-ma (or A-u-ma) of Yalung and (3) Jomo Mangchungma of Mangkhar.[35]

LINEAGE HOLDERS

'Lineage holder' is here defined not only as a person who holds the main teachings (secret precepts and the like) from a particular teacher, but one

32 Olkha is a region within Lhokha (a general name for the area around the great bend in the Brahmaputra river). It is unfortunate not to be able to further identify this patron/disciple. Even her proper name is not known (but it is certainly possible it was preserved in one of the many biographical accounts of Gampopa). Although Gampopa had already spent some time in Olkha before, he met this woman patron during one of his lengthy retreats in Olkha after the death of Milarepa (therefore, in the late 1120s or 1130s).

33 Their names are listed in *gCod tshogs* 1985: 94; in Kollmar-Paulenz 1993: 200, 244, 248; in Chos-kyi 1992: 233 and in Savvas 1990: 73. Even their names are spelled in very different ways. It might prove possible to put together scattered pieces of information about Gyanema (whom I believe to be identical to the first of the 'four daughters', Lablung Drotsa Gyen).

34 On Ladu see Edou 1996: 91, 93, 108–10, 114–15, 145, 154, 196n. 42; Gang-pa 1992: 285; Kollmar-Paulenz 1993: 71, 144 and Savvas 1990: 71. There is confusion in the sources as to whether her father Tonyon Samdrub was Labdron's son or her great-grandson. On Lantogma see Edou 1996: 115, 163, 196n. 42; Gang-pa 1992: 320 and 'Len-sto-ma' in Kollmar-Paulenz 1993: 198. A daughter of Tonyon by the name Namkha Gyen is said to have shocked Jigten Gonpo into taking monastic vows by running into his presence naked (see Roerich 1976: 597; Jigten Gonpo was known for being extremely scrupulous about avoiding even the least physical contact with women). Padma dKar-po 1968: 426 mentions, without listing any individual names, a group of Tonyon's disciples called the 'eighteen daughter *siddhās*,' and says that from them the Women's Cutting (*mo spyod*, i.e. *mo gcod*) lineages spread. There is considerable confusion about Ladu and Lantogma in the sources, which requires sorting out. Lantogma may belong to a later century.

35 This is based on Mang-thos 1988: 131.

who also passed them on in a lineage significant for posterity. Apart, of course, from Labdron and Zhama, one of the most intriguing female personalities in this category was one Jobum, important for holding a place in the transmission of the Kālacakra tantra of the Dro system. Her location in the lineage clearly places her in the twelfth century. Her father's name was Dharmeśvara (a Sanskritized form of his Tibetan name Chokyi Wangchuk), while her grandfather was Yumo,[36] both of them very important figures in the early history of Kālacakra in Tibet. Her brother, Semo Chewa Namkha Gyaltsen, although he suffered in childhood from serious speech and hearing problems, went on to master the extensive Kālacakra commentary known as *Vimalaprabhā* and the practices of the Six-Limbed Yoga. The brief account of Jobum in the *Blue Annals* translates as follows:

> The daughter of Dharmeśvara was Jobum. In her childhood, she was urged by her mother to study magic (*mthu*) and destroyed many enemies. After that she practised the Six Limbed Yoga, and during that same incarnation became a saint (*'phags-pa-mo*) of equal fortune to the naturally born yoginīs.[37]

She appears in a—for the most part—quite standard lineage of the Dro system of Kālacakra by Tsewang Norbu, where a single line, with added refrain, is devoted to each lineage holder. Her line reads: 'Chief of all who live their lives in the sky [the *ḍākinīs*], [attainer of the] rainbow body, Jobumma. [Refrain:] I pray to you, hold me in your thoughts with compassion. You hold the lineage; bless me to have a life comparable to yours.' (Kaḥ-thog 1979)[38] She is preceded in the lineage by her father, and after her comes her student Jamsar Sherab Ozer, although it is curious that she is not mentioned in the role of teacher in the latter's biographical account

[36] Yumo studied directly with the Kashmiri Kālacakra master Somanātha. Some of Yumo's Kālacakra treatises, although falsely attributed to others in the published version, have miraculously survived. See Stearns 1999: 44–5 for more on Yumo and his treatises. Stearns (1996; 1999) has written the most valuable studies of the Six Limbed Yoga. For Yumo's Kālacakra treatises, which have been mistakenly published under the authorship of Buton Rinchen Drub, see Yu-mo 1983, and note (on p. 13, line 1) that Jobum does occur in a lineage prayer (*not* by Yumo) appended to the first treatise (although it spells her name *Ma-1 Lo-'bum*).

[37] Based on 'Gos 1974: 675–6; see the English translation in Roerich 1976: 768.

[38] Checking the lineage of the Dro system in the 'record of teachings received' (*thob-yig*) by the Seventh Dalai Lama (Dalai 1983, vol. 11: 222), one may observe that Tulku Jobum (nothing here indicates her gender) is indeed included. Still, there is a footnote attached informing us that the name does not appear in the Dro lineages as included in some seven other *thob-yigs*, including those of Buton and Tsongkhapa. The Seventh Dalai Lama places her immediately after Drubtop Namkha O (described in the footnote as a shaven-headed white [robed] tantric) and immediately before her brother Semo Chewa. One of the earliest sources for the lineage, 'Phags-pa 1968: 191, column 3, also excludes Jobum.

in the *Blue Annals*, where he studies instead with her brother Semo Chewa (Roerich 1976: 769–70).[39]

The most detailed biography of Jobum was found in the Kālacakra history by Tāranātha (1575–1635). It runs as follows:

Of the three children of Chokyi Wangchuk, there were two who served animate beings. The Lady Lhaje Jobum was renowned as being the emanation body of Indrabodhi's Lady Lakṣmīnkāra.[40] She had such great knowledge that she had thoroughly mastered the tantras and commentaries of the Kālacakra. In her younger years she engaged in all kinds of activities. When she became a young woman, at her mother's urging, she practised the Yamāntaka Gesture of Vanquishing and beheld his visage. She coerced Life Lord (*Tshe-bdag*) and Great God Blazing Glory (*lHa-chen dPal-'bar*) into her service. She practised life magic (*srog-mthu*). She made magical displays, hail and so forth. She spent all her time on this. The magical powers of her coercive mantras were extremely great. During her thirty-sixth year (i.e., age thirty-five) she was suffering from a severe illness which convinced her that nothing was of any importance apart from realizing the way things truly are. She meditated on the Six-Limbed Yoga which she had learned from her father and during the first day she completed the ten signs. In the seventh day, the internal winds dissolved into the central vein. She became a great woman *siddhā* (*grub-thob chen-mo*). In her retreats she would go entirely without human food for about half a month or about a month, but her physical strength would become much better. She stayed in rock shelters at Sinpori, and travelled in areas impassable to humans, meditating. She was able to stop outbreaks of contagious diseases simply by pronouncing the Power of Truth. A simple touch of her hand would free the sick from their sicknesses. These and other such signs [of her accomplishments] became known. (Tāranātha 1983: 17–8)

About her dates, or how long she lived, we are told nothing, only that she died before her brother Semo Chewa.

I was also able to locate a brief reference to Jobum in a defence against critics of the Nyingma school, one attributed to the famous Longchenpa (1308–63). The general context is an argument that many members of other schools have benefited greatly from their study of Nyingma

39 Jobum is not mentioned in the brief account of the early Dro system lineage in Bu-ston 1965: IV 61–5. A slightly later Kālacakra history, dated to 1360, mentions her only as a teacher of some relatively minor practices and precepts to (her brother) Semo Chewa. Here she is called 'father's lady Emanation Body Jobum'. Here, again, she is left outside the main line of transmission (folio 38 verso, line 1; the author of this work, I now believe, must have been a disciple of Dolpopa and not Dolpopa himself; for bibliographical details see Martin 1997: no. 89). Even more confusing, calling her 'father's lady' (*yab-kyi lcam-mo*) would seem to imply that she was Dharmeśvara's sister or wife (*lcam-mo* may serve as an honorific in both meanings).

40 Indrabodhi, although the name often appears so in Tibetan sources, ought to be corrected to Indrabhūti. For Lakṣmīnkāra, 'one of the founding mothers of Tantric Buddhism', see Shaw 1994: 39, 110–13, *et passim*.

Woodblock print portrait of Machig Jobum
(From Ngag-dbang 1983, p. 77)

teachings, in particular the Great Perfectedness. In the narrower context, it seeks to show that Kunpang Chenpo (this is a way of referring to the founder of Jonang Monastery, who lived 1243–1313) received Nyingma teachings. It says, 'Then he requested the Royal Manner Anointment initiation from Machig Jobum, the daughter of the great *siddhā* Yumo.' (Klong-chen 1977: 168)[41] This is quite a puzzling statement, first because nothing that we know connects Jobum to Nyingma teachings, and second because of the obvious chronological problem. I would suggest that the author of this work has confounded Jobum, the (grand) daughter of Yumo, with another person with the same name. One candidate might be the wife of Nyangrel Nyima Ozer, whose name was Jobumma, or the male Nyingma teacher Taton Jobum (1124–74), or a person (male?) Nyantob Jobum (1235–73).[42] Only the last-named would solve the chronological problem, but this person also was, being connected with the

[41] Despite the tone of the discussion here, there is evidence that the Kālacakra lineages had a considerable number of exchanges with Nyingma teachers. Germano 1994 has attempted to excavate evidence of some of the doctrinal and practical cross-fertilizations that have become obscured in the (generally lineage specific) histories.

[42] There was also the wife of Trulshig Darma Senge (1223–1303, a practitioner of Peacemaking) named Jobum (Roerich 1976: 960). Clearly, Jobum (-ma) was a rather common name during these and subsequent centuries.

transmission of Cakrasamvara, free of any apparent Nyingma connections. This unsolved and perhaps insoluble problem is offered as an example of the confusions of identity that we find so often in the sources, and we take our leave of Jobum with some reluctance, since there must be more literary sources about her somewhere. For the moment, we have done our best.

The fifteenth and sixteenth century teachers Tsangnyon Heruka, most famous for compiling the life and songs of Milarepa and Pema Karpo, the Fourth Drugchen incarnation and perhaps the most important intellectual of the Drugpa school, both belonged to lineages of the esoteric ear-whispered teachings called the Rechung Ear-whispered Transmission (*Ras chung snyan brgyud*). This lineage included two women, Machig Ongjo and Kunden Rema (a.k.a. Yeshe Kunden, daughter of Dhara Śrī).[43] Only the former, Ongjo, belonged to our period. Since one biographical source (which provides only a few biographical details, however) has been translated (Allione 1986: 213–19),[44] we will not translate it once more, but rather summarize and add some further sources.

The Rechung Ear-whispered Transmission was a special tradition centred on Cakrasamvara and Vajravārāhī. Some of its teachings were received by Rechungpa from the Indian Tiphupa, and not from his main teacher Milarepa (some parts of these teachings were in fact given by Rechungpa to Milarepa). It was certainly esoteric in the sense that it existed independently of the public arenas of Buddhist teaching, and could freely pass inside monastery walls and out again. Its existence outside the institutions, as well as its deliberate fostering of 'individual' spirituality, made it rather suspect in the eyes of some of the more scholastic leaders, for example Chag Lotsawa.[45] One consequence of this independence of monastic institutions was that its lineage members continued to include laypersons. Another consequence may be that it had less problem accepting women as bearers of the blessings of the lineage.

The one independent biographical source would appear to have been written by Ongjo's follower in the Rechung transmission, Zhang Lotsawa.[46] Her outward life is covered in just a few lines, which tell us that she was born in Uyug, that her family had achieved great wealth in both

[43] The story of Kunden Rema has been translated in Allione 1986: 221–31.

[44] The translation is generally quite well-done, but there are so many explanatory elements added to what the Tibetan actually says, that it would better be described as a paraphrase.

[45] See Martin 1996a: 33–4 for more on Chag Lotsawa's polemic.

[46] I have two cursive manuscripts to work with. They are not identical in content, but I have combined them rather indiscriminately in the following summary. They are located in *bDe mchog* 1983: 285–8 and *bDe mchog* 1973: 175–6. The latter source, which is the one used by Allione, is somewhat less detailed.

field and livestock agriculture,[47] and that she belonged to the Gyamo clan. She was extremely sad during her youth, refused to remain in the household life and escaped to the mountains. She 'entered the door of religion' (she took lay vows) and studied and reflected on many of the esoteric precepts, but most importantly, she met Khyung Tsangpa. He said to her, 'You are a reincarnation of the Total Knowledge Sky-Goer Determa',[48] and with compassion accepted her as a disciple. She received the ear-whispered teachings three times, the first time as a layperson, the second and third times as a fully ordained nun.[49] Of her degree of attainment after receiving and practising the esoteric precepts, one of the manuscripts says, 'An extraordinary realization of the way things are took birth in her mind.' The remainder of this 'biography' illustrates how she brought to perfection in her life the six transcendent qualities of generosity, disciplined conduct, patience (including tolerance and longsuffering), energetic application, meditative absorption and insight. She realized these virtues, universal to Mahāyāna, within the tantric realm of the Vajrayāna.

Only one of the manuscripts says that Ongjo received the one-to-one transmission (*chig-brgyud*) from Khyung Tsangpa. In fact, Khyung Tsangpa also passed the ear-whispered transmission teachings on to three men, one of whom had the name Gedingpa. But these three along with Ongjo were all teachers of Zhang Lotsawa (d. 1237). Zhang Lotsawa, who had many teachers, first studied with the three men, but had some doubts. Pema Karpo's sixteenth-century history says, 'When he had some doubts because no text was forthcoming, Gedingpa told him,

[47] The expression used is *bod 'brog 'dzom-pa*. This means '[sedentary] agriculture and [nomadic, or rather transhumant] shepherding combined'. This is one of those interesting cases where the word for 'Tibet', *Bod*, is applied specifically to the farming areas.

[48] It is probable that the manuscript has misspelled the name *bDe-ster-ma*, 'She Who Grants Bliss'. This is known to the Kagyu tradition as the name of Tilopa's spiritual 'sister' (*sring-mo*), a sky-goer who offered him guidance throughout his life. On her, see for example Padma dKar-po 1968: 246, 248. One manuscript says that Khyung Tsangpa accepted her as a disciple with compassion (*thugs-rje*), while the other says he did so with affection (*[b]rtse-ba*). Although not *necessarily* different in meaning, there is certainly a difference in tone, since the latter may connote kindly affection of a less spiritually refined and more familial kind. Even though we will note some later sources which suggest that she and Khyung Tsangpa had intimate relations, there is really no overt sign of this here, in the primary source of the later literature about her.

[49] This statement, which appears in only one of the manuscripts, is quite significant, since the word *dge-slong* (notably lacking the feminine ending '*-ma*') is used. This is one of the few pieces of evidence we have that women were receiving (or at the very least keeping) the complete *bhikṣuṇī* vows in those times. This point will be discussed further in the section on nuns. Note also how one source says that, ending at age thirty-three, Machig Labdron had been a '*vollkommene Nonne*' (Kollmar-Paulenz 1993: 142), a 'perfect nun' (but as we will see later on, she is said to have had a child in her thirtieth year).

'Machig Ongjo is the lama's consort (*gsang-yum*). It seems she has [the texts]. Go to her.' He went to her twice, but she did not speak, let alone say what she had. Meanwhile he went and took complete ordination from the Great Pundit of Kashmir and studied the monastic rules. Only then did she very happily grant him the precepts.[50]

The *Lhorong History* has nothing to add to Ongjo's biography, of which it gives brief extracts, but it does tell in a different way how Zhang Lotsawa received the ear-whispered transmission from Ongjo, 'He went to the presence of Machig Angcho three times, but the first two times she did not grant [the precepts]. The third time, she said, '[Khyung Tsangpa] told me to give them to a suitable vessel, and that means you.' She gave him the initiations and guidance instructions of the ear-whispered teachings as well as the Revered One's personal books and sacramental objects. Then she made a prophecy.'[51]

The only passage about Ongjo that seems to be in some degree independent of all the other sources which stem from the only biography there is, is a brief one in a sixteenth century history already cited above. Notice the very unusual rendering of her name:

> The Heart Disciple of Khyung Tsangpa by the name of Machig Kongcho was born in Uyug. From her youth she had very great faith and compassion. When she went to the presence of Khyung Tsangpa she heard the complete precepts of the ear-whispered transmission, and countless good qualities were born [in her]. She helped many fortunate disciples such as Zhang Lotsawa, and then departed for the sky life. (Sangs-rgyas n.d.: 76b.3)

Although they might fall outside the chronological boundaries set for us, we should at least mention two other women lineage holders, Machig

50 Based on Padma dKar-po 1968: 509.

51 rTa-tshag 1994: 127; with summary of Ongjo's life at 119–20. This account is somewhat elaborated in Zhang's biography composed by his own disciple (contained in bDe-mchog 1983: 308–9). Here the objects he received from Ongjo are clarified. The personal books of Khyung Tsangpa were 'codified' (*bkod-pa*) by himself (a different manuscript, however, says it was codified by Milarepa) and the 'sacramental objects' included a set of the six ornaments (worn by male wrathful deities) and elixir pellets. For several years she did not perform the initiations and neither did she explain the more profound precepts. She made a mysteriously worded prophecy which seems to say that he would have to wait until his hair reached his knees, when a student of the great man would arrive and the sky-goers would extend an invitation (?). One may consult the *Blue Annals* (Roerich 1976: 443–4 and 446), but be aware that this text offers no more than a summarized form of the biographies. Note, too, that the few entries in biographical dictionaries devoted to Ongjo simply copy the *Blue Annals*. It is curious that the *Blue Annals* (and sources based on it) say that she served as a tantric assistant (*shes-rab-ma*) during the performance of initiation rites. The source on which this is based says no such thing, although one of the manuscripts does say (at the same point in the story) that, quite to the contrary, she served as a Vajra Master. The other manuscript says that (she or someone else?) 'performed the initiation'.

Rema and her spiritual granddaughter Dzema.[52] It seems that Rema must at least have been born sometime in the twelfth century. She was a direct disciple of the Indian teacher Mitrayogin, an historically shadowy but nevertheless extremely popular figure in Tibetan literature.[53] She passed the lineage of the 'Cutting the Flow of Saṁsāra' (*'Khor-ba rGyun-gcod*) teachings on to a man called Trulshig, who in turn passed them on to Dzema of On. Mitrayogin's dates are unsettled, but based on his presence at the beginning of the building of the Great Maitreya image (80 cubits high, or about 120 feet) at Trophu, he must have come to Tibet sometime in the late twelfth or early thirteenth centuries. We may attempt to be more precise, in that Trophu Lotsawa (1172–1236) invited Mitrayogin to come to Tibet when the former was in his twenty-sixth year. This means he must have been invited in 1197, some seven years before Trophu welcomed the Kashmiri teacher Śākyaśrī (1127? or 1140?–1125?) to Tibet in 1204.[54] Rema would have met Mitrayogin, who stayed in Tibet only eighteen months, in 1198 or 1199.

The *Lhorong History* has by far the most detailed account of her life, but gives her name as Rebma:

> Machig Rebma Darma Changchub received the name [Rebma] from her native area. She met with Lord Kunden Repa [1148–1217] and requested all the secret precepts. Then she did the practices single-pointedly. Her realization reached the point that is like when both the blade and the whetstone disappear. Scholars rank her by saying, 'She is a great yoginī who clearly did realize the way things are, emptiness.' She had unrestricted clairvoyant abilities, and knew that there would come to a fisherman in the lower Je valley [in Tsang] named Lukye a child who would be a reincarnation of Dampa Rinpoche.[55] The morning that child was born, she carried him to the first feeding ceremony[56] and then she raised him. Later he

[52] The story of Dzema, not told here, is found in Roerich 1976: 1039–40. Although here it is obviously a proper name, it may be interesting to know that the noun '*re-ma*' (also spelled *re-rma, re-dma', ri-ma* and *res-ma*) is said to be an obsolete word meaning 'woman' (see bTsan-lha 1997: 892–3). One woman disciple of Phadampa was named Rima (Roerich 1976: 916) although for purely chronological reasons she cannot be identified with the present Rema.

[53] The study of the biographies of Mitrayogin will prove a difficult but rewarding effort. There are numerous variant manuscripts, most of them based on a series of miraculous events in his life. Five unpublished manuscripts are described in van der Kuijp 1994: 602, and several more have been published. Also unpublished but potentially quite valuable for research on Rema and Dzema and their circles are some manuscript collections of Trophu Lotsawa's writings and translations (see van der Kuijp 1994: 600).

[54] On these figures, see especially Jackson 1990 and the review by van der Kuijp 1994. The Kashmiri teacher is said to have died in his ninety-ninth year.

[55] I suspect this is an oblique reference to the death in 1195 of Gyaltsa Rinchen Gonpo (1118–95), leader of the Trophu lineage and disciple of Ngok Do-de.

[56] Called here *rkan-mar* or 'palate butter', since butter is applied to the newborn's palate. Pats of butter may also be given to women experiencing a difficult delivery; see Pinto

would turn out to be an unimaginably great *siddhā* known as Chegom Dzongpa Sherab Dorje who would found and reside in a monastery at the rock of Khakyong in Tanag, and thereafter be called Khakyong Drakpa. In later times, this same Machig Rebma would clear away obstacles for this very person. The Six Treasuries of Dohā [songs single-handedly translated by Vairocana] were obtained from Lama Zhang by Tsongton Gompa and, just like the latter, this one [Chegom] mastered them.[57] When it is said that this person [Chegom] met with Tsangpa Jo-se,[58] it is referring to the memories of five hundred rebirths found in the biography. Some say that it refers to Kunden Tsangpa, while others say to a disciple of Kunden. This requires more research. This person's Buddhist compositions were very fine and many, and the Dharma transmission has continued until now (it is said). What this refers to is the fact that this person had two transmissions going back to some masters of the Kadampa. This person had many students including Dromton Lhariwa, Sangye Balampa,[59] Sangye Dulwa and the *siddha* Hum Barwa.[60] Hum Barwa had a transmission lineage [list of names omitted]. There were many other transmissions as well, but they are not recorded. (rTa-tshag 1994: 336–7)[61]

LEADERS OF POPULAR RELIGIOUS MOVEMENTS

Sometime in the decades before or after the year 1100, two women led broadly-based religious movements. Literary sources place them in groups variously characterized as 'The Four Children of Pehar', 'The Six Black Yogis', or 'The Four Total-Knowledge Sky-Goers.' Their names were Shelmo Gyacham and Zhangmo Gyating. Although all but one of the

1999: 167. Butter has a number of special usages in Tibetan rituals, particularly in the lay rituals associated with the new year, where it seems to be associated, quite rightly, with richness and prosperity.

57 A mistake in the text (*do-ra* instead of *do-ha*) made this passage incomprehensible until locating a parallel passage in rTa-tshag 1994: 205, which has the more correct reading and specifies that it was exactly Chegom Dzongpa who received the teachings from Tsong Gompa. The Lama Zhang mentioned here is of course Zhang Yudragpa (1123–93), on whom more will be said later on.

58 This means the spiritual son of Tsangpa (and Tsangpa often forms a part of Kunden Repa's name, in forms like Kunden Tsangpa). I believe this refers to Kunden's nephew Trophu Lotsawa, as the spiritual son of Kunden Tsangpa.

59 Balampa was a renowned teacher of the Tsalpa school born at the end of the twelfth century or beginning of the thirteenth.

60 That he was a student of Chegompa is confirmed in Roerich 1976: 1025.

61 Part of the problem with translating this passage is that it is in the form of a commentary on an unidentified text. Various photographic copies of manuscripts of the Lhorong history have begun circulating in recent years, and they may have better readings for this passage. Nowadays Chegompa is primarily thought of as a member of the Kadam school. For arguments about Chegompa's connections with Machig Rema and the Trophu lineage, those interested are referred to Sørensen 1999. This study includes further sources for the story translated here.

sources provide them with dubious reputations, some even denying their human embodiment by 'spiritizing' them, and although nothing survives in terms of self-representation, it is clear that they were widely followed during their times, and their movements may well have continued into the fourteenth century. Their stories have already been told elsewhere (Martin 1996a and 1996b), so it will suffice to say that, like so many of the women mentioned here, one or both of them were in (or came into) close relationships with Phadampa and his circle.

TEACHERS

There would seem to be little point to this particular category, since so many of the women mentioned above did have teaching roles. Here it is just a category used to include some of the more obscure figures who do not fit in one of the others, and who happen to be mentioned in the role of teacher. One of these was Kalden (or Kalden Tso), daughter of Ten-ne. Two sources tell us that she passed teachings on to Rok Sherab O (1166–1244) (Roerich 1976: 946; Chos-kyi 1992: 214). This probably occurred during the first two decades of the thirteenth century, since Ten-ne was extremely old at the time, perhaps also blind.

It seems Cheton Gyanag (1094–1149) received teachings from one Jomo Nyangmo (Roerich 1976: 128, 1005).[62] These teachings belonged to the system of Great Perfectedness known as Kham Aro.

Two women are mentioned by Zhang Yudragpa (1123–93) among his many teachers. One, Majo Dron-ne, is likely to be the same as the Jomo Dron-ne mentioned in a previous footnote. She gave Zhang teachings on the direct introduction [to the nature of mind] according to the Ke'u Tsangma system. Zhang's mother was herself an ex-nun who evidently preserved her association with her former convent. The *Lhorong History* provides some unique information. It says that his mother was Shumoza Mangkyi, as is well known in many sources, but adds in a footnote that

[62] Nyangmo as a proper name is not very specific, and could be used to refer to any woman from the region of Nyang. One Nyangmo was among the twenty-four women disciples of Phadampa (Roerich 1976: 918), but there is no reason to believe that she should be identical to the teacher in the Kham Aro system. This Aro system had one of the most obscure transmissions in all of Tibetan religious history (see Karmay 1988: 93, 126, 208). In the twelfth century, Phagmo Drupa was searching for a teacher and at one point requested Aro precepts. Afterwards he said, 'It is no help. It has nothing to offer but quiescence meditation (*zhi-gnas*)' (O-rgyan-pa 1972: 283; cf. Roerich 1976: 556). The only published texts of the Aro system I know of are in Kong-sprul 1978 vol. 1: 311–78, although these texts do not include Nyangmo in their lineages (to be sure, a woman named Zurmo is to be found in the Zur system's Great Perfectedness lineage, but she must belong to the fourteenth century).

the name Majo Yangmo also occurs.[63] When she was evidently still a nun, a woman who was recognized as a Total Knowledge Sky-Goer named Majo Rama prophesied to her, among other things, that she, Mangkyi, was like the *bhikṣuṇī* Prasannaśīla who became the mother of Vasubandhu and Asaṅga,[64] that she must take up the household life since it would be a great benefit to the teachings. As a consequence of this prophecy, Zhang and an elder brother were born. When Zhang was four (i.e. three), he asked his mother what Majo Darma was like. His mother told him how, while she was in the stomach of Majo Sangye Kyi, the latter would recite the *Names of Mañjuśrī*, that when Majo Darma was born she knew it without studying, that she was known as a sky goer and natural yoginī who was able to interpret the words of the text. Then Zhang and his mother went together to Ne'udong to meet her. Zhang recited a brief text for the assembled nuns on the nature of mind. Majo Darma was the first to recognize him as a tulku (*sprul-sku* 'emanation', Skt. *nirmāṇakāya*) and foretell his future greatness. She was not only his first teacher, but also his first disciple (so says the *Lhorong History*). Years later when she died, it was Zhang who made the necessary arrangements for her funeral and cremation.[65]

NUNS

It has often been suggested that the lineage of fully ordained nuns might never have been instituted in Tibet, and in recent publications this idea seems to have become an article of faith with a life of its own.[66] We have already seen that Ongjo did become a fully ordained nun, a *bhikṣuṇī* (*dge-slong-ma*). If we may be permitted to use an example that lies outside our time frame, in a history of his monastery Tsele, Tsele Gotsangpa

[63] I could not find any other source for the name Majo Yangmo. However, the only known manuscript of the rare history by dGe-ye (folio 36; for bibliographical references see Martin 1997: no. 140) supplies Zhang's mother with the 'similar' name Majo Yagma. On the title Majo see the previous discussion.

[64] Her story, although quite fascinating, belongs to an Indian Buddhist context. For English language sources see Chimpa 1990: 155 and Tsonawa 1985: 26–7, 33.

[65] Most of the material for this paragraph is from rTa-tshag 1994: 181–3. The story has been told briefly, without the benefit of the *Lhorong History*, in Martin 1996c: 65. The text recited by Zhang, entitled *Mind Meditation: Six Meanings of Enlightened Mind*, has been translated in Martin 2001.

[66] For examples see Tsomo 1989: 121; 1996: viii-ix and Campbell 1996: 5. The translators of Kongtrul 1998: 26 attribute to Kongtrul the idea that 'the ordination of nuns was never introduced into Tibet'. What Kongtrul in fact says is, '...since the nun's ethical conduct is not observed in Tibet at this time, [the subject] will not be discussed here.' (ibid.: 126) Kongtrul was referring to his own times in the late nineteenth century. Other references to the literature may be found in Havnevik 1989: 45, 210.

(b. 1608) tells this story of a fully ordained nun (who may, with more research, prove datable):

> Chamo Jetsunma Konchok Tsomo took the complete vows from Je Mikyo Zhab, and became an actual *bhikṣuṇī*. She faultlessly practised all the minutest rules of the Vinaya. In Zhongkha Convent, in the midst of over a hundred nuns (*btsun-ma*) she taught the Dharma. Her life span and her practice were brought to perfection and she was honoured with the prostrations and offerings of all the people of Dag valley. (rTse-le 1979: 327)[67]

While there may have been Tibetan-born nuns already during imperial times (I have not really looked into the question), there were surely both nuns and nunneries during the time of the Second Spread, as newly published evidence would indicate. The daughter of King Yeshe O named Lhai Metok, who took (unspecified) nun's vows herself, 'instituted the custom of women (*bud-med*) becoming nuns (*btsun-ma*)', founded a nunnery called Trewel, and provided for its maintenance (Vitali 1996: 55, 60, 110, 178, 209, 274).[68]

In reading the English translation of the *Blue Annals* it is important to realize that the translation 'nun' is used to cover a number of Tibetan terms, including 'jomo', 'majo' and 'tsunma' (*jo-mo, ma-jo* and *btsun-ma*). While these terms are likely, in most cases, to refer to ordained women—in fact, nuns—none of them necessarily imply the full ordination of the *bhikṣuṇī*. Three mentions of nuns occur, for example, in the stories of Dzeng (1052–1168) and his disciple Dzeng Jo-se. Dzeng was conceived when his mother, named Tsarguza Kyi-de, when she had been a nun (*btsun-ma*) at Tangchung in the Yarlung valley and was forced to descend from her vows by the eldest son of the Tangchung 'Emperor' (Roerich 1976: 176). A nun (*ma-jo*) named Dowa, among others, requested Dzeng to teach the Vajra Bridge, while the mother of Kunsang (a disciple of both Dzeng and Dzeng Jo-se) is said to have studied religion with a 'mad nun' (*ma-jo smyon-ma*) named Samdrub (Roerich 1976: 188).

These nuns may or may not have been *bhikṣuṇīs*, but *bhikṣuṇīs* probably did exist in those days, despite the not-quite-total silence of the literary sources on this point.

---

[67] Dag valley is equivalent to Dagpo, a major region in the eastern part of central Tibet, to the north of the Brahmaputra river.

[68] This evidence was not available to earlier authors such as Gross 1993: 86, who could—quite mistakenly as it turns out—state, 'It is uncertain whether nuns' ordination was ever transmitted from India to Tibet, but certainly it was not transmitted during the second diffusion of Buddhism from India to Tibet, in the tenth and eleventh centuries, and if it ever had existed in Tibet, it had died out by then.'

ENCOURAGEMENT AND DISCOURAGEMENT: WOMEN'S SPIRITUALITY IN THE CIRCLE OF PHADAMPA

One general observation that might be made is that the majority of these women had some direct contact with Phadampa Sangye, or at least with his immediate circle of followers (Jobum and Ongjo being the foremost exceptions).[69] Phadampa, a native of the region of Andhra on the eastern coast of south India (his father was a sea captain), is said to have visited Tibet a number of times, but it was only during his last visit, after going into retreat at Dingri Langkhor, that his fame spread over the Tibetan plateau and people flocked to see him from far distant valleys. Although he still used intermediaries or 'interpreters' such as Kunga when people came to ask him questions, there is also evidence that he knew Tibetan quite well, that he spoke in Tibetan and was able to translate Indian texts into Tibetan by himself (the colophons to these works use the word 'self-translated' [*rang-'gyur*], indicating that he did it himself without working with a Tibetan), although these translations were then scribed, proofread and corrected by native speakers. Few other Indian teachers in Tibet have been credited with such translations (another is the Vairocana mentioned above). He was known for strange and highly symbolic utterances and behaviour, and knew how to deploy a gesture or interjection to cut more directly through the illusions brought by his listeners. He was famous for his parables, paradoxes and riddles. Much to the discomfort of conventionally minded Tibetans, he seems to have been naked, or nearly so, when he gave most of his teachings.[70] He must have been one of the very few to provide Tibetans with an opportunity to communicate directly with an Indian Buddhist tantric master.

69 The percentages might very roughly be estimated at sixty per cent for Phadampa and his circle (including followers of both Peacemaking and Cutting), as compared to thirty per cent for the wider Kagyu group, and ten per cent for all the rest combined. Despite my best efforts, not a single religiously significant woman could be identified within either the Kadam or the Bon sects during the times. One reason Phadampa might have supported women's spiritual education is the fact that, among his fifty-four *siddha* teachers in India, about ten were women (see Roerich 1976: 869 and Chos-kyi 1992: 21, for lists). It is noteworthy that the Peacemaking literature employs explicitly gender-inclusive language when referring to Phadampa's teachers, calling them 'the fifty-four male and female *siddhas*' (*grub-thob pho-mo lnga-bcu-rtsa-bzhi*). Lists of their names have been compiled in an unpublished paper by Kurtis Schaeffer (personal communication). By way of contrast, the much better known set of eighty-four *mahāsiddhas* only included four women.

70 We know that he did not wear clothes because his followers would sometimes beg him to put some on (see, for example, Kun-dga' 1979 vol. 2: 212). As in India, this religious nudity is meant to demonstrate transcendence of the 'social self', the casting off of worldly concerns, and, in spite of the apparent paradox, the ultimate in modesty. In earlier iconographical representations, he is usually depicted seated with a cloth loosely coiled about his lower body.

Based on the literary remains of his school, he was surely an advocate of a kind of women's liberation, both in the spiritual and mundane senses of the word. He taught the highest teachings to men and women alike, but for women in particular he demanded the courage to break free of the household life and to stop slaving for their husbands.[71] 'A woman who cannot leave the household life behind and who produces Dharma I have not seen.' 'A woman who cannot cast the household life to the winds will not get Dharma.' 'A beggar woman without a husband is happier than a wife of a bad husband.' 'Women cannot have Dharma, [but] if they are to get Dharma, they have to cut off their connections to the household life. Even if they were to get Prince Tse-de[72] for a husband, they would just be high class slaves.' 'Women who practise Dharma need a bone in the centre of their hearts [they need courage].' What other teacher in Tibet of those times was telling so many women to break free of their servitude to house and husband to seek the highest spiritual liberation?[73]

It follows that in Phadampa's circle, more than others, the spiritual potential of women would have been recognized. There is one text, perhaps the finest literary monument from our era of concern on the spiritual abilities of women, entitled *Answers to the Questions of the Twenty-Four Jomos, together with their Stories*. It is contained in a wonderful old manuscript collection now available in a five volume reprint edition (Kun-dga' 1979; for convenience, we will just call this entire collection the *Peacemaking Collection*). The original manuscript, with an undeniable and unrivalled importance for understanding the Peacemaking teachings, dates from no later than the late thirteenth century (some of its titles do

[71] There are several dozen possible examples of such advice that he gave to particular (named) women in a single volume of Kun-dga' (1979 vol. 2) alone. The following examples are from pages 407, 412, 415, 420 and 422. 'A bone in the centre of [their] hearts' (*snying gi dkyil du rus pa cig*) plays with the Tibetan word for 'courage' (*snying-rus*). It is worth noting that Phadampa demands that men have courage, too (Kun-dga' 1979 vol. 2: 189, for example). He was also of the opinion that Tibetans of spiritual accomplishment are so few primarily because they are servile and do not take matters into their own hands (Kun-dga' 1979 vol. 2: 221).

[72] Tse-de was a king of the western Tibetan kingdom of Guge. He probably ascended the throne in about 1057 CE, and was especially famous for the religious council he held in 1076. For more historical details see Vitali 1996: 72–4, 317–33.

[73] It would of course be valid to ask, what really is the gender difference? If women who break free of worldly concerns can advance their spiritual practice, isn't this equally true of men? Another question lies behind these questions, which is, what allowances are to be made for religious and spiritual practices for laypersons in general? Despite the now common generalizations to the contrary, there is evidence that early Buddhism did encourage lay practice of meditation (it is not just a modern concept; on this point see Samuels 1999). Phadampa taught a form of meditation-based Buddhism with no prerequisite training in syllogistic reasoning and sophisticated scriptural exegesis, and therefore much more accessible to people in general.

date to the mid-thirteenth century). It was kept until recently at Dingri Langkhor as a kind of 'speech receptacle', an object of worship, a 'relic', even, of the early lineage. It consists in large part of a collection of teachings put together by Kunga, who is said to have received the one-to-one transmission from Phadampa, and it was Kunga who composed the text on the jomos. The *Peacemaking Collection* deserves a full study not practical here, and we may hope that someone will undertake the task of overcoming the problems due to its old orthography and vocabulary and do just that. The stories of the twenty-four jomos have long been available in English, based not on the original, but on the later *Blue Annals*, which quite possibly made use of the very same manuscript we have today.[74]

Just because it is so clear that, more than any other group, the circle of Phadampa supported women's religious practice, it is all the more surprising and even dismaying to find more as well as less negative statements on women's spiritual potential. There is a tenuous but nevertheless crucial distinction between men saying that woman have it bad, a statement with which many women of past and present would agree, and saying that women *are* bad. I believe at this stage of my research that Phadampa himself had not unequivocally crossed that line. His actions in teaching women clearly show that no matter how unfavourable women's home lives might be to spiritual practice, if they are freed from their household duties they are capable of pursuing enlightenment. But it does not necessarily follow that his followers followed suit. Even the text on the twenty-four jomos, composed by Kunga, mentions that women are of 'small accumulation'. Perhaps, but only perhaps, the intention was to say that they had little learning, although it could also intend that their accumulation of merit and full knowledge, and hence their spiritual status, was low. In the following I adduce other statements from the early *Peacemaking Collection* to lend support to the latter interpretation.

74 The Tibetan text is found in Kun-dga' 1979 vol. 4: 302–23. The author, Kunga, explicitly states that he has written down this account as a 'message for the women of future generations' (ibid: 314). A large part of it was more or less reproduced (often abbreviated, with minor changes and omissions) in the Tibetan text of the *Blue Annals* translated in Roerich (1976: 915–20) with the life of Kunga following (pp. 920–3). Incidentally, this text has what may be the earliest known reference to 'carrying corpses to the mountain' (*rir skyel*), which is what we, not Tibetans, call 'sky burial'. The *Peacemaking Collection* as we have it was probably first put together (by adding to a nucleus already formed by Kunga and Patsab) by Zhigpo Rinchen Sherab (1171–1245) in 1210, although this original was done in gold letters (see Roerich 1976: 953), and the manuscript we have today would have been prepared, on the basis of the earlier one, but with three added titles, near the end of the same century. The miniature drawings have most unfortunately not been reproduced well, and in most cases have simply disappeared.

For example, consider the commentary that takes up the entire fifth volume of the *Peacemaking Collection*, commenting on interviews Kunga had with Phadampa.[75] Of its fifty-five chapters, the ninth is entitled 'Showing how, women being bad receptacles, the thought of practising [religion] dawns with difficulty'. We will start with the words spoken by Phadampa to Kunga, which is translated completely, while the much more lengthy commentarial treatment is excerpted.

'It is as if the likes of women were cut off from the inheritance of the Buddha.'

Kunga: 'But what about the saying that, in an enlightened mind, there is no gender (*pho mo*)?'

'First, their rebirth is low (*skye-ba dman*) by virtue of not having accumulated the accumulations. In their bodies there is opposition. Because they have no bone in their hearts [no courage], they are unable to do the practices. In their youths, without remembering Dharma, they do everything they can to start a family. When they are old, although they may wish to do something, their bodies are unable. If they take renunciation vows, they are shadowed by the habit. [But] then, if birth and shape are good, they are picked out once more. The women who have obtained independence (*rang-dbang*) are few.'[76]

The commentator elaborates these statements with typical commentarial pedantry under ten different categories spread over several pages. It is far from certain that these elaborations would have been countenanced by Phadampa himself (and it definitely post-dates our period of preoccupation), which makes it less interesting for present purposes. A few of the more remarkable passages must suffice in the present context.

The likes of women are bad receptacles [for the teachings]; they clearly place their trust in the causes of suffering. Having little sorrow for their lot in saṁsāra, since they view suffering as an ornament, they do not escape from household work, and get no chance to work on Dharma… It is because they have no escape (*bud*) from routine chores, that they are called 'women' (*bud-myed*) …[77]

[75] The colophon to this commentary tells us it was authored by one Mikyo Dorje, teacher of the person who had the manuscript volumes constructed. I will save my arguments about this problematic identity for another place.

[76] For the passage with Phadampa's words about women in the 'root text', the *Heart Mirror* (*Thugs kyi me long*), which is a compilation by Kunga of various interviews he had with Phadampa, there are at least two other textual witnesses. One is in Dampa 1985: 217–18 and the other in Kun-dga' 1979 vol. 2: 184. It may be useful to look at the wider context of the passage, since Phadampa, immediately before and after casting doubts on the spiritual possibilities of women, has some sceptical things to say about the local Dingri people, about Tibetan Buddhists in general ('just seeing these Tibetan Buddhists makes me depressed…'), and about the worldly concerns of followers of the Kadampa sect.

[77] A different etymology for the word *bud-med* (the 'y' belongs to a now obsolete orthography) has been proposed in Klein 1995: 51, 'those not to be put out (*bud med*) because a woman is not to be left outside the house at night' (cf. Campbell 1996: 31–2). Modern

'Because they have not accumulated the accumulations, they take low rebirth.'[78] This means, first, that because their bodily receptacles are inferior, the minds that rely [on those bodies] are also inferior. Their minds being of limited scope, their thoughts are incapable of anything more than minor objectives.

He makes part of his argument the idea that women are subject to thirty-two diseases that men do not have, and since their possible physical sufferings are greater, their minds are more prone to emotional afflictions: 'Women's bodies are vessels of pain, and women's minds are vessels of suffering.' Commenting on women's lack of independence, he does make use of an unfortunate animal metaphor:

The receptacle for finding one's way to heaven and liberation is the precious human body. Even those who do find human rebirth, if they are simply born as women, they turn into the unadulterated [nature?] of animals, so their nose ropes are lost to others [i.e., they lose their independence]. While the attainment of independence is rare [for anyone, for women] it is more rare, [and they are] extremely few.

He ends by quoting a verse from an unspecified *nītiśāstra*,

In their youths they are kept by their parents,
as young women by their husbands,
in old age by their children.
Women do not obtain independence.[79]

If women are indeed handicapped by their bodily sufferings, lack of courage, and social position, there would seem to be two different responses here, one by Phadampa and one by the man who elaborated on his comments. Phadampa's response would probably be that, on an individual

---

academic discussions of the word almost invariably take their point of departure in Das 1973: 872, which supplies a Tibetan-language etymology of unspecified origins that is not translated correctly. Instead, it ought to be translated, 'Because their [gender] signs do not protrude [*bud*] outward, they are called 'women' [*bud-med*].'

78 The words *skye-ba dman* would appear to provide an etymology of a very common Tibetan word for 'woman', *skye-dman* (sometimes spelled *skyes-dman*). Phadampa never seems to use the word *skye-dman*, most frequently employing the word *bud-myed*, as is true also of the earlier Dunhuang documents. Therefore it might seem that the word *skye-dman* had not yet gained currency in Phadampa's time, although this point needs further study. It is likely that the word *skye-dman*, used as a 'description' of women a few times (in the form *skye-ba dman*) in the *Peacemaking Collection*, achieved the status of a substantive noun only subsequently. Nowadays, there is considerable pressure to do away with the term entirely. Given its essentially derogatory etymology, this would be an excellent idea. See also Changngopa forth coming.

79 Kun-dga' 1979, vol. 5: 94–102. I have not yet identified the source of the *nītiśāstra* verse. A *nītiśāstra* is a text of advice in favour of ethical conduct in worldly affairs, frequently addressed to members of royalty.

basis (not, *nota bene*, as part of any programme of social reform), their bodily sufferings need to be alleviated, they need encouragement, and above all they need emancipation from their particular social situations. But his commentator crosses over the line. The alleged handicaps are given such weight and emphasis one wonders whether he would have found teaching Buddhist spirituality to women worth the bother. Both men agree that the reason for low birth as a woman is that one has not 'accumulated the accumulations', and although neither explicitly draws this consequence, this would imply a lack of spiritual cultivation in previous lives, and could mean that such a person would not be considered suitable for the higher meditative precepts, like Great Seal (Mahāmudrā) or Great Perfectedness, which are often said to require prior cultivation.

There are still a number of tensions tending toward contradiction in both men's positions. For example, if women are in fact inordinately suffering entities, it is still the case that suffering itself is, along with impermanence, the strongest motive for the Buddhist quest. Suffering, including in particular bodily sickness and pain, is not a necessary block to spiritual progress, but might, to the contrary, be directly employed as an expedient (*lam-khyer*) on the path.[80] Therefore, if it is in fact the case that women have greater suffering, they would be even more driven to undertake spiritual disciplines and faster in reaching spiritual goals than men are. Even the nagging concerns of the day-to-day life of householders would not necessarily have to bar them from spiritual development.[81] Padmasambhava could even say, in a passage in which he prophesies Yeshe Tsogyal's future rebirth as Machig Labdron, 'The basis for realizing enlightenment is a human body. Male or female—there is no great difference. But if she develops the mind bent on enlightenment, the woman's body is better.'[82]

[80] A separate text on the practice of 'taking happiness and suffering on the path' (*skyid sdug lam-khyer*) attributed to Śākyaśrī is to be found in the *Blo sbyong brgya rtsa* collection, and this text is the evident basis of a more recent one by the Dowa Drubchen III (Thondup 1990: 117–29). The same practice appears embedded in a large number of other Buddhist texts and in fact might be considered universal to Vajrayāna. Phadampa himself could say (in Kun-dga' 1979 vol. 4: 131), 'Pain grants realization. Pain is a goad for perseverance. Pain brings mindfulness of death. Pain makes us lose confidence in our illusions. Because of pain we do not think our present life is permanent. Pain makes us turn away from worldly preoccupations…' and later on the same page, 'Without suffering, there will be no revulsion [from saṃsāra].'

[81] Thondup 1986: 82: 'For them the household life is a method of practice to transform every source of experience in life as the means of enlightened attainment.' See also the text translated in Thondup 1990: 130–41 on a tantric method for making daily activities take part in the path to enlightenment.

[82] Quoted from Nam-mkha'i-snying-po 1983: 102, following Willis 1984: 14.

CONCLUSIONS AND A RECOMMENDATION FOR HISTORIANS

Contemporary western feminisms find their necessity in their own cultural past, and their justifications within the current socio-ideological atmosphere. It may not even be very fruitful to compare the 'semi-' or 'proto-' (?) feminism of Phadampa's circle with any or all of the feminisms of the present. Still I think it would be fair to say that Phadampa himself (along with some members of his immediate circle), more than any of his contemporaries in Tibet, advocated a particular kind and degree of women's liberation with strongly Buddhist characteristics. His 'feminism', unlike most modern feminisms, was not aimed at emancipating all women from a socially endemic inequality, nor did it demand for women economic or occupational parity with men. It simply made individual emancipation from women's social conditions prerequisite for spiritual emancipation. In so far as the spiritual emancipation and socio-religious recognition of women is an issue for today's advocates of feminism, they may find in Phadampa one historical man with whom they could possibly forge an alliance, even if an uncomfortable one.

There are just a few less momentous conclusions that we would hazard to make, and a few possible objections to answer at the same time. We know that women's status in eleventh to twelfth century Tibet was not high. We may know this from at least two angles. One angle would be to listen to the words of Phadampa himself, as a rather critical and outspoken outside observer (both as a man and as a foreigner with considerable experience of Tibetan culture). Another angle would be to simply observe the relative scarcity of historical evidence about women. If women did have identical opportunities for education and employment to men in those days, we ought to find just as much written about women as we do about men.

Taking a cynical view, it might be argued that most of the women who did gain prominence for spiritual realization and religious leadership gained this recognition because of their family connections. The lives of Machig Zhama, with her illustrious religious family; of Jobum, who received her spiritual lineage through her family lineage; and of others could be brought forward to support this argument. Although I believe that this is a line of thinking worth testing against the evidence, other women did not belong to charismatic or privileged families (for example, Labdron's father may have been a semi-nomadic chief, but she was orphaned in her early teens). If a number of prominent women did have such connections, it might, however, suggest little more than that, generally speaking, family connections played a strong role in achieving social recognition for sanctity or leadership. This would also hold true (in equal degree?) for men.

Another cynical observation might be that all or nearly all these women belonged to esoteric orders with little public exposure. Despite some arguable truth in this, Zhama is clearly one who had a great deal of public exposure, even widespread fame, during her later life. Some of the others probably were recognized for their sanctity at the very least in a specific locality. Their transmission lineages might have been quite restrictive and exclusive, but the sanctity they achieved was palpable to those who came in contact with them, even to those with no inkling about their secret teachings.

Momentarily taking leave of the Tibetan for the general Buddhist realm, it is well known that Buddhist scriptures sometimes recommend that in order to strive for enlightenment, women ought to first transform their bodies, either miraculously in the present life, or 'naturally' in a subsequent rebirth, into bodies of men.[83] It is also well known that Buddhism frequently recommends, at a particular stage of spiritual training, meditations on the foulness of women's bodies (along with the foulness of human bodies in general, particularly dead ones). These meditations are bent on making men more realistic by deconstructing the illusions projected by male desires on the bodies of women, to make it possible to eventually achieve freedom from the entanglements of the desires themselves. Although clearly androcentric (women are rarely explicitly advised to perform foulness meditations on men's bodies), this practice is not misogynistic, or if it is misogynistic it is misogyny aimed at illusions about women, not at women as they (truly?) are.[84]

83 Passages in the *Peacemaking Collection* (Kun-dga' 1979, vol. 2: 191; vol. 5: 257) would suggest that 'having turned into a man' (*khyo gar gyurd nas*) is considered there to be a psychological rather than a bodily process. The woman in question who 'turned into a man' was born to the Jim clan in Mangyul with the name Chogyen, although here and elsewhere she is generally referred to as Gyagoma (she is the one mentioned in Roerich 1976: 919, which should say that Rozenma married as a bride into the family of Gyagoma, not that she *was* her bride). Her name surfaces frequently in the biography of Phadampa during his stay in Dingri, although she also spent much time in the Kathmandu valley. At one point (Chos-kyi 1992: 61) he granted her profound precepts including the direct introduction to seeing awareness in its nakedness (in its irreducible simplicity). Shortly before Phadampa died, he passed on some of his personal possessions to her, including a robe and a skullcap. In many cases she is called Gyagom or Gyagompa, which might lead to the mistaken idea that she was in fact a man (as indeed occurs in Roerich 1976: 914). With further study the *Peacemaking Collection* will certainly prove a rich source for still more accounts of women's lives.

84 For more about gender transformation and foulness meditation (there is now a considerable literature) see the recent works of Havnevik 1989: 27–31, 163–5; Hopkins 1998: 41–3, 114–17; Sunim 1999; Wilson 1996: 77–110, and literature cited therein. For Buddhist Mahāyāna scriptural sources on women, including accounts of gender transformation, the most important book, still unsurpassed, is that of Paul 1985.

Finally, a few significant points for historians—if we want to learn more about women of a particular time period, it will be essential in the future to use historical sources composed in, or as close as possible to, those very times. Later sources, because of their greater distance from the realities of the times of which they speak, tend to idealize, regularize, encapsulate and at times reinterpret the past according to the lights of their own times. One effect of this is that there is likely to be less about women in, say, a fifteenth century source about the twelfth century than there would be in a twelfth century source. From a historian's angle, those places where women's (and not just women saints') lives do surface in the traditional historical sources are precisely those places where we may glimpse the kinship and gender concerns of the traditional historian. Understanding these concerns may open a window on the larger social conditions of the times, through which might emerge insights that no contemporary history writer can afford to dismiss or miss. Knowing the past, like knowing women (or religion, or life, or oneself…) may involve struggling through any number of illusions projected by both self and other both past and present. There are many barriers in the way, which is not to say that we should allow ourselves to be discouraged.

THE AUTOBIOGRAPHY OF A MEDIEVAL HERMITESS: ORGYAN CHOKYI (1675–1729)

Kurtis R. Schaeffer

Orgyan Chokyi was a nun and hermitess from the south-eastern corner of the Tibetan cultural region known as Dolpo, the highland region of the Nepal Himalaya immediately west of Mustang. Born in 1675 to a father afflicted by leprosy and a mother who did not want her, she died prematurely at the age of fifty-five when a wooden beam fell on her head during a ritual in 1729, fatally wounding her.[1] This woman from Himalaya was the author of a striking example of what is perhaps the most intriguing form of Tibetan Buddhist literature—the spiritual autobiography.[2] Autobiographies by women were uncommon in Tibet. Out of the over 150 Tibetan autobiographies currently known only three or four are by women, and among these the autobiography of Orgyan Chokyi is the earliest by some two centuries.[3]

[1] The number of modern works dedicated to Buddhism in Dolpo is considerably less than those devoted to Mustang, or the more eastern Sherpa regions. Snellgrove travelled through Dolpo in 1956 and stayed there again in 1960–1. Ch. 3 (pp. 70–163) of Snellgrove 1989 is one of the most enjoyable accounts of mid-twentieth century religious life in the region. Snellgrove 1967, from which we hear more below, is probably the most important work on Buddhism in Dolpo to date. A detailed and fascinating ethnographic account of Tarap, the south-eastern corner of Dolpo, was carried out in the mid-1960s by Jest 1975. Samuel 1993: 322–4 typologizes Dolpo under the 'remote agricultural pattern', in which 'there are sometimes small communities of *trapa* [monks] and *ani* [nuns] but there are rarely monastic *gompa* [monasteries] of any size. The leading religious practitioners are hereditary or (less often) reincarnate lamas, often of the Nyingmapa order. Communities of part-time *chöpa* [religious practioners] who are noncelibate and do agricultural work as well as their religious duties are also common.' As a general starting point Samuel's characterization is useful, but it must not discourage particularization through continued historical and anthropological study. Other recent contributions to the historical study of Buddhism in Dolpo include Ehrhard 1996 and 1998 and Mathes 1999. Pictures of many of the religious structures of Dolpo can be found in Snellgrove 1967 and 1989 and Mathes 1999. Jest 1981 provides an overview of Tibetan Buddhist monuments of the Nepal Himalayas.

[2] Orgyan Chokyi has, to my knowledge, been briefly mentioned twice in modern scholarly literature: in Ehrhard 1998: 9 and 13 and Jest 1974: 306–7.

[3] See Gyatso 1992: 470 and Havnevik 1997: 357. Gyatso 1998: 282 cites Tashi Tsering, who mentions a 'post-twelfth century' autobiography by one Sonam Peldren. This is most

Like no other genre of Tibetan literature, autobiography holds the potential to reveal the most intimate details of the religious life in its full spectrum—from evanescent experiences of realization to the mundane sufferings of daily life in troubled times. Yet this genre of literature is also an important instrument of religious edification and inspiration and as such is always based upon conventions drawn from centuries of Buddhist narrative literature. Orgyan Chokyi does not disappoint the reader on either account; she writes the story of her quest for the eremitic life in vivid and gripping terms, in simple and direct words which evoke the hardships of daily life in Dolpo while never losing sight of the fundamental themes of Buddhism.

I focus primarily on the conventional and doctrinal aspects of Orgyan Chokyi's life-story rather than the cultural history of Dolpo in her time, with full awareness that life and writing cannot be so neatly divided. The next two sections of the chapter deal respectively with life and writing of the hermitess and the connection between suffering and gender in her poetic songs.

According to Orgyan Chokyi the female body is itself *saṃsāra*. Women's bodies themselves are—in her terms—the round of rebirth and suffering, the negative pole in the dualistic system of bondage and enlightenment which constitutes the Buddhist predicament of human existence.[4] There is a unique rhetoric of the body in this woman's autobiography and I hope to make this clear by comparing it with the rhetoric of suffering in a contemporary man's autobiographical writings. While we cannot make any broad claims about the interplay between gender, rhetoric and religious experience based upon the writings of two individuals, we can fruitfully use such a comparison as a means to orient further studies. This line of inquiry is part of a larger endeavour to look at gender as an important aspect of Buddhist religious life in different times and places and to relate this to transcultural Buddhist themes.

In the final section I extend the discussion of Orgyan Chokyi to women and Buddhism in Dolpo. The aim here is to provide specific, though limited, details on what we can learn about medieval women's religious lives in the Himalaya from the writings of their contemporaries. While Orgyan

likely the three-part autobiography of Sonam Peldren (bSod-nams dPal-dren n.d.) All three of these were written in collaboration with one Rinchen Pel, who integrates his questions about Sonam Peldren's experiences with her responses. I have not been able to date this work yet.

4 My concern here is to understand the viewpoints of Orgyan Chokyi herself on gender and suffering as expressed in her autobiography and not to develop a theory of gender in Buddhism. It should go without saying that I do not intend the following analyses of her writing to refer to Buddhist women's experiences in general.

Chokyi's autobiography is a rare example of a woman's autobiography, it is part of a common literary heritage of life-writing which includes contemporary Buddhist masters from Dolpo, Mustang and other regions of the Nepal Himalaya and ultimately stretches back to the biographies of Milarepa that spread throughout the Tibetan cultural world. These biographies and autobiographies capture the personal suffering and the spiritual achievements of great Buddhist practitioners in order to teach and inspire the readers and listeners of these works.

ORGYAN CHOKYI AND HER AUTOBIOGRAPHY

The life-story of Orgyan Chokyi is at present the earliest datable Tibetan woman's autobiography and thus holds an important place among Tibetan autobiographies.[5] It was composed some 220 years prior to the autobiography of Jetsun Lochen Rinpoche (1865–1951) (Havnevik 1997: 356). The autobiography of Sera Khandro is also a twentieth-century composition.[6] Unlike the work of Jetsun Lochen, Orgyan Chokyi's autobiography does not specifically claim to have been written down by anyone other than herself. The majority of women's life-stories in Tibetan currently known owe themselves either entirely or in part to the efforts of male disciples or descendants. The biography of the first abbess of Samding nunnery, Chokyi Dronma (c. 1422–55),[7] was the work of a close male

[5] However, if we are willing to consider the 'delog' (*'das-log*) literature—accounts of those who have travelled to hell and back—as a part of the autobiographical tradition as a whole, then the 'namtar' (*rnam-thar*) of Lingsa Chokyi may be the earliest autobiography; Epstein 1982: 80, dates her to the sixteenth century. Her story is certainly told in the first person. See Gling-za 1977: 410–11. The singular focus of these tales, namely the trip to hell and the ethical message brought back for the sake of the living, sets them apart from those autobiographies which seek to relate the events of one's life in this world among the living. Still, the narrative traditions of the delog need to be examined in relation to the biographical and autobiographical traditions as a whole.

One thing is sure, the delog literature is the one place where women have written or been written about more than men. Indeed the percentages are astounding; if we take the fourteen delog namtar listed in Epstein (1982) and add to them the story of Dawa Drolma recently translated in Delog Dawa Drolma 1995 (or is her name Dawa Dronma [*Zla-ba sGron-ma*]?; the Tibetan folio reproduced opposite p. 1 of the translation clearly has Da-dron [*Zla-sgron*]) we find that nine out of fifteen, or sixty per cent of delog biographies are by or about women. The reasons for this deserve more attention. See Pommaret 1989 for a full study of delog literature.

[6] See Havnevik 1997: 357 where, citing an unpublished paper by Tashi Tsering, she says that Sera Khandro was born in 1892.

[7] These dates are tentative. Her biography (*Ye shes* n.d.) gives her birth year as a tiger (*stag*) year. According to the late sixteenth century *Bo dong chos 'byung* of Chime Ozer, translated in Diemberger and Wangdu 1997: 111, she died at age thirty-four. We know that she was present at the death of Bodong Chokle Namgyal (1375–1451) and thus the tiger year would seem to be 1422.

student, although it does contain passages that are said to be the direct speech of Chokyi Dronma herself.[8] The biography of Mingyur Peldron (1699–1769)—daughter of the great treasure finder, Terdak Lingpa (1646–1714) and renovator of Mindrol Ling Monastery after the Dzungar invasion of 1717—is likewise the work of her disciple Khyungpo Repa (1715–*c.* 1782) (Khyung-po 1984: 234–7). Orgyan Chokyi's story is different in other respects as well. It is not a work of learned literature such as the biography of Chokyi Dronma. It lacks the poetic flourish of Jetsun Lochen's long work (Havenvik 1997: 361, 1999; Rig-'dzin Chos-nyid 1997: 318–19), or the eloquent and tradition-laden accounts of Mingyur Peldron's previous embodiments. It is not organized in terms of the exoteric-esoteric-secret (*phyi nang gsang*) divisions of spiritual autobiography, as is the story of Sonam Peldren. Orgyan Chokyi was not the daughter of a great teacher and she was not born into an aristocratic family. She was the daughter of farmers in the village highlands of the remote valleys of the Himalaya and she was reared and educated in these same valleys. Her autobiography reflects her humble origins—and this is precisely its strength, for her story is replete with inspirational examples drawn directly from the lives of its traditional readers.

The autobiography consists of ten chapters, an introduction and a brief conclusion. A list of the chapter titles will reveal the major concerns of the work:

(Youth)
1. How a mountain of suffering arose in her youth
2. How she was a goat-herd and was sorrowful
3. How she cut her hair, herded horses and impermanence arose

(Mid-life)
4. How she requested religious teachings and understood the stillness and movement [of the mind]
5. How she went on pilgrimage to Kathmandu and Mt Kailash offering prayers
6. How she worked in the kitchen and was in mental anguish

(Later life)
7. How she quit the bustle, meditated and recited *oṃ maṇi padme hūṃ*
8. How she lived in solitude and joyous experiences dawned upon her

[8] Our copy of *Ye shes* n.d. is missing the last two folia and thus the colophon. Nevertheless, the author refers to himself as 'I' (*kho-bo*, f. 2a.3) and reports the words of Chokyi Dronma in which she uses the feminine pronoun *kho-mo*. Still, the vast majority of the biography is the work of the male author. See Diemberger and Wangdu 1997: 32–7 and 110–14 for a recent summary in English of the Dorje Phagmo lineage.

9. How she preserved the commitment and vows and opened the three doors

(Death and funeral proceedings described by disciples)
10. How she pointed out impermanence through death
(O-rgyan Chos-skyid n.d.a: 1b–2b)

As the chapter titles suggest, the two overarching themes of the work are suffering and impermanence. Orgyan Chokyi described suffering in social, bodily and karmic terms. From the 'mountain of suffering' that was her early family life to her untimely death, the pervasiveness of suffering and impermanence was described again and again.[9]

Although the autobiography mentions her age only seven times and contains only one specific date, the basic chronology of Orgyan Chokyi's life can be constructed by comparing her writing with that of her teacher, Orgyan Tenzin (1657–1737).[10] From her earliest memories of her early life, roughly 1675–85, we are confronted with scenes of a difficult high mountain farming life, made no easier by parents who did not care for her. Until age ten she was in the care of her parents and does not appear to have travelled far from home. In 1686, at age eleven, she became a goatherder and thus ranged through the hillsides of her homeland. As a teenager she took ordination—she does not say specifically which vows she took—under Orgyan Tenzin, beginning a teacher-student relationship which would last until her death, more than three decades later.

At the age of twenty, in 1694, she moved from herding goats to horses. One year later she entered into a difficult and intensive period of study and meditation which lasted for much of her twenties. Her late twenties and thirties appear to receive little attention in the autobiography, although this must have been the period in which she went on pilgrimage to Kathmandu. In her late thirties and early forties she lived at Nyima Phug—'Sun Cave'—a site of bustling religious activity in Dolpo. The last three years at Nyima Phug were spent in solitary retreat, but as the establishment grew it became more difficult to maintain her solitude. In 1724, at the age of fifty, she moved to a more isolated retreat at Tandru. It was here that she spent the last years of her life alone, visiting nearby communities occasionally to perform rituals and spend time with her female friends. It was during one of these visits that she was fatally injured by a falling

[9] The question of precisely what sources went into the development of Orgyan Chokyi's descriptions of suffering and women is an open one. In general terms, the songs of Milarepa, so popular among the faithful of the Nepal Himalaya, must have played a role. See, for instance, the story of Mila's female disciple Peldar Bum in Chang 1999: 136–48.

[10] See Ehrhard 1998 for a discussion of this master's life and travels.

wooden beam. After eight days of attempts by her well-wishers to heal the wound on her head, she died at the age of fifty-five, in the year 1729.

The introduction to Orgyan Chokyi's story of her life contains an explicit testimony of the difficulties women encountered in trying to produce religious literature. As in so many cultures, women are barely represented in the vast corpus of Tibetan literature. Even though it is abundantly clear that women have played important and varied roles in the religious life of the Tibetan cultural world, they have never been in positions of authority sufficient to contribute substantially to the traditions of writing in which men have so excelled. The following passage illustrates what might be a prototypical scene lying behind this imbalance. Orgyan Chokyi writes:

> [I, Orgyan Chokyi] said: 'I have good reason to write a few words on my joys and sufferings. Therefore I pray of you master, write it down.' When [I] said this [the master] said: 'There is no reason to write a liberation tale for you—a woman.' And thinking on this woman's words he added: 'You must be silent!'
>
> Many tears fell from my eyes. I did not myself know how to write. I said, 'If I knew how to write, I would have reason to write of my joys and sufferings.' Later, when I was dying, amazing omens of my death arose and I thought: 'I have been struck with the spiritual instruction of the *ḍākinīs*.' The impediment of not being able to write disappeared and I wrote. (O-rgyan Chos-skyid n.d.a: 2b)

Thus, in violation of her master's wishes, Orgyan Chokyi began to write the story of her life.[11] Although she claimed ignorance of writing before the benevolent influence of the *ḍākinīs*, she mentioned elsewhere that she received instruction in writing from a senior nun.[12]

Orgyan Chokyi was born to parents who did not want a girl. She relates that they were hoping for a boy and when she was born her mother was depressed. Her mother was generally antagonistic toward her. Early in her childhood her father was stricken with leprosy. This caused him to act resentfully toward her and thus she found only misery from her parents. Her descriptions of her early life centre mainly around her tormented family and her work as a goat-herder—both of which caused her profound grief—and her meetings with monks and nuns. These meetings were the only encounters which brought her solace as a youth. Nuns and monks intervened on her behalf when her parents beat her and they

11 Jetsun Lochen also encountered strictures against writing; see Havnevik 1998: 101.

12 This is a not uncommon trope in the spiritual autobiographies of western women. See Myers and Powell's engaging study (1999) of Madre María de San José (1656–1719), p. 312: 'She frequently states, "I don't know how to write." While these comments participate in formulaic claims to modesty and ignorance, they may also reflect María's awareness of the gap between her own often vernacular style and that of more learned, polished texts published with ecclesiastical support.' I think much the same can be said of Orgyan Chokyi.

complimented her early on for her sense of compassion. The following, somewhat abridged, translation of chapter one of the autobiography provides some idea of the tone of the work as a whole (O-rgyan Chos-skyid n.d.a: 3b–8b):

BIRTH AND EARLY LIFE

Father's name was Drangsong Phuntsok. His ancestry was Sepa. His place was Zolung. He was a Buddhist, but he [also] practised the Bon religion. In terms of exoteric, esoteric and secret qualities he was a scholar. When all the patrons had faith and reverence, my consciousness was residing in Father's body and then went into the womb of my mother, Kunga Sangmo. My mother's ancestral line was Gyamo. Her place was Peson. Nine months later they were hoping for a boy, but a girl came and Mother was depressed. They gave me the name Kyilog, 'Happiness Dashed'. Then Father was stricken with leprosy. [I] sang this song of Mother's suffering:

> [Homage to] Father, Omniscient Master and Avalokiteśvara
> A nun, I'm not leaving the door of religion.
> But if I was a lazy trouble-making son with no religion
> Would mother want this boy instead of my religion?
>
> In so many bad stories it is a daughter that comes:
> [Mother said]:
> 'Great yogin, fantastic Lord Drangsong Phuntsok,
> Boasting of drawing up the channels and vital winds: look at this girl!
> The shame and depression are unbearable.'
> A nun, I'm not going among the masses.
> This girl will not show herself to people, but take refuge in the mountain crag.

Many such sorrowful songs were sung.

Sufferings of youth

Now I will speak of the sufferings of [my] youth: Mother said she hated me. She would say to me, 'Girl, you tell awful stories!' The people said that I did many unkind things and because of this untold mental anguish came [to me]. As I remember now, from five to ten years of age there were suffering, yelling, unnecessary beating and the food was not good. Untold mental anguish came [to me].

Father Drangsong was covered with leprosy and was at the end of his rope. He was miserable. He said he hated me. Everybody saw this and there were many who said, 'What a pity!'

I went to Peson, but Mother was not there. In Shapku the monk Kunga Pendar and Ani Peldzom saw me. 'Kyilog, girl come here!' they called and they gave me some soup that was like water. They both cried [when I told them my tale]. 'What suffering has come to you, girl!' they said. I told them a long sad tale and they said 'What a pity!'

Ani Peldzom drew a wash tub for my face and said, 'Girls should not suffer in mind so!' Then I said, 'May [I] never be born into laziness and strife in all [my] future lives.' She brought solace to my mind. I was feeling both joy and sorrow and I cried a great deal.

Learning to weave

Father was covered with leprosy for about five years. One night he was hitting me, Drolma the monk and Phuntsok the yogi said, 'Drangsong, this girl is not the cause of your leprosy. Do not act like this; be kind.' Untold mental anguish came to me.

Then there was no one to carry father's leprous corpse away, so [somebody] said, 'In the little valley make an offering house and bury him secretly.' Mother worked like a donkey. Her woollen [clothes] were filthy and covered with manure. 'Take it away!' [She] said. So I threw the pile of wool in the fire. Well, Mother heard this and said, 'If a low-born girl does not know how to work with wool, from where will happiness come to you?' Then she threw a spindle at [my] head and I was sad and cried a lot.

Being around Father was miserable, [but now] I thought, 'Now Mother will still not be nice to me', and I was in mental anguish. Then Ani Peldzom said to Mother, 'You should not hit a small girl like that. Be kind, go slowly. You need to teach her how to work with wool.' Then she left.

Then I learned how to weave. But I could not remember [anything] and Mother threw a weaving shuttle at my head. Much mental anguish came [to me]. Then I learned something of working with wool, but I didn't know anything about weaving. Since my body was not strong I couldn't even work in the fields well. I did not know what to think. One day Mother looked at me and said, 'Learning spinning and weaving is for you. Do not create this mental suffering.' I thought, 'Mother is right.'

These are a few tales from the mountain of suffering that arose in [my] youth.

Orgyan Chokyi's outlook on life was no doubt greatly influenced by these early experiences of family dysfunction. Yet it appears that the presence of a few compassionate individuals also had a lasting effect on her feelings of empathy toward other beings. Her early descriptions of the suffering she endured as a small girl give way in later chapters to lamentations for the nanny goats and mares who had lost their offspring. She writes (ibid.: 8b):

One day I went to Ratso Ruri. As I was going through the thick woods, a thorn became stuck in my leg and I stopped to remove it. A nanny-goat had had a kid and it was about seven days old. Suddenly an eagle swept out of the sky and carried the kid away. The nanny-goat looked into the sky and wept. I also looked into the sky and wept. Some herders said, 'Every year a kid is carried away by an eagle. Don't weep!'

Then one day I was going from Dolpo to the border of lowlander territory when the nanny-goat was carried away into the sky. I wept for the mother and the kid. Kunga Pelsang the monk came and said, 'Do not weep. The mountain will be disturbed.'

During the middle period of her life Orgyan Chokyi concentrated primarily on her experiences in mental training, receiving religious teachings,[13] going on pilgrimage,[14] and doing housework. While she spends a great deal of time later in the autobiography describing her personal struggles within the master-disciple relationship and the long process of meditative development, she does not spend much time recounting the teachers of her lineage or the teachings she received, a characteristic feature of men's descriptions of their early maturity.[15] She worked as a horse keeper, she went on pilgrimage to the Kathmandu valley and she received Nyingma teachings from her master. The major and continuing crisis of her life revolved around her intense desire to practise meditation in solitude, which was in direct tension with the socially dictated requirement that she work in the kitchen of her village monastic complex. Orgyan Chokyi makes it clear that the domestic duty she was forced to perform was a major obstacle to her spiritual advancement.[16] She describes the mental challenges of contemplative practice and in an extremely down-to-earth way detailed her many question and answer sessions with her master.

The will to get away from the mind-numbing hardship of manual labour in order to advance her contemplative practice is the major theme of the later chapters of her story. It took her a number of years to succeed after pleading with her master on numerous occasions. The uniqueness of her request is suggested by the fact that Orgyan Tenzin himself describes her urgent request in his own verse autobiography.[17] The later chapters of the autobiography dwell on her joyous experiences in solitude at Sun Cave and Tandru, where she eventually spent almost a decade in meditation retreat. Merely to be able to devote her time to meditation was an

[13] The religious teachings she received included the *Byang gter* and the *Ma ṇi bka' 'bum* .

[14] Most of the action in the chapter dedicated to her pilgrimage itinerary is centred around the Kathmandu valley, although the title of the chapter includes Ti-se (Mt. Kailash).

[15] The comments of Myers and Powell 1999: 313, on medieval Hispanic women's spiritual autobiographies could also fit the case of Orgyan Chokyi: 'Most male religious writers recall a period of formal education in which they learned Latin, rhetoric, philosophy and theology, followed eventually by the religious vocation; women, by contrast, write about experiencing the divine without formal training beyond submission to a practice of the basic tenets of the faith.'

[16] Her descriptions stand in stark contrast to the whimsical impressions of monastic kitchen life evoked in Aziz 1976.

[17] O-rgyan bsTan-'dzin 1985: 29.6–30.1. This episode occurred sometime between 1706 and 1722; see ff. 27.4 and 33.3.

unqualified success for her and she expands on the pleasures of her retreat cave. The freedom to sequester herself in retreat was the culminating success of her life; indeed she had been working toward autonomy for most of her life.[18] She narrates the simple and basic freedoms which her new life as a hermitess afforded her (O-rgyan Chos-skyid n.d.a: 70a):

> Before, when I was tending the kitchen fire, I had to get out of bed by lamp before dawn. Now I do not have to get up at dawn if I do not want to. If I want to take soup, I am free to do so when I am hungry; I am free to eat when I think of it. I can wear clothes on the path and I can go naked when I am in my cell practising [meditation]… Serving myself (*rang-g.yog*), self-empowered (*rang-gi byed-dbang*), I have escaped people. I have attained autonomy (*rang-dbang*).

During this time she struggled through the meditative and visionary practices of the Great Perfection (*rDzogs-chen*) teachings.[19] Although she was personally involved in the teachings of the Nyingma school, it is not the past masters of this school to whom she looked for inspiration. Rather, she evoked several great women of the past as her inspirational models, including Nangsa Obum, Machig Labdron and Gelongma Pelmo.[20] She also described her efforts at building a community with other nuns in southern Dolpo. Much of the narrative is taken up with dialogues between her primary female superior, the great meditator (*sgrub-chen-ma*), Ani Sonam Drolma, or between her and her sisters in religion.[21] This is the beauty of the autobiography; Orgyan Chokyi speaks about her personal religious life, a life which we come to see as intimately bound with the lives of her female companions.

[18] See Ortner 1996: 131, where she tells us that the search for autonomy was a primary motivation to become a nun among Sherpa women during the mid-twentieth century.

[19] She describes her experiences of *thod-rgal* visions ('supreme vision', 'direct crossing') and the difficulties she has in interpreting these visions with her master. On *thod-rgal* in the autobiographical poetry of Jigme Lingpa (1730–98), see Gyatso 1998a: 202–6.

[20] The story of Gelongma Pelmo was retold throughout the Tibetan regions of the Nepal Himalayas by such women *ma-ṇi-pas* as Jetsun Lochen; see Havnevik 1998: 89. Her story is also important in popular nyungne fasting rituals among the Sherpa (Ortner 1989: 181). See also Ortner 1978: ch. 3. It is likely that Orgyan Chokyi also heard the story of Gelongma Pelmo in the context of this fasting practice; her autobiography mentions several occasions in her later life on which she and other village women sponsored fasting rituals. For classical Tibetan versions of the story of Gelongma Pelmo, see the first story in the histories of 'nyungne' lineages. (Martin 1997: entries 98, 109, 295, 385)

[21] There are at least ten different nuns, or 'ani' mentioned by Orgyan Chokyi: Ani Peldzom, Ani Drubchenma Sonam Drolma, Ani Tsuga, Ani Tsering Kyebma, Ani Nyishar, Ani Dzompa Kyi, Ani Kunga Chokyi, Ani Drubamo Pelden Drolma, Ani Kunga Drolma and Ani Chosangmo. Other women, primarily patrons, are also discussed at length. Compare these with the long list of women's names in Madrong 1997: 87–9. The term *jo-mo* for 'nun' does not occur once in Orgyan Chokyi's work and *btsun-ma* only infrequently. 'Ani' is the term of choice.

In 1729 Orgyan Chokyi was performing the fasting and prayer ritual called 'nyungne' (*smyung-gnas*)[22] with other nuns of her community when a log fell on her head and killed her. By the end of her life she must have been fairly well-known in the area, for her teacher Orgyan Tenzin mentioned the great sadness felt by the villagers of Tadru as they prepared her reliquary stupa.[23] By the time her autobiography was being reproduced by faithful patrons such as the nun Ani Sangmo of Samten Ling, she was considered an emanation of Guhyajñāna herself—primordial wellspring of the Mahākaruṇika teachings (O-rgyan Chos-skyid n.d.a: 57a).

At the close of the ninth chapter, we leave the words of Orgyan Chokyi and move to her disciples' description of her last days. At this point we discern the presence of a scribe or an editor.
The editor added this comment at the end of chapter nine:

> The above are the many words spoken by the *ḍākinī*, [Orgyan Chokyi] herself. This is a condensed account. Some prose passages were put into verse; nothing else was changed. If the life-story of the *ḍākinī* were to be written [fully] from the beginning, it would be merely a copy of the life story of Nangsa Obum [the famous heroine of the Tibetan opera]. (O-rgyan Chos-skyid n.d.a: 78b–79a)

This is a remarkable statement given the great dissimilarity of these two works; the tale of Nangsa Obum belongs to a group of narratives dedicated to people who have died, travelled through the land of the dead and returned to impart ethical teachings to the living through coercive examples of what awaits them in hell if they do not follow the Dharma. Perhaps the emphasis on ethical teachings found in the two life-stories

22 This fasting ritual appears to have been as important in late seventeenth century Dolpo as it is today throughout the Nepal Himalayas. Watkins 1996 describes women's participation in nyungne in her ethnographic account of Nyeshang, to the west of Dolpo. The fourteenth/fifteenth century history of nyungne by Joden Sonam Sangpo (Martin 1997: entry 98) explicitly states that this practice is beneficial to women: 'If a lowly woman performs the fasting ritual once, when she dies she will be reborn as a bodhisattva who dwells on the first level and will turn her back to saṃsāra' (see Jo-gdan n.d.: 9a.6). And yet even here the success of women is held to be less than that of men; according to Jodan Sonam Sangpo, if a male animal hears the spell (*dhāraṇī*) associated with this ritual three times he will be reborn in Sukhāvatī heaven, skipping the human state altogether. But if a female animal hears the same, she will not go straight to Sukhāvatī, but be reborn as a human (see Jo-gdan n.d.: 10a.2–5).

23 See O-rgyan bsTan-'dzin 1985: 34.4. This passage allows us to date Orgyan Chokyi. She died when Orgyan Tenzin was seventy-two, in 1728/9. In her autobiography the year of her death is said to be a *bya* year, which can only be 1729. She lived fifty-five years by Tibetan reckoning, or fifty-four in western terms and thus she can be dated 1675–1729. Orgyan Tenzin, like his friend Tenzin Repa, mentions the female practitioners he encountered on his travels, among whom was a faithful nun at Sadul Temple on the southern border of Dolpo (see ibid.: 84.4).

led this anonymous editor to draw a parallel between Orgyan Chokyi and Nangsa Obum, rather than any similarity in the course of their respective life narratives.

When so many autobiographies and biographies of Tibetan men are but pallid recapitulations of the forms of their teachers' life-stories and those of their teachers before them, it is sadly ironic that Orgyan Chokyi's unique work was apparently cut short by a scribe because of its perceived similarity with a work of the past.

Suffering, saṃsāra, and gender

In what follows I would like to look more closely at several of Orgyan Chokyi's songs on suffering and impermanence. These songs indicate the tone of the autobiography as a whole and they exemplify her views on the relationship between gender and suffering. For Orgyan Chokyi suffering is affected by gender, or suffering is gendered. According to her the very nature of suffering is explicitly associated with the female body in the autobiography. This is one of the most important points that can be drawn from this work in terms of the broader study of Buddhism and gender. But her words cannot be understood in isolation. Was this gendering of suffering something unique to Orgyan Chokyi, or does it occur across a range of Tibetan Buddhist writings? I suggest that this strong equation of suffering with the female body was a distinctive feature of Orgyan Chokyi's writing as a woman. She characterized suffering differently from her male contemporaries precisely because of her experiences as a Buddhist woman.

The context in which the autobiography of Orgyan Chokyi is placed here is at once more broad and more limited than life in Dolpo: the ongoing Buddhist discussion of the nature of suffering.[24] As we shall see, much of her life-story is dedicated to describing the various forms of social, mental and bodily suffering which she endured during the course of her life and which led her to the religious vocation. Suffering—and its particular Buddhist partner, impermanence—are in fact the crucial themes of her autobiography. The topic of suffering is of course central to Buddhism and it links the writings of this eighteenth century woman to what is traditionally held to be the first teaching of the Buddha himself, the first of the four noble truths: the existence of suffering.

The assumption of a close relationship between women and suffering has long standing in Buddhism. Early Buddhist literature presents a list

[24] Lichter and Epstein 1983 provide an excellent overview of the nature of suffering and happiness in their study of karma as understood by Tibetan Buddhist laity.

of unique situations of women's suffering; the *Samyuta Nikāya* names five of these: (1) leaving blood after marriage; (2) menstruation; (3) pregnancy; (4) giving birth; (5) waiting upon a man (Harris 1999: 54). As several writers have noted, women were often associated symbolically with the evils of saṃsāra.[25] Less often do we find so pronounced an equation between the sufferings of women and the nature of saṃsāra as we do in the songs of Orgyan Chokyi.[26] While it is certainly clear that in the Buddhist tradition both men and women are subject to the miseries of saṃsāra, women, according to Orgyan Chokyi, must suffer precisely because of their bodies. On several occasions she employed stories of animals to emphasize this point. Her early experiences herding goats and sheep fostered in her a profound feeling of empathy for the beasts she looked after. Sold to butchers, eaten by wild cats, lost over the cliffs of the Dolpo mountain highlands, the sufferings of animals became for the young working nun symbolic of the sufferings of all beings. The sufferings of female beasts of burden, 'dzomo' (*mdzo-mo*), provided especially poignant circumstances for lamenting the misery of mothers. Orgyan Chokyi sang the following song after witnessing a dzomo trying to save her calf from the attack of a mountain lion. The rescue failed and both mother and offspring were killed. Orgyan Chokyi became distraught and she began her sorrowful song, mourning the loss of her dzomo. But she took the scene one step further, allegorizing the calf's fate as a powerful commentary on the fate of all women, or at least all mothers. Yet even here she did not stop; the intimacy with which female beings encounter suffering links them closely to saṃsāra itself, so much so that for Orgyan Chokyi the female body, human or otherwise, is in fact saṃsāra. The song makes the equation clear:

> Alas, alas, Bodhisattva of Mercy,
> May you look upon all beings with compassion.
> Three days past this dzomo was here; today, gone.
> I look at this and melancholia flares bright.
> The enemy of four legged beasts leapt up,
> Life wrested from this mother dzomo and calf.

[25] According to Paul 1989: 6, 'Symbolically, woman represented the profane world, saṃsāra. Perhaps more detrimentally, women were potential obstacles in actual life to man's spiritual growth.' This last observation applies to Tenzin Repa's comments on the deleterious affects of association with women. See also Harris 1999: 55: 'When woman or the feminine is used in a symbolic or metaphoric way, it is more often linked with *dukkha* and *saṃsāra* than with the holy or mystical.'

[26] This point requires further cross-cultural comparative research. Wilson 1996: 71 argues that in early Indian Buddhist narrative '....similes constitute *saṃsāra* as feminine and entrapment in *saṃsāra* as a male dilemma...' This is not the case in Orgyan Chokyi's equation of saṃsāra and the female body; she is not concerned with the dilemmas of men, but with her own spiritual dilemma.

Humans, horses, dogs, all beings,
Male and female all think alike,
But the suffering of life comes to females as a matter of course.
I could do without the misery of this female life.
How I lament this broken vessel, this female body.

I could do without this female body with its misery.
Ranting thoughts dwell in this woman's body.
From within the body, spreading outward,
From the centre of the mind misery comes unchecked.

Like the dzomo protecting her calf,
They give up life for their children.
This female body is itself saṃsāra—the round of existence.
May I attain a male body and keep the vows,
May I never again be born in the body of a woman!
(O-rgyan Chos-skyid n.d.a: 17a)

As a natural outgrowth of the equation of female bodies with saṃsāra, Orgyan Chokyi included several prayers to be reborn a male.[27] In the following song she laments the fate of the horses she herds, chastising the stallions for their indifference to their mates and championing the hardships of mares.

When I ponder our female bodies
I am sorrowful; impermanence rings clear.
When men and women couple—creating more life—
Happiness is rare, but suffering is felt for a long time.

May I not be born again in a female body.
May the mare not be born as a mare.
The steed follows yet another mare.
When I see the shamelessness of men,
[I think:] 'May I be born in a body that will sustain the precepts.'

When acts of desire are committed, suffering must follow.
When I see the mare suffering, melancholia flares.
Behold us with mercy, Lord of Compassion.
Let me not be born a woman in all lives to come.
When I ponder the suffering of beings, melancholia flares.
(O-rgyan Chos-skyid n.d.a: 15a).

The prayer to be reborn a man comes up again in the chapter on pilgrimage. Indeed, other than a list of places at which she prayed, this prayer forms the central element of the chapter. Here she prayed fervently while walking around the great stupas of the Kathmandu valley, Bodhnāth and Swayambhūnāth:

27 Von Fürer-Haimendorf 1976: 136 and 148 notes that several nuns at Bigu nunnery in Nepal also expressed a wish to be reborn male. See also Havnevik 1989: 163–5.

In the presence of both stupas I prostrated, made circumambulations and offered aspirational prayers. 'I, Orgyan Chokyi…' I would say and make prayers to the gods, the three jewels and the stupas.

Then, at the close of *Samāntabhadra Prayer* or whatever prayer I knew [I would pray]: May the sins and obscurations of all six classes of beings who have ever been my kind mother and father in the unending saṃsāra of rebirth—be purified and may they complete the two accumulations [of wisdom and merit].

May I never be born in a female body in any rebirth. Having attained a male body, may I be able to sustain pure conduct. (ibid.: 38a)

In these songs and prayers Orgyan Chọkyi seems to internalize all that has been negatively claimed of women in Buddhism. However, we can see something more going on in the autobiography than simple internalization, which is a subtle use of gender transformation that actually extols women's ability to practise the Dharma.[28] Orgyan Chokyi's suffering as a woman allowed her to see and teach more directly. If, as she states, the very nature of a woman is suffering, then women know best about its nature and how to eradicate it. Women are experts in suffering, she might have said and who better than a woman like Orgyan Chokyi to explain its workings?

Further, in this single song Orgyan Chokyi criticizes the actions of men in marriage while at the same time praying to be reborn as a male: 'When I see the shamelessness of men [I think,] "May I be born in a body that will sustain the precepts."' From elsewhere in her work we know that a male body is implied here. She did not merely pray to be reborn as a male; she would be a male capable of sustaining the precepts, the ethical and spiritual teachings of Buddhism. The implication of the paradox is this: with her intimate knowledge of suffering from the perspective of a woman—embodied in the saṃsāric female form—she would use a male body better than the men around her in the spiritual quest. Knowing what she knew, she would not waste the opportunity a male body provided, like so many horse-like men did. Her prayer to be reborn a man contained a scathing critique of the inability of men to use their advantage in the practice of Dharma. Her message thus addresses both a male and female audience and one can only wonder how her thinly veiled animal allegories struck the men of her religious community.

A further move can be seen in the autobiography too: the muted critique of her male masters through the absence of praise. A conventional feature of Tibetan spiritual autobiographies is the effusive praise of one's masters. Orgyan Chokyi recorded many meetings with her master, Orgyan Tenzin, when she first became a nun. Nevertheless, she is all too

[28] See Bynum 1991: 16–17: '….Marginal and disadvantaged groups in a society appropriate that society's dominant symbols and ideas that revise and undercut them.'

restrained in her descriptions of their encounters and he is often represented as being either mocking or somewhat elusive. Given that her story begins with her master forbidding her to write at all, it is little wonder she does not expend too many words in his favour. In the context of Tibetan autobiography, the muted tone she adopts with regard Orgyan Tenzin hints at a relationship of antagonism, one about which she had mixed feelings.

We can say then that Orgyan Chokyi made rhetorical use of the perceived lower status of her gender.[29] Throughout the verse and prose sections of the autobiography she used gender as a teaching aid to emphasize the first noble truth, impermanence. She accomplished this through the most personal and concrete example she could have used: her own body. And her greatest weakness was in fact a great strength: her suffering as a woman permitted her a powerful insight into the nature of the first noble truth and an inspirational rhetoric of suffering.[30]

As the final verses of the work show, the lesson of her life lay precisely in its ability to encourage others to ever more involvement in the religious life. Though her story may be subtly critical in its portrayal of the relation between gender and spiritual efforts, it also upholds the value of traditional Buddhist practices. Her autobiography is, in the end, one long exhortation to practice, in which the scenes of her life offer the reader or listener a powerful model to emulate in the ongoing struggle to live according to the Dharma.

With Orgyan Chokyi's songs in mind I would like to turn for a moment to the songs and autobiographical writings of her male senior contemporary, the Drugpa Kagyu master Tenzin Repa, who—though born in Muktināth—spent the better part of his mature religious career in Dolpo, very near Orgyan Chokyi's homeland.[31] Both writers evoke the passage from

29 But I do not want to say that the trials portrayed are simply a matter of pedagogical rhetoric. Again I am inspired by Bynum 1991: 235: 'We must never forget the pain and frustration, the isolation and feelings of helplessness that accompanied the quest of religious women. For all her charismatic empowerment, woman was inferior to man in the Middle Ages; her voice was often silenced, even more frequently ignored. Not every use of the phrase 'weak woman' by a female writer was ironic; women clearly internalized the negative value placed on them by the culture in which they lived.

30 See Myers and Powell 1999: 313: 'While taking part in the rhetoric of humility and ignorance on the one hand, women's reiteration of this "lack" on the other hand had a strategic benefit, pointing up how formal education had not interfered with or tainted the visionary's experience an intuitive knowledge of God.'

31 The life and writings of Tenzin Repa deserve a separate study. Snellgrove 1967 announced his (apparently never realized) desire to undertake a full study of this master. Snellgrove 1989 discusses the task of finding and copying the collected works of Tenzin Repa. Aris 1979 mentions him briefly as a treasure-finder in Kutang. Ehrhard 1994 discusses Tenzin Repa's comments on the sacred landscape of Muktināth, Ehrhard 1996 makes note of his collected works and Ehrhard 1998 mentions his relationship with Orgyan

suffering to freedom as a theme around which to organize their autobiographies. Both describe the traditional themes of hardship and mishap as crucial moments in the spiritual quest. Both were part of a tradition of religious poetic songs which sought to express the human experience in tangible and moving ways, a tradition whose greatest hero is of course Milarepa. However, while Orgyan Chokyi portrays suffering primarily in terms of the female body, motherhood and domestic life, Tenzin Repa's representation of suffering is offered in more general social terms, emphasizing social hypocrisy on a large scale and the inevitability of death.[32]

We must view the songs of both Orgyan Chokyi and Tenzin Repa in the context of the fundamental Buddhist teachings on suffering, the four noble truths. The first of these describes the basic existential predicament of human life, which is that there is suffering, and suffering is the result of craving and change:

> This is the noble truth of suffering: birth is suffering, aging is suffering, sickness is suffering, dying is suffering, sorrow, grief, pain, unhappiness and unease are suffering; being united with what is not liked is suffering, separation from what is liked is suffering; not to get what one wants is suffering; in short, the five components of psychic and physical life and their obsessions are suffering (taken from Gethin 1998: 59).

Tenzin Repa's characterizations of suffering resonate with this definition, formulated some two millennia before him. He finds inspiration for songs and teaching in meditations on the inevitability of death and the uncertainty as to when it will occur. He dwells upon aging, sickness and death in often vivid terms:

> Some die as they leave their mother's womb,
> Some die old and infirm, some in their prime.
> Some are burned by fire, some swept off by floods,
> Some are killed by enemies, some struck down by thieves,
> Some of little faith pass away in despair.
> Who does not die once they are born? (bsTan-'dzin 1971h: 19b.6)

Chokyi's teacher, Orgyan Tenzin. Schuh 1995 translates the genealogical section of one of his autobiographies and discusses the history of his family estate, Rabgyal Tse, the fortified castle of Dzong, ruins of which still stand in the Muktināth valley. Mathes 1999 mentions his activities around the holy mountain of Shelgyi Riwo Drugdra. Photographs of the castle of Dzong can be found in Snellgrove 1979: fig. 15 and Jest 1981: figs 38 and 39. Jest 1981: 68 mentions a statue of Tenzin Repa upon the main altar of the temple atop the ruins of Rabgyal Tse, but I was unable to locate this statue when I visited the temple in March 1999.

32 Although the selection of Tenzin Repa's songs presented here is necessarily limited, the following remarks are based upon an overall reading of the some one hundred songs and autobiographical writings contained in his collected works.

Throughout Tenzin Repa's song we see a rhetorical use of suffering as both an instructional and inspirational theme. Tenzin Repa relates how he himself found strength and mental clarity from the stories of the suffering endured by Milarepa—the archetypal cotton-clad yogin—and the other Kagyu masters of the past as he was tormented by zombies in a delirium of sickness (ibid.: 19b.6). So too is his own story of perseverance in the face of human misery meant to inspire his students. The dramatic conclusion to the song emphasizes this point:

> I cannot remember a single moment of happiness
> Until I was twenty years old.
> If I were to speak in detail of this,
> Even my enemies would be brought to tears.
> Such is the life-story of a cotton-clad. (ibid.: 47a.6)

His vision of suffering also encompassed the social realm. On several occasions he laments the hypocrisy of the religious scene in central Tibet with a mixture of sarcasm and sadness, contrasting it with the serenity of his hermitage in Dolpo, Crystal Mountain Dragon Roar:

> While those bastions of religion in central Tibet make merry,
> And temples are plundered for the sake of their estates,
> Disputes of petty philosophical sophistry flourish.
> As I beheld these ways my heart longed for solitude,
> To Dolpo, to Dragon Roar I fled.
>
> Royal families rage in evil with their armies,
> Dukes just lust for wealth by exacting tax
> Commoners and serfs are struck down by plague.
> As I beheld these ways my heart longed for solitude,
> To Dolpo, to Dragon Roar I fled. (ibid.: 52a.4)

Here we encounter a very different range of vision from that of the songs of Orgyan Chokyi; where Tenzin Repa was concerned with being kidnapped by crooked traders, the timeless inevitability of death for all beings, or the pan-Tibetan hypocrisy of religious life in this degenerate age, Orgyan Chokyi was occupied with smaller, more local and personal forms of misery. She wept over the fate of a young calf, she lamented the fact that her parents wished for a son but only got a daughter and, most significantly, she equated saṃsāra—the realm of suffering itself—with her own body, with the female body. Tenzin Repa's concern covered the translocal network of institutional religion, extending from his home all the way to the great monasteries of central Tibet. He looked outward to the political structures that impeded spiritual practice. He talked of faraway places, places connected to his local religious scene only indirectly. This was quite the opposite of Orgyan Chokyi's interiorized and microsocial lamentations.

One of Tenzin Repa's short autobiographies was composed at the behest of his students and provides an inspirational model of perseverance against the misery of life. The introduction to the song evokes a typical beginning of an auto/biographical project; his disciple, Karma Tenzin, asks that his master's teachings be anthologized and that he composes a small autobiography. Tenzin Repa demurs at first, but then acquiesces:

> At that time Karma Tenzin asked, 'Wouldn't these teachings spread if they were collected and written down?' [The Master said,] 'If I had them in mind, I would do so.' [Karma Tenzin] said, 'Well, since very few of your teachings can be written down as examples, please give a summary of your ancestry, your family, your mother's and father's names and status, your homeland and your life until you ventured toward the Dharma.' The great yogin said, 'Many other instructions and life-stories have already been written. What use is there [now]?' Again [Karma Tenzin] said, 'If we don't ask for your life-story [now], there will be no opportunity later. So please tell us your life in full to guide both myself and these other faithful. If your mind is tired, we really only need root verses.' (ibid.: 46a.3)

Then the song begins and the life of Tenzin Repa is added to those of his spiritual forefathers. This passage is in vivid contrast to the introductory scene of Orgyan Chokyi's autobiography; while Tenzin Repa fights off his disciples' requests to speak even a few verses of his life, Orgyan Chokyi has to plead even to be allowed to write in the first place. While Tenzin Repa complains that his life-story will be just like the many masters of the past—but then goes on tell of his life anyway—Orgyan Chokyi's tale is cut short at the end because a scribe or an editor deems it too similar to one of the few women's life-stories which preceded it.

A song of joy should conclude this look at Orgyan Chokyi's songs for, as is also true in the songs of Tenzin Repa, she had much to say about the pleasures of solitary life. Both spoke of their joys as well as their sufferings and both spoke of a love for their natural surroundings. But the two hermits sought solace from different aspects of their common social world. While Tenzin Repa fled from the hypocrisy of large scale religious institutions, Orgyan Chokyi made it clear that for her freedom is liberation from domestic duties, from the kitchen and all the petty interpersonal misery that made up her life before she was able to sequester herself at Sun Cave. She sings in praise of her small cave:

> This pleasant nook of mine, my rocky cave,
> Is a small place for meditation and reciting *maṇis*.
> There is neither rain nor snow, no unpleasant things here—
> They are cut short by this one-cornered cave.
>
> Above, no thunder—what a joyous place.
> In front, clear blue water, like offering water,
> Many trees, like a banquet display,

Water and trees aplenty, a joyful, auspicious place,
From east to west, Tibetan valleys replete with food.
Whatever I ponder here, my spiritual experience is heightened.

Hearing the teachings of the guru and buddha,
Gaining experience through the strong faith of a beggar woman,
The joyous experience of non-conceptual radiant bliss—
These are mine, Chokyi's joyous spiritual experience.

Solitary, alone and looking after reality,
Free from the chatter of the common people,
Serving religious women of a similar faith—
These are mine, Chokyi's signs of joy.

Far from the kitchen of the residence hall,
Free of the cross speech of the jealous kitchen mistress,
Here, the melody of *maṇi* prayers—
These are the signs of joy for this beggar, myself.
(O-rgyan Chos-skyid n.d.a:. 63b)

ORGYAN CHOKYI IN CONTEXT: RELIGIOUS WOMEN IN MEDIEVAL DOLPO

Though there appear to have been few women writers in Dolpo, it is clear that there were many women who were religious practitioners and patrons in the seventeenth and eighteenth centuries; specific references to the presence of such women in the religious life of Dolpo can be culled from other writings. The male religious leaders of the Nepal Himalaya often mention their female students in their autobiographies,[33] and these writings should be used as sources for the history of religious women. We must be aware, however, the possibility (if not the probability) that writings by men do not give voice to the experiences and concerns of women in the manner in which they might express themselves.

One example can be found in the collected songs and teachings of Taktse Kukye Mipham Phuntsok Sherab, a Drugpa Kagyu master active in Mustang at the end of the seventeenth century. He gave teachings to a number of women, including nuns,[34] noblewomen[35] and a queen.[36] His

33 This is certainly not always the case. It is unfortunate for the present research that the biography of the early sixteenth century master, Namdrol Sangpo (b. 1504), contains nothing of relevance on the religious activities of women during his era (see bSod-nams Blo-gros 1985). For a study of the teaching traditions to which Namdrol Sangmo was heir, see Ehrhard 1996.

34 See sTag-rtse 1971a: 4a.3 where a Jomo Mangkhama is mentioned and f. 7.6 for a Jomo Sangye.

35 Ibid: 27b.1 mentions Dagmo Peldzin Pangmo and f. 27b.4 mentions Dagmo Norzin

36 Ibid: 30a.1 mentions one Gyalmo Tridze.

collected works were in fact printed in Lo Mustang under the patronage of the noblewoman, Jetsunma Phuntsok Lodro Tsomo, to whom he also gave religious teachings.[37]

We might also mention the Dolpo master Chokyab Pelsang (1536–1625), whose autobiography is one of the most fascinating glimpses into the social history of his time (see Snellgrove 1967 v. 1:125–82). The description of the deadly clan feuds in which the family of Chokyab Pelsang was involved provides a harrowing vision of the stormy times in which many of these Buddhist masters lived. His autobiography reveals several items of note regarding women's institutions in Mustang during the late sixteenth and early seventeenth centuries. He had a number of female students and founded at least two convents.

Sometime during the end of the sixteenth century the king of Jumla[38] called on Chokyab Pelsang to end a feud at the village of Khangkar in Mustang. After successfully settling this violent conflict the local chiefs professed their strong adherence to the Dharma and asked him to set up several religious institutions, including a nunnery. He reported the village chief's request: 'In particular, the women are not models of religious action, but only of worldly action. So please cut the hair of many of them and establish a nunnery.'[39] This comment on the religious capabilities of the women of the village is ironic when read in the context of the concurrent quarrel between male leaders and the violent fighting that had taken place at Khangkar in the 1540s (ibid.: 88–92). Shortly after this, Chokyab Pelsang narrated that he set up a monastery and another nunnery near Gami, a village in Mustang and that 'many girls had their hair cut and entered the door to religion' (ibid., v. 1: 154; v. 2: 122).

This type of attention to the places where women are mentioned should accompany our studies of the writings of the male masters of this area. It is a truism to say that women were active in religious life; but it is not redundant to point out the specific language that is used to describe them, the actions that they undertook and—if we can think of this in separate terms at all—the actions of women which men saw fit to describe in their writings. Religious women are described in the writings of Dolpo

[37] See sTag-rtse 1971b: 7b.4–5. More than half of the colophons in Taktse Kukye's some thirty works mention this woman.

[38] From the sixteenth to the eighteenth centuries the royal line at Jumla held an uneasy and difficult rule over much of the high western Himalayan region, including Dolpo, Mustang and Muktināth. The complex history of Jumla in the politics of the western Nepal Himalayas from the sixteenth to the nineteenth centuries has been detailed in Schuh 1994 and 1995. Ehrhard 1998 has discussed the role of the Jumla royalty in the patronage of the Tibetan Buddhist temple of Sadul Gonpa, located on the primary route between Mustang and Jumla on the southern border of Dolpo.

[39] See Snellgrove 1967 v. 1: 153, for a different translation; also Snellgrove 1967 v. 2: 120.

men as nuns (*jo-mo, btsun-ma, a-ne*),[40] laity, patrons (*yon-bdag-ma*), noblewomen (*dpon-mo, btsun-mo*), queens (*lcam-mo, rgyal-mo*) and practitioners (*rnal-'byor-ma, grub-chen-ma*). They travelled from all around Dolpo to meet their teachers and they also travelled from Mustang, from Jumla and even from Sikkim further east to receive Buddhist teachings.[41] But if it is fairly easy to perceive the presence of religious women in the medieval Nepal Himalaya, it is another matter entirely to glimpse their attitudes toward religious life.

We learn much of the religious attitudes of women in Dolpo and Mustang—as well as the attitudes of male religious leaders toward women—from the autobiographical writings of Tenzin Repa. Although I have found no indication that Orgyan Chokyi ever practised under this master, it is clear that she knew of him, for she is listed among the patrons who contributed to the printing of his collected works. Tenzin Repa taught many women and seems in general to have been supportive of women's religious practice. We know that nuns were living at Shey monastery, Tenzin Repa's establishment in northern Dolpo, for its monastic code—put into writing sometime during the late eighteenth or early nineteenth century—includes a number of rules for women as well as men (see *Shes sgon* n.d.: 7b, 9b, 10b, 11a).

Tenzin Repa's writings reveal, however, a tension between this support and his views on the nature of women. Although he did give religious teachings to women, he nevertheless held them to be heavily subject to their desires and associated them explicitly with saṃsāra. The paradox that characterizes Tenzin Repa's notion of women is brought out powerfully in his reply to a noblewoman and others who wanted him to stay in Muktināth and presumably to settle down and marry. He refused, saying he was a yogi and that he must be away from women:

> I, a yogin free of desire,
> Know that [women] are emanations of the beautiful goddesses
> Daughters of gods, of Brahma and Indra.
> Still, I will not prolong saṃsāra by amassing sins.
> Women are known to be receptacles for the seeds of saṃsāra,

40 The term *dge-tshul-ma*, 'novice nun', is rare in these works from north-west Nepal, and not surprisingly I have yet to see the term *dge-slong-ma*, 'fully ordained nun', used to refer to any woman other than the nun and folk hero, Gelongma Pelmo. The specific vows taken by women in these regions during the seventeenth and eighteenth centuries are not clear yet and I have used the term 'nun' in a broad sense. See Karma Lekshe Tsomo 1999: 178 for a discussion of these terms in Ladakh.

41 The autobiographies of Padma Donrub (1668–1744), Padma Wangdu (b. 1697) and Orgyan Tenzin (1708–c. 1767) (this master is different from the teacher of Orgyan Chokyi) all contain numerous references to nuns, laywomen and patronesses, and should figure in a longer survey of the type begun here.

> The beautiful and desirous noblewoman is carried away by life.
> The seed of saṃsāra, [she] spreads sloth and quarrel.
> I, a yogin, will head to the lonely mountain.
> (bsTan-'dzin 1971h: 21b.1)

We do find some admission that men are responsible for their own behaviour toward women, as when he gave advice to his disciples who were going on a three to four year pilgrimage to central Tibet, Lapchi and other holy places. Amidst discussions of holy places and proper prayers, he issued this warning: 'Don't follow women around like dogs!' (ibid.: 21b.1)

We can also get some idea of the regional religious community of which he was a part by examining registers of those who donated money for the printing of his collected works. These various works were printed at different times, but it is likely that the collection of some 206 printing blocks (which David Snellgrove viewed at Shey Monastery in 1961) was assembled shortly after Tenzin Repa passed away in 1723. The names of over a hundred faithful donors are listed—people from all walks of life. Lamas, officials, monks, nuns, lay patrons, nobles, nomads and the queen of Mustang—all contributed money to the printing of their master's words. They hailed from all parts of Dolpo, from the nomadic pastures to the north, as well as from his homeland in Muktināth. Nearly a third of the donors were women: nobles, royalty and female renunciants. We can note briefly that out of the seventy-one patrons of the printing of his *Secret Biography* twenty-eight are identifiable as women. These included the queen of Mustang, Pelden Tsomo, an elder nun teacher (*dge-rgan-ma*) named Zopa Sangmo, two nuns (one *btsun-ma* and one *a-ne*), among those whose social positions are explicitly stated.[42] The *Oral Instructions* had fewer female patrons, with roughly fourteen women out of seventy-eight donors. Orgyan Chokyi is present in both of these lists.

Certainly the most important passage in the works of Tenzin Repa for the present discussion is his report of the complaints of women who are struggling to practise meditation, but who are frustrated with the social restrictions by which they are bound. While staying at Dragmar, one of the most famous places along the Nepal-Tibetan border associated with Milarepa, Tenzin Repa listened to the troubles of a group of female meditators (*grub-chen-ma*) and bestowed upon them several teachings. It

[42] We also find a *dge-tshul-ma* patronizing a work on meditation (bsTan-'dzin 1971g: 9a.2). The term *dge-tshul-ma* occurs much less frequently in this literature than the other terms for female practitioners mentioned above. It would appear that this woman is Chokyong Sangmo (see bsTan-'dzin 1971g: 9a.5). She also appears in the donor colophon of Tenzin Repa's secret biography (bsTan-'dzin 1971e). See also the letter given to 'male and female religious practitioners' (*chos-byed pho-mo*) in bsTan-'dzin 1971c: 12b.5.

is remarkable in and of itself that Tenzin Repa felt compelled to include the words of several of his female disciples in his anthology of songs and all the more so for the content of the small passage:

> Further, they said: 'When we hear the teachings of a great spiritual adept, we are leaky chimneys; overpowered by the inability to do the right thing, we forget these arcane teachings and so these days we have no certainty. No matter what you do in this nun's body, there is suffering. Our parents are old and we are not able to leave for very long and even if we could go into retreat for a short time, we don't have anyone to remove obstacles and watch over us… Please give us a written instruction on how to meditate in calm abiding, on how to perform the Dharma, and bestow upon us a vow for a retreat.' (bsTan-'dzin 1971h: 42a.5)

This rich glimpse of the concerns of hermitesses attempting to meditate in the caves of Milarepa suggests that these women were self-critical of their status as women, exhibiting an internalization of negative Buddhist conceptions of women reminiscent of Orgyan Chokyi's prayers to be reborn as a man. It also reveals an open dissatisfaction with the family structures inhibiting their ability to practise meditation, also a major theme in Orgyan Chokyi's life-story. We can further note that these women were literate, as they specifically requested a written teaching. What is finally suggested by this passage is that these women were not part of a stable community of religious practitioners which effectively supported their efforts. They asked, they pleaded to Tenzin Repa—an itinerant yogin—for guidance and mentoring. But of course we must remember that this is the second-hand report of Tenzin Repa (or a disciple acting as a scribe or an editor) and thus the tone of the passage may represent a variety of competing perspectives. In the context of the activities of religious women in Dolpo just presented, Orgyan Chokyi's life is probably not unique; women were involved in a variety of religious vocations in the medieval Nepal Himalaya. They were nuns and patrons, temple keepers and hermits, queens and goatherds seeking religious perfection. What singles out Orgyan Chokyi is that she was able to write her story. From humble beginnings on the fringes of Tibetan culture, she achieved what few women have in Tibetan history: the telling of her own life.

Orgyan Chokyi is unique on another account as well: the strong equation she makes between the female body and the key term in the Buddhist view of human life in its unenlightened state, saṃsāra. Her portrayal of suffering in strong bodily terms contrasts with Tenzin Repa's social critique. Both of the figures use suffering as a theme to tell their life-stories and to inspire their followers. But the difference is nevertheless profound. Tenzin Repa is concerned with social forms of suffering—the violence levelled against commoners by lords, the hypocrisy of the large monastic establishments in central Tibet, the stark realities of mortality.

The fact of his male gender is not an explicit issue for him in his portrayal of suffering. Being male as opposed to female is simply not a cause for suffering and is thus not a powerful rhetorical tool with which to instruct about suffering. By contrast, for Orgyan Chokyi to be female (as opposed to male) is to be saṃsāra embodied. Orgyan Chokyi thematizes gender to such an extent that it is the most significant symbol of suffering in her life-story.[43] It is also the most powerful rhetorical theme of her autobiography and, I believe, the main reason why the story of Orgyan Chokyi was able to speak so strongly to her descendants.

It is important to remember that Orgyan Chokyi and her contemporaries were not lost to oblivion in their native land; indeed they were forerunners of traditions that continue to the present day. Tenzin Repa was instrumental in establishing the monastery of Shey in northern Dolpo (*Shes sgon* n.d.) and it was his incarnation whom Snellgrove met when he stopped at Shey in 1956 (Snellgrove 1989: 137). Orgyan Chokyi was still celebrated in Tarap in the 1970s with a yearly festival of dance and song (Jest 1974: 306–7). Her fame and respected status is evidenced by Orgyan Rigzin (late eighteenth century) in the following verse of homage:

> Yeshe Tsogyal, Dorje Phagmo, Guhyajñānā, Machig, Tronag,
> Nangsa, Lingsa, Bhikṣuṇī Śrī,
> Noble Tārā and Orgyan Chokyi,
> To mothers, sisters and *ḍākinīs* I give praise in faith.
> (O-rgyan Rig-'dzin 1983: 9.3; 54.3)

Thus does Orgyan Rigzin praise his spiritual ancestry or, more particularly, his female spiritual ancestors. He creates a lineage of some of the most renowned female figures of the Tibetan Buddhist world, the mothers and sisters whom Orgyan Rigzin places alongside his male masters in his verses of homage. Yeshe Tsogyal, famous as Padmasambhava's wife; Dorje Phagmo, abbess of Samding Monastery; Guhyajñānā, enlightened source of the Mahākaruṇika teachings (see Roerich 1988: 1026); Nangsa Obum and Lingsa Chokyi, folk heroes of Tibetans for centuries; Bhikṣuṇī Śrī, the medieval Indian nun so loved in Tibet as the founder of the fasting rites practised to the present day - all of these women are

[43] Again, see Myers and Powell 1999: 329 on medieval Hispanic spiritual autobiography: 'There is no gender-linked ambiguity about the man's worthiness to be a subject. In general, men's accounts do not employ sex as a category for establishing the significance of the story or its outcome. Gender is not even discussed… Accepted as normative, the male subject's masculinity is literally unremarkable. In narratives about women, by contrast, gender is a central concern. In fact, much of the drama in these narratives—and the justification for taking time to attend to a woman's life, whether one's own or someone else's—derives from the amazing spectacle they present of a woman managing to live a praiseworthy life in spite of her sex.'

exemplary models of Tibetan religious women. All of them have inspired women and men to practise the Dharma for centuries, their stories told again and again, and by Orgyan Rigzin's time Orgyan Chokyi was counted among them.

There are several further implications of this work for the study of Tibetan cultural history. One of the most important defining characteristics of Dolpo, Mustang and other regions in the Himalaya where Buddhism flourished is their position as border communities. While it is obvious that the Himalayan range forms a geographic border between the high plains of the Tibetan plateau and the lowlands of the Gangetic plain in India, the mountains also have helped to maintain cultural, political and ethnic boundaries. Recent scholarship has drawn attention to local traditions of Buddhist life in Dolpo and the different regions of northern Nepal, but we still must heed the words of Gene Smith, who suggested more than thirty years ago that 'It is important to see what was occurring in Dolpo within the broader picture of the trends that were also predominant in the richer Mustang and throughout south-western Tibet.'[44]

The border as a theme around which social and religious concerns were voiced is predominant in the writings of Buddhist writers, from Kailash in the west to Dolpo and Tsari. A variety of related topics come into play in the literature from the borderlands including ecumenism between certain groups, the search for hidden lands with their promise of religious freedom, the critique of religious institutions in central Tibet, fear of violent political persecution, the slandering of scholasticism at the expense of personal spiritual experience, and a serious questioning of ethnic identity.

In the present context I would add that in our continuing studies of the history and literature of these regions, we must certainly include gender as a category of analysis; if men felt marginalized from the centres of religious power in central Tibet, did women feel the same? Did they feel this marginalization in the same ways, or did they have different concerns? I have shown that Orgyan Chokyi most certainly expressed her discontent with the social roles in which she was compelled to practise in somewhat different terms than her male contemporary. Tenzin Repa's borders were between central Tibet and his mountain homeland, between institutionalized religion and the eremitic life. And those of Orgyan Chokyi? Perhaps they fell between her body and her bodhisattva vow, between the monastery kitchen and the small cave, between the great tradition of men's life-writing and her struggle to speak for herself. But this is only one example. Future studies must seek to ask the question anew in terms both specific and broad.

[44] Smith 1970: 1. This call to action has been cited by Jackson 1984: 19 and Ehrhard 1996: 26.

We are fortunate that the life-story of Orgyan Chokyi has come down to us, for it allows us a view of religious life in the Nepal Himalaya hitherto inaccessible. The biographies and autobiographies of men from this area simply do not address the same concerns for the spiritual implications of gender and suffering, or the religious life of women to be found in this work. As such, this autobiography should be seen as an important source for the cultural history of the Tibetan borderlands, a history which takes into account human experience at all levels of social life. The study of the history of women and the cultural construction of gender in Tibet—and in Buddhism as a whole—can do no better than to rely on the firsthand accounts of such writers as the hermitess from Sun Cave.

Part II

MODERN TIBETAN WOMEN

FEMALE ORACLES IN MODERN TIBET*

Hildegard Diemberger

I am the one called Targo of the North.
This root is free of rottenness
And its uppermost part has not dried up.
I am the great god of the world, it is said.

I am known as the first god who spoke
After having possessed [a medium].
If you do not know the god Takyong,
Or know by name the protector of religion,
[Then know] the names Changtsen Targo Dablha
And Targo Gungtang Ringmo.

On the peak is a covering of snow
On the white snow is the glistening of the sun
Its mid-parts are the place of the practice of religion:
Known by some as Takyong,
Takyong in fact is Changtsen Takyong,
King of the gods of defence.

There is a fast horse bearing the box of the gods
Whose movement is faster than the blue water.
There is a place of snow-melt waters
And waters from the mountain slates,
The homeland where demons and spirits reside.
There are ritual items like the mirror of religion
And a throng of divine queens (*btsun-mo*).
[Where] the sun shining on the snow is visible,
Can the numerous bears be seen?

Above are the horns of wild yak;
antlers of deer are his crest.
The head of Takyong reaches the celestial spheres.

It is said that I am a relative of Dingri Gangmar
As well as Abopho Gangtsen, Goyang,
Gomchung Dragtsen, Trengge Dragtsen
and others.

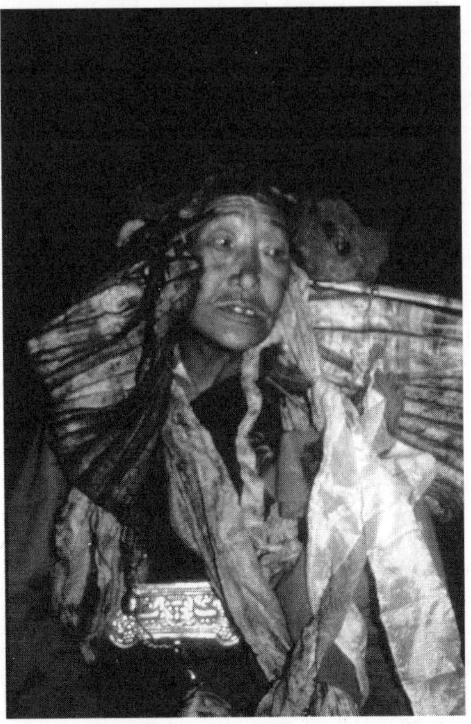

Female oracle in southern Lato. (Photo: H. Diemberger 1998)

> If I did not know the names of all the great gods,
> I could not be said to have power,
> To be able to rule or protect living beings…

I first heard the song of the mountain deity Targo and its emanation Takyong in 1999 during a visit to a nomadic area of southern Lato in south-western Tibet.[1] The songs of Targo and Takyong have probably been sung in that valley for centuries; they belong to a kind of religious cult which predates the modern state, the Buddhist religion, and perhaps even the kinship systems which have been associated with Tibetans since history has been written. This song tradition, with its echoes of the mountain cults of ancient Tibet, has survived in the practice of oracles even if it has been reshaped and redefined in Buddhist terms over the centuries.

[1] Given the sensitive nature of the oracles' phenomenon in contemporary Tibet I have occasionally chosen not to disclose the locations and names of people.

Now it even includes a set of communist phrases and features of contemporary Tibetan life in the People's Republic of China.

On the occasion that I witnessed, the singing of these words by the oracle signified that the god had entered the medium. He introduced himself in a deep voice, speaking through an elderly lady who was shaking and sobbing. The oracle was surrounded by a crowd of nomads in a black tent pitched in a remote nomad encampment. It was late at night and she had arrived there from a small temple just beyond the mountain ridge, having been called to consult the gods on behalf of a nomad in the camp who had been taken ill. She had agreed to come to the encampment despite the fact that these practices had recently been reclassified by the authorities as superstitious (*rmongs-dad*).

Before beginning the song, she had first arranged a series of cups filled with offerings and mirrors on the family altar. She had unwrapped an old headgear (*rigs-lnga*)[2] from a bundle and placed it on her head, and then put on a coat made from multicoloured strips of cloth, very similar to the prayer-flags which festoon high passes. During these preparations she talked with the family about the problems that had led them to call on her. She also exchanged a few words with an elderly man whom she evidently knew well, and who would act as 'translator' during the session. He would present the questions to be asked to the gods and interpret their answers, especially in the case of uncertainty.

When the oracle was ready she lit a butter-lamp and consulted three round mirrors that had been stuck in a cup filled with grain. She would use these to see which god would come to her and to get some preliminary indications about the divination. As soon as the visions in the mirror allowed her to establish contact with her main god, she started the prayer of invitation, trembling and breathing faster until the chant gave way to a different voice, that of the powerful god of the north: Chang Targo. The person who had requested her intervention immediately offered a white scarf to the god, putting it around the woman's neck. The first few lines were sung in a language that was incomprehensible, and the assistant begged the god to be communicative. Accordingly the god switched to a Tibetan dialect spoken by the To Drogpa, the nomads of the western and northern areas of Tibet. This is also the language of the area where this mountain god is said to reside. Although different from the local dialect, it could be understood by the participants at the divination.

The questions posed to the deity primarily concerned health problems. Other people in the crowd, however, took the chance to consult the god about kinship issues, the condition of dead relatives and problems connected with their work. Each person was given a reply indicating some

[2] Headgear depicting the five buddha families.

sort of ritual therapy. Before the god left, a man in the crowd took out from the fire something that looked like a thick red-hot iron knife. The elderly woman took it in her hands and licked it repeatedly without scalding herself, a sign that she was still in a non-human state. After the god departed, she lay motionless for some time, exhausted by the experience.

She is one of numerous oracles whose divination practices feature in the life of villages and nomad encampments in present-day Tibet. Like many others, she is a woman. But who are these oracles? Why do they still practice divination despite various persecutions and prohibitions, and how have they become agents of the renewal of divination practices after 1980? Why do they seem mainly to be women? Is there a specific female competence connected with this function, or is it a non-gendered role? Does the female connotation of these traditions represent a modern development, a feminization of this practice, or is it a traditional practice that has come increasingly to the fore in the contemporary context? This chapter is an attempt to address these questions in a provisional way by looking at the life-stories and practices of the oracles that I encountered during field trips in the Tibet Autonomous Region (TAR),[3] and by corroborating these with historical records and ethnographic material from other areas. I shall look at woman oracles from two perspectives: in the first part I shall explore their experiences and practices, in the second their relation to religious and political institutions and popular movements.

WOMEN AS ORACLES

Even though I am focusing on female oracles it is important to remember that they are just one element in a tangle of intertwined female and non-female traditions. Not all oracles are female. Nor can those oracles who are female be seen as operating in a well-demarcated religious field of action. On the contrary, aspects of the oracular phenomenon among women can be seen in other related traditions—notably those of the Gesar bards, female tantric practitioners, and women who have, while under some form of spirit possession, initiated political movements. These aspects can range from the use of specific rituals, to the kind of deities involved, to religious experiences related to spirit possession, to

[3] The data on which this article is based was collected by my colleague Charles Ramble and myself in the period 1997–2003 during a number of research expeditions in central Tibet in the framework of a co-operation with the Tibetan Academy of Social Sciences, Lhasa. I wish to thank the Austrian Science fund, the Austrian Academy of Sciences, the Italian Ev-K2-CNR Project and the British Academy for funding the research on which this article is based, as well as Robert Barnett, Hanna Havnevik, Janet Gyatso and Caroline Humphrey for their valuable comments.

the place that sacredness acquires in the life-story of a woman. Here I highlight those features which associate oracles with tantric and epic traditions but I will not be able to analyse them in detail. Rather, I shall focus on the religious and political significance of the oracular practice both in the past and in contemporary Tibet. In particular I show that in specific circumstances the overcoming of a personal crisis in the life-story of an oracle leads to an ability in dealing with personal and collective crises, for which the oracle can be praised or blamed, and either integrated and controlled by the state or persecuted.

The oracle I saw in southern Lato belongs to a category of oracles known variously as 'lhaka' (*lha-bka'*), 'lhabab' (*lha-'bab*), and 'lhaba' (*lha-pa*), or 'pawo' (*dpa'-bo*) and 'pamo' (*dpa'-mo*). These are the local oracles and are usually seen by the Tibetans as clearly distinct from the highly institutionalized oracles known as 'kuten' (*sku-rten*), despite the common features shared by these traditions. The local oracles can still be found throughout Tibet, both in rural and in urban contexts. Some are 'old' oracles who received their initiation in the so-called 'old society' and who, having survived the Cultural Revolution, have restarted their activity with the few ritual items they could rescue. The majority are new practitioners, some who have 'inherited' their gods from their ancestry and some who were possessed in the wake of a personal crisis.

The investigations we have been able to carry out on this kind of local oracle are still preliminary and limited by the conditions of research. These conditions have produced on the one hand a fragmentary documentation, and on the other hand a considerable breadth of perspective which has permitted limited comparative analysis. This comparative framework has allowed us to focus on a number of elements which appear to be significant and which seem to create a recurring pattern. The life-stories, the religious practices and the ritual items of all these oracles are in fact fairly similar throughout the TAR and can be found both in Ngari in western Tibet and in Nagchu in the north, as well as in Dingri to the south and in the Lhasa area. There are however significant local variations as well as horizontal cross-regional differences between oracles of different generations. The older practitioners have a clearly defined relation to Buddhist institutions. They are evaluated socially according to whether or not they were recognized by lamas, and their gods, narratives and ritual practices are structured according to traditional and commonly shared beliefs. Presumably because of the absence of lamas in rural Tibet, the oracles of the current generation have more often been initiated by other oracles or they are said to have been initiated by gods directly. Their status therefore depends exclusively on their local reputation for competence and ability, and their practices and narratives reflect an extensive process of creative adaptation to the new context.

In the area of Lato, which I was able to explore systematically, fifteen oracles were identified. Of these, three were elderly women who had been recognized by lamas, while two were elderly women who had not been acknowledged by a lama and accordingly had very limited standing in the community. The other ten were younger practitioners of whom seven were women, all with varying degrees of significance for the community. These findings concur with Barbara Aziz's work in Dingri, where all of the four lhaka oracles she mentioned were women (Aziz 1978: 253n.). None of these oracles were regarded as belonging to one of the highly institutionalized or state traditions of mediumship. In Ngamring, however, people told me the story of one medium of this kind, who at one point had been recognized directly by the government and who had then been granted an official appointment. This was a man.

In principle oracle traditions can be both gendered and gender-neutral according to the context. Some geographical variations can be perceived: for example, our investigations in U, Tsang and Ngari indicate a predominance of women in central and south-western Tibet and a predominance of men in north-western Tibet, with variable situations in northern and north-eastern Tibet. But this is just an impression. In general the traditional high oracles and the oracles integrated into monastic institutions seem mainly to be men, while oracles operating at the village or nomad-encampment level are mostly women.[4] Nebesky-Wojkowitz, who gives a detailed classification of high-ranking oracles, affirms this observation:

> The male mediums are by far in the majority. While those of the male mediums, who are supposed to become the mouthpieces of the chief gods of the *'jig-rten-pa'i-srung-ma* class, occupy important places within the system of Tibetan Buddhism, there are on the other hand only one or two female mediums of some importance. (Nebesky-Wojkowitz 1975: 409)

This view presumably reflects the social origin of his informants and the emphasis they placed on the category of practitioners who were considered to be the most important oracles.

In contemporary Tibet and in people's current recollections of the period before 1959, however, women are more often seen as constituting the majority of oracles. These accounts emphasize those traditions defined by Nebesky-Wojkowitz as the 'lowest ranking mediums, who are regarded to be mouthpieces of deities belonging to the classes of the *gzhi-bdag, klu*, and other protective deities of local importance (ibid.: 413). It was these oracles, who were part of territorial cults and whose significance was largely local, who were probably the most numerous in earlier times. The majority of the oracles who did not flee into exile in 1959 and

[4] A comparable situation was observed by Volf in Ladakh. (Volf 1994: 218–19)

who survived the Cultural Revolution belong to this local class. The political changes that led to the disappearance of the high oracles thus seem to have enhanced the number and the significance of these local forms of possession, with their greater involvement of women. These ranged from the resumption of traditional practices to the revitalization or even the reinvention of traditions. Attitudes towards oracles in contemporary Tibet, however, show considerable ambiguity, influenced perhaps by the conventional Buddhist view of village oracles as low and worldly and only tolerable insofar as they bring some benefit to common people, and by the more or less condemnatory attitude of the Chinese authorities. Not surprisingly, popular views, even among the patients of oracles, seem to vary between faith and scepticism.

Some of the main questions concerning the tradition of female oracles can be illustrated by the history of the medium who I heard sing the song of Targo. Born in the late 1930s in a poor family, she had been sent at the age of fifteen as a daughter-in-law to a nearby encampment. She had been unable to tolerate the new situation and had escaped, only to be forbidden to return by her own family. She found shelter in a small monastery at the top of a hill tended by a couple of monks. Here she dedicated herself to religious practice for some years, until she fell in love with one of the monks, and had a child by him. Apart from the practical difficulties surrounding the birth of a child born out of wedlock, the episode was also considered to have shamed the whole community. It was at this time that she became ill and appeared to be mentally ill. She was thought to be on the brink of death. Local doctors were unable to help, and she was taken to a nearby village to consult the oracle of Shar Nyanchen Tanglha. This oracle recognized in her the signs of spirit possession, and identified the presence of the god Chang Targo and his local emanation Takyong. He then opened her channels of energy (*rtsa-sgo phyed-pa*). Following the advice of this oracle, she was taken to a Sakya lama who again opened the energy-channels, enabling her to receive another protective god called Namkha Drolma. Thus she became an oracle herself.

This took place in 1976, in secrecy, since the persecution of oracles during the Cultural Revolution had only recently diminished, and there was still a great deal of anxiety. In May 1980, however, the visit of the reformist Chinese leader Hu Yaobang to Tibet introduced a more tolerant climate, and led oracles, as well as other religious practitioners, to become more confident and to take a more public role. And this is what she did. Even though she did not belong to a lineage which transmitted these skills from one generation to the next, her ability led her to acquire certain renown, even beyond her own community. In the late 1990s she lived with her grown-up daughter and her husband. At that time, she was constantly on the move, either visiting religious communities or families who needed her help and had become respected for her skills at diagnosis and at imparting advice. In many relatively inaccessible areas where healthcare is completely out of reach, oracles still remain the first and only persons to whom people turn in crises, especially those involving health.

From this life-story we can see the importance of the oracles's experience of crisis. The nature of such crises is reflected first of all in the concept of the 'god's sickness', which is considered to be cured when the oracle learns to manage the experience of spirit possession. The god, in fact, is said to enter the body along the energy-channels and if these are not purified, the person may be affected by a variety of mental and physical illnesses. Uncontrolled visions, voices, fainting, weakness, and the experience of a death-like state are the most common symptoms. In addition to the sensation of a divine element, a human and social dimension of this critical moment can often be perceived in the life-stories. These seem to reflect individual responses to social constraints, which are likely to be more relevant in those cases involving women who transgress rules and consciously or unconsciously refuse to adhere to patterns of expected female behaviour. The element of crisis can potentially spill beyond the personal to the social and political. The role of a personal crisis in the formation of an oracle appears to be much more prominent in cases where oracles do not belong to acknowledged lineages. In this case the identification of acute illness or behavioural aberration as spirit possession is the only available kind of empowerment, irrespective of whether or not it is subsequently recognized by a Buddhist lama. In contrast, in the case of oracles who represent lineages, a crisis is expected and appears to conform to more ritualized models both in practice and in the associated narratives.

The crisis plays an important role not only in the personal development of the oracle, but also in situations in which she or he is called to intervene. In fact, clients approach oracles when hounded by uncertainty during decisive moments. This seems to reflect the very etymology of the word 'crisis' from the Greek *krino*, 'to decide'. It concerns the situation in which decision-making cannot rely on a predictable cultural response, and is confronted with equally valuable alternatives. This might occur in the case of sickness, or in kinship transactions or in political upheavals. The god speaking through the oracle is considered to be a master of the future as well as of hidden aspects of past and present, able to construct a mental 'map' of orientation for effective decision-making. The god—and the life-experience—endow the oracle with extraordinary insights in understanding critical situations. The divine presence and the oracle's performance enable the consulting crowd to be involved in a process of collective reflection. Oracular activity can be considered not only related to the extraordinary faculties of the oracle, but as a function of the oracle's competence emerging from a whole network of human relations and needs.

Those who seek consultations with the deity take an active role through their involvement in the process of interpreting the responses, which are often enigmatic. The oracle is not a solitary religious practitioner with a purely private relation to the sacred. The séance has a collective dimension even when this is not as formalized as in the cases in which an oracle intervenes in major collective rituals. Furthermore the entire activity of the oracle, in time, articulates with specific social and cultural dimensions. The life-stories of oracles are often narrated at the time of a séance as well as in other moments and come to represent an integral part of the phenomenon. They reproduce, in narrative form, the empowering moment of the oracle's original crisis, and the process of its overcoming. In other words, these recitations re-enact the social recognition of the oracle's acquisition of power and the changes that have accompanied her or his life-itinerary.

This wider frame of reference defines the social dimension in which a consultation takes place. It situates an oracle as an individual healer, a political adviser or even as a symbolic figure of collective religious and political aspirations, in local or ethnic terms. It is therefore a phenomenon that is intrinsically connected with the religious and social context in which it has emerged and is practised. Whenever the direct link to a certain geographical context is severed by distance, as for example in the case of oracles who have migrated to an urban context or have left Tibet, the reference to this broader landscape is recreated by the recitation of narratives. This is especially significant for local deities, unlike higher and more abstract gods, who are generally situated in a cosmos created by their own iconographical appearance and mythology.

Stories of 'old' female oracles

I came across an example of the 'old' type of oracle—that existed before the Chinese administration was fully introduced in central Tibet in 1959—when I was travelling in northern Lato. There I met a woman in her seventies who was considered a very powerful oracle and was highly respected even by the local traditional doctor. She was living in a small farming village and her skills were in demand throughout the area among nomads and farmers. She was one of the few surviving and active oracles who had been recognized in the former period and who had already operated as an oracle in those times. When I met her, she was a grandmother wearing thick glasses, speaking in a low voice in the local dialect. To an outsider she appeared to be a simple farming woman, and it was hard to imagine her otherwise. She too, however, draped herself in a multicoloured costume and began to beat a drum, jumping, sobbing and shouting in order to allow gods to manifest. She gave this account of her entry into the role of an oracle:

'In the old society, when I was a little girl, I used to look after the animals. At the age of thirteen or fourteen I often felt various invisible presences when we would be up in the pasture areas. These beings used to play with me, pull my clothing, or touch me. Sometimes I could even see them, or sometimes I just felt some strange presence. This continued for two years. Then I fell ill. I went to some monasteries and took part in various religious ceremonies, and this brought some relief. After that I could see these spirits more clearly and understand better what was going on.

'Then I was taken to the lama of Phuntsoling. He opened the door of my energy-channels (*rtsa-sgo*) and declared that I was allowed to be possessed by gods in order to bring benefit to living beings. I was fifteen. So I started to go into trances in order to heal people. I also started to perform the practice of sucking diseases from the body (*'jip*).

'My main god, the "owner of my energy-channels" (*rtsa-bdag*), is Targo. Both Targo and Tanglha possess me regularly. I have never been to the north to see Targo, but I can see the Targo mountain, the lake (Dangra Yumtso), Ombu and the Targo river in my mirror.

'Targo has stupas of crystal,[5] stupas of silver and stupas of brass. When he comes he introduces himself in detail and answers all questions. However, if he is not asked to introduce himself in detail he will just say: "I am Targo coming from such and such place."

'This god used to possess other people in my family before me. My paternal uncle was an oracle and before him a lady of his lineage used to be an oracle. My paternal lineage stems from a nomad area not far from here.

'When I was performing my task as oracle in the old society, all kinds of people used to come. Subsequently no cadres came, and even if they did come I would refuse to be asked about political things. Formerly the local political leaders used to consult me and they would ask also about the situation of the country and would ask me for advice on what to do. One of the ones who used to come was the official X, and I gave my prediction to him that the Chinese would come and that he and his followers would be defeated. Then all of them escaped.

'During the Cultural Revolution I had to stop the sessions and all my ritual items including the headgear (*rigs-lnga*) were destroyed. I could only save the mirrors. Everything was taken away from my tent, even the stove. Life was also difficult because the gods were still there and I could feel them, but I could not let them speak. When some religious freedom was allowed I started to practise again.'

Here we can see the familiar biographical features of the life-story of an oracle. First she was visited by undefined entities that appeared in the

5 She used the word *shel*, literally meaning 'crystal' and 'glass', but perhaps alluding to gold.

form of visions, voices, presences and touches. Then the sickness manifested itself in an unbearable way, so much so that she was taken to the monastery where she got some relief. However she was cured only after being taken to the lama of Phuntsoling, who eventually opened the door of her energy-channels and declared that she was allowed to be possessed by the gods in order to bring benefit to living beings.

In this case, the woman had just resumed an established local tradition. She had oracles in her ancestry, recognition by the Buddhist authorities in the 'old society', and a reputation for imparting valuable advice. She therefore had an impact reaching far beyond that of a healer in individual cases. At the time of our research she was well-known throughout the area. Despite her conscious avoidance of political commentary, she still represented a problem for the local administration, since in her case the implementation of the recent official bans on oracular practices would be widely unpopular.[6]

'New' oracles

The oracles who have no pre-Chinese history emerged in a very different context, where revived traditional features have been mixed with newly introduced social practices of Chinese origin and a considerable amount of individually created practices. One such oracle that I met was an energetic woman of about forty living in a small farmers' hamlet. She emerged after the Cultural Revolution and was never recognized by a lama, but has retained local respect on account of the wisdom shown in a number of difficult cases, although not everyone in the community considers her to be a true oracle. In her very simple house only the presence of a few common ritual objects such as a bell, a double-headed drum (*ḍamaru*) and a couple of newly printed sacred texts indicate that the house-owner might be involved in some religious activity. Despite the books she is completely illiterate. The only item that suggests her function as an oracle is the mirror that she uses for divination.

'Until twenty-nine, I was a road-worker. At that time my mother died; my father had died when I was a little girl. So then I came back to the village. I have many brothers and sisters who are already married now and have their own families. Since I spent most of my life working on the road or taking care of them I never married. When I was thirty-two, after my return to the village, I fell ill. It was as if I had gone insane. This lasted for a year or more. I did not go to see any lamas, but I went to visit the oracle of Tingto [?]. I visited her nine times. Then before dying the oracle said that I had the god's sickness, opened the door of my energy-

[6] After the banishment of the Falun Gong movement in 1999, there has been all over China a tighter control over religious groups labelled as superstitious.

channels and said that I would be possessed by her own god, Tingto Jarog [?], the spirit "owner" of a cliff not far from here. After a short while the oracle died. Since then I have been falling into trances upon request. The requests come from people who ask me about illnesses or about problems with hail and crops. Sometimes I say embarrassing things about people. One time a thief came to me. I saw that he was a thief and I said it. Then he admitted it. Now I spend my life going to different places, in response to requests from people.'

The impact of this kind of oracle—especially if they do not have any precedent within their family—is usually very local unless they prove to have exceptional abilities. They are the most numerous among oracles and are usually completely ignored by local administrators, who in many cases are unaware of their existence.

Oracles and collective feelings: mother and daughter, ladies of the lake

The relation of female sacrality to the landscape and to the community can often be perceived within the family sagas of oracular lineages. These narratives reflect the transition from a traditional context to a new one. One such account is given of a woman whom I shall call Y, who is considered the '*dākinī* owner' (*mkha'-'gro bdag-po*) of a holy lake. She is a nun and is not herself an oracle but her mother was one, and the women of her lineage used to be possessed by the goddess who was the 'owner of the lake' (*mtsho-bdag*), a goddess who is said to be in essence the same as Drabchi Lhamo [?]. This old nun inherited from her female ancestry a special relationship to the lake, the ability to prophesy and her charismatic position. She was regarded with great respect, not only by the local community, but also by people in the nearby city of Lhasa, so she was often consulted on difficult matters. The narrative concerning the sacred lake, together with its prophetic dimension, constitutes part of her sacredness, just as it had done for her mother, and can be seen as directly linked to the ancient notion that a kind of soul (*bla*) resides in features of the landscape (see Karmay 1987: 100). At the same time, this narrative reflects the impact of modern Tibetan history on the locality:

'Our lake is called a 'soul-lake' (*bla-mtsho*) of the country. Nowadays it is said that there is not much to see there. Previously, this lake used to give good prophecies. It has been there since time immemorial. When the People's Liberation Army came and some canals were constructed to bring water to some areas, they went there and dug out the ground. Still they did not manage to get the water out of it. But now the lake is gradually drying up.

'When a divination was made about how I came to have a connection with this lake it turned out that I am a serpent spirit reborn (*klu*). In fact whenever I go there the lake gives some signs and prophecies. If I do not go there the lake does not produce any images. Unfortunately, now I cannot go there. In the past, the "owner of the lake" used to possess my mother. When I go to the shore of this lake and offer incense I have visions that I see in the lake. They are not dreams or anything like that. It is the same as (the lake) Lhamo Latso.

"The goddess Owner of the Lake" (Tsodag Lhamo) is the territorial god (*yul-lha*) of this place. She used to be worshipped at the fifth sliver of the moon. Before, there used to be a mountain covered with trees producing small red fruit. It was of a type that is called a *se*.[7] During the Cultural Revolution these trees were uprooted. Afterwards some people tried to eat the fruit. They vomited and died.

'On the top of the hill there used to be a deity (*rgyal-po*). He is the same as Nechung but he did not possess people. The goddess, however, used to possess people often, but only women. My mother used to be possessed by her. Usually this faculty was passed on from mother to daughter or at least among the female members of the family. My mother was the last oracle.

'Once, when my mother was still alive, two communities started to fight over this holy lake. The other community said that the lake was theirs and was called X, while our community claimed the same lake and called it by a different name. The fight became serious. Then the other community threw the corpse of a dog into the lake, chanting malicious mantras at the same time, and the lake started to dry up. When my mother was possessed by the goddess she realized that the corpse of the dog had been thrown into the lake and she managed to take it out. So the lake stopped drying up. Now the lake has started drying up again, but we do not know the reason. The other day monks from a neighbouring area went to the lake to try to have some vision, but they did not have any. These days the lake does not show anything any more.

'We used to go there in the fifth and sixth months, and we used to burn incense in a special place. Then a vision would appear predicting future events. Before the uprising,[8] a Rinpoche went with me to the lake. While we were there, five elephants appeared in the lake. On each elephant there was a jewel, and on one of them was the Rinpoche himself, but he fell from there into the water. When he saw this, the Rinpoche said: "I will not stay [i.e., live] more than another fifteen years. And in these fifteen years I will not be able to stay in Tibet, I will have to be in India." And he said: "Count and see!" In fact he died fifteen years later in India. Now his reincarnation is there in India and is very skilled in reading holy books, just like a "doctor of philosophy" (*dge-bshes*).

'This lake is full of blessings (*rtsa chen-po*). For several years it was possible to prevent people from throwing plastic and polluting things into the lake so that the lake could stay pure. Now nobody cares. I do not say anything. I keep silent.'

Here one can see the significance of the lake and of the local landscape in the personal and collective imagery of the community. The natural feature participates in the history of the community. The lake that once used

[7] Possibly *se-bo* or *se-'bru* meaning 'pomegranate'.

[8] Probably the rebellion led by the Chuzhi Gangdrug in 1958–9.

to give signs and prophecies and whose visions tantalized the oracle, now remains a powerful symbol of a sacredness that has been lost. Its silence now speaks of its defilement.

The idea of protecting sacred environments and communities from defilement is a recurrent theme in the practices of oracles. In this sense they are thought of as embodying collective interests, a function which is also expressed by their association with certain features of the landscape regarded as significant to the community. Even though Y was not a practising oracle herself, she has been endowed with a special relationship to the sacred landscape and to the collective interests of the community. Such virtues can be seen as constituting the background to her own life as a very charismatic nun. This standing became significant when she took the initiative after the visit of Hu Yaobang in 1980 to reconstruct her nunnery. Her renown enabled her to gather around her a new community of nuns and the necessary funds and support. Her nunnery, however, faced serious difficulties in the late 1990s.

> 'When I was thirteen I was ordained as a nun and entered the nunnery. In 1959 the nunnery was severely damaged, and then in the Cultural Revolution it was totally destroyed and all the nuns were dispersed. But I still remained. When the policy of freedom of belief (*chos-dad rang-mos-gyi srid-'jus*) was introduced, I went around seeking alms and I managed to put together this nunnery. I raised the matter with a Rinpoche, and once I got his approval I started begging. Then I requested permission from the county authorities, and they agreed. So I was able to start construction.
>
> 'At that time the Panchen Rinpoche was still alive [before 1989]. When the nunnery was rebuilt it had an assembly hall, eight pillars in size. We made statues and arranged to have a set of the canon. Gradually more and more nuns came and rooms were built for them. It took a lot of work, but the nunnery became quite nice. Now it is all gone. There were many nuns. They were all dispersed.'

This nunnery was closed down and partially destroyed during one of the recent campaigns that implemented the restrictive religious policy that was introduced by the government since 1994.

WHAT IS AN ORACLE?

As the cases described in ethnographic literature and the examples mentioned above show, oracles and traditions connected with them have assumed a kaleidoscope. A few constant elements remain, however, as markers of this form of sacredness. Among these are the oracle's life-story, the trance, the experience of initiation and the use of ritual objects such as the mirror. Of these features still to be found in contemporary Tibet, several are similar to those of the traditional oracles in Tibet described by Stein (1986: 125 ff.) and Nebesky-Wojkowitz (1975) as well those described in recent anthropological studies in Nepal and India (Berglie 1980, 1989; Samuel 1993: 291 ff.; Day 1989; Schenk 1993, 1994; Volf 1994). These elements seem to constitute a pattern by which people identify an oracle and relate themselves to this religious practice. Under the new social and political conditions, however, a process of simplification seems to have taken place. This might be related to the diminished role of Buddhist institutions and to the disappearance of the literary traditions connected with oracular practices. Thus the affirmation and transmission of oracular customs at present depends exclusively on oral traditions—the local narratives that accompany and shape the resuming or the reinventing of local traditions. In particular, missing ancient paraphernalia are always superseded by oral narratives on how they were lost during the Cultural Revolution and in some cases on how they were substituted by modern items. The scanty use of ritual paraphernalia in contemporary Tibet compared with the practices described by Nebesky-Wojkowitz, Stein and anthropologists outside Tibet is significant. In fact this radical simplification raises its own questions, such as why it is the mirror rather than any other ritual item that has been retained or even adventurously 'rescued' by most oracles, and also which items were obtained from where.

Local definitions

The idea of the medium, defined in various ways in different localities, always includes the implication that a human being can be possessed by a god and that the god speaks through the person possessed. These notions are implied by the terms 'lhabab' (*lha-'bab*), which means literally 'god-descending' or by the term 'lhaka' (*lha-bka'*), or 'god's speech', terms already present in Dunhuang material and associated with Bonpo and pre-Buddhist practices (see Stein 1986: 160; Nebesky-Wojkowitz 1975: 428). It is the latter semantic connotation that encourages me to use the term oracle—which entails the notion of 'speaking'—as a general label, despite certain misleading implications.[9] Other terms like 'kuten' (*sku-rten*) imply the idea that the medium is a 'receptacle', a 'physical basis'

[9] The Dalai Lama underlines this view:

> Another point to remember is that the word 'oracle' is itself misleading. It implies that there are people who possess oracular powers. This is wrong. In the Tibetan tradition there are merely certain men and women who act as mediums between the natural and the spiritual realm, the name for them being kuten, which means literally, 'the physical basis'. Also, I should point out that whilst it is usual to speak of oracles as if they were people, this is done for convenience. More accurately, they can be described as 'spirits' which are associated with particular things (for example a statue), people and places. (Dalai Lama 1999: 232–3)

for the god, but this is an honorific form and is usually restricted to the high level oracles. The ancient but still common terms 'mopa' (*mo-pa*) and 'moma' (*mo-ma*) that signify a male or female diviner can also be used. 'Mopa' and 'moma' however refer to practitioners employing various kinds of divination and not necessarily to that obtained through spirit possession. The titles 'pawo' (*dpa'-bo*) and 'pamo' (*dpa'-mo*), for men and women respectively, can be rendered as 'hero' and 'heroine'. They can refer to oracles as well as specific gods of a heroic nature and in some cases are connected to the bard-mediums who orate the Gesar epic.[10] These terms are also used for mediums who embody other kinds of gods as well, and it is possible that the labels refer to perceived qualities of the individual medium.

The notion of heroism can also relate to the life-journey and to the making of a medium which is invariably characterized by a confrontation with supernatural forces and social liminality, which the medium in some sense transcends. The personal crisis primarily represents a point of transition in the experience of oracles. It serves, like an initiation, to allow them to enter a different stage in their lives, and to allow them to diverge radically from their expected social trajectory. Only after overcoming this critical period successfully can a medium take over his or her social function. This period of crisis reflects a fundamental confrontation with danger, an experience that the Tibetan medium shares with Nepali and Central Asian shamans (Sagant 1996: 397). There is thus something 'heroic' in the life of these people[11] which distinguishes them from the other members of the community and which is socially acknowledged. This impalpable difference is remarkable when no other visible distinction of rank or religious function distinguishes them. Otherwise they are simple lay people leading ordinary lives.

The life-story and divine sickness

The period of crisis in the life of an oracle is usually defined as 'god's sickness' (*lha-nad*). In the case of women there are mainly three phases in their lives during which this is liable to occur. The first of these is puberty, during which the gods start to manifest themselves. The family of the girl takes care of her and tries all possible methods to have the god's sickness identified and the opening of the energy-channels performed,

10 On this kind of oracles see also Berglie 1983.

11 'The word *dpa'-bo* (with the female form *dpa'-mo*, sometimes written *'ba'-mo*) indicates, in colloquial Tibetan, magicians or mediums who are "popular" or lay, i.e. who do not belong to the lamaist or bonpo clergy. The word is significant. It translates the Sanskrit *vīra*, the heroes or the saints who both distinguished themselves for their bravery and their perseverance' (Stein 1959: 332).

thus healing the sickness through the mastery of spirit possession. More frequently, god's sickness occurs in women just after marriage or childbirth. Both the family the girl has married into and her natal family feel responsible for her and try to sort out her case, unless specific events in her life have separated her from one or the other of these families. Sometimes a god's sickness episode allows her to redefine and renegotiate kin relations, while in other cases it can end up with the girl renouncing family life. Finally, there are certain contexts where fertility is considered incompatible with the god's presence. In these cases the woman can become possessed by spirits only after menopause.

Both men and women sometimes refer to specific events not connected to life-phases that have precipitated the incident of god's sickness, such as the death of a family member, or some incident that has led to a prolonged absence from the village or local community. In many cases the outbreak of the sickness is related to a difficult personal situation and the appearance of the god creates a real or supposed threat to life that brings about a complete redefinition of the situation. During the period of sickness the gods manifest themselves as undefined presences, dreams, or voices which are not yet understood or identified. That process can take place only through the ritual of opening the energy-channels. In some cases the divine presences take the spirit of the medium on a dream journey, while in others the future medium enters into a near-death state. Nebesky-Wojkowitz compared this phenomenon to shamanic illness (Nebesky-Wojkowitz 1975: 538 ff.), thus identifying one of the many features that connect Tibetan oracles with Central Asian shamanism.[12]

During this period of illness people surrounding the future medium are usually described as confused or scared. They try to consult traditional doctors and lamas in the hope of finding a cure for the patient. The god's sickness appears to be a clearly identifiable condition for Tibetan traditional doctors and lamas. In northern Lato, I was told by a practising Tibetan doctor, or 'amchi' (*em-chi*), that qualified traditional doctors can recognize cases of god's sickness, and consider them to be outside their own competence. Traditionally they would refer immediately to a lama. However this became impossible during the Cultural Revolution and immediately afterwards, since at that time spirit possession was illegal and it was not possible to declare this sickness for what it was, or to find a lama who could treat it. The same doctor told me that in the 1970s he had difficulties with a sick girl because he recognized that she was suffering from this illness but it could not be declared as god's sickness. Eventually

[12] This kind of comparison has been undertaken in later studies as well, but the scanty material available so far has made this approach somewhat tentative (see Samuel 1993: 8).

she was able to find an oracle who opened her energy-channels, thus allowing her to recover from the condition and to become an oracle herself.

The god

Many gods can take possession of a medium. Until a ritual of initiation has been carried out, it remains possible for all kinds of spirits to appear. Some of these deities are malevolent, but these will be prevented from entering the medium once the ritual of opening the energy-channels has been carried out. Usually there is one main god who appears during the god's sickness, and this presence is later recognized as the 'god-owner of the energy-channels' (*rtsa-bdag*). This god will accompany the oracle throughout her or his life as a spirit-guide and will be the entity that controls access by other gods or spirits of the deceased. It is with this main deity that an oracle establishes contact before going into trance, usually by means of a mirror.

The deities who most frequently possess local mediums are territorial deities—those who inhabit mountains, rocks, lakes or springs, and who in many cases are worshipped by local communities.[13] Either as the sacred focus of a community or as a minor deity related to one of the main local deities, the god who speaks to the people directly through a medium is considered to express collective interests. From a Buddhist perspective these deities are considered to be of low stature, belonging to the worldly sphere and still involved in mundane issues. Only deities who have not yet passed beyond the worldly sphere are said to possess people. This opinion, reported also by Nebesky-Wojkowitz (ibid.: 409), is still dominant, both among clerics and lay people. Those rare oracles who claim to embody very high gods are regarded with great suspicion.

An alternative view holds that only deities who were not bound by oath by Padmasambhava or later lamas can possess people. This perspective is much more controversial and often reflects recent or even on-going negotiations between the followers of local deities and local Buddhist clergy. In the area surrounding the abode of the mountain god Dingri Gangmar two oracles exist, one embodying the mountain god himself and one embodying his minister. The first one incarnates the higher god but has

[13] The relation of the deities possessing a medium to mountains and rocks is the most common. In some cases, especially in that of a serpent spirit (*klu*), the deity can have its seat in a lake or in a spring. It can even be a mythological lake. In the area surrounding the Tandrug temple there are four serpent spirits associated to a mythical lake, and the spirits are believed to have been subjugated and the lake drained during the construction of this Buddhist temple. The four serpent spirits have been possessing women of that area until 1959 (Hazod forthcoming).

much lesser standing than the second one, who is possessed by a minor god. The first one was never officially approved by a lama, the second had her initiation performed by a great Sakya lama at the beginning of her practice and was reconfirmed by a famous Nyingma lama after having resumed her activity in the 1980s. The difference between the two oracles might be related, among other things, to the history and the ritual practices of these mountain deities. Until 1959 Dingri Gangmar used to require animal sacrifices from the local communities and from the local military camp. This arrangement seems to have been a controversial issue for several generations between Buddhist representatives and local communities, and led to various attempts at mediation. Practices of this kind were stopped abruptly by the introduction of the 'Democratic Reforms' in 1959 and whatever had survived was annihilated by the Cultural Revolution. It was only with the advent of the 1980s that the communities surrounding this mountain were able to resume their ritual practices and with them the relevant debate. The territorial cults could not be fully resumed, however, because of two factors: the acknowledgement of major changes which had taken place in the communities themselves, and the intervention of an important lama of the Nyingma school who was then living in exile. The latter declared that rituals entailing animal sacrifices were not to be resumed and were to be stopped if they were still being practised, since they contradicted Buddhist principles and since the deity in question had been bound by oath to observe Buddhist beliefs.

The debates concerning both the status of the oracle and the practice of animal sacrifices have deep roots in local cosmology. According to ritual texts and local mythology the mountain god Gangmar has four ministers, one in each of the four directions. These ministers, except for the eastern minister Zurra,[14] do not require animal sacrifices and are not considered to be bound by oath. With the revival of local rituals in the 1980s all practices had to be redefined and re-negotiated in light of the new circumstances and this prompted various strategic choices. The lama who condemned the traditional sacrifices in the 1980s was the same that reconfirmed the female oracle as a vehicle for the southern minister Serchung. This allowed a successful re-negotiation between a local cult and a mainstream Buddhist tradition. The other woman oracle, despite the presence of several oracles in her family history, was never recognized by any lama as a medium for Dingri Gangmar, for this god is not allowed to possess people. She has, accordingly, only a very limited standing in the area.

The identity of the 'owner of the channels' is very important in the process by which an oracle becomes defined and is directly linked to the

[14] On Gangmar, his ministers and the relevant sacrifices see also Diemberger and Hazod 1997: 261–82; Diemberger 1998: 43–54.

medium's original tradition, to that of her or his community and to that of the person who opens their energy-channels. This might be one and the same god, but this is not necessarily the case. There can be more than one owner of the channels, and often overlapping of traditions. These combinations might consist of two or more mountain gods, or of Buddhist deities or even historical figures mixed with local mountain deities.[15] One oracle that I was told about had both Nyanchen Tanglha and the spiritual master Dromton (1004–64 CE) as 'owner of her channels', but these deities were described as being in their essence identical (*dngos-po gcig*). Educated people often consider incongruities of this sort as proof of a deception. In fact this mixing of deities and historical figures indicates a thin layer of Buddhist terminology applied to territorial rituals.

Initiation

The ritual of initiation presumes the presence of energy-channels (*rtsa*) in the human body. In some accounts these correspond with the descriptions found in Tibetan medical literature. In other cases traces of different perspectives are evident. These energy-channels can be entered by divinities of any kind, including evil deities or spirits of the dead, and this can create various problems, such as insanity. Such an idea allows us to conceptualize what may be defined in western terms as a 'psychic pathology' also as a form of possession—a bad one. It also allows one to understand why the borderline between good and bad possessions seems to be blurred.

The energy-channels are entered during episodes of god's sickness, but at that stage neither the identity of the deities nor their means of entry are clear. The cure for this sickness is usually attributed to the opening of the door of the energy-channels so that the access of the god in the future will not be obstructed. The popular perception is that impurities in the energy-channel are responsible for aberrant behaviour. Once these are ritually purified, possession is considered to be under control and confers upon the oracle an extraordinary competence in helping the other living beings. It is very difficult to obtain detailed descriptions of this ritual because it is considered a highly secret procedure (see Volf 1994: 98 ff.) The 'door' is usually considered to be located in the fingers, or sometimes in the head, and the main function of the ritual is to purify the energy-channels. It is said to be impurities in these channels that cause the ailments of the god's sickness.

A lama performing the ritual assesses the background of the oracle, identifies the main god and 'blocks the door' to prevent entry by malevolent spirits. The ritual also includes some form of training or giving of

15 See also the case of the Tenma at Drepung (Changngopa 2002 and Havnevik 2002).

instructions, but since spirit possession is considered to be a faculty of divine origin, directly transmitted by the god, the idea of training is considered contradictory and the ritual is usually described in terms of cleansing.

A lama who has some experience in opening the energy-channels told me that the relationship between the god and the oracle is a spontaneous one.[16] In principle the main task of the lama is to assess the oracle and the nature of the possession. If this is good there is little to be done, if the possession is of a dangerous kind then a ritual intervention is necessary. But this is then a ritual for 'closing the energy-channels' (*rtsa-sgo 'gag-ba*). The opening of the energy-channels does not need to be carried out by a lama: it can be done by an oracle or by a god. In such cases the tradition is performed completely outside Buddhist institutions. When the god is said to have opened the energy-channels himself, this is usually related to a kind of self-mastering of the god's sickness by the new medium, a process that involves a lengthy series of procedures in the attempt to purify the channels. In the Dingri area, one young oracle, who was in a state close to death for some time, gradually recovered by performing religious practices and then by going on pilgrimage. During the pilgrimage she was possessed by the gods of every holy mountain she visited, but by the end she mastered her spirit possession. She achieved some renown because of her ability, but the fact that she had not been initiated by a lama led to an ambivalent status in her community.

Divination with mirrors and lakes

The mirror is one of the most important among the instruments of an oracle. An oracle usually sets up one or three mirrors in a cup full of grains and consults them before falling into trance. This allows preliminary contact to be established with the main deity, the 'owner of the energy-channels'. Sometimes, for minor purposes, only this divination is performed and no trance is necessary.

In many cases a mirror is the only ritual instrument that an oracle rescued from the Cultural Revolution. At the same time it may also be the only ritual instrument handed down from one generation to the next within a lineage. In some cases the resumption of oracle practices around 1980 is associated with narratives of the more or less extraordinary

[16] The training of oracles is, however, mentioned in the written texts, especially where the higher oracles are concerned. The notion of divine transmission is most relevant in the case of local oracles, where it resembles the directly acquired knowledge attributed to the shaman in the Mongolian context. 'Being a "shaman", on the other hand, was not in essence a social role or a profession but was seen as an ability, something that anyone could be endowed with, women as well as men.' (Humphrey 1996: 139)

Female oracle in Tolung. Diagnosis by the use of a mirror. (Photo: C. Meazza 1998)

reappearance of the mirrors. In Phadrug, for example, all the ritual implements of a local oracle had been lost during the Cultural Revolution. When some villagers discovered her mirror and gave it back to her, she started her public performances again. This event became part of her narrative as the act by which the community invited her to resume her traditional function.

The mirror is called *ling*, and the origin of this term is somewhat obscure.[17] It is an instrument which allows an oracle to see into other dimensions, not only the divine dimension of the gods, but also those of other places and other times or even the innermost recesses of a human being. It literally allows the oracle—and the clients—to reflect on a certain situation and discover its hidden aspects.[18]

17 Berglie in his study of Tibetan mediums in exile reconstructs this term as *gling*, meaning 'world' or 'continent'. If this is correct, it indicates that the mirror provided the medium with a view of the world. This object is reported as one of the most important ritual items of an oracle (Berglie 1976: 85–108).

18 This process allows access to forms of knowledge and interpretation of reality that can be compared to that of shamans.

> … not only is reality exactly what shamans and other practitioners are aiming to discover, but they proceed from basic concepts of the nature of human, animal and material existence in the world, which might well be shared by anyone anywhere. These are never entirely lost sight of in the contentious or mythic versions discovered by shamans, since

Mirror divination has an ancient history in Tibetan narratives: it was used by Padmasambhava for the subjugation of local deities[19] and also by the Chinese princess Kimsheng Ongcho on her way to Tibet.[20] The practice of divination through reflective surfaces recalls similar practices among shamans of Central Asia, and it can also be found in Indian and Chinese traditions. The reflecting surface allows the gods to express themselves, with the oracle acting as an intermediary who can also provide the relevant explanation while in a lucid state. The mirror is often closely associated with the use of a lake as a site of prophecy, and in fact some oracles also practise divination by observing the surface of sacred lakes, or they describe such lakes as appearing in their mirror during the divination process. This aspect emerges clearly from some of the cases mentioned above. It does not seem a coincidence therefore that in the account given by Bellezza, an oracle, who on giving up her practice, threw her mirror into the lake Mapham (Bellezza 1997: 319).

The association between mirrors and lakes exists at a local level as well as in the most prominent forms of divination employed in the search for incarnations. This has also been described by the Dalai Lama:

> In some cases, the identification process involves consulting one of the oracles or someone who has power of *ngon-shé* (clairvoyance). One of the methods that these people use is *Ta*, whereby the practitioner looks into a mirror in which he or she might see the actual child, or a building, or perhaps a written name. I call this 'ancient television', it corresponds to the visions that people had at Lake Lhamoi Lhatso, where Reting Rinpoché saw the letters Ah, Ka and Ma and the views of a monastery and a house when he began the search for me (Dalai Lama 1999: 238).

In general the mirror seems to be a powerful symbol for the entire divinatory ability. This can be seen in the narratives on rescued mirrors connected to the resuming of traditions, in the importance attached to mirrors inherited from ancestors, in the significance of mirrors handed over by oracles or by lamas and eventually in the destruction of mirrors indicating the end of an oracle's career. Finally the consultation of the glittering surface of sacred lakes became the symbol of divination as such, even more than its equivalent the mirror. Contemporary official narratives concerning the modern version of the search for reincarnated lamas in the TAR show that the consultation of sacred lakes became one

---

one finds that the latter are not entirely random but are related to salient aspects of the everyday concepts (Humphrey 1996: 359; see also Boyer 1994).

19 See *dBa' bzhed* folio 12a,b (Wangdu and Diemberger 2000); Orofino 1994: 612–28.

20 See *sBa' bzhed* (Stein 1961: 2–3; Chinese edition p. 3); *rGyal rabs gsal ba'i me long* (Sørensen 1994: 356–7).

of the procedures advertized by governmental bodies to underline the fulfilment of the relevant ritual requirements.[21]

The trance

The trance as such is described by terms such as *lha bzhugs-pa* or *lha-'bab*, which define the god as 'residing' within the oracle or 'descending' into him or her. A number of ritual practices precede the arrival of the god: a meticulous process of putting on the costume and arranging the altar, a presentation of ritual offerings, the carrying out of divination and prayers of invitation. The ritual implements may include a drum, a multi-coloured costume and headgear (*rigs-lnga*). None of these items is regarded as essential and in some cases, for those who have lost everything in the Cultural Revolution, the medium might carry out the trance in ordinary clothing. In these cases the items are often superseded by the narratives regarding their loss. In other cases either modern substitutes have been created or can be purchased.

Many of the ritual items are typical of the tantric tradition. For example the most common headgear, a crown that depicts the five buddha-families, can be found on statues of the Buddha, in the headgear used by tantric lamas, and in some funeral rituals. In all these cases donning the headgear implies a transformation into a divine state. For oracles too it represents the onset of such a state, which in their case indicates the presence of the god.

After the offerings have been completed, the oracle starts the chant of invitation (*spyan-'dren*). The entry into trance is indicated by trembling, yawning, or rapid breathing. The arrival of the deity is marked by a radical change of voice and sometimes by quite extreme behaviour such as jumping and wild shaking. The language and the behaviour of the medium

21 See for example the report in *Xinhua* (New China News Agency), 16 January 2000:

...Following the passing away of the Sixth Reting on 23 February 1997, the Tibet Autonomous Regional government and Lhasa city government formed a leading group to search for a reincarnated boy soul, aided by a leading search advisory group composed of senior Tibetan monks, and began the search according to religious rites and to the traditions of searching for a boy soul. Over the past year, the search group, composed of the Reting Temple's monks, who, according to the indications of divination and of observation of a lake, conducted searches among 670 children in 31 townships and villages in eight of Tibet's counties. It found the basic traits of Sonam Puntsog, son of Yangqing and Rumu, domiciled in Azha Village, Lhari County, Nagqu Prefecture, who was born in the Tibetan calendar year of Fire Ox, were in accord with the indications of divination and of the observation of the lake. The discovery was later reported to the state Bureau of Religious Affairs under the state Council for approval. The state Bureau of Religious Affairs entrusted the autonomous regional government to formally approve Sonam Puntsog the reincarnated boy soul of the Sixth Reting Living Buddha.

Female oracle in Tolung in trance. (Photo: C. Meazza 1998)

reflect the character of the god, who usually introduces himself or herself with a short self-description. A dialogue then takes place between the people and the god through an assistant who acts as a 'translator' (*lo-tswa-ba*). In contrast to the divination process, during which the medium is a conscious and active intermediary, in the trance consultations, the translator acts as the intermediary between the human being and the gods. The medium is considered to be absent—she or he has lent the body and has no consciousness of what is happening. Usually the main god appears first and the various other gods come in sequence afterwards. In principle any god could possess the oracle depending on which deity a petitioner would ask for: the medium is just a means, a human vessel. Even if unplanned intrusions are possible, usually the control exerted by the owner of the energy-channels and the authorization by the lama prevent inappropriate spirits from coming into one's body. Replies are sometimes clear and sometimes enigmatic, and are often given in verse: for example, 'There is nothing which cannot be realized, you ought to keep to the very roots of Tibet.' Such answers make the role of the translator crucial for the first effort at interpretation. Further efforts at interpretation will be made by the petitioner and by the audience. Thus the oracle will generally be only one element of the collective system that ultimately produces a verdict that allows the consulting party to take a decision concerning the matter that was raised.

During the trance the oracle may carry out healing practices such as sucking (*'jib*).[22] This involves extracting the cause of the patient's sickness by sucking it out of their body. The cause is then spat out in the form of a dark substance that is then shown to the people attending the séance (see also Schenk 1993: 335; 1994: 45,128). In some sessions non-human knowledge is underlined by magical action, as we saw earlier with the handling of the red-hot iron. Nebesky-Wojkowitz (1975: 420) describes high-level oracles twisting swords and performing other displays of superhuman abilities. The combination of charismatic performance skills with an altered state of consciousness give the participators in the event a sense of being in contact with non-human dimensions. This can to some extent explain the effectiveness of these events. At the end of the trance the oracle collapses into unconsciousness. In some cases, oracles cover their face with a cloth to make the transition of identity even more explicit.

Women oracles as healers and political advisers

The importance of crisis is apparent not only during the process by which men and women become oracles, but also in the situations in which they are called upon to act. In general, they are consulted when petitioners are experiencing crises or transitions of some kind. Questions to oracles might thus include not only health problems but also issues about kinship, household management, weather or work; occasionally they are also consulted about local political issues. The main task of an oracle is to understand the origin of a sickness by identifying the disturbances that have damaged relations between the patient and any divine or human being. This task can be seen as closely linked to the notion of 'defilement' (*grib*; the word also means 'shade' in its non-religious use) and to the necessary purification process that must follow. The diagnosis might include a denunciation by the god of various actions taken by the local people or refer to some transgressions of community mores. The god can be very aggressive and may even insult the patient, who will be very apologetic. If the patient is accompanied by members of his or her family, the entire family might apologize collectively. Finally the god prescribes a number of rituals to be performed. Sometimes the oracle also recommends some herbal treatments in addition to the prescribed rituals, but these are regarded as ancillary and are not considered to be within her main area of competence.

The reputation of an oracle does not depend purely on success in curing illness. Not all the issues brought to the consultations can be resolved

22 The term *'jip* is used to indicate a specific ritual practice and is derived from the verb *'jib-pa* meaning 'to suck'. This practice is also described by Volf 1994 in the Ladakhi context.

successfully, and an oracle's credibility will depend on his or her ability to address a problem accurately, even if it involves acknowledging an inability to resolve it. In one case that occurred in an urban context, an oracle prescribed a certain ritual 'therapy' for a man who was ill, and she announced that he would recover in due course if he followed her instructions. At the same time, without being asked, she addressed the wife of this patient and advised her to go to a hospital because her 'life-potential' (*srog*) did not look promising. Three months later it turned out that she had liver cancer, and she died shortly afterwards. This case was not seen as a 'failure' of the oracle. Despite her inability to cure the woman, her recognition of the woman's serious physical condition gave her credibility.

Oracles are assumed to be able to cure only certain kinds of health problems; in others they are just expected to give good advice. Traditional Tibetan doctors and oracles can be seen as complementary, and in some cases a similar relationship can be seen between oracles and local modern medical institutions, where the latter exist. It is more common, however, to find that co-operation of this sort has been blocked by doubts about the quality or trustworthiness of an oracle or by ideological objections implying that oracular cures are unscientific and old-fashioned.

The evaluation of the effectiveness or credibility of oracles is based, in practice, only on their reputation, and there are frequent reports of oracles pretending to heal illnesses that they are unable to handle. As Samuel puts it, 'In a society where shamans are common and culturally valued, the risk of self-interest and exploitative behaviour on the part of the shaman is a real one' (Samuel 1993: 472). Only subtle mechanisms of 'reputation building' can constitute a form of social regulation of this phenomenon, and these mechanisms become completely ineffective in the event of major social and cultural upheaval. Under these circumstances representatives of modern medicine, and of the state, tend to produce generalized criticisms of these practices as being no more than frauds.[23] Although this may sometimes be true, this perspective does not take into account the cultural complexity of oracles. It can also be argued that in many peripheral areas oracles might still be the only ones able to give people reasonable advice in the event of a crisis. This might include advising the sick person to travel to a hospital.

Besides her role as a healer, an oracle is often asked about family problems or community issues; even legal matters such as unsolved criminal cases and the transgression of local rules might be among the questions presented during a consultation. In such cases the impact of an oracle's verdict can be significant for how a community deals with a particular

[23] It is therefore often defined as part of feudal superstition and thus condemned (see Ye 1996).

person or group. Such cases can be extremely sensitive and, while the possibility of intentional deception can never be excluded, an oracle is usually careful to handle these cases in the most judicious way possible unless she or he wants to risk a dramatic loss of reputation. This is true at all levels—stories of the price paid by high and famous oracles who had given what was considered wrong advice to the Tibetan government on political issues are well-known (see Nebesky-Woykowitz 1975: 451 ff.) Local oracles can find their decisions challenged in a similar way by traditional leaders and administrators in their area.

The skills attributed to an oracle include a deep knowledge not only of local religious customs but also of social and interpersonal relations. This ability is usually said to have been acquired from the deity, but relates also to the oracle's personal history and to the overcoming of a crisis in her own life, especially in the case of women this is often combined with a reluctance to accept social expectations. The period of crisis with its physical threat and social liminality seems to provide an oracle not only with a peculiar perception of the sacred, but also with the basis for a different and broader understanding of the human and social reality in which she or he is immersed. In fact liminality enables her to reflect on social constraints from the 'outside' after having challenged them. Thus the gender connotation associated with female oracles lies in providing domains where women can engage actively in the process of decision-making that concerns not only themselves, but the community as a whole. The recognition of the network of human and divine relations as a system to be dealt with allows the future oracle to acquire a new identity and to recognize her own fields of agency instead of being a passive element in kinship transactions, as is especially the case for young women. Through training and subsequent experiences as a healer, or even as political diviner, the oracle has the opportunity to deepen and improve her knowledge and wisdom. In the case of male oracles the life-crisis and the subsequent achievement of a new identity is also a critical point in their evolution as oracles, but the process does not include the challenges to the social expectations and the forms of classification which are specific to the female oracle's experience of life.

The set of skills that allow an oracle to intervene in decision-making for individuals in a situation of crisis seems to give oracles a basis for commenting on political situations as well. Since the wisdom granted to oracles by their possessing deities is considered to impart extraordinary knowledge, local decision-makers sometimes used them in cases of controversy to ascertain factors that might otherwise remain unknown to the political leadership. The competence of an oracle seems in fact to be a knowledge that has allowed people to reflect on hidden layers of the society. The device of consulting oracles for decision-making was used not only traditionally, but tends to persist in outlying areas. Here it is possible to encounter, occasionally, modern administrators who do not seem to regard these practices as contradictory to official ideology. Decision-making in the communist system, like in any modern state, is often a highly sophisticated procedure requiring complex interpretation of political instructions that may be obscure, vague or simply difficult to apply to local conditions. It can therefore be argued that for contemporary cadres the process of consulting these traditional sources of knowledge might simply be a way to show respect to traditional customs formerly used by village headmen. And oracles, irrespective of their divine attributes, often prove to be judicious advisers and useful channels for local opinions. They can even use phrases like 'the earth belongs to the Communist Party and the sky also belongs to the Communist Party, thus make a good relation with comrade XYZ'. In the formulation of a specific verdict, such pronouncements blend concrete political advice, modern political ideology and ancient cosmology. They also indicate in a very pragmatic way that it is better to establish good relations with everyone within the earth and the sky.

MEDIUMSHIP AND FEMALE COMPETENCE

Spirit possession is accessible in principle to anyone, whatever their sex or social background. The most important factor seems to be individual vocation, although the presence of oracles in one's ancestry seems to be regarded as a highly favourable indication of competence. Certain lineages are clearly defined as either male or female, but more often male and female oracles can occur at random within the same ancestry. In certain contexts, however, there seems to be a predominance of women and sometimes even an exclusivity of women. One case in which the medium's role is considered to be exclusively female can be found in a Tibetan community now situated within Nepali territory not far from the Tibetan border.[24] No monasteries exist in this area and the local politico-religious leadership is in the hands of 'big people' (*mi-che*), namely traditional village headmen (*rgan-po*) and lineages of lama and 'lhabon' or 'lhaven' (*lha-bon*).[25] The social fabric in this community is based on patrilineal clans and women are expected to marry patrilocally, although there are more uxorilocal marriages than might be expected. A number of oracles exist in this community, all of whom are women. For this

[24] The community known as Khumbo or Nawa inhabits an area known as Beyul Khenpa Lung or 'the Hidden Valley of the Artemisia' (Diemberger 1992).

[25] Lhabons are priests dealing specifically with clan deities and territorial deities.

community it would be inconceivable to think of a male oracle. The role of the oracle is explicitly defined as an exclusively female domain.

The oracular tradition here is regarded as originating from Dingri, some miles to the north, within the modern Tibetan polity. One of the main spirits invoked in local sessions comes from there; the others are all local mountain gods. Oracles are usually consulted in cases of sickness, or at funerals in order to serve as vehicles for the spirits of the deceased. These women are excluded from the ritual of sharing the cup, a procedure through which people express their membership in the community and their position in its hierarchy. The women oracles are excluded because they 'have the god', a condition that renders them dangerous even though they are highly respected. They will give opinions to anyone who consults them about a problem, but normally they hardly express any views on issues regarding the whole community. Their focus is on disentangling individual situations. When there is a serious conflict which threatens the coherence of the community, the opinion of the gods speaking through the mouths of the oracles is likely to be regarded as more significant than the opinion of any lama, whatever his status. It is thus not infrequent for these women to be given the final word on the location of a temple, and to articulate the opinion of the community on unpunished crimes or on any misbehaviour by the religious leadership.

The difference between the roles of the oracle and the lama points to a specifically female area of activity. In contrast to the standardized and repetitive ritual pattern of the celebrations held by lamas and lhabons that reaffirm the relation of the community to its territory, to its ancestry and to the Buddhist cosmology,[26] the oracle's intervention is unpredictable. There seem to exist two complementary, sometimes competing, discourses that engage with the religious entities of the landscape and recall the Inner Asian social and cultural context. As Caroline Humphrey puts it:

> There are at least two ways of being in the landscape, which are simultaneous possibilities for any Mongol group. Each combines its own sense of place with spatial awareness … The two landscapes engage different notions of energies-in-nature and the social agencies by which such powers may harnessed to human benefit. One is that of the chief or ruler, and the other is that of the shaman… Very briefly, chiefly agency derives from patrilines of males which constantly reconstitute themselves as 'the same' through generations, and they are successful in so far as they can prevail upon the powers in the land, which are anthropomorphized as kings and warriors, to produce fertility, health, and prosperity among people and livestock. Shamanist agency, on the other hand, acknowledges and celebrates difference… (Humphrey 1995: 135–6)

26 The lhaven or lhabon evokes the territory in terms of long lists of toponyms, whereas the lama mentions only a few of them and places them in relation to Buddhist divinities. For a detailed study of this ritual see Melcher 2000.

And further:

> ... the distinction between the chiefly/Buddhist and the shamanic world-views rests on radically different theories of empowerment. Both chiefs and Buddhist lamas derive their legitimacy from social processes: from genealogical descent, from political or military structures, from teacher-pupil lines in the Buddhist system, and so forth. Shamans, on the other hand, think of themselves as acquiring their abilities not so much from social training as directly from the energies of the world, conceived as spirits who decide who is to be a shaman. (ibid.: 151)

In the small community of the Nepal-Tibetan borderland it seems that the competing discourses are gendered. Like a Mongolian shaman, the oracle speaks of difference, constructing an incidental and situation-specific landscape of divine and human relations. The god articulates in a very individual way what is not already defined as the order of the world, and which should be passed on in an unchanging way from one generation to the next; it is a discourse of disorder, restoration of order or perhaps even of differing orders.

It seems that the work of the oracle is directly related to the fact that these women are by definition outside the politico-religious ranking system, that they have a deep knowledge of the kinship-network as patrilocally married wives, and that they have a direct experience of the processes of life as mothers. Both at an individual level as well as at a community level these women seem to be expert at conflict resolution and at negotiation since they allow tensions and hidden emotions to be articulated, especially on the part of those who have the least power. They enact a function that gives voice to the voiceless, and they articulate many dark aspects of a community which are considered conflictual and thus impure. The connection of conflict with impurity—a connection which is spelt out in a local saying that 'birth, death and conflicts are defiling (*grib*)'—is also a connection with female aspects of life, since the womb is considered impure, as is the newly born child up until the time it is ritually purified. Female oracles are able to speak of this hidden but omnipresent and life-giving dimension of existence.[27]

While the conditions of a marginal Himalayan village community cannot be transposed to the Tibetan context, there do seem to be features in common. When in Tolung, in central Tibet, a female oracle possessed by Nyanchen Tanglha passed purifying incense-fumigations between her parted legs, it evoked the link between the female womb, impurity and purification. This is just one of many symbolic acts which associate women as sources of life with a specific religious function: the oracle.

[27] On the notion of defilement (*grib*) and the relevant mythology and social practice, cf. Schicklgruber 1992.

This act also brings out the ambiguous relation between fertility and defilement. Here, oracles are not only accessible to women but seem to employ a specific female approach to social orders and disorders. The sacredness of a female oracle seems, in fact, to be deeply shaped by a woman's experience of life and by the religious and social categories that construct gendered identities. This regards not only her life-story but also her oracular practice. A specific female area of competence can be seen for example in the marriage customs from Dingri (see Aziz 1978: 428). Here female oracles intervene by getting possessed when the bride is separated from her parental household—emotionally speaking the most traumatic moment for the young woman. As in the above-mentioned community, young daughters-in-law are common clients and it seems that the oracles serve to diffuse the tensions surrounding marriage arrangements and kinship relations.

These women explore the margins of social discourse and become authors of alternative social scripts that allow for conflict renegotiations. Their actions enable other women in the community to explore the ambiguities around impurity and disorder. Ultimately women are not merely identified with the domain of impurity but more importantly also with the ability to give an expression to impurity together with all that belongs to the realm of the interdicted. In contrast to the small community of the Nepal-Tibetan borderland, in most areas of Tibet the female dimension of oracles seems to co-exist and overlap with non-gendered and male forms of oracular tradition.

Indeed, from historical sources we know that in ancient Tibet spirit possession had a central position in the political system and that women had an important role in embodying this institution. During differences among the leadership, when critical decisions had to be made, female diviners are reported to have determined the outcome.[28] This was, however, a limited and contextual power, just like that of the female oracle,

28 Both the political relevance of spirit possession—especially in time of crisis—and the intervention of female mediums is suggested by a passage given in the *dBa' bzhed*. This narrative regards the conflicts between Buddhist and Bonpo during the youth of King Trisong Detsen. At that time ominous events afflicted the kingdom after the chief minister Mazham banned and persecuted Buddhism. The critical situation is reported as having been sorted out by the intervention of diviners:

> As far as Zhang Mazham is concerned, after receiving great omens of death, female diviners (*mo ma*) who were given some reward [by enemies of the minister] said: 'The divination for the king is very inauspicious (*bla'i sku phya ngan no*)', then [the minister] was sent to be buried alive (*gson khung du stsal*) as a ransom (*sku glud*). As the omens and the divinations (*mo dang ltas*) of the superior and inferior [people] corresponded, it was said that the Chinese idol was threatening or harmful.' (*dBa' bzhed* 4b–5a, Wangdu and Diemberger 2000).

lhakama (*lha-bka'-ma*), of the Nepal-Tibet borderland, or that of the Mongol shamans whose 'shamanist landscapes' became decisive only in time of weak power of chiefs and elders—those who expressed the 'chiefly landscapes' (Humphrey 1995).

Contemporary Tibetan reality suggests that only in certain contexts does spirit mediumship become a female domain. Popular opinion on this usually distinguishes between a few high and institutionalized oracles that are predominantly male[29], and female oracles that are generically associated with the ideas of 'low', 'lay', 'local' and 'numerous'.[30]

An immediate opposition is evident in the very notion of 'low' and 'high' level oracles. Low level local oracles are generally indicated with non-honorific terms such as 'lhakhama', whereas the high oracles are usually referred to with honorific terms like 'kuten'. Thus there seems to be a two-level perception of oracles, not unlike the distinction between peripheral and central spirit possession proposed by Lewis (1971). This model, which has been applied in a comparative study of spirit possession, sees peripheral spirit possession as a female domain and central spirit possession as a male domain. This model has been applied to other Asian contexts such as Nepal (Gellner 1994: 27–48) and China (Strickman 1982: 55). Does the Tibetan double-level classification of oracles correspond to Lewis's model representing two distinct forms of the phenomenon? And does this dichotomized classification reflect a specific perspective on other classificatory oppositions like centre versus periphery, monastic institution versus lay world, and so on?

At a first glance Lewis's model would seem to be applicable to the Tibetan context. At one level, the female life-giving principle is ideologically appropriated under the rubric of female impurity. Hence female possession is seen as a vehicle for the representation and 'solution' of conflicts at all levels of society. At another level the role of spirit possession in the political and religious process appears to be identified with male strategic domains insofar as it serves to preserve the established system of social and moral norms and values.

A more careful analysis shows that Lewis's model proves to be insufficient. Even if a dichotomized classification of spirit possession seems to

---

This passage does not only indicate that the diviners decided to eliminate the anti-Buddhist Great Minister through their 'consultative' power but also shows that an omen could be manipulated and that lower and higher levels of specialists of divination existed.

29 'In general even though the majority of oracles (*sku-rten-pa*) are men, there are also a few women' (dBang-'dus and Zha'o ha'o 1992: 28; cf. Changngopa 2002; Havnevik 2002.). The main state oracles like Nechung and Gadong are men. The Gadong oracle, for example, is transmitted patrilineally.

30 The great number of local female practitioners is not only stated by common people but seems to be reflected in the official statements regarding superstitious practices.

exist in Tibet, Tibetan social practices disclose tendencies that are nuanced. The distinction made by Tibetans is reflected in the terms they use to differentiate one kind of medium from the other. These categories seem, however, to be more than abstract classifications. They appear to constitute a field of social negotiation. This is why it is often difficult to draw a typological borderline, and it might even occur that an oracle belonging to the 'lower' kind is recognized at a 'higher' level, and changes position in the hierarchy. Furthermore an oracle might be considered low and marginal by someone from Lhasa while having a high standing in the local community.

Similarly, an oracle might be seen by someone from Lhasa as transgressing certain Buddhist moral values but might be seen locally as contributing to the preservation of the social and religious order. The way in which the status of an oracle is shaped and reshaped reflects, therefore, the cultural and political dynamics that link the lay world to Buddhist institutions and local realities to the state. Therefore the phenomenon must be seen contextually. The traditionally decentralized character of the Tibetan state accounts, in fact, for the co-existence of very different religious traditions and viewpoints as well as for fundamental differences in other features of the society, such as concepts related to kinship systems and political power (Samuel 1993: 139 ff.). It would seem therefore that the classificatory opposition of periphery and centre is entirely based on the specificity of local contexts. Indeed, the Tibetan context challenges not only the notions of a central and a peripheral spirit possession but also the very conventional idea of a centralized state opposed to a periphery.[31]

Another opposition that is challenged by the Tibetan context is that between centralized, normative Buddhist institutions versus various types of religious practices associated with the lay world. In particular the blending of pre-Buddhist practices with tantric forms of belief has led to the construction of hybrid forms of female sacredness.[32]

31 This applies to the idea of a geographical, political and cultural periphery. To my surprise I encountered among rural communities of central Tibet religious traditions and phenomena that can be seen as very heterodox from a Buddhist point of view, while other areas belonging for example to Ngari might display stronger tendencies to conform to traditional Buddhist norms (see Ramble forthcoming).

32 Two distinct yet overlapping aspects can be seen: on the one hand territorial and ancestral cults imply a gendered notion of defilement (*grib*) that is opposed to the notion of honour and prestige (*dbu-phang*) bestowed by the gods. Oracles seem to deal to large extent with this form of impurity. This kind of view is mainly rooted in a lay politico-religious context and is common in Tibetan and Tibeto-Burmese societies (Sagant 1990). In the Tibetan context, this perspective merges with tantric beliefs that reflect a female impurity and sacredness that originally derives from Indian traditions and reflects ancient Indian society.

This process is reflected in the way in which oracles combine items taken from tantric traditions such as headgear with ritual functions typical of territorial cults. This blend is especially striking and sometimes contradictory in communities that have a weak link to centres of politico-religious power and literacy. In these contexts terms taken from the tantric lexicon such as 'khandroma' (*mkha'-'gro-ma* , 'sky-goer', Skt. *ḍākinī*) or 'naljorma' (*rnal-'byor-ma*, Skt. yoginī) can be used to define a female medium as an alternative to ancient terms like 'lhakama' which point to the pre-Buddhist roots of oracular practice.[33] However, the ritual context is to a large extent shaped by territorial cults.[34] This blending of tradition is reflected also in the different layers of interpretation of the landscape: for example lakes that can be seen as the seat of certain territorial deities can also be described as reproducing female tantric deities such as Vajravārāhī and Vajrayoginī.[35] The process whereby these traditions are merged in one way or another is not value-neutral. It is marked by disparities in the relations of power between the various religious institutions at various points in time, as can be seen in the ritual practice of Buddhist lamas subjugating local deities. This process can be strongly gendered[36]

Here there is a specific association of social and ritual impurity with women and low castes. Rituals implying confrontation with impure things and events can be seen as the source of sacred power by virtue of the endeavour to overcome social conventions. This Indic origin is for example mirrored in the names of tantric female deities in the *Hevajra Tantra* and the *Tattvasamgraha* (Tsuda 1978: 167–231) whereas the attitude to impurity can be seen for example in practices like the Cutting rite (*gcod*) (Gyatso 1985: 320–41).

[33] I could see this phenomenon in remote areas of southern Lato and among Tibetan communities of the Arun valley. Something similar has been reported by Nebesky-Wojkowitz for Chumbi valley, Sikkim and Bhutan (Nebesky-Wojkowitz 1975: 425 ff).

[34] See also ibid.: 427. It is well-known that animal sacrifice is a highly controversial practice. It can reflect both heteredox tantric rituals as well as pre-Buddhist cults. In all the cases I could witness or on which I received first-hand accounts, the animal was offered to a territorial god, usually a mountain.

[35] Namtso Lake is one of the most common examples. Here numerous layers of interpretation of a ritual practice merge: the protective territorial deities of the local nomads, the Bonpo deities, the Buddhist deities, the lake seen as shaped like Vajravārāhī, and so on. All these interpretations are imposed on something more ancient to which the numerous petroglyphs bear witness.

[36] There are numerous examples of this, such as the case of the ritual subjugation of the sacred mountain known as Ama Pujungma, 'Pregnant Mother', in the Nepal-Tibet borderlands. This mountain is considered by the local Tibetan ethnic community to be a seat of fertility and was subjugated at the beginning of this century by a lama who came from Tibet and placed a statue of Guru Rinpoche in the part of the mountain that corresponded to her genitals (Melcher 2000). In a broader sense this gendered connotation is also expressed by the famous myth of the demonness embodying Tibetan territory who had to be pinned down by Buddhist temples (Gyatso 1987: 33–51).

not only in the mythology but also in the ritual practice connected with sacred places.[37]

The relationship between Buddhist institutions and forms of popular religiosity like oracles—a mixture of antagonism and complementarity—seems to have shaped the religious life of Tibetan communities through the centuries. But was this a one-way process, whereby pre-Buddhist phenomena like female oracular traditions were influenced and redefined in Buddhist terms, or might there have been a similar reshaping of Buddhist practices by pre-Buddhist forces as well? And if this was the case, as it seems to have been, were the women who became famous tantric practitioners influenced by the existence of female oracular traditions of pre-Buddhist origin? Such questions can only be answered through a detailed study of the relevant biographical material, which is beyond the scope of the present discussion. In general, local oracles appear to be more rooted in oral traditions, whereas tantric women have based themselves on concepts and practices that stem from the Buddhist literary traditions of Indian provenance. These, however, bear the traces of folk religious traditions of ancient India that included various forms of divination and spirit possession.[38] Thus, local oracles and tantric practitioners can be seen as belonging to two distinct traditions which have been converging and intertwining for centuries. It can also be argued that the Tibetan women who appropriated Buddhist tantric teachings benefited from a pre-existing social space for female sacredness: in this sense they can be seen as having been influenced by the religious role of women in the ancient territorial cults.[39] It is probably not a coincidence that Dingri,

[37] The pilgrimage to Tsari is a striking example of how discourses on gender and body can shape this kind of ritual practice (see Huber 1994: 350, 371).

[38] Some of these features are discussed by Berglie 1983 and Orofino 1994: 612–28.

[39] Historically speaking it is well-known that mountain deities were central in the politico-religious system of the early Tibetan kingdom as it emerged from the preceding confederation of patrilineal clans (*rus*). Apart from famous categories of mountain gods such as the *sku-bla* and the *phywa*, there were also classes of female spirits that were related to various features of the landscape such as the *mu-sman* and the *klu-mo*. All these deities were considered to have direct influence over the life and the power of the royal family and the ministers as well as over the well-being of the community in general (Macdonald 1971: 295). These deities were not only the focus of the royal cults but used to communicate to human beings through various forms of divination and spirit possession. Their mediums were women, or at least some of them were, as it is attested by divination texts such as P.T. 1047 (ibid.: 274 ff). It seems that the practice of divination was common at all levels of society and used to influence very important governmental decisions as well. Even if information on this subject is fragmentary, the great political and controversial relevance of divinatory practices can be perceived from the royal edicts of the eighth and ninth centuries. A. Macdonald concludes: 'It seems therefore that the edicts confirm the existence of a body of specialists in divination attached to the royal court or the government…it is through these diviners that the opposition to Buddhism was expressed on several occasions.' (ibid.: 288)

an area that is rich in female oracular traditions, also produced many great female tantricists.[40]

In this highly articulated and heterogeneous context, the role of female oracles has apparently been more than peripheral. These various female religious specialists seem often to have reached degrees of power and competence that reflect the existence of social spaces for female agency in male-dominated politico-religious spheres. But these also provided space for contesting gendered identity at an individual level. These sacred women seem again and again to have raised claims on domains that were traditionally non-female. This was expressed in their challenges to the kinship system or to the political and religious establishments, just as the first Dorje Phagmo was able in a slightly different context—that of tantric Buddhist women—to abandon her royal civil life and undertake an extraordinary religious career. She is reported as having become a *bhikṣuṇī* (*dge-slong-ma*), a female fully ordained member of a monastic order,[41] and was also able to establish a tradition of female religious dances (*'cham*) conscious of its innovative character (*Ye shes* n.d.: 80). She also became the first of a long reincarnation line of female spiritual masters who have been heading the monastery of Samding up to the present day and who embody the tantric goddess Vajravārāhī.[42]

[40] These are figures such as Machig Zhama, one of the founders of the Path and Result (*Lam-'bras*) and Pacification (*Zhi-byed*) traditions, concerning whom see Martin in this volume. The first Samding Dorje Phagmo, Chokyi Drolma, is also a later remarkable example. She was born in the fifteenth century as the daughter of the king of Gungtang and married into the ruling family of southern Lato. Later she became a companion of Bodong Chokle Namgyal, devoted herself to religious practice in Porong Pemo Choding, a monastery in the Porong area not far from Shekar, and then moved to Samding and Tsari (see *Ye shes* n.d. and 'Chi-med n.d.). Incidentally, both women feigned insanity in order to leave family life and devote themselves to religious activity. In a different framework, this recalls the divine sickness that allows the female oracle to redefine her identity in new, sacred terms. Eventually both became associated with sacred lakes in local narratives, respectively a sacred mythological lake in Kharta (see Diemberger and Hazod 1999:34–51) and the lakes in Yamdrok.

[41] *Ye shes n.d.* folio 60b '*...sde snon gsum pa chen po rje btsun chos kyi dbang phyug las kyi slob dpon mdzad/ dad pa' i dge mdun grangs dang mtshan nyid yongs su rdzogs pa'i dbus su tshigs phyi ma dge slong ma'i dngos por bsgrubs nas/ lhag pa tshul khrims kyi bslab pas thugs kyi bum pa gang ste/ 'gro ba thams cad kyi mchod gnas chen por gyur te... bod kyi dge slong ma thams cad kyi dbyid du gyur ba...*' (The great Denon Sumpa Jetsun Chokyi Wangchuk acted as teacher [*slob-dpon*], at last she became a fully ordained woman amidst a number of monks of faith and full realization. Then she completed the Spiritual Vase as taught by Lhagpa Tsultrim and became an object of devotion for all living beings...She became like the spring of all fully ordained women...)

[42] The Gungtang Princess Chokyi Dronma became the first Samding Dorje Phagmo and her story and that of the next four reincarnations are mentioned in the *Bo dong chos 'byung*, a sixteenth century text written by the tantric partner of the fourth Samding Dorje Phagmo that narrated the history of the Bodong tradition. However, Chokyi Dronma was also

Once these sacred women were acknowledged, however, they were usually confined within institutions that provided them with a non-ordinary identity. The same institutions privileged discourses of common, non-gendered interests, aiming at the local or the religious community. These women may have represented a discontinuity, but the narratives about them ultimately relocated them within the dominant gender and religious ideology.

ORACLES, BUDDHIST INSTITUTIONS AND THE STATE: DIFFERENT LEVELS OF INTEGRATION

We have seen from the life-stories of oracles that spirit possession is apparently rooted in an individual's overcoming of a life-crisis as well as in an ancient religious function. This seems to have been related to territorial cults and was a key element in the resolution of conflicts and in local decision-making. The co-existence of oracular traditions with Buddhist institutions has led not only to the marginalization of oracular practices but also to various forms of integration and control. This happened within the central Tibetan government as well as at the local level.

Integration, control or repression of oracles used to happen in various ways according to the specific context. As mentioned above the most common way in which oracles were sanctioned by and integrated into Buddhist institutions was when lamas would 'open the energy-channels' of the prospective oracle. This involved careful examination of the case and the giving of clear instructions about which divine beings should be allowed to enter, and on how this ability was to be used 'for the benefit of all living beings'. The performance of such a rite conferred upon the oracle a kind of religious authorization and immediate social recognition.

This was the most common and easily negotiated way in which oracles were integrated into the Buddhist framework, albeit in a marginal role. The higher oracles were subjected to a much stricter and somewhat repressive process of institutionalization by the central government. The need to control oracles seems to have been prompted by a sense that the local forms of negotiation and incorporation were insufficient. Indeed it was possible, as we have seen, for oracles to remain completely outside the Buddhist tradition by having their channels opened by another oracle or by the gods.

The extent to which oracles were integrated into Buddhist institutions was therefore only partial. On certain occasions the complexity of the

---

recognized as the third in the line of Dorje Phagmo reincarnations that started with Yeshe Khandro Sonam Drenma before Samding became its seat and the Bodongpa tradition its religious affiliation (see *Ye shes* n.d. and Tashi Tsering 1993).

oracle practices, and probably the inadequacy of local forms of integration and control, prompted the Tibetan government to intervene directly. In an interview a former low-level official of the Tibetan government from Rutok (western Tibet) gave a description of one such intervention in his youth some seventy years earlier:

> 'When I was some twelve years old, the government sent an order that oracles had to be tested, probably because they felt that there were too many of them around and that not all of them could be considered trustworthy. All the oracles of the area were summoned. There were sixty-one. Two thirds of them were men, one third of them women. They had to write their name on pieces of paper that were then folded and put in a bowl. Those who could take out their own name would be approved, while those who could not were to be designated as fakes. Only two men managed to pass the examination. One really managed to take out his own name. Another said that he could not take out his name because it had already been taken out by somebody else and his claim turned out to be true. All of them except for these two were said to be fake and their ritual items were confiscated. But after a short time most of them started to practise again.' (Ngari, August 1998)

In Lato there was a similar test for oracles. One informant could remember oracles having to describe an object that had been placed in a box: those who could not give the correct answer were said to be fakes. He also recalled a man who was recognized as a high oracle and given a title and some land by the government. From then on this man was considered to be a high level oracle and he was called a 'kuso' (*sku-gsol*) or 'kuten' (*sku-rten*). In this case too, all the other oracles had their ritual items confiscated. Nebesky-Wojkowitz (1975: 419 ff.) described more elaborate tests for higher oracles. The oracle's relationship to Buddhist institutions and to the Tibetan government through initiation rituals and examinations seems therefore to have created a system of layered institutionalization which determined the 'centrality' or 'peripherality' of an oracle in society. These mechanisms of control were likely to express gendered discourses. But to what extent this was so is still to be assessed.

It is well-known that at the time of the Fifth Dalai Lama oracles came to occupy significant positions in the establishment, since they were of primary importance in installing new reincarnations as the head of state. The prominence of high-level oracles like Nechung, Gadong, and Lhamo Chokyong in political and religious affairs goes back to this era. These oracles seem to have been important to the Manchus as well. Some of the high Tibetan oracles were later sanctioned by the Qing emperors in the eighteenth century. In a 1792 decree the emperor Qianlong confirmed the use of oracles in selecting the Dalai and Panchen Lamas.

> At the time of recognising the successor of a high *sPrul-sku*, ceremonies for obtaining divine inspiration [*lha bla'i lung-babs*] having been first performed

according to the former custom, the name of each of the boys whose claims are under consideration are to be put into the golden vase and the Ta-la'i Lama or the Pan-chen Er-te-ni and the Great Minister Resident in Tibet in public assembly shall draw out a wooden name-tablet and so recognize the *sPrul-sku*. (Richardson 1974: 77)

Richardson observed that this order included a reference to the Lhamo Chokyong, one of the main state oracles. This was mentioned generically in this text as previously existing 'ceremonies for obtaining divine inspiration' along with the newly introduced customs. Richardson points to a passage from the Chinese version of the same decree that was translated by Stein in which this process of reform was seen to 'improve their religion without changing their custom; straighten their policy without changing their convenience' (ibid.: 78). This indicated that from a Chinese perspective a subtle process of negotiation with pre-existing customs was considered important in establishing and maintaining imperial rule. Even when drastic changes were introduced, continuity with the past needed to be constructed.[43]

This policy towards pre-existing customs and leading figures in the Tibetan establishment was part of the Qing consolidation of its expansionistic aspirations, which included gaining control over the western border areas of the empire. In contemporary times we can discern continuity with this tradition. The appointment by the modern Chinese administration of traditional figures like the Dorje Phagmo to an honorific position in the Political Consultative Conference and in the Congress is an example. This continues the tradition of co-opting religious leaders, including those who are women.[44]

43 The Qing used strategically the pre-existing links between Tibetans and Mongols. They adopted Tibetan Buddhism as a political device in affirming control over the various Mongol groups. The construction of the Jehol temples (250 km to the north-east of Beijing) by Emperor Qianlong who took Tibetan models as a source of inspiration is especially significant in this respect (see Chayet 1985). While Tibetan Buddhism was strategically promoted under the Qing emperors, shamanism was to a large extent repressed. However a few shamans were formally institutionalized in a way that eliminated the most spontaneous and less controllable forms of this sacredness (see Heissig 1970:338–48; 1953; Stary 1977: 28; Humphrey 1994: 208 ff). Repression and partial integration of shamanism by the Qing state show certain parallel features to what happened with Tibetan oracles in the same period.

44 A body such as the Political Consultative Conference is usually seen as having no power, as illustrated by the nicknames associated with its members, such as 'kitchen corner' (*thab-zur*) or 'decoration' (*rgyan-cha*). In fact it is probable that this institution was at least at one stage endowed with a more significant role than merely one of expounding state propaganda. It might have represented a *trait-d'union* for the Chinese administration with those political and religious dignitaries and with their traditional networks which have been dispossessed by the new administration but which still have to be taken into account in the practice of local administration and policy-making. In that sense this body, at least in times

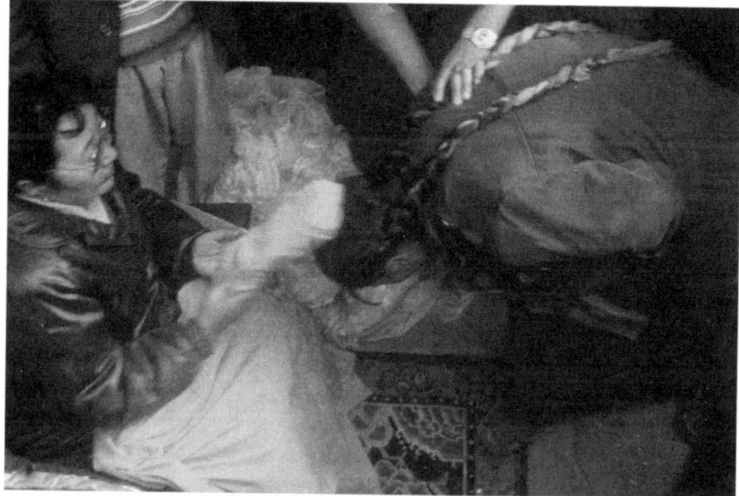

The twelfth incarnation of Dorje Phagmo, Dechen Chodron, blessing a pilgrim with a holy text. Dechen Chodron is vice president of the People's Congress of the TAR. (Photo: H. Diemberger 1996)

According to the pattern described above, the traditional sacred women of Tibet were either co-opted or repressed. The Dorje Phagmo, like other female religious authorities from less famous reincarnation lines,[45] was given a new political identity in contemporary Tibet,[46] but all the great oracles of the past were excluded from the new system, either because they went into exile or because their institution ceased to exist.[47] The new

when there was a functioning United Front policy such as in the 1950s and 1980s, might have had a relative and informal but real role as a consultative agency.

[45] One example is the sixth reincarnation of Gungru Yeshe Khandro at Dragkar of Gengya in southern Amdo. From 1979 she was given various positions such as member of the standing committee of the Political Consultative Conference of the Tibetan Autonomous Region of Southern Gansu and others (see Tashi Tsering 1994: 27–47 and Chayet 1994: 292).

[46] She occupied positions like chairman of the Political Consultative Conference of the TAR, vice-chairman of the People's Congress and various others. On the Dorje Phagmo see also Barnett in this volume.

[47] In contrast to the consultation of oracles, the consultation of lakes curiously remained part of the protocol carried out by the state-appointed commission in charge of the search of reincarnated lamas, as for example was the case for the reincarnation of the Sixth Reting Rinpoche, publicly announced in January 2000. The various forms of divination, including the consultation of lakes and oracles, were traditionally carried out by high lamas in charge of the search.

regime did, however, adopt the Qing mode of incorporation for a remarkable female practitioner who can be seen as closely linked to oracles: Yumi a famous Gesar bard, who was made a member of the Political Consultative Conference of TAR in the early 1990s. This appears to be the only concession in this direction. Yumi is a bard (*'bab-sgrung*)—she received her ability as a divine gift in very much the same way as an oracle is possessed by a personal deity and was initiated with the ritual of 'opening the energy-channels'.

The traditions of bards and of oracles are drawn from a common background and use similar expressions, as has already been noticed and discussed by Stein 1959. In fact Gesar, the famous hero of the Tibetan epic, appears again and again in the most unpredictable ways, as a kinsman of local gods or even as the putative author of petroglyphs and prehistoric items in local explanations of ancient human remains. The account by Yumi regarding her own life and initiation can be seen as parallel to that of many oracles:

> 'In the year in which my father died I was sixteen, and it was in this year that I started to fall into trance. In that year I had gone to the mountain pastures with two other girls. I went to sleep and I dreamt about a black lake above and a white lake below. From the black lake a person riding a black horse appeared. He had a black face and was wearing a headgear (*rigs-lnga*). He was a holding a black greeting scarf (*kha-btags*). He tried to capture me and I immediately cried "*Aba, Ama!*" ("Father, Mother!") At that time a beautiful girl wearing a headgear appeared from the white lake. She was holding a white greeting scarf. She was fighting with the black man. Then this black man was defeated by this beautiful girl and his face was full of blood. Then this beautiful girl asked me: "Do you want to go to the place of your parents or do you want to go to the white lake?" I answered that I preferred to go to my parents' house, and that I did not want to go to the white lake. Then this beautiful girl offered me the white greeting scarf, put it around my neck and tied a knot in it. Then she said, "Go to your parents' place!" Exactly at this moment I woke up. The other two girls woke up as well. I arrived home at dusk and on the way there was a bird called *gobo*. With his wing he beat my shoulder. Then I immediately felt a little strange. After I arrived at my house I could not speak a single word. I had become sort of mad. Then my father and some relatives called a doctor (*em-chi*) but he could not say anything about my disease. Then my father said "My ability to recite epic verses under divine inspiration (*sgrungs-ba*) is passing now on to her (*'bab*)". He sent back the doctor and said: "This girl should not be touched!" I remained in this state for about one month without being able to speak. Then we invited one precious lama from Rabten Gompa who is a relative of ours to come and open the energy-channels. After having the ritual performed by this lama, I could tell a lot of Gesar stories such as the "great fortresses (*rdzong-chen*)" and the "forty-eight little fortresses (*rdzong-chung*)" and so on. Then my story came to be known in Lhasa. Then when I was nineteen I was taken to Lhasa by the Tibetan People's Publishing House.'

Her practice, however, does not imply any form of divination and her appointment could be a reflection of the role given by the state to the Gesar epic as a leading symbol in its efforts to encourage the revival of Tibetan culture during the 1980s.

From the material at our disposal, it seems clear that the traditional process of institutionalizing oracles privileged men, especially in the case of monastic and state oracles. Women were not, however, completely excluded from these higher levels, and one of the main oracles of the Tibetan government, alongside the oracles of Nechung and Gadong, was a woman known as the Drepung Tenma. She used to live in a small village to the east of Drepung monastery, just outside Lhasa, and was appointed by the Tibetan government to the level of a fourth rank official. She was allowed to go into trance in the great hall of the Drepung monastery as well as in the Dalai Lama's residence, a concession allowed to no other oracle but Nechung and Gadong. Her position was passed on within the women of her family. The last Drepung Tenma is called Lobsang Tsedron. She practised as an oracle until 1959. After the uprising she moved to Phenpo but was later invited back to Lhasa at the suggestion of Ngapo Ngawang Jigme, at that time vice-chairman (of the Political Consultative Conference). Here she has been leading a civil life up to the present day (dBang-'dus and Zha'o ha'o 1992: 28–31; Changngopa 2002: 245–59; Havnevik 2002: 259–89).

In the contemporary exile establishment this exceptional inclusion of a female oracle at the highest levels of decision-making has been continued, in this case through the incorporation of a new and spontaneous occurrence of the phenomenon. The new oracle is a woman who left eastern Tibet after a number of prophetic dreams and then made a pilgrimage to Mt Kailash. There she became possessed and decided to flee to India in order to become an adviser to the Dalai Lama. She was initially regarded with some scepticism in the exile establishment but she was soon acknowledged as a medium of the deity Tsering Chenga. She was recognized by the Dalai Lama and has regularly been consulted on exile government as well as personal affairs such as the other state oracles.[48] Female competence is therefore still acknowledged even at the highest level, despite the usual male dominance.

SPIRIT POSSESSION IN MODERN TIBET: TRADITIONAL CUSTOMS AND LEGAL DILEMMAS

In contemporary Tibet the loosening of the control that local Buddhist institutions and the Tibetan government had formerly exercised over

[48] There is still great interest in oracles in the exile community. The Dalai Lama has elaborated on his consultations of an oracle for advice (Dalai Lama 1999: 232–4).

spirit possession resulted in what seems to be an increase in 'lower level' oracles—especially those who base their competence on spontaneous forms of spirit possession. The abilities of these oracles can vary widely and the evaluation of them now depends on their social reputation and individual views. These oracles intervene through various means in individual and collective affairs, and the TAR administration has reacted to them in different ways. Some of these reactions, which varied widely in the different phases of modern Tibetan history, reflect the long and complex history of China's dealings with spirit possession and divinely inspired millenarian movements (see for example Strickman 1982: 55; Feuchtwang 1992), while others reflect the influence of Marxist or atheistic approaches.[49]

During the Cultural Revolution, for example, oracles were seen at a local level as the embodiment of old customs that had to be destroyed. They were thus in much the same position as monasteries and temples. An unknown number of oracles and local religious practitioners did not survive the Cultural Revolution, and it is very common to hear local accounts of oracles who died in 1966 or 1967. A considerable number of oracles, however, ceased their activity and survived, later resuming their practice when the expression of local traditions became acceptable again. In the early 1980s, when the state was somewhat tolerant, there were cases where this rehabilitation was even legally sanctioned. Thus, in one case concerning a woman oracle, the Shigatse Intermediate Court issued a legal document reversing a Cultural Revolution ruling that had been passed against an oracle by a Ren bao zu (People's Protection Group) under the Shigatse Cultural Revolution Committee in 1970. The document describes the original verdict given against the woman. She is mentioned as a Tibetan of a poor family background acting as oracle (*wupo*) in X County. Since she had been accused of reactionary criminal activities she had been condemned to five years in prison, commuted to house arrest. It then gives details of the original verdict and, as part of a China-wide process of general rehabilitation for those persecuted during the Cultural Revolution, declares that none of these actions is any longer to be regarded as a criminal offence in the legal climate in China in 1980.

> The former decision regarding the accusation that 'the defendant by practising divination and oracle activities, with the help of servants, used superstition for cheating money and profiting from the labour of the masses' was revised. Although this item is to be considered as superstition, it cannot be considered a

49 The scholar Niu xin fang (1983: introduction) gives a typical argument supported by the tenets of Marxist class struggle and dialectical materialism against the 'freedom of religion' to believe in gods and demons.

crime…The former decision regarding the accusation that 'after the peaceful liberation of Tibet, the defendant still persisted in keeping reactionary positions holding to the already broken banner of religion. In the name of healing patients practised reactionary activities cheating money' was revised. This item can no longer be considered a crime (quoted from a legal document in Chinese in possession of the oracle).

As a result of the new liberalization policy the practice of spirit possession was to some extent decriminalized as a part of traditional beliefs. Since the whole complex of traditional cultural activities was considered under the rubric of 'gomshi' (*goms-gshis*), or *xi guan* in Chinese, a term that means 'traditional custom', the state implicitly admitted that these practices were acceptable, at least at a local level. It also encouraged research into these phenomena, and publications on the subject gradually appeared. For example, one of them narrated the history of the female oracle Drepung Tenma (dBang-'dus 1992), while another described the situation found by the researchers in a part of the Nagchu area:

There were a number of lhapa among the Amdo tribes (*bu luo*) before. If lhapa is translated into Chinese it can be rendered as *shen han*, 'god-man'. Before the Cultural Revolution there were at least two lhapa in each *xiang* of Do ma qu of Amdo county. There were even six or seven lhapa in Madeng xiang (*dMar-steng Shang*) of Zhasa qu (*sKra-za Chus*) of Amdo county at that time. The main function of lhapa in the tribes was that of treating illnesses. The main way of treating illnesses by lhapa is to take it away or suck it with the mouth or the palm of the hands. While sucking the sickness the lhapa usually uses a greeting scarf or a black cloth or multicoloured pieces of cloth from the drum… (Ge-lai 1993: 272).

The text goes on to describe in detail the oracle practices which the researchers found in the area in the 1980s (Ge-lai 1993: 272–9). At this time traditional local oracles were not seen as threatening or as socially disruptive. They were just part of Tibetan culture.

This exploratory and sometimes exoticizing attitude was gradually replaced by a more controversial view, the elements of which were already visible from the early 1980s. The researchers who were recording the survival of Tibetan traditions and the cadres who tolerated traditional customs in their areas were acting within the policy formulation known as 'nationality special characteristics' (Ch. *min zu te si*),[50] which entitled Tibet and other nationality areas to certain local relaxations with regard to central policy.[51] But there was also a different policy within the

[50] See for example *Xizang Ribao* 1991. At one point the article advocates, 'The special characteristics of the Tibetan region must be recognized and there must be special measures and flexible methods…' The notion of 'special characteristics' was increasingly attacked after 1992 (Barnett 1996: 20).

[51] Hu Yaobang during his famous visit to Tibet in 1980 underlined that the first task facing

establishment that continued to regard spirit possession as belonging to the category of feudal superstition (Ch. *mi xin*; Tib. *rmongs-dad*). This was a particular concern, especially when it appeared to be a device used by dishonest people to deceive and take advantage of others. This view has shaped current Chinese legal discourse on the matter since the early 1980s, and has left the way open for such practices to be treated as criminal offences. According to Article 300 of China's revised Criminal Law, passed in 1997:

> Whoever organizes and utilizes superstitious sects, secret societies, and evil religious organisations or sabotages the implementation of the state's laws and executive regulations by utilising superstition is to be sentenced to not less than three years and not more than seven years of fixed-term imprisonment; when circumstances are particularly serious, to not less than seven years of fixed-term imprisonment.
>
> Whoever organizes and utilizes superstitious sects, secret societies, and evil religious organisations or cheats others by utilising superstition, thereby giving rise to the death of people, is to be punished in accordance with the previous paragraph.
>
> Whoever organizes and utilizes superstitious sects, secret societies, and evil religious organisations or has illicit sexual relations with women, or defrauds money and property by utilising superstition, is to be convicted and punished in accordance with the regulations of Articles 236, 266 of the law.

Much stricter penalties, including death, had been decreed in the previous version of the law that described those who used feudal superstition as part of any 'counter-revolutionary' project that might be designed to threaten the state or its integrity.[52] Linking spirit possession to counter-revolutionary activity was not explicitly stated any more in the law of 1997. However the Chinese authorities remained extremely concerned about this kind of potential connection. This is reflected in the separate law concerning cults passed in 1999 on the occasion of the crackdown on the Falun Gong movement.[53] This legal position perhaps reflected the

Tibet was 'To exercise nationality autonomy in the region fully—that is to say, to let Tibetans really be masters of their own lives' and further 'To make efforts to develop science, culture and education…' This approach shaped the Chinese Tibet policy in following years (see Wang Yao 1994: 285–9).

52 'Whoever organizes or uses feudal superstition or superstitious sects and secret societies to carry on counter-revolutionary activities' is guilty under Article 99 of the Criminal Code (or Criminal Law) 1980.

53 See for example Associated Press 1999a:

> As Falun Gong followers quietly protested for a sixth defiant day on its doorstep, China's legislature approved an anti-cult law today to quash the banned spiritual movement and punish group leaders. The law was passed 114–0 with two abstentions by the executive committee of the National People's Congress. It makes leaders of Falun Gong and other

ancient view in China of spirit possession as a potential means for the expression of political feelings, and the historical experience of messianic movements that had jeopardized the state in the past.[54]

The legal and practical ambiguities regarding spirit possession can often be seen in the attitude of local cadres who are supposed to deal with them. Already by 1981–2 there was evidence of a restrictive reaction to certain religious movements then taking place. In Nagchu Prefecture in the early 1980s a movement called the Heroes of Ling emerged, whose leaders claimed to be embodiments of Gesar and other heroes of the Tibetan epic.[55] They achieved initiation, just like oracles, through 'opening of the door of the energy-channels' (translated as 'primal veins'). An internal document later published in the west[56] reports these events with a comment by Yin Fatang, then the Party Secretary of the Tibet Autonomous Region:

> Pentse went to see So-phun who claimed to be the legendary Gesar. He was in Serwa Me-me Commune of Serwa District, in Tsonyi Dencho Group. So-phun, holding Pentse's right hand, remarked: 'If you hold the spear in your right hand and point it upwards, the sky will turn, and if you point it downwards, the earth will tremble.' He continued with prayers of this nature. Since then, it is claimed that Pentse had his 'primal veins' opened, or became possessed.

This case seems to have been regarded as particularly threatening because it involved multiple possessions, a phenomenon which is very rarely encountered by oracles.[57]

---

groups labelled cults liable for prosecution for murder, fraud, endangering national security and other crimes, the government's news agency Xinhua reported…

[54] The methods which the Party has adopted to deal with sects are basically those employed by their imperial predecessors, and it is clear from the historical precedents that the authorities should exercise some caution lest they experience the same reaction to repression. Just as several of the sectarian uprisings during the Ming and Qing Dynasties have been ascribed to an explosion of frustration at official intolerance, so too there are signs that over-zealous attempts to stop illegal religious activity in the contemporary era have sometimes served to incite revolt. Thus even in 1980 several members of the Pu Ji Tang ('Hall of Universal Succour') in Henan's Huaiyang County stormed their local brigade office in protest at the closure of their own sutra hall, and set up a makeshift temple in the office itself. In August 1988 a group of more than 1,000 villagers in Fujian's Shouning County destroyed the local Public Security Bureau in twelve hours of rioting caused by official attempts to stop their religious procession (Hilary 1992).

[55] For a detailed description and discussion of this movement see Schwartz 1996: 227–9.

[56] Hilary 1992; see also Schwartz 1996: 227.

[57] Cases of multiple possessions are more likely to trigger reactions from the state. Even if it seems to have been a very rare event, this kind of phenomenon seems to have taken place also under the Tibetan government. There is the report of one case that involved the highly controversial cult of the deity called Shugden. Shuguba gives a detailed description

> Immediately after returning to Kangnyi Commune, Pentse made water offerings to the altar in the chapel, pretended to be possessed by a deity and allowed people to see him in a trance. Some onlookers were so frightened that they trembled. When Pentse saw them trembling, he told them that they were ready to have their primal veins opened.
>
> Then, using the 'primal vein opening' method, the Heroes of Ling movement was expanded …
>
> Ever since the emergence of the so-called Heroes of Ling movement, there have been widespread instances of people pretending to be possessed by deities and demons, spreading rumours to dupe the public and causing damage to people's productivity and livelihood.

Other initiates are said to have referred to 'China's harmful influences' and to 'the evil deities of the dark forces'. 'In this way,' the document claims, 'they openly instigated rebellion … and attempted to destroy the friendship between the nationalities.' Yin Fatang's commentary locates the origin of this movement in the excessive relaxation of political education and discipline.

> One reason why the illegal Heroes of Ling movement had emerged in Kangnyi Commune is that the leaders of this Commune are scattered and powerless, lacking common convictions and unity of action.
>
> Second, since the introduction of the 'responsibility system' in production, there has been a lapse in the political education of the people. Instead of attending public education sessions, most evenings were spent in narrating and listening to the Ling Gesar stories.
>
> As a result, people came to have a good deal of faith in King Gesar of Ling and his heroes. In this situation, when people like Pentse pretended to be possessed by deities they had invoked it was difficult for most people to differentiate between legally approved religious faith and the illegal form of authoritarian blind faith. Distinguishing right from wrong became difficult and preventive sanctions became ineffectual.

It seems therefore that on the one hand, the state was trying to impose a clear-cut separation between illegal superstition and legal religion that would be acceptable within certain well-defined terms.[58] On the other

---

of a delegation sent by Lhasa in the 1940s on the occasion of an uprising of monks in Shitam Gompa near Chamdo. These monks believed that they were possessed by Shugden, referred to by Tsipon Shuguba as a local deity, and used this as a pretext for riotous behaviour. They arrived at Chamdo Labrang and broke down the doors and smashed them up. They were later arrested. The four instigators were given two hundred lashes each. Their normal human screams proved that their possession was a fake. They confessed that they had destroyed a thirty-foot statue of Padmasambhava at the Nyingma monastery on their way to Chamdo and forced the locals to give them food. The instigators were punished and the cult was banished (Carnhan 1998: 88–92).

58 Regarding popular religious beliefs and cults, Ye Xiaowen, then director of China's Nationality and Religious Bureau under the State Council, called for tighter controls to be

hand, nationality cadres in Tibet, as in other nationality areas like Inner Mongolia, seem to have tried to use the notion of 'local custom' as a strategic category. This allowed them to deal with this kind of cultural phenomenon in the more negotiated way that had been endorsed by the notion of 'special characteristics'. Since then the reform period has, in the view of some writers, come to an end, with reforms regarded as having been a failure (Sharlho 1993). This has led to increasing constrictions on the space available for discourses promoting local difference.

In the 1990s new policies that stressed standardization within the country in the name of economic development have become increasingly prominent. A stricter control on local customs and on those phenomena that can be seen as superstition has increasingly been implemented.[59] This can turn into a source of tension and legal inconsistency, so that local cadres find themselves unsure about how to handle phenomena which they used to tolerate as harmless parts of the traditional life of the community but which according to current interpretations of Chinese law need to be officially condemned, with measures which can lead to loss of popular support. This situation applies not only to Tibetan administrators but also to Chinese cadres stationed in rural areas, who need at least a minimum of local consensus in order to run their communities. The problem is due

---

implemented in a 1996 statement referring to 'new species, sub-species, mutations and bogus species of religion'. He argues:

> How is folk belief to be defined? Can it be regarded as a religion? There are many different views. In my opinion, the central idea of folk belief is about ghosts or gods, the soul or fate. It is a mixture of the traditional patriarchal and ancestral idea; the primitive, crude religious belief and ancestor worship plus folkways and customs, folk culture, superstition, as well as actual social and cultural life and social psychology. At the present time, folk beliefs are rather active in the coastal areas. We face an urgent task of investigation and study as to how to guide and manage them (Ye Xiaowen 1996: 137).

59 See for example the report by Yang Zhenglin published by a Chinese regional newspaper from Tibet (*Xizang Ribao* 2000), which states that due to 'the recent rise of feudal superstitious activities in the rural and pastoral areas….Dinggye County Political and Legal Committee' has prompted the departments concerned 'to carry out a concentrated and vigorous drive to ban and rectify such activities which were affecting social stability' on the basis of 'thorough investigation and study'….Since the middle of April 'a drive to ban and rectify such activities in every township and village in the county' was launched. 'Six mass meetings in the places where six witches lived' were convened so that 'State Council's decision on banning illegal cults and the relevant state policies, laws, rules, and regulations' could be explained and the masses could be educated 'in eliminating feudal superstitious ideology, getting rid of bad customs and habits, and advocating scientific, civilized, and healthy ways of life'. It is also reported that 'musical instruments and vestments used in superstitious activities' were confiscated and 'two of the witches who had done a lot of harm' were taken into custody, and that the other four were entrusted to the County Public Security Bureau 'for acceptance and education'. It is also said that subsequently 'these women realized that their activities were unlawful, and transformed their thinking'.

not so much to the feeling that the community might have towards its own oracles as it is to the sense of interference by the state in the life of the community.

FEMALE SPIRIT POSSESSION, COLLECTIVE FEELINGS AND POLITICAL CLAIMS

The revitalisation of oracular traditions since 1980 has in most cases been individualized. But in some cases spirit possession has taken on a more collective role, both in constructive as well as in destructive ways. The feeling that ethnic aspirations have been betrayed or repressed seems to have been a key element in some cases, where constructive initiatives were transformed into aggressive political opposition. In addition, the general prohibition of certain objects of devotion seems to have had the effect of increasing their relevance, ethnicizing something that might originally have been endowed with a merely local relevance. Thus in some cases the repression of local religious practices tended to promote the use of pan-Tibetan symbols and rituals. These were endowed with additional significance and were sometimes transformed into expressions of resistance: from the display of photographs of contested important lamas, to certain rituals of incense-burning, to practices related to Gesar. Both repression and resistance contributed to re-designing the 'stage' of cultural and political interaction along the lines of ethnic confrontation. Remarkably, a link between repressive excesses and rampant development of 'superstition' was also denounced in communist terms and from a communist point of view in the early 1980s.[60] The most vivid example of this can be seen in the case of the Nyemo uprising of 1969.

The Nyemo revolt and the divine bird of Gesar

Nyemo, a flourishing valley between Lhasa and Shigatse, has a long history for Tibetans as the place of origin of the great translator Vairocana, and as an area where the legendary eighth century teacher and adept Padmasambhava subjugated local spirits whom he encountered on his way from Nepal to the seat of the Tibetan kings. Later a number of monasteries of various traditions were established in Nyemo and these have co-existed with local cults of much older origin up to the present day. Spirit possession was practised in the area, but female mediums, most of whom were operating mainly as healers, stopped their activity during the Cultural Revolution and have not since resumed it in any visible way.

60 A Tibetan text which was written by a Chinese scholar before the Cultural Revolution but could be published only afterwards, attacks certain forms of fanaticism as modern superstition and saw in the excesses of the Cultural Revolution the root for the increased superstitious activities. (Niu xin fang 1983, introduction)

It was in this area that a young nun called Tinley Chodron, who was considered to be possessed by a divine entity, led an abortive revolt in 1969. The mythological figures invoked by the followers of this movement were those of the Gesar epic, which although often interrelated with local mountain cults also have pan-Tibetan relevance, as we have seen in the very similar case of the Heroes of Ling. The revolt started as a conflict that was not at all unusual within the context of the Cultural Revolution. Fights that appeared to be initially between revolutionary groups attacking cadres, then became fights between the two main factions, mainly led by Chinese, the Gyenlog and the Nyamdrel.[61] Tinley Chodron and her group were at first seen as part of these conflicts, but their role was rapidly re-evaluated. The group captured and killed fourteen Chinese cadres and soldiers and seems to have triggered a chain of revolts in neighbouring areas that were drastically repressed. A Tibetan who witnessed her execution in Lhasa later that year gave this account of the uprising:

'Ani Tinley Chodron was about twenty-eight and was from Pusum village in Nyemo. It is said that she was an emanation of Labja Gongmo, a holy bird in the Gesar epic. When she started this movement she proclaimed herself to be an emanation of this holy bird. She gathered many people around her, of whom some men were her partners and were given titles of Gesar's brave counsellors such as Denma and Gyatsa …

'She led the uprising. When the Chinese army came all these people escaped to remote places in the mountains. When the army arrived, there were only women and children remaining. Then the army said to them: "Let the men come down and nothing will happen to them." Then a few people believed this and started to come down. And in fact nothing happened to them. Later most people came down and the main men were caught and taken to prison.

'All these people were later executed by the Chinese government, some in Nyemo, some in Lhasa. The Ani [Tinley Chodron] was executed in Lhasa. Even some people who were marginally involved, like some old farmers who happened to be in the villages where the Ani held some meetings, were killed as well. A primary school teacher who was used by the Ani for writing things was considered one of the main people responsible for the uprising and was also killed. In Lhasa they were taken around by truck preceded by soldiers armed with machine guns. Besides the Ani there was an old man who had a long beard and standing long hair. He was covered with tsampa [roasted barley flour]. I was wondering how it could be that a tsampa miller could be a leader of the revolt …

'At the beginning the Ani seems to have described herself as part of the Gyenlog. At that time everywhere there were the two groups of Gyenlog and Nyamdrel fighting each other, but her issues were quite different …'

[61] During the Cultural Revolution factional fights became visible in a most violent way. All over Tibet two main groups were confronting each other claiming that they were defending Mao and his true thought (see Tsering Shakya 1999: 314 ff).

Both the exemplary punishment meted out to those involved in the uprising and the Tibetan narrative recollection of it reflect a distinction between the ways in which this movement and the factional fights then going on were viewed. In fact there was a qualitative difference in this movement that prompted its drastic repression. At the time, although the fights between the Nyamdrel and Gyenlog groups were leading to casualties every day, the army had been ordered not to interfere. However, this changed when what originally looked like a Gyenlog attack on local cadres was reappraised as something threatening Chinese national interests. This shift was probably triggered by the ethnicization of the movement, indicated by its primarily religious discourse.[62]

A political oracle

Individual spirit possession and collective practices associated with political movements are usually quite distinct from each other. Oracles, however, retain their roles as traditional specialists for dealing with impurity, conflicts and tensions in the local community. In certain circumstances they are liable to locate these issues within a broader context and to refer to the Tibetan community in terms of its ethnic rather than its local identity. This kind of situation seems to arise when there is an idea of crisis applying to Tibetanness as such. In this sense a continuum can be perceived between these very different forms of spirit possession, from individual healers to possessed bards, to various hybrid forms that mingle territorial cults with tantrism, to political oracles, to religious leaders of messianic movements. Spirit possession, however, is not a cause of such incidents, but just one of the many ways in which such collective emotions can be expressed.

One example of such a highly ethnicized situation is an incident involving an oracle named Drolma Tsamcho who was sentenced to eight years in prison in Lhasa in 1993. Her practice as an oracle had started in 1979. A woman from the same village who then went into exile gave this account of the case:[63]

> 'She had often been—as she continues to be—in constant trance, believed to be a medium of a local deity, in which state she had made pointed face-to-face accusations against culprits. She would point at the nose of the guilty persons, against persons guilty of causing damage to the well-being of her village, those

62 The incident led by the young nun Tinley Chodron was described as widespread. The millenarian movement was reportedly fuelled by rumours of her possession by a local deity and her acquiring supernatural and magical powers (ibid.: 345).

63 Interview at the Refugee Reception Centre, Dharamsala, 22 February 1994. The interviewee, a woman from the same village as Drolma Tsamcho, asked to remain anonymous.

committing theft and robbery, Chinese "running dogs" elements, those slaughtering or capturing innocent wildlife, and she would object to or try to stop such practices.'

Somehow she seems to have seen herself as a defender of the collective interests of the community, as she perceived them to be. As long as her activity was confined to the interests of individual cases and of the local community, Drolma Tsamcho's impact remained localized, and officials did not attempt to intervene. At a certain point the scope and perceived meaning of her activities seem to have changed:

In 1993, Dolma Tsamchoe [Tsamcho] reportedly toured seven villages around Rutok where in front of assembled crowds she shouted 'Tibet is independent', 'His Holiness the Dalai Lama, and not the Chinese, is the Supreme Leader of Tibet, the Land of Snow', 'Independence of Tibet is coming soon, all Tsampa-eating Tibetans, unite!' etc. She was believed to have raised the above slogans while in the stage of a trance. (*Tibet Human Rights Update* 1994)

According to this account she seems to have shifted her discourse from addressing interests of the local community to that of the community in its broadest sense: the Tibetans as a people. This took place during a brief period of relative relaxation in central Tibet following the suppression of political unrest in the late 1980s. She probably expressed emotions that were acute and widespread at that time because they were reinforced by narratives regarding the protests in Lhasa and their repression, which had led to a considerable number of deaths. According to the account by her fellow-villager, however, she did not really manage to raise a movement in the countryside, apparently because other villagers were too afraid of possible consequences. The local authorities were still remarkably reluctant to intervene, and only when authorities of a higher level were called in was legal action taken against her.[64] Her activity had by then acquired a new profile which prompted the severe punishment by the authorities. According to the same fellow-villager,

She went to a nearby village with X and Y. In this village she called a meeting and asked the villagers to raise their hands if they wanted Tibetan independence. Many people raised their hands, but nobody shouted slogans (which she had asked them to do). In the course of about six months X went around many villages calling meetings and asking people to raise their hands and shout slogans. In the first week of the fourth Tibetan month of 1993 [May 1993] Drolma was arrested.

[64] 'Because the god-fearing local authorities did not know what to do about it, the head of her Work Brigade reported her actions to the … district authorities, who in turn reported the matter to the "Tibet Autonomous Region (TAR)" authorities. Under direct orders reportedly issued by the "TAR" authorities in Lhasa, she was arrested…' (*Tibet Human Rights Update* 1994) This reluctance by the local officials might have been as much due to fear of the deity as uneasiness about intervening against an important person in the community.

After two months, Drolma was sentenced to eight years imprisonment. She was charged with spreading political propaganda in the villages and calling on the villagers to resist the regime. She was considered a very serious case. The authorities feared her much more than those who took part in the big demonstrations in Lhasa. She was trying to create protest in the countryside.

A Maoist oracle

Most examples of oracles that expressed powerful collective political feelings were associated with ethnic resistance, as an expression of Tibetan identity. This is not, however, the only form of political discourse developed by oracles. I also heard this story of an oracle who became a fervent follower of Mao and combined in her own way allegiances that seem completely contradictory:

X was born as the first daughter in a rather irregular family. Her father soon disappeared and she grew up with her mother and her younger half-sister. As a young girl she was sent by her family to assist an old and blind lady oracle in the shrine of a local deity (*btsan*) in Lhasa. Before dying the old oracle opened her energy-channels and the young girl took over the function as oracle of the shrine. Then the big upheaval came and the girl became an ardent follower of Mao. She considered him her 'root-lama' and had pictures of him all over the place. With her working brigade she started her own 'Long March' to meet the Great Helmsman, but the journey was interrupted by the outbreak of the Cultural Revolution. Some cadres advised her to return to Tibet where she became a political activist. Even though she had stopped practising spirit possession in the traditional framework in 1959, the spirits were said to have continued to visit her throughout her life. Until her death in the 1990s she remained a dedicated follower of Mao.

Sacred empowerment and reconstruction

Finally, oracles can be one of the forms of sacred empowerment that represent collective feelings to a significant and even organized degree, but in a way that does not oppose the political system, most notably in the form of encouraging reconstruction projects and other forms of cultural revitalization. These forms of reconstruction usually take place in a negotiated framework in which local authorities and religious representatives agree on the forms of cultural revitalization that are described in modern and acceptable terms such as social welfare. In most cases this allows the community to work towards its own common interests, and even towards development and strengthening its cultural and social identity. In such a context the sacred empowerment of formal or informal leading figures in the community can function as the shared banner for the reconstruction of the 'world' of a community following a period of extensive material and spiritual destruction.

Female oracles in many cases represent, as in the past, a peripheral phenomenon that articulates within a local context the oppression of individual conflicts and subaltern people. But they seem to represent much more than this as well. Their traditions can be seen as involved in more central forms of spirit possession and in the female sacredness embodied by tantric women. Oracular traditions seem thereby to acknowledge various levels of politico-religious female agency, which presents a female specificity but is able to move into traditionally male spheres. Despite some overlap with the Buddhist celibate traditions of Tibetan nuns,[65] this sacredness differs from that of the nuns: its references and forms of expression seem to be rooted primarily in the religious experience of the lay world, centred on territorial cults and intermingling Buddhist and pre-Buddhist elements.[66] Spirit possession has thus taken on peripheral and central forms over the centuries, and the various oracular traditions have redefined themselves and re-negotiated their identity in more or less Buddhist terms in surviving the major political and religious changes that Tibet has undergone in its history. The contemporary situation represents a continuation of this mode of adaptation to prevailing norms.

That many oracles in contemporary Tibet are women seems to be a consequence not only of the disappearance of the higher level oracles through exile or prohibition, but also of the fact that the ability to resolve personal life-crises and to deal with social liminality by means of spirit possession seems to be connected to a female experience of life in a privileged and specific way. This spontaneous and usually local dimension of spirit possession has always been the aspect of that practice which was least dependent on Buddhist institutions, and it seems now to be the root of much of spirit possession in contemporary Tibet. In contrast to the various forms of institutionalized religion, this form of religious practice seems to be nourished by the experience of crisis. This applies not only at an individual level but also to the community, whether it is defined as a local entity or in its broadest senses as an ethnic identity.[67]

The reason for the persistence of local oracular tradition lies in part in its relative freedom from transmitted traditions and in its correspondingly

[65] From this point of view also nuns have been playing a very significant role (see Havnevik 1989; 1994: 259–66).

[66] It accompanied thus the reemergence of territorial cults that have since been closely connected with the construction of a local and ethnic identity in Tibet (Karmay 1994: 112–20).

[67] Tibetan reality confirms Lewis's observation that: 'It seems that peripheral female ecstatics may often have pioneered new religions. Women seem to have played a major, if much ignored role in religious change and innovation' (Lewis 1975: 155–6). However it seems to contradict the notion of a 'peripheral' spirit possession as female and distinct from a male 'central' spirit possession; this distinction can, at most, be identified with gendered tendencies and can vary according to viewpoints.

Female oracle in northern Lato. (Photo: H. Diemberger 1998)

greater dependence on individual responses to exceptional personal and social conditions. The social impact depends on the extent to which the community acknowledges the medium as a mouthpiece of the gods who embody its communal or territorial identity; or even in some cases its identity as members of one or other Buddhist sect. It is this, the highly adaptive and spontaneous character of spirit possession, which makes it a kind of phoenix. To the confusion of government officials whose task has been to contain them, oracles were capable of constant re-emergence and recovery from banishment, whether that attempt at repression be Buddhist or communist in origin. At the same time, in terms of gender roles in Tibetan society, the tenacity of female sacredness within the oracular tradition raises the question of how much of the female agency shown by Tibetan women in crucial situations has been drawn from and nourished by the thousand or more years of such female sacredness, which has existed and still exists in the local communities and occasionally also in the higher circles of Tibet.

OUTSTANDING WOMEN IN TIBETAN MEDICINE*

Tashi Tsering

Tibetan literature preserves records of many famous female personalities, including secret consorts and daughters of tantric yoginīs, ordained nuns, female reincarnates, wives and daughters of rulers, and daughters of defrocked monks and nuns. Many others were also highly educated, but are not as widely known because they maintained a very low profile in the community. This chapter concerns itself with biographical accounts of three female medical practitioners. The institutional complex for medical education sets the context for the description of the lives of the three protagonists.

EDUCATION AND MEDICINE

All the academic institutions administered by the Tibetan government were set up solely for males. For the lay aristocrats, a school 'Finance Bureau: Excellent Structure' (Tsikhang Phuntsok Kopa) was founded by Desi Sangye Gyatso in 1699. It was meant to train them in accountancy, law and general supervisory skills before they took administrative responsibilities within the Tibetan government. Likewise, the education of the future monk officials of the Tibetan government was done in the 'School of Sciences in the Potala' (Tse Rigne Lobdra) established by the Seventh Dalai Lama Kalsang Gyatso in 1754. The medical college situated on the Chakpori hill in Lhasa and called 'Place for Dispensing Knowledge to Benefit Sentient Beings' (Chakpori Dropen Rigcheling Dratsang), established by Desi Sangye Gyatso in 1696, and the 'Astro-Medical Institute' (Mentsikhang, also often called 'Medical Institute'),

* Translated from the Tibetan (bKra-shis Tshe-ring 1994) by Sonam Tsering. The Tibetan text should remain authoritative if there are any disparities between the two versions, with the exception of a few updates that have been inserted relating to events postdating the publication of the original. I express my deepest gratitude to Nadja Breton who not only polished the English, but also gave the vital *bla srog dbugs gsum* to this article. The phonetic rendering of several of the Tibetan names correspond to how the persons themselves write their names in English.

set up in 1916 during the reign of the Thirteenth Dalai Lama Tubten Gyatso, provided educational opportunities only for monks of the different religious schools, mainly from the monasteries of Sera, Ganden and Drepung, and also for personnel of the army.

Nonetheless we know from a variety of sources that female physicians existed. The first part of this chapter deals mainly with female physicians before the Chinese invasion. Such women were not formally trained in any government-administered institution. However, since coming into exile in 1959, both men and women have had equal opportunities to study various fields of science in accordance with modern educational systems. The entry of women into a new institutionalized educational set-up helped produce many scholars and graduates of repute. The second part of this chapter relates the life accounts of some famous women physicians trained in the traditional art of Tibetan medicine, who graduated from medical institutes in Tibet and in exile after the Chinese invasion.

The seventeenth century text *gSo dpyad sman gyi khog 'bugs* narrates how in the fourth century CE the Indian physicians Bichi Gache (=Vijay Rama?) and Bilhama Gadze, widely known as the King and Queen of Medicine, travelled from Bodhgayā to Tibet to propagate the art of holistic healing, as prophesied by Ārya Tārā (sDe-srid n.d.: 108Na4). Upon arrival in Tibet, they came across a twenty-year-old lady bearing the signs and marks of a *ḍākinī* and her ailing mother. On seeing the physicians, the lady cordially invited them into her house to check her mother's condition. Having nursed her mother according to their advice, the lady then made a *maṇḍala* offering of one thousand golden coins and uttered the following praise:

> O! You, the two supreme emanated physicians,
> Embodying great compassion,
> Hail from the sacred land of India.
> As foreseen by the saviour Tārā,
> You spread the light of medical science in Tibet.
> It is for sure that you, whose kindness
> Equally spreads to the kings and subjects of Tibet,
> Are the speech-emanation of the deity of medicine,
> The one who allays all painful ailments and diseases.

The lady also spread to the people the news of the arrival of the two physicians, who happened to be siblings, and who had come a long way from India to cure sickness and disease afflicting the people of Tibet. As the Tibetan king Lha Totori Nyantsen (b. 374 CE; he received Buddhist texts and mantras in 433 CE) heard of their arrival and their dissemination of the healing tradition, he invited them to his fortress, Yumbu Lakhar. Nine cushions were stacked on top of each other to form a seat for the two honoured physicians. The king then made an offering of one thousand ounces of gold to each of them. After touching their feet with his forehead as an expression of deep respect, the king offered his queen, Yikyi Rolcha, to Bichi Gache. The two physicians remained in Tibet for two years.

The account continues by stating that the royal queen, Yikyi Rolcha, gave birth to Dungi Torchogchen. After the two physicians returned to India, this Dungi Torchogchen served as personal physician to Lha Totori and later to Trinyen Sugtsen. Trinyen, during the later phase of his life, was attended by the physician Lodro Chenpo. His wife was Tsangpay Lulenma. In another seventeenth century text, the biography of the senior Yutok (Jo-bo 1982) believed to be the founder of Tibetan medicine, we find a list of the Tibetan kings, together with the names of their personal physicians and the physicians' wives.

Lodro Tsungme served as personal physician to Drongnyen Deu. His wife was Gawa Pelde. Lodro Rabsel was the personal physician of King Takri Nyansig. His wife was Pelkyi Zijima. Lodro Gyaldzo was appointed to Namri Songtsen. His wife was Lodro Sangmo. Furthermore, King Songtsen Gampo (617–650) also had a special physician, Lodro Shenyen, whose wife was named Konchok Sangmo. (Historical texts also clearly describe the Chinese princess Wencheng Kongcho's expertise in medicine and astrology.) The physician Dreje Gyagar Vajra and his wife Ga Kyongma attended both King Gungsong Gungtsen and King Mangsong Mangtsen. The physician Khyungpo Dorje served as physician to Dusong Mangpoje Lungnam Trulgyi Gyalpo. His wife was Gyasa Chokyi Dronme. Yutok Nyingma Yonten Gonpo (708–833), whose wife was Dorje Tsomo, served as personal physician to the kings Me Agtsom and Trisong Detsen. (During the latter's rule, the Chinese princess Kimcheng Kungchu is said to have brought treatises on Chinese medicine to Tibet.) The physicians Bumseng, Pelbum, and Gaga, who shared a wife, Lhamo Peldren, served as physicians to the kings Mutig Tsenpo, Mu-ne Tsen and Mutri Tsenpo. The kings Ralpachen and Tri Darma's personal physician was Yutok Drogon, whose wife was named Jojam Norbu Sangmo. Odrung was looked after by Yutok Jose Pel, whose wife was Phuntsok Norbu. King Pelkhortsen was treated by his physician Yutok Jampa Tugje. The kings of the Tibetan royal lineage and the descendants of Yutok kept very good relations, which can be likened to the spiritual bonding of method and wisdom (*thab-shes zung-'brel*).[1] Lhacham Deva Peldren, the wife of Yutok Sarma Yonten Gonpo (1126–1202), was born to Pema O, the wife of the aforementioned Khyungpo Dorje (Dar-mo 1982: 339). It

[1] Jo-bo 1982:65–6; see also Dil-dmar 1993. I doubt the account of the physician Bichi Gache and his sister Bila Gadze's visit to Tibet and their dissemination of the art of healing

is very tempting to say that all the wives of these Tibetan physicians also practised and knew the art of traditional Tibetan medicine.

WOMEN MEDICAL PRACTITIONERS

Lato Jomo Namo[2] one of the nine who was chosen because of '(favourable) karma from previous training' (*sngon-sbyang las-'phro sad-pa*) was amongst 'the fifty-eight[3] propagators [of Tibetan medicine]' (*dar-byed lnga-bcu rtsa-brgyad*) who appeared before the fifteenth century,[4] and also one of the many exemplary female physicians.

Those of the later periods include Taykhang Jetsunma Jampel Chodron (*c.* 1882–*c.* 1959)[5], the younger sister of Taykhang Jampa Tubwang, who

---

during the reign of the twenty-eighth Tibetan king Lha Totori Nyanshe. I consider it a fabricated history of Tibetan medicine and a mere imitation of the tale that surrounds the spread of Buddhism in Tibet, which is also associated with King Lha Totori Nyanshe. Since there are still doubts about the accurate history of the physicians from Dungi Torchogchen up to Yutok Champa Deleg, including Yutok Nyima, closer study needs to be undertaken. One of the problems concerns the way names are rendered in the old biographical texts. It is evident that the names of physicians serving during the years of Lha Totori Nyanshe's rule up to the twelfth century suggest modern usage and do not observe the patterns of the sixth to the eleventh centuries. Early Tibetan names begin with a clan and/or family name, and end with a personal name of varying length. They sound slightly unfamiliar to a modern Tibetan ear, but the names listed in the above-mentioned sources appear rather standardized, as they were in later periods. I also feel that the names of some of the physicians' wives seem like a translation of typical Indian names, rather than being names of Tibetan origin. This story may, however, indicate that at the time of the advent of Buddhism to Tibet during Lha Totori's reign, Indian medical experts may have come to Tibet.

2 sDe-srid n.d.: 152Ba5 describes the spread of *Jo mo sna mo mde'u ldum bcos* (the pill therapy of Jomo Namo) as among fifty-six various cures newly designed by physicians residing in the four directions and those in complete seclusion. Dil-dmar 1993: 722 mentions the techniques of Lato Jomo Namo as one of the nine who were chosen because of (favourable) karma from amongst the fifty-eight propagators. He also considers *Jo mo sna mo mde'u ldum bcos* as one of fifty-five ways of healing taught and practised by great physicians of the four directions and those remaining in seclusion (Dil-dmar 1993: 720).

3 sDe-srid n.d.: 153Ba1–155Ba4. Since sDe-srid n.d. lists eighty-one as belonging to the group of the fifty-eight propagators, whereas Don-dam 1976 counts only forty-eight, further research needs to be done on this group. For an enumeration of the fifty-eight propagators, see Appendix I below.

4 This dating is based on sDe-srid n.d. 155Ba4: 'The glorious deeds and activities of the so-called fifty-eight propagators of Tibetan medicine were so great that it put even the lively waxing of the moon to shame. However, in later years there appeared only two prominent masters, Chang and Zur, who clearly elucidated the difficult points concerning *rGyud sde bzhi* (*the Fourfold Tantra*) in particular, and the other medical treatises in general.' Since this text locates the fifty-eight propagators of medicine before the arrival of Chang and Zur, i.e., Changpa Namgyal Draksang (1395–1475) and Zurkar Nyamnyi Dorje (1439–75), it is evident that the fifty-eight propagators should be dated not later than the fifteenth century.

5 Kungo Trekhang Khenchung Tubten Tsephel, New York, personal communication.

was the personal physician of the Thirteenth Dalai Lama; Khando Yanga (1907–*c.* 1973); Shingmo Sa Lhamo (b. 1916),[6] the consort of Dilgo Khyentse Rinpoche; Tashi Paldon (died in Pemako around 1959),[7] the niece of Terchen Barwe Dorje; Rinzin Wangmo,[8] the daughter of Dru Jamyang Drakpa, a famous lama from eastern Tibet (Kham); Dasel Wangmo (b. 1928)[9] of Minyak Dotsang; Phurbu Dolma,[10] the daughter of the great physician of Derge Gonchen monastery; Lobsang Dolma Khangkar of Kyidrong; Tinley Dolkar (1931–56) and Tinley Paldon (b. 1939), daughters of Rinzin Lhundrub Paljor (1897–1979), of Nyarong Shag[11] in Lhasa; Drungtso Tsering Peldren (b. 1965) of Bumtang, in Bhutan,[12] and Tsewang Dolkar Khangkar (b. 1959). It appears that there have been many notable female medical practitioners in the three regions of Tibet and in Sikkim, Bhutan and other neighbouring Himalayan areas.

From those mentioned above, I shall, with my limited knowledge, narrate the life stories of three important physicians: Yangchen Lhamo (also known as Khando Yanga of the Zur tradition), Lobsang Dolma Khangkar from Kyidrong, and her daughter Tsewang Dolkar Khangkar.

I do not have much knowledge about other female practitioners of medicine; hence this choice of three is determined by my own access to information. Likewise, the provision of an equal number of seats to both male and female candidates at the Astro-Medical Institute in Lhasa in 1963, and later in Nagchu, Ngari, Chamdo, Derge, Dzo-ge, Ngawa and Golog, should definitely have produced many experienced female physicians. The biographical accounts of these contemporary physicians wait to be written.

Khando Yanga

Yangchen Lhamo, affectionately known as Khando Yanga, was born in Pemako on the first day of the first month of the Tibetan Iron-Sheep

[6] Personal communications from Semo Dingo Tsang Chime Wangmo of Paro, Bhutan and Kungo Juchen Tubten Namgyal of Dharamsala.

[7] Personal communications from Venerable Bardo Tulku, Karma Triyana Dharma Center, Woodstock, New York; and Karma Dragpa, caretaker of the Library of Tibetan Works and Archives.

[8] Namkhai Norbu, Dharamsala, personal communication.

[9] Alak Zenkar Rinpoche, New York, personal communication.

[10] Pewar Rinpoche, Bir, Himachal Pradesh, India, personal communication.

[11] The household of the Nyarong Shag family from Lhasa is widely known by the name 'Ru Emchi Tsang of Nyemo'. Some of them are held to have served as personal physicians to the previous Karmapas and also to a couple of Goshri Gyaltsab's reincarnations at Tsurphu monastery.

[12] See *Kuensel* (Bhutan National Paper) 1993: 4.

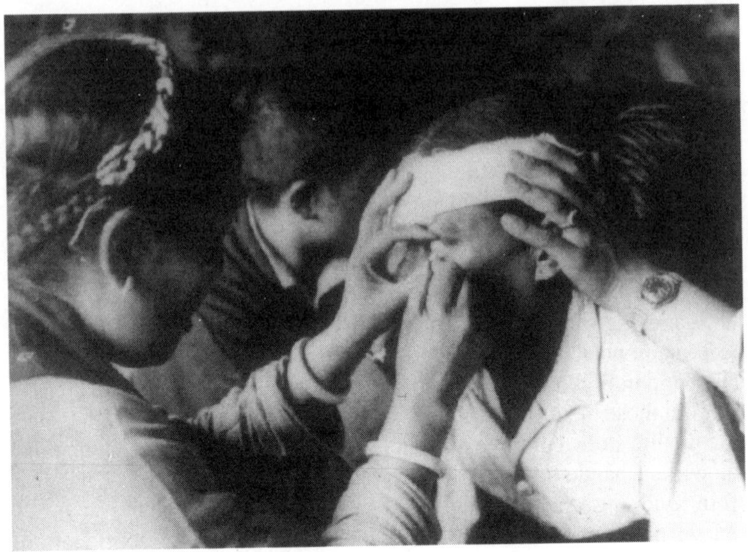

Dr Kando Yanga treating cataract in Sikkim, c. 1950. (Tashi Tsering, personal collection)

Year (1907).[13] A year before, her father Ngawang Drakpa Tinley Jampa Jungne,[14] the seventh incarnation of Jedrung of Yangon Labrang (Kham Riwoche), and her mother Tsultrim, daughter of the Ngom Sagang Depa family from Chamdo, travelled to Pemako in 1906 to reveal 'treasures' (*gter*). Her father Jedrung Jampa Jungne was renowned for his wide knowledge of the sūtras, the tantras and other fields of studies. He is more famed yet for his skill in Tibetan medicine.

After Jedrung's return to Riwoche from his purported visit to Pemako, the young Yangchen Lhamo was introduced to basic training in reading and writing later supplemented by a higher training in Tibetan grammar and poetry. She undertook a rigorous study of Tibetan medicine and gained a special ability to memorize fifteen or more folios from the medical texts in just a few hours.

When she reached eleven years of age, her father Jedrung Jampa Jungne, accused of having kept in the past a suspicious relationship with the Chinese Manchu Regiment Lu'u-cun, was banished to the Takring region of

13 This section is based on Byams-pa 1990: 443–7 and on my own notes. See also Adams and Dovchin 2000.

14 Jedrung Jampa Jungne's works have been published by two different publishers: rJe-drung 1974–5 and rJe-drung 1985.

the Changtang and was kept under the custody of Takring monastery. During that time, Tsetrul Ngawang Pelden, the thirtieth hierarch of Chang Taglung monastery, sought permission from the Thirteenth Dalai Lama to invite Jedrung Jampa Jungne to Taglung monastery. At the consent of the Thirteenth Dalai Lama, Jedrung was relocated in Taglung. Thereafter, the Medical Institute in Lhasa, with the permission of the Thirteenth Dalai Lama, sent two physicians to seek special teachings on Tibetan medicine and its practice from the highly learned Jedrung. In return, Jedrung requested that his daughter be taught the technique of 'opening the eyes' (*mig-'byed*), i.e. cataract operation, at the Medical Institute.

Yangchen Lhamo's working life as a doctor began at the age of thirteen from when she was able to conduct urine analysis and pulse examination, she began working as a capable doctor. Later, when she travelled to the Medical Institute in Lhasa for higher training, Khyenrab Norbu, the personal physician to the Dalai Lama, showed great interest in her. After he decided that she was the girl to whom he would teach the cataract operation techniques, he made her undergo the required training at the institute. On completing her training, she took up the task of curing many blind people, especially the poor and destitute in Lhasa and in the Chamdo region. Her kindness was legendary. It is said that she treated her poor patients, and provided them food if they could not afford it, though she herself was not wealthy. She helped those coming from outside Lhasa to find accommodation, often contributing to rent when needed. She especially helped to cure those afflicted by disorders caused by an 'imbalance of wind' (*rlung*).

She later married Karma Tsultrim Namgyal, the sixth incarnation of Nedo Karma Chagme, with whom she had two daughters, Yeshe Wangmo and Ngawang Peltso. Since then, she has been known as Khando Yanga. In the year 1948, Jigme Wangchuk, king of Bhutan, sent a special envoy requesting Yangchen Lhamo to help perform a cataract operation on him. During her stay in Bhutan, Yangchen Lhamo cured the king's ailment and took up an extensive work of providing treatment and medicine to the people living in the kingdom. Her fame spread to both Bhutan and Sikkim. Following her return to Lhasa, the physician Khyenrab Norbu honoured her with a first position certificate in 1951 for her high expertise and unwavering service in the field of cataract treatment. She was also accorded the privilege of working with the renowned physician Ngawang Phuntsok in organizing free medical camps to treat patients in eighteen districts including Taktse, Reting, Maldro, Drigung and Zangri. From 1951 to 1953, Yangchen Lhamo managed to help more than three hundred blind patients in those regions regain eyesight. She also treated patients in the area adjoining Chamdo, Riwoche and other places in eastern Tibet while passing by both ways on a trip to her native place in 1956. On her return to Lhasa in 1958, the physician Khyenrab Norbu enrolled her in the Medical Institute. Thereafter, she served at the institute as one of its permanent staff.

It is a known fact that traditional treatises on Tibetan medicine including the classic *Fourfold Tantra* (*rGyud bzhi*) provide an extensive discussion of diagnosis and treatment in gynecology and pediatrics. It is also evident from the past that many physicians have made great efforts to preserve this ancient tradition. But, from the seventeenth century onwards, Tibetan medical practice was dominated by monks and lay tantric practitioners, who would not get into close contact with women. As only female practitioners would deal with specific diseases of women and children, and as there were not many of them, this part of the Tibetan medical practice had fallen into relative disuse. Some even condemned women training as medical practitioners. However, Khyenrab Norbu's encouragement helped in making Yanga a female physician of high repute whose mastery over a myriad of ailments and their cures is still remembered.

Following the Chinese invasion and occupation of Tibet in 1959, Yangchen Lhamo resumed her work at the Medical Institute as an employee of the People's Republic of China's government with all related provisions and privileges. During her stay at the Institute, she treated those who came to her clinic, and also paid house visits to attend to patients in more serious conditions under the direction of her teacher Khyenrab Norbu.

With the establishment of a special wing for women and children at the Medical Institute in 1962 Khyenrab Norbu appointed Yangchen Lhamo as the first director/chief medical officer of the women and children section. As the number of women and children seeking consultation increased, Khyenrab Norbu entrusted Yangchen Lhamo with the task of training more gynecologists and pediatricians to meet the rising demand. She was also asked to compile from her extensive experience a text dealing exclusively with diseases afflicting the women and children of Tibetan society. She also considered it her responsibility to increase the special quota for female applicants at the Medical Institute. In 1963, when new candidates were enrolled for the preservation and development of the Tibetan medical tradition, the Medical Institute witnessed an increased number of female candidates applying for formal training during its annual recruitment.

In 1964 Yangchen Lhamo presented a paper on disease and ailments relating to women during a seminar held at the Medical Institute in Lhasa. Her experience and in-depth knowledge of Tibetan medicine as expressed through her writings won her and her institute wide recognition.

In 1966 she was subjected to severe torture and struggle-sessions (*'thab-dzing*) against fake charges. On 7 July 1968 the Chinese arbitrarily used force against the young Tibetans near the Jokhang temple in Lhasa, leaving many arrested and more injured. When Yangchen Lhamo voluntarily treated and distributed free medicine to the injured Tibetans, she was once again tried for her 'anti-nationalistic' action towards the communist regime. She died around 1973. The family medical lineage is carried on by her son, the physician Jampel Kunkhyab, who is now in Lhasa.

Lobsang Dolma Khangkar

Lobsang Dolma Khangkar[15] was born as the only daughter of Dingpon Tsering Wangdu[16] in the family of Khangkar[17] in Dra,[18] Lower Kyidrong, in 1935. Because Dingpon Wangdu did not have any male successor to his clan, he educated his daughter as he would his son. After taking in a bridegroom (*mag-pa*),[19] she was made to assist her father in various affairs such as levying taxes, and running the administration.

At that time, one of the two Kyidrong district governors, Dragtonpa, provided special opportunities to young Tibetans of the region: a two-year intensive training in higher studies including Tibetan grammar under the tutorship of Pelbar Geshe Lungtok Nyima Rinpoche (1893–1985) (from now on abbreviated as Pelbar Geshe Rinpoche), at the sacred hermitage of Rab-nga Riwo Pelbar Samten Phug, and also at the Phagpa Wati Sangpo temple in Kyidrong. In 1955, when Lobsang Dolma was

[15] The life account up to the year 1958 is solely based on the information provided by the State Astrologer Dragton Champa Gyaltsen. Events spanning between the years 1959 to 1989 were personally related to me by Lobsang Dolma at irregular intervals since 1984. Some of the information has been collected from my interviews with her husband Norbu Chophel, personal attendant to Kyabje Trichang Rinpoche. For written information see Pasangs 1988; Mullin 1978; and Josayma and Dhondup 1990. I also relied upon dPal-ldan 1988, a manuscript in my possession.

[16] He was from a triple unbroken lineage of Kyidrong: a lineage of *lding-dpon* (ruling family of one of the nine territorial sections of Kyidrong); a lineage of *grong-sngags* or *dbon-po* (lay tantric practitioners); and a lineage of *sman-pa* ('doctors'). Born in 1891, he died in 1958. He married Tsewang Sangmo (1914–92), daughter of the Kyikhang Damcho household. During the late phase of her life, she renounced worldly life and was ordained as a nun, and known as Lobsang Dechen.

[17] The description of how Khangkar Dingpon acquired the name of its paternal clan and family is presented in 'Ba'-ra-ba 1970: 90–2, which narrates the biography of one of the most respected figures in the Dra Khangkar lineage.

[18] The place refers to Mangyul Kyidrong in the lower Ngari region. Located in the eastern end of the sacred dwelling of Arya Wati Sangpo, at the furthest 'dra' (*grwa*; lit. 'corner' or 'end') of the land, where Songtsen Gampo placed four hundred monks to worship, it is called Drapa.

[19] She married Tsering Wangyal of Dongna (who later came to be known as Dozur or Dokar Zurpa) household of Lungnag Shelkar in Tsang in 1952. One of their sons died as an infant. Their other three children—the boy Dorje Gyaltsen and the girls Pasang Gyalmo and Tsewang Dolkar—were born respectively in 1953 (died in the mid-1960s), 1956 and 1959.

Dr Lobsang Dolma and her family members in Dalhousie, c. 1968. (Photo: Elite Studio, Tashi Tsering, personal collection)

twenty-one years old, she attended with her husband a complete course on Tibetan grammar. The exercises she composed during her exams showed her to be an outstanding student.

In 1956, at twenty-two, Dolma and her husband received a two-month special training in astrology from Pelbar Geshe Rinpoche at his residence in Rab-nga Samten Phug hermitage. In the winter of 1957 and the beginning of 1958 she received teachings on Buddhism and Tibetan medicine from Pelbar Geshe Rinpoche at Dragkha Tegchen Ling, also known as Petsel Ritro, situated near Kyidrong Samten Ling monastery.

During this period she sought higher knowledge about Tibetan medicine. Given the increased need for physicians in the locality along with his concern for his daughter, Dingpon Wangdu invited a medical practitioner named Changpa Dingpon and occasionally an eastern Tibetan physician[20] living in Kyidrong. At the Dingpon's request, they compounded medicines, which were distributed free of cost to the patients. The need

20 This Khampa physician was Drugyal Tsangdrub, who was trained in the Zur tradition of Tibetan medicine of Kham Riwoche. He was very close to Riwoche Jedrung Champa Jungne and his daughter Yanga. While he was in Kyidrong, he was invited by the chieftain of Drongpa. Besides Drugyal, Lobsang Dolma also studied under the guidance of Gen Rigzin, a direct disciple of Master Pema Chogyal (1876–1958), of the Tsibri retreat centre who in turn was a direct disciple of Mahāsiddha Sākya Śrī (1854–1919), who imparted the teachings of Naro Chodrug, Trulkor, Cho and other fields of studies. She also received teachings on the art of holistic medicine from the physician Pelden from Shekar.

and significance of medical practice at that time motivated the Dingpon to encourage his daughter to learn Tibetan medicine from Pelbar Geshe Rinpoche. After mastering the subtleties of the traditional art of healing, she rendered service to the people as a full-fledged physician.

In 1959 she travelled to Sertang, on the border between Nepal and Tibet. She later moved to Bentser, which lies between Sertang and Shabru, and undertook rigorous meditation involving the supplication of Vajrayoginī seven hundred thousand times.

In 1961 she reached Pathankot, north India, with two thousand other Tibetan refugees. With the rehabilitation provided by the Tibetan government-in-exile, she could earn her livelihood by working in road construction for more than a year in Palampur, Manali, Lalethang, Chalithang and Lahoul.

At the beginning of 1962, when the Tibetan government-in-exile established a separate institute of Tibetan medicine, Dolma, along with many other Tibetan workers from Manali, visited Dharamsala to seek blessings from His Holiness the Dalai Lama. When they were allowed a day to visit the nearby temples, she and five or six of her friends from Kyidrong sought blessings from Trijang Rinpoche (1901–81), the junior tutor of the Dalai Lama. After the brief audience, Rinpoche asked her to stay back. Then handing her a bottle labelled 'Dorje Rabjom', he asked her what it was. As she explained the curative power of the medicine in detail, Rinpoche enquired about her educational background, especially in medicine. Rinpoche realized that she had undergone formal training in the traditional science of medicine and advised her to join the Medical Institute under the wing of Tibetan government-in-exile. She remained grateful to Rinpoche. Later she approached the Council for Religious Affairs of the Tibetan government-in-exile that was responsible for the Institute, but her request for admission was declined on the ground that it was inappropriate to accept female candidates for medical courses. Although deeply disappointed, she offered some of the treatises on medical science and medicinal ingredients she had brought from Tibet to the Institute, and then returned to her work on the roadside near Manali.

In 1963 she visited Dharamsala to see her mother and her children. With the help of Rikha Tsetay, who was then a staff member of the Council for Education, she obtained a job of foster mother and Tibetan language teacher at a girls' transit school in Ghurkhari, Kangra. During her year stay at the school, she taught Tibetan dances, songs, and skipping-songs, and also volunteered as a nurse.

In 1964 she moved with her husband to Dalhousie, where both worked as foster parents at the Central School for Tibetans. Since her foster

Dr Lobsang Dolma practising at her clinic in Dalhousie, c. 1971. (Tashi Tsering, personal collection)

children affectionately referred to her as Ama Lobsang Dolma, other Tibetans, as a sign of respect, also called her by the same name till the end of her life.

In 1969, while working as a foster mother at the Central School for Tibetans in Dalhousie, she took to collecting herbs and plants of medicinal value, which were growing in abundance on the mountains of Dalhousie and the nearby Champa and Peldar regions.

The advice of Trijang Rinpoche, and the outcome of a dream-divination conducted by Pomra Geshe Bayu Lobsang Gyaltsen[21] (1910–74) of

[21] According to Chadab Gen Ngawang Tabke (personal communication) Geshe Lobsang Gyaltsen was born in Bayu Nyadrong Tsang family of Terong in Gyaltang Pombor Gang in Kham in the year 1910. At his monastery he studied under Gyaltsen Shakya Rinpoche, who was both a teacher at the monastery and also his personal tutor. In Tibet he received religious teachings from many high lamas including Kyabje Ling Rinpoche, Kyabje Triyang Rinpoche, Dragri Dorje Chang, Zhungpa Lhatsun Rinpoche, and His Holiness the Fourteenth Dalai Lama. In India, he sought religious teachings from Trehor Kyorpon Rinpoche and other great masters. After coming into exile in 1959, he continued his studies at Buxa Daur and successfully completed his Geshe Lharampa degree in 1963. Then he went to Gyuto Dratsang, the Upper Tantric College, and perfected his tantric practice. He passed away on the twenty-fifth day of the third lunar month in 1974, at the age of sixty-five. Bayu Geshe's disciples include Ven. Lobsang Ngodrub, ex-abbot of Sera Mey monastery, and Geshe Rabgyal.

the Upper Tantric monastery concerning the need for her to practise medicine to benefit the sick and poor, provided the inspiration for her to resume her service as a Tibetan medical doctor. She made a start with the good wishes of Geshe Bayu, who was her first patient.

In 1970, she resigned from her work at the Central School for Tibetans, Dalhousie, and rented a small room in the school's cleaner Swaran Singh's house where she set up a private clinic.

By the end of 1970, her clinic was crowded with monks, local Indian residents and Tibetans from the nearby school and staff from the Tibetan handicraft-centre waiting for her treatment. Her growing reputation at this time might be compared to that of 'the six physicians who earned instant fame', who represent one group among the fifty-eight propagators of Tibetan medicine before the fifteenth century.

When the senior physicians of the Tibetan medical centre in Dharamsala, Tro Gawo Gyurme Ngawang Samphel Rinpoche (b. 1932), Kurung Peltsewa Norlha Phuntsok Dradul (1932–72), personal physician to His Holiness Sakya Trizin Rinpoche, and Yeshe Dhonden, personal physician to the Dalai Lama, who were then serving as resident physicians, all resigned from their responsibilities, the Council of Religious Affairs dispatched an order summoning Lobsang Dolma to Dharamsala. Later she was invited by the directors of the Medical Institute, Ngawang Namgyal and Gowo Lobsang Tenzin. She also received repeated invitations from Jetsun Pema, the younger sister of the Dalai Lama and director of the Tibetan children's village, who then had the medical centre under her care. On request from various Tibetan authorities and concerned people, she and all her other family members moved to Dharamsala. On 5 July 1972, Amala joined the medical centre to serve as its principal physician and her husband Dozur Tsering Wangyal joined the centre's pharmaceutical unit (Menjor Khang). Medical Institute 1973 reports: 'To avoid a predicament such as a further decrease in number of patients coming to the main clinic, Lobsang Dolma was purposely invited from Dalhousie. Subsequently, she resumed her service as a consultative physician from July 5, 1972.'

Both the medical centre's pharmaceutical unit and the clinic were efficiently supervised by Tsona Gontse Jamyang Tashi and Lobsang Dolma respectively. Patients from all parts of India and abroad flocked to the place. It was even rumoured that she would be the next personal physician to the Dalai Lama.

Lobsang Dolma went abroad several times. In December 1974, she visited Jeffrey Hopkins of the University of Virginia in the United States to give lectures and conduct demonstrations of some aspects of Tibetan

Dr Lobsang Dolma with the second and third batches of female medical students in Dharamsala, c. 1976. (Tashi Tsering, personal collection)

medicine and medical practice. During her three-month trip, she visited more than ten major hospitals and twelve universities including Harvard, Yale, and Richmond. Then in 1978 she visited the Vajrapani Institute in California for three months with permission from the Dalai Lama. During her trip, she visited the University of Wisconsin and gave an intensive training on Tibetan medicine for two weeks. Then she conducted a ten-day workshop in Zurich on the invitation of the Jungian Institute of Psychology. At the behest of the Exile Tibetan Cabinet Office and at the invitation of the World Health Organization, Lobsang Dolma travelled to Australia to participate in the International Conference on Traditional Asian Medicine held at the Australian National University, Canberra, from 1 to 7 September 1979. She later toured other cities including Sydney and Melbourne, where she gave training on diagnosing the conditions of auditory nerve cells, epilepsy and the traditional pulse-reading techniques. She also held more introductory classes on Tibetan medicine and practice.

In 1975 her husband Dozur Tsering Wangyal died. Later, she married Norbu Chophel, the personal attendant to Trijang Rinpoche. On 15 July 1976 she took the vows of a laywoman (*dge-bsnyen-ma*, Skt. *upāsikā*) from Yongzin Trijang Rinpoche.

On her return to Dharamsala on 1 September 1978 from her visits abroad, the director of the medical centre, Tsewang Jigme Tsarong, handed her a notice which read:

Since Lobsang Dolma has been continuously on leave since the beginning of the year, Tsering Dorje, a physician from a branch clinic in Ladakh, has been duly appointed to her post. It was also noticed that Lobsang Dolma has not reported for work, even a month following her return from abroad. With a selfish attitude that gave personal gain greater priority in her daily work, she disregarded the general rules and regulations of the employees of the medical centre. With the negative impact and detriments far outweighing any consideration of the other staff, the members of the medical centre, after prolonged tolerance and understanding, unanimously resolved to suspend her from her present duty.[22]

As instructed by the order, she left the centre.

She then oversaw the construction of a new building to house her private clinic and residence. Yongzin Trijang Rinpoche laid the foundation stone and consecrated the site purchased in the vicinity of Mcleod Ganj. On completion of the work, Rinpoche named the clinic White Mansion of Joy (Dekyi Khangkar).

On 1 March 1979 Kamal Shamsher Singh, deputy commissioner of Dharamsala, inaugurated the clinic. Other dignitaries were present. Even Tsewang Jigme Tsarong, director of the medical centre, attended to express his wishes by offering traditional white scarves on the occasion.

In mid-October 1982 she fell seriously ill, after which her health deteriorated. At her request, Yongzin Ling Rinpoche, throne-holder of Ganden and senior tutor to the Dalai Lama, conducted a divination rite that foretold immediate complications but eventual recovery. She performed all the religious rituals suggested by Ling Rinpoche and also performed special ceremonies for the destruction of evil spells. After the culmination of the ritual practice, Amala Lobsang Dolma, as if by miraculous resurrection, gradually recovered from her serious illness.

Then at the invitation of Namkhai Norbu, Amala attended the First International Convention on Tibetan Medicine in Venice from 26 to 30 April 1983, and later at Arcidosso from 2 to 7 May 1983. Other attendees at this conference included such physicians and officials of the Tibetan Astro-Medical Institute as Tro Gawo Rinpoche, Tenzin Chodak (personal physician to the Dalai Lama), Namlha Taklha, director of the Institute, and Jigme Tsarong. During her two-week stay in Italy, she treated many women and children and gave talks on various gynecological and pediatric problems. She also demonstrated Tibetan healing practices. Then she travelled to Holland where she stayed for a month at the request of the Dutch Foundation for Tibetan Medicine.

[22] See Medical Institute 1978; also refer to *Tibetan Review* 1978.

As an expression of gratitude to the monastic community for their prayers and rituals, which appeared to have resulted in a miraculous recovery, Amala visited various monasteries in south India to pay homage and make offerings. During her trip to Mundgod, she visited an old and infirm people's home and treated the old and sick by providing free treatment and medicine. At the request of the Regional Tibetan Women's Association (RTWA) in Mundgod, she undertook to support the expenses for detergent cakes, washing accessories, and wages for workers for the old and infirm people's home. She also agreed to arrange for a group of women to wash clothes at the elder people's home once every month. This is evident from the report of annual expenses of the RTWA in Mundgod. Until her last breath, she never failed to send towels and soaps every year to the old people living there. In 1984, when the Tibetan settlement in Mundgod faced a scarcity of drinking water, Amala, in response to the proposition made by Gyaltsen Chonden, donated money for the installation of a boring machine for the settlement and two sheds housing water pumps for the elderly people. In the same year, she set out on a pilgrimage to Nepal. Although she went all the way to see her teacher Pelbar Geshe Rinpoche, she failed to meet him as he was on a strict meditation retreat in the mountains of Yolmo.[23]

In 1985, she received a letter from Pelbar Geshe Rinpoche, who was then residing at Nyanang Phelgyay Ling monastery, expressing his regret over not being able to see Amala and her husband Norbu Chophel during their previous pilgrimage, and inviting them to his place then. As soon as they received the letter, they set forth to Nepal by flight from New Delhi on 20 January 1985. When she approached Rinpoche the next day at his residence at Phelgyay Ling, he expressed a deep appreciation for her

23 Although she was not able to see Pelbar Geshe Rinpoche, the signed letter handed to her read:

Dr Lobsang Dolma, born in the line of Dra Khangkar Grwa in Kyidrong, has been practising this holistic art of healing even during the time of her forefathers. At a young age, she studied all fields of sciences in general, and medicine in particular, from the prominent physician Tsering Wangdu, who was the most distinguished medical practitioner in the region. Besides studying the art from this renowned physician, she also laboriously studied poetry, grammar and composition besides medicine and astrology under my care during her stay at Kyidrong Dzongshar School in 1957. Owing to the proper conditioning of her previous karmic disposition, she turned out to be exceptionally intelligent, with an unwavering faith and conviction in Buddhism. And because of her genial behaviour and her rich experience in the art of healing and medication, she is regarded as one of the most outstanding and prominent physicians. I pray that the doctor, with a caring and compassionate mind, always strives to alleviate the suffering of illness and diseases of all living beings. I also pray that the pains and sufferings come to a natural end. Written on the 12th day of the first month of Tibetan Fire-Mouse Year 2111, corresponding to 15 March 1984, by Pelbar Lungtok Nyima from Yolmo Gegye Retreat in Nepal.

service to humankind by providing treatment and free medicine. He said that he felt overwhelmed with the good news about her philanthropic and pious nature. Rinpoche presented her with a bowl of longevity pills (*tshe-ril*) and a pouch full of Tibetan tuber (*gro-ma*).

After she took charge of her private clinic, Amala completed the construction of her residential building in a very short time, which later drew more than a hundred patients each working day. She credited all her success to the blessings of her spiritual benefactors. As an expression of her gratitude and to ensure further success in her endeavour, she offered on each first working day after the New Year the earnings of the day to Trijang Rinpoche, and later to his young reincarnation. She offered free medicine to patients who came to seek treatment and advice, including young male and female students, monks and nuns, army personnel, and local Indian and Tibetan religious practitioners.

Given her success and lucrative returns for her service, she would jokingly express her gratitude to Tsarong and the other concerned staff, without whom she might still have been working for the Medical Institute at the meagre salary of five to six hundred rupees. She would often say how her suspension from the Medical Institute turned out to be a blessing in disguise. She was very generous with her hard-earned profits and used them for charitable purposes such as organizing free medical camps, primarily to help needy Tibetans, Ladakhis and other Indians.

She conducted a free medical camp for nearly a week at the tourist hotel in Pathankot. Then she held a two-week-camp at Amritsar at the request of the chief priests of the famous Golden Temple, Satwan Singh and Kulwant Singh. Later the Mahabodhi Society and Dawa Samten, manager of Kunga hotel, invited Amala to Calcutta, where she stayed for two weeks. In the same year, she was a guest at Yogi Mahajan's Ashram in New Delhi. She again visited Amritsar, where she attended to patients at the Mahesh Chopra Memorial Hospital for two weeks. Then she organized a free medical camp at Jalandhar for ten days.

In August 1985, acquiescing to the insistent request from her private students Rinzin Dhondup and P. Namgyal, she toured various places in Ladakh including Nubra and Saspol. She also set off on a week trip to the Tibetan settlement of Puruwala. Later, she held a seven-day medical camp at the dining-hall of the Tibetan Homes Foundation, Mussoorie. She also conducted free medical camps in other Indian locales.

In 1986, at the request of the deputy commissioner of Hamirpur and the Lions' Club, Amala conducted a two-week camp, where she gave free treatment and medicine to Hamirpur residents. Then on 22 February 1988, when the young incarnation of Trijang Rinpoche was enthroned at Ganden Monastery, Amala conducted free medical camps in honour of the young rinpoche. During the camp, which lasted for nearly five days, she not only treated monks from Drepung and Ganden along with lay Tibetans and Indians, but also provided them with a two-week dosage of medicine free of cost. In 1988, she stayed for four days at Kyidrong Samten Ling, a Tibetan monastery near the Bodhnāth stupa of Kathmandu. There she attended to sick patients, especially Tibetans residing in the vicinity.

The students to whom she taught Tibetan medicine and who continue her legacy at present include the physicians Pasang Gyalmo, Tsewang Dolkar, Khyunglung Thogme Thinley Dorje, and Purang Tsewang Namgyal.

During her service at the medical centre since 1972, and later at her private clinic from 1978 onwards, she made laborious efforts to compound new medicines that would cure more serious illnesses and diseases. Like most Tibetan physicians, she also felt confident in nature's ability to cure even dreaded diseases such as cancer. These physicians believed that a mere quote from the classic medical treatise, *The Fourfold Tantra* (*rGyud bzhi*), was enough to substantiate that claim:

> How can it be true
> That means and result are unrelated?
> Because all beings evolve from the four elements,
> Because all ailments to be cured arise from the four elements,
> And because all curative medicines are compounded from the four elements,
> Is it not the case that body, ailments, and medicine are of the same nature?
> What is affected and what causes the affliction
> Are related like base and branch,
> While what cures and what is cured
> Are related like meritorious deeds and karma (g.Yu-thog 1984: 675).

She produced the Yutok Deter, the only Tibetan contraceptive pill. Likewise, around 1980, Amala and other Tibetan doctors asserted their ability to cure sexually transmitted diseases and AIDS, basing their confidence on a quote from the same classical medical treatise:

> At the time when the five hundred eons come to an end
> When the evil spirits let out unforeseen harm,
> When the sky-dwelling *ma-mo* demonesses bring illness to the world
> And when the hedonist spells harm through magical substance,
> Thou shall protect thyself and also others (g.Yu-thog 1984: 863).

However, the medical insight that Amala gained from her years of experience helped her to accept her limitations. She confessed her inability to cure AIDS by hanging a public notice in her private clinic which read: 'I have no medicine to cure AIDS.'

During that period many Tibetans and Indians from nearby villages or far-off cities who turned up in Mcleod Ganj without fail paid a visit to

Dr Lobsang's clinic for a check-up or to seek advice. Most of the patients who came for consultation were Indians. Since that time she has been considered one of the most experienced Tibetan physicians of the contemporary period.

In 1981, when the Toepa Welfare Association (Toepa Kyidug) was newly established in Dharamsala, she lent a large sum to the association, and was its chairperson from 1984 till 1987. In April 1985, when the Toepa Association offered a long-life ritual to the Dalai Lama during a religious teaching at Bodhgayā, she served as chairperson of the advisory board for the Long-life Preparatory Committee, and was also one of the principal donors. She served in the capacity of the association's advisory board member till the end of her life.

At the same time, when the Tibetan Women's Association (TWA) was re-established according to the wishes of the Dalai Lama, she served as one of the appointed members of its advisory board. She gave a major monetary contribution for the first general-meeting of the body of the TWA held in April 1985. Besides, she generously donated a fair sum of money for freedom movement activities and social services in Dharamsala.

With her fame as an experienced and eminent physician of Tibetan medicine spreading far and wide, she was listed in *Encyclopaedia of Women in India*, published in India (Vashishta 1976:73), *The World Who's Who of Women*, published in Cambridge, England (Kay 1982: 213), *The International Who's Who of Intellectuals* (*The International* 1985: 288), *Five Thousand Personalities of the World* (*Five Thousand* 1986: 152) and *Asia's Who's Who of Men and Women of Achievements and Distinction* (Bhushan 1986: 209). On 15 July 1989, Doordarshan, India's official television network, screened a documentary film featuring Lobsang Dolma entitled 'India's Foremost Practitioner of Tibetan Medicine' as a part of its series *India Alive*.

Lobsang Dolma's written works include *Dr Lobsang Dolma: Tibetaanse Geneesekunde* published in Holland in 1985; *Lectures on Tibetan Medicine*, published by the Library of Tibetan Works and Archives, Dharamsala in 1986; and many articles on Tibetan medicine.

In 1988, she ordered a three-foot-high gold-plated brass image of Vajrayoginī, which she offered to Tugje Ling, a nunnery in Kyidrong. She also offered representations of the Buddha's body, speech and mind to various monasteries and incarnate lamas.

In the following year of 1989, when Amala was at the peak of her career, she fell ill. Lamas and oracles were consulted and rituals performed accordingly. However, despite the rituals, medications, and the care of her family members, she eventually succumbed to the deteriorating illness on 15 December 1989, at the age of fifty-four. Her husband

Norbu Chophel and the other family members who survived her made large offerings in order to accumulate merit for the deceased. Offerings made to Ganden Monastery included twenty-three precious religious paintings (*thang-ka*) containing images of the Buddha, the sixteen Arhats, the four Guardian Kings, the Upāsakā Dharmatala and Hwa-shang. The pictures were mounted on brocade cover, with carved silver coverings that weighed ten silver *tolas* each. In addition, and out of devotion, they conducted various post-funereal rites and made other offerings for accumulating merit.

After her death, the clinic was renamed the Dr Dolma Memorial Clinic, and was managed by her elder daughter, Pasang Gyalmo, who simultaneously worked as its head physician, while Norbu Chophel supervised the collection of medicinal herbs and other ingredients, and also ran the clinic's pharmaceutical unit. Togme Tinley Dorje served as junior physician at the clinic. As envisioned by the late Dr Lobsang Dolma, the clinic still continues to provide free treatment and medicine to monks, nuns, Indian ascetics and students. More than three thousand patients annually make use of the facilities offered there.[24]

OTHER FEMALE PHYSICIANS TRAINED RECENTLY IN TIBET AND IN EXILE

In Tibet, when a co-educational system was first introduced in the Astro-Medical Institute in 1963, around thirty-five seats were allotted for male and female applicants. The lists of women trained to become doctors include Phuntsok Wangmo from Derge (b. 1966) and Dekyi Pedron from Lhasa.[25] So far, I have had no access to any information about other female doctors in Tibet.

As for the exile community, it was in 1960 that the Dalai Lama gathered around him experienced physicians including Yeshe Dhonden (b. 1927), a physician from Gongkar Shedrub Ling, to Dharamsala. In 1961, the first batch of trainees was organized under Dr Donden and Tro Gawo Rinpoche, and comprised monks from Namgyal and Sera monasteries. At around the same time, the Dalai Lama summoned Akhu Lodro Gyatso (1910–85), an astrologer of the Kālacakra tradition, from Tashi-khyil monastery in Amdo, and set up a school for Tibetan astrology. On 29 June 1963, the Dalai Lama named the Institute's medical school

24 For more details, see Pa-sangs 1988; Mullin 1978; and Josayma and Dhondup 1990. I am also dependent upon dPal-ldan 1988.

25 She is daughter of Dr Tinley Paldon Nyarong Shag, who is an expert in curing *grum-bu* diseases. According to Dr Kungyur Nyarong Shag, his niece Dr Dekyi Pedon is carrying on as the unbroken seventh generation in the lineage, which produced many experienced physicians.

'Tibetan Traditional Medicine-Dispensing School' (Bokyi Rigzhung Menchin Lobkhang). Later in 1967 when the medical unit was combined with the astrology unit under one administration, the Dalai Lama renamed the Institute as the 'Central Astro-Medical Institute to Benefit Sentient Beings' (Dropen U Mentsikhang).

The second batch of students was summoned on Tibetan New Year's day of 1969 and included both male and female candidates. From 1960 to 1971, the medical centre was managed by the Council for Religious Affairs. From 1971 to 1976 it was managed by the Office of the Tibetan Children's Village, and from 1976 onwards the Private Office of the Dalai Lama took charge of it. From 1981 onwards, the Institute functioned under the supervision of the Health Department of the Central Tibetan Administration. During this period, numerous women were trained at the Institute; their names are listed below in Appendix II.

Tsewang Dolkar Khangkar

One of the outstanding current young Tibetan female physicians is Tsewang Dolkar Khangkar,[26] the daughter of Lobsang Dolma discussed above. Despite her young age, she has already earned considerable fame in the field of Tibetan medicine.

At a very young age, Dolkar Khangkar was admitted to the Central School for Tibetans, a boarding school in Dalhousie, and later to Dalhousie Public School, where she received her elementary education. At a time when the fame of her mother spread all over India, the Pomra Geshe Bayu predicted that Dolkar Khangkar, who was then merely five, would one day become a very good and famous doctor. In mid-1972, when her mother was invited to work at the medical centre, she and the rest of her family relocated to Dharamsala. There she was admitted as a student in the Centre's third batch (1973–8). Since adverse circumstances compelled her mother to terminate her job as the centre's chief consultant physician, she and her older sister Pasang Gyalmo felt uneasy and left the centre even though there was only less then three months left for their final exams to be completed.

Dolkar Khangkar later married the famous historian, poet, journalist, and nationalist K. Dhondup. They have had three daughters: Tsering Yangchen (deceased) in 1978, Sonam Peldron in 1980, and Dechen Dolma in 1982.

In 1978, when her mother Lobsang Dolma toured the West to give talks and training, Dolkar Khangkar attended to patients at the clinic along with her sister. She also made several trips to the mountains to

[26] Josayma and Dhondup 1990. I have also known her and her family from 1964 onwards.

collect medicinal plants and other essential ingredients. Through the advice and inspiration of Pomra Geshe Bayu and her mother, she had the opportunity to open the first Tibetan clinic under the auspices of the Gangadaya Haitibhai Charitable Trust Clinic in New Delhi, and serve as its chief Tibetan physician.

In October 1983, at the invitation of State Finance Minister Nyulle, she travelled to Nagaland, where she organized free medical camps in association with the Lions' Club and the Rotary Club. Since then, she visited Nagaland on four other occasions. She also went to Calcutta several times to treat patients. At the initial stages, patients who came for treatment were mostly Indians, but gradually foreign ambassadors and diplomats in Delhi visited her clinic as well.

In 1984, she quit her job at the charitable clinic and opened a private clinic for Tibetan medicine and healing in New Delhi. From mid-1986, when Dekyi Khangkar could not meet the ever-growing demand for medicine in Dharamsala, Dolkar Khangkar opened a new pharmaceutical unit in New Delhi. Soon after, she led the members of the unit on their first trip to the mountains of Manali and Lahoul to collect medicinal plants and herbs. To be more precise about the types of plants and herbs and their medicinal value, she consulted an eminent local physician-cum-botanist, Tashi Tsering, also known as Sunder Singh (1922–86), and his disciple Kolong Wangdu.

Since 1984 she paid periodic visits to Bombay and at the request of residents of Bombay, she opened a Tibetan clinic at Oshiwara Tarapore garden, Andheri West in Bombay in 1986. On 3 October 1987, Doordarshan broadcasted a documentary on Dolkar entitled 'A Face in the Crowd'. On 12 July 1989, the Bombay daily *Dharm Yug* brought out an exclusive article on Dolkar Khangkar with extensive coverage of the traditional Tibetan art of healing. Later she appeared in other papers in English, French, German, Russian, and many regional Indian languages. In August of 1993, the Liberté Tibet Association in France, produced a film on Lobsang Dolkar entitled 'Lady Doctor'. Dr Dolkar also received many awards.[27]

With the number of patients increasing steadily from big cities like New Delhi and Bombay, as well from other places such as Mongolia, Bulgaria, Yugoslavia, Poland, Sweden, Africa, Pakistan, and the Middle East, her fame gradually spread in many places in the world.

During June and July of 1993 and 1994, she explored the mountains and valleys of Manali, Rothang and Lahoul in search of medicinal plants

[27] For more detailed information about both Tsewang Dolkar and her mother Lobsang Dolma Khangkar, see Khangkar and Lamothe 1997.

with a group of fifteen to seventeen from places like France, Japan and Lithuania. She also taught Tibetan medicine and the art of identifying medicinal plants during that trip.

Among all the physicians brought up and trained in the exile Tibetan community, Dr Dolkar is one of the most noteworthy for her diagnostic expertise. She is not only skilled in the art of compounding medicine, but she also takes great care during the blending process to avoid adulteration. Her knowledge and skill in the production of herbal medicine is exceptional. Her philanthropic nature is evident not only through her contribution in the field of traditional medicine, but also through her specific services rendered to the downtrodden and poor.

Whenever interested students and researchers come to her, she first refers them to the personal physician of the Dalai Lama and other senior physicians. It is also evident from her deep knowledge of astrology that her skills and expertise are not confined to Tibetan medicine.[28]

On 20 August 1998, Dr. Dolkar was awarded the 'Bharat Nirnâm Affiliation Certificate' by the All India Organization to promote and take up constructive programmes in all walks of life, based in New Delhi. In the same year she published her own work on Tibetan medicine (Khangkar 1998). On 1 December 1999 Dr Dolkar was awarded yet another prize, the 'Gem of Alternative Medicines'.[29]

Appendix I. THE FIFTY-EIGHT PROPAGATORS OF TIBETAN MEDICINE

translated from sDe-srid n.d.: 153Ba1–155Ba4

Of those who are famous, one is as learned as a paṇḍit, one is as pervasive as the sky, two are as famous as the sun and the moon, nine served as physicians to noble rulers, ten have emanated in various forms to serve entire beings, six are renowned for their scholastic knowledge, ten are as famous as the Medicine Buddha, nine have positive karma as residues from previous training, ten are able to conduct complete examination and analysis, six have achieved fame overnight, five have achieved fame unexpectedly or instantly, two are skilled in experimentation and examination,

[28] The brief biographical sketch above is based on my own first-hand observation of her life. There may be many other such promising female personalities in the field of medicine in India, Nepal and Bhutan, but I do not have information on them.

[29] For more detailed information about both Tsewang Dolkar and her mother Lobsang Dolma Khangkar, see Khangkar and Lamothe 1997.

two are as popular as kings, nine are like the core of a structure, and fifty-five are renowned crusaders of medicine. Among these myriads of great beings, the first one is the great translator Rinchen Sangpo, the second one is Kyebu Melha Chagdum, and the third ones are the dyad Nyangmen Lotsa and Tongmen Tagchung. The fourth comprise three triads: Beji, Cheje and Ugpa from the Upper region; Yutok, Drangti and Minyak from the Central region; and Nya, Tong, and Tazhi from the Lower region. The fifth consists of the ten exalted ones: Orgyan of Changlung Budtra, Darton Gendun of Chang, Khulung Gochen Mentsun, Rongton Chosang, Tratsang Druglha, Summen Joso of Urto, Drapa Ngonshe, Zhangton Ziji Bar of Yarnga, Burto of Nyal and Ochen Tulku of Kham. Those listed in the sixth section are: Konchok Kyab of Mangkhar Chelung, Gyatso Chagdor of Nyangto, Gyaton Jozung Rutsam, Kareg Tsangmen Dorje, Pomen Chape, and Tongmen Sengdrak. The seventh section comprises ten notable physicians: Yutok Yonten Gonpo, Tazhi Shakya Dar, Gyangkar Minyak Sakyong, Jangmen Lewe, Rogchung of Nyangto, Bamen of Shang, Langdro Jemen of Zhalu, Chemen Jodor, Cheje Tri-o of Gungtang Menlungpa, and Gewa Bum. The eighth section comprises nine other physicians: Jomo Namo of Lato, Tognyi of Lato, Mebar from Kham, Lhundrub Lodro of Samye, Gyina of Bumtang, Kugtsal of Lhodrag, Lhakhang Rashag Terton, Gyalwa Tramdrug, and Kunga Dondrub of Dranyedo. The ninth part consists of ten great personalities: Zemen of Purang, Ozer Phen of Lato, Ngogmen Gyongpo of Gyankar, Shershag of Nyangto, Dzongdol of Phenpo, Yogmen Tashi of Dromto, Darso of Urto, Pelseng of Nyal, and Senge Zhangro of Yarlung, Chokyi Gyaltsen. The tenth part has six persons: Drakpa Dorje of Nyangri, Nyenpa Tashi Dorje of Tolung, Chigmen Gawo of Yarto Gyewo, Tseseng of Mekhab, Tashi of Nyalmen, and Marpa of Yarlung. The eleventh part lists five people: Menkar of Shang, Menag of Shang, Shagrampa Nyima Pel of Nyemo, Gontang Pakshi of Yarlung, Loton Yontan of Gyere. In the twelfth part is the dyad Tsonseng and Bare Lhaje, experts in the *byang-khog* and *thur-dpyad* traditions. The thirteenth is Drangti Gyalnye Kharphug. The fourteenth section comprises nine masters including Shenton Yeshe Lodro of Darding. And finally the fifteenth part consists of fifty-eight propagators including Lotsawa Zhazer Chen. The deeds of these great physicians increased as greatly as the waxing of the moon during the first fortnight.

Appendix II. WOMEN TRAINED AT THE MEDICAL INSTITUTE IN DHARAMSALA

The list was provided by the Medical Institute in December 2001; the students' medical degrees are given in parentheses.

The second batch of students to graduate from the Institute (1969–75) included five female trainees: Dawa Dolma (Menram Dringwa), Kyizom Buti (Menram Chungwa), Tsering Chokyi (Menram Dringwa), Sonam Lhamo (Menram Dringwa) and Kunsang Dolma (deceased).

The third batch (1973–8) also included five women: Chungla (Menpa Kachupa), Pema Yangzom (Menram Chungwa), Yeshe Khando (graduated with the students of the sixth batch in 1989, Menram Dringwa), Pasang Gyalmo and Tsewang Dolkar. Gyalmo and Dolkar could not appear for their final exam in 1978.

The fifth batch (1982–6) had ten female students: Ani Thubten Chokyi (Menram Chungwa), Tamdin Sithar (Menpa Kachupa), Dawa Chodon (Menram Chungwa), Kyizom (Menram Chungwa), Tenzin Kyipa (Menram Chungwa), Pema Yangchen (Menram Chungba), Phurbu Dolma (Menram Chungwa), Karma Dolma (Menram Chungwa), Pasang Lhamo (Menram Chungwa) and Yangchen Tso (Menpa Kachupa).

Group photograph of the second and third batches of female medical students of the Tibetan Medical Center, Dharamsala, c. 1976. (Tashi Tsering, personal collection)

The sixth batch (1983–7) had six female students: Tenzin Kyizom (Menram Chungwa), Nyima Yudon (Menpa Kachupa), Dawa Buti (Menpa Kachupa), Chodon Kyizom (Menpa Kachupa), Kunsang Dolma (Menram Chungwa), and Changchub Dolma (Menpa Kachupa) (See Pa-sangs 1988; see also sMan-pa 2000).

The seventh batch (1987–91) also had six female students: Pasang Dolma, Lobsang Dolkar, Tsering Tsomo, Pema Yangzom, Ani Tenzin Chodon, and Pasang Dolkar. (The students from the seventh batch to the eleventh batch graduating in 2001 all obtained the degree of Menpa Kachupa).

The eighth batch (1988–92) included seven female students: Tashi Yangchen, Ani Tsewang Palmo (Ladakhi), Ani Tenzin Yangkyi (Kinnauri), Kesang Dolma, Kesang Dekyi, Tenzin Yangdon and Tsewang Dolma (Ladakhi).

The ninth batch (1992–96) included twelve female students: Dekyi Tsomo, Chungdag, Tamdin Sangmo, Tashi Lhamo, Jamyang Dolma, Dekyi Sangmo, Tenzin Yeshe (Ani Nyidon), Tenzin Changchub (Ani Yangchen), Tsering Lhamo, Konchok Palzom, Dekyi Yangzom and Sonam Dolma.

The tenth batch (1993–97) included five female students: Ngawang Chime, the reincarnation of Dakar Jetsunma, Yangchen Dolkar, Kunsang Tsewang, Sonam Wangmo and Kunga Dechen.

In the eleventh batch (1997–2001) included nine female students: Dechen Chodon, Thubten Dolma, Chime Dolkar, Lhagpa Dolma, Migmar Lhamo, Choying Dolma, Pema Dolma, Pema Tsetso and Pema Sangmo.

In the twelfth batch (1998–2002) there were seven female students: Namgyal Lhamo, Dechen Chodon, Chonga Lhamo, Rigzin Sangmo, Tatiana Tchoumitova (Buryat Russian), Khorlo Batojargalova (Buryat Russian) and Nergui Dolgorsure (Mongolian).

WOMEN IN THE PERFORMING ARTS

PORTRAITS OF SIX CONTEMPORARY SINGERS

*Isabelle Henrion-Dourcy**

Studies of pre-1959 and contemporary Tibetan performing arts are so scarce that any endeavour to assess comprehensively the role of gender in this field is still premature.[1] The aim of this chapter is to provide some preliminary descriptive landmarks and raise a few questions. To my knowledge, the specific focus of women in the Tibetan performing arts has never been studied formally until now, either in English, Tibetan or Chinese,[2]

* This chapter could not have been written without the help of Tashi Tsering (Amnye Machen Institute), Puchung Tsering and Tsereng Dondhup (Brussels), Tenzin Gönpo (Paris) and Laetitia Luzi for factual information. I am grateful to Yungchen Lhamo, Dadon and Choying Drolma for their kindness and collaboration during our regular transcontinental telephone conversations. I thank Fernand Meyer and Françoise Lauwaert for their generous intellectual support and patient reading of the different versions of this study, and finally Heather Stoddard, Steve Jones and Ashu Conrad for their useful comments on the first draft of the text.

[1] For overall yet lapidary descriptions see Norbu 1986; Tethong 1979 and Lhalungpa 1972. For an ethnomusicological approach see the pioneering work of Crossley-Holland 1986 and Helffer 2000 (which includes a bibliography on pp. 116–23). Also see Henrion-Dourcy 2001 for a thumbnail presentation of the Tibetan secular musical genres and an updated bibliography of the major studies in specialized fields of the Tibetan performing arts. It also contains a bibliography provided by various scholars on their respective fields of research.

[2] This comment could be updated with further research. Looking through *Bod ljongs sgyu rtsal zhib 'jug* and *Xizang yishu yanjiu*, the Tibetan art studies journals published in Lhasa, or even in *g.Yu-mtsho* from Dharamsala, I have found no article on women in the Tibetan performing arts, except one small point (bDe-smon 1987: 2). In this article, the author mentions whom she considers to be the most renowned female singers of Tibet at the time: the folk-singers Chung Putri and Anan, the Gesar epic bard Yumig [probably = Yumen], the lute player Chushur Yeshe Drolma, the singer of peasants and labourers' songs Mowo Tagcho, and finally the 'musical theatre' actress Ama Lhagpa. I am grateful to Tashi Tsering for having drawn my attention to this article. Most of these women were in their sixties and over at the time. I will evoke each of them in this chapter, except Mowo Tagcho, about whom I have not been able to gather any information so far. We can assume from the description of her in this short quote that she was an elderly lady who sang mostly socialist songs. I have added to this list Tseten Drolma, Dadron and Yungchen Lhamo, who are by far the most famous female singers of the younger generation.

but there are occasional articles[3] on individual female performers in newspaper interviews,[4] obituaries (Le'u kre jun 1998),[5] and even websites.[6] This lack of interest does not reflect a gender bias in the Tibetan performing arts: in this field women are neither absent nor prominent: not absent in the sense that they equally share the spotlight with men—they sing, dance and play instruments just like men do, both publicly and privately—and not prominent in that they are not more numerous or important than men, and it is not the major expressive field of women.[7] Nevertheless, it does not imply that the gender of the performers is meaningless, that women are interchangeable with men, or that women's performances and status are exactly the same as men's. Repartee songs[8] and circle song-dances, spread throughout Tibet, clearly acknowledge male and female parts. Expectations of body language, behaviour and assertiveness are different between the sexes, both in singing and dancing, but a focused ethnography is needed to examine the matter closely, whilst keeping in mind the wide variations throughout the Tibetan-speaking regions.

Ellen Koskoff (1989: 1–10) summarizes in two questions a gender approach to ethnomusicology, which can here be extended to the whole of the performing arts. First, Koskoff asks how the gender ideology of a society affects musical thought and practice. She alludes to 'separate expressive spheres' and a specialization of musical genres along the sex divide, and also to the musical activities surrounding the primary social roles of women: childbirth, childrearing and work, and also sexuality. Charlene Makley (1997: 13) and Barbara N. Aziz (1987; 1988) have already underlined the 'discrepancies of existing images of the female in Tibet' (Aziz 1987: 72) and questioned the epistemological validity of assuming *a priori* a coherent and essentialized gender ideology applicable to

3 Plus the administrative biographies kept in the work units for Tibetans living under Chinese rule, e.g. Chos-'phel 1997.

4 Since Dadon and Yungchen Lhamo live in exile, there are quite a few interviews of them (especially Yungchen Lhamo) in the western media. I have reproduced a few important references in the bibliography. There are interviews of Tseten Drolma and Ama Lhagpa in *Xizang Ribao* (Tibet Daily) at the end of the eighties. These articles are mentioned without precise reference in Hu Xiangze and Cheng Ping 1995 and Le'u kre jun 1998:119.

5 Nearly all the obituaries in *Dranyen* and *TIPA Newsletter*, published by the Tibetan Institute of Performing Arts of Dharamsala, are about male rather than female performers.

6 See the web addresses for Dadon, Yungchen Lhamo and Choying Drolma at the end of this chapter.

7 The Tibetan Women Association in Dharamsala, created by the government-in-exile to promote women's issues, has summarised in its website the different fields of activity of Tibetan women, but makes no mention of singing and dancing, or performing arts as a whole (see http://www.tibet.com/women/index.html).

8 See the bibliography for references on these repartee songs.

the whole of the Tibetan speaking peoples; they suggest instead to examine local processes. Second, Koskoff asks how music reflects or affects gender relations. Koskoff refers to situations where musical practice is an active agent in transforming, reversing or mediating gender relations, pointing to issues of power and social and cultural identity. Out of the three concerns that appear central to gender studies, namely (dis)empowerment, gender interrelationships and the constitution of male and female identities, researchers need to examine which are the most useful guidelines relevant to the specific Tibetan empirical context. The assumed theoretical framework should not warp the social processes it examines, or contort the observed data and overemphasize questions that do not appear salient, either voiced or unvoiced, in the local ethnographic context. The intention of this chapter is therefore to try and let the data speak for themselves with no other methodology than interpretive analysis.

In trying to circumscribe an image of Tibetan women in the context of 'performing arts' (taken here in a loose sense, encompassing activities such as storytelling, singing, dancing and instrument playing, carried out by specialists and non-specialists), two approaches immediately come to mind: a literary analysis, and a performative study. First, one could look at the lyrics of the songs, dramas, epics and folktales (whether traditional or contemporary), to try to bring out recurrent images of the female. This would imply the handling of an immense corpus of data in Tibetan including the innumerable compilations and local anthologies published in Tibet and China since the 1980s, and which are still to be mapped out by Tibetologists (there are nevertheless some important surveys in English, relying on research done before the 1950s or among exiles). I am not aware of a corpus of songs exclusively sung by women, an arena for voicing womanhood or social criticism where women would tell of their experiences of being women: mothering, domestic violence, access to education or political participation (Koskoff 1989; Robertson 1989; del Valle 1993). Women, like men, sing many songs in Tibet, but can a song be called a 'female song' just because it is sung by a woman? Does that necessarily entail an organic, inbuilt relationship between the two parts, conveying feelings specific to women? Songs were, and still are, an important means of expression amongst low-literate sections of the Tibetan people. There were songs like the pre-1959 Lhasa 'street songs' (Goldstein 1982) that can be considered an outlet for social and political frustrations, but they were the appanage neither of women nor of men. We can nevertheless underline here the relative outspokenness of Tibetan women in their songs, as also for the love songs, which they sing to/with men.[9]

[9] See, e.g., the repartee songs. An ethnographic example is the following anecdote related by Diemberger (1993: 109) from the Khumbo region of north-east Nepal: 'One

The second, performative approach would be an ethnographic analysis *in situ*, combining an observation of choreography, costumes and body practice, a sociological study of performers on and off stage, a role specialization between men and women, and also an examination of the relationship between the performers and the audience, as well as the wider cultural setting. For various reasons, having access neither to the data of the first approach, nor to the fieldwork[10] of the second one, I have compiled notes from my previous fieldwork in Lhasa and extant secondary sources in Tibetan, Chinese and western languages to propose a first empirical delineation which examines in which performance contexts Tibetan women have held a notable place, and to portray six prominent contemporary performers. These are merely the first pieces of a puzzle (I have no ambition for regional comparison, generalization or theoretical elaboration).

TIBETAN PERFORMING ARTS IN CONTEXT

Women's role and importance in the Tibetan performing arts are to be understood only if contextualized in the wider understanding of the place ascribed to performing arts in Tibetan society and culture, both before the Chinese takeover and under communist rule, since 1959 (at least in central Tibet). The onset of communist rule marks a sharp fracture between two radically divergent ideologies and societal organizations.

Considering the performance of songs and dances before 1959, Buddhist scholars make a clear distinction between sacred and secular genres, echoing a contrast often made in the Tibetan context between literate and popular culture.[11] With an ideological focus on spiritual liberation,

---

evening in a tourist area close to Mount Everest, a girl invited a Sherpa boy by singing: "I have a nice camera but I haven't got a film. Have you got a nice film? If you give me your film we can make nice photos." The boy, who did not have a film and did not look as if he was likely to have one, was rather confused and surprised by the question. Then the girl made it clear to him that he *did* have the nice film…'

[10] I more recently completed a PhD thesis in anthropology on the musical theatre of lhamo based on fieldwork in Lhasa and South Asia from 1996 to 1999 (Henrion-Dourcy 2004). I must acknowledge that gender issues have not, to this day, appeared salient in my own investigations, or rather, I have not decided to focus on this perspective.

[11] It is interesting to note that both the two reconstructed images of Tibetan 'traditional' society—one put forward by Dharamsala, with orthodox religion-centrism, and the other by the Chinese communists, along the Marxist divide between mass and elite—assume an inherent polarization in Tibetan society, as if there were two distinct cultures within Tibet, a popular culture and a literate culture. While holding some truth, it is a caricatured depiction of the past. As far as my experience in the Tibetan performing arts goes, this polarization appears more in discourse than in the more interwoven practice. Whether as sponsors, amateurs or even performers, high-ranking religious figures would indulge in, for example,

the clergy and the literate elite in general, have tended to look down upon activities that distract the mind from the noble path to enlightenment. Perhaps therefore, Tibetans themselves have paid little attention to their performing arts, not considering them a worthwhile area of study, nor an enviable activity to engage in (this comment does not apply to monastic music and dances, which clearly do not belong to the same category, and, whilst sometimes spectacular, are thought of as religious practice). This minimization was coupled with effective contempt if performing was a livelihood, since that meant being a roaming beggar, such as the 'bheda' (*'be-dha*) of Ladakh, the 'ralpa' (*ral-pa*) of Kham, some 'dranyen' (*sgra-snyan*) (lute) players, and some 'lhamo' (*lha-mo*) actors in central Tibet.[12]

In this context, women's status was the same as men's. It was not the activity of the performers that was despised, but their vagrancy, the absence of an anchor in a piece of land (or an estate), which entails that they had to beg for their food. If performance was just a side occupation, then performers were not looked down upon. The divide is not so much between 'professional' and 'amateur' (the same quality lhamo performances could be given by the two types of actors, who would have a very different social status), but between 'livelihood from roaming' (*sa-zhing med-pa*) and 'livelihood from one's own fields' (*sa-zhing yod-pa*).

Though anecdotal and peripheral compared to the vital nexus of Tibetan culture, songs and dances are, in practice, on the long and winding path to liberation, clearly acknowledged for 'making this life happy'. The complexity of Tibetan performing arts lies in the fact that they appear with an irreducible terminological, regional and contextual diversity. There is also the supplementary complication arising out of the very difficulty to localize them in Tibetan civilization: they are both everywhere and nowhere in particular. Most of the songs and dances in the Tibetan context are participatory,[13] i.e. with no divide between performers and

---

lhamo or other songs and dances, with absolutely no second thought for partaking in this amusement.

[12] Such contempt did not extend to other specialized performers, who were not considered as beggars: the 'gar' troupe of the Dalai Lama, amateur lhamo actors in general, and 'tashi sholpa', a style of lively songs and dances evoking auspiciousness. The 'nangma' musicians of Lhasa, which comprised full-time musicians as well as *dilettante* aristocrats and wealthy merchants, were considered in various ways according to their livelihood. Likewise, the social status of the epic bards depended not upon their activity, but upon their social origin and means of livelihood: 'If the bard (*sgrung-mkhan*) was an incarnate lama or from a well-to-do family, then he had an elite status; but if he was from a poor family background, then he was no more then a beggar' (Tashi Tsering, personal communication). Moreover, Rig-'dzin 1999: 37 claims that the Gesar epic was qualified as a 'beggars' bawling' (*sprang-po'i ku-co*) before 1959.

[13] I am grateful to Ashu Conrad for introducing me to the conceptual distinction between participatory and presentational genres, which she takes from Nahachewsky 1995: 1.

spectators. Singing and dancing have been informal, shared by all, an unprofessional part of Tibetan culture, and not clearly isolated from the rest of the social fabric. Basically, all social gatherings, whether picnics (which could rightfully be considered a Tibetan national sport) or formal parties or even ritual festivals, were and still are punctuated with songs and dances, the young ones imitating the old, with varying attention from the participants.

Some work songs were more frequently sung by women, because of their more significant participation in these activities. In the same way, women were usually the beer-vendors (*chang-ma*). Even for more formalized presentational genres (i.e. those that differentiate spectators from performers), such as lhamo, ralpa, 'gar' (*gar*; 'court-dances'), and instrumental music, carried out by semi-professional specialists, there was no specific institution for learning the style. Performing was not considered an art in its own right. There is rarely a conception of being an 'actor' or 'singer' as a profession. There was no phenomenon of fame for any 'artist', whether male or female, except perhaps some lhamo actors.

The Chinese communist rule has meant an unprecedented intrusion of a centralized totalitarian state with a pervasive political ideology into the Tibetan performing arts, as occurred in the whole of China. Virtually any performance became a political statement, and, in time, tried to adjust to the successive waves of cultural policies that shaped China over the past fifty years. For performers, it meant the emancipation of the sphere of performing arts from its traditional context, and the professionalization of performing as a formal job within work units ('folk'-singing and -dancing continued in informal situations, but with varying degrees of tolerance by the government: acceptance (1950–66), total ban (1966–78), or revitalization (1978–). For female professional performers, it meant a status, a salary, and a training in China, or later Tibet, equal to those of men. Maoism propelled gender equality, which also meant an enforced androgyny for the female on the stage during the more radical period of the Cultural Revolution. Roughly, two periods can be singled out. The first would be the Maoist era, which exalted the social role of the performing arts, viewing them clearly as a vehicle of propaganda, creating and instrumentalizing dramas and songs to spread the ideological doctrine of the state, framed in Sino-Soviet theatricality and realism. The omnipresent warlike class struggle meant for the minorities a near annihilation of any distinct cultural identity, whether for literature, painting or performing arts. Participatory genres vanished or became staged to provide a politicized display, and presentational genres were formatted along a pan-Chinese model (Tung 1987; Meserve 1979).

The second period is the post-Maoist era. With the opening of China to foreign influences through commerce in the 1980s came the revitalization of minority cultural traits (and nationality issues) in China. This led, on one hand, to a systematic compilation, folklorization, and to some extent standardization of the revitalized amateur genres (after a near-twenty-year ban) (see Trébinjac 1997; 2000), and on the other hand, to the reframing of the political content of the performances. What it displayed was a gradual liberation from communist ideology, but did not let go of the historical discourse of Chinese recent history, and featured the Han-chauvinist portrayal of its 'happy' minorities as backward simple people, living close to nature and emblematic for the Chinese of their own exotic Other (Harris 1997: 169), which also meant an 'erotic' Other (Gladney 1994). Henceforth, the image of the women on the stage regained some femininity, but framed in an exaggerated sensual 'noble savage' fashion. Nowadays, alongside the government presentational productions, 'traditional'[14] participatory and presentational genres have managed to find some place to co-exist, which adds a new layer of complexity to the issue of the current state of the Tibetan performing arts. But what appears striking is the significant role of performing arts as identity markers. They are tied up with issues of national and cultural self-presentation, to the Tibetans themselves, to the Chinese and to the westerners, for troupes as much from the People's Republic of China (PRC) as from the diaspora. Nowadays, Tibetan performing arts take on a growing importance on the international stage, as the Tibetan Institute of Performing Arts (TIPA, Dharamsala), as well as groups of monks (showing a secular display of ritual genres; see McLagan 1997) and individual performers such as Yungchen Lhamo and Choying Drolma bring awareness about, and export, Tibetan culture in the West mainly with the popular performing arts. Willingly or unwillingly, Tibetan performing arts have become increasingly tied up with politics.

Noticeable loci for women in pre-1959 song and dance

The most noticeable participatory performance locus for women in pre-1959 contexts is that of the 'ceremonial beer-servers', the 'trungshuma' (*khrung-zhu-ma*). They were called to entertain the guests at parties with beer and songs, and one of the main occasions when they were called, especially in central Tibet (above all in Tsang), was weddings. In this role, we still see them nowadays.[15] Tibetan weddings are usually lengthy

[14] 'Tradition' is used here as a convenient shorthand, since I do not have the space to discuss the influential work of Hobsbawm and Ranger (1983) on 'the invention of traditions', which has debunked the illusions of authenticity in claims of the traditional. We might say instead 'performing arts as they are widely held to have existed before 1959'.

[15] As I have seen in Tibet. Diehl 1996: 102–5 has observed two groups of these women in Dharamsala, and gives a few pictures of them.

and copious parties where both men and women sing, but there seems to be a role specialization in the sequential unfolding of the celebration. Men are generally responsible for the more ceremonial songs, like the alternating song competitions when taking the bride to her new home, and the 'explanations' (*kha-bshad*) describing the family, the structure of the house and the virtues of the region (Aziz 1985: 123–5) which contain many historical and mythological allusions. But when it comes to the partying, women seem to hold a prominent entertaining position. This role specialization echoes a popular saying: 'To the men, culture and knowledge. To the women, intelligence and [a talent in] maintaining a nice appearance.'[16] It is as if, once the world is set by the speech of men, it is entertained through the art of women. When the family members can afford it, they hire one or several 'ceremonial beer-servers'. They are not professional, but experienced ones acquire a regional renown, and a respectable family will prefer these. In all cases, they should be renowned for their pleasant ways, for being lively, talkative and speaking softly in everyday life, as they are going to be in contact with all the guests and manage the party. They have to come a few days beforehand to be instructed by the family on what to do and who is who. Their responsibility is to provide a joyful atmosphere, sing drinking songs to the guests, respect the etiquette of the seating rows, and dispose all the presents in the storeroom. There are usually two of them, sometimes more if the party is big. The best ones sing a different drinking song to each guest and, when all are served, they put on a little show of singing and dancing, sometimes accompanied with a lute.[17] They try to make all the guests participate. Therefore, they must have a large repertoire. Both the family and the guests remunerate them.

In pre-1959 Lhasa, the ceremonial beer-servers were found in another context, much more formal, as much for dress code as for etiquette: the hostesses of the Yasor pageant that was held at the end of the new year celebrations. The event consisted of a military parade and competitions organized by the Tibetan government, representing seventeenth-century Mongol soldiers (see Karsten 1983 and Richardson 1993: 31–3). Each Yasor general had a retinue of fourteen servants, among whom there were

16 *Bu la shes bya yon tan / Bu mor shes pa rnam pa*. I am grateful to Puchung Tsering for informing me of this popular saying. It is somewhat difficult to translate, as the categories of *shes-bya*, 'all that there is to know', and *shes-pa*, 'perceptive intelligence', connote a literate background that seems incongruous here. It may well be that *gzhis-kha*, 'temper, or nature', is to be read here instead of *shes-pa*. The second part would then become, in a slightly looser translation: 'to the women, temper and grace'.

17 The 'dranyen' (*sgra-snyan*) is a plucked lute with an unfretted neck found in folk-music throughout the Himalayas. In central Tibet, these lutes generally have six strings tuned in pairs.

three sorts of maids of honour, who were ranked according to the complexity and lavishness of their dress and jewellery: first, the 'beautifully adorned girls' (*rgyan-bzang-ma*),[18] selected from the (aristocratic) household of the Yasor, who were clad in the most splendid costumes of the Lhasa noble ladies of the highest rank. The etiquette prevalent in Lhasa at the time was that out of the sixteen types of ornaments of female jewellery, which could never be worn all at once, noble women would normally wear five ornaments for usual parties (Yuthok 1990: 321–5). But the beautifully adorned girls put on the maximum, i.e. twelve ornaments at once (ibid.: 185–6). The second maids of honour were the ceremonial beer-servers and then came their maids. Their role was to offer 'chang' (barley beer) and 'tsampa' (roasted barley flour) to all the guests in strict observance of the feast's protocol.

With regard to the presentational and specialized repertoire of Tibetan performing arts, court dances (gar) and a lively style of songs and dances evoking auspiciousness, 'tashi sholpa' (*bkra-shis zhol-pa*), were exclusively male. Men were the main performers in Tibetan musical theatre (lhamo), in the various types of songs of specialized beggars generally playing the lute or the fiddle (*pi-wang*), and also in the Gesar epic (*ge-sar sgrung*) as ralpa performers and 'nangma' (*nang-ma*) singers, but in these genres there were prominent female actors and singers as well. As the first three women portrayed in the next section represent the first three genres, I will delve only into the last two here.

The ralpa were wandering performers from Kham, travelling also through central Tibet, sometimes as far as to India and Bhutan. As for other roaming groups, their troupes were often family-based, with both men and women performing and sharing an equally low social status. The ralpa mixed formal narration, songs, dances, acrobatics and small excerpts of plays depicting important parts of the biography of Milarepa, who they claimed as their founding figure. Very little is known to this day about ralpa performances,[19] and most of this tradition has vanished. From the extant performances reconstituted (and folklorized) by the TIPA and in Tibet, one can see a division of labour between the men, who do the formal narration (*ral-bshad*) and the acrobatics, some of which involve swords; and the women, whose most striking appearance is the

[18] For photographs of the richly adorned *rgyan-bzang-ma* see Bell 1992 facing p. 275; Richardson 1993: 32; Harrer 1955: 176–7; Harrer 1997: 102; Tsarong 1995: 30 and Tung 1980 (book cover and plate 110). This last picture is reproduced in Yuthok 1995: 176–7 and Dunham, Baker and Kelly 1993: 90. See also a drawing by Topden in Moon 1991: 211. For a detailed account of the whole ceremony see Karsten 1983: 123, 133, 135.

[19] For further information on ralpa see mGon-po 1998; bKra-shis 1991; and Ngag-dbang 1988–7.

tumbling dances with hand drums. Both men and women sing the songs (*ral-gzhas*).

Nangma,[20] the elegant music played in instrumental ensembles, is known mainly for its role in the aristocratic parties of Lhasa, alongside the related style of 'toshe' (*stod-gzhas*), songs originally from western Tibet, but played in large parts of central Tibet. These styles were not confined to official picnics. They are still extensively played nowadays, and stand as a hallmark of Tibetan music altogether. Before 1959, different groups played nangma and toshe, but the most renowned one was the Nangme Kyidug, the association of nangma musicians based in Lhasa, that was disbanded in 1942. Members of this guild, which featured alongside former beggars,[21] common people, Tibetan Muslims, and dilettante performers like aristocrats and wealthy merchants, comprised only a few full-time professionals, some of whom were women: Acha Yitsa, a Hui Muslim specialised in nangma songs, and Sonam Kyidzom (see below), dedicated to toshe songs and dances, as recalled by Zholkhang Sonam Dargye (Zhol-khang 1991: 155), who was part of the guild. Women playing this kind of music were not despised. On the contrary, they were assessed by their skills, and they also had to be charming and beautiful (*mdzes-ma*).

Among the performers of this repertoire of songs, we find some of the 'label-girls' or 'lambar' (*lam-'bar/lam-bar bud-med*), the notorious prostitutes known under derogatory nicknames, mostly given to them by angry wives.[22] Although they were real Lhasa celebrities (but not known

20 For photographs of musicians playing nangma music see Richardson 1993: 89; Tsarong 1997: book cover and Henrion-Dourcy 2001: 454. For a historical and musicological description, as well as for bibliographical references see Samuel 1976 and Henrion-Dourcy 2001.

21 For a short biography of the last teacher of the troupe see Henrion-Dourcy 2001.

22 *Lam-'bar* is held to be a Tibetan phonetic adaptation of either 'number' or 'label' in Indian English. In the middle of the twentieth century *lam-'bar* came to mean 'brand, trademark' in Lhasa. For instance, there is the case of the Indian soaps sold on the market: since the Tibetans could not read the trademark in a foreign language on the soap cover, they called the soap by the animal pictured on the paper: *rma-bya lam-'bar*, 'the peacock brand [soap]'. Indian army issue cigarettes were called *sa-bzhu lam-'bar* 'the lantern brand' after the drawing on the cover. Tashi Tsering has drawn my attention to the use of this term in several advertisements published in the *Yul phyogs so so'i gsar 'gyur me long* (*The Tibet Mirror*), the Tibetan periodical published in Kalimpong between 1925 and 1963. For example, a wool carding-comb was advertised as *lug lam-'bar* 'the sheep brand' (*The Tibet Mirror* VI, 9, 1 [October 1932]: 8) for nearly twenty years, and we find it some time later as *bal-ma lam-'bar*, 'the brand of the woman spinning wool' (*The Tibet Mirror* XVIII, 11, 1 [October 1950]: 6). Another box features an advertisement for batteries named Estrela in English, and termed *skar-ma lam-'bar*, 'the star brand' in Tibetan (*The Tibet Mirror* XXII, 3, 1 [July 1954]: 4). The same principle of analogical nicknaming, or labelling, also applied to people very much *en vue* in the streets, namely prostitutes: Khata Lambar, who was also selling

Nangma and toshe singers and dancers at aristocrats' picnic in Lhasa. The Nangme Kyidug Music Association main female performer, Acha Yitsa, between two of the 'label-girls': the Crow on the left, and the Cat on the right. British Lhasa mission, Sir Basil Gould, 1936–7. (British Library)

nationally, their fame was perhaps limited in later days to Lhasa, Shigatse, Darjeeling and Kalimpong), only the elders remember them now, and very few young Tibetans have heard of them. Some of them (e.g. the Cat and the Crow, so labelled after their physical features) were also proficient singers and dancers,[23] and were invited to entertain the Lhasa jetset with nangma and toshe during the lavish picnics of the Tibetan government and the lay officials, thereby contrasting with the roaming

---

'khatas', Tibetan ceremonial scarves; Sha Pa-le, whose mother was selling 'shapale', or meat-stuffed bread; Jutta Lambar was probably selling *jutta*, the Hindi word for shoes; Natug Lambar, who was probably often seen with 'natug', nose mucus, on her face. Lugo Lambar 'Sheep Head Label', and her daughter Lugtrug Lambar 'Child of the Sheep Head Label' were living in Kalimpong. The most famous ones were named Angu Lambar, 'Dove Label' after the grey colour of her dress, and Gutsig Lambar 'Nine Syllables Label', who was a very good lhamo singer, and the lhamo songs are versified in generally nine syllables per line. I thank Tashi Tsering for the first information and subsequent explanations on the subject, Norbu Tsering (Lapa-la), the lhamo master at the Tibetan Institute of Performing Arts (Dharamsala), for sharing his good stories of life in Lhasa in the 1940s and 50s, and Nicolas Tournadre for helping me explore the various possible interpretations of this term.

[23] It is Phorok Lambar, 'Crow Label' and Zhimi Lambar 'Cat Label' who sing nangma and toshe songs on the Basil Gould recordings (see discography).

beggars who went round common people (see section below on Chung Putri). These nangma singers were for that period high-class courtesans, and gossip would spread swiftly in Lhasa about which aristocrat had succumbed to whose charms. Importantly, not all the nangma performers were prostitutes, and not all the prostitutes, actually very few, were nangma singers. Only one of them was part of the Nangme Kyidug: Cat Label, whose real name was Sonam Kyidzom from Lhasa, and whose singing apparently evoked the cat's mewing. Crow Label, i.e. Phurbu Drolma (*c.* 1912–*c.* 1966), was originally from Shigatse.

Her nickname is said to derive either from her face with a long nose, or from the dark complexion of her skin. Wheel Label was also from Shigatse: she was a libertine from an artistocratic family, but was not a singer. Interestingly, their daughters inherited their nicknames: Crow Label's daughter was known as Child of the Crow, and Wheel Label's daughter was known as Child of the Wheel, also known as Lady Daughter—as she was the child of an aristocrat. When they were not playing for the jet set of Lhasa, they played and sang with Kyomolung lhamo actors and other infamous Lhasa figures like Lutsa (1916–83),[24] a Tibeto-Nepali who ran a sort of 'tavern' where one could drink beer, listen to music, smoke opium and meet women (see Norbu Tsering 1999: 43). The following women were also famed in the same social environment, but were not qualified with such 'label' names: Migmar and Norzin Seldron, of whom only their names are remembered, and Anan of Lhasa (*c.* 1911–95),[25] who had one lame leg, but her dancing was apparently so stunning that it was not perceptible. The most illustrious of these dancers was undoubtedly Chushur Yeshe Drolma.[26] She was probably born in the village of Chushur, some thirty-five miles south-west of Lhasa, around 1915 and died in Lhasa in 1992. Her beauty was by all accounts irresistible, as were her kindness and generosity. Prostitution at that time did not seem to entail the same cynical commodification as in contemporary Lhasa. Not only was Chushur Yeshe Drolma a singer, but she could also play the lute (see discography for a recording of her playing in the 1980s). Two songs that circulated in Lhasa in the 1940s and 1950s bear witness to her prominence on the public scene:

> Chushur Yeshe Drolma,
> For one silver crown, how many times will you let me [lie with you]?

[24] See his obituary in *Dra-nyen, Newsletter of the Tibetan Institute of Performing Arts* 8,1 (1984): 37.

[25] For a recording of Anan made in Lhasa in the 1980s see Discography.

[26] For a photograph of Chushur Yeshe Drolma see *Drikung* 1998: 27. She was identified as the second singer from the left by Norbu Tsering (Lapa-la), lhamo master at the Tibetan Institute of Performing Arts in Dharamsala.

Even if the princess of Sakya
Gave me a better deal, I wouldn't want her![27]

Handsome young men, it is pointless
To go to Changseb Shar [where she used to live?] this year.
Chushur Yeshe Drolma
Has got a hammer and tongs in her hand.[28]
[This could mean that she was from a blacksmith family, i.e. of low birth.]

SIX CONTEMPORARY FEMALE SINGERS

The following six women have been selected because of their notoriety amongst the general public of Tibet Autonomous Region (TAR) Tibetans, at least those from Lhasa, and their significance in the respective genres they are performing. The three first ones, Ama Lhagpa, Chung Putri and Yumen, appear on the list of the most renowned female singers of Tibet in bDe-smon (1987). They embody 'traditional' presentational musical genres of Tibet, i.e., respectively, musical theatre, folk-songs and the epic tradition. I have completed the portraits with three women presenting 'new' types of songs: the political singer Tseten Drolma and the pop singer Dadon, whose social impact in the TAR, for both of them, has been the strongest; and finally Yungchen Lhamo, who is, despite the fact that not many people have heard of her inside Tibet, the first Tibetan artist to have made a name in the West. Interestingly, all these women are singers or performers of 'traditional' song-and-dance and there do not seem to have been female instrumentalists, dancers or theatre actresses who have achieved such renown in contemporary Tibet.[29] They are all professional

[27] *Chu shur ye shes sgrol ma / ṭam kar ga tshad gtong ga / sa skya'i rje btsun sku zhabs / khan pa rgyab kyang mi dgos //*. One *ṭam-kar* was a currency unit equivalent to fifty silver coins (*dngul-srang*) in pre-1959 Tibet. This song must have been composed in the 1950s, when the Sakya princess was living in Lhasa; see Sakya and Emery 1990: 128–32.

[28] *Da lo lcang gseb shar la / pho gzhon theg blos mi 'dug / chu shur ye shes sgrol mas / tho skam phyag na bsnams bzhag //* (I am grateful to Tashi Tsering for showing me these two songs).

[29] Contemporary dance, instrumental western music and realistic theatre (or cinema) are three genres of western/Chinese import that are extremely recent in Tibet, and have been very slow to take up the liking of the Tibetans. There are some famous male actors, but no famous male dancers. China's Tibet website (http://www.tibet-china.org), in its politically-motivated search for exemplary Tibetan women, mentions two prominent Tibetan female dancers, whose names are not known to the general public, and who may currently be working in mainland China: Tsering Sangmo and Drolma. According to this website, Tsering Sangmo is a member of the Chinese Dancers' Association and of the Council of the Chinese Society of Ethnic Dances. She was sent to Beijing's Central Minorities Institute in 1959 to train in dancing, becoming the first Tibetan woman to be educated and specialise in this field. Chung Putri was probably one of her teachers. She graduated in 1965, and pursued a career of performer and choreographer, which apparently won her prizes. She is said to have

performers, and all come from the TAR.[30] All these women have been or are stars, which is both rare and atypical for Tibetan performers.[31]

I have not been able to meet any of these women. Two of them have already died. The following portraits do not constitute complete life-stories that were reconstructed using ethnographic methodologies. I had to rely on secondary sources, most of which were published in the PRC. Due to the relatively uninformative, inconsistent and unreliable nature of these sources, I have tried to complete the stories of their lives with opinions voiced by Tibetans in Lhasa. I have been able to interview the last two women by phone, as they live in the West, and thus gather more data about their lives. With such a disparity in the quality of the information at my disposal, I have tried to draw for each of these six women an overall trajectory, examining their education and social position, and have attempted to contextualize their lives socially and historically. A self-oriented perspective (an 'ethnography of personhood' or a 'practice theory of self') would certainly have yielded deeper insights and given voice to these women's choices, and would have told more about their 'struggles to constitute themselves as particular kinds of actors and persons vis-à-vis others within and against powerful sociopolitical and cultural worlds' (Skinner and Holland 1998: 3). This focus on agency could have thrown some light on how their gender has affected their lives, work and

---

travelled in different regions of Tibet to research traditional dances, and to have written a dance manual. Drolma is Tsering Sangmo's student, and is said to have won several prizes within Chinese national competitions. The website comments in this way about her: 'She has brought new life to the Tibetan dances, using techniques of exaggeration and distortion. She blends Tibetan folk-dancing traditions using taps and revolutions with other styles, and has evolved the Tibetan dances from original self-entertainment to an unrestrained dancing with aesthetic bearing and a strong national flavour.' Hanna Havnevik informed me of a mention and a photograph of another dancer, named Pelkyi, in *Xueyu zangjia nu* 1995: 101.

30 I have heard of no outstanding female performer in India. The Tibetan Institute of Performing Arts (TIPA) of Dharmasala trains and features professional actors and singers, but has invested little attention in the individual merit of the performers, stressing instead their social (as well as political) roles as holders and preservers of a cultural tradition. The biography of the TIPA lhamo master, Norbu Tsering, the only one of its kind, was written by a westerner (Antonio Attisani; see N. Tsering 1999). A few young actors have worked with western film crews for the international productions that have recently come out about Tibet (*Seven Years in Tibet, Kundun*, and *Himalaya*). A few talented and committed singers have left TIPA and perform Tibetan songs in the West (Chaksampa, Tenzin Gönpo, Gangchenpa, Loten, Garpa and others), but there does not seem to be any strong personality standing out at this moment, even less so among the women. See Diehl 1997: 153–4 and 2000: 224 for an examination of gendered discrimination amongst the Tibetan exile performers.

31 This is not an elitist choice on my part, but information was more accessible and easier to gather on them than on performers with a lower profile.

feelings, and whether they are typical or atypical Tibetan women. Therefore, the following portraits should be regarded as mere previews.

Ama Lhagpa: a lhamo prima donna[32]

Ama Lhagpa was born in Lhatse in 1909 and died in Lhasa in 1997. She performed lhamo (musical theatre) for about eighty years in the most important lhamo troupe of Tibet: the Kyomolung troupe, which was later integrated into the governmental Tibet Opera Troupe.[33] She married successively the three most prominent actors of the troupe, of whom the last two were teachers, and has held the leading heroines' roles of lhamo for her whole career.

Her mother, named Metok, was regarded as a stunning beauty, and sang songs and played the lute in the Shigatse region. Ama Lhagpa never knew who her father was, but rumour says she was the child of a Shigatse aristocrat (Chos-'phel 1997: 1). Her mother later married a merchant from eastern Tibet and went to India, where she died early and left Lhagpa as an orphan at the age of three. She was then taken care of by another woman, who roamed the region singing and playing the lute to beg for food,[34] and Lhagpa followed her on the streets and in chang taverns, performing whatever she could, given her small age. When the Thirteenth Dalai Lama fled in exile to Darjeeling (1910–12), the Kyomolung lhamo troupe was disbanded. This troupe was mostly composed of landless roaming actors, but they were based in Lhasa for part of the year. Although

[32] Sources: Bod-ljongs 1980; Chos-'phel 1997; and Le'u kre jun [Liu Zhiqun] 1998. Liu Zhiqun was the Chinese director of the Tibet Opera Troupe from 1977 to 1989. Of utmost importance were the comments by Norbu Tsering (Lapala), the lhamo master at the Tibetan Institute of Performing Arts (Dharamsala) and Ama Dachung (Bylakuppe, stepdaughter of Ama Lhagpa), who were actors in the same lhamo troupe until 1960, and by contemporary lhamo actors who have been taught by her. For recordings of her singing, see the HMV references of the Basil Gould mission in the Discography section of the Bibliography.

[33] For the institutions pertaining to the performing arts, I have chosen to employ the English translations as they usually appear on documents published in China, in order not to create terminological confusion. Therefore, I speak of the Tibet Opera Troupe (Bojong Lhamo Tsokpa; Chin. Zangju Tuan); Tibet Song-and-Dance Ensemble (Bojong Lugar Tsokpa; Chin. Xizang Gewu Tuan); Central Minorities' Institute (Chin. Zhongyang Minzu Xueyuan) in Beijing; National Music Conservatory (Chin. Zhongguo Yinyue Xueyuan) in Shanghai; Central Minorities' Performing Arts Troupe (Chin. Zhongyang Minzu Gewu Tuan; Tib. Trungyang Mirig Lugar Tsokpa) in Beijing; and Association of Literary and Art Circles (Chin. Wenlian; Tib. Tsomrig Lhantsok).

[34] It is unclear whether this was a second woman (Le'u kre jun 1988) or if this is a description of her own mother playing the dranyen and singing songs (Chos-'phel 1997). It is interesting to note that female wandering musicians were not a rare ocurrence in the Tsang region at the time (see also Chung Putri's life-story).

Lhamo performer Ama Lhagpa, Lhasa, c. 1990. (Collection Tibet Opera Troupe, Lhasa)

it was not an official state troupe, it held a prominent place vis-à-vis the other lhamo troupes of Tibet. The actors were the only professional, or rather semi-professional, lhamo perfomers in the country. Their only official duty was to perform for the Dalai Lama during the Shoton, the summer lhamo festival organized in Lhasa by and for the Tibetan government. Other troupes were called for the same duty, but the Kyomolung was by far the most popular, being famous for their lively and attractive style of acting, and its actors enjoyed close relationships with the Lhasa jet set. This position did not enhance their low social status, but the Tibetan government bestowed upon them the prerogative to co-opt any potential actor that they met on their wandering tours across Tibet.

In 1913, as the Thirteenth Dalai Lama was back in Lhasa, the Tibetan government ordered the Kyomolung to be reconstituted, and all the scattered performers were gathered. It was on their way back from Nepal that the two Kyomolung actors Drolma Tsering, a.k.a Dronla, and her husband Lobsang, a.k.a. Tsangmo Gyau, stopped in a chang tavern in Lhatse. They spotted the young Lhagpa and thought that this child could become a lhamo actress. They adopted her for one silver crown (*rdo-tshad*)[35] and

35 Currency unit of pre-1959 Tibet: one *rdo-tshad* or one *ṭam-kar* equals fifty silver coins (*dngul-srang*). According to old Tibetans, one could buy at the time, for one *rdo-tshad*,

intended to bring her with them to Lhasa (ibid: 1). As the actors enrolled by the Kyomolung were usually promising young boys, this adoption was probably a way to come to Lhagpa's assistance. Given the poor status of wandering actors, her maternal relatives never tried to find her, and her foster-parents never told Lhagpa about her origin.

Lhagpa was taken to Lhasa on horseback, a journey that must have lasted ten days, and she was immediately incorporated into the life of the troupe. She trained with the famous Kyomolung teacher Migmar Gyaltsen[36] and performed in public from the age of eight, starting with the smallest roles any lhamo beginner would do: the mime of animals, the first song of the fairies (*oṃ maṇi padme hūṃ*) and the children roles, gradually taking more important parts. From the age of fifteen, and for the rest of her life, she was given the main female roles in the plays: Sukyi Nyima, Nangsa, Yindrok Lhamo, Drowa Sangmo and Mande Sangmo. When she was very young, she married Yangden Pao,[37] one of the most striking actors of the troupe, famous for his jokes on the stage and the witty nicknames he made up. When another actor, Tashi (Dondrub) from Sakya, became a member of the troupe, the two soon became lovers. They left the troupe and went to live on their own for one year. They were then taken back by the Kyomolung troupe and they married when Lhagpa was nineteen years old. It is said that, before he met Ama Lhagpa, Tashi had a powerful voice but his performing was not very good, and that it was Ama Lhagpa who trained him privately in singing and dancing. She must have been an excellent mentor since Tashi soon became the teacher (*dge-rgan*, i.e. director) of the troupe. Like most wives of the Kyomolung actors, she performed lhamo with the troupe, except for formal occasions like the Shoton in Lhasa, or at performances in monasteries.

Ama Lhagpa is said to have been particularly succesful on stage, and she was even allowed to perform in front of Reting Rinpoche, then the regent of Tibet (1933–41), from whom she is said to have received good tips, as it was usual that the sponsors of performances tipped their favourite actors. Her voice was said to be extremely clear, and her distinctive glottalizations (*mgrin-khug*) in the lhamo songs were particularly easy

approximately twenty *khal* (i.e. more or less 280 kg) of barley, and one yak cost about two *rdo-tshad*.

[36] For a biography of three famous actors of the Kyomolung troupe see Henrion-Dourcy 2001: entries 'Dvangs-bzang, A-lce'; 'Mig-dmar rgyal-mtshan' and 'Nor-bu tshe-ring'.

[37] Yangden Pao, alternatively called Lenden Pao, was the son of a Chinese soldier *en poste* in Lhasa and a Tibetan woman who acted as a servant in the Kyomolung troupe. His mother tongue was Tibetan and he couldn't speak Chinese at all. Both he and his sister Acha Shilog (her name indicates that she 'came back from the dead' after a serious illness) were prominent lhamo actors in the Kyomolung troupe.

and effortless. She thus shared the wandering lifestyle of the lhamo troupe, and went to perform for mainly aristocratic and monastic sponsors in Kongpo, Tsang, and even Sikkim and Kalimpong. Because she was the teacher's wife, she was sometimes called 'Acha Tashila' (Elder Sister Tashi, from the name of her husband). They had one son, who died of measles. She was invited as a ceremonial beer-server at the Dalai Lama's mother's mansion on two occasions, thanks to her becoming manners and proficiency in singing the lhamo songs. The British mission, under Basil Gould, made in 1943–5 the only recordings of lhamo before 1959 (see Discography). Most of the tracks excerpted from *Drowa Sangmo* and *Sukyi Nyima* are sung by Ama Lhagpa, so there exists a trace of her voice and singing style. Although the Kyomolung troupe did not have much contact with the Chinese at the time, she was apparently called 'the Tibetan Mei Lanfang' by Chinese observers in the 1950s (Le'u kre jun 1998).[38]

The death of her husband Tashi in 1960/1 was the death of the last 'traditional style' teacher of the Kyomolung troupe. That apparently made her so emotional that she was unable to perform. In 1961, after a two-year-break, the once wandering Kyomolung actors were compelled to enter the governmental Tibet Opera Troupe and carry out a full-time job in a communist work unit, alongside Chinese technicians and other Tibetan 'folk-experts' (see section below on Chung Putri). Lhamo stories and acting techniques started to be revised along political lines, but not yet to the far-reaching extent as during the Cultural Revolution. As part of this trimming process, two senior Kyomolung artists were sent at the beginning of the 1960s to Shanghai's Music Conservatory, to 're-educate their voices'. Ama Lhagpa was selected, together with Ama Tsering,[39] the newly appointed teacher of the troupe. He became her third and last husband and died in 1985. They had to be accompanied by a translator. Ama Lhagpa and Ama Tsering were then in their fifties—by lhamo standards old actors on the verge of retirement. The policy of sending young artists to complete their formal education in China was implemented at a later stage. At the end of the 1960s a few teenagers were sent to learn the model operas in Beijing. Compared to the usual case for artists from

38 Mei Lanfang (1894–1961) was one of the most famous actors of Beijing opera (*jingju*) of pre-communist China, who specialized in female roles. See Duchesne 1994.

39 'Ama' is an affectionate nickname that was given to him, probably by his mother. He was born in Drigung, where he was a prominent actor in the local amateur lhamo troupe. After his talent had been noticed he was asked to join the Kyomolung troupe around 1948. He was also known by two nicknames: Ama Trasil 'Ama with Tinkling Jewels [inlaid in his face]' (but this is also a Tibetan corruption of the English 'amethyst'), hinting at the sparkle in his eyes; and Ama Seril 'Ama Yellow and Round' (unknown etymology). He had been trained by Tashi to become his successor as a teacher of the lhamo troupe (see Grongkhyer 1996).

other performing arts work units in Tibet, very few singers from the Tibet Opera Troupe have been sent for musical education in China (none since the 1970s), maybe because of the catastrophe it entailed for Ama Lhagpa. In Shanghai, it was a fashion to exercise and massage the throat vigorously, and Ama Lhagpa recalled bleeding in her larynx (ibid., 4). One day, the two Tibetan singers received a telegram telling them to go back to Tibet immediately. They were required to perform the renewed version of the *Chogyal Norsang* story, which was to be set up for the first time in an abbreviated form, on a stage, with lighting, make-up, scenography, and all the paraphernalia of 'modern' productions. But Ama Lhagpa had totally lost her voice, and she never completely recovered.[40] Not only had she lost vocal power, but she could not get rid of the (by lhamo experts' standards) distasteful tremulations that had appeared in the *sostenuto* parts of the songs.

After the upheavals of the Cultural Revolution, Ama Tsering and Ama Lhagpa were asked to teach the new recruits of the troupe. Although her voice was broken, she had the 'rights of a senior artist' (*sgyu-rtsal-pa rgan-gras kyi thob-thang*) and was given the rank of 'national first level performer' (*rgyal-khab rim-pa dang-po'i 'khrab-ston-pa*).[41] She was also given formal positions, such as Honorary Chairman of the Performing Arts' Association of the TAR (Bojong Dogar Tuntsok Tsandzin Truzhi), and she was made a member of the Chinese Association of Expert Performers, Tibet Branch (Trungo Dogar Khechan Bojong Yanlag Tuntsok). With the old generation of Kyomolung fading away, she was the last remarkable 'holder of the tradition' (*rgyud-'dzin*), and she fulfilled the need for a public image of 'woman, popular and artist', typical of the oppressed masses. Above all, she legitimized the changes that lhamo had gone through since the 1960s. In 1993, she received the first artistic award of the Jomolangma Foundation.

Ama Lhagpa's main ascribed role was thus to mediate past and present: 'She not only advocated a faithful transmission of the knowledge, but also improved the genre, and perfected the art of lhamo...which involved movements on the stage and psychological impersonation' (Le'u kre jun 1998: 118). Interestingly, this role does not appear in her biography written by a Tibetan, when he concludes with her following words:

40 This is not the only occurrence of a Tibetan singer who lost her vocal abilities after being trained in China. This also happened with Lhamo, a Ba Serkhang (Amdo Chabcha) singer, who is now in Switzerland.

41 Work units in the PRC started in the 1980s to classify their workers according to experience and merit into four ranks, most workers falling into second and third ranks. In the Tibet Opera Troupe, Ama Tsering and Ama Lhagpa are the only two artists to have achieved such ranks to this day.

'My greatest regret is that I haven't been able to transmit my knowledge to the younger generation, before I was too old, either in writing or in recording' (Chos-'phel 1997: 4). What is poignant is that, in lhamo, the ascribed emblem of 'tradition' was an old lady with a broken voice. She nevertheless influenced all the younger lhamo professional generation, inside the work unit and at the art school, thereby providing a formal education that radically departed from her own informal experience.

It is difficult to assess how gendered was the precedent that Ama Lhagpa created for lhamo. What we know of pre-1959 lhamo stems mainly from Lhasa accounts, where lhamo was made popular with the official Shoton festival, featuring only male performers. So the idea developed that lhamo was the appanage of men, who played both male and female roles,[42] and indeed the most renowned troupes, except the Kyomolung, were exclusively male. Yet there were small-scale or family-based troupes in villages who did also incorporate actresses, who would sometimes even play the male roles. Ama Lhagpa, for instance, was famous for her impersonation of the prince Chogyal Norsang himself. And some female lhamo lovers from Lhasa also gained enormous popularity just by the quality of their voice, singing lhamo *en dilettante* without ever performing (e.g. Lhadron, Tsenyi Lhamo, Chagtra Ani, Drapchi Yangdzom, Lubug Chime Drolkar and Drungdo). Women were not allowed to play lhamo in monasteries because it was considered improper for them to exhibit bodily movements in front of monks. Neither were they allowed to perform in front of the Dalai Lama during Shoton. There was a danger for them to 'lose their minds' (*sems-pa shor*) and give up their vows. This did not, however, prevent Ama Lhagpa from playing in front of Reting Rinpoche, as we know from her memories, and also in front of the Karmapa and the monks of Sera when they invited Kyomolung lhamo actors to their picnics outside the monastic compounds. Rather than pioneering the advent of women on a lhamo stage, Ama Lhagpa initiated the widespread professional performance of women taking up female roles. From her time onwards, many women became professional performers, and now they also became state workers, with a salary and status equal to men's, according to the gender policy prevalent in China at the time. Ama Lhagpa had experience, respectability and credibility, and she became the most celebrated actress in post-1959 Tibet.

We may wonder how men enacted female roles before that period. Rather than having recourse to make-up[43] or to psychological impersonation,

42 For a literary analysis of the image of women in the lhamo plays see Chayet 1993: 150–3 and Paul 1982: 188–220.

43 Although Richardson (1993: 98) recalls that the heroines played by young men were 'heavily rouged and powdered'.

since this was neither developed nor favoured in the traditional acting technique,[44] the acting technique itself was gendered. A character in a lhamo play is evoked through the two types of artistic language constituting the lhamo technique: the melody and the dance. Each main character has one or a few set melodies that belong to him, and a set way of moving across the stage, especially upon his first appearance. Virtually, there are different melodies and dances for all the characters from all the lhamo plays, which are not interchangeable. Yet they are subdivided into two main genres, at least in the Kyomolung tradition: male (*pho-gdangs*) and female (*mo-gdangs*) melodies, and male (*pho-'khrab*) and female (*mo-'khrab*) dancing. As for melodies, the male way of singing should be louder, more assertive and with an open throat. The initial voice positioning (*skad-gtong*) at the beginning of each song features rougher sounds like 'ööö'. The female way of singing is softer, quicker, and involves squeezing the muscles in the throat. The initial voice positioning features finer sounds like 'êêê'. That is why the feminine roles were usually taken by the young male performers (Tsering 1999: 18–21). As for dancing, the male movements are wide and ample, whereas the female movements involve keeping the limbs close to the body, avoiding raising them too high. The ritual introductory section of lhamo performances features three types of characters, amongst which are the hunters and the fairies, who have specific male and female movements. It is said that 'the female movements of the fairies look like the spinning of wool, and the male movements of the hunters look like the shooting of an arrow: on the right side, the man takes the arrow out from the sheaf, and on the left side, he takes out the bow'.[45] When asked about the typical qualities of a male and a female leading role, it is generally said that boys should be elegant and heroic and girls should be charming and considerate (Zhol-khang 1992: 19); in short, they should have the eight virtues of beauty.[46]

[44] It remains so today for amateur troupes, but not for state-supported troupes. The leading figures can express only minimal expression and feeling (confined to stately gestures), and the lesser figures are allowed freedom and comedy.

[45] Zholkhang Sonam Dargyes, personal communication, quoting a popular saying. On the gendered symbolism of the arrow and the spindle, see the famous article by Karmay 1998: esp. 147–53 on mythology pertaining to marriage.

[46] Zhol-khang (ibid.) writes of the *mdzangs-ma'i yon-tan brgyad*, 'the eight virtues of the learned woman'. This classification is probably of Indian origin (Rakra Tethong and Tashi Tsering, private communication). Allione 1984: 131 lists them together with the five flaws of a woman: 'The five bad qualities of a woman: (i) thinking about other men after marriage, (ii) lack of generosity, (iii) wanting to do what cannot be done, (iv) wanting to do what should not be done, (v) killing her husband. The eight good qualities of a woman: (i) friendliness, (ii) always having male children, (iii) doing what should be done, (iv) ability to do any kind of work, (v) not being jealous of other women, (vi) speaking meaningfully, (vii) having faith in the Dharma, free from wrong views, (viii) even if her husband is not there, she does as he likes.' *Bod rgya* 1987 gives *mdzes-ma'i yon-tan brgyad* ('the eight

Finally, we find important references to women in two key moments of the history of lhamo: first in the legend of origin of the theatrical style, and second in the circumstances of the restart of the Kyomolung troupe at the end of the nineteenth century. Oral tradition ascribes the founding of lhamo in the fifteenth century to Tangtong Gyalpo, a prominent tantric scholar and yogin. As he was trying to collect funds from spectators in order to build iron-chain suspension bridges, he purportedly trained some of his workers to perform a show mixing edifying Buddhist stories with popular songs and dances. The bridge-workers he instructed were, so the story goes, seven young women (more exactly, seven relatives which the oral tradition unwaveringly refers to as 'women'). Unfortunately, the story does not tell us why, at a later stage, most of the performers were male.[47] But they were obviously not all male at the turn of the twentieth century, since the regeneration of the Kyomolung troupe is attributed to a woman, Ache Dangsang. Together with her husband Pema Tenzin, she founded a village lhamo troupe in the vicinity of Lhasa that bore her own name, 'Dangsang Lhamo'. This troupe became so successful that it supplanted what was then the official Kyomolung troupe in the Shoton festival while keeping its name. This troupe brought a more lively style to lhamo, with an active way of singing the songs, and with more joking on the stage. It is this troupe that contributed to the immense popularity of lhamo in Lhasa in the first half of the twentieth century. It became the first (semi-) professional opera troupe of the country, conferring a wandering lifestyle unto the actors. Folk-tradition evokes images of Ache Dangsang's large size, unconventional demeanour, strong personality and facial pilosity. A song was popular in Lhasa at the time:

> [Although he performs as one,] Pema Tenzin is not a king.
> If he was a king, why would he beg for tsampa?

---

virtues of beauty'), which are slightly different from the ones provided by Allione: (1) to never be overcome by the three mental poisons, even without the company of a man (*skyes-pa med kyang nyon-mongs kyi dbang-du mi-'gro-ba*); (2) to feel a heart closeness with her husband (*khyim-thab la snying nye-ba*); (3) to give birth to many children (*bu mang-du btsa'-ba*); (4) to 'keep her body unchanging', i.e. not to give herself to other men (*lus-tshugs thub-pa*); (5) not to talk too much (*smra ba mang po med pa*); (6) to be honest (*sems drang-ba*); (7) to keep affection and friendship for a long time (*phyi thag ring-ba*); (8) to be active and 'to have clean hands', i.e. not to steal anything (*las-la yang zhing-lag-'bras gtsang-ba*). I thank Fernand Meyer for researching for this reference.

47 Tashi Tsering has found a puzzling dictionary entry for the term *a-che lha-mo* (*sic*), which brings a new element into the gender issue of the theatrical style. Sogpo Geshe Chodrak (1898–1972) was a Buriat who came to Tibet as a monk at around the age of twenty-five (he disrobed at fifty) and stayed there for the rest of his life. He compiled a dictionary in the 1940s, where one reads for *a-che lha-mo* the definition 'men disguised as women' (Sog-po 1980, vol. 2: 1160). This proposition is rather uncommon, but it is now impossible to assess the sources or experiences that lead him to such a claim.

[Although she performs as one,] Ache Dansang is not a fairy.
If she was a fairy, why would she have a moustache?[48]

Although composing songs on the conspicuous personalities of Lhasa was very common (e.g. as those composed about the famous lhamo actors Migmar Gyaltsen and Norbu Tsering) I am not aware of any song composed about Ama Lhagpa.

Chung Putri: the folk-singer of Tibet[49]

Chung Putri or 'Little Putri' was born in a poor peasant family in Tong-mon near Lhatse (western Tibet) in 1920,[50] and she died in Lhasa in 1985. Since the 1960s, she has become the most important old-style folk-singer of Tibet. As with Ama Lhagpa, she became an orphan quite young, at the age of seventeen. Since she could not rely on support from any remaining family, she went to Shigatse to live on her own. Here she started to sing and dance folk-songs to earn her living. It seems that semi-professional musicians in pre-1959 Tibet were at first resourceless beggars. Such musical beggars[51] were spread all over central Tibet, but especially in the Tsang region, where they wandered with their lutes, sometimes in small families. Chung Putri was apparently talented and gifted with 'a very clear voice'. In Shigatse she met Pema (d. 1975), who was a roaming musician from Kongpo Giamda. He was nicknamed lingbu Pema, 'Pema the flute [player]', as he was an excellent instrumentalist: he not only played the flute, but also the lute and the fiddle (*pi-wang*). They married and performed together: she sang, and he played the instruments. They went begging with their daughter across vast distances, from Chamdo to Nepal, including nomad areas. They went to Nagchu, Kongpo, Lhasa, Lhokha, the Tsang province, and also to Kalimpong, India, Sikkim and Bhutan. Chung Putri is said to have tried to learn songs from each of the regions where they travelled, thereby building up a vast repertoire of local folk-songs.[52] She could even sing lhamo, especially the role of Nangsa in

[48] *Padma bstan 'dzin rgyal po yin dvogs med/ rgyal po yin na rtsam pa slong dvogs med/ a lce dvangs bzang lha mo (alt. mkha' 'gro) yin dvogs med/ lha mo yin na kha spu (alt.: a rag) yod dvogs med//* (Source: old lhamo lovers from Lhasa and exile, as well as Bod-ljongs 1980: 8 and Grong-khyer 1995)

[49] Tian Liantao 1996: 1–14. The preface of his book on Tibetan folk-songs summarizes the life-story of Chung Putri, the woman who taught all of these songs to him. For a recording of her singing see Discography.

[50] A Tibetan informant from Lhasa who personally knew Chung Putri reckons that she was born in 1925.

[51] *gzhas-ma 'khyams-po* for a woman, and *gzhas-pa 'khyams-po* for a man.

[52] It is of course impossible to know whether we can give credit to this part of her biography, or whether it was written later to conform to a Chinese ideal of folk-song compilation throughout all the different regions of Tibet by Tibetans themselves.

Folk-singer Chung Putri, Lhasa, c. 1984. (Collection Tibet Opera Troupe, Lhasa)

Nangsa Obum. They learned nangma and toshe in Lhasa, where they settled for a while, although they never performed with the Nangme Kyidug. Her vocal technique was purportedly inspired mainly from the singing style of the Tsang region, but she is said to have mixed several Tibetan traditions.

Chung Putri was apparently already well-known in the 1950s. In 1956 she and her husband joined the Shigatse 'literary and cultural arts team' (*wengong tuan*), at the same time as the young Tseten Drolma, who started her career in this troupe. Their involvement in communist performing arts work units is thus relatively early. In 1957–9, they were sent to teach Tibetan dance at the Beijing Dance Institute,[53] and then at the Central Minorities Institute, Arts Department. They returned to Lhasa in 1960, and became a part of the regional Tibet Song-and-Dance Ensemble and the Tibet Opera Troupe, where they worked as performers and teachers together with Ama Lhagpa. Hu and Cheng (1995: 105–10) mention two other important figures from the emerging folk-scene of the time, Ngawang Khetsun and Tsamten. At the time, there were so few Tibetan teachers alongside the few Chinese teachers in these work units that they taught in both work units, but Chung Putri's main responsibility was as a teacher in the Tibet Opera Troupe. In the Tibet Song-and-Dance Ensemble, Chung Putri's main student was Tseten Drolma.

53 Beijing wudao xueyuan, called 'xuexiao' nowadays.

Some Tibetans reprove Chung Putri for mixing the local songs' styles, or for giving in to the Chinese expressive amplifications of the melodic line of the songs, but she is generally well-considered by Tibetans, as 'she had no choice'. She played an important role in the 'emergency rescue' (Ch. *qiangjin*, Tib. *myur-skyob*) of the folk-songs in Tibet during the relaxation at the beginning of the 1980s: she recorded one cassette of nangma and toshe (see discography) together with Anan and Chushur Yeshe Drolma (two of the label-girls mentioned above). The Chinese musicologist Tian Liantao's compilation of *The Essence of Tibetan Traditional Music* (Tian 1996) is actually his writing down of Chung Putri's remembered repertoire. Other pre-1959 female semi-professional singers, like Anan or Chushur Yeshe Drolma, were also active in the revitalization of traditional songs after the relaxation, but never worked in government work units. Chung Putri is the only one to have been enrolled by the state, probably because the two former singers had a repertoire limited to nangma and toshe, whereas Chung Putri acquired a wider spectrum of songs.

The context in which we have to understand Chung Putri's life trajectory is the state-initiated endeavour to compile, stage and later folklorize the traditional genres of folk-songs. She lived through the first wave of this movement, when singers became professionals for the first time, when the songs and dances were polished on a stage with lights, costumes and choreography, and performers sent to China. It is unknown how she manoeuvred in the sinicization of the songs. Chung Putri also filled an important gap. She epitomized the culture of the frustrated masses in a communist ideology and was 'elevated' from the status of beggar to that of a respectable artist working for the society. The fact that she was a woman was positive for her as it was for Ama Lhagpa, since Maoism regarded women as an oppressed category that required emancipation. But, most importantly, in the relaxation period at the beginning of the 1980s, she was part of the polemic about who was the legitimate holder of the Tibetan musical tradition. What was the 'tradition' like, anyway? On the one hand, musicians like Chung Putri, Anan and their following (see discography), represented a glorification of the 'popular' culture, the spirit of the illiterate masses. On the other hand, musicians of the arts department of Tibet University, like Zholkhang Sonam Dargye and others, coming from an aristocratic and literate background, who had an extensive experience in the Nangme Kyidug or the gar troupe before 1959, but disappeared from the public eye for twenty years, came with their own interpretation of the same songs, with a different speed, different lyrics and a different emotional tonality altogether. The intense discussion between Tibetans from Tibet and from exile on cultural authenticity and transmission legitimacy is notorious, but it overlooks internal dissent within Tibet itself.

Yumen: archiving the Gesar epic in research offices[54]

Yumen's story sheds light on a different facet of the governmental 'emergency rescue' project, that of the Gesar epic, which is 'one of the [Chinese] state's key social sciences project',[55] with specialized offices, full-time researchers in Tibet and in mainland China, and various (inter)national conferences. There are roughly speaking two kinds of bards (*sgrung-mkhan*). First, those who have learnt the epic through listening to another bard (*thos-sgrung*), or sometimes by reading the printed text of the epic. They are by far the most numerous, and it is through them that episodes of the epic have reached all the Tibetan regions. Second, those, mostly illiterate, who receive the text through spiritual revelation, in a trance (*'babs-sgrung*). Yumen, who is today the most celebrated Tibetan bard alive, is held to be a representative of the latter, which is the most valued type of epic narration in Tibet. These 'inspired' singers generally come from pastoral areas in Changtang, Kham and in the Golok region, thereby addressing a totally different part of the Tibetan civilization from what has been evoked until now. Nomadic culture is deeply imbued with the Gesar epic: personal names and environmental features constantly refer to Gesar's mythology, atmosphere and characters; rocks in the mountains are held to be Gesar's saddle, drum, drumstick, bow, arrow or horse footprint. His concubine is said to be born in a place near where Yumen was born. Therefore, these 'inspired' singers all come from areas where the epic is cognitively very alive.

It is difficult to know whether there were many, if any, female bards before 1959. Yang Enhong (1995), out of one hundred epic narrators surveyed in the 1980s, has written twenty-six life stories of 'inspired' Gesar bards, in which two women are included: one is Yumen and the other is 'Zhuoma Lancuo' (Drolma Lhamtso?) from Derge in Kham (Yang 1995:

54 Sources: Byams-bzang 1985; Chab-'gag 1993; Giraudon 1999; leaflet of the CD published by Koch (see Discography); Yang 1995, 1999; Rig-'dzin 1999 and gCod-pa 2000. I am extremely grateful to Geoffrey Samuel for generously sharing with me his unpublished translation into English of several chapters of Yang 1995. The chapter devoted to Yumen («Tamen chu zi tongyi pian wotu. Ji yige jiazu de sanwei yiren Yumei, Luoda, Quzha» ['Singers nurtured by the same land. Three singers from the same clan: Yumen, Lodar, Chodrag'], pp. 158–176) constitutes the longest and most focused account of Yumen's story, as well as that of her father and of her relative, both epic bards. The story of Yumen in gCod-pa 2000 is very close to Yang 1995. I have not been able to interview Yumen.

55 According to China's Tibet website: http://www.tibet-china.org. See also Rig-'dzin 1999: 35 and Yang 1995 who states that the 'rescuing' of the Gesar epic was part of the Chinese national five-year-programmes in the eighties.

349–53). There are also a few bards reading from printed texts mostly in Amdo (Qinghai province), for instance the female bard Nama Dorje (gCod-pa 1992).

Yumen was born in 1957 (Yang 1995; Koch n.d.; and gCod-pa 2000: 117) or 1959 (Byams-bzang 1985: 115 and Giraudon 1999: 82) in a nomadic family from Rongpo in Kham,[56] which has known other bards: her father Lodar was a famous 'inspired' bard, and one of her relatives (Chodrak) started to recite the epic in 1966, a few years before she did.[57] From the available materials at my disposal, Yumen's experience and career offer a stark contrast with those of her father. When Yumen's father was young, the nearby monastery organized a Gesar competition where they called him and another bard for one month. They had to sing separately, with monks writing down their versions and comparing them. Yumen's father won the competition and became a local celebrity. He was invited to the home of the Sog district commissioner (*rdzong-dpon*) to sing for three months and was well-treated and lavishly paid. He sang mostly at home during the night, but also in other places. His audience would give presents in kind. He was also sometimes called by Tibetan officials to come and sing in Lhasa before 1959.

Following a recurrent scheme for the transmission of knowledge to 'inspired' bards, Yumen developed the skill to recite through a spiritual crisis. I compiled the following account of her spiritual initiation from secondary sources.[58] When she was sixteen, she fell asleep while minding the yaks and had a dream where she saw a red-faced demoness coming from a black lake trying to pull her into the water. As she was struggling, a fairy wearing a five-lobed crown came from a white lake to rescue her and to teach her Gesar's heroic deeds to transmit them to all the people of Tibet. A young boy came out of the white lake and together with the fairy he bathed her in the lake. They gave her stones and nine threads of horsemane, and claimed that Yumen now belonged to them. When the fairy disappeared in the white lake, a divine bird came. It took her to the platform of celestial burial and pecked a piece of flesh from her shoulder to offer to the gods. Yumen woke up in pain. After this experience, Yumen was violently ill, mute, or spoke incoherently with a fixed stare. She spent over a month in her bed, and then two months in hospital. Scenes of Gesar and his generals' battles would appear in front of her. There are claims that an incarnate lama from the nearby Rabten Monastery was

[56] It lies now in Sog county, Nagchu prefecture, bordering the Chamdo prefecture.

[57] For these two bards see Byams-bzang 1985: 114–15 and Yang 1995: 158–76.

[58] Yang 1995; Giraudon 1999; Koch n.d.; and gCod-pa 2000: 118–19. See also Gyaco 1988: 102–3 for a short account of Khatse Trapa Ngawang Gyatso's (1906–86) similar experience, at the age of nine.

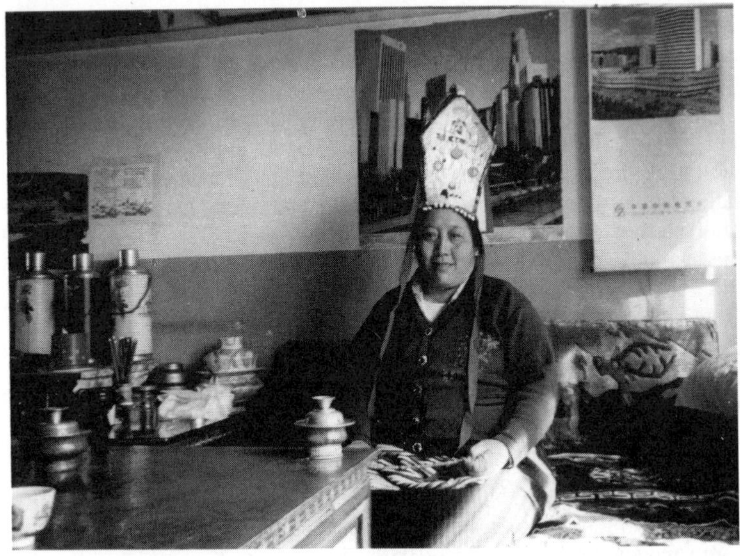

Epic bard Yumen in her home at the Tibet Academy of Social Sciences, Lhasa. (Photo: H. Havnevik 2000)

secretly invited to her bed, to chant scriptures and perform the prescribed ritual for her.[59] This is not verified, however, as the lama was apparently in prison by then. She recovered a few days after his visit and was able to recite the songs of the epic. Her father had a premonition of his death and died soon afterwards.[60] He left her his spectacular bard's hat (*sgrung-zhva*), from which some ornaments and jewels were lost during the Cultural Revolution. This hat plays an important part in the bard's trance, and Yumen's father had never parted from it in his life. Yumen soon gained some fame, and the local people gathered meat, butter, tea or money to invite her to sing.

Yumen first came to Lhasa in 1977 to work in the Tibetan People's Publishing House (Byams-bzang 1985: 115), then she worked for the Tibetan Association of Literary and Art Circles for five years. In 1983, she was employed by the 'TAR Gesar Emergency Rescue Office',[61] where

59 The ritual of 'opening the channels' (*rtsa-sgo phye*). For more on this topic see Hildegard Diemberger's chapter in this volume.

60 Yumen was sixteen years old at the time. Byams-bzang 1985:115 writes that Yumen's father died when she was thirteen.

61 Bo Rangkyong Jongkyi Lingdrung Nyurkyob Zhung Lekhung. It is housed at the Tibetan Academy of Social Sciences. There is a similar office at Tibet University: Bojong Lobdra Chenmoi Gesar Zhung Lekhung.

she probably joined illustrious bards like Drakpa, Samdrub, Tsewang Gyurme and Khatse Trapa Ngawang Gyatso. She lived and worked at Tibet University, until she moved to the Tibet Academy of Social Sciences around 1990, to which she is still attached. After being a herder and an epic bard, Yumen thus became a government employee.[62] This work entails the recording of her reciting more or less an hour a day in front of specialists. None of her recordings have been distributed commercially, contrary to what was the case for other bards of the 1980s, whose cassettes can be found on the Barkor. Yumen's repertoire is enormous, although she is still illiterate.[63] Before each recitation, she does a preparatory ritual, letting her rosary slide through her fingers and then she enters a trance by summoning the gods. She closes her eyes partially to see the scenes. She claims that all the stories are given to her by the gods, conferring unto her a sacred duty, that of propagating the deeds and merits of Gesar to all the people. Yang 1995 reveals the hardships of her life, after an early break-up with her husband, with whom she has had a daughter. She appears at the beginning of the film *The Saltmen of Tibet*, by Koch (1998), of which the CD *12 Treasures* (see Discography) is the soundtrack and most of the tracks feature her singing the epic. She was invited abroad, e.g. to France in 1999 for the *Biennale de la Poésie*, but it never materialized.

I do not have reliable or first-hand information about the fate of Gesar bards since the beginning of the communist regime. I assume that the reciting of the epic, as a manifestation of the 'old' culture of Tibet, underwent a total ban during the Cultural Revolution. Since the 1980s, like bards from Sichuan, Qinghai and Gansu, Yumen has participated in all the major stages of the Gesar 'emergency rescue' project[64] in the TAR. The website of the Chinese government on Tibet (http://www.tibetchina.org) states:

> [Since 3 April 1980 (Rig-'dzin 1999: 38)], concerned organizations were established by the State Minority Nationalities Affairs Commission, the Ministry of

[62] Rig-'dzin 1999: 38 describes the position of Yumen as 'the complete rights of a middle level professional intellectual'.

[63] The available secondary sources estimate in various ways the extent of Yumen's repertoire: according to Geoffrey Samuel personal communication, Yang 1995 writes of 70 episodes, including 18 major drung, 48 minor drung, and a few episodes. Koch n.d. mentions 37 volumes. Rig-'dzin 1999: 44 lists nineteen episodes that Yumen has recorded, which amount to a total of 682 hours, out which seven episodes (212 hours) have been transcribed but not published. gCod-pa 2000: 121–2 lists the thirty episodes that Yumen is able to recite.

[64] For a summary of the chronological phases of the 'emergency rescue' (*myur-skyobs*) of the Gesar epic, the state of publications, recordings and translations, together with an assessment of the repertoire of its most famous singers and a bibliography of the extant articles on the subject, see Rig-'dzin 1999.

Culture, the Chinese Academy of Social Sciences, and the China Folk Artists' Association, as well as related departments in Qinghai, Sichuan, Gansu, and Yunnan provinces and the Tibet, Inner Mongolia, and Xinjiang Uighur autonomous regions, in a bid to complete the massive but far-reaching cultural cause of preserving the Gesar epic … and documenting the great intelligence and spirit of initiation of the masses.

Research offices were set up in Beijing, Chengdu, Lanzhou, Xining and Lhasa. The first 'National Conference on Gesar' was held in Chengdu in April 1980, which enticed the TAR party committee to give some means to its research offices. Forty bards, including Yumen, were singled out in Tibetan-speaking regions. Rig-'dzin (1999: 36) states that the following offices of the TAR have been involved in the Gesar 'emergency rescue' project: the Ministry of Propaganda, the Cultural Affairs Office, the Tibet Publishing House, what was to become Tibet University, the Tibetan Academy of Social Sciences, the Literary and Art Circle, and the *Tibet Daily* newspaper. The three main aims were to document the life-stories of the bards, to research the epic tradition, and to publish their recitations. The bards were given offices in the Tibetan Academy of Social Sciences and Tibet University. The three following National Conferences on Gesar took place in Beijing.

In August 1984, the venue moved to Lhasa, where Yumen participated at the first national performance of Gesar singers.[65] This event was staged at the time and place devoted to the Shoton festival of the past, when lhamo plays were given in the Norbulingka, the summer palace of the Dalai Lama. The 1984 Gesar performances were a huge public success, and the audience gathered en masse in the Norbulingka gardens. In 1986, Yumen was invited to Beijing for the next national Gesar conference. She was also invited to the First International Symposium on Gesar in Chengdu in November 1989, to the second one in Lhasa in 1991 (Karmay 1995: 7),[66] and to the third one in Inner Mongolia in 1993.

Along similar lines as what was shown with Ama Lhagpa for lhamo and with Chung Putri for folk-songs, Yumen's story offers a viewpoint on the involvement of the PRC state in Tibetan performing arts. In the case of the Gesar epic, the state has likewise, since the 1980s, encouraged a folklorization in the form of stage productions, as well as a compilation of what it considers 'oral literature'. But due to the specific literary characteristics of the epic, both in content and in mode of transmission, the 'emergency rescue' of Gesar also displays features of its own.

65 Organized by the TAR party committee, the Ministry of Propaganda, and the Tibetan Academy of Social Sciences.

66 Karmay was present and makes the following comments on Yumen's performance: 'She… represents a younger generation of bards. There is something less professionally authentic about her' (1995: 7).

As for the folklorization process, a difference can be made between, on one hand, theatrical adaptations of excerpts of Gesar stories by professional actors who are not epic bards, and, on the other hand, the recitations of the bards themselves on a stage. The first case has given rise to complex shows involving a combination of singing, dancing and acting, and the use of flamboyant costumes and stage props, as with the Qinghai Performing Arts Troupe in 1980 and 1983, and two small shows of the Lhasa City Performing Arts Troupe.[67] A TV series revolving on Gesar themes was also shot in the 1980s. Another show of the Lhasa City Performing Arts Troupe featured a solo by the famed comedian Tubten,[68] who played the role of a Gesar bard, wearing the bard's hat and describing it, accompanied with an orchestra of instruments in the background. As for the second case, bards have been invited to perform solo with microphones on a stage in front of large audiences, like in 1984 at Norbulingka, during nomads' festivals (the Nagchu horse races, for example) and during the various academic conferences. In the case of Yumen, I am not aware of the yearly amount of her public recitations outside her work duties, and whether she still does any 'old-style' recitation, as when the bards were invited to the house of private sponsors to recite a particular episode in front of a limited audience.

The compilation of the whole Gesar epic is one aspect of the state-initiated project to rehabilitate and write down all the oral folklore in China after the massive destruction during the Cultural Revolution. This has produced voluminous local anthologies of songs, stories, dance descriptions and musical notations. But the Gesar case is different from the other forms of oral folklore compilation. First, the research concerned with the epic has not been confided to local-level compilers, as is the case for folk-songs, but to entrusted Tibetan and Chinese academics holding high profile 'scientific' seminars. Second, the mode of transmission of the epic is not entirely oral. Tibetans had started to write down passages of the epic, at least since the eighteenth century, in manuscript form and block prints. Some episodes were actually composed as a literary creation by important lamas, and then read and recited together with the

[67] The Lhasa troupe created in 1980 a small show based on the 'The war between Khache and Ling' episode (Thub-bstan 1993: 686) and in 1982 another one based on the 'The war between Mon and Ling' episode (ibid.: 688).

[68] Tubten was born in Lhasa in 1939. Educated as a monk in Kundeling monastery in Lhasa, he disrobed to become a professional actor, singer and dancer in 1954. He has been the director of the Lhasa City Performing Arts Troupe for at least the last twenty years. He is very popular in the TAR for his performances mixing songs and acting (*gzhas-ma-gtam*) and his humorous dialogues (*dgod-bro'i gtam-gleng*) with Migmar. See his autobiography in Thub-bstan 1993 and bKra-shis dPal-ldan 1991–2.

other episodes. Thus, the Gesar epic already circulated in a scriptural form in Tibetan society.

The main difference between Gesar and other oral literature collected in Tibet is the very content of the epic, i.e. the fact that it represents a monumental world view, a comprehensive depiction of the cognitive, social, and material aspects of an important part of Tibetan civilization. Since the publication of Gesar epic texts in Lhasa in 1979, the Chinese government has encouraged Tibetans to read their secular literature in order to discourage the demand for religious books. In order to comply with the ideological requirements of the time, Gesar was reframed as a proto-socialist hero breaking the yoke of tyrants and rescuing the downtrodden, instead of the military conqueror or the religious figure he appeared as earlier. Moreover, although the epic also features many Buddhist elements, its lively descriptions of pre-Buddhist beliefs and practices came to epitomize the secular literature of Tibet. Therefore, the widespread publication of Gesar stories has contributed to redefine the terms of Tibet's cultural, if not national, identity. Gesar is now regarded as a paragon of moral virtue and patriotism, 'a symbol of cultural nationalism among the Tibetans, especially in the provinces of Kham and Amdo today' (Karmay 1995: 6; see also Samuel 2002).

This wide diffusion through printing has entailed a progressive disappearance of epic narrators in Tibet. As the older 'inspired' bards have faded away, Yumen has become the most renowned specialized bard alive in the TAR today.[69] She has been given formal recognition and promotions. Her gender has been an important asset. It has given her the same positive discrimination as in the case of Ama Lhagpa and Chung Putri. Yumen holds official positions in the TAR Chinese People's Political Consultative Conference and in the TAR Popular Arts Association (Jong Mangtro Gyutsal Tsokpa). Such privileges Ama Lhagpa and Chung Putri would certainly have been given as well, but the policy of co-opting public figures and artists came into effect after their heydays. It still remains to be seen how much this institutionalized performer is able to manoeuvre within the system.

Tseten Drolma: the golden voice of the Party[70]

Everyone in Tibet knows the name Tseten Drolma. Her story shows the radicalization of what was started with Chung Putri: the ultimate instru-

69 She is the only bard cited in Rig-'dzin 1999: 38, as the older bards have now passed away. Yang 1995 gives details on other bards alive and concludes that, despite the fact that there are a few young 'inspired' bards emerging in the 1990s, the number of bards in Tibet is now very small.

70 Dran shang cun 1983; Caidan Zhuoma 1989; Hu and Cheng 1995; Barnett and Conner

mentalization of songs by the communist party. Tseten Drolma has emotionally and significantly marked a whole generation of Tibetans, if not of Chinese as well. She started by singing all the revolutionary songs of the 1960s and she symbolizes the Tibetan commitment to the Party. Still to this day she performs patriotic songs at high profile public meetings.[71] This political loyalty has granted her a considerable number of honorific positions within Tibet and China, but she is generally considered a 'running dog' (*rgyugs-khyi*), i.e. a collaborator, by Tibetans.[72] She could be termed 'the most famous Tibetan in China', right after the Dalai Lama. Not only is she 'the voice' of the Party, she is also 'the mouthpiece' of the government, since her political duties extend far beyond singing, and make her a kind of representative for the Tibetan people, both in China and abroad. She was trained in China from early on, and sang mostly in Chinese, although her songs were also translated into Tibetan. Nowadays, her CDs are purchased mainly by Chinese customers. Amongst Tibetans, they are the usual gifts that work units distribute to their workers, who usually immediately and dismissively throw them away.

Tseten Drolma was born in May 1937 in Shigatse, the youngest of three daughters in a family of 'serfs, but a little bit well off' (Hu and Cheng 1995: 6). Her mother, a servant in a noble family, and a famed beer vendor (*chang-ma*), was apparently married with four brothers in a polyandrous family. The first one, who died in 1950, was a peasant on a Tashilhunpo estate. The second one, a goldsmith, to whom Tseten Drolma felt particularly close, was fond of lhamo and folk-songs, and she received her musical inclinations and first training from him. The third one was a local small scale trader and mule driver. The last one was a peasant and herded the household livestock, and also taught her many songs. Her musical foundation therefore resides in her family. In 1956 she was enrolled in the

---

1997: 100–1; 223; Barnett in this volume; Li'o tung phan 1995; Liao Dongfan 1995. The source I used most extensively is Hu and Cheng (1995), which is an example of flowery Chinese political eulogy. The book was compiled to commemorate the thirty years since the foundation of TAR. The authors probably did not interview her, and perhaps never even saw her. It is a very formal and superficial account of her life: list of journeys and performances, lists of the lyrics of her songs, political statements she made on tour and printed in newspapers, and history of the Tibetan Song-and-Dance Ensemble. No place is given to her experiences, inner motives and feelings. There does not even seem to be a chronological, let alone thematic, thread through the enumeration of her deeds. Therefore, this portrayal is largely perfunctory.

[71] She sang the song *Kha btags nyi mar 'phul ba* (*Offering a Khata to the Sun*) at the national minority sports games in Lhasa in 1999.

[72] The general assessment is actually not as radical, because Tibetans would also say that she did not have the choice, or that she tries to manoeuvre within permitted limits. See also Barnett in this volume.

Political singer Tsetsen Drolma. (From Daixan 1995: 91)

army's Wengong Dui (literary and cultural arts team) in Shigatse, where she met Chung Putri. She participated in the first competition of the 'Youth Delegation of Tibet to Show Love for the Motherland' (Gyalche Zhonui Tundrok Tsokpa). The success she had by rendering nomads' songs led her to join the Shigatse branch of the 'Tibetan Youth Co-operative Troupe for the Love of the Motherland' (Bojong Gyalche Zhonui Rigne Nyamdrel Tsokpa), comprising six thousand people throughout Tibet. She was then enrolled formally in the Shigatse Arts' Team (Rigtsal Rukhag). The songs of the time mixed Tibetan and socialist images, like the following one:

The Golden Grassland[73]

On the grassland of the eastern mountain, a white camp has been set up.
In a white tent, a golden table is placed.
On the golden table, a jade bowl is put.
The jade bowl ornamented with dragon drawings is full of the milk of the snow-lionness.
This clean and fresh milk is offered to Chairman Mao.

[73] Ch. *Jinse de caoyuan*, Tib. *gSer gyi rtsa thang*.

Tseten Drolma married Namgyal Dorje, an Amdowa from Kokonor lake, who had come to Shigatse as a bodyguard of the Tenth Panchen Lama. Thanks to her early communist commitments, she was sent with her husband in 1957 to the Tibet Public School[74] in Xianyang, about which Robert Barnett and Victoria Conner write (1997: 100): 'The school prepared a large number of cadres and professional technicians for the task of "carrying out democratic reforms and socialist construction" in Tibet.' Tseten Drolma sang a few times at the school celebrations and it was decided that she could fulfil her political duties as a professional singer. She was sent to study (1958–63) in the National Music Conservatory in Shanghai, set up in 1956 by the central government and the Ministry of Culture. She was enrolled in the 'Nationalities' Vocal and Instrumental Class' where she learnt to combine Chinese and Tibetan ways of singing, mixing her teacher Wang Pingsu's teachings with the Tibetan 'gyurkhug' (*'gyur-khug*), the vocal ornamentation held by Tibetans to be the hallmark of their tradition.[75] From this time on, Tseten Drolma has been reputed to have 'a golden voice'. Indeed, she seems to have a remarkable voice. Although it has been trained in the 'Chinese' *bel canto* style, her voice has kept its Tibetan characteristics, and no other singer has managed this combination.

The very first time she attracted national attention was in 1959, when she participated in the celebrations of the tenth anniversary of the founding of the PRC in Beijing. She performed in Zhongnanhai and sang *The Song of the Emancipated Serfs*[76] in front of Mao Zedong, Zhou Enlai and other party and state leaders. This song was to become one of the main songs of the Cultural Revolution in Tibet, and conferred to Tseten Drolma a role she has kept throughout her professional life: that of symbolizing the Tibetan devotion and gratitude to the Party and to China, and of telling again and again about the miseries of pre-1950 feudal life in Tibet. To bear witness to these ideas, she always uses her own life story as a model in her public statements, in an accurate or a reconstituted fashion. In 1960, she participated in the the third meeting of the nation's art workers, where she was the youngest representative, and in 1961 she joined the Communist Party. In 1963 she went to the the former Soviet Union as a singer of a visiting troupe, and in 1964 she joined the chorus of *The East*

[74] Ch. Xizang gongxue, Tib. Bojong Chinyer Lobdra. In September 1965, the name was changed to Tibet Minorities Institute (Ch. Xizang minzu xueyuan, Tib. Bojong Mirig Lobdra).

[75] On the technicalities of Tseten Drolma's voice training and changes in Shanghai see Dran shang cun (1983).

[76] Ch. *Fanshen nongnu ba gechang*, Tib. *Yar langs zhing bran gyis glu dbyangs len*.

is Red (*Dongfang hong*). She sang the following song, which was to become another landmark of the Cultural Revolution in Tibet:

The Brilliance of Chairman Mao[77]

The light of Chairman Mao has reached the snow mountains like the sun from the East.
Since then the Tibetan people have started a life of happiness.
Chairman Mao, people's protecting leader,
We wish for you to live 10,000 years without obstacles.

It is said that Tseten Drolma was equally impressed each of the ten times she met Mao, and her biography is replete with the patriotic statements she alledgedly made at these occasions. She also met Zhou Enlai often and went to his home frequently (Hu and Cheng 1995: 67).[78]

All the propaganda songs of the 1960s were about Mao, but what made Tseten Drolma one of the most popular singers in the whole of China during the 1960s is that she was chosen by Zhu Jian'er,[79] a prominent communist composer, to sing *Love Song for the Party* and *On the Golden Hills of Beijing*. He let her keep her unique voice, and did not force her to adopt the vocal style of the other revolutionary singers. These songs had spread everywhere in China, and that made a name for Tseten Drolma.

On the Golden Hills of Beijing[80]

The light of the golden mountain in Beijing
Shines far and wide in the four directions.
Chairman Mao is the bright golden sun.
What a warmth, what a kindness,
Lighting up the hearts of the emancipated serfs!
We are striding along the broad and happy socialist road.

The first political position she held was as a member of the Fourth National Conference of the CPPCC[81] in 1964. Her unfailing patriotism over the next thirty-five years was to be recompensed by numerous other

77 Ch. *Mao zhuxi de guanghui*, Tib. *Ma'o kru'u zhi'i 'od gser* . She sang it both in Chinese and in Tibetan. It was created by the Chinese PLA arts' team in the 1950s, when they entered the Batang area. They adapted a traditional song from Kham that was played with a *piwang* (fiddle), and put new words to it. Tseten Drolma did a cover version of it, with some coaching from Chung Putri.

78 There are widespread rumours in Tibet that this particular closeness was actually an affair between Zhou Enlai and Tseten Drolma, and they call the singer Chalmo Tseten Drolma ('Tseten Drolma the Whore'). After Zhou Enlai's death, she sang a song entitled *The Children of Tibet miss Zhou Enlai*, including at a few official celebrations.

79 Zhu Jian'er is a Chinese musicologist who studied in Moscow between 1955 and 1960. See *Chime: Journal of the European Foundation for Chinese Music Research*, 12–13 (spring–autumn 1998): 220.

80 Ch. *Beijing de jinshen shang*, Tib. *Pe cing gser gyi ri la.*

81 Chinese People's Political Consultative Conference.

political positions as mentioned below. In 1964 she was sent back to Tibet to join the Tibet Song-and-Dance Ensemble, where she became an icon. She learned more nangma and toshe songs from her teacher Chung Putri, and went to perform for nomads, in army camps and in co-operatives. In 1967, during the Cultural Revolution, she went to Nepal to perform with the China-Tibet Performing Arts Troupe. That was the only performance the troupe did, because the Tibet Song-and-Dance Ensemble, like all the work units in this chaotic period, was disbanded. Tseten Drolma was engaged in a propaganda team called 'Mao Zedong's 23 May Ideas Propaganda Team' (referring to Mao's Yan'an speech on 23 May 1942). She worked on farms and herded livestock, and performed from time to time. The Cultural Revolution was undoubtedly her time of glory. Her songs, mainly in Chinese, but also in Tibetan, were nearly the only ones by a Tibetan singer to be diffused on loudspeakers all over Tibet. Most of her songs were melodically based on Tibetan folk-songs (*gzhas* and *sgor-gzhas*), but sinicized with an expressive change of rhythm and harmonized accompaniments. The themes were invariably praise songs to the Chinese Communist Party, Mao and the People's Liberation Army, describing 'the happy new life of the emancipated serfs and the great victory of building a socialist country'. In 1973 she participated as a representative for Tibet in the Tenth National Representatives' Conference of the communist party in Beijing.

After the Cultural Revolution, and until now, she has been invited as a representative for Tibet to many Chinese official cultural meetings. She was the head of the Tibet Song-and-Dance Ensemble, and led all its tours to China.[82] She was expected not only to sing the Cultural Revolution favourites, but also to render stereotyped patriotic statements. Most of these tours were coupled with an economic mission, as well as a political one: to show the 'positive changes of the peaceful liberation of Tibet'. The 1984 Tianjin tour was aimed at acknowledging the city's financial help in building Lhasa Theatre (Ch. Lasa juyuan), the biggest and most modern venue of Tibet, and the building was also planned to house all the official political meetings. Indeed, just before the twentieth anniversary of the foundation of the TAR, forty-three large-scale aid projects supported by Chinese cities and regions were under way. Other projects were added in 1991 so as to make 'the Sixty-four Aid-projects for TAR'. During the 1994 tour in Macao, two Macao companies (Zhongtian and Hu) invested

[82] In November–December 1980 to Kunming; in May 1984 and May 1987 to Tianjin; in September 1987 to Wuhan; in June 1988 to Hangzhou, organized by the Tibet Developement Fund, with Tibetan performers from TAR, Qinghai, Sichuan and Yunnan; in December 1993 to Shaoshen, the hometown of Mao, to commemorate the centennial of his birth; and in April 1994 to Macao.

RMB 200,000 to found the 'Tseten Drolma Art Foundation' (Tseten Drolmai Gyustal Tebtsa), 'in order to train and support young artists, mainly Tibetans, to spread and develop the national culture and arts' (Hu and Cheng 1995: 176). When Hu and Cheng wrote (ibid.: 130) about Tseten Drolma touring the Chinese cities, she was likened to a bridge easing co-operation between Tibet and China. The authors used similar imagery when they described her touring over thirty countries worldwide with Chinese and Tibetan performing arts troupes and described her songs as a a prayer scarf (*kha-btags*) uniting the whole world (1995: 141).[83] Even abroad, she sang the Cultural Revolution favourites, *On the Golden Hills of Beijing* and *The Song of the Emancipated Serfs*, which apparently delighted the overseas Chinese, but provoked strong opposition from the Tibetan and western audience.[84]

After being the head of the Tibet Song-and-Dance Ensemble, she was promoted to be an important cadre, as deputy director of the TAR Cultural Bureau. But she is still called for important singing performances, and is still often seen on TV, both CCTV from Beijing, and XZTV from Lhasa, as when she was called to Beijing to replace Dadon, who had just defected to exile, for the Chinese New Year show. With the release in 1994 of a revival album of *The East is Red* performance (*Dongfang hong*) of the 1960s, widely purchased throughout China, the three or four songs that she sings on that CD have again strengthened her name all over the Chinese territory.

Tseten Drolma's unflailing patriotic and communist commitments over the last forty years have earned her important political recognition.[85] Her positions have included: member of the national committee of the CPPCC (Beijing), from 1964 until now (4th-8th conferences); vice-chairman of the Tibet CPPCC (since 1987); member of the CCP committee of

[83] Her first performance abroad was in 1963 in the former Soviet Union, followed by Mongolia (1965), Nepal (1967), Romania and Yugoslavia (1976), Sweden, Norway, Finland, Denmark and Iceland (1978, as leader of the Tibet Song-and-Dance Ensemble), the USA (1979, as member of the Chinese Women's Association), Australia (1982, with a delegation of Chinese artists), Congo, Zaire and Cameroon (1984, as leader of a delegation of Chinese artists), the USA and Canada (1992), England, France, Germany and Italy (1994), Austria (1994, where she sang *On the Golden Hills of Beijing*, reportedly bringing the audience to tears), and also Poland, Indonesia, Cambodia and Mexico.

[84] According to Calkowski (1997: 55), when the 'Zaxi Luge Tibetan Dance Group' performed in North America in 1992, western members of the audience came draped in Tibetan flags and were beaten by private security guards hired by the Chinese sponsors of the event. I also heard, but this report is not confirmed, that when she sang *The Brilliance of Chairman Mao* in Canada in 1992, Tibetans in the audience booed her performance and started to sing against her with the original lyrics of the song in Tibetan.

[85] For a good summary and chronology of her titles see Barnett and Conner 1998: 100–1; 223.

the TAR vice-chairman of the Chinese Musicians' Association (since 1978); executive vice-chairman of the Chinese Federation of Literary and Art Circles (since 1988); chairman of the Tibet Federation of Literary and Art Circles; member of the standing committee (1978), deputy (1983), and then presidium (1986) of the National Peoples' Congress (Beijing); permanent member of the TAR People's Congress; and deputy director of the TAR Cultural Bureau (1983 to at least 1993). Though impressive, these positions are nonetheless merely ornamental, as position and power do not coincide in the Chinese political structure.[86] Most public figures, especially famous actors and singers, are given honorary positions,[87] though of a much lesser importance than that of Tseten Drolma. She has also received a few awards: the 'First National-Level Golden Song Prize' in 1989 (the year when this award started); the 'Golden Melody Cup of the Five Continents (of China)' in 1990; and the 'Golden Prize of the Jomolangma Literary and Art Foundation'[88] in 1993. Tseten Dolma has been for twenty years the only celebrated Tibetan female singer working in a governmental work unit, but since the mid-1980s she has been followed by a younger generation of singers, such as Dekyi Metok,[89] from eastern Tibet. She worked as a first class singer in Sichuan and now performs in Lhasa.

[86] 'The Chinese system of elite politics has its own particular characteristics. One of those characteristics is that the two concepts of "power" and "position" are not automatically related…. In the Chinese system, a high position does not necessarily bring with it power, and, similarly, the exercise of power does not require a formal position or office. In Tibet, this distinction is most readily apparent in the case of those … who hold positions in the government or in the CPPCC which entitle them to considerable privileges and social prestige but which do not in practice enable them to participate in the decision-making process' (Shakya 1997: 2). See also the chapter by Barnett in this book on the gyencha (*rgyan-cha*) and on Gao Shizen, a Tibetan dancer of the PLA 18th Corps who later acquired political positions.

[87] Yumen, Tubten (a famed comedian, director of the Lhasa Performing Arts Troupe), and directors of amateur lhamo groups, are also integrated in the (at least) city level CPPCC. Ama Lhagpa and Chung Putri would also have been integrated in these honorific organizations, but the policy of co-opting public figures like the artists was not *en vogue* during their heydays (they were retired and very old ladies when this process started). Other prominent female singers working in governmental work units, but from a younger generation than Tseten Drolma's, have also gained seats in the National People's Congress in Beijing, like Tsamcho Drolma from Lhokha (see Lho-kha 1987: 106) and Dzomyang Drolma (mentioned in Daixan 1995: 101).

[88] 'To help Tibetan culture and arts to flourish, the local [Tibet] Federation of Literary and Art Circles and the Cultural Department [Bureau] have set up the Qomolangma Literary and Art Foundation through Tseten Drolma's proposition and efforts. In August 1993 the foundation held its first awards ceremony, at which Tseten Drolma and other leaders awarded 32 writers and artists and an artists' collective the Qomolangma golden Image Prize, the highest honor for literal [sic] and artistic achievements in the Tibet Autonomous Region' (from China's Tibet website, http://www.tibet-china.org).

[89] See Tshe-rdor (1995) and a brief mention and photograph in Daixan 1995: 101.

Hu and Cheng (1995: 186) provide just a few superficial comments on her private life: 'In her house, she put a Tibetan carpet on a Chinese sofa' and they report that a picture of her holding hands with Zhou Enlai is hanging on the wall (ibid.: 137). Her husband has acted as a secretary for her, keeping all the archives of her journeys and statements. He also took care of their two children, a boy who studied in Xianyang like his parents, and a daughter.

On the whole, Tseten Drolma is given more importance by the Chinese government than by the Tibetans themselves. In her own way, she was also a mediator, between the CCP and the Tibetan people, through her patriotic displays. The significance of her gender is difficult to discern in this political context: for the Chinese, she could have been Mongolian or Uighur, but would it have meant the same if she had been a man? Significantly, she was the only Tibetan singer of this genre of songs during the Cultural Revolution, and she was a woman. She therefore cannot be compared with any male counterpart. It may have been that these political songs were received much more easily when sung by a woman.

Dadon:[90] *the tumultuous search for a Tibetan pop style*

The last two singers to be mentioned here have chosen exile, which adds a new layer onto the question of their political and cultural identity. Dadon can be considered the most important pop singer of the TAR, despite her relatively short career (1987–92).[91] Young Tibetans nowadays will mention her first when asked to name their favourite Tibetan pop singer. Contrary to their neglect of Tseten Drolma, people do talk about Dadon, at least in Lhasa, and show that they relate to her songs and experience. She is considered a model by young female singers like Jamyang Kyi and Dechen Wangmo, and the latter one is nicknamed 'the second Dadon'. The fact that Dadon was a professional singer employed by the Tibet Song-and-Dance Ensemble and that she defected to exile in 1992 constituted a political gesture that added to her fame, but she had already left a significant mark in Tibetan society by then. For sure, Tibetan pop was and is just one part (maybe not even the most prominent, given the importance of the Chinese karaoke scene) of the music played in the TAR. Lhasa, in particular, has a variegated 'soundscape' (Diehl 1997: 122) creating in the streets aural clashes between Chinese political songs, pop songs from the PRC, Taiwan and Hong Kong, Hindi film soundtracks, western classical and rock music and Tibetan 'traditional' tunes,

90 Sources: widespread comments by Tibetans, her website, personal telephone conversations, and *Tibet Press Watch*, May 1993: 3–5.

91 Other important names are the two male singers Jampa Tsering from Lhasa (mid-1980s/mid-1990s) and Yadong from Derge, who made his breakthrough after 1995.

Pop singer Dadon, c. 1988 (cover of her second album).

whether in cassettes, CDs or DVDs (see also Adams 1996). What is often said about Dadon is that she 'looks in front, not behind'. Her story appears as a tentative and experimental path to find a contemporary pop style for Tibet, with many rebounds, as we will see.[92]

Dadon (short for Dawa Drolma) was born in Lhasa around 1968, the elder of two daughters. Both of her parents were major performers in the Tibet Song-and-Dance Ensemble. Her father, a Khampa employed as a singer in the troupe, became a government employee, as manager of the Lhasa Theatre (the Juyuan) where high-level officials held their meetings. Her mother, Tsering Drolkar, was also a singer, a contemporary of Tseten Drolma. Dadon was fairly privileged with her educational opportunities: she was recruited in 1980 to the Central Minorities Institute, Music Department, in Beijing. She followed the same path as her mother,

[92] Lhasa dwellers generally use the Chinese term *liuxing gequ* for 'pop songs', showing the effective penetration of Chinese vocabulary into the Tibetan language. There are nevertheless Tibetan equivalents, such as *dar-bzo che-ba'i gzhas, dar-khyab glu-gzhas*, and *gtong-bde'i glu-gzhas*. For a general commentary on the status of pop songs in Tibet, their effects on and relationship with Tibet's 'traditional' songs, and the importance of TV programmes in this phenomenon, see sMan-grong 1991: 79–80.

who had been sent there herself to learn dancing at about the same age, twenty years earlier. Dadon learned to play the violin and the piano, and she read Chinese musical theory. She did not study singing, but she already excelled when singing at the school celebrations. She graduated in 1985 and went back to Tibet, where she was appointed to play the violin in the Tibet Song-and-Dance Ensemble.

As Dadon found it neither fulfilling nor demanding to play in the Ensemble's orchestra, she started in 1986 to sing Chinese pop songs in karaoke bars, as an extra occupation. Her model, for both style and vocal technique, was the Taiwanese Deng Lijun, widely known as Teresa Teng. This singer was immensely popular all over China at the time, as she was the first pop singer to reach fame in the PRC at the beginning of the 1980s. Coming back from Beijing, Dadon felt that she belonged to a new generation of Tibetans, with new ideas, and she felt a need for a music that the youth could relate to (she calls Tseten Drolma's songs 'old songs'). Hearing a smuggled cassette of a band called Rangzen Shonu (1988) was apparently an eye-opener to her.[93] In 1987, Dadon, with other members of the Tibet Song-and-Dance Ensemble, started to integrate a flavour of Tibetan traditional melodies within a Chinese pop frame (rather than the instrumentalized and sinicized versions of Tibetan folk-songs that existed until then). Her musical style, as it still stands now, even on her American CD, can be called 'Asian pop', with a catchy rhythm on a rhythm box and an electric keyboard. Dadon is technically speaking not the first to attempt a pop style for Tibetan songs,[94] but she is its first professional, public, and significant figure.

More than in melody, it is in lyrics that Dadon's songs have brought the most far-reaching renewal. Moving away from the enthusiastic socialist praise songs (Tseten Drolma, since the 1960s), or stereotyped and folklorized traditional songs (Yeshe Drolma,[95] since the beginning of the

93 *Rang btsan gzhon nu* (Freedom Youth), who published the first cassette of *Modern Tibetan Folk-songs*, were influenced by western rock songs in 1988 (see Diehl 1998: 219).

94 The very first attempt at a 'modern' (rather than pop) style in Tibetan seems to be that of Tibetan students coming back to India after studying agriculture in Norway in the late 1960s, copying what they had seen there, with groovy dance steps and fingers' snapping. The first substantial composition of 'new' songs seem to be that of Tubten Samdrub (Sam), of the Tibetan Institute of Performing Arts (Dharamsala), around 1971–3, with the song *Rig 'dzin dbang mo*, on the LP album *Padma thang*; see Diehl 2000: 208. Tseten Drolma (on the CD mentioned in the discography) and other singers from Tibet did a cover version from this song, thereby indicating a musical bridge across the 'iron curtained mountains'. In Tibet itself, Dadon was not the only one to propose a new type of songs, but she was in the first generation of such singers, and she was very young, very influenced by the Chinese pop scene, and perhaps the most daring of the singers at the time.

95 Yeshe Drolma was born in Chamdo (Kham) around 1960. She studied in the Central

1980s), Dadon's lyrics are new compositions.[96] She uses direct language close to spoken Tibetan, not a hermetic literate language. Her songs articulate themes and symbolic images dear to Tibetans: Buddhist devotion and love for Tibet's environment and majestic beauty. Following the upsurge of romantic love in Chinese pop songs (Ch. *qingyin yue*, 'soft music'), her songs are the first occurrences of intimate feelings (Tib. *nang-gnas ldan-pa'i gzhas*) in Tibetan contemporary music. But the emotional tone of her 'love songs' delves more into sadness, and they are called in Tibetan 'dranlu' (*dran-glu*), which means songs of both 'remembering' and 'missing': missing one's lover, parents or country. These songs gave voice, for the first time since the 1950s, to a feeling of grief amongst Tibetans, emerging after the hardships of the previous twenty years.[97] This is probably the reason why this barely out-of-teens girl became so popular so quickly, among both young and old in Lhasa. There had been a few non-professional singers expressing these themes before, but she was the first professional government employee to have sung these feelings with such a high public profile. She participated in TV shows as well as in national song competitions. Her very first Tibetan pop song has never been recorded on a cassette, but she sang it publicly. It was a sad song about missing Tibet, promising that 'after three or four years (I will come back)'. It actually contained a hidden word play, quoting inconspicuous words from a speech the Dalai Lama had just made in India for Tibetans inside Tibet.[98] The following song is her first 'hit':

My Dondrub Tsering[99]

In the land of high snowy peaks / I have left my beloved Dondrub.
Whenever I remember Dondrub / The freedom of the religious practitioner is discarded.

Minorities Institute in Beijing, and was then enrolled in Beijing's Central Minorities Performing Arts troupe. She preceded Dadon by a few years, as she made her breakthrough at the beginning of the 1980s, but they don't belong to the same repertoire of songs. Dadon's fame revolves mainly around Lhasa, because she comes from that city, but Yeshe Drolma is more famous in other Tibetan regions. Yeshe Drolma sings mostly Tibetan traditional folk-songs formalized and rearranged in a Chinese instrumentation, sometimes even translated into Chinese. She sings in both languages about sightseeing, Himalayan landscapes and Tibetan customs. She has also composed a few songs of her own.

[96] Her albums also feature folk-songs like *Tshe ring lags so.*

[97] This feeling of depression is not limited to music, but is also found in literature (see Dondhup Gyal's experience in Stoddard 1994 and Robin 1998) and in painting (see Gongkar Gyatso's experience, in Harris 1997: 169).

[98] *Lo gsum lo bzhi rjes la* ('after three or four years [I will come back to you]').

[99] *Nga yi don grub tshe ring* (lyrics and music by Penor. From her first cassette album *The Beautiful Melodies of the Young Dadon* [*Zla gzhon snyan dbyangs*]).

Oṃ maṇi padme hūṃ hṛīḥ / My Dondrub Tsering
[Lama and supreme beings in heaven] / Please look down on human beings.
Even though I hold the sacred Dharma in my heart / I never have the chance to meet the supreme beings.
To the poor and the objects of compassion / Don't send obstacles into their lives
In the future, in the *maṇḍala* of karmic connections / Dondrub and I are bound to meet.

This song not only contains the ubiquitous mantra of Avalokiteśvara '*Oṃ maṇi padme hūṃ*', sung for the first time[100] in a pop fashion (as was later copied by the Chinese Dadawa; see below), it also came out right after the September 1987 demonstrations in Lhasa, the first public display of discontent with Chinese rule in Tibet since 1959. Tibetan listeners started to provide, undercover, a second reading of who 'Dondrub' was, namely the exiled Dalai Lama, the emanation of Avalokiteśvara. At that particular time, this song became a momentous expression of frustration, despondency and longing for the exile leader. Though not intended in that way, the following song was also interpreted to express in music the sorrow that fear forbade to express publicly after the demonstrations:

I Sing What is in my Heart[101]
As I sang a sad song, I missed my kind parents [later interpreted as the Dalai Lama].
Whatever I had in my heart, I have sung it with this song.
My girl's heart is full of sadness, this year is the saddest of all.
Not only am I sad, but the birds in the sky are also sad.

Some songs also display a more positive outlook:

Yesterday's Sun[102]
You have gone through a long night / With no cursory word nor sadness
Not even attachment / This world is developing day by day.
[Yesterday's sun has set forever]
But today's sun, that is rising now / Is showing a new smiling face.
You have gone through a long night.
Because the frozen snow has melted / Great happiness and faith arise in you.
Glorious spring is growing now because of natural karma.

100 Technically speaking, it was done for the first time by the Ladakhi singer and Bollywood actor Phonsok Ladakhi on the album *Oṃ Maṇi Padma Hūṃ: In Buddha, His Teachings and His Community, I Take Refuge* (Lyrics by Lama Thupstan Tsewang Balingpa, music by Phonsok Ladakhi, produced by Dorji Tenzen and Om Dojudwhia), *c.* 1984. This Ladakhi music was not known in Tibet, and Dadon had not heard it.

101 *Sems don gzhas nas btang yod* (lyrics and music by Penor. From Dadon's first cassette album *The Beautiful Melodies of the Young Dadon* [*Zla gzhon snyan dbyangs*]).

102 *bZhud pa'i nyi ma* (lyrics and music by Monlam Dorje). From her first album (see previous footnote).

Yesterday's sun has set forever
[But today's sun, that is rising now / Is showing a new smiling face].

Since the purpose of karaoke bars was enjoyment, Dadon sang (mostly) Chinese light songs at night, and she did this in order to train her voice. She also sang with her mother. But these melancholic songs were recorded on cassettes and sold to the general public. Because it was the first time the authorities found such songs on the market, the censors were caught off-guard. But after her first album, all the lyrics writers were asked to first seek approval from the regional Cultural Affairs Bureau.[103]

As there started to be too much political stirring in her private life, she decided to leave Tibet for a while and went again to China. She paid the fees herself for refresher courses in vocal music for one year (1988–9), at the Beijing Minorities Institute. She also went to Shanghai's Music Conservatory for a while. Her vocal technique changed to some extent after this training, but she resumed with the content of her songs when she went back to Tibet. Between 1988 and 1990, she participated in three national contemporary song contests, broadcasted on CCTV to the whole of China. Each time, she sang both in Chinese and in Tibetan, and she ranked among the first ones. The most important breakthrough was in 1990, when she paid for her own participation in a national CCTV contest in Beijing. Tibet's regional Cultural Affairs Bureau did not select her, but she won important recognition in China. She subsequently recorded albums to be distributed in the whole of China. She says this success increased awareness about Tibet among the Chinese audience. She was the first Tibetan singer to win such national-level awards in her category of songs, offering to the Chinese a change from the committed and patriotic Tseten Drolma, the only reference to Tibet available at the time. 'Not only was I able to tell [the Chinese] that we Tibetans are not incapable as they think but I was also very proud to [be] able to fulfill the void for my people on the Chinese stage for singing…Hence, most Chinese and Tibetan people know that I am one of the good singers from the high land' (*Tibet Press Watch* 1993: 5). The following song is a Lhasa favourite. It features once again a *double entendre* of who her 'parents' stand for, but that was a later interpretation by Tibetan listeners:

Beloved Country[104]

My beloved country / Happy divine Lhasa,
Whenever I see the Kyichu river in Lhasa / I remember the faces of my parents.
Ah, Lhasa, happy country.

103 Ch. *Hong hua thing*, Tib. *Rig gnas thing*.

104 *brTse ba'i pha yul* (lyrics by Sonam Tsering, music by Dorje. From Dadon's second cassette album *My Beloved Country* [*gCes pa'i pha yul*].

Whenever I see the Kyichu river in Lhasa / I remember the faces of my parents.
The faces of my parents / is like the bright and clear moon.
Missing my coutry / is like missing my compassionate parents.
If only I could repay / the kindness of my parents.
I offer all my prayers and wishes to you forever.
Please see to it / that my hopes come true.

In this period, and as was the case for China, television seems to have played an instrumental role in spreading the pop style in Tibet (see sMan-grong 1991: 80). Nearly all of her songs are tributes to the typical beauty of the Tibetan surroundings, as most Tibetan songs are anyway, but some of her songs were tinted with an 'extra touch' of pride, of a distinct cultural identity. She did a famous cover version of *The Blue Lake*, a song composed in Amdo on a poem by the *enfant terrible* of Tibetan literature, Dondrub Gyal:[105]

The Blue Lake (Kokonor)[106]

E-ma [How amazing!]
The Blue Lake is the prestige of [our] nationality and the honour of the motherland.
When it is rippled by blue waves, the ducks are delighted.
When the Blue Lake is frozen at the edges, the ducks are depressed.
E-ma, you are a witness to [our] history and a hope for [our] nationality.
You are the truth of happiness and the hope for the future.
E-ma, the Blue Lake is the happiness of the fatherland and the protector of [our] nationality.
When the Blue Lake is petrified with ice, the golden-eyed-fish dissolve in the lake.
When the ice melts at the edges of the Blue Lake, the lucky sheep start to delight.
E-ma, you are happiness for the present and hope for the future.
You are the owner of the destructible world and the prestige of the fatherland.

She did another cover version, which looks quite daring if we do not know that it is actually a song by Deng Lijun, which she translated into Tibetan. As the lyrics were attributed to a Chinese writer, she was not under suspicion, but she nevertheless replaced the original 'Huanghe' (Yellow River) of the first line with the Tibetan 'Tsangpo' (Brahmaputra):

Dragon[107]

The water we drink is the the water of the timeless Tsangpo.
The roads we walk on are the remains of the roads hollowed out by the hands of our forefathers.

105 On Dondrub Gyal and his crucial importance for contemporary Tibetan literature see Stoddard 1994; Bhum 1995; and Robin 1998.

106 *mTsho sgnon po* (lyrics by Dondrub Gyal, music by Makye Chopa Tar). From her cassette album *My Beloved Country*. She rearranged this song on her American CD.

107 *'Brug* (song by Deng Lijun, translated into Tibetan by Dadon). From her cassette album *My beloved country*.

The prestige of one thousand generations is maintained by wandering after leaving home,
When we look at the instructions left by our ancestors, tears are shed easily.
We can tolerate misery, but not bend our heads down.
Hardships have erased any vestige of magnificence on the past life that crumbled into dust,
Hardships have made [us] yearn to look outward every year we live.
The time when the eternal big turquoise dragon is dragged from his sleep
Coincides with our time right now.
Dragons, shoot off to the heavens whilst shouting a vigorous call!

On the whole, Dadon did not write her songs herself, as the roles of lyricist, composer, singer and stage director are very often separate in the Chinese performing arts work units. The names of the lyricists and composers that appear most frequently on her cassettes' cover are: Penor, Monlam Dorje, Ma-a-lu, So-ma-ni (two Tibetan Muslims) and Peljor, all of them employed by the Tibet Song-and-Dance Ensemble. So, this new musical trend did not develop outside the governmental system, but within it. These musicians, most of whom have been trained in China, belong to a regional level work unit, and the recordings were made and produced within the governmental Tibet Audio Publishing House (Bojong Dranyen Pardrun Khang).[108] Even after her escape the lyrics of the new songs were published in Lhasa literary magazines such as *Tibetan Literature*.[109] This bears testimony to the political climate of the end of 1980s: the nascent Tibetan pop, of which Dadon was the main and promising icon, found itself at a historical confluence of two requirements: the Chinese state's policy on nationalities, and the Tibetan surge for expressing an identity of their own in a relatively liberal period. On one hand, Tibet had to appear modern: it fulfilled the government's need for a token cultural and material advancement in its minority areas, and so the new pop songs, which on a superficial level were the same as everywhere in China, were seen as a progressive trend in 'backward' Tibetan society. On the other hand, whilst trying to express a distinctive Tibetan character, the singers could not afford to hit frontally the political line of the regime, hence *double entendre* was often the recourse. But it would be misleading to see in Dadon (or any singer, she argues) a political singer:

'By then I had no idea that what I was doing was political. I was just doing things spontaneously, without asking myself many questions. If you want to move other people, you have to sing from your heart. Express the feelings and speak the truth.

[108] Although most of contemporary pop in Tibet seems to be organized within governmental work units (Tibet Song-and-Dance Ensemble, Tibet Opera Troupe, Lhasa City Performing Arts Troupe), there are some autonomous, sometimes undercover productions of traditional songs recorded on house recorders and sold on the Barkhor.

[109] See Bibliography. The lyrics for the three albums of Dadon were published in *Bod kyi rtsom rig sgyu rtsal* 1993–4 (82–5); 1993–5 (104–8); and 1993–6 (77–81).

I always say that I don't know anything about politics. I say things as I feel, like any regular Tibetan.'[110]

Tibetanness was most visibly expressed in the Tibetan language of the songs (although Dadon also sang many songs in Chinese) and in the Tibetan dress worn on stage, for the TV, and on cassette covers (Dadon is always pictured in chuba, and so is Tseten Drolma after the 1980s). This contrasts with the Chinese pop scene, where the singers, very much according to American models, appear either with hardly any clothes on, or with blue jeans and sun-glasses.

Dadon's songs were spread mainly through cassettes and TV shows, but there were also concerts with the Tibet Song-and-Dance Ensemble. Due to her reputation, although we can by no means talk of a 'star-system' in Tibet, she was called to sing some solo songs in the Ensemble performances.[111] Some people saw her as groomed by the government, from a very young age, to express the new ideological reframing of the minorities by the state, and she did express the momentary convergence of two diametrically opposed interests: that of the Chinese state and that of the Tibetan people. But given that she actually paid herself for her vocal training and for her TV pop competitions, it was only later that she became acknowledged and used by the government. Her experiments were first tolerated by the government, but afterwards she was treated and regarded as a prominent figure by the Chinese. Involvement in the pop scene did bring substantial profits to these musicians, but no professional recognition: she was still officially considered a low-level violin player in the Tibet Ensemble, and she found many administrative hurdles that blocked her way because of the dissident political involvement of some of her entourage. She was invited to perform for official celebrations, such as the important live shows for New Year on CCTV (in 1991 and 1992) in Beijing, a popular program that the whole of China would watch. She subsequently recorded songs in Chinese in the CCTV studios, and even four sets of records for a Japanese company. Thus she became a star in China as well.

Although Dadon was seen in a favourable light by the communist regime, as the years went by, her songs (and lyrics writers) caught more and more of the attention of the authorities, as with this song:

Your Image Appears Stronger and Stronger in my Mind[112]
In front of the Potala / There were three magnificent stupas

110 From my interview with Dadon, 2 October 2000.

111 With economic liberalization, the Tibet Song-and-Dance Ensemble needed to find money by other means than through state support. Dadon was called to sing, as she would draw the crowds, but she was ordered to sing special songs, not the ones recorded in her cassettes, but lighter in content.

112 *Sems la lhang lhang dran byung* (lyrics by Peljor, music by Dawa). From her third cassette album, *Tibet and Myself* (*Gangs ljongs dang nga*).

When the flags were fluttering in the wind / The sound of the bells was so pleasant.
Stupa Drago Kaṇi[113] / Your image appears stronger and stronger in my mind.
All the people (like us) who have faith / need a support [for that] faith.
As an ornament of the beautiful Lhasa / we need Drago Kaṇi.
Stupa Drago Kaṇi / Your image appears stronger and stronger in my mind.
The glittering golden light of the Potala / Drago Kaṇi, the door of the country:
As we entered through that door / we saw the ancient and elegant city.
Stupa Drago Kaṇi / Your image appears stronger and stronger in my mind.
For all of us who have faith / we need a support for our faith.
On the ornament of the beautiful Lhasa / We need the stupa Drago Kaṇi.
Stupa Drago Kaṇi / Your image appears stronger and stronger in my mind.

I will Make the Donations (for it)[114]

Looking down from the Potala / I remember the stupa Drago Kaṇi.
To see no gate for the country / Saddens my heart tremendously.
The stupa Drago Kaṇi / used to be the beautiful ornament of Lhasa.
Please rebuild this stupa / I will make the donations for it.
The warm and pleasant radiance of the sun / warms the heart of the people.
The stupa Drago Kaṇi / used to be the beautiful ornament of Lhasa.
Please rebuild this stupa / I will make the donations for it.[115]

She published six albums between 1987 and 1992,[116] which amounts to about forty songs. As she could not hold her unsteady balance for too long, she escaped to Dharamsala by road in April 1992. She was five months pregnant at the time. The reason she consistently gave for absconding to India was that she started to get into trouble because of her new songs, which apparently did not receive the approval of the Cultural Affairs Bureau any more. Her main aims in India were to get an audience

[113] Drago Kaṇi, 'stupa of the Kaṇi type situated in Drago (a passage way between two hills at the foot of the Potala palace)' (Bod rgya 1987: 7). *Kaṇi* is a technical architectural term for a four-(or two)-passage-way-stupa (*kakṇi sgo-bzhi*) related to the Indian king Kaṇiska (first century BCE). This particular stupa stood at the foot of the Potala palace and marked the entrance into the city of Lhasa. It was destroyed during the Cultural Revolution and rebuilt in the 1990s.

[114] *Zhal 'debs nga ras 'bul chog* (lyrics by Peljor, music by Lobsang Samten, from her third album *Tibet and Myself*).

[115] This stupa was eventually rebuilt.

[116] It is not easy to ascertain a discography for Dadon, as not all the songs she sang are recorded, and she didn't distribute some of her cassettes because of the bad quality of the recordings. Whilst in Beijing for the CCTV competition, she recorded albums in Chinese just for the Chinese market, and also with a Japanese TV company. But, as far as the TAR market is concerned, she published, in chronological order, three albums at Tibet Audio Publishing House, i.e. *Zla gzhon snyan dbyangs* 1–2–3: 1) *The Beautiful Melodies of the Young Dadon* (*Zla gzhon snyan dbyangs*); 2) *My Beloved Country* (*gCes pa'i pha yul*); 3) *Tibet and Myself* (*Gangs ljongs dang nga*). All of these three albums were translated into Chinese, so that makes six in total. I have not been able to ascertain the publication dates for any of these albums.

with the Dalai Lama (and a blessing), and use her voice and fame for the Tibetans instead of the Chinese government. She also had to reframe her discourse of national identity in exile, with overt praise songs for the Dalai Lama.

Dadon had fled an ambivalent situation in Tibet, and she met again with ambiguity in Dharamsala. Her place in the Tibetan exile community was not easy to find, probably due to the ambient conservatism in Dharamsala's cultural self-presentation (see Diehl 1997: 136–9), and to the lack of interest of the exile institutions and community in who she was in Tibet and what her defection could mean in India. On one hand, she was rather wrongly seen as a cultural worker groomed not to displease the Chinese government, so, seen from the exile establishment, a traitor to her own culture. Her vocal technique was dismissed as Chinese. On the other hand, the exile community did not know her enough to understand the significance of her arrival. Her escape to India could have been transformed into a very potent and symbolic defection, but it did not quite work out. She was taken care of by the private office of the Dalai Lama, which tried to let her join TIPA, but she felt uneasy with the other artists' background (in musical education, for example). Her high profile was nevertheless acknowledged at the beginning, as she was asked to sing three times while she was in Dharamsala in 1992: for the Dalai Lama's birthday, at a Central Tibetan Administration staff picnic, and at a Tibetan Children's Village anniversary festival.

Dadon stayed more or less one year in Dharamsala, then moved to Switzerland for three months. She was asked to sing a song for 'A Tribute to Tibet', held in Washington in April 1993. It was a big event, organized by the International Campaign for Tibet, hosted by Harrison Ford, with the Dalai Lama, United States congressmen, businessmen and prominent Tibetan community members. Later on, the Hollywood star Harrison Ford helped her secure an American visa, and she finally settled in the United States, near New York. After the concert, she declared on the Voice of America, to be broadcasted back to Tibet: 'In the future I will endeavour not to waste the great expectations of our great leader, the Dalai Lama, and of my Tibetan brothers and sisters. I will make an extra effort toward my study and to popularize Tibetan pop songs throughout the world.' (*Tibet Press Watch* 1993: 5)

Given the small market for pop in the Tibetan language in the west, her endeavour has been somewhat difficult. While in the United States, she has mainly studied English, and has performed in a theatrical piece *Moon Goddess* with a troupe of high school actors telling her own story. She performed at various Tibetan benefit concerts, the most famous of which was the 1997 Tibet Freedom Concert in Randall Island, where she sang *sKyid ma skyid* ('Happy not Happy'), a song for which she composed the music. It has a definite western rock flavour, both in the melody line and in her voice, which is now low-pitched and rough like singers in the West. This is the third change that her voice has gone through in her search for a Tibetan pop style. But we find again in the lyrics an overall gloominess:

Happy not Happy (excerpt)[117]
… There is no choice but to leave my homeland behind.
My happy place is held by others.
… One sad heart and two sad hearts.
Sorrow both day and night.
There is nothing but sadness.

She published a CD in Tibetan (see Discography) in 1997, featuring this song, a prayer of long life to the Dalai Lama, a nomad's song and two cover versions of her songs from Tibet (*Blue Lake*), but very few people have heard it given the confidential distribution of the album. Her most important appearance is in the Paul Wagner film *Windhorse* (1998), where she acted more or less her own role as a pop singer in Tibet. Whilst in America, she takes care of her two sons and involves herself in the Tibetan cause with a self-declared strong feeling of nationalism.[118] She tours schools and universities to talk about the political situation of Tibet, putting forward a rather secular agenda of human rights (compared with the more spiritual agenda of Yungchen Lhamo; see below). She sees her concerts as opportunities to inform westerners on the hardships Tibetans face back home: the political repression, the massive Chinese demographic input, the children who freeze to death whilst crossing the mountains into exile, and also her distress at not being able to go back to her

[117] English translation given in the CD leaflet; see Discography. The lyrics were composed by Tawo Lobsang Pelden.

[118] Text on the back side of this CD:

How does it feel to have one's country ripped like a carpet from underneath one's feet? To grow up witnessing ancient temples demolished, devout monks and nuns tortured, and one's mother tongue overtaken by the language of an invading nation? I am Tibetan, and I stand for the freedom and independence of my homeland. I sing in Tibetan language, drawing from the rich traditions of my parents' and grandparents' generation [sic]. I sing about what all Tibetans wish for: respect, self-determination, and the freedom to maintain our ancient cultural and spiritual practices, values and beliefs. In Tibet, I used my music as a subversive language to inspire hope and pride in my fellow Tibetans. In 1992, I left Tibet determined to meet our exiled leader, His Holiness the Dalai Lama. I left Tibet so that I could contribute to his efforts to win international support for human rights in Tibet. Now, I am here in the United States, where freedom of speech and religion and political autonomy are taken for granted. I am asking your help, on behalf of all Tibetans. Support my efforts, and together we can end the cultural genocide of my people (1997).

country to meet her relatives. She has projects to continue her work to find a suitable pop sound and image for Tibet, 'not as outdated on the world stage, and more real in feelings' and record new albums, one to be distributed in Tibet itself: 'songs that would give strength to my fellow Tibetans in their resistance to keep their cultural identity, and avoid their giving in to sinicization.'[119] We may wonder whether the Chinese authorities will let her music be distributed. After her escape though, her songs have not been banned in Tibet,[120] but withdrawn from official shops, and available from the black market. Her songs have also been re-recorded with other singers on commercial DVDs.

Dadon's life-story shows the imbrication of at least four issues. First, her aspirations whilst in Tibet: as she sang the first significant songs with a Tibetan flavour after the Cultural Revolution, she navigated carefully within the PRC for a modern, yet Tibetan pop style to be accepted. Second, her defection signalled the impossibility of realizing her aspirations within the PRC. Third, the difficulty of finding, or even creating, a place for her in the exile community. And fourth, her voice changes, which exemplify the difficult search for a modern tone in Tibetan singing. She changed her voice three times: first copying Deng Lijun, then after her vocal training in Beijing, then again on her last American CD.

Yungchen Lhamo: a Tibetan diva for a western audience[121]

Yungchen Lhamo is the first singer introduced here who has not gone through a formal education or employment in Chinese schools and work units. She is also the Tibetan performer who has achieved the most popularity in the West. Drawing a parallel with Dadon is quite tempting: they are both born in Lhasa and escaped to India in the same period, but their backgrounds and trajectories are totally different. Their significance is located at different places and different times: Dadon's heyday was in Tibet in 1987–92, Yungchen Lhamo's rise began in the West in 1995. When Dadon arrived in India, she was an experienced professional, while Yungchen Lhamo built her artistic carreer in exile. One is extremely famous in Tibet, and unknown in the West; the other one is a world music star, but few people are aware of her work inside Tibet and amongst exiles in India.

Their musical repertoires are also quite distinct, but they are both deeply committed to a form of Tibetanness whilst in exile, mediated by a

119 From my interview with Dadon, 8 October 2000.

120 Except her songs *Nga yi don grub tshe ring* and the *Stupa Drago Kaṇi* songs, in the nangma bars of Lhasa after 1996.

121 My sources for this section include personal telephone conversations with Yungchen Lhamo, her two websites and press clippings, Tobden Tsering 1997 and *Bod kyi* 2000.

World music singer Yungchen Lhamo, c. 1995. (press kit photograph)

relationship to the western media. Both see their songs, following the line set by the Dalai Lama, as a means to engender international awareness of Tibet, to let the world know of Tibetans' non-violent struggle to win international recognition, and preserve their cultural traditions. Whereas Dadon's agenda is more secular, both in her lyrics and in her involvement off-stage, Yungchen Lhamo delves more into Buddhist themes: she considers singing as an offering and a spiritual practice. The bulk of her songs, which can be termed 'Buddhist devotional songs', consists of *a cappella* singing of mantras and standard prayers. Following the trend set by Nawang Khechog, she carved out a style that is now widely copied by Tibetan singers addressing western audiences.[122]

[122] Compare, for example, Namgyal Lhamo (Holland) and Yangdu Tso (Belgium). Nawang Khechog is a self-taught musician. Educated in India, he became a monk and

The two crucial elements of the life narrative of Yungchen Lhamo, that uphold both her artistic choices and her present involvement in aid work, are her childhood and her walk over the Himalayas to flee into exile. She was born in Lhasa around 1964, the fourth child in a family of six. Her family was poor, patriotic and strongly Buddhist, keeping a vivid memory that her grandmother had been sent to a labour camp for having helped Tibetan freedom fighters in 1959. Both her parents were monastics who defrocked after the communist takeover. Once again, her musical inclinations are to be found in her family, this time in an exclusively female line. First, it was her grandmother who bestowed upon her the predestined name of Yungchen Lhamo, 'Melodious Goddess', as she thought that this child was 'born with an amazing voice, and that she could help people with her talent'.[123] Second, it was her grandmother and her aunt who transmitted to her an embodied fondness for, and a repertoire of, traditional and religious songs. Yungchen Lhamo did not have access to education at all, as she was sent to work in the fields at the age of five, and then in a wool factory at fourteen. She remembers hardships from that time: little food and a lot of work.

As Yungchen Lhamo's life aspiration was to meet the Dalai Lama, she escaped from Tibet with her boyfriend, just after the 1989 Lhasa demonstrations, in order to receive the exiled leader's blessing. As for the great majority of escapees, her walking journey was difficult, and she arrived in Dharamsala with the feeling of having lost everything—her country, her family, her friends—and of arriving in a place where no help and no contacts were waiting for her. 'The only thing I had with me at the time were the clothes I was wearing and my faith. The only thing one can never lose is one's heart'.[124] This experience of material and affective deprivation was, amongst other things, the reason why she developed a minimalist style of *a cappella* singing.

---

meditated for a while in the Dharamsala mountains. In the early 1980s, he married an Australian woman, and migrated to Australia and eventually to the United States in the mid-1990s. He became quite famous in the New Age scene (he played with Joan Baez, Philip Glass, and Kitaro) by playing the transverse flute and the didgeridoo. Since the late eighties, he has sprinkled his concerts to western crowds with speeches about the inherent Tibetan sense of peace, the importance of compassion and long life prayers for the Dalai Lama (see Norbu 1992 and *World Tibet News* of 12 July 1995; 12 May 1997 and 26 January 2001). Technically speaking, he is the first Tibetan musician to have acquired international fame, with a music geared towards the western market. The album *In a Distant Place* (2000) that he created in collaboration with R. Carlos Nakai, William Eaton, and Will Clipman, mixing Tibetan and native American music, was nominated for a Grammy award in 2001 in the New Age section.

123 Interview with Yungchen Lhamo, 9 August 2000.

124 Ibid.

While in India, from 1992, she toured the Tibetan settlements with a group of ex-political prisoners, to perform shows about the political situation in Tibet. She joined the Tibetan Institute of Performing Arts for some time. In 1993, she moved to Australia with her Australian husband, a musician who became her manager, and had to leave her son born from a first marriage back in Dharamsala. Her singing career started there within the Dharma centre she was attending in Australia, where the quality of her voice was noticed and where she was requested to sing the prayers of the meditation sessions. This eventually led to her first recording in 1995, an *a cappella* singing of prayers with samples of Namgyal monastery monks' chanting in the background: *Tibetan Prayer* (see Discography). This album also contains folksongs and her own compositions. She participated in the Womad[125] festival in Adelaide and, still in 1995, her record won the Australian Record Industry Award (ARIA) for best album of world music. She toured Australia, which was but the start of a (western) world career: she attracted the attention of Peter Gabriel, a famous musician and record company owner, who re-recorded her album under the title *Tibet, Tibet* in 1996, for his Realworld Records company, one of world music's most prominent and widely distributed labels. From then on, she has been on tight performing schedules all over the world, touring solo in sixteen countries like a *diva*. She also participated in numerous high-profile musical events like concerts in the Carnegie Hall, the Lilith Fair (featuring American women singers), the Tibet Freedom Concert (Randall Island, 1997), and the London Royal Festival Hall, each time sharing the spotlight with major celebrities. She performs totally alone on the stage and sustains her audience's attention just with the power of her voice and her presence, an experience that may be rather unsettling for a western audience. One of her regular features is to sing on top of a stretched *OṂ* drone by the audience.

For her concerts, she has always kept her solo performances, but in 1998, for her second CD (*Coming Home*) with Realworld, she departed somewhat from her first minimalist orientation. Here, she experimented with the producer Hector Zazou, mixing her mellifluous vocalizations with computerized sounds, instrumental music, deep-toned monks' chanting and a Tuva singer's throat singing sample, which gave a New Age tinge to her style. Her list of concerts is most impressive, with an average of sixty concerts a year since 1995, and a peak of one hundred concerts in 1999. Her thick press book bears witness to countless interviews with the media. She has thus discovered the paradoxical experience of professional exhilaration, yet entailing some sacrifices in private life: the

125 Womad (World of Music, Art and Dance) is a label that was owned then by Realworld Records and organized international world music tours.

much-coveted (western) world-star lifestyle also has its share of perpetual yet luxurious homelessness, and has led to the separation from her son in India. It is not so much the Chinese state or the government that this last Tibetan singer has had to come to terms with, but the demands of the western record industry.

Yungchen Lhamo's music is introspective, an emotive mix of personal sorrow and spiritual longing. The general tone is again one of melancholy, but contrary to the style of Dadon, it rests more on her *lamentoso* type of melisma than on the lyrics themselves. Her main themes are praises to the Dalai Lama and aspirations for world peace, but also exile and separation from both her family back in Tibet and her son in India:

Heart[126]
Little boy beloved from the bottom of my heart,
Please make prayers that we come together, please make prayers.
If you, Dalai Lama, are a Wish-fulfilling Jewel [one of his titles],
Please make prayers that we will meet.
I feel a little sadness in my heart; Mother and Father are so far away,
A day feels longer than a year.
Ah! Wish fulfilling Jewel; please make prayers that we will meet [again].

She also re-arranged a few traditional songs, but her main style is to compose new melodies on famous mantras and standard Buddhist prayers:

Happiness Is…[127]
oṃ maṇi padme hūṃ
oṃ maṇi padme hūṃ
All the phenomena that are held to be happiness in this world,
are just like a dream that holds no truth [in reality].
May the [meaning of the] sacred Dharma, which is peace and truth,
be achieved soon.
oṃ maṇi padme hūṃ.

Her new songs are imbued with political and Buddhist symbols, but always refer to the root image of the Dalai Lama:

The Three Regions of the Tibetans[128]
In the land of happy Tibet live Tibetan brothers from the three regions.
All of us are from the same parents, the same flesh and bone.
Lama Tenzin Gyatso, your kindness is as vast as the sky.

126 Entitled *Heart* on her second Realworld Records CD, *Coming Home* (1998). The author of the lyrics is not cited, but is probably Yungchen Lhamo herself.

127 Entitled *Happiness Is…* on her second Realworld Records CD, *Coming Home* (1998). Standard Tibetan prayer on a tune composed by Yungchen Lhamo.

128 Entitled *Per rig chog sum* (*Bod rigs chol gsum*) on her second Realworld Records CD, *Coming Home* (1998). Author of lyrics not cited.

In Lhasa, the land of jewels, there are four everlasting seats.[129]
The core of the four seats is the Protector,
Lama Tenzin Gyatso, your achievements are as bright as the shining stars.
In the lotus of the everlasting seats, meditation caves were everywhere [?].
Leader emanating from the assembly, Lama Tenzin Gyatso.
Your kindness will last as long as time will exist.

With the longing for a lost country, a constant reference to the religious way of life of Tibetans, and the Dalai Lama as dominant icon, Yungchen Lhamo wields the three core identity markers of contemporary exile Tibetans (Harris 1997: 160–1). But her approach is personal in that she departs from the singing of religious melodies, and creates her own style, integrating her international experiences in her singing as time goes by. The melodies she composes cannot be called Tibetan, and her voice is not recognized as typical by the Tibetans themselves. '[In Australia] I had to change in some instances the melody and the way I use my voice to inspire an emotion in the people so that they would understand the meaning of my songs.' (T. Tsering 1997: 26). This points to the recurrent and crucial concern amongst Tibetan exiles about the 'Tibetanness', rather than authenticity of the singers' voices. It seems difficult for Tibetans to determine the criteria to ascertain when a voice is or is not Tibetan. There needs to be 'a Tibetan feel', which may rest upon a natural, unforced use of the voice, and a legato in the throat when changing notes (*'gyur-khug*). Anything else is dismissed as Chinese. This discussion actually affects the reputations of all six singers described in this chapter,[130] but has been more prominent for the two last ones, as they are born in the TAR and confronted with exile. Yungchen Lhamo does assume her role as an innovator: 'My singing is totally different from Tibetan traditional singing. It is my creation. But my voice is Tibetan.'[131] Her references to Tibetan Buddhism diverge from Dadon's concerns for a free Tibet and the rooting of a cultural identity different from the Chinese. Her aspiration is less focused and wider: universal peace. She sees her singing as the sharing of an individual and spiritual experience, with the wish that it may benefit everyone. Her minimalist *a cappella* singing is related to the deprivation she felt upon her arrival in India, and to the fact that she considers herself self-made, through the sole power of her faith and her hard work. The imagery of her albums display Buddhist symbols: the mantra *oṃ maṇi*

[129] Either the three seats of Ganden, Sera and Drepung, plus the Jokhang, or the four monasteries located in the four cardinal points of Lhasa: Tsechogling, Tsemonling, Tengyaling and Kundeling.

[130] For example, Choying Drolma is considered to have a traditional and 'typically' Tibetan voice.

[131] Interview with Yungchen Lhamo, 14 August 2000.

padme hūṃ is engraved on the CDs, destined to make listeners earn merit through its rotation. There are also pictures of symbolic ritual accessories widely diffused through Tibet networks in the West: a buddha statue, the wheel of life, the vajra and the bell. Moreover, although she was never a nun, she considers her practice of singing a particular ritual:

'When I sing, I am visualizing that I am making an offering of song to all the highest spiritual beings and, pleased by it, they shower down blessings on everyone who actively listens to the songs. I hope that people can feel it and that the blessings can inspire them to think of their own spirituality—something that many people tend to forget about and ignore. I hope that when people hear my songs they feel inspired—that is the reason why I sing.…This is in our religion. My art is a form of offering. Any art, if it makes people happy, just one or many people, is a form of offering.'[132]

Finally, another of her Buddhist commitments is to seek to bring not only emotional, but also practical benefit to people through her singing. That is why she created the Yungchen Lhamo Foundation in 1999, to use her renown and raise funds for 'the betterment of Tibetan women and their families'. So far, this aid-work has meant sponsering an exile government school (TCV) in Bir, near Dharamsala. Her aims reach further, however, as she wants to sponsor young and poor Tibetan women refugees in education, job training and the arts. She says this enterprise stems from her childhood experiences rather than from an explicit gender discourse regarding the Tibetan community. She believes it is important to train women as teachers and in health care as role models for young girls, 'to establish an infrastructure of informed women teaching and empowering each other, … to foster a school of art where women can develop their artistic potential through traditional and contemporary art forms, …to make sure that no child is forced to work instead of attending school, that no woman is forced to compromise herself to find opportunities to work or study …' (the quotes are from her website; see below).

The last two issues which she attributes to Tibetan Buddhism, that of ritual and that of practical benefit to the community, resonate with the work of another Tibetan female singer, Choying Drolma.[133] She also

132 Interview with Yungchen Lhamo, 14 August 2000.

133 Choying Drolma was born in 1971 in Kathmandu in a family of Khampa refugees. She is a nun in Nagi Gompa (Kathmandu), where she has studied with her main lama Tulku Orgyen Rinpoche. She terms her songs 'religious songs' (mainly *gcod* prayers, mantras, and other prayers). She has recorded three CDs, the first two containing compositions of western musicians on top of her recitation of prayers, which gives a New Age feel to the integrated whole. Her last album presents her *a cappella* ritual recitations, much in the style of monks' recordings like the Gyuto monks, Lama Karta (Belgium) or Lama Gyurme (France). She also appears, as does Yungchen Lhamo, on the CD *Voices of Asian Women* (Singapore).

sings solely for a western audience and is marketed in the same world music and New Age category as Yungchen Lhamo. Choying Drolma entered this scene under much acclaim with her collaboration with the guitarist Steve Tibbets in 1997 (see Discography). She also sings standard Buddhist prayers and mantras, mainly from the 'Cutting' (*gCod*) tradition, which is in itself a complex and profound ritual. In contrast to Yungchen Lhamo, however, she is a nun from a formal monastic background, and she uses traditional tunes transmitted to her by her lama. She considers her performances, carried out with her ritual accessories (drum and bell) whether for CDs or for concerts (fifty concerts in the west in 1999), as meditations in public.

'I think that I was born gifted with a good voice. I always loved singing, it makes me happy, as it does for my listeners. I don't think it is contradictory to the fact that I am a devoted nun. Singing is for me a way to help people. In this way, I can bring support to people.'[134]

As with Yungchen Lhamo, Choying Drolma uses her renown and the benefits of her concerts to implement practical support in community work.[135] She founded the Nuns' Welfare Foundation of Nepal, with a Tibetan nuns' school, Arya Tara school, as her first project. She is strongly critical of Tibetan society as androcentric, privileging the education of males over that of females, and holds education to be the most powerful social tool. Choying Drolma also has her own views about the monastic system of Tibet:

'I am inspired by the work of Mother Teresa. I am practical. I don't think that all the monks and nuns should stay in their monasteries and study all the time. The base of the monastic system is the fundamental relationship between the monastic community and the lay community, which they must help. Nuns are now able to serve the community much more than before. They should be involved in community work like hospitals and teaching. Their role is to inspire people to lead a better life… Tibetans are amazed that a nun like me takes so much responsibility in the world… The most important thing for Tibetans, which makes them approve of my work, is that my melodies are entirely traditional.'[136]

The fact that Yungchen Lhamo performs only for westerners (and in a few Asian countries like Singapore and Japan) entails a particular relationship with both the westerners and the Tibetan exiles. With the

[134] From my interview with Choying Drolma, 14 September 2000.

[135] A similar case of combining concerts and community work can be seen in Japan with Pema Yangjien (*sic*), a Tibetan woman from a nomad family of Sichuan province, who married a Japanese man. Upon settling in Japan, she performed Tibetan songs and dances, lectured about Tibet, and raised funds for building schools back in her homeland. See *World Tibet News*, 24 February 2001.

[136] From my interview with Choying Drolma, 14 September 2000.

westerners, both her musical performances and her media interviews have led her to assume a role of cultural ambassador of Tibet.[137] First, from a musical point of view, she is the earliest major Tibetan singer in the western music industry, so she feels responsible for the whole image of *the* Tibetan 'tradition' of songs, the interest influential producers may subsequently vest in what this 'tradition' has to offer, and the reliability of its artists. She has created a precedent that can possibly launch a fashion, yet her songs are not 'traditionally Tibetan' (she nevertheless argues that her voice is typically Tibetan).

Second, she is called to sing for, and represent, Tibet at various high-profile meetings, like for the Fiftieth Anniversary of the U.N. in 1995, attended by Secretary-General Boutros Boutros-Ghali, and again in 2000 for the U.N. Millennium Peace Summit, and also for numerous international CD compilations. On the stage, like Dadon, she talks about the predicament of Tibet between her songs, but in spiritual more than political terms, delving into compassion and a sense of individual as well as world peace. She sees interviews as means not to talk about herself, but about the situation of all her people. Her political involvement for her country is not so much the content of her songs, but the very fact that she does sing these religious songs, 'because when I was in Tibet, just singing devotional songs meant risking arrest and imprisonment'.[138]

More than the attack of her country, or the repression of human rights and culture (Dadon's current cause), Yungchen Lhamo shows an attachment to a way of life and a religion that are under threat, a divergence which illustrates the inherent Tibetan diglossia 'in negotiating a secular nationalist agenda on the political front, and a religious cultural project on the other hand' (Harris 1997: 161). Just one of her songs explicitly merges Buddhism and a patriotic feeling:

In my Happy Homeland[139]
In my happy homeland, I remember the peaceful freedom,
I remember the heroes of Tibet, their bravery and their courage.
You have sacrificed your life, but the true fruit of justice will ripen.
But the true fruit of justice will ripen. May we meet again and again.
When the enemies tortured [you], you did not bend your mind nor bow your neck.
For the sake of the Buddha's doctrine, and the purpose of universal peace.

137 The official position of TIPA certainly makes it more of a formal cultural and political ambassador than Yungchen Lhamo (see T. Tsering 1999: 14, 18–20), but they do not perform in the same circles of venues, and TIPA has had a more limited impact than Yungchen Lhamo.

138 From my interview with Yungchen Lhamo, 14 August 2000.

139 Entitled *sKyid pa'i pha yul phyogs la* on her first Realworld Records CD, *Tibet, Tibet* (1996). Author of lyrics not cited.

When peaceful freedom will be recovered, we will enjoy peaceful happiness. When we will enjoy peaceful happiness, the heroes [who sacrificed their lives] for peace, will be victorious.

She defines 'being Tibetan' in rather open and experiential terms:

'My grandmother, when she told me to sing Tibetan songs instead of Chinese ones, gave me something really precious: a feeling of being really Tibetan. Being Tibetan doesn't come from words; it is something my grandmother and my mother put inside my heart. Who you are is inside of you .... Whatever I say, the Chinese will say it is politics, although I don't think of myself as a politician. I just speak the truth about the Tibetan situation. Actually, about spirituality and family. This is my message.'[140]

But this ingrained feeling of being Tibetan has led her to make professional decisions with political connotations:

'When I was called to perform in Singapore, they told me that I had to say I was Chinese. I said no, I am not Chinese. Even if a place in the world is special, I would rather not see it than say I am Chinese. Then I performed there and I demanded they say I am Tibetan. My concert was a real success. The media then said that Dadawa was a fake; she's not real Tibetan, but Chinese.[141] In contrast, here is a real Tibetan. This is my work: letting the truth come.... Then some

[140] From my interview with Yungchen Lhamo, 14 August 2000.

[141] 'Dadawa' is a hybrid Sino-Tibetan pseudonym meaning 'Big Moon'. Her real name is Zhu Zheqin and she is Han Chinese, born in Guangzhou in 1971. She studied in Shanghai's Music Conservatory and teamed up with composer / producer / music professor He Xuntian. Her music is sometimes likened to a 'Chinese Enya'. It is the first Chinese-produced computerized music of its kind, and it is apparently Warner Music's first one-million-selling CD in Asia. After having spent a few months in Tibet, she released two albums evoking Tibetan cultural traits: monks' chanting sampling, reference to sky burials, mantras, nomads, monasteries, the Sixth Dalai Lama's love songs... (Dadawa, *Sister Drum*, Ufoco Group, Shanghai, ISRC CN-E02–94–338–00/A.J6, 1994 also released by Warner Music for western countries; Dadawa, *Voices from the Sky*, Ufoco Group, Shanghai, 0630 18768–2, 1997, also realeased by Warner Music for western countries). She did a short tour in the West around 1996, probably cut short by the strong polemic that arose on the ethics and politics behind her music. Tibetan exiles (see Chopathar 1998, especially the bibliography) immediately dismissed her music as a propaganda tool used by Chinese authorities: a mockery of Tibet's sacred traditions, assimilated in a superficial manner by the very government that represses them, to blur the distinction between Tibetan and Chinese culture. 'In fact all the lyrics are a cultural nightmare...; the CD portraits Tibet as unique, mystical, ancient, backward and romantic, but not necessarily a different country' (Tenzin Gelek, cited in *World Tibet News*, 27 February 1996). What Dadawa's dispute signals here is that, due to the political and colonial context of the Chinese takeover in Tibet, any Chinese artistic attempt at being 'inspired by Tibetan mysticism' immediately arouses political suspicion on its authors, rightly or wrongly. Dadawa is quite popular within PRC, and a ballet featuring clichéd images of Tibetan nomads and monks has been created on her first album by the Zhejiang performing arts troupe in 1998, broadcast a few times on national television. On the poetics and politics of Dadawa's music see Upton 2002.

producer in Singapore wanted to do a CD with famous Asian female singers. They wanted to put Dadawa on the same CD as me. I said: "If Dadawa is on, I am not on." Then they took her off. I always have to fight! I don't mind that she is a Chinese singer, but she wears nuns' robes, and even I don't promote myself like that.'[142]

Yungchen Lhamo's international recognition does not affect her ambivalent position in the exile Tibetan community. She is rarely broadcasted on radio programmes for Tibetans like on VOA, RFA or VOT, and her musical style does not emotionally speak to Tibetans. But those who know about her envy what they think is her happy life while touring the world, and resent her for making money from singing religious songs. Keila Diehl (1998: 228–34) has singled out not only problems of social status and money for musical 'artists' in exile, but also, and perhaps most importantly, the impractical consequences of the Buddhist (and socially shared) expectations of extreme personal modesty. These involve the systematic downplay of solo achievements and ambition, the little attention paid to authorship, and the disapproval of any behaviour that appears self-praising. Such expectations may provoke not only a paralysis of individual initiative, but also a conservative rejection of innovative daring individuals. 'Fundamental to this resistance to public exposure is the stigma in Tibetan society of being set apart from the group, whether voluntarily or unvoluntarily' (Diehl 1998: 234). Despite her involvement in community work with the Yungchen Lhamo Foundation, being famous is still not easy, and has put Yungchen Lhamo in a situation of isolation vis-à-vis the society she supposedly represents. This solitude is perhaps another aspect of what Clare Harris (1997: 160) has coined 'struggling with Shangri-la' for the painter Gongkar Gyatso. For Tibetan creators who have gone into exile, the sense of belonging has become problematic: whereas exile feels more like home in spiritual and political terms, it also entails feeling culturally displaced and misunderstood in that very context. This 'Lhasa girl' knows where home is, yet there is no place that feels like 'home'.

The Lhasa Girl[143]

You are the Guide to boundless peace; you are the Leader of world peace
You are the Saviour of all people, the Protector, the Dalai Lama.
My birthplace is Lhasa. I, the Tibetan girl,
Am offering a beautiful garland of little songs.
Please look at them, Leader of All.
In my ordinary body, my mind is happy like a garden of flowers.

142 From my interview with Yungchen Lhamo, 14 August 2000.

143 Entitled *lHa sa bu mo*, from her first Realworld Records CD, *Tibet, Tibet* (1996). Author of lyrics not cited.

This offering of delightful songs [is like the best of flowers], it shines brightly amongst the stars in the sky.
Whether old, young, man or woman, everyone has the same aspiration for happiness.
Everybody should show respect and affection, have modest behaviour and good manners.
In every single place in the world, may there be shows, dances and games to watch.
I make prayers for the glorious peace to come.

Given the geographic (Lhasa-centred), thematic (focused on professional high-profile artists rather than other women who have had less direct impact on Tibetan society) and methodological (not having been able to meet and observe any of these women) limitations of this research, I will not attempt a general assessment of the situation of women in the Tibetan performing arts. Nevertheless, I might raise the following question: what is the significance for these six personalities of being female Tibetan singers? From the outlines of their personal trajectories and looking at what they stand for, the only factor we can find in common is that their vocal talent was a natural gift, and that their musical foundation always lay within their family. Rather than sharing other common features, these women represent different facets of Tibetan singing traditions, and how these fared in the second half of the twentieth century.

Singing always is more than just producing melodious sounds. Music is as much a vehicle for politics as it is for pleasure, as it crosses between the realms of public and private use. More than different aspects of Tibet's singing traditions, these women represent different periods of Tibet's recent history, and we can see how all six women form a tiled historical bridge, from Ama Lhagpa's tipping by Reting Rinpoche to Yungchen Lhamo's websites and jet-lagged world career. The lives of all of them also appear traversed by contradictory tensions stemming from their problematic political positioning. They have been involved willingly or unwillingly in presenting a cultural message, holding a public position in the community, representing their nationality, mediating between past and present, Tibet and China, and Tibet and the West, yet failing to fully be acknowledged by all Tibetans, from both Tibet and Dharamsala. All these life-stories have been caught up in the redefinition of what it means to be Tibetan, both within Tibet and in exile, and in the negotiation of a professional and cultural identity within the new social forces of contemporary Tibet. And what appears specific to the Tibetan context here is the tension between two epochs and the difficult negotiation of modernity. In their own ways, each of these six women has had to come to terms with the same question: how to be at the same time 'modern' and 'Tibetan'?

If, from the available information at my disposal, ethnicity issues have appeared to have precedence over gender issues,[144] I would strongly suggest a more self-focused 'ethnography of personhood', to 'locate [not only] persons in history [but also] history in persons' (Skinner and Holland 1998: 3). Selves are grounded in history and mediated by culture, but, in a constructive view of self, they can mark themselves in history and culture. It would be worthwhile to try and see how these women are both constructed by, and resist dominant discourses. This personal approach may throw light on their struggles to constitute their personal identity, and maybe then their gender would seem a major defining factor. Strikingly, nearly all the songs sung by these women have been written by men. The women I have been able to interview (Dadon and Yungchen Lhamo) have shown some discomfort in stating explicitly how their gender has influenced their lives let alone truly appreciate the connotations of my question. What has appeared salient so far is the role of these women as mediators who, like the pre-1959 ceremonial beer-servers[145] evoked at the beginning of this article, have eased contact between people with discrete charm and grace.

Websites for contemporary Tibetan singers

Choying Drolma: http://www.choying.com
Dadon: http://www.moonsite.com/dadon/
Yungchen Lhamo: http://www.yungchenlhamo.freeuk.com
Yungchen Lhamo: http://www.tibet.org/yungchen/
Also see the Tibetan government in exile's website on «Performing arts worldwide»: http://www.tibet.com/Artist/index.html

144 See for example Tseten Samdup 1994: 20: 'Tibetan women today play a more dynamic role in both the cultural and political activities in the community.... These women see themselves more as political activists than feminists.'

145 My proposition to see a continuity between the contemporary singers and the ceremonial beer-servers finds an echo in the fact that at least Tseten Drolma and Dadon have sung in public 'beer songs' (*chang-gzhas*), typical of the ceremonial beer-servers. But it may also just be a case of singing old favourites to the audience.

THE BODY OF A NUN

NUNHOOD AND GENDER IN CONTEMPORARY AMDO

Charlene E. Makley

THE MARGINALITY OF NUNS

In the intimacy of a conversation among female friends, a nun I was interviewing poignantly portrayed the way local gossip worked to marginalize nuns in the Tibetan community of Labrang:

> Tsomo and I were sitting on her bed in her tiny one-room home, and Karma was standing in the doorway listening. I asked Tsomo if people in Labrang didn't like nuns. She replied:
>
> 'They don't like nuns, you know; the laity here, if a monk is going by, say [here she uses honorific verb forms as a sign of respect], "Ama, a monk went by, take off your hats!" That's how they act. As for nuns, they compare us to Muslims and stray dogs!'[1]

Nuns in the Tibetan Buddhist monastery town of Labrang in south-west Gansu province, China, were widely considered to be interlopers. Thus, Tsomo's analogy here was particularly apt: like the Muslim Chinese who were settling in increasing numbers in town, and the dogs that did not belong to any household but scraped out a living between public spaces and family courtyards, Tibetans in Labrang most generally saw nuns as the embodiment of inappropriate otherness within rapid socio-economic changes.[2] Tsomo's portrayal of lay gossip about nuns encapsulated both the derision from locals that effectively refused and silenced nuns as public and ritual actors, and nuns' private indignation at what they felt was the fundamental injustice of such scornful talk about them.

[1] All personal names that appear in this chapter are pseudonyms.

[2] For the most part, nuns in Labrang steered clear of any public roles, including overt anti-state protest. As a result, they were subject to far less state scrutiny than monks. This contrasted sharply with the situation around Lhasa, where nuns were at the forefront of non-violent protest in the late eighties and early nineties, and the state regularly targeted nunneries for political education, investigation and closure (see Devine 1993).

This chapter focuses on the difficult and ambiguous roles of the burgeoning communities of Buddhist nuns in this town which placed the huge monastery and its monks at the centre of its economic and ritual life under the wary supervision of the Chinese state. Since the reopening of the monastery in the early 1980s, unprecedented numbers of young women went to Labrang to join the three (re)building nunneries there, much to the irritation and disapproval of local Tibetans. I deliberately foreground the nuns' situation here because their very marginality in the Tibetan community, and the processes by which they were constructed as such, so compellingly elucidate the contested core of the community—the gendered boundary between lay households and the monastic community. Drawing on fieldwork conducted among Tibetan nuns, monks and laypeople in Labrang in 1992–6, I demonstrate the ways in which nuns' bodies were the objects of particularly intense contestation and scrutiny because they represented a direct challenge to the gender ideals that structured the community as a whole, at a time when it was under siege by intensifying assimilation pressures.

My approach to gender in the study of Tibetan societies differentiates me from some feminist writers about Tibet who explain social inequities like the low status of Tibetan nuns by cordoning them off from the 'ultimate truths' of a Buddhism actually based on gender equality.[3] This type of move ultimately reproduces discursive boundaries between 'sacred' and 'profane' contexts so salient in studies of Buddhist Tibet as well as in religious studies in general. In practice, such boundaries are often deeply gendered, and, as Ursula King argues, truly considering gender in relation to religion *entails* a view of religion as completely (re)constituted in the everyday workings of social lives (King 1995: 3). Grounding an analysis on this insight then requires a focus not on pre-existing religious 'truths' or 'beliefs' per se, but on how people (including the researcher) work to construct, contest or negotiate them in larger socio-political contexts.

Eschewing a notion of gender as the cultural inscription of 'masculinities' and 'femininities' on a universal binary of male and female-sexed bodies, I draw on theories emphasizing the essential 'performativity' of gender.[4] Thus I focus on the practices through which people (often unconsciously) reiterate or contest gendered subjectivities in relation to particular sex-gender systems, which partially sustain empowered bodies in any social interaction. In this view, then, gender is a not an identity fixed in internal mental states, but a 'surface politics of the body' (Butler 1990: 336). In contrast to analyses of gender relations that treat social

[3] See Klein 1985 and Gross 1993 for paradigmatic examples of such explanations.

[4] See, for example, Butler 1990 and 1993. Also see Epstein and Straub 1991. For an overview of these developments in feminist anthropology see Morris 1995.

actors as already constituted men and women, this approach opens the way to discover the often inharmonious multiplicity of subjectivities with regard to particular notions of sexed bodies. But I demonstrate that a focus on the gendered body as a 'boundary maker' (Zito 1994: 117) between centres of power and the peripheries of the Labrang Tibetan community is a way to discern patterns in the dense cultural politics of everyday life there.

This perspective on the politics of gender performance illuminates the particular significance and social effects of scandalous gossip about nuns in Labrang. Such talk both directly responded to and critically depended on the bodily performance of monasticism as a particular type of gender identity. In fact, the contestations articulated in gossip about nuns were inseparable from those transpiring everyday in the bodily performance of nunhood. For that was where local Tibetans identified and distinguished nuns from monks despite the gender-neutral appearance of their monastic costume, what I refer to as their 'monastic androgyny', at the same time as nuns (silently) insisted on their status as equivalent ritual actors, resisting efforts by locals to erase them as such. The analysis serves to demonstrate that for Tibetans the move to monasticism, especially in recent years, has been most importantly about ritually transformed gendered bodies, not doctrine on paths to Buddhahood or even levels of monastic vows upheld. Ultimately I show that the cultural politics surrounding the nuns' gender ambiguity in contemporary Labrang effectively marginalized them from the ritual and economic life of the town even as they insisted on staying and succeeded in carving out a small ritual niche for themselves.

PRECARIOUS BOUNDARIES: ASCETICISM AND SEXUALITY

In the following paragraphs, I provide a brief history of the particular sex-gender system that developed in Labrang among Tibetans. This section is structured around two Tibetan proverbs well-known in the region. The first goes like this:

> Labrang is the place to worship monk-teachers/
> In the meantime it is the place to look for lovers.[5]

[5] *Bla brang nga bla ma mjal sa red/ de zhor gi rogs pa btsal sa red/* Proverb cited for me by a Tibetan lay women friend in the course of a discussion of sexuality in Labrang. Proverbs (*gtam-dpe*), usually structured in parallelisms that express basic conceptual similarities and oppositions, were a vital part of local Tibetan culture. They are rarely written down (although several collections of 'Tibetan proverbs' have recently been published in Qinghai, Gansu and elsewhere), but are passed along through frequent citation in everyday interactions and in more formal rhetorical exchanges such as comedic duets (*kha-shags*), and speeches.

I cite this proverb to emphasize the extraordinary regional status of Labrang as the site of (seemingly) conflicting gender ideologies. Labrang is a frontier town situated at the very edge of the grassland steppes and the eastern extent of Tibetan settlement in China. Since the founding of the famous Gelug monastery of Labrang Tashi Khyil in the Sang river valley in 1710, Labrang has been both an edge of empires and a powerful centre of religious and political economic life. As a sacred 'power place' or pilgrimage site and seat of the Jamyang Shepa lineage of incarnate lamas, the monastery expanded to house over three thousand monks and its influence encompassed patron villages, nomad tribes and branch monasteries.[6] By the early twentieth century, the tightly integrated religico-political system preserved loyalty to the Buddhist order over regional and even ethnic difference, keeping competing Chinese regimes at bay. As a Gelug monastery, the sacred prestige of its monks and lamas was grounded in an ideal of a particularly strict asceticism relative to other Tibetan Buddhist schools. But Labrang was also a teeming frontier trade town on the eastern extent of Tibetan settlement in China with a culture of open sexuality relative to other, more rural Tibetan regions.

The monastery, as principal landowner and political power in the region, could arbitrate gender by fining monks and laity for transgressions of dress and behaviour when crucial sacred or political boundaries were at issue. But the close juxtaposition of male asceticism with relatively open (hetero)sexuality in Labrang actually encapsulates the (oftentimes hidden) symbiotic relationship between asceticism and sexuality, a key aspect of the gendered culture of the body which runs throughout Tibetan culture.[7] As I describe below, despite discourse to the contrary a relationship of mutual dependence between monasticism and lay life was actually the basis of the sex-gender system that both structured social life in Labrang and created inherent tensions within it.

The second proverb condenses this system down to its ideological core:

> The place where a young monk goes is a monastery/
> The place where a young girl goes is her [new husband's] home.[8]

[6] According to Pu 1990, before 1958, Labrang monastery rented 21,700 square mu (*c.* 3580 acres). The 900 or so households in the surrounding villages were all tenants. Labrang monastery had 36,500 head of sheep in the Xiahe county region, 7,400 head of cattle and 9,540 horses, and rented 5,100 house. Add to that the monastery's business in high interest loans, commercial activities, donations from laity, fundraising by monks, and most capital and property was controlled by Labrang.

[7] Tibetan Buddhism, in its emphasis on tantric forms of yogic practice which crucially utilize sexual metaphors based on a notion of a dichotomy of male and female-sexed bodies, perhaps epitomizes this more than other Buddhist cultures (see Campbell 1996, and Samuel 1993).

[8] *Ban de 'gro sa sgar red/byis mo 'gro sa gnas red/* Proverb collected by Wang Qingshan.

This saying describes ideal gender trajectories of Tibetan men and women for the reproduction of society and religion: the parallel movements of young men to the sacred space of the monastery, and young women to the mundane space of patrilocal marriage. This spatialized gender polarity crucially worked to reproduce the distinction between monastic and household realms. But because monasteries and households relied on each other for economic support and ritual services, this Buddhist-inflected gender polarity reveals a radical predicament at its heart: celibate monasticism posits a polarity of male and female-sexed bodies and requires their separation in a denial of (heterosexual) sexuality,[9] yet it critically depends on their relations for the reproduction of its own numbers and the lay economy which supports it.

In the Labrang region this predicament had particularly difficult consequences for women. The rural economy placed great labour demands on lay households, and with men seen to be responsible for ritual and political economic affairs outside the household, Tibetan women (in both farming and nomad communities) were responsible for the majority of household labour and childrearing. The particularly strong emphasis on male monasticism and the crucial importance of women in the rural economy help explain why, despite a definite shortage of marriageable men, only a tiny minority of young, never-married women, about 80–100, entered monastic life in Labrang before the communist victory in 1949.

The communists brought unprecedented socio-political transformations to the region. The remarkable reach of the communist party-state (CCP), especially during the Maoist years between 1958 and 1978, meant that for the first time in centuries a competing sex-gender system had become ascendant in Labrang. With the forced closure of the monastery

---

See Makley *et al.* 2000. According to Jäschke 1991, the term *ban-de* means a Buddhist priest or practitioner in general. Among Amdo Tibetans in Gansu and Qinghai, the term has taken on the colloquial meaning of 'young male novice' or 'young monk,' a boy (usually aged seven to thirteen years) who has taken the most basic level of vows and resides at a monastery. In Labrang, such boys are referred to as *mu-phrug*.

[9] To date there is very little information on homosexual practice in Tibetan Buddhist monasteries, but some scholars assert that traditional monastic codes singled out heterosexual activity as the paradigmatic form of sexual transgression. For example, Zwilling 1992: 209 argues that the Vinaya (books of monastic discipline) punishes all intentional sexual misconduct with a hierarchy of punishments for monks and nuns, but homosexual practices were considered less grave offences: '...in a certain way homosexuality, not to speak of homoerotic friendship, is not entirely incompatible with the monastic life, in that it presents no temptation for the parties involved to forsake the order to which they are committed, nor does it lead to family encumbrances many must have joined the sangha to escape.' See Goldstein 1964, and Goldstein *et al.* 1997 for accounts of homosexual practices in Tibetan Buddhist monasteries in the Lhasa region during the first half of the twentieth century.

and the organization of households into collectives, Tibetans, as many elders told me, initially experienced these transformations as an extraordinary assault on the very foundation of their social worlds: the integrated system of household and monastery. Importantly, this assault targeted Tibetan women as a pivot between state, household and monastery by urging their 'liberation' through the dissolution of monasteries, marriage reform, and their participation in so-called productive labour. The zenith of CCP regulation was reached during the Cultural Revolution with the state's unprecedented attempt to eradicate the performance of gendered ethnic difference among Tibetans. All Tibetans at that time had to adopt a kind of communist androgyny by wearing the blue-grey unisex Mao suit signifying encompassment by and service to the state.

The recovery period since the death of Mao in the late 1970s brought further transformations at the same time as Tibetans attempted to recuperate traditional practices. With the re-opening of the monastery and the dissolution of the commune system, gender became a crucial site upon which social boundaries were negotiated and newly foregrounded identities were recreated and shored up. The (partial) retreat of CCP regulations had ambiguous effects for women as many Tibetans evinced a resolute conservatism about gender, insisting again on the spatialized gender polarity that relegated women to affairs 'inside' the household (*nang*); and men to those 'outside' the household (*phyi*). And yet, with the decline of monastic power to regulate bodily performance, and the increased influence of state-sponsored feminism among young women who grew up under CCP rule, more unmarried young laywomen than ever before migrated to urban areas seeking jobs. Many such women resisted pressures to get involved in long-term dating relationships and attempted to delay marriage in order to postpone the limitations such relationships entailed for women.[10] Meanwhile, young men in great numbers as well as monks indulged in the amusements of the emerging pleasure market. The traditional commerce in compensated sex with Tibetan women, now construed by the state as a degenerate crime needing eradication, had re-emerged,[11] and ethnic others (including foreign and Han Chinese tourists, and Han and Muslim merchants), as well as state agents, converged on Labrang to pursue oftentimes clashing interests.

10 In addition, a trend toward neolocal marriage in the valley was giving some young women relative freedom from the traditional dominance of the mother-in-law in the household.

11 The most successful women could bring in thousands of yuan a month, especially during festival seasons. This was several times the average salary of a government cadre in town, and it provided them with a large disposal income to buy the accoutrements of modern femininity—cosmetics, jewellery and leather jackets.

THE FOUNDATIONAL NATURE OF SEX

In that tiny mud and straw room on the hill, the wind whipping down the valley past the door, I continued my interview with Tsomo. I had asked her about her marriage eighteen years ago, and she told me how it had been arranged by her parents, how she had not agreed to it, but they had forced her to go live with her new husband. Her husband beat her so badly and often during the five years of their marriage, she told me, that even though she had two young children, she could stand it no longer and decided her only recourse was to become a nun, something she said she had aspired to since girlhood. I asked how she was able to leave, and she said her husband never knew, she just secretly fled and didn't write for two years. No one could do anything about her decision because 'if you become a nun', she said, 'the state and your husband have no recourse.'

In the ferment of these massive transformations in Labrang, Tibetan households and the state both targeted women's bodies, their labour, reproduction and sexualities, as a site for resistance to and regulation of change.[12] Nunhood for young women, as Tsomo so aptly put it, was a space of recourse, albeit a deeply contested one, from both the demands of husband/household and the projects of the state.

Like my nun friends Tsomo and Karma, most nuns were young, and from relatively impoverished farming regions outside Labrang; and unlike Tsomo, most had never been married. According to my estimates, there were about two hundred nuns affiliated with the Labrang nun communities in 1995, at least eighty per cent of whom were under the age of forty. This was over twice the number of nuns reportedly living in Labrang just prior to the communist victory in 1949.[13] By contrast, there were almost eight hundred state-recognized monks in the monastery, not to mention the hundreds of young monks who lived in and around the monastery informally seeking religious teachings there. Most of these young nuns had come to join two separate Gelug nunneries that were

[12] For more detailed discussions on such everyday difficulties for women in China see Makley 1999; Barlow 1994 and Gilmartin 1990.

[13] See *Gannan* 1993: 47, and Geng 1993: 217. My estimated current population of nuns in Labrang is based on numbers given me during interviews with the heads of all three nunneries for both nuns attending assembly and nuns in training, adjusting for the arrivals of new nuns and the larger numbers I arrived at based on my own count. Numbers of nuns reported in books either only include nuns attending assembly, or since there is some confusion about the boundaries of the nunneries, they conflate numbers of some and leave out others. These numbers and my own estimates do not include another class of Tibetan 'nuns': older, post-marriage and menopause women who take basic vows, don robes and devote themselves to worship practices in the last years of their lives in order to ensure a better rebirth. These 'nuns' usually live in households, or become itinerant pilgrims. They are peripheral to the nunneries in town and do not participate in their daily routines and rituals. Thus, they have a very different relationship to the laity.

historically attached to the monastery, as well another Nyingma nunnery newly established there in the late 1970s.[14] During the Cultural Revolution, as with the monastery itself, the two original nunneries were closed. The nuns (numbering about eighty) were forced to wear lay clothes, grow their hair and return to the villages where they were urged to marry. According to Tsomo, the 'best' of such nuns kept their vows and remained nuns 'at heart', until they were able to return to Labrang in the late seventies and revive their communities.[15]

Such elder nuns were the main teachers of nunneries, and they passed down their teachings and traditions of ritual practice. However, a decade and a half after the reinstatement of 'freedom of religious belief' in China, this generation of stalwart elder nuns had gradually dwindled until only a handful of them remained. Thus, without the mentorship of elder nun teachers, many of the young women who went to Labrang in pursuit of traditional education as nuns did not have the historical connection to local Tibetans which would have supported their authority as religious specialists. In addition, partly because of the historical prestige and power of male monasticism in Labrang, and partly because young women growing up in this relatively urbanized trade centre were less likely to be drawn to the disciplined and insular lifestyle of a nun, most Tibetan residents I talked to were adamant that no self-respecting Labrang woman would become a nun.

Indeed, I never met a nun whose natal village was one of those historically attached to the monastery as tenant farmers and ritual patrons (i.e. part of the 'four patron tribes' of Labrang). The closest were several young nuns from a nomadic pastoralist tribe historically under Labrang about twenty-five kilometres north of the town.[16] In contrast to nuns' rural home regions, Labrang had relatively well-funded schools.[17] In

14 According to the Vinaya, nun's communities were always supposed to be under the ultimate direction of monks. In Tibet, many nunneries were attached to monasteries in this way and were constituted by female devotees of a particular lama, who acted as their patron and advocate at the monastery. However, such nunneries, including the ones at Labrang, had great autonomy in the day-to-day running of the community (see Ortner 1983).

15 These nuns initially benefited from the state's desire to make Labrang a model revitalized Tibetan monastery in the early eighties. With the advocacy of the Sixth Gungru Tsang, the only female incarnate lama and now a lay cadre, nun elders were able to secure a small amount of the state funds allocated for rebuilding. This process pitted the nun communities against each other as they vied for precious funding. The oldest nun community was disenfranchised as a result because they had no elder nuns or lama patrons to advocate for them (see Makley 1999 for a more in-depth account of this rebuilding process).

16 One of these young nuns told me that it was embarrassing to be so close to her home region because she was always running into people she knew.

17 Labrang had state-run elementary, middle and high schools divided by ethnicity. It was one of the few places that had a Tibetan high school, supported by the Sixth Jamyang

addition, the valley was increasingly urban. That is, much of the land previously under cultivation had been given over to state and residential development. Many families in villages formerly subject to the monastery were now landless, squeezed by new state demands for property tax and what they perceived as runaway inflation in the marketplace. Thus, daughters were encouraged to seek some education or participate in wage labour in order to ease the burden on families with no avenues for subsistence production or capital for entrepreneurial projects.[18] Whereas in Labrang, the transformed political economic context had opened up some leeway in gender roles for women, nuns I spoke to experienced their rural home regions as places where the reassertion of traditional gender practices most unequivocally disadvantaged women.[19]

The three separate nunneries in Labrang had different histories and relationships with the state, the monastery and lay households. However, a certain gendered politics of the body resulted in the display of an extraordinary antipathy for nunhood in general among Labrang residents, and a studied distance from the nuns regardless of their particular affiliation. In our interview, Tsomo and Karma lamented that it was an especially difficult time to be a nun in Labrang, and they described the derision they often encountered on the streets from laity and young monks alike.[20] In my discussions and interviews with lay Labrangites, most men and women evinced utmost ignorance about the lives of nuns in town, at the same time as they repeated, with gleeful delight or righteous indignation, scandalous rumours that emphasized nuns' bodily transgressions as wilful violations of monastic vows, such as secret

Shepa, where students could learn to read and write Tibetan. Han Chinese students had been enrolled by 1995, however, and teachers included Muslims and Han. Meanwhile many rural regions outside of Labrang still did not have electricity, much less schools. Families who would spare a child for schooling usually chose boys and had to send them to schools in township seats. See Bass 1998.

18 The number of girls in school in Labrang still trailed that of boys, and far fewer girls went on to higher education than boys. In addition, I found that in families where daughters were allowed to be in school, parents, depending on their financial means, often 'adopted' a younger girl, usually a poor relative such as the child of a distant cousin or niece, or hired a maid (Ch. *baomu*) to do all the household labour and take care of any young children.

19 Historically, Tibetan women have been most disadvantaged in farming communities relative to women in nomad and urban communities (see Makley 1997).

20 Since young monks and older married women were structurally the categories of people most directly threatened by nuns' presence in town, it is not surprising that nuns most often cited these people as frequent purveyors of derisive gossip about them. Young monks directly competed with nuns for scarce lay support (see below), and older married women were the ones who missed the labour of daughters the most. Indeed, I had close relationships with many such matriarchs in the villages surrounding the monastery, and they were the ones who expressed the most disgust and vituperation when the subject of nuns was raised.

liaisons with laymen and monks.[21] Gossips invariably cited these stories as evidence of nuns' inherently suspect motivations and efficacy as religious specialists. In the course of these and other interactions with lay and monastic Tibetans, it became apparent to me that nuns' bodies, as templates for the display of an ambiguously gendered monastic identity, had taken on new significance for Tibetans living in the transformed political economic context of contemporary Labrang.

In the face of great changes that threatened the foundations of Tibetan social worlds, gossips drew on traditional assumptions about sex attributes to critique and resist nuns' (implicit) claims to have altered their genders by taking on a form of virtuous monastic androgyny. In my many discussions about gender with Tibetans of every stripe, I discovered that when my interlocutors were attempting to explain the spatialized gender polarity that relegated women to 'inside' and men to 'outside' affairs, they frequently appealed to a law of embodied karma. This notion linked the discourses of disparate people from indignant young laywomen and nuns to highly placed monks in the monastery.

Karma (*las*) is the driving mechanism of the basic Buddhist theory of transmigration that, importantly, posits a particular relationship between mind/consciousness and body upon which all paths to Buddhist liberation are based. Mind and body are separate but intimately interconnected: the body acts as a temporary basis (*lus-rten*) for a mind-consciousness that moves from lifetime to lifetime within a gradation of six possible forms of existence, from hell-beings to gods. A consciousness achieves rebirth in better or worse body-forms according to its accumulation of merit or demerit through past deeds. In Buddhist thought, the human body is precious, since it is the only chance in the six types of rebirths to choose, through Buddhist practice, a route out of the endless suffering they entail. But it is also polluting. The body is seen to contain compulsions to attachments and desires that hinder progress on the path. Thus most liberation paths advocate transcending the body by viewing it as empty of any inherent, enduring existence, and seeing it as nothing but a temporary, defiling heap of component parts.[22]

21 However, in recent years due to the perception of an increasing lack of discipline among monks, and perhaps the influence of state propaganda warning against 'charlatan' monks who dupe the masses, the laity in Labrang did express great doubts and suspicions about the motivations of the large numbers of young monks coming to town. But these suspicions were not framed in terms of considerations of the body as they are for nuns; instead they tended to focus on mercenary motives and the selfish seeking of prestige. In addition, scandalous behaviour on the part of monks was not constructed as typical of monkhood in general as it was for nuns.

22 Hence the colloquial Amdo Tibetan term for the body: *phung-po*, lit. 'heap'. Tantric Buddhism, which advocates a quicker path to enlightenment through secret practices

According to this logic, then, the body of a particular rebirth critically influences the capacities of the mind to learn during that lifetime, and therefore ultimately to master the body and materiality in general through ritual power. Significantly, in practice among Tibetans in Labrang and elsewhere, rebirth as a human was fundamentally bifurcated: sex differences were seen to produce different mind-body relationships and to result in basic proclivities that differentiated male versus female abilities to progress on Buddhist paths. To the embarrassment of many of my interlocutors, in the face of the Chinese state and some Buddhist rhetoric claiming the equality of the sexes, the female body was still widely seen to be a lower rebirth, associated with more suffering, and the result of an inadequate accumulation of merit from past lifetimes.[23] Thus in Labrang, gender differences and consequent socio-political inequities were consistently referred to a bottom-line 'time-lapse morality' (Keyes 1986: 87) associated with the body: males have more merit from past lifetimes and thus enjoy great social advantages in this lifetime. In all my discussions about gender with Tibetans, even laywomen and nuns who expressed righteous indignation about their low status would not challenge this.[24]

Importantly, the basis for the lower status of the female body was the assumption that the female body, burdened by such physiological suffering as menstruation and childbirth, more tightly circumscribes the mind than a male body.[25] This corporeal circumscription of women then

---

accessible only to a very small minority of (mostly male) practitioners, is a partial exception to this.

[23] *skye-dman*, lit. 'low birth', is a word, albeit not in wide colloquial use in Labrang, for 'woman'. My Tibetan interlocutors, men and women, were often embarrassed by the stark hierarchy expressed by this term, and women especially objected to its very pejorative connotations, even though most did not challenge the sex-gender hierarchy underlying it, referring instead to the basic difference between men and women as men's greater accumulation of merit. For other discussions of the use of this term among Tibetans see Aziz 1987; Havnevik 1989 and Changngopa forthcoming.

[24] Only one young urban laywoman explicitly challenged this belief to me, and insisted that she, for one, was not going to pray for a male rebirth. The fundamental hierarchy of sexed bodies, I would argue, helps explain the proliferation of still-current cultural practices among Tibetans in Labrang which were concerned with the relative value of sexed bodies—the rituals for women to pray for male rebirths for themselves and their unborn children, legends, rites and recent stories evincing a fear of male to female transsexual change, and the texts and legends replete with stories extolling the virtues of female to male transformation. For the rare discussion of these practices among Tibetans, see Aziz 1978 and Huber 1994. By contrast, foreign feminist advocates for an 'androgynous' Buddhism emphasize the small group of Mahāyāna texts which explicitly argue for the irrelevance of sexual difference vis-a-vis Buddhist enlightenment and state that a female adept need not be transformed into a male in order to become a Buddha (i.e. Gross 1993).

[25] Indeed, words for 'woman' in Tibetan related to bodily attributes far outnumber those for men.

extended to explain their appropriate enclosure in social realms associated with the household, labour and reproduction. Among a wide variety of my Tibetan interlocutors (women as well as men), women's minds were considered to be basically narrow or small (*sems chung-gi*) versus men's minds,[26] and thus they were seen to be less able than men to exert control over bodily compulsions and emotions, to concentrate and as one monk friend put it 'to think things through'. Women's bodies were therefore more closely associated with a sexuality requiring containment and regulation. Hence the foundational nature of what I call a 'sexual-karmic polarity' among Tibetans in Labrang: the division of bodies into hierarchically arranged primary categories of male and female, indexed in everyday usage by the phrase, 'the two, males and females' (*pho mo gnyis*), established females as essential conceptual and economic support for the superiority of male agency. Women *qua* female bodies were the entailed other for males' ability to achieve relative freedom from the body in more prestigious pursuits associated with the mind. And this logic was the basis of the spatial binaries that were the backbone of Tibetan social structure and ethnic identity in Labrang: female/body/inside/profane/household :: male/mind/outside/sacred/monastery.

MONASTIC ANDROGYNY AND GENDER AMBIGUITY

Hence the dilemma and danger represented by women's performance of monastic identities. From the perspective of ordinary observers, what linked the disparate women in Labrang considered to be 'nuns' ('ani', 'jomo'), and rendered them all but indistinguishable both from each other, and, significantly, from the men considered to be 'monks' ('akhu', 'trapa'), was the unisex monastic costume of maroon skirt, outer robe, sleeveless blouse, traditional felt or wool boots and shaved head.[27] This costume produced ritually marked bodies richly symbolic of a Buddhist cosmology. Most importantly, it marked a conventional and prestigious rite of passage in which an individual ideally renounced the selfish pursuits and attachments of sexuality, family and personal gain by taking various levels of vows corresponding to one's level of commitment to the discipline and Buddhist scholarship they required.

According to the system of monastic regulations first codified in India, the pious individual could choose to take the five basic vows (not

26 This does not preclude, however, the ability of women to learn and broaden the scopes of their minds through Buddhist or secular education, but Tibetans still insisted on upper limits to women's mental capacities vis-à-vis men.

27 Unlike in other Buddhist societies, Tibetan nuns most often wear the same monastic 'uniform' as monks, although nuns will sometimes wear a bodice under their blouses to hide the breasts (see Bartholomeusz 1994).

to drink alcohol, kill, steal, lie, or engage in sexual activity) and achieve the status called 'genyen' (Tib. *dge-bsnyen*, Skt. *upāsaka*).[28] One was considered a 'getsul' or novice monastic (Tib. *dge-tshul*, Skt. *śramaṇera*) if one pledged to refrain from ten basic offences.[29] Finally, a 'gelong' or fully ordained monk (Tib. *dge-slong*, Skt. *bhikṣu*) was one who committed himself to approximately two hundred and fifty vows aimed at regulating daily life in minute detail. Somewhat similar ordinations for women were instituted in early Buddhism, but it is debated whether full ordination of nuns as 'gelongma' (Tib. *dge-slong-ma*, Skt. *bhikṣuṇī*), was ever brought to Tibet. For Tibetans, a monastic ideally embarked on that career out of the pure intention to emulate the altruism of a bodhisattva and help all sentient beings attain enlightenment.[30] That orientation, as well as the commitment to refrain from non-virtuous behaviour, speech and thought, were the moral bases for the monastic community's ability to serve as a 'field of merit' for the laity.

However, in practice the boundary and relationships between lay and monastic communities were actually far from fixed in such ritualized vow-taking. Instead, the ongoing construction of the crucial boundary between lay and monastic worlds was fundamentally an issue of bodily performance—a ritual transformation carried out by and on bodies that for Tibetans most significantly indexed an individual's changed relationship to sex and sexuality. Just as Keyes (1986) found for Thai Buddhists in rural Thailand, I found that for ordinary Tibetans in Labrang, monasticism was most widely and basically associated with the vow to maintain (a certain construction of) celibacy, and engaging in heterosexual sex was the reason most often given (apart from the state-enforced returns during

[28] These five vows add the pledge to refrain from drinking to the vows to refrain from committing the four gravest offences in Buddhist ethics. People could take these vows temporarily for a particular ritual period such as annual fasting rites known as 'nyungne' (*smyung-gnas*) or attempt to uphold them permanently, as did many elderly folks accumulating merit before their deaths. Some of the more pious added three more vows and pledged not to wear ornaments, sing or dance, or sleep on high beds.

[29] These ten vows add the pledge not to eat at unscheduled times and not to handle money to the eight basic vows listed in the next note.

[30] Beginning at the novice level, monastics in Tibet take the bodhisattva precepts, pledging not to harm sentient beings, to seek full enlightenment and to help them attain enlightenment in addition to the levels of vows outlined in the Vinaya and delineated above. Since many of the vows in the Vinaya texts regulated aspects of lifestyles specific to ancient India, Tibetan monastics were also subject to their monasteries' own monastic 'constitutions' (*bca'-yig*) that enumerated rules and regulations for their own communities. These were not usually part of ordination rites in which vows are taken in the presence of a teacher and a quorum of fully ordained monks. Instead, they were often passed along orally, maintained and enforced by the monastery disciplinarian. For discussions of monastic constitutions in Tibet, see Ellingson 1990 and Cabézon 1997.

the radical years) for a monastic 'falling back' to lay life. In Labrang, however, the performance of a gendered monastic identity was the most important determinant for if and how the laity took one to be a field of merit, not adherence to or level of vows taken. This perspective, I argue, helps to sort out some of the confusion in foreign writings about Tibetan monasticism that attempt to reconcile a Buddhist monastic ideal with the actual proliferation of social roles and apparent behavioral license of monastics in Tibet. It also helps explain why such a situation did not necessarily threaten or render 'contradictory' the relationship between laity and monastics historically.

I found that for Tibetans throughout the community, the basic defining feature of a monastic was the public renunciation of family life and (heterosexual) sex marked by shaving the head, donning the monastic costume and leaving home, a status designated by the idiom 'one who has renounced and left home' (*rab-tu byung-ba*).[31] And that status was first entered when one became a monastic neophyte after pledging before a lama to uphold various levels of basic vows.[32] Thus, contrary to the way scholars such as Charles Keyes and Tessa Bartholomeusz (1994) describe Buddhist monasticism in India and south-east Asia, and what Giuseppe Tucci (1970; 1988) argues for Tibet, for ordinary Tibetans in Labrang, the most important boundary between lay and monastic status was not that between novice and fully ordained but that between a 'householder' (*khyim-pa*) and 'one who has renounced and left home.'[33]

This is the transformation that was both marked on the body and acknowledged as worthy of respect through linguistic (use of honorific) and non-linguistic (bowing, removal of hats, etc.) deference practices. As my monk friend Konchok put it in my formal interview with him, if one

31 This phrase is perhaps best glossed in English as 'one who has gone forth', or by the Chinese term *chujia ren* (lit. 'one who has gone out of the home'). Another Tibetan term (*spong-ba-pa*) refers to one who has renounced all worldly affairs, and is closer to the English term 'ascetic'. Such a person lived in a small hermitage with only the bare necessities. This was actually a tiny minority of monastics in Tibet.

32 Since in Tibet, the majority of monks were traditionally brought to monasteries as children, there were several levels of monastic neophyte status before the level of 'official' monastic novice or getsul. This was not as important for nuns in the region because few were brought to nunneries as children.

33 Tucci 1988: 110, assuming Indian Buddhism as a model, states that both genyen and getsul are lay vows, and only a gelong is a 'monk'. While I can see that Tucci was trying to point up the disparity between the monastic ideal and social reality by arguing that only a minority of monks were fully ordained in Tibet, his distinction between lay and monk vows does not at all correspond with the perspective of most ordinary Tibetans, and misses the social complexities of how monasticism was actually performed and acknowledged. This is not to argue, however, that Tibetans did not recognize a distinction between novice and fully ordained monastic status.

takes the five genyen vows, one is still no different from a householder because *no one knows*. In his view, the vows in that case were only for oneself—to increase one's own store of merit. For him, only one whose renunciation of household life was publicly performed (*rab-byung*) qualified as a monastic motivated by altruism. Konchok's view summarized a perspective shared by most ordinary Tibetans—the words for male and female monastics in everyday usage were applied to all those who donned the monastic costume.[34]

From this angle then, I follow Keyes to assert that Tibetan communities like Labrang, in which celibate monasticism has been so powerful and attracted such a large percentage of the population, are a particularly striking case of societies where the normative sex-gender system is made up of three, not two, separate gender ideals articulating in different ways with an assumed dichotomy of male and female-sexed bodies. Monasticism in Labrang was a third gender because it was a passage to a cultural status with its own social functions that was crucially defined by altered relationships to sex and sexuality.[35] This passage was marked by rituals and the performance of a kind of monastic androgyny, that is, the adoption of a generic monastic costume that eschewed the emblems of gendered lay statuses—hair and hairstyles, ornaments and gendered dress.

Indeed, Tibetan naming practices, forms of address and use of terms for monks and nuns indicate this new gender status. Upon taking the novice vows, monks and nuns are given a new name by which they will thereafter be called. Further, there is no colloquial term in everyday use for 'women' encompassing nuns and laywomen, or for 'men' encompassing monks and laymen. In addition, normally appropriate kin terms are usually eliminated in everyday speech when people refer to or address monks and nuns. A monk or a nun is thus no longer a 'brother', 'sister', 'son', or 'daughter', but 'ani' or 'akhu' (literally 'aunt' and 'uncle', kin terms which encode respect entitled to elder relatives). If I pressed them, people could be induced to clarify their familial relationships to monastic

[34] This is, after all, how the English words 'monk' and 'nun', and the Chinese words *heshang* and *nigu* are used, and thus the reason why such translations are so susceptible to over-simplifying the actually complex social disparities among people who don the robes in Tibet. While there is a change in monastic costume in Labrang to indicate scholarly achievement and monastic office in the monastery, there is no major change in everyday costume to signify neophyte versus fully-ordained status, nor is there one to indicate relative adherence to vows. Although the 'monastic constitution' of a college of another famous Gelug monastery, Sera in Lhasa, states that novices should wear 'imitation' robes, while fully-ordained monks should wear 'real' ones (see Cabézon 1997: 347). In Labrang today, no such distinction is widely apparent.

[35] See Shapiro 1991: 264 and Morris 1995: 581 for discussions of this definition of a 'gender'.

relatives, but I could be confused when people talked about 'their ane, or akhu', not knowing if they were talking about an aunt or uncle, or a nun or monk relative. More than once, friends corrected me, as if it was disrespectful, if I referred to their monk or nun sibling as 'your brother', or 'your sister'. They would insist that the sibling, even if younger than them, was 'my akhu' or 'my ani'.

At first glance, this gender status, what Keyes calls a '*saṅgha*-gender',[36] would seem to stand in a mediating relationship to those of layman and womanhood. The monastic androgyny of such a person, especially in the Labrang region where male and female renunciants wore the same costume, would seem to embody the elimination of a male-female polarity and the polluting heterosexuality and desirous attachments it entailed. In Keyes' words, such a gender would not be determined by 'natural' sex attributes. Instead, it would represent the possibility to transcend them by subjecting the self to certain forms of discipline and making progress on a path to ultimate liberation from the suffering they cause. Indeed, in our formal interview, Konchok was very concerned to argue for this view of monasticism, saying that once a person took the vows of a novice the importance of sexual difference would 'lighten' or decrease in importance (*pho mo gnyis ka yang rgyu red*).

Monastic androgyny would thus seem to epitomize the radical potential of a Buddhism, touted especially by foreign feminist Buddhists, based on gender egalitarianism. But as Jennifer Robertson notes in an insightful article, practices of androgyny scramble conventional gender markers so as to both 'undermine the stability of the sex-gender system premised on a male-female dichotomy and retain that dichotomy by either juxtaposing or blending its elements' (Robertson 1992: 419). In other words, practices of androgyny ostensibly negate gender differences but their social significance and impact always rely on references to existing gender ideals. Thus recourse to androgyny can open the possibility for a kind of resistance, all the while retaining a cultural logic of gender hierarchy that grants primacy to maleness or masculinity. As such, monastic androgyny in Labrang was not a form of transgressive gender ambiguity that parodied more prestigious and normative gender ideals. Instead, it was itself a performance of the ultimate ideal, a gender status both fundamentally subject to a hierarchical male-female polarity, and containing within it a latent threat to that arrangement, a threat that emerged in ways specific to particular historical contexts. As the second proverb cited above so clearly stated, for Tibetans, the move from household to monasticism was paradigmatically for males only. Thus I argue that, as it was played out in everyday interactions, *monkhood*, not

36 *Saṅgha* is the Sanskrit term referring to the monastic community as a whole.

monasticism in general, was the third gender status in the sex-gender system actually operative in Labrang.

Monastic androgyny notwithstanding, Tibetans throughout the community did not consider the monastic costume and shaved head to indicate a state of sexlessness. Instead it was clearly gendered masculine. From this perspective, monkhood was not fundamentally a repudiation of masculinity, but the renunciation of those aspects of lay manhood that were most seen to hinder progress on the path, i.e. heterosexuality and responsibilities to the household. The model monastic career was actually the perfection through discipline of the basic good traits said by Labrangites to inhere in the male sex; it was the ideal destiny for lay masculinity, a superior masculine gender status first entered through the rite of passage of neophyte ordination.[37] By contrast, in the Labrang region, the ideally lay status of females was performed through the 'letting down the hair' or coming-of-age rite (*skra-phab*, Ch. *shangtou*) in which sixteen to seventeen year old girls donned the headdress of an adult woman and were presented to the community as sexually mature and marriageable.[38]

When viewed in this way, nunhood in Labrang can be seen not as an ideal gender status but as a conventional form of 'gender-crossing' that emulated a masculine societal ideal. As such, it represented upward social mobility, and thus it has historically been considered to be a socially possible or understandable move that was nonetheless more vulnerable to failure than that of monkhood.[39] While monks' performance of

[37] From this angle we could view 'tulkuhood' ('tulku', *sprul-sku* = incarnate lama) as a possible fourth ideal gender status. A logical outcome of the sacred as male, it is another distinct cultural status with its own functions and an altered relationship to sexuality. Since tulkus are said to be emanations of already enlightened beings, they enjoy much more latitude in sexual behaviour than do monks, and, especially nowadays, they do not necessarily become monastics. Such a status could be said to mediate between lay and monastic masculine ideals. Some young Gelug tulkus take ordination, while many resist pressures to become monastics, and many local Gelug tulkus defrocked during the Maoist years never returned to monastic life. Yet most, (to varying degrees depending on personal charisma and the politics of the recognition process) enjoy reverence and respect from constituencies of laity, regardless of their sexual activities. For the sacred as male in Christianity, see Børresen 1995.

[38] This rite of passage for girls was widespread in Amdo regions. Li Anzhai (1992) says it was not held in Kham regions to the south. In Labrang, there was no equivalent rite of passage for lay boys. The rite for girls was clearly based on presenting girls as good prospects for a patrilocal marriage, because the girl was dressed in her finest, the ornaments in her hair indexing the wealth of her family. The girl then visited all the homes in the village, where neighbors and relatives presented her with money and gifts that helped to bolster her 'dowry', the property she would take with her to marriage. However, as Li Anzhai noted, girls did not necessarily marry immediately after undergoing the rite. The rite also made girls 'socially sexual', that is, they could then (discreetly) take lovers.

[39] Versus for example the much more radical and rarely, if ever, seen move of a lay male taking on lay women's appearance and roles.

renunciation did not make them essentially less male (it was not seen to 'neuter' or 'feminize' them),[40] nuns' renunciation ironically destabilized their femaleness. Nunhood was thus a far more ambiguous gender identity than monkhood. Nuns embodied, more so than monks, the tensions inherent to Buddhist monasticism between the mutability of gender and the relative immutability of sex—they teetered on the boundary between monastic and lay worlds. Whether or not a woman could successfully inhabit such a status was, I argue, specific to particular historical contexts.

THE POWER OF GOSSIP: RE-SEXING NUNS

This perspective, better than arbitrary distinctions made by feminist Buddhists between an ultimately egalitarian religion and actual social realities, explains the historically inferior position of nuns in Buddhist societies. The Buddha is said to have decreed that allowing an order of nuns would ultimately contribute to the earlier dissolution of Buddhism, and monastic rules proliferated to place nuns under the ultimate direction of monks and to regulate nuns *vis-à-vis* monks and the laity.[41] In contemporary Labrang, nun's bodies, ritually inscribed in the same way as monks, represented a particular condensation of these gendered tensions. To the laity, the nuns' bold androgyny and resemblance to monks loudly claimed equal status with male renunciants, regardless of the level of vows or learning achieved. Tsomo and Karma explicitly referred to this claim when they emphatically agreed in our conversation that it was unjust nuns were treated so differently from monks because after all they had all publicly renounced the mundane world by taking the (initial) vows of ordination and donning the maroon robes.

Thus in the Labrang region, because most families resisted the movement of daughters to monasticism and raised them not to consider it as a possible career, nuns' bodies indexed this strong oppositional agency (of which all nuns I spoke to were very proud). Unlike most monks, women who chose to become nuns had to persevere into adulthood against the hardships of great social opposition.[42] However, the nuns' stories of brave escapes from villages by night and lonely journeys to Labrang demon-

40 In the past, when men wore various types of robes in lay life, the contrast between lay garb and monastic costume was not as striking. Now that lay men most often wear pants and shirts, the association of monastic robes with skirts and femininity embarrassed some young monks.

41 Fully ordained nuns ended up with over 150 more vows than fully ordained monks.

42 However, due to frequent labour shortages, families past and present have resisted sending sons to monastic careers, especially when there were few sons to inherit land and property. In recent years, the relative prestige of secular education and careers and new economic opportunities in Labrang and elsewhere have increased, luring many young men away from monastic careers with their families' blessings.

strated how they benefited from the performative power of monasticism—crossing the threshold to monasticism by publicly donning the costume and shaving the head is a ritual passage with consequences, regardless of the level of vows taken. For males or females, leaving the robes for lay life was not only a social embarrassment, but it was also bad karma. I found that most nuns' families ultimately respected their decisions and ended up supporting them with annual gifts of food, money and help buying or building houses, once their daughters had proved their commitment to monasticism through perseverance (Tsomo's family was an exception).[43] And nuns in Labrang generally did not participate regularly in their families' agricultural work, only returning to visit once or twice a year (usually during the new year holidays in February and March).

Nunhood for young women from impoverished farming regions was a traditional refuge in the transformed times of the post-Mao era. They could escape the demands of household and labour in regions where arranged marriage and women's responsibility for the majority of farm labour were again the norm. And they could leave home villages where women's illiteracy rates still hovered around eighty per cent, and pursue rare opportunities for an education relative to urban women.[44] In such a context nunhood was for them the most available goal on which to project their widened aspirations for self-improvement relative to previous generations. Further, in the past few years, the withdrawal from households and childbirth into voluntary celibacy also represented a refuge for poor women (the ones most vulnerable to enforcement) from the state's increasing regulation of women's bodies through enforced birth control and sterilization.[45]

[43] I heard a few stories of violence in which family members came to Labrang and forcibly returned women to household and marriage, but this was actually relatively rare. Significantly, the stories I heard in which violence was involved were cases in which the would-be nuns had already married. Gossipers about nuns generally reserved the most vituperation for such women. Interestingly, narrators tended to dwell on the initial humiliation of the returned women because of the incongruity of their shaved heads in lay contexts.

[44] According to Duan 1995, relying on statistics from the 1990 census, 2/3 of the 180 million illiterate people in China were women. More than half of school-age girls unable to go to school were in the 10 provinces and autonomous regions in west China, particularly in impoverished ethnic minority areas. Duan cites statistics published by the State Education Commission saying that only 63.9 % of school-age girls were enrolled in Gansu, 70 % in Ningxia, and only 37.2 % in Qinghai, while the national average was 96.8 %. In an otherwise comprehensive survey of the state of secular education in Tibetan regions, Bass (1998) barely touches on the issue of gender disparities in access to education. She notes only that in 1990 84.2 % of women in the TAR were illiterate, or 73.3 % of the total illiterate population (p. 206).

[45] As many observers monitoring China's draconian birth control policies have pointed out, implementation varied widely with locale. I found that in Tibetan regions, the degree of

However, young nuns coming to join any of the three nunneries in Labrang were dismayed to find themselves the target of particularly vehement disdain expressed in scandalous gossip about nuns in general, a disdain they had never experienced in their home regions. Nuns encountered such intensified resistance from locals largely because the body of a nun was more visible than ever before, not only because nuns were more numerous,[46] but also because due to increased demands on Tibetan women to uphold the duties of lay femininity, the monastic androgyny they performed was more starkly oppositional and problematic than before. Further, bodily performance, in the form of ritual, gesture, speech patterns, and ethnic or state-inflected dress, had taken on new significance as local identities in a frontier region under siege had to be continually buttressed against competing interests. The nuns' androgyny in this context then ironically recalled the communist androgyny of the radical years because both posed a threat to the household-monastery system by claiming the irrelevance of sex differences and exhibiting the movement of women out of the household.

Nuns' emulation of monks was now too close for comfort; their androgyny claimed ritual equivalence at a time when their repudiation of femaleness could ill be afforded—when the reassertion of the stable realities of a male-female sexual-karmic polarity was deemed essential to the survival of the Tibetan community. Scandalous gossip about nuns thus

---

strictness depended mostly on the whims and personalities of local cadres. Laywomen and nuns from some regions told me the local cadres were fairly lenient and did not enforce mandatory sterilization, while others told me that in their regions in recent years enforcement had increased, with cadres rounding up village women who were registered as having had two to three births and taking them to local clinics for sterilization. Not surprisingly, women in farming villages were more vulnerable to enforcement than nomad women. My interlocutors told me that in some cases, families were required to pay for all or part of the operation for which recovery took months and severely limited a woman's ability to work. In such places, they said, women pregnant over quota were known to flee to nomad regions to escape forced abortions and have their babies. In Labrang, the enforcement of female sterilization emerged as a definite class issue, with poor village women subject to sporadic round-ups, and wealthy or connected women able to avoid mandatory sterilization by bribing local cadres.

46 Nuns in Labrang were more numerous for a variety of reasons mentioned above. Another reason was that the Nyingma nunnery drew a new pool of young nuns to Labrang. Leaders of all three nunneries told me in interviews that young nuns, some as young as eleven to twelve years, joined their communities every year. In 1995, there was a housing shortage for such new nuns, and many lived with nun roommates, or rented spaces in lay households, hence also their increased visibility in public spaces. In addition, some young nuns came to Labrang only to take vows, and then returned to their home regions to join or start communities there. As one of the nun leaders of the Nyingma nunnery told me, the influx of young nuns would only increase in the coming years when both they and the larger Gelug nunnery had the added cachet of new assembly halls.

worked to defrock them; gossips resolutely *re-sexed* nuns by sharply differentiating them from monks, and by claiming the uncontrolled and hence negative corporeality of females to be typical of all.

Such talk, as many of my nun friends said, was the most important thing that limited their aspirations for learning and advancement, keeping them timid and silent in public and afraid to fundraise among the laity or seek teachings from monks or lamas. In our separate interview, Karma complained that nuns had to be extremely careful in their public comportment because one mishap among nuns would be the talk of the town for a long time to come.[47] And this, she declared, was far disproportionate to the much larger number of young monks in Labrang who were publicly visible indulging in once forbidden (or at least hidden) leisure activities. Indeed, during my fieldwork, the most frequently and vehemently cited of rumours was the story about the misdeeds of a nun and her beautiful nun daughter, referred to as Jomo Sangtruk, who were said to still be living in Labrang. According to gossips, the latter began an affair with a monk, and after she became pregnant the two retired to lay life and she opened a shop. My monk friend Konchok, who told me this story more than once, said that when it first happened, the story was on everyone's lips, and to this day laymen talked about the former nun's great beauty and joked about having liaisons with her.

I heard no parallel story about a monk that was told as frequently or throughout as many social contexts as this one. And even though there was a fallen monk in the story, the focus was entirely on the instigating misdeed of the beautiful nun and the eroticization of her body. This story was so frequently cited in conversation because, I argue, it encapsulated the important gender politics operating on all nuns in recent years. The body of Jomo Sangtruk epitomized the dangers (and allure) of a female body outside of the social controls of the household domain, dangers that in Labrang had ironically come to be associated most closely with the body of a nun. Indeed, in the contemporary context, nunhood represented the most radically oppositional of gender transformations. The body of a nun indexed a determined resistance to intensified pressures against a monastic career from both household and state. Further, it displayed a resolute decision not to participate in gender practices sponsored by the

[47] All three nun communities enforced strict rules concerning public behaviour: nuns could not be seen in public places like restaurants, movies and video shops, they most often did not go out alone and never at night, and they could not interact one-on-one with monks. Nuns frequently caught at such activities were liable to be expelled from the community. Indeed the heads of one of the Gelug nunneries told me they had expelled one nun in recent years, and I knew of another who had been expelled from the Nyingma nunnery. This was in sharp contrast with monks in town because of the sheer numbers of monks attracted to Labrang and the reduced power of the monastery to discipline them.

state and the media that offered the limited choices of a secular male-female hierarchy.[48]

Thus, local gossip about nuns operated to reject unequivocally the '*saṅgha*-gender', a term coined by Keyes, to refer to the implicit claim of monastics to have transcended sex difference, claimed by young nuns in town and to reassert their status as females—as women whose bodies critically circumscribed their mental capacities and rendered them more suited to household labour and reproduction. The citation in everyday conversations of scandalous stories about them cast aspersions on nuns' religious motivations, and worked to confirm widespread views that such young women chose to become nuns not out of altruism or the desire for Buddhist enlightenment, but primarily due to considerations of the body: they could not find husbands because they were disfigured in some way, or they were lazy and wished to escape household labour.[49] Ritual efficacy among Tibetans in Labrang was thus fundamentally gendered. The male body, connoting great stores of merit, and more amenable to mental and ritual mastery, was empowered to conduct efficacious ritual, while the female body was not. I was often told when I asked whether a household hired nuns for ritual services that nuns were 'useless' (*phan-thogs med-gi*, lit. 'without benefit') to them; and nuns from all three communities complained that on the few occasions when nuns were hired, there was a great disparity between monks and nuns' wages for such services.

To the laity, hard-pressed by labour shortages, increasing inflation and fierce competition for their support from a wide variety of religious specialists, the nuns' resemblance to monks represented the moral burden of another potential 'field of merit' to support. Through their scandalous gossip, they summarily rejected that burden by constructing nuns as morally unworthy of support, thus justifying their unprecedented neglect of nuns relative to the past and their choice of monks (regardless of whether or not they were fully ordained) as more ritually efficacious for them.[50] In

48 Further, except in very circumscribed ritual contexts (such as conventional humorous interludes in large-scale monastic or lay propitiation ceremonies in which lay male actors will dress as women), there was no radical cross-dressing among Tibetans, and no openly oppositional transgender or homosexual identities.

49 While my interviews with nuns revealed that they did indeed find nunhood a refuge from the often crushing demands of farming labour especially, all nuns I spoke to emphasized their great religious aspirations as their primary motivation, and most told me how they had aspired to a religious career from very early ages—sometimes a decade or so before the traditional age of marriage (at 17–20 years). In addition, monks I spoke to were just as likely as nuns to talk about monkhood as an escape from hard labor and the demands of marriage; and I never heard the same suspicion of monks' motivations from the laity (see Ortner 1983.)

50 In contrast to the past, when the Gelug nunneries could count on some regular support from the religious patrons of their main lamas, my nun friends told me of their difficulties

the context of scarcer resources within that increasingly crowded, narrow valley, there was little room for the exceptional generosity required to support nuns' more 'unfocused merit-making' (Gutschow 1997), and most chose to invest precious funds in supporting the indispensable ritual mediations performed by monks in the monastery or in private homes—so much so that during the first few months of the lunar year, when ritual obligations were given to families by lamas to ensure prosperity in the coming year, there was a shortage of monks to meet lay demand for chanting services to fulfil them.

However, in recent years, nuns in Labrang had acquired a ritual role that served specific merit-making goals of the laity. Since lamas continued to assign 'nyungne' (*smyung-gnas*) fasts to laity seeking solutions to particular problems, while laity were less willing to undergo such a difficult practice, and monks would not do it on the grounds that it took away from their studies, laity 'entrusted' (*bcol-ba*) their nyungne obligations to nuns exclusively.[51] This is the widespread fasting practice Tibetans believe was established by Bhiksuni Lakshmi, a great eleventh century Indian Buddhist nun and devotee of the Bodhisattva Avalokiteśvara. In a rite focused on that deity, all nuns in Labrang fasted during the two weeks of the waxing moon on alternate days, taking no food or water for twenty-four hours and observing (ritualized) silence on those days except to chant mantras and the rites and prayers of the fast.[52] As Roger Jackson has put it, such a fast '…makes for a retreat whose intensity and difficulty is comparable to that of the austere retreats in Zen monasteries' (Jackson 1997: 274).

All nuns I spoke to emphasized that generating merit by taking on vows to refrain from eating and talking on behalf of lay sponsors was their primary source of income. For most nuns, who could hope for only a few hundred yuan and several sacks of flour once or twice a year from their families, the meagre income from their occasional nyungne jobs represented a significant boost to their personal subsistence they could not refuse. Thus, in addition to the gruelling semi-annual two-week

---

nowadays in fundraising among the laity in Labrang, recounting how heads of households would sometimes shoo them away by saying they were tired of all the fundraising by monastics. Most nuns had to go to regions far afield to have any luck with lay donations for personal or community-wide support.

[51] Several lay friends of mine who had grown up in the region told me that lay participation in nyungne rituals since the recovery period had never come close to that before the communist victory, especially during the two annual nyungne festivals.

[52] The Gelug nuns in Labrang practice the nyungne rite outlined by the seventh Dalai Lama, Kalsang Gyatso (1708–57). For an English translation see Thubten Zopa Rinpoche and Churinoff 1995.

nyungne retreats that all nuns in the Labrang communities endured, many nuns took nyungne vows over two-day periods for hire several times a month—what amounted to young women having to starve themselves in order to eat.[53]

Nuns in Labrang were thus a field of merit of sorts to the laity, but the ritual power associated with that role required them to harm their bodies to the detriment of their minds, a role for which, as females, they were always already suited. Despite their pride in their ability to persevere through many fasts and in their integrity in upholding the nyungne vows without the supervision of lay sponsors, all nuns I spoke to lamented the serious toll it took on their bodies (which were not well-nourished to begin with) and on their ability to study. As Karma put it in our interview, 'If one is not observing nyungne, then one can do anything! During my fieldwork, it seemed that my nun friends, young and old, were always fasting. It was hit or miss whether a nun I was visiting was pledged to silence, not to mention strong enough to play host to me and talk about her life. Nuns were frequently ill, much more so than the lay population. They were very aware that their illnesses (usually prolonged and often very serious) were the result of their frequent fasting and the consequent weakening of their bodies over time. While fasting, they complained, they could do nothing but lie around weakly and chant prayers, and it took several days afterward to recover the energy required to read and memorize texts.

Thus it is that the particular ambiguities of the gender status inhabited by nuns in Labrang produced an ironic situation. Nuns were entrusted with upholding vows that were supposed to control and purify body, speech and mind on behalf of a community less inclined to take them on, and yet, in scandalous talk about them, they were reviled as quintessential female bodies out of control. The suffering of nuns epitomized that of Tibetan women in general: their important yet silent part in maintaining the now-precarious boundary between lay and monastic worlds was never acknowledged with public prestige or power.

53 Unlike monks in the main assembly of the monastery in recent years, nuns could not expect any financial support from their assemblies, although they did benefit from occasional gifts of food, or from pooling practices in which nuns in the assembly contributed food for communal feasts. Nuns in training, i.e., those who had not passed the exams for memorization of the prayers and rites of the communities' ritual calendars, could not participate in this. Further, as monks, nuns and laity all told me, nuns were paid much less for nyungne services to laity than were monks when they perform ritual services for lay households. Nuns only made about 5–10 yuan each, plus a little butter or bread, for a two-day fasting rite, while monks were paid 15–30 yuan each per day of chanting, plus meals and tea.

THE DANGEROUS BODY OF A NUN

In contrast to the elder nuns who prior to communist intervention enjoyed a modicum of lay support, the laity in contemporary Labrang was more adamant about the gendering of ritual efficacy because young nuns embodied a more pressing threat to the inner sanctum of Tibetan gendered worlds. This was not only because they were from regions outside of Labrang (although that made them easier to dehumanize), but it was also because the agency they exhibited was necessarily a more oppositional one—their sheer perseverance in the face of unprecedented pressure against a monastic career required a more conscious resistance to competing state and traditional Tibetan gender ideologies. Their larger numbers in recent years also pressed in on lay donors, sharpening competition for scarcer resources in the narrow valley, thus compelling choices inevitably made in favour of monks.

Most importantly, however, I argue that the body of a nun in Labrang was a fulcrum on which turned Tibetans' to regulate and resist change amidst an unprecedented clashing of gender practices in town. Nuns in Labrang were outsiders in multiple senses: they not only came from regions outside of Labrang, but their bodies also represented an anomaly to the sex-gender system now vital to sustaining Tibetan identities under siege. And since the state had begun implementing childbirth quotas among Tibetans, Tibetans in such 'frontier' regions, beleaguered by the encroachments of Han and Muslim Chinese settlements, and whose traditional male authorities had diminished in numbers and real power, felt an even greater sense of urgency. The 'monastic androgyny' of young nuns thus displayed the particularly galling choice of marriageable women to refrain from childbirth and labour when both were in extraordinarily precious supply.

To recall the words of my nun friend with which I opened this essay, in order to understand how nuns in contemporary Labrang could be homologous to dogs and Muslim Chinese, we need to see nuns as icons for ominous and polluting outsiders whose assault on the Tibetan sex-gender system had in very recent years reached crisis proportions for Tibetans. Tibetans feared that the delicately balanced relationship of sexuality to (male) asceticism was no longer symbiotic, but predatory—the boundaries traditionally keeping sexuality in check and in service to monasticism seemed to be wavering and the lure of new gender practices threatened to diminish the number of young men willing to renounce and the number of young women willing to support them.

Nuns like my friends Tsomo and Karma were acutely aware and privately pained at the unjust irony that they were the most frequent targets of scandalous gossip, despite their celibate lifestyles. But for the most part they had to suffer that indignity in silence. For they found themselves with few resources to really resist what their ritually marked bodies had come to represent. Eminently visible as females who had consciously renounced the household and crossed into a traditionally masculine gender status (*versus* laymen and women whose bodies did not necessarily mark their resistance to traditional gender practices), nuns were easily targeted as the objects of angry opposition to larger patterns of changing gender practices which locals experienced as baffling and multifarious. In this way, gossip about nuns attributed to them great power—not in ritual efficacy, but in the potential to disrupt the spatialized gender polarity that reproduced the vital symbiotic relationship between monastery and household, the very core of Tibetan social worlds.

WOMEN AND POLITICS IN CONTEMPORARY TIBET*

Robert Barnett

It is March 2000. In an office in New York a Tibetan woman is speaking rapidly, recounting memories of her past, pulling from a shoulder bag faded copies of documents once issued to her by offices in Lhasa. She is talking about a demonstration in that city that she had seen some twelve years earlier. She recalls monks being badly beaten and arrested, and then a crowd of laypeople gathering to call for their release; she mentions a policeman filming the protestors from the roof of the police station; she describes the women at the back of the crowd carrying stones in the laps of their 'panden' (*pang-gdan*), the multicoloured aprons worn by married Tibetan women, and handing them to men to throw at the police cameras, to stop their faces being filmed. Finally she describes the crowd burning down the police station, the monks escaping, and armed police opening fire.

Her immediate concern in telling this story is to convince United States immigration officials that she is indeed from Tibet, a place which in this account is a site of fierce antagonisms between the state and the nation or nationality to which she feels that she belongs. She is at a critical juncture in her life: speaking no English and barely literate, she has somehow made the journey, without legal papers, from her life as a pavement seller in Lhasa to a new life of some kind in the United States, where she is now applying for asylum. But she stands accused of fabricating her claim to have lived in Tibet, or even to be Tibetan; if her story is found false she faces deportation. Apart from her memories and her papers, it is only her body that now remains to represent what is Tibetan about her, and it is not believed. She resists the accusation of deception by what we might call 'performing her nation', in this case by presenting a narrative that establishes her as part of the extended Tibetan body politic and identifies her within a history of nationality oppression and resistance. It is a narrative of Tibetanness in which women have a special role.

* I am indebted to Jeanne Marie Gilbert and Kelly Washburn for their editorial assistance on this chapter, and to the Fonds zur Förderung der Wissenschaftlichen Forschung (Vienna) for their funding support.

For me, it is her recollection of the role played by women in that demonstration that is significant, initially because it confirms that she had, in fact, been there. Accounts of that event can be bought from tutors in New York to be memorized by asylum seekers, but there is little mention in the popular reports surrounding that 1987 incident of the instrumental part played in that event by women, and so her story is unlikely to have been manufactured.[1] But her choice of this remembered image from that episode is of wider significance: it emphasizes the role of women in that protest in Lhasa so many years before, and the gendered aspect of political practice in Tibet in general. In addition, it recalls, in the action she has chosen of bodily moving herself to another place, the way in which the political process is carried out on and within the bodies of those involved.

It is with such considerations in mind that I attempt in this chapter a preliminary description of the activity of women politicians and political activists in contemporary Tibet, focusing on Lhasa and the Tibet Autonomous Region (TAR), as it is now called,[2] and particularly on the period since the mid-1980s when a new phase of politics, and of women's politics, emerged. Resistance in the dramatic sense of physical confrontation with the state is only one form of politics, and it is a project which several writers have warned against romanticizing,[3] just as others have shown the dangers of heroizing the downtrodden, the 'subaltern', or ethnic and gender minorities.[4] My initial endeavour, therefore, is not to

1 The role of women in this incident was briefly noted in one western newspaper article under the sub-heading 'Many, Many Women Crying', which cited an unnamed Dutch tour-guide as saying that 'there were people breaking up pavement stones, men and women' (*New York Times* 1987). The moment when the demonstration escalated from a static crowd throwing stones at the police to an active movement burning police vehicles came when a laywoman walked out of the crowd and broke the windows of a police car (personal observation).

2 The Tibet Autonomous Region was formally established only in 1965, delayed by the 1959 uprising and widespread armed conflict. In this chapter I have been able to discuss events only in the TAR, which includes the central and western parts of the Tibetan-inhabited area now under China, and not in the eastern Tibetan areas of Kham (western Sichuan) or Amdo (part of Qinghai), where about 52 % of the Tibetans within China live.

3 'In order to avoid the essentialisms and pitfalls of these other representations, an alternative feminist perspective must begin from a view of local situations, of experiences of empowerment or disempowerment shaped within local cultural categories in relation to larger social contexts' (Makley 1997: 13).

4 'This situation also complicates the postcolonial attempt to rescue the agency of the subalterns. Subaltern agency is often a legitimate moral device appropriated for intellectual representation against power. In due course, it is also essentialized, failing to differentiate the diversity within the subaltern agency… Without documenting the nature of domination and its resistance, silences, complicity and displacements, above all the hybridity of social reality, we risk naturalizing the communist discourse of nationality policy. To say the least, as I have shown, China's nationality policy emerged out of the debris of conflict between class and ethnicity, and was predicated on the imbrication of class struggle and ethnic equity' (Bulag 2000a).

focus on the drama of resistance but, looking at political activity as narratives in which the protagonists seek to modify the power relations within which they find themselves, to describe various forms of contemporary women's politics.

There are two primary areas of female political assertion that have appeared most visibly in Tibet since the early 1980s. One is the participation of women in oppositional and outlawed political action, in the form of demonstrations, pamphlet distribution, the promotion of underground organizations, and so on; the other is the emergence of a new group of Tibetan women in the formal leadership apparatus established by the Chinese Communist Party in Tibet in the years since the first Chinese troops arrived there in 1950. Between these two poles are many other spheres of female activity in politics of a great variety of kinds—in informal politics, in networking, in patronage formations, in workplace, domestic and localized decision-making, in choices about whether to leave for exile, and so on. We do not know, for example, how Tibetan families reach decisions about their children's education—since 1990 these have led to some 16,000 children being sent to China for their secondary schooling and some 5,000 others being sent illegally to schools in India[5]—but if these have been made primarily by women, this would be just one example of an area in which women would be making decisions of great significance for the future development of their society. But of these forms of everyday politics we have as yet only limited knowledge.

There are obvious differences between the two groups—the establishment élite and the underground resistance—most notably that the women in formal politics are involved in state discourse, while the dissident women activists are openly opposing it. On the one hand, the formal politicians have little choice, once they are in that system, other than to confine themselves to ritualized statements of loyalty, although as we shall see, their statements may be interpreted variously precisely because of the limitations within which they are produced. The dissident women, on the other hand, seem to have chosen voluntarily to use rituals of another kind, perhaps to make their statements more effective as political challenges. With the activist women we can in general be guided, as readers, by their explicit statements of intent and purpose, but with the women working within the state system we are involved in the interpretation of signs and indications which may not reflect their intentions. In either case, these interpretations indicate the existence of an important subculture of Tibetans in Tibet who, shaped largely by the open protest of the

[5] Bass 1998: 150, 152, 158. An exile government official claimed that 1,500 children fled to Nepal in the first quarter of 2001, nearly ten times the average (interview broadcast by the BBC World Service, 30 April 2001).

activists, read these signs in oppositional ways. Operating as reader-narrators in a highly political process of re-interpretation, they thus produce narratives about their leaders that redefine and undermine the ritual hyper-uniformity of the state.

In this essay there is an intentional disjuncture between the two main categories that I invoke, those of the élite women and the female activists. It leaves a conceptual space which I suggest could, if we but knew enough, be filled by the as yet untold histories of women who work through low key, everyday activities and who seem in general not to have constructed themselves as significant, or to have communicated narratives about themselves, or to have constituted themselves as groupings.[6] The binary arrangement which I have chosen is intended also to raise doubts about the romanticizing tendency to see one as opposed to the other, and to question any certainties about who we think is fighting whom. Tibetan women in resistance do not, as far as I know, cite élite co-opted Tibetans as opponents, still less as enemies, nor consider it necessary to know if their leaders share their religious beliefs. Whatever their political views, they share with the élite women a common ethnicity as well as gender, and a common sense of history. The feminist observation that as women they share doubled forms of diminution, being reduced in status and power both by their gender and by their nationality, since they are viewed as a minority by the state,[7] is relevant here, but in either case the ethnicization of contemporary Tibetan history, and of Chinese politics, pushes these groups together.

The issues that in general these women raise in their protests and discussion are not gendered, despite the distinctive ways in which they carry out their politics: it seems that in Tibet the urgency of the national question has so far overridden other issues, so that the stated concerns of women are similar to those defined by men.[8] Both groups—the élite

[6] This is partly because to do otherwise would be to put their initiatives at risk. But it is also because that space has been appropriated by the state, which promotes women involved in social construction and enterprise as model citizens. The gap between official praise and imprisonment for these women can be narrow, as is shown by the case of Rebiya Kadeer, widely praised in official media until 1996 as the leading Uighur business woman in Xinjiang (East Turkestan). She was a member of the Xinjiang Political Consultative Conference and ran the '1,000 Families Mothers' Project', designed to help Uighur women develop their own small businesses. She was sentenced to eight years in prison for sending copies of a public newspaper to the United States (Human Rights Watch 1999 and 2000).

[7] Havnevik notes an additional source of inferiorization for nuns: 'Tibetan nuns are … subjected to a triple subordination. First they are discriminated against by the Chinese, secondly they are women within a patriarchal society, and thirdly they have to adjust to a monastic structure made by monks for monks' (Havnevik 1994: 266).

[8] 'Women's struggles in Tibet and even in exile are not a women's liberation struggle but mainly part of the Tibetan nationalist movement' (Tsering Tsomo 1994). Makley

women with their focus on Tibetan culture or economy and the underground activists with their attention to questions of sovereignty and rights—thus appear to be addressing Tibetan rather than specifically female issues. The considerable impact of the 1995 UN Women's Conference in Beijing on women in the Chinese and Tibetan élite seems not to have changed this focus on ethnicity.[9] Even criticism of China's birth control policies seems not to be viewed as primarily a women's issue: in formal politics women cannot challenge these policies because the state has made them part of its core programme of required compliance and thus placed the matter beyond debate, while in illicit, oppositional and exile politics this issue has been handled as much or more by men than by women.[10] In the latter case birth control policies seem to have been considered primarily in terms of their implications for the nation or the nationality rather than because of their impact on women. Issues of women's employment and status, such as the drift of rural women into urban domestic labour and the growth of prostitution in Tibet, are likely to become more relevant to women as disparities in social wealth are increasingly exacerbated by the advance of market economics and globalization in Tibet. In the meantime the focus seems to be on cultural identity rather than gender equality, on contesting ethnic rather than sexual inferiorization.[11]

---

comments: 'When writers turn to representing Tibetan women's resistance, the focus is on these highly visible laywomen and nun dissidents, as counterparts to male actors… In these representations then, the "nation" is still the most authentic unit for the "political", and asymmetric, gender relations among Tibetans themselves, or the different ways Tibetan women experience oppression by the Chinese state, are glossed over' (Makley 1997: 10). Li Xiaojiang has a developed discussion of this issue, and of the experience of Chinese feminists faced with western funding and academic intervention (Li 1999).

[9] The 1995 UN Conference led a number of Tibetan women intellectuals in Tibet to initiate research into women's conditions in the labour force in Tibet, and into issues of female drop-out from schools (in 1990, the percentage of girls students in Tibetan primary schools was 30 % lower in year three than in year one, according to the TAR Social and Economic Statistical Yearbook 1990), and one woman in Lhasa started a development project focused on women's issues.

[10] In the West much of the strongest rhetoric on this issue seems to have been initiated by western men—for example, Kerr 1991 and Moss 1995. For a Tibetan view from within Tibet see below the discussion of P and her mostly male group of pamphleteers, who raised the birth control issue because 'historically Tibet had six million people in total but now the Tibetan population has become less'.

[11] The growth of commercial sex work is sometimes seen as a nationalist issue also. A satirical verse circulating in Lhasa goes '*guo qu hong se niang zi jun sha bu jue / jin ri huang se niang zi jun sha bu wan*'—'In the past the Red Army of Women could not be extinguished, but now the Yellow Army of Women cannot be extinguished.' The Yellow Army, also called in some versions the '19th Corps' (the 18th Corps was the unit of the People's Liberation Army that led the 1950 invasion/liberation of Tibet), refers to Chinese commercial sex workers in Tibet.

In this chapter I try to explore a number of themes which seem to be discernible in the stories of these women, particularly questions of space, ritual and the human body, and the relations of these to each other within the particular political context in which they found themselves in the TAR in the last fifteen years of the twentieth century. The first group, that of formal politicians, exists in the places constructed by the state to add authority to its messages—conference centres and offices, meeting halls and the media (all media in Tibet are state-owned)—but it has no permission to express its own unsanctioned interests there. It is trapped and immobilized within this public space. The second group—specifically the nuns who have staged demonstrations in the Barkor—is denied access to almost all areas of formal expression but seizes another public space, one which is small, informal and overcrowded but which has much greater symbolic value to Tibetans, their primary audience, especially Buddhist Tibetans. This space is the Barkor, the circular alleyway that surrounds the Jokhang temple in the heart of Lhasa, which includes an important market area, and which is seen by many as the historic, ritual, religious and commercial centre of Tibet. The activist nuns, by their performances of their identity in this specific location, have feminized this space, at least as a site of ritualized protest—that is, they have led to the practice of protest in this area becoming popularly identified with certain modes of behaviour associated with them as women. As we shall see, this group has also reshaped two other state-defined spaces—the prisons of Drapchi and Gutsa. The first existed in official statements as a site of model correctionism and humanitarianism, and the second has still never been acknowledged in public by the state as existing. Both have now been reconstructed by the narratives that underground activists have projected depicting them as sites of state brutality and torture. As we shall see, women, and especially nuns, have had a particular role in this process.[12]

The re-contraction of public space and discourse in the late 1980s in Tibet, after a five- or six-year period of relative expansion,[13] seems to me to be related to the elements of ritualization which can be discerned within the political practices pursued by the forms of female politics I discuss here. Politics in the modern Chinese state, in the sense of the expression of organized power through social forms and practices, is

[12] Havnevik stresses the innovative and assertive aspects of this phenomenon: 'Today, with even the nunneries in ruins, young nuns have, so to speak, to create their own roles as nuns. They copy tradition, but they also transform it by combining it with new elements called for in a situation of critical urgency; they become political nuns' (Havnevik 1994: 265).

[13] In 1980 Hu Yaobang, then China's party secretary, led a delegation to Tibet and announced widespread local reforms (see Goldstein 1995 and Shakya 1999: 380–9).

anyway a highly ritualized affair, albeit within a relatively austere aesthetic. Titles are conferred along with privileges and endowments, repeated gatherings are held in appointed places to hear formalized recitations, formulaic expressions of loyalty are made to patriarchs and canonical texts, and a symbolic apparatus of meaning is constructed around certain phrases, institutions and practices which is accessible primarily only to adherents. Elements of political ritual exist in all cultures, and certainly were central to the practice of politics in Tibet and China before their respective 'liberations', but ritual of this kind seems to have acquired a special role for women participants in contemporary politics in Tibet. As I try to show, both the élite female politicians and the street-level women activists are seen as communicating meanings through the repetition and formalization of otherwise trifling actions which have been adopted from predominantly masculine forms of public politics. It is not necessarily the case that only women do this—many collective entities seek to adapt existing structures and rhetoric to convey their meanings—but the ritualistic type of adaptations used by these two groups seems to be related to the restrictions that they faced, and, in my view, may even have resulted in a feminization of areas of Tibetan political practice.

Both categories of women can thus be seen as involved in the same project: contributing to or creating narratives and rituals which are performed within the interstitial public spaces of Tibet which, by means of a 'politics of difference', sustain or promote certain notions of the nation and the nationality.[14] In their various ways these women are, like the women who broke and carried the stones that were thrown during the Lhasa demonstrations of October 1987, inventing or conveying strategies which might appear to observers to be secondary but are in fact formative, and by means of which Tibetans at the present time, to borrow a phrase, perform the nation.

WOMEN IN FORMAL POLITICS: APPEARANCE, STATUS, POWER

The women who work in the co-opted élite appointed by China to administer or lead the Tibetan areas are encountered by the public in highly formalized locations, such as in meetings broadcast by the state television

[14] Bulag 2000a; see also Golan 1997: 75–93 and Siu 1993: 19–43. I am using 'nation' here with deliberate ambiguity so as to include the Chinese sense of *minzu*, a people or ethnicity. What Havnevik says of the nuns and religion could also be said, albeit in a very different way, of the élite women and their involvement in formal politics: 'Without doubting the religious motives of young Tibetan nuns today, one can believe that more than religion is involved when they choose to embrace monastic life. Becoming a nun in Tibet today is more than a commitment to religion, it is a commitment to the survival of the Tibetan people and culture' (Havnevik 1994: 261).

channel, and they live in guarded government compounds behind closed walls. If heard at all in public or in print, they principally express in formulaic language statements of loyalty to the Chinese state and to certain state-approved notions such as stability, development and the superiority of the Communist Party. There are few records, as far as I know, of these women's personal views: since formal politics in China works on the basis of publicly expressed consensus by its leaders, their survival in power depends on their skill in avoiding, at least in public, the expression of non-uniform ideas.

In popular discourse, however, some of these leaders, including some women, seem to be regarded as trapped in these spaces against their wills. This view appears to be based not so much on a notion of coercion—these women were not forced to take up their positions—as on a perception of institutional decay: the party that they had joined in earlier times is seen as having progressively betrayed the ideals and commitments which it offered at the outset, and those within it have no safe way of leaving their positions, let alone of expressing their ideas. This view, clearly part of a project to reclaim these politicians for a Tibetan narrative, rests on a notion of public service, which sees these leaders as having taken up their positions strategically in order to maximize the benefits extractable from the state for their community. In this view they are seen as frontline negotiators with the centre on behalf of the local. Although in the 1960s and 1970s Tibetans of serf or nomad origin had been energetically proclaimed to be natural allies of the Chinese and the Party—with the result that in the 1980s they were assumed (at least by outsiders) to be leftists opposed to religious or cultural reconstruction—the class origins and former ideologies of these leaders seem now to be disregarded by those involved in this process of nationalist re-interpretation, just as they have been forgotten by the state. These leaders, among whom the older ones are known to have suffered terribly from the regime, not only during the Cultural Revolution, can therefore acquire popular esteem just because they have persevered in office despite the difficulties of official politics in China.

The popular regard for those in the élite who survive in political life seems to be related to the awareness that many of them are powerless. The modern Chinese state has gone to great lengths to construct political institutions the task of which is to provide multiple layers of visible confirmation to the appearance of consensus, while maintaining at the same time a suitable display of cultural difference; it thus requires 'different' people, such as Tibetans and former aristocrats, to work within these institutions and to carry out this role.[15] In what are now called 'nationality

15 The expression of difference has been officially encouraged in China at certain times and not at others. In the TAR these times of difference are associated mainly with the 'co-

areas'[16]—those areas like the TAR where non-Chinese peoples have traditionally lived and where they have in theory been granted local autonomy by the modern Chinese state—the pressure to display both consensus and the state's tolerance of difference is even greater, especially at times of tension or unrest, because of the long histories of dissent in these area, above all in Tibet. There is thus a constant pull between universalizing rhetoric (such as class struggle or patriotism) and rhetoric that affirms the separate identities of social groups and nationalities.[17]

The incompatibility between the state's claims of difference (nationality leaders are entitled to express difference and to disagree) and of consensus (all leaders agree), and the perception that many high level leaders have no access to the decision-making progress, contributes, as far as I can tell, to the conviction that 'all Chinese statements are lies', a view which can frequently be heard in Tibet.[18] This in turn creates space for the

---

operation' period of 1950–9, and the 'reform and opening up' period from 1979 to about 1987; these dates are approximate.

[16] The term *minzu*, 'nationality' or 'nation', has come to be used in China as a synonym for the more loaded phrase 'minority nationality' or *shaoshu minzu*, although the majority group, the ethnic Chinese or the so-called Han, are technically considered to be a nationality too. Since the late 1990s all official translations in China have changed to using 'ethnicity' or 'ethnic' in place of 'nationality' or 'nation'.

[17] Bulag demonstrates this conflict in his study of the Chinese Communist Party in Inner Mongolia in the 1940s, an experience which re-shaped Chinese nationality policy. 'Demarcating Inner Mongolian territorial boundaries for the purpose of autonomy, winning the relative autonomy of Mongol herdsmen from the Chinese, universalizing class struggle in land reform, and prevention of Chinese peasants from struggling against Mongol "landlords", all rested on the discourse of group difference as well as a revived subaltern identity. Taking advantage of conflict between class theory and practice with regard to ethnicity, Inner Mongolian Communist officialdom succeeded in framing a signifying strategy in which Mongols, especially pastoral Mongols, the symbolic centre of Mongol identity, were recognized as a distinctive culture that warranted a boundary. This continued as a valid argument which Chinese leaders were prepared to accept not only because their universalized land reform and class struggle had produced great 'deviations', which Mao and other leaders came to deplore, but also because Inner Mongols, as a role model for soliciting support from other ethnic minorities in China and/or incorporation in a future 'unified China', had to be treated leniently.' By the mid-1960s the policies of difference had come to be seen by the Party in a universalist light, and as threats to the state (Bulag 2000b).

[18] This view applies to officials' statements and meetings rather than to individual Chinese, and it varies over time, as shown in these remarks given by a nun who escaped to India in 1991: 'I didn't know that the Chinese were lying to us. I used to trust them. They say a lot during the meetings. But later when we were in prison and came face to face with their policy, only then I learned about their fake policy. When we talked to one another, then all the lies came out. I used to trust what the Chinese told us. My parents used to warn us a lot. I have a maternal uncle who was one of those who fought against the Chinese just before the invasion, and killed many Chinese. He was arrested later by the Chinese. He had two sons and the Chinese told them that they were releasing him and called the two sons and the other relatives, but when all of them went there for his release, right in front of their eyes, he was

idea that Tibetan official statements might be coerced, and have subversive intent. It leads also to the view commonly encountered among Tibetans, and surely many Chinese too, that there is no necessary link in the Chinese system between privilege and power; in other words, the language of difference is seen as cosmetic. The Party is perceived as having given power in general to those who most resemble it ethnically and socially, while having appointed to high position people from non-Party or non-Chinese groups who will confirm its opinions publicly in return for the benefits of high status, but who may in fact have little or no opportunity to exercise power.

The distance between prestige and power is especially marked among nationality leaders, and is doubly so in the case of female nationality leaders. It has been particularly apparent since the late 1980s, and is likely to get wider because the emphasis on difference as a strategy for ensuring sectoral support and productivity in the early 1980s (which produced Hu Yaobang's reformist nationality policies and their promises of enhanced autonomy for nationalities) has been replaced by a discourse about modernization which regards as a serious obstacle any assertion of difference in the political or economic spheres rather than in the cultural domain. The area of allowed difference has therefore contracted, and in addition, a discourse of progressivism has been projected in which the implicit point of aspiration or destiny is ethnically Chinese.[19] Both anti-imperialism and socialism, the earlier engines of Chinese communist legitimacy,[20] are seen in retrospect by Tibetans as having been colour-

---

shot dead. So my parents tell us these things, but we used to tell them that the Chinese would not do such things, and that their polices are good. But later, slowly, we learned the truth. They always tell us lies.' I am grateful to Ellen Bruno for allowing me to use this material from her interview which she conducted in Dharamsala, India, in 1992. The interviewee asked to remain anonymous (personal communication).

19 'The Party's own developmental discourse creates hierarchies both of class and ethnicity through an official social evolutionist schema that tortuously justifies the superiority and inferiority of different groups. In China, Han are anointed as the nationality of destiny, equated with the Chinese Nation (*zhonghua minzu*), while all minorities are classified as being located at various lower stages and exhorted to "catch up" with the Han' (Bulag 2000b). See also Sautman 1997. In February 2000 Jiang Zemin announced a theory of 'three representations', the second of which requires the party 'to represent the progressive course of China's advanced culture', read by some as suggesting that advanced culture is Chinese. According to Li Lanqing, then the politburo member in charge of culture in China, 'in order to become cultural workers who can always represent the course of China's advanced culture, we must lead the people to... become builders of advanced Chinese culture' (Xinhua 2000).

20 'In *1950–51*, the Chinese proclaimed that they were "liberating" Tibet to free it from *imperialist* influences, not the serf system' (Goldstein 1986: 109; emphases are in the original).

blind, at least at the time of their inception in the 1930s and the late 1950s respectively. Modernization, on the other hand, which is the current source of official legitimation rhetoric, discriminates in its Chinese form between the advanced and the backward in ethnic terms.[21] At the same time, it erodes the politics of gender, which, like health and education provision and other forms of affirmative action politics, had anyway been decimated by the withdrawal of the 'iron rice bowl' era of social welfare after 1978, and especially by the 1992 'Spring Tide' reforms of Deng Xiaoping. Both women and nationalities thus stand to lose political access in the modernization project.[22]

The political structure of the Chinese state consists of four main bodies—the Communist Party, the military, the government and the National People's Congress (the NPC)—plus a fifth one known as the 'Chinese People's Political Consultative Conference' (the CPPCC). It is this organization which epitomizes status without power. The task of the CPPCC is to represent the views of people and groups who are not or cannot be members of the ruling party—for example, religious leaders, former capitalists and aristocrats, and those who are 'socially influential'. Its members are appointed by the United Front, the high level Party department which is in charge of forging alliances with non-Party elements, and in return for extensive social benefits they issue regular statements endorsing official policies. The CPPCC, wrote a Chinese official after leaving for the west, 'is purely a "front"; it has no offices or staff and its work is done entirely within the United Front Work Department. The position of the CPPCC chairman is purely honorary.' (Tong 1995)[23] Nevertheless, the women who seem to be most often presented in official discourse as examples of female participation in political life, especially in discussions about women from the non-Chinese nationalities, are those holding positions in this body.

[21] Implicit references to the debate over this historic shift can be found in articles about 'Baba' Goranangba Phuntsok Wanggyal: 'Although his argument that equality is cause and unity effect was objected to and attacked by some, it was approved and adopted by leaders such as Peng Zhen, Chairman of the Central Committee, and was written clearly into the clause of socialist national relationship in the Constitution "equal, unified, and mutually beneficial socialist national relationship". National equality must be placed before national unity. This is not making a mountain out of a molehill, but it is rather an expression of a crucial element in nationality affairs, and a matter of highest principle.' (Zla-ba'i 1999)

[22] 'While females have made considerable advances since the party came to power in 1949, in many areas they have lost ground with the demise of egalitarianism. The capitalistic-style changes accompanying China's transition from a centrally-planned economy to one driven by market forces have left urban women discriminated against in employment, education and even their domestic lives.' (UPI 1996)

[23] Tong Zhan worked as a staff member in the United Front offices in Beijing throughout the 1980s.

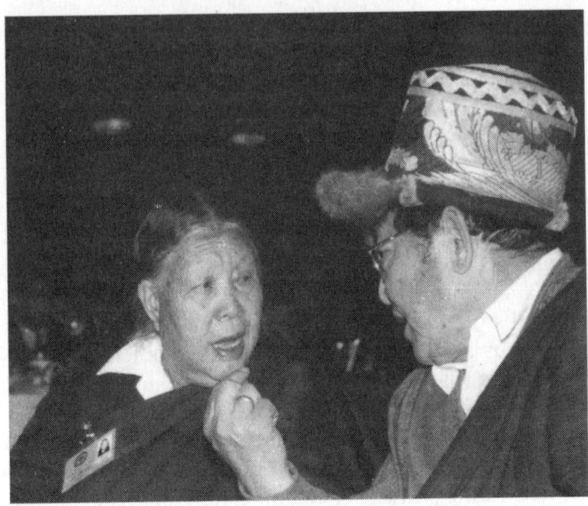

Yabshi Sonam Drolma, mother of the Tenth Panchen Lama. (From Daixan 1995: 46)

The Tibetan women in the CPPCC have been appointed to their positions generally by virtue of their marriages, titles or birth in the traditional system. These figures have included the late sister of the Dalai Lama, Yabshi Tsering Drolma; the mother of the Tenth Panchen Lama, Yabshi Sonam Drolma;[24] the wife of the former cabinet minister, Ngapo Ngawang Jigme, Ngapo Tseten Drolkar;[25] and Dorje Phagmo,[26] the most

24 Chinese: Yabxi Suolang Zhoima or Raoxi Suolang Zhouma, born in April 1916 in Dowi, Qinghai. In March 1954 she was made Director of the Lhasa Patriotic Women's Federation and from 1956 she was on the Preparatory Committee for the Autonomous Region of Tibet (PCART), and a member of the All China Women's Federation. From 1959 to 1965 she was a member of the Committee of the TAR Branch of the CPPCC, and again from 1980 onwards. In 1988 she was made a vice-chairwoman of the TAR Branch of the CPPCC and in 1993 she became a member of the CPPCC National Committee.

25 Chinese: Ngapoi Cedain Zhoigar or Apei Caidan Zhouga, born in November 1919 in Lhasa. In March 1954 she was made a deputy director of the Lhasa Patriotic Women's Federation and in 1959 she was put on the Standing Committee of the TAR Branch of the CPPCC, and on the Standing Committee of the TAR Preparatory Committee. She was a deputy to the National People's Congress in 1964, 1975, 1978 and 1983. From 1965 till 1985 she was chairwoman or vice-chairwoman of the Tibet Women's Federation and from 1978 a vice-chairwoman of the All China Women's Federation.

26 Dorje Phagmo Dechen Chodron (Ch. Samding Doje Pamo Deqing Quzhen) is the twelfth incarnation of Samding Dorje Phagmo (some sources count her as the fourteenth). She was born in 1937 (not 1942 as in some accounts) in Nyemo. She was Director of Religious Affairs of the Gyantse Office of PCART from 1956 to 1959, but in 1959 fled for a few months to India. After her return to Tibet she was made a vice-chairwoman of the Tibet

prominent female tulku, or incarnate lama, in Tibet, whose position was a state function in pre-invasion Tibet.[27] These women sometimes hold national level positions as well as positions in the local Tibetan CPPCC or in its parliamentary equivalent, the National People's Congress (the N.P.C.), the function of which is seen as broadly similar, although it does in fact pass acts of local legislation. Ngapo Tseten Drolkar, for example, held a Beijing-level appointment from 1978 onwards as vice-chairwoman of the Chinese Women's Federation; this too was widely seen as entirely honorary. Occasionally, during the more moderate policy phases of the 1950s and 1980s, the élite women in this category have held high but still cosmetic positions in the local government as well as in the token bodies of the NPC, the CPPCC or the Women's Federation. But since these bodies are perceived as being at the privilege end of the political spectrum, their members are referred to in common parlance as 'gyencha' (*rgyan-cha*)—'jewellery' or 'ornament'.[28] This term can be applied to men as

---

Branch of the CPPCC in 1961 and again in 1965. She was a member of the TAR People's Congress, and a vice-chairwoman of the TAR Congress in 1984, 1988 and 1993. She re-appeared as a CPPCC vice-chairwoman in the TAR in 1977 and remains in that position, and since 1988 has been on the Standing Committee of the National CPPCC as well. From 1982 to 1986 she was a vice-chairwoman of the Tibet Branch of the Buddhist Association of China.

[27] Note also Tangme Konchok Pelmo (Ch. Tangmai Gongjue Baima), born 1919 in Lhasa and until recently a vice-chairwoman of the Tibet CPPCC. She was born into the Sampho family, which included the 7th Dalai Lama. She was vice-chairwoman of the Lhasa Women's Federation in 1962–6 and 1980–3 and vice-chairwoman of the Tibet CPPCC in 1983–97.

[28] A similar term is used to describe women politicians in Mongolia: *chimeg*, meaning 'decoration', 'ornament' or 'beauty'. The use of the term in Mongolia has shifted with the advent of a democratic system there. According to Tumursukh, the term is now used (for example) to criticize women in parliament who have no input in policy-making, or it can be used by ultra-conservatives to denote the proper behaviour of women politicians, which in this view should not include actual involvement in power. The ultra-conservative politician Dashbalbar apparently used the term in this approving sense in reference to two prominent Mongolian women in the Soviet era: 'In the last 70 years, one could say that Yanjmaa *guai* and Udval *guai* participated in state affairs. But Yanjmaa *guai* was a *chimeg* of the state as the spouse of the leader Suhbaatar. She did not have any substantial state power. She was the slave of the state … The same is true of Udval *guai*. She was a beautiful, serene mother, a calm and modest manager, and a dignified lady, but she was not a member of the politburo or a member of the ministerial council. She was mainly involved in social work and again was a *chimeg* of the state. Being the column of the state and being the *chimeg* of the state are different matters. That women were members of the central committee of the Party or deputies of the People's Great *Khural* does not mean they had state power. There were women who modestly fulfilled their duties, enjoyed high reputation among the people, and had the right feelings for the state!' (*Zasgiin Gazryn Medee* 1996: 4) The notion of women as political decoration thus shifted in meaning from Tibet, where it is still used to criticize the refusal of the political system to share power, to contemporary Mongolia, where it is used to

well, but as members of a nationality granted fictive autonomy and as members of a gender granted supposed equal participation in the political process, these Tibetan women leaders are doubly ornamental.

This perception of women leaders as adornments within one or other official narrative, even though it is largely based on the empty role of the CPPCC and is not in fact always correct, seems to colour all views of women and most other Tibetan leaders in Tibet. As a result, the action of the state in drawing attention to these women and this institution as a sign of its inclusiveness serves only to reinforce a widely-held perception of the exclusion of nationality and women leaders from the decision-making process. In fact, the popular view that high status positions are not connected to power, especially for Tibetans and in particular for Tibetan women, reflects the picture given by statistics. Since it was founded in 1959 about eighty per cent of the CPPCC's leaders in the TAR have been Tibetans,[29] but if we look at the formal political élite as a whole—leaders at prefectural level or above in the five main ruling bodies—we find that, according to my calculations, on average Tibetans held 30.2% of the positions in the formal élite during the thirty-seven years after the arrival of the Chinese in Tibet in 1950. This figure contrasts awkwardly with the proportion of Tibetans in the population of the region, which is put officially at around 97%.[30]

A similar picture can be seen with the leadership of the 'mass organizations' in the TAR, a relatively minor and numerically insignificant

---

attack emerging gender equality. For a discussion of the role of women in Mongolian politics see Tumursukh 2000. I am grateful to the author for her assistance with this material.

29 The Preparatory Committee for the Tibet Autonomous Region decided on 6 July 1956 during its sixth session (when it was still a 'consultative' body) that a Tibet branch of the CPPCC would be established, but the first session of the 'Tibet Regional Committee of the CPPCC' began only on 12 December 1959, suggesting that the party had some difficulty in mustering sufficient leading social figures to take part. A Tibetan branch of the NPC was not formed until September 1965 (see Conner and Barnett 1997).

30 The charts show TAR leaders as if they had one position each, but in fact most—except for Tibetan CPPCC leaders—had more than one leadership position (on average 2.3 each) in different agencies, mainly because most also held senior Party positions. Most members of the military are also members of the Party élite, and vice versa, so these two categories are largely interchangeable in this table; but the members of the CPPCC, the mass organizations and the government élite listed here are those who had leadership positions only in those institutions, and not in the Party or military. If double counting is allowed for, the percentage of Tibetans in the CPPCC élite for this period is 68.7%, in the government 34% and in the Party 21%. I have extracted this information by indexing the 10,000 positions listed in the *Zhongguo gongchangdang Xizang zizhiqu zuzhishi ziliao 1950–1987* ('Materials on the History of the CCP in the TAR 1950–87'), 1993. I have discussed the data for 1987 to 1992 in Conner and Barnett 1997, but neither more recent data nor detailed data for the eastern Tibetan areas are available.

grouping constituted by labour, women and youth—the Trade Unions, the Women's Federation and the Youth League. In this area of the administration, which also has negligible political power or status, Tibetans constituted about 58% of the leadership in the years from 1950 to 1987. In the bodies that actually exercise power in the Chinese system—the military, the Party and to some extent the government—about 13%, 23% and 43% of leaders respectively were Tibetan in that period. In other words, these statistics support the popular perception that the more powerful the institution, the less Tibetans have been involved in leading it.

The official narrative about gender equality in China in the Maoist era—that 'women hold up half the sky'[31]—has also been marked by a conflict between universalism and difference, and by a discrepancy between rhetoric and implementation.[32] The constitutions of the new China had guaranteed women 'equal rights with men in political, economic, cultural, educational and social life' from as early as 1949, and in late 1953 women were promised equal pay for agricultural work.[33] Political participation also increased: by 1956 some 12% of the deputies at the NPC were women, and since 1975 that proportion has been steady at around 21%. These statistics are, however, misleading, first because they mainly represent ideological imperatives imposed as part of ultra-leftist projects which in fact otherwise suppressed feminist initiatives in favour of class struggle,[34] and second because in bodies which are closer to the sources of political authority than the NPC more recent figures show considerable declines in women's participation. By 1978 only 5% of

[31] Mao's slogan was disinterred by Jiang Zemin after the UN Women's Conference—he used it in a message published by *China Women's News* in March 1996, adding that the government's determination to achieve equality of the sexes was 'an important indicator of the civilization of society'. In a commentary, *China Women's News* said, 'What modern women need most is real and just equality in lieu of gifts on International Women's Day. The bulk of the laid off workers are women, female college graduates find it difficult to secure jobs, and rural women who fail to give birth to a boy are so ashamed they cannot hold their heads up high' (UPI 1996).

[32] As one Chinese feminist scholar put it, 'louder thunders but little raindrops' (Li 1999: 47).

[33] The first commitment to gender equality was in Article 9 of the 1949 'Common Programme', which is regarded as the first Constitution of the People's Republic. The 1953 'Resolution on Developing Agricultural Producers Co-operatives' set the principle that 'equal pay for equal work should be the rule for both men and women' (Liu and Wu 1986: 534).

[34] 'The gains in social rights and equal social status were making a sharp contrast with the exceptionally awful quality of life women endured.' (Li Xiaojiang 1999: 48) 'The Resolution on Tasks of the National Women's Movement in the Future' approved by the Second National Women's Conference in 1953...was the last time when the word 'movement' appeared publicly in documents of the Women's Federation... From September 1957 to September 1983 the All China Women's Federation had not issued any documents or decisions specifically relating to women. Women's work conducted at the level of the State and government almost stopped completely.' (Li Xiaojiang 1999: 67n. 2 and 5)

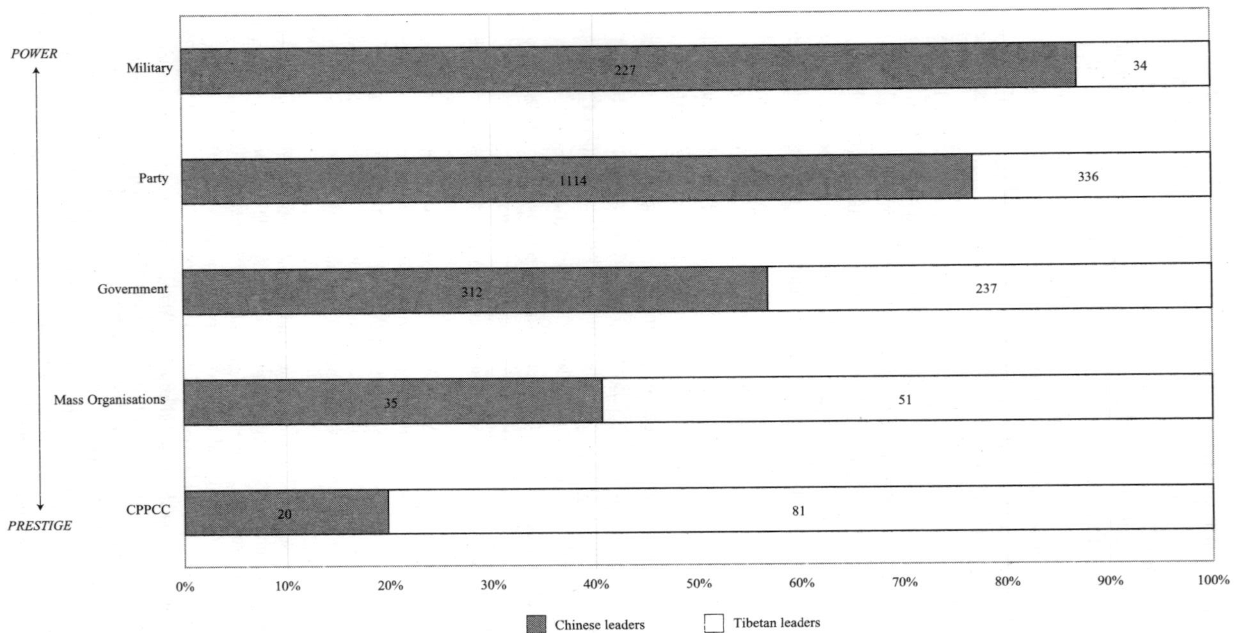

Chart 1. Tibetans in the TAR Leadership, 1950–87.

communes had a woman leader, compared to 70% of Agricultural Production Co-operatives twenty years earlier; in the Standing Committee of the NPC the proportion of women had fallen from 25% in 1975 to 12.69% by 1993, despite the rise in the overall number of woman deputies. In the Central Committee of the Chinese Communist Party, a far more significant body, the proportion of women members had dropped from 10.26% in 1973 to 6.35% by 1992 (Riskin 1997: 47).[35]

It is not therefore surprising that in the TAR there is a popular view, according to Tibetans with whom I have talked, that Tibetan women have a negligible role in the élite, or no role at all. Research seems to confirm this: there were no Tibetan women in the Party leadership at all before the Cultural Revolution. In the period from 1950 to 1987 as a whole they represented only 6.05% of the total TAR élite; even if women of Chinese and other nationalities were included, the figure would be only 7.52%. As with the Tibetan men, in percentage terms the women only have a significant presence in the two least powerful and smallest institutions, the CPPCC and the mass organizations. Even then, their presence in the mass organizations is misleadingly large, because that category includes the Tibet Women's Federation, to which Tibetan women must by law be appointed as leaders. At the decision-making or 'power' end of the spectrum, the picture is very different: in the Party only eighty-two Tibetan women achieved élite positions in nearly four decades, compared to 1,358 men, and only twenty-one women held such positions in the government.[36]

[35] The proportion of women in the Central Committee of the Communist Youth League showed a similar fall from 25.1% in 1982 to 15.15% in 1993. 'Although the White Paper claims that women are participating in general social affairs and quotes the figures of women in the National People's Congress and the Chinese People's Political Consultative Conference, it is generally known that these two bodies are only rubber stamps to the CCP policies. As for the Communist Party that holds real power, there are over 7 million women party members, comprising 14% of the total membership; but in the Political Bureau, not one of the 20 bureau members and the two alternate members is a woman. This might not be a bad thing for the women's movement, because having women in top power positions does not mean any guarantee for women's interests, since those women would be representing not the interests of the majority of women, but the interests of a minority élite' (*October Review* 1995).

[36] These figures for prefectural and provincial-level women should be compared with public official reports, although this is difficult because these usually list women at county level and above. 'In 1998 female deputies to the Tibet Autonomous Regional People's Congress made up 20.09 per cent of the total. Now Tibet has 573 women cadres at or above the county level, and some Tibetan female judges, procurators, police officers and lawyers for the first time in Tibetan history' (Xinhua, 1999). 'The number of women cadres [in the TAR] is 19,510 (up to December 1993), which makes up 32.3% of the whole region's cadres...Among all women cadres, Tibetan and other minority nationalities women cadres account for 19.7% [3,843] of cadres' (Publicity materials for the UN Women's Conference, TAR Government, 1995).

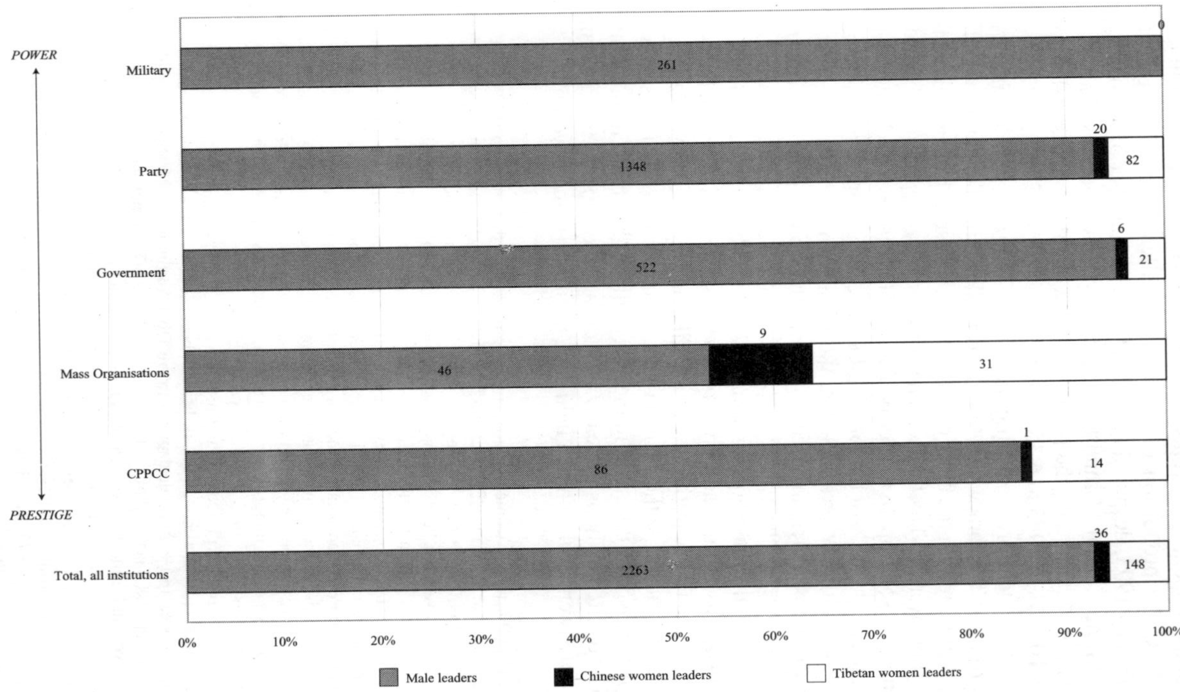

Chart 2. Women in the TAR Leadership, 1950–87.

This small cohort of 148 women leaders within the TAR over some forty years includes not only the women running the Women's Federation, but also those who have been appointed to fulfil regulations which require that at least one vice-governor in each province-level body (such as the TAR) and one deputy commissioner in each of its seven prefectures must be a woman. It also includes the number allocated to what we might call sub-nationalities—the peoples formally regarded as, broadly speaking, Tibetan but classified since the 1950s as separate peoples, such as the Monpa and the Lhopa—where we find that the required positions representing those groups in the NPC and elsewhere are often held by women, thus fulfilling both reserved quotas at one go.[37]

This use of women to represent minorities reflects more than constitutional manipulation. There is a widespread overlap between gender politics and nationality politics in state discourse (and popular discourse) in China, especially since the early 1980s, in that nationalities and other forms of difference are frequently feminized and eroticized (Harrell 1995; Gladney 1994). Thus, in what is perhaps the standard official textbook on nationalities in China, sixty of the book's eighty-three photographs of the non-Chinese consist of young women in their local ethnic costumes (Ma Yin 1989).[38] Representing the nationalities in this way not only characterizes them as colourful and female, but implies also that they are consensual and non-threatening; this in turn suggests that they can be expected to acquiesce in being depicted as backward and accordingly to accept being awarded high status positions without demanding power. It is not surprising, therefore, that there is a counter-narrative in Tibet and other nationality areas which argues that there are no Tibetan women in positions of power within China. This view is not, however, strictly correct: a closer analysis of Tibetan women's roles in the élite suggests that, as with men, at certain times and in certain sectors some women leaders do approach positions of significance.

One form of such analysis was provided to me by a Tibetan informant within the party who categorized the women leaders in the TAR élite according to a generational model. This is the method used by official

[37] Sherab Tsomo (Ch. Xirao Cuomu) has represented the Monpa (Ch. Menba) nationality in the TAR Congress and in the TAR Party Committee since at least 1983, and has held various honorary positions, such as vice-chairwoman of the TAR Women's Federation; she is currently a deputy director of the TAR Religious and Nationalities Affairs Commission. Yangchen Lhamo (Yangjin lamu) has represented the Sherpa nationality in the TAR Congress since 1979, and probably comes from the Dram area of southern Tibet. Yacho (Yajiu) represented the Lhopa (Lopa) nationality (not the Gewa as given in some official texts) in the TAR Congress from 1979 onwards. These women are widely seen as 'gyencha'.

[38] I have included the cover photographs in this count. Gladney 1994: 93 gives similar statistics.

party historians of the leadership, dividing leaders according to their date of entry into the political process, with the highpoint of value being entry during the pre-liberation period. In Tibetan accounts, however, it is commonly intersected by a counter-narrative which divides these leaders according to traditional Tibetan perceptions relating to their place of birth or to their affiliation to a particular leader or institution.[39] The groupings that my informant used were Babas, Central Tibetans, Cultural Revolution women, Horpas, and a 'new' group.

The Baba group consists of Tibetans brought from Ba, the area around Batang, or from other areas of Kham and eastern Tibet, by the 18th Corps of the PLA's South-Western Military Command when it advanced in 1950 from Chengdu into what became known fifteen years later as the TAR. The most prominent woman from this group, which, other than during the Cultural Revolution, dominated the TAR leadership until the mid-1980s, is Gao Shizhen. Gao—her Tibetan name is not known—was only about eleven years old when she arrived in central Tibet with the 18th Corps as a member of its dancing troupe.[40] Other leading Baba women who came to central Tibet from Kham at this time, and who later were given high positions after the 1959 uprising which led to the flight of the Dalai Lama and many nobles to India, were Lhagdron,[41] Lanzhen[42]

39 This categorization is similar to that which I have used, again following Tibetan models, in a paper describing the TAR élite (see Barnett forthcoming).

40 Being a member of a dancing troupe is not in this case derogatory, as it was in the case of Mao's wife Jiang Qing, since Gao was a child at the time.

41 Lhagdron (Ch. Nazhen) came from Batang. She travelled with the 18th Corps of the PLA to Lhasa in the early 1950s and held senior positions from 1959 until she retired in the 1990s. She was a member of the Standing Committee of the Tibet Federation of Trade Unions from March 1959 to May 1966. She was made a vice-chairwoman of the Tibet Women's Federation when it was first formed in June 1960 and remained in this position until December 1979, apart from a seven year period (from 1966 to 1973) during the Cultural Revolution when the Federation was not functioning. She was chairwoman of the Tibet Women's Federation (and secretary of its Party Group) from November 1979 till December 1986. She was a committee member of the First TAR People's Congress, which met from August 1965 until May 1966, and was on the Standing Committee of the TAR People's Congress from August 1979 to May 1990. Her highest position was as a member of the Third TAR Party Committee, which met from November 1983 to October 1987.

42 Lanzhen, whose Tibetan name could be Lhagdron or Namdrol, is also said to have come from Batang, although this report may be a confusion with Lhagdron/Nazhen. Lanzhen was one of six Tibetan women on the 56 member TAR Party Committee from 1971 (female representation was much higher in all fields during the Cultural Revolution—the next party committee, after the Cultural Revolution had ended, had only five Tibetan women among 101 members, excluding alternates). She was on the Standing Committee of the Party in Shigatse from 1972 to 1983 but her only other leadership positions were in the Shigatse Mass Organization and Youth League system from 1981 to 1984 (as party secretary), the Shigatse Women's Federation 1973–6 and 1980–7 (chairwoman), and the TAR Women's Federation 1973–86 (committee member).

and Lobsang Chodron.[43] The Babas are generally thought of as having been highly motivated, principled and Tibetan-oriented, and as having had the potential for considerable political influence in more moderate periods because of their historic links to the liberation era, if they chose to use them.

The central Tibetan group consists of slightly younger women who were born in central Tibet and who belong to a generation which took no part in the 'liberation' itself—they were educated in colleges in mainland China (notably the 'Tibet Public School' near Xi'an) from the mid- or late 1950s onwards, as the new Chinese administration began to prepare its first group of local Tibetan cadres to replace or supplement the eastern Tibetans. Although not all of its members are viewed as purely token, the process of promotion has been much slower for this group than it had been for the Babas: Tsering Drolkar, born in Lhokha in southern Tibet in 1943 and sent to study in Lanzhou in the Chinese province of Gansu in 1955, is the most prominent of this group. She became the first Tibetan woman to be made a vice-chairwoman of the TAR government. But this happened only in 1994, some thirty years after the TAR was formed.[44]

The Cultural Revolution group consists of women who were rapidly promoted for ideological reasons in the late 1960s, usually after they had been recognized locally as 'model workers'. Most notable among these are Pasang, who was one of the deputy Party Secretaries of the TAR for thirty years from 1971 (she was the only woman to hold such a position in Tibet),[45]

[43] Lobsang Chodron, after working in Gyantse, probably under the patronage of the Chinese leader Yin Fatang, became Deputy Secretary of the Lhasa City CCP in 1972, vice-chairwoman of the Women's Federation from 1977, and later a vice-chairwoman of the CPPCC and chairwoman of the Lhasa City People's Congress.

[44] Tsering Drolkar (Ch. Cering Zhuoga) belongs more precisely to a sub-set of the central Tibetan cadres trained in the 1950s—that of the professional/technical cadre group, those whose education and work was in technical or professional fields before later in their careers they were drafted into political work. Born in Tsetang, Tsering Drolkar was trained in medicine at the North-West Nationalities Institute in Lanzhou and was employed in public health work, becoming deputy director of the TAR Public Health Department in 1971, deputy party secretary from 1979 and director in 1980. She became a member of the TAR Party Committee in 1983.

[45] Deputy Secretary Pasang (Ch. Basang) was born in March 1937 in Gongkar, Lhokha, in southern Tibet. She joined a unit of the PLA in 1956 and was sent the following year to study at the Tibet Nationalities Institute. In 1959 she joined the CCP, and was for a time a minor county official in Lhokha until September 1968 when she was made a vice-chairwoman of the newly established TAR Revolutionary Committee. She was given a national position on the CCP Central Committee in 1973 and has served notionally on the Central Committee since then, even though most leaders of this era were purged after Deng came to power. From 1979 to 1983 she was a vice-chairwoman of the TAR government and from 1971 she was made a deputy party secretary in the TAR Party Committee and later was also

Tsering Lhamo[46] and Yangdzom.[47] The group included women such as Chang Weiwen (Pasang Pentok), later Deputy Director of the Supreme Court of TAR, Yang Aiwu (Yangchen), who was on the Lhokha Party Standing Committee in 1973–6, and Hong Ying, a member of the Chamdo Party Committee from 1972 to 1980. Many of these women took counter-traditional, counter-gender names in Chinese—the last three names given here mean 'Protect the Cultural Revolution', 'Love Battles' and 'Red Hero'; they represent a 'universalising' period when class struggle replaced any assertion of nationality differences and when women from peasant or serf backgrounds were rapidly promoted into the political process as part of an egalitarian project. But, apart from Pasang, who remained as the highest-placed woman in the region but with no actual power, these women generally disappeared from the political élite in Tibet when the Cultural Revolution ended in the late 1970s, along with other Cultural Revolution appointees throughout China: the permitted assertion of difference in China which re-emerged at that time had ceased to privilege the admission of women into the leadership.[48]

A fourth group consists of women connected by birthplace or circumstance to Raidi or other male leaders from the Hor or, more specifically, the Nagchu area of northern Tibet who dominated the TAR élite until 2003. One woman Horpa leader is Karma, now in her 40s, who trained in the Central Party School in Beijing and was a deputy governor of Nagchu Prefecture and is now head of the TAR Women's Federation; another is Yumen (Ch. Yumi), who holds a senior position in the CPPCC by virtue of her standing as a leading bard or reciter of the Gesar epic.[49] We know

---

made a vice-chairwoman of the Tibet Branch of the CPPCC. She held these positions until she retired in 2002.

46 Tsering Lhamo (Ch. Ciren Lamu) was a farmer from Nedong county, Lhokha prefecture. In November 1968 she became a vice-chairwoman of the TAR Revolutionary Committee, where she was one of the three representatives of the Gyenlok or 'rebel' faction among the Red Guards. In the early 1960s she became famous as a labour model for farmers while she was the leader of a working group or brigade in her hometown, Kyepa. In the 1980s she retired from political affairs. Her position was regarded as ornamental and she was said to have been put in a position where she could not carry out any significant work.

47 Yangdzom (Ch. Yangzong) was a farmer from Gyatsa county who in 1968 became a member of the TAR Revolutionary Committee, where she was one of the Gyenlok representatives. In the 1970s she gradually disappeared from the political scene. She was a 'mass deputy' on the Lhokha Revolutionary Committee of 1969–76, and a member of the First TAR Party Committee of 1971–6.

48 In particular, those leaders who were part of the Gyenlok faction suffered from the ascendancy of the Nyamdrel faction after the Cultural Revolution, so that few Gyenlok supporters retained significant positions after the transition; Raidi, for example, was associated with the Nyamdrel group.

49 Her name is spelt *g.Yu-sman*, literally, 'turquoise medicine' (see 'Yumi' in Liu and Chen 1991: 138 ff).

Dekyi Drolkar, deputy major of Lhasa City and former head of Lhoka prefecture. (Daixan 1995:50)

little of this group, however, except for anecdotal reports that Horpas are popularly regarded by Lhasa people as even more misogynistic than other Tibetan groups and are therefore rumoured to have encouraged the appointment of even fewer women to power than leaders of the other groups. This may also be due to the fact that currently Horpa appointees often have more than nominal authority and once elevated to the élite their positions can sometimes be more than token.

The fifth group in this model is perhaps the most important to this analysis. It consists of women leaders who received their education after the end of the Cultural Revolution and who are mostly still at deputy prefectural or even county level.[50] Among this group are second generation

[50] The women who were regarded as significant at prefecture level within the TAR in the late 1990s were Dawa (party secretary of the TAR Party School), Dekyi Tsomo (Ch. Deji Cuomu, head of the TAR Culture Bureau until 2001—see following footnote), Sonam

Tsering Lhamo, a national 'model farmer' who became a vice-chair of the TAR Revolutionary Committee during the Cultural Revolution. (Daixan 1995:56)

(Ch. Suolang, head of the TAR Foreign Affairs Office, and a former deputy governor both in Shigatse and in Nagchu Prefectures), Kyi-kya (Ch. Ji jia, head of the Physical Culture and Sport Commission), and Ma Zebi (head of the TAR Civil Affairs Bureau; she is a member of the Hui or Chinese Muslim nationality). The 'new group' women of note at deputy prefecture level are Dekyi Drolkar (Ch. Deji Zhougar, a former doctor born in 1944, now deputy mayor of Lhasa City), Tsung-la (deputy governor of Shigatse Prefecture), Sonam (Ch. Suolang, deputy head of the TAR Culture Bureau), Lhamo (Ch. Lamu, deputy President of the Tibet Academy of Social Sciences), Dekyi (Ch. Deji, secretary of the TAR Communist Youth League) and Tsering Yudron (Ch. Ciren Yuzhen, vice-chairwoman of the TAR Federation of Literature and Art). Dekyi Drolkar, a former doctor at the Lhasa Municipal hospital, has already appeared in the western media, marking herself as a future rising figure ready to create her own story: 'The way they [the separatists] believe is too much. I am not against their religion. For me there is no question that Tibet is part of China. I cannot feel any contradiction between my nationality and my citizenship. Ninety-five per cent of the Tibetans think like me,' she told a German journalist (Juergen Egar, as reported in *Neues Deutschland*, 2 May 1997).

Babas who have been brought up in Lhasa, as well as the children of aristocrats and intellectuals allowed entry into the education system and given, briefly, some official positions after their parents were freed from prison or marginalization in 1978 or shortly after. The way in which women's involvement in formal Tibetan politics will be popularly characterized in the future depends on how this group is perceived by local Tibetans, a perception which the women members of the cohort can potentially generate themselves by modifying the political conventions within which they are bound. This new generation was described by my informant as 'gradually rising, and still too early to assess', but we can guess that it is probably meritocratic in its composition, likely to be educated and internationalized, informed about the implications for women's politics represented by the 1995 Women's Conference, mindful of the tastes of power and opportunity offered to Tibetan leaders briefly in the early 1980s, and aware that narrow ideological positions have proved to be dispensable in China when set beside economic imperatives. At the same time, they are faced with powerful universalizing doctrines, widely held in their peer group both in China and worldwide, which offer either state nationalism (with its privileging of the drive for stability above all) or China-style modernization (with the offer of wealth for the urban élite) as political ideals which displace and marginalize expressions of difference. The direction of women's politics is therefore likely to depend on the paths chosen by this little known group of women power-holders in Tibet.[51]

THE INTERPRETATION OF WOMEN IN POWER

The political system in China, especially in nationality areas, thus produces a popular differentiation between status and power, while at the

[51] Within these main divisions there are a number of women who are regarded as intellectuals or artists; their careers show the high positions available to such figures. They include two of the women at deputy prefecture level—the writer, Dekyi Tsomo, director of the TAR Culture Bureau; she was identified in 1994 as the deputy secretary general of the TAR Party committee and in September 2001 as the second-most junior member of the TAR Party standing committee, making her only the second Tibetan woman to be a member of the most powerful body in Tibet. Unlike her predecessor, Pasang, her position is unlikely to be purely ornamental. Another is the folklorist Tsering Yudron, vice-chairwoman of the TAR Federation of Literature and Art, who was on the Nagchu Party Committee from 1983 and a deputy governor of Nagchu Prefecture. The best known and most senior of these women is the singer Tseten Drolma (Ch. Cedain Zhoima), who was born in June 1937 in Shigatse, and is vice-chairwoman of the Tibet CPPCC, executive vice-chairwoman of the China Federation of Literature and Art and a member of the TAR Party Committee. She joined the CCP in 1961, studied in Shanghai Conservatory of Music until 1964 and was on the CPPCC National Committee from 1964 and on the Standing Committee of the N.P.C. from 1978 to 1987. She was deputy director of the TAR Cultural Bureau in 1983–93, but she belongs to an older generation promoted in an ideological era for propaganda purposes (she fronted the PRC's tenth anniversary concert in 1959), and her positions are seen as purely decorative.

same time enforcing a ritualized mode of discourse which makes it difficult to ascertain from the outside which is which, let alone who thinks what. It is, in other words, a text which presents narratives of autonomy and consensus, but which is widely read as a story of powerlessness and deception, since its unity is presumed to conceal a wide divergence of private views. This contradiction creates the social space for the emergence of contrary or interstitial popular accounts which see some leaders, if they are skilful or particularly daring, as manoeuvring within the system, without apparently dissenting, in order to privilege a particular interest group or principle other than that then promoted by the state. There is thus a corresponding tradition of close interpretation by which local Tibetan 'readers' assess the political loyalties or significance of these leaders and by which they see these leaders in a way not wholly unconnected to the women involved in resistance politics. Interpreted through the ways in which they carry out the formal political rituals required of them, and read within the context of their histories of action and inaction, some of the women leaders in formal politics are perceived as performing the nation while at the same time performing the state

Some of this process of popular interpretation will be based on the pursuit by those leaders of certain ideals that might seem normal or even statist to outsiders, such as opposing corruption, illiteracy or bureaucratic inertia. Since Chinese officialdom has been widely viewed in Tibet, as in much of China, since at least the late 1980s as corrupt and self-serving, the state's promotion of these ideals is seen as purely nominal. A leader who pursues these objectives in more than a token manner can thus be regarded as criticizing the Chinese state, and so might be seen as praiseworthy, distinctive or even subversive. This is especially true of women leaders, since they are perceived as having even less access to power than men and therefore as more courageous if they pursue such issues. If these practices and reforms are linked to a specifically Tibetan discourse, they receive an even higher rating in this process of popular re-evaluation. In such cases, these leaders, including some women, can be reconstituted by these readings as undeclared champions of a specifically Tibetan identity acting within the confines of state discourse.[52]

Much of this hermeneutic process derives from a sense of history. Many of the women in our first group, the leaders from Batang and the eastern areas of Tibet, for example, have histories which suggest greater complexity than might be articulated by their formal positions or statements,

52 This is, of course, a Tibetan view. One Chinese view of the practice of politics by Tibetans sees this in opposite terms, as exaggerated complaints used by them to increase support and subsidies from the central authorities. This has been described to me by a Chinese informant in the form of the proverb, 'the child that cries loudest gets the most milk.'

and of which many Tibetans will be aware. Among the Baba women leaders, for example, were some who may have been communists from an early age, and who were never aristocrats, so that they appear to fit the profile of the revolutionary convert who benefits from China's entry into Tibet. But in fact, these same women have close relatives who were Christians, or who were educated in missionary schools in Batang, and others who were or are among the most senior lamas advising the Dalai Lama; others had relatives who later became leading members of the parliament in Taiwan.[53] These histories constitute a reservoir of popular knowledge that is but one of the many forces that, as we will see, fracture and dissect the binary ideological categories of patriot versus enemy, or of loyal citizen versus separatist—categories which are promoted by the state and widely accepted by outsiders.

Equally, the women of the third group, those promoted during the Cultural Revolution, occupy a new and highly equivocal historical position in the light of the popular re-readings that have emerged since the 1980s. Those women are typically assumed to have come from poor or serf backgrounds and accordingly to have leftist inclinations, for the very good reason that they stood to gain most from the Chinese takeover of Tibet. The current regime, however, has given up socialist ideals in practice and no longer provides for the collective interests of the dispossessed—in many rural areas in Tibet, for example, the Chinese regime is seen as having scarcely relieved pre-invasion conditions of poverty,[54] especially since it now offers little or no free access to education or health. It is therefore equally true of these Cultural Revolution 'model women' that, as the term model implies, they were also used as 'gyencha' by the state, albeit to provide token authentication for a system that promoted a socialist ideal rather than the current reformist system that sees itself as inclusive rather than class-based, and as celebrating difference. It appears, as a result, that some women from this generation have come to be seen within Tibet not as rigid pro-Chinese collaborators or ideologues left behind by shifts in state ideology but as fellow-Tibetans exploited and discarded by an alien political system which has consistently used women and nationalities

[53] The previous Ling Rinpoche, former Ganden Tripa (head of the Gelugpa school of Tibetan Buddhism) and senior tutor to the present Dalai Lama, was from a Batang family; the same family included a prominent Christian doctor, as well as the leading Tibetan representatives in the Guomindang parliament in Taipei until the mid-1990s. The best known example of category-crossing within families is found in the case of Ngapo Ngawang Jigme and Ngapo Tseten Drolkar, since among their children are Tudao Dorje, deputy minister level in the State Nationality Affairs Commission in Beijing, and Jigme Ngapo, head of the Tibetan section of Radio Free Asia in Washington.

[54] Tsering Shakya, talk at Columbia University, May 2000.

Pasang, Deputy Party Secretary of the TAR, 1971–2002. (Daixan 1995:44)

as decorations for its attempts to retain local legitimacy and to remain in power.

A tradition of particularly close re-reading of this kind has accumulated around the figure of deputy secretary (Ch. *fushuji*) Pasang, the one female survivor of the Cultural Revolution generation who remained in power. It provides in itself an example of the ambiguities surrounding even the most unlikely candidates for re-interpretation. Pasang was by far the most senior of all Tibetan women leaders in the TAR, or, indeed, in China. She held positions on the central committee of the CCP in Beijing from the early 1970s for three decades—an extraordinary record of political survival, especially given that almost all of her political generation in China was purged when Deng Xiaoping came to power. She is imagined by many outsiders as the archetypal Cultural Revolution serf-radical, largely uneducated, repeating rehearsed texts to preserve her position and holding leftist ideas in line with her origins as a liberated serf. She is usually seen, therefore, as a willing but feeble figure within a system allied to the former serf class which promotes Chinese rather than Tibetan interests.

Tibetans in Lhasa with whom I talked in the late 1990s, however, offered a very different view. To many Tibetan intellectuals and others, the leftist regime of 1960s China represents in recollection much stronger ideals of public welfare, free education, social concern and dedication than its successor, and leaders from that earlier era are accordingly thought of as less corrupt or venal than their modern counterparts; Pasang clearly benefits from that perception and is seen accordingly as having idealistic and therefore purer motives. The particular representation of her that emerged in the late 1990s, however, was not necessarily based on any knowledge of her views or private remarks, but on microscopic interpretation of details within or at the margins of the political rituals of leadership. These details had mostly to do with her lifestyle. Tibetan interpreters pointed to her living accommodation, which was in standard official quarters, meaning that she had not appropriated any personal funds to build or purchase her own property. Further, they reported that her rooms were sparse, with no ornaments or luxuries, and that her eating habits were meagre, indicating a personal avoidance of luxury or excess. She never married, but had nevertheless adopted a Tibetan child as her daughter; this was read as a sign of being a caring person. There were even some anecdotal reports that she may in fact have been quite competent in written as well as spoken Tibetan. Additionally, she is said to have sent her adopted daughter to an ordinary school and to have insisted that she learn Tibetan there. Finally, she is known to have given her personal support for development projects in remote rural areas of the TAR.

In other words, the story of Pasang has been, or is being, completely rewritten. I do not mean to suggest that these signs are being read by dissidents or intellectuals in Tibet as elements of a pro-independence text in Pasang's story: no one inside Tibet, as far as I can tell, constructs political categories among officialdom in such crude or unlikely terms, least of all among leftists. And I do not know if this re-interpretation is widespread: in theory it may be limited to a group of Lhasa intellectuals, of whom my informants were a part. But it seems to me that the story of Pasang told by these readings is one which is almost indistinguishable, other than in the area of religious practice, from the depiction of a Tibetan nun: celibate, austere, ethical, caring and committed to supporting Tibetan culture and the Tibetan people. This representation thus locates her in a framework that is strikingly similar to that which we will later see projected of themselves by the women resistance activists, one that is based on self-denying dedication to Tibetan culture and the national community. There is no assumption here that the shared territory between the resistance nuns and Pasang is about affection for Buddhism or any other religion, let alone seeking independence: what this view of Pasang shares with the view of nuns is an idea of communal difference or mutuality, something which we might call 'Tibetanness', as opposed to 'Chineseness'. Whether

Pasang or any other female leader is a former serf or a nun, or whether these women belong to a former aristocracy or to a communist élite, is largely secondary to the way they are now being understood and the way their stories are now being told. In these accounts what seems to matter now is not these leaders' ideological histories nor their specific political programmes, but whether they are perceived to be 'Tibetan', whatever that term might mean at different times and to different people. Similarly, although the arrested nuns are Buddhists and are demanding political independence, it appears that they are seen primarily as Tibetans expressing Tibetanness, and as such are not dissimilar from the newly reinterpreted women political leaders.

This point can be illustrated even more vividly by an incident in a little frequented Tibetan tea house in Lhasa in the year 2000: seeing a small photograph of Pasang, three Tibetans, all students at the local university, stood up, folded their hands and bowed their heads. They did this, they explained to me, because it was well known that Pasang was a 'lhamo' (*lha-mo*). This term describes a goddess or local deity found not only in Buddhist but also in pre-Buddhist and specifically Tibetan elements of the Tibetan religious system. Although Pasang is a communist, and although the students were forbidden to hold religious beliefs or to engage in religious practices such as revering or believing in goddesses, she had been reinscribed by them into a specifically religious and Tibetan system in which both she and they are covert and unstated partners by virtue of their shared national and ethnic histories. In this case, Pasang as an ideal woman leader has been beatified and Tibetanized not so much (or not only) as a secret figure of self-denial, but as an embodiment of a local deity, and as a part of the forbidden local pantheon.

The women leaders and the activists therefore are both regarded, at least in this view, in terms of a residual view of the ideal female political protagonist as a paragon of self-denial and purity of motive. This role is embodied in contemporary Tibetan society prototypically by the nun, but it now seems to be perceived in certain women political leaders as well. This is not only the case among nationalists: a similar morality seems to be applied to women by the political establishment. Karma, the former deputy governor of Nagchu Prefecture who was thought to have been relatively powerful because of her links to the dominant Horpa group, is said to have been demoted in 2000 because she had an affair with a junior official. I cannot say for sure that a male leader would not be required to adhere to the same standards,[55] but it seems probable that abstinence and

55 The only recent case I know of where a male leader was demoted on grounds of alleged sexual impropriety was that of Jampa Tinley, director of the Tibetan Medical

moral probity are unequally demanded of women leaders even by other members of the CCP élite.

The process of close interpretation takes place even with the clothes that Tibetan women wear. Nuns express a specifically Tibetan identity through their clothes and their shaved heads, both of which, as we will see, were explicitly denied them by the state after 1990 once they had been arrested.[56] A statement of a similar sort is popularly inferred from the clothes worn by many of the re-interpreted women political leaders as well. Pasang and Tsering Drolkar always appeared in Chinese-style clothes until about 1985. Pasang now appears in western style clothes, typically in subdued colours and unfashionable fits. In her case these clothes are not now seen as demonstrating Chineseness or western influence, but are read as a sign of her austerity despite the lure of modern wealth, recalling the earlier political idealism associated in retrospect with the Cultural Revolution era during which she rose to high position. But since the mid-1980s Tsering Drolkar and Gao Shizhen have sometimes appeared in Tibetan chubas, the distinctive traditional gown or wrap, together with the panden, the traditional woman's apron.[57] Since the end of the 1970s, wearing national costume is not seen as subversive for Tibetans, and has often been encouraged: Tibetans were explicitly asked to take up this practice by Hu Yaobang, then China's leader, in a carefully scripted performance of tolerated difference at the height of the reform moment in 1980.[58] It is still, in fact, required uniform for high Tibetan 'gyencha' the former aristocrats and traditional dignitaries, mainly in the CPPCC, whose role is to announce difference while declaring consensus.

School, but this accusation was made publicly by an aggrieved party and seems to have served an unrelated political agenda; in any case, his position was not at all commensurate with that of a senior leader like Karma.

[56] Sometimes the nuns were able to turn expectations about their clothing to advantage. One woman, formerly of Chubsang nunnery, described how she was able to evade the police after the Norbulingka demonstration in August 1989: 'There were twenty-five of us. Nine nuns were arrested. Each nun was arrested by one *Wu Jing* [armed police]. Many of us were able to run away… I escaped into the crowd. Soldiers came to arrest me but I went to a toilet and hid. Then I and my friends who hid in the toilet, we took off our nun's robes and dressed in lay clothes. The Chinese were not able to arrest us.' (Interview in Dharamsala, 29 September 1990) The women used hats or in some cases wore wigs to cover their heads.

[57] Tsering Drolkar's son, Junjian, which is also a Chinese term meaning 'Build the Army', is said to have changed to a Tibetan name at about the same time.

[58] 'Hu Yaobang came to Tibet in May 1980 but at that time you could not find any Tibetan clothing in the shops. So he ordered Tibetan clothes to be produced and sold publicly. In one meeting he announced: "Why don't you dress in your traditional Tibetan costumes which are so beautiful, why are you wearing Chinese clothes instead? Why don't you wear the beautiful and colourful Tibetan apron?"' (Anonymous interview, Lhasa, 2000)

But for other leaders, who are thought of as having positions with a higher quotient of power than those in the CPPCC, small gestures are more closely scrutinised, and the wearing of clothes was never such a simple choice. This was especially true after Hu Yaobang was removed from his position as general secretary of the Communist Party in 1987: his protégé, Wu Jinghua, a member of the Yi nationality who had taken over the role of party secretary in the TAR in 1985, was dismissed one year after his mentor, apparently in large part because he had worn a Tibetan chuba at public events; this was seen as having taken the idea of a united front too far.[59] In such conditions the wearing of a chuba is seen, for women leaders as well as for Wu Jinghua, as the symbolic communication of some affiliation or ideal, and becomes part of a popular narrative of identity assertion.[60]

There are, of course, reverse interpretations in some cases. Gao Shizhen, for example, has been described to me as 'a leader who did nothing, nothing special happened, she merely made her living', which suggests she is seen as having made no effort to differentiate herself from her Chinese appointment, despite her choice of clothes. Tsering Drolkar is frequently criticized popularly as an opportunist. Dawa, party secretary at the TAR Party School, a cadre with a Cultural Revolution history, and wife of a former Lhasa party secretary, changed from a Chinese to a Tibetan name,[61] but is rumoured to have written a famous private letter to Jiang

59 Wang Xiaoqiang, before 1989 an adviser to Zhao Zhiyang on Tibet policy and a key supporter of Wu Jinghua, gives a sympathetic view of Wu's decision to wear Chinese clothes: 'In 1987 when [Wu] appeared in Tibetan costume at the anniversary celebration of the Tibetan Autonomous Region, he was hailed enthusiastically, bringing the house down among all the Tibetans. This symbolic behaviour had much greater impact than huge amounts of money.' (Wang Xiaoqiang 1994: 291; see also Shakya 1999: 402 and Goldstein 1995) Tibetans are still expected to wear ethnic costume for public events, but the borders of acceptable demonstration of difference are fluid, and in one case in 1991 a Tibetan was imprisoned for three years for saying to his friends 'This year during the Kalachakra…we should put on our Tibetan national clothes.' (Administrative Detention Order, 26 September 1991; see TIN 1992a)

60 Similar interpretations are made of even smaller details of political ritual: the way a certain woman leader has been known to shake hands during official meetings, the fact that Pasang is said to read her speeches with deliberate flatness since 1987, or even the reports that Tsering Drolkar shouted too loudly at foreign and exile opponents during the 1995 Beijing Women's Conference (this was interpreted by some Tibetans as indicating that her criticisms of her opponents were largely conventional). Even Tseten Drolma, the famous singer who became a national symbol of Tibetan devotion to the state and to its leader by singing a eulogy to Mao at a Beijing ceremony in 1959, has been described to me as intentionally undermining that role by repeating the same song at each appearance instead of inventing new songs to describe new leaders.

61 Dawa was deputy director of the Education and Culture Bureau from 1974 until 1986, and was later promoted to be director and party secretary of the TAR Party School; until

Zemin criticizing other Tibetan cadres in 1997; Jiang, without naming the author, used the letter to justify a stringent crackdown on secret religious belief among Tibetan officials.[62] But even in this case there are versions of this episode circulating in Lhasa which say that Dawa's letter was deliberately misquoted by the Chinese leadership, and that she had intended to expose corruption, not religious belief.[63]

The Tibetan nationalists' practice of close interpretation has a much more solid basis than might at first appear: it does not arise out of some dreamy sense of hopefulness, but out of careful attention to the details of Chinese political rhetoric in Tibet. Since October 1991 Chinese political leaders in the TAR have made repeated if veiled accusations that among Tibetan cadres lurk an unknown number who are secretly disloyal to the state. 'We must pay particular attention to a small handful of dangerous elements who have passed themselves off as upright persons with an ulterior motive and have mingled among us,' warned TAR Party Secretary Chen Kuiyuan in 1997, clearly referring to Tibetan officials and members

---

that time she had used the Chinese name Mao Weihua ('Mao Protect China'). She is said to have received an MA degree from the Central Party School in Beijing.

[62] There are many accounts of the genesis of the 1997 anti-religion drive among cadres in the TAR, all of which source the campaign to a letter from a TAR Party member. One account I received described it as follows: 'Last year the Central Party held a meeting on Taiwan at which a document was presented which had been issued by Jiang Zemin regarding Tibet, in which it was mentioned that a party member from the TAR had sent a letter to Jiang Zemin stating that there are many problems of a financial type within the TAR government officials, and adding that many of the Tibetan [cadres] still have huge faith in the Dalai. So Jiang Zemin then had referred the case to [deputy premier] Hu Jintao who in turn instructed [TAR Party secretary] Chen Kuiyuan to look into the matter. The document issued by the Centre was dated 31 July 1997. And as a result of that there was a specific document by the TAR government which just came out. And it is entitled Document 106. The document specifically states that Party members and cadres are misusing state funds for private purposes such as housing and cars, and that therefore investigations and inspections must be launched... this seems to be specifically aimed at the Tibetan cadres, because the Chinese cadres build their houses or have cars in their home areas, and so these things that they do are less visible than those done by the Tibetans... The document also deals with the Party members having strong religious beliefs and having faith in the Dalai Lama, having photos and altars at home [and they are now] being ordered to remove their altars and photographs from their homes.' (handwritten document, September 1998)

[63] There are other, less equivocal cases: two women leaders of the county-level administration in Tolung Dechen were said to have been responsible for the order to demolish all of Rakhor nunnery in the summer of 1998 except for the assembly hall. In October 1997 the Rakhor nuns had refused to sign papers condemning the Dalai Lama at the end of a three month 'patriotic education' drive led by nine officials, according to an anonymous handwritten account from the area (handwritten document, Aug. 1998). Two older nuns were arrested on 9 November 1997, and on 20 November the 79 other nuns were ordered to leave the nunnery and to return to their homes. One local account accused two women leaders, Drolkar *shen-drang* (Ch. *xianzhang*, 'county leader') and Nyima Drolma of initiating the demolition. See also TCHRD 1998c and 1998d, and TIN 1998b and 1999b.

of the CPPCC. 'There are certain individuals… who were trusted by and received special treatment from the Party and government for many years, rebelled against the Party and country at the crucial moment, and stabbed the party in the back.'[64] It is the Party leaders who are the most active in this hermeneutic enterprise, and the nationalist 'readers' are responding to the indications within Party rhetoric as well as to the details of public rituals.

The process by which political actions are subjected to interpretation is, therefore, neither simple nor unidirectional, and it can change quite rapidly over time, from place to place and from one person to another. It reflects an attempt by the interpreters to deconstruct formal political rituals as if they were texts with hidden political meanings that only they, by virtue of their nationality, can read. These interpretations do not necessarily tell us about the views or intentions of the women who are being re-interpreted. It is, however, not the case that these accounts of significant political action are seen as resistance in the sense in which that term is used to describe pro-independence movements: the process of producing counter-narratives, whether initiated by the readers or the protagonists, is certainly more subtle than that story would allow. But in a much more nuanced sense, all these actions and readings are a form of resistance to what we might call an institutional or systemic attack on one or other aspect of identity, or to a growing tendency within Chinese politics to promote universalizing rhetoric and policies. This form of resistance might be as small as the use of the word 'gyencha' to undermine the use of Tibetan dignitaries by the state to support some fictive official ideological position; it is a 'politics of the weak' like that James Scott described among peasant populations (Scott 1985 *passim*) but, which in this case is found within the élite.

Between the two extremes, from the use of the word gyencha to the demand for independence, lie many everyday, unglamorous and often non-discursive actions, often of little apparent consequence except to those immediately involved. In these actions women assert specific

64 'Tibet party leader justifies religious policies, denies 'rumours' of personnel changes', Tibet People's Broadcasting Station, 1997. In this speech Chen gives the example only of Chatral Rimpoche ('Qiazha'), the abbot of Tashilhunpo monastery imprisoned for communicating with the Dalai Lama, but adds that this was 'not an isolated case'. The first statement of this kind that I have found was 'Some Party cadres, including some leading cadres, have mixed in among the local people and no longer believe in Marxism and socialism… They openly believe in Buddhism and regard the Dalai Lama, a political exile, as their spiritual support.' Cited from *Tibet Daily*, Reuters 1991. I discuss other examples of the drive to identify 'hidden reactionaries' in Barnett and Spiegel 1996 and in Barnett 2000, and suggest that it has been the key force in policy formation in the TAR since the early 1990s.

identity in one way or another, in a process that might broadly be called political however personal it may be. From this point of view, Pasang's empty living quarters and Tseten Drolma's monotonous paean to Mao become, through this process of popular re-interpretation, not so remote from the Tibetan women demonstrating for independence, setting up businesses in Lhasa, sending their children to India, or emigrating under false documents to the United States. All of these stories are narratives which tell of self-determining action by these women; through their performance of these actions, these women are interpreted by their constituents, with or without their acquiescence, as taking part in a shared idea of the nation and its future. In other words, they are seen as representing a larger, collective story by which Tibetans, in particular Tibetan women, contest the perceived erosion of Tibetan identity.

CONSTRUCTIONIST POLITICS

Resistance is only one form of political activity, and the assertion of identity is only one type of political objective. The form of politics that we might call constructionist—the strategic pursuit of practical achievements in lieu of suspended or inadmissible larger objectives, such as building schools or encouraging rural development—is frequently seen among TibeHtans as more important and effective than any form of confrontation. Since this approach is within permitted state parameters, it is pursued by many Tibetans both from inside and outside Tibet, and in fact it may be a more significant area of commonality among Tibetans in general than issues of Tibet's political system or status.[65] Constructive initiatives of this kind might be interpreted by some as indications of a specifically Tibetan narrative; this happens particularly in the case of a leader who takes part in a project such as funding or encouraging the repair of a monastery or the building of a school. These actions, again, are not forbidden, since in the post-1980 era Tibetans are allowed to display aspects of their culture and identity. But this dispensation applies primarily to gyencha women and much less to men and women in positions of relative power, especially those in the Party, who officially must become atheists. The fact that accounts circulate of Pasang supporting such activities is therefore of some significance.

[65] Reported on, for example, by Janet Upton regarding local funding of schools in Amdo. (paper presented to the Brandeis Conference on Development, May 2000) Well-known Tibetans who have been involved in major projects constructing schools or clinics in various parts of Tibet include Tashi Tsering, the late Chime Dorje, Akong Rinpoche, Namkhai Norbu and Dragyab Rinpoche. In 1987 the Panchen Lama and Ngapo Ngawang Jigme founded a non-governmental organization with offices in Beijing and Lhasa, the Tibet Development Fund, to carry out projects of this kind.

Tibetan women are certainly significantly involved in such activities and probably in very crucial ways. Dorje Phagmo, for example, a vice-chairwoman in the CPPCC, is often praised for her reported efforts to reconstruct the monastery at Samding where her predecessors were based; by such accounts she, like Pasang, is rescued in the popular imagination from the apparent subservience of her public position. But it is on unknown women in the villages, schools and offices of rural Tibet that the effectiveness of such projects might most depend. An illustration of this can be found in the account given by a twenty-two year old woman called Nyima Drolma, shortly after she fled to India in 1997. She described graduating from a junior secondary school in Tsetang and then, after two years of unemployment, being finally sent in 1995 with another woman to run, without training, a primary school in a rural village:

'We were told that in the past there had been a teacher. But when we reached there, there was no teacher. The classroom was very dusty and it was falling into ruins. … While I was there, for those one and a half years, no one came [from the county education bureau]. When we first reached the school we heard that some inspector was going to come. But no one came. Actually it doesn't at all look like a school, it is just some kind of dilapidated building, a building in ruins, and the village was on one side of the river and the school was on the other side of the river, so it was in a way very isolated. I heard that the school had been constructed in 1992. It was not very well built, so sometimes when we had a little bit more rain the walls would collapse. We complained many times because of what happened and because the schoolhouse is very isolated and most people cannot get there, and are scared to stay there at night. But we two had to stay there, we had nowhere else to go, we had to live in the school itself. And there was no electricity. We frequently complained about this, that there was no electricity and that the students were not coming. And then they [the education bureau] said that they were going to send a lantern, a kerosene lamp. But no kerosene lamp came and no inspectors came.'[66]

The account given by Nyima is bleak: we should expect this, since it was presumably such conditions that led her to give up her life in Tibet and to decide to move to India.[67] That decision to emigrate is in itself, perhaps, a kind of self-determining politics on an individual level, and one that about five hundred girls and women from Tibet, or some twenty per cent

66 Interview by TIN researcher in Dharamsala, 25 April 1997. I express my gratitude to all the TIN interviewees, researchers and those who helped them for their work over ten years of research and interviewing in Nepal, India and elsewhere.

67 The conditions in Nyima's school are similar to those depicted in a rural Chinese school by Zhang Yimou in his feature film *Not One Less*, based on the novel by Shi Xiangsheng, released by Sony Pictures Classic in February 2000. In that film the school situation is redeemed by a TV station in a nearby town which organizes an appeal to help the under-resourced rural teacher.

of the total, have taken each year since at least 1990, when records started to be kept of Tibetan refugee arrivals in Nepal. In Nyima's account it is not a decision born of laziness or curiosity, since she describes efforts at assertion, at promoting Tibetan well-being, and at trying to change the local conditions that she, her colleague and the villagers were faced with: it is an important account of why political action in Tibet of the most fundamental, non-subversive kind, can be so fruitless for those who engage in it. Most of her efforts concerned attempts to mobilize the local authorities over the fact that there were only four pupils in the school when they arrived. The two young teachers complained about this to the local authorities but received no response, so they made a survey of the school-age children in the village and found that there were about one hundred, of whom they excluded thirty whose parents were dependent on the children's labour for survival. The methods they used to attract the other seventy were not particularly liberal—they tried to get the village leader to fine the parents of truant children one yuan a day in cash or in kind. But this fine was only levied once, because the families were too poor to pay. They succeeded in getting between fifteen and twenty children to attend;[68] several were able to graduate to a higher school later.[69] In addition, the two teachers appealed to the county bureaucracy which had sent them to the schools, and which paid their salary of 120 yuan (then about US $14) a month:

'If you walk to the county offices it takes about eight hours, and we walked, once every month, because our salary was paid on a monthly basis. Sometimes they would ask us: "Do you have any problems?" Now, we cannot tell them our personal problems, because they can't help us. But we told them about one problem in the school, that is that the parents are not sending their children to the school. Then they would say: "Okay, we will come and ask the parents to send their children." But of course nobody came.'

Nyima's narrative is thus largely a complaint about the bureaucratic response to the efforts of the two teachers, and an indication of systemic collapse in the educational system. But it also illustrates in passing the

[68] Although statistically girls in Tibet and China are shown to be disadvantaged in the education system—apparently because their families withdraw them for domestic labour—Nyima noted that this does not apply in the first 2–3 years of schooling: 'There are more girls than boys. Because boys, they look after the cattle, their family needs them to look after the cattle. And girls, they generally do the farming, and [so] after some time they are withdrawn from the school. That is probably because at a young age you can't do farming, you need strength. So that may be the reason.'

[69] More of the children would have graduated, but during the eighteen months Nyima worked at the school the local official responsible for administering the exam never turned up to give the test.

extent to which she and her colleague were able to invent their own solutions to some of the difficulties they faced:

> 'When we first reached there, there were no chairs, tables, absolutely no furniture, and the floor was not concrete, it was just earth, and there was lots of dust everywhere. So then we complained and we told them that it is very dirty for the students to sit on the dusty floor. Then later they [the county education bureau] gave us one table and one chair. There was just one wooden board [to use as a blackboard], it was not even black. So later on what we did was that we collected batteries, we broke them, and there is that black carbon inside. So we sort of rubbed the carbon on the board and made it into some kind of black [paint]. We collected [the batteries from] the village garbage. With a lot of classes, after three days the blackboard would fade out again to white. We would use about seven to eight batteries per week. There is some white substance in them which is jellyish, but the black is totally dry. Children would break the batteries and grind the black powder and we, the teachers would mix it with liquid, with water and then rub it onto the blackboard.'

Although her story is couched in oppositional terms, as a critique of the local authorities, it is a demonstration of constructive politics rather than of resistance in the classic, gestural sense. Such narratives are largely missing from popular Tibetan accounts of self-assertion or identity construction, partly because accounts of women like Nyima are generally co-opted by the state to serve its discourse about model workers and so on, and partly because the narratives produced by those involved in the politics of resistance are more dramatic; there may be little or no popular regard for the work of these local figures, particularly the women. Unlike the resistance activists, among whom we must include the activist nuns in particular, women involved in everyday efforts do not see themselves as important and do not produce or disseminate a narrative which locates them either in the politics of construction or resistance; they rarely mention what they do, and see it just as work. The role of Nyima Drolma and her brief but significant attempt at educational transformation in a Lhokha village should, however, not be understated: whether constructed as part of Chinese state modernism or as Tibetan cultural renaissance, it lies at the core of politics in Tibet, a core in which many women whose stories we do not know are almost certainly involved.

BODY POLITICS: NUNS AND PHYSICAL RESISTANCE

The larger, visibly enacted modes of women's political activity in Tibet are those acts of physical disobedience which have become well known to us as a result of reports of demonstrations and imprisonment provided by many Tibetans, including many nuns themselves, mostly after their escape to India. They have been described by Hanna Havnevik in her study of Tibetan nuns, the most important work on this subject, and by Ronald Schwartz in his study of demonstrations,[70] and from time to time have been recorded in the western press as well. Those acts of female confrontation with the state, which have led to about one quarter of Tibetan political prisoners being women, are best known through the series of street protests staged by Tibetan nuns. These began in their most recent form on 19 December 1987, when some fifteen women from Gari Nunnery walked three hours from their nunnery to the Tibetan capital and then entered the Barkor, the circular alleyway surrounding the Jokhang Temple. There they raised their voices and waved banners in protest at 'the continued oppression of the Tibetan people by the Chinese' until the police arrived a few minutes later.[71] The five who did not evade capture on that occasion were imprisoned for one month and eleven days; once released, they staged other demonstrations and went back to prison, this time to serve much longer sentences.[72] Over the next six years some 325 other nuns from twenty-eight nunneries are known to have been arrested,[73] almost all of them for staging brief, politicized circumambulations of the Lhasa Barkor. All these women, except a tiny number who

[70] See Havnevik 1989; Schwartz 1994; and TIN 1991. The discussion of activist nuns in this paper, as in some of the other pieces cited here, is an amplification of an outline report I wrote in 1989 (Barnett 1989). Devine 1993 discusses much of this material, and some incidents are described by Craig 1992. A report by Steve Marshall on nuns in prison was due for publication by TIN in late 2000 but was not available when I was writing this paper; likewise, a major study of exile Tibetan women by Losang Rabgay ('En-gendering Tibet: Nation, Narration and the Woman's Body in Diaspora'), submitted for a PhD to London University (SOAS) in 2004. For an example of press treatment of this subject see *Philadelphia Inquirer* 1966.

[71] Interview with two participants, November 1988. The reasons given by the women to the police were more carefully constructed: 'They asked why we came to demonstrate. They were insistent but, because I was unsure of the situation, I found it very difficult to reply. When I was asked why I was at the demonstration, I gave answers such as, because His Holiness lives in a foreign country, and because the Dalai clique is continually referred to. I said that this is unbearable for me to listen to, which is why I took part in the demonstration'.

[72] The first five nuns detained in this campaign were Gyaltsen Dekyi, 30, from Phenpo; Gyaltsen Norbu, 27, from Phenpo; Ngawang Drolma, 23, from Phenpo; Ngawang Champa, 24, from Phenpo; Gyaltsen Wangchuk, 27, from Lungsho; Gyaltsen Chotso, 26, from Taktse, all from Gari nunnery and caught in the Barkor on 19 Dec. 1987. There are some reports that this demonstration or a similar one by Garu nuns took place on 15 December but this is probably an error. Gyaltsen Chotso had not in fact taken part in the protest—she arrived too late—but when police came to the nunnery and asked who had taken part and supported independence, she voluntarily turned herself in and was arrested as if she had been one of the participants (interview in Kathmandu, 25 September 1991).

[73] See Marshall 1999: 32, 36. A further 79 laywomen are known to have been imprisoned for political offences in this period, about 20% of the female total. The real figures are likely to have been much higher, because of the difficulty of getting information about arrests in the period 1988–90, or generally for arrests outside Lhasa at any time.

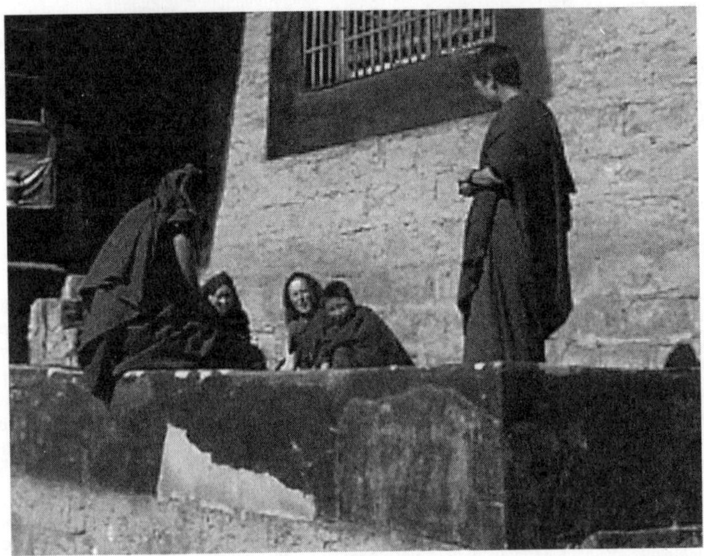

Gari nunnery. (Photo: R. Barnett, 2000)

escaped arrest, went to join the Gari nuns for the next several years in the various prisons and detention centres of Tibet.

There seem to me to be three main narratives surrounding these events. One is that which we as observers can try to shape from the various accounts of the incidents themselves, how they took place, and what effect they seemed to have had. A second can be formed by looking at the chronology and timing of these incidents. A third is that told by the nun-participants themselves after their release from prison and their escape to India.

From the first perspective, the observer's view, the nuns, by repeatedly exposing the state's inability to accept criticism, can be seen as having transformed demonstrations in the Lhasa Barkor into events of charged and cumulative significance, making them similar, in effect, to rituals. The October 1987 incident had signalled the emergence of a new mode of political action for the 10–15,000 Tibetans who took to the streets in protest over the following ten years.[74] There had been a history of resistance and opposition among Tibetans since the Chinese invasion, including a guerrilla movement until 1974, and before the Chinese authorities took over the running of Tibet in 1959 there had been a sub-culture of popular criticism of the traditional Tibetan government as well as occasional violent conflict.[75] But the street protests of 1987–96 differed both from those and from earlier protests against Chinese rule. First, they relied consciously on mainly non-violent methods—besides the one that the asylum seeker in New York and I saw in October 1987, there were only two incidents in Lhasa out of the 180 reported (including 35 from other parts of Tibet) where stones were thrown or Chinese property was set on fire.[76] Second, these protests rapidly became highly ritualized and symbolic. This was largely due, as Ronald Schwartz has demonstrated (1994), to the fact that the participants chose in most cases to imitate the traditional religious practice of circumambulating the Barkor, but it was

[74] This figure is from my records for the period 1987 to 1996 only, and does not include 53 reported demonstrations about which there has been no confirmation, or 37 protests which were not specifically calling for independence or political objectives, or the small number of demonstrations since 1996.

[75] Goldstein describes the use of political satire in poetry among laypeople before 1959 (Goldstein 1982). He also describes a number of monastic clashes with the state (which included the monks of Drepung Loseling defecating over the Dalai Lama's flowerbeds in 1921), most notably the Kundeling and Reting incidents, which led Lhasa to the brink of civil war (see Goldstein 1990; also Aris 1987).

[76] The reference in Goldstein 1995, to the 10 December 1988 as 'a third riot' is incorrect, since it did not include any violence by the demonstrators. The shootings by police of the two lead demonstrators in that incident were in effect assassinations, since they were at point blank range and were not provoked.

not just the religious reference that distinguished these acts of protest. Very quickly they came to impute to certain actions in the Barkor a burden of implicit political significance, so that any raising of a fist or voice there—and certainly every sign of response by the security forces—came immediately to indicate in a compressed form a political statement about Tibet's claim to independence, even without words or slogans being spoken. This made the protests extremely powerful at conveying meaning, so much so that news stories would be carried in the international media, originating from local Tibetan reports, concerning a brief protest by a single Tibetan in Lhasa. The newsworthiness of protests in Tibet, unlike so many other situations, came to be judged not by the number of participants but simply by the fact that an incident had occurred. The state also imputed additional significance to these incidents by the manner of its response: an entire repertoire of security methods was worked out and implemented from May 1990 onwards just to deal with the phenomenon of the Barkor protest,[77] so that by 1993 a western tourist was able to report having seen three incidents of successive solo protest in the Barkor, apparently planned so that one began only after the other had finished: the last one was ended by police arrests within four minutes of the first one beginning.[78]

The transformation of these demonstrations into incidents of added significance seems to have been largely due to the repeated protests staged by nuns: modelling themselves on the example of the single Barkor demonstration by the monks in October 1987, in the following six months the women staged five incidents of this kind before the men turned again to the method of the Barkor protest.[79] Through the act of regular, consistent repetition, never including other tactics such as stone-throwing, the nuns turned the practice of demonstrating in the Barkor into the principal and indeed iconic mode in which modern Tibetan resistance has been performed: the politicized and non-violent circumambulation of the Jokhang temple. In general, accounts of Tibetan protest in this period focus on large-scale incidents led by men, but in fact much of

77 I have discussed these in some detail in Barnett 1992.

78 The incidents took place on 4 June 1993 in the Barkor Square in Lhasa (Interview with 'P', Kathmandu, 9/10 June 1993).

79 The monks carried out a protest on 8 October 1987, in front of the government offices, outside the Tibetan area of Lhasa; the next incident staged by them was an impromptu protest in front of the Jokhang temple on 5 March 1998 which turned into a major incident that led to hundreds of monks running round the Barkor. This began as a small confrontation with a group of leaders at a public ceremony, not as a circumambulation, and included stone throwing from early on, so it was of an entirely different character from the Barkor protests carried out by nuns. Apart from this incident, there seem to have been no street protests in Lhasa between October 1987 and May 1988 other than those by the nuns.

the form and character of recent Tibetan protest, as it has been viewed both among Tibetans and in the international media, and particularly its associations with non-violence, derives from practices established by women.[80] The nuns used their inclination to non-violence, and perhaps in doing so their gender, strategically: by being publicly beaten and arrested, they exposed the police to greater public scorn and forced the security forces to act out the oppression they were being accused of, since there was never in the nuns' protests any trace of violence which the state could use to justify the police or military response to their demonstrations. It is perhaps not coincidental that from as early as December 1987 nuns seem to have been perceived by the security forces as particularly problematic because of their determination to stage protests, so much so that in some cases groups of nuns were arrested or intercepted for even walking towards the Barkor: in a famous case in 1993 a group of nuns from Gari nunnery were arrested on the way to the Barkor and given sentences of up to seven years without having carried out any actual protest.[81] Women thus seem to have been responsible for transforming the nature of this form of protest by stylized repetition so that it acquired enhanced ritual, symbolic and political potency; they took a largely masculine practice and turned it into a much more potent and charged form of challenge to the state.

At the same time these events also seem to have changed the way in which nuns were perceived in the Tibetan community. Perhaps in part because the nuns had never been involved in the violence which marked three of the larger protests, their political statements seemed to have been viewed as of special import and significance by other Tibetans. In addition, not only were the politically active nuns coming from a group

[80] The practice of protesting in the Lhasa Barkor was not the only form of public protest, and there were several attempts, led mainly by laymen as far as I can tell, to invent other strategies of protest after 1987—the 'human rights' protest by students in December 1988, tax disputes in the early 1990s, the 'food prices' demonstration of May 1993, and the sabotage campaign of 1995 to 1997, all of which were more or less veiled forms of opposition to the Chinese presence in Tibet. But these modes of protest were not much repeated and never acquired the symbolic force of the Barkor 'circle of protest', as Schwartz 1994 has called it.

[81] The group of 12 women from Gari nunnery, sometimes known (with two others arrested ten days earlier) as 'the Gari Fourteen', were arrested on 14 June 1993 for taking part in a pro-independence demonstration. There are no reports of protests that day, and the nuns are thought to have been arrested even before they began to demonstrate. They received sentences of up to six or seven years, apart from one minor. The Chinese authorities said the women had been sentenced 'for incitement to subversive and separatist activities' (PRC Government 1994). One of them—Gyaltsen Kalsang, age 23, from Nyangdren—died in February 1995, apparently as a result of prison beatings or abuse (Barnett and Spiegel 1996). The Chinese authorities said that she died of 'serious tuberculosis meningitis' which she had already contracted before going to prison (PRC Government 1998).

traditionally regarded as inferior in Tibetan society as women and in the religious hierarchy as nuns, but they were all, as far as we know, from poor, usually rural backgrounds, and so were of inferior social standing in class and educational terms as well. Paradoxically, this might have inversely increased their standing when viewed as protestors, because their motivations (to cite a traditional Buddhist notion) were more likely to be viewed as pure, since they were not perceived as likely to have any secondary agenda behind their actions.[82] If indeed these women were traditionally looked down upon, by demonstrating in this particularly consistent and tenacious way, nuns in Tibet, at least in the Lhasa area, reconstituted their reputation and standing as Buddhists or as Tibetans among large sectors of the community.[83] They may thus have changed, through their rituals of disobedience, the general narrative about their position in Tibetan society; whether this change is extensive or lasting remains to be seen. But this change was not merely discursive: there is also a practical and strategic explanation for the respect that the resistance nuns acquired, and for the political, social or ritual value that seems to have been attached to their protests. That explanation can be illustrated by looking at the narrative formed by the timing of their protests.[84]

Chronology of protest: re-asserting challenge

The chronology of women's demonstrations, the second perspective from which I want to view these events, is based on the historical shape that open political resistance in Tibet took after 1987. It was built around a single phenomenon: the fact that a small incident staged around the Lhasa Barkor by a group of monks was known to have the potential to trigger a much larger incident involving significant numbers of laypeople,

[82] Gutschow (1997) suggests that in Zangskar, Ladakh, nuns were seen as having purer motivation than the monks, but were thought to be less powerful in terms of being able to convey merit or other spiritual goods. Havnevik 1994, and Schwartz 1994, along with others, have noted nuns as being seen as having less pure motivations.

[83] The 1999 feature film *Lungta* 'Windhorse', written by a Tibetan exile, Tubten Tsering, and filmed by an American, Paul Wagner, heroizes the role of activist nuns and their effect on other women in Tibet. A brief and heroic demonstration by two nuns in the Barkor leads to one of them being severely beaten in prison, and to one of her female relatives deciding to abandon her career as a pop singer and to flee to India. The film is partly a biographical account of the famous Lhasa pop-star Dadon, who plays the lead role in the film. Dadon left Tibet in 1992, at the height of her career (see Isabelle Henrion-Dourcy's chapter in this volume).

[84] The chart shows reported pro-independence demonstrations in Tibet, divided by gender. There were several cases where monks and nuns were more or less equally involved in an incident—these are shown in this chart as half a protest in each category—but generally nuns organized and staged their incidents alone. I have not divided the major incidents by gender, since both women and men were involved in large numbers in those events.

especially if the police were seen arresting, beating or shooting the monks. This is what had happened on 1 October 1987. It was these major incidents staged by laypeople in response to the arrest of monk demonstrators which indicated the widespread loss of political compliance among the population in Tibet, or at least in Lhasa, and a collapse of the state's claim to have a consensual system of governance in Tibet. It was such incidents, probably because they featured an open alliance of lay and monastic interests, which forced the authorities to reconsider and later to change their policies. This phenomenon of lay response happened on three occasions besides October 1987: on 5 March 1988, 10 December 1988, and 5 March 1989.[85] On these days the entire city centre was dominated by protest, and the armed police (and, in the last case, the army) were called in and allowed to open fire, killing a number of protestors. Each incident was followed, as one would expect, by the imposition of particularly restrictive measures by the authorities in the Lhasa area.

The political significance of the smaller, clerical demonstrations therefore seems to have been that, apart from their symbolic impact, they had the potential to trigger these large and essentially uncontrollable movements of spontaneous lay support. Each protest by nuns in the Barkor would therefore have represented to the security forces and to political leaders a potential major threat quite disproportionate to the numbers involved. That in fact this threat of escalation never materialized from a women's demonstration is probably not due to lay Tibetans caring less about the way police treat nuns rather than monks, but to contingent factors—the incidents which led to lay involvement often involved thirty or more monks, while the women's protests were often smaller; the four trigger incidents took place on festival days or around anniversaries, when large numbers of people were present in the Barkor and not expected to attend their workplaces (and so could not be identified just by checking records to identify workplace absentees); the police on those four occasions, until they were trained in different tactics in 1990, beat the monks conspicuously in the street or opened fire on them. Never-

[85] There are reports of a major protest against the imprisonment of three monks in Kardze (Ch. Ganzi) in western Sichuan on 31 October 1999, involving 3,000 people, according to exile claims (Associated Press 1999b). TIN put the number of participants at around 300 (TIN 1999c). There were some major incidents of a different kind, such as a demonstration involving 1,000 laypeople in Lhasa on 24 May 1993 ostensibly protesting against food prices, but this was not triggered by monks or nuns, they did not enter the Barkor, and they avoided explicitly political demands, at least for the first few hours; police opened fire with tear gas, killing one person, but did not use live ammunition. There were also important rural protests, notably one at Kyimshi in Chedeshol, about 45 miles south of Lhasa, on 27 May 1993, and another by about 150 monks at Ganden monastery, about 30 miles east of Lhasa, on 6 May 1996. These did not greatly effect the situation in the capital.

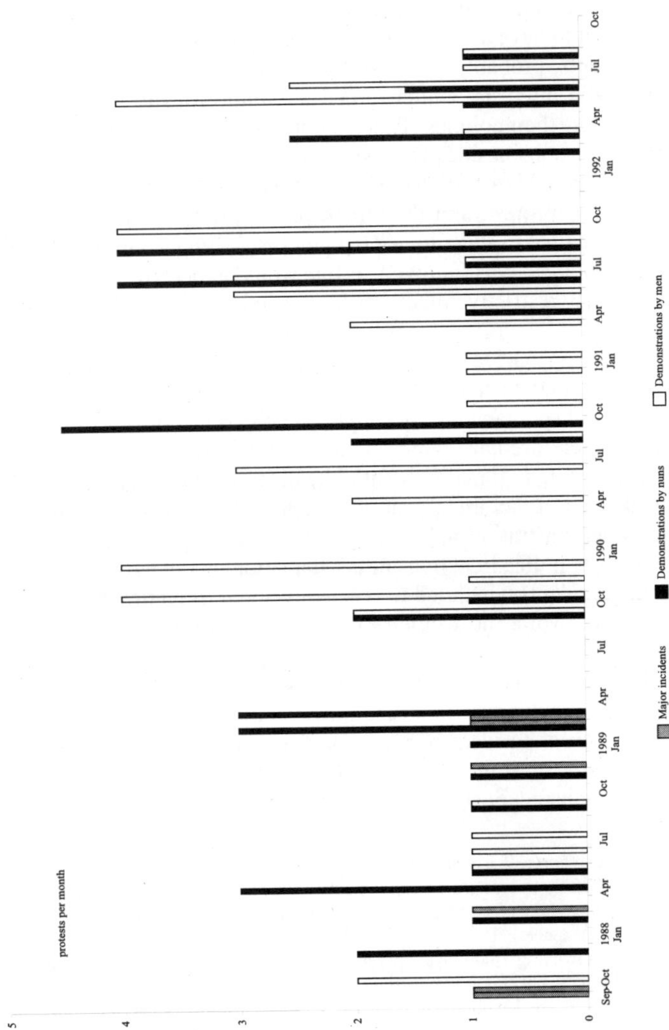

Chart 3. Street Protests by Nuns in Lhasa, 1987–92.

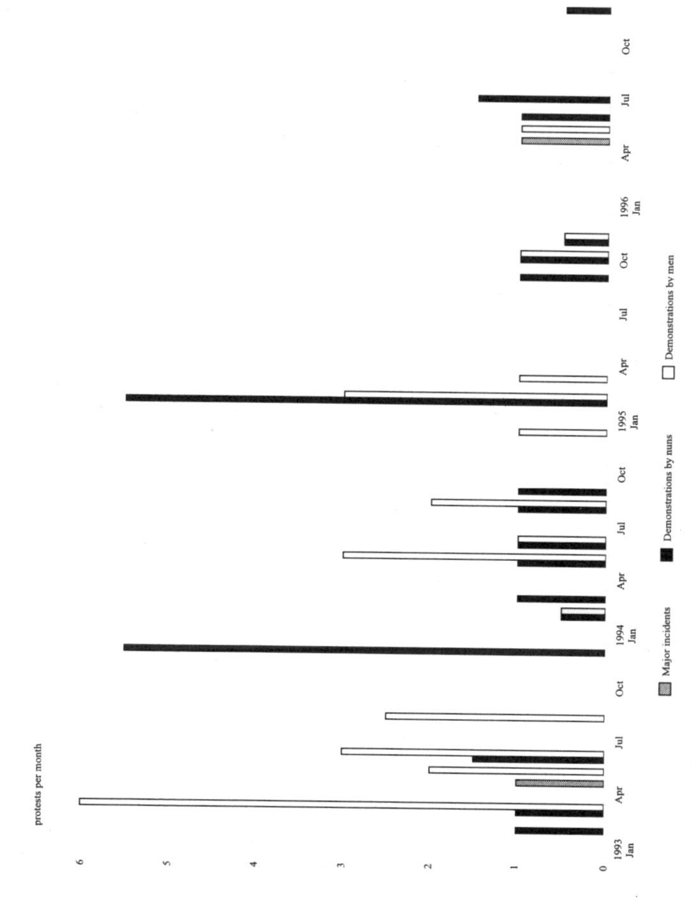

Chart 4. Street Protests by Nuns in Lhasa, 1993–6.

theless, we know of these factors only with hindsight: at the time any of the women's protest would have been viewed as potential seeds of major unrest, and the participants received rapid and aggressive treatment as a result.

The weeks and months immediately following each of these four major incidents—those in which several hundred or more laypeople became involved—were among the most dangerous times to stage any kind of protest, however small, and the times when, it seems, monks and others avoided taking to the streets to express dissent. But it is exactly in these periods of heightened tension after a major protest that the nuns' demonstrations seem to be clustered. Thus there were two protests by nuns in December 1987, three in April-May 1988 and five in January-February 1989, each in the period of high tension following a major confrontation. In the last two cases the nuns who staged these mini-protests were the first to risk taking resistance to the streets again following the shooting of demonstrators one or two months earlier.

A second pattern of nuns' protest shows in the clusters of incidents they staged immediately preceding the anniversaries that fall on 10 March, 27 September or 10 December (these days mark earlier protests in 1959, 1987 and 1988 respectively) on which major incidents were usually expected to break out. There were clusters of nuns' protests just before the 10 March anniversary in 1989, 1992, 1993 and 1995, and around the 27 September anniversary in 1989, 1990 and 1991. These were widely perceived by other Tibetans at the time, rightly or wrongly, as preparations or encouragement for others to mark the coming anniversary by showing that the security forces could or should be challenged.

An even more conspicuous pattern occurs in the period from 1990 onwards, during which there were no major incidents of the joint lay-religious kind seen earlier, perhaps because police tactics had become more sophisticated by then. In this period the clusters of women's demonstrations took place after long periods of silence from the Tibetan opposition in Lhasa, at least in terms of street incidents. Thus in December 1993, when there had been no street protests for five months, women from different nunneries staged five demonstrations; in June and July 1996, following six months of silence on the streets of the capital, they staged another three. During 1995 and 1996, the last two years during which street protests were a regular mode of opposition in the capital, twenty-two of the thirty-four demonstrations in Lhasa—two-thirds of protests in that period—were staged by nuns.

Thus it appears that each time a major incident of unrest provoked a more determined effort by the authorities to deter the populace of Lhasa from protest, or that the interest in staging protests flagged, it was the nuns who sought to show that the authorities could still be challenged by these acts of resistance. The continuance of protest during periods when tension was at its highest, and when the danger of such actions was at its greatest, appears to have been in almost all cases a result of initiatives by women, so much so that it could be imagined that without them the practice of Lhasa street protest in this period might otherwise have only been a pattern of erratic, possibly violent episodes or have fallen into disuse.

In their role as protestors, these women acquired a relative respect that may have led for a time to them being seen within their community as models of nationalist courage and religious principle. The chronology of these events suggests that such a perception was based on or reinforced by the timing and frequency of their demonstrations. Like the woman who first stepped forward from the crowd to ritually damage the police vehicles in the October 1987 protest, or the women who provided the stones at that time which made the police flee, the initiatives taken by these women, rightly or wrongly, changed the tone or level of the situation, and helped transform the protests into incidents of greater significance and power. These women may or may not have changed the political situation in Tibet—some Tibetans and others argue that the strategy of street protests was counter-productive, since it encouraged further state repression[86]—but to some extent they can be seen as having rewritten the narrative within which other Tibetans see protest in general and nuns in particular. The women may not be seen by men as initiators in this story, but it is likely that they are recognized as quintessential proponents of some of the ideals and aspirations of Tibetan political opposition. In other words, we could say that by their actions the women, and the resistance nuns in particular, feminized Tibetan protest: they not only re-characterized it as an act of non-violence, which it had not much been till then (*pace* western and exile press reports) and identified it to a large extent with the feminine, the religious and with ritual, but also located women as formative in the generation of political protest.

The activist nuns (many nuns were not, of course, involved in open protest) did not, however, limit their initiatives to re-enactments of the Barkor protest. In one particularly resonant incident in September 1989, for example, twenty-five women from Shugseb and Chubsang nunneries staged a demonstration in the middle of an official event—an opera performance during the Shoton or Yoghurt Festival—in the Norbulingka park in Lhasa in front of the political élite. There were at least two subsequent occasions in following years when the nuns, on occasion joined by

[86] A view of this kind was put forward by a group of young Tibetans at a panel discussion held at the Tibet Foundation, London, 2 September 1998.

a small group of monks, tried again to disrupt the Norbulingka Shoton.[87] This tactic of disrupting official events in front of the leadership, reminiscent of British Suffragette strategies in the early twentieth century, is very rare even in China, besides the events of April to June 1989. Apart from the monastic protest of March 1988, which involved the much safer proposition of several hundred monks disrupting a semi-religious ceremony within the precinct of their own temple, it has been little seen in Tibet. But the real site of women's initiative in methods of resistance has not been on the streets, but in the prisons of Lhasa.

Women in prison

If we look at the accounts given by women activists after their escape to Nepal or India, a somewhat different picture emerges from that of proponents of a feminized street ritual.[88] Their own accounts tend to focus not on the causes of their protests or their ideals for the future, but on the state's response to their dissent and, in particular, on the conditions of prison life. This is largely because these accounts were given, at least initially, in response to questions posed by exile and western researchers and interviewers (including those whose work I have cited here). Many of these are dominated by the politically disingenuous traditions of human rights reporting and propaganda, and represent the typical limits of that approach, for example by inviting their subjects to confine themselves to certain forms of narrative (principally, in human rights discourse as often used in the Tibet case, to portray themselves as victims of abuse). But whatever the reasons, the nuns on arrival in exile tended to produce, as a group, a narrative that directed attention to the problem of imprisonment. Their initial reasons for doing this, and also the major interests of the interviewers, were generally to depict the prisons as sites of brutality. But

87 Nine of the 25 women demonstrators at the first Norbulingka protest were caught. They were sentenced without trial on 11 September 1989 to up to three years' re-education through labour for 'participating in the splittist activities on 2 September in the Luobu Linka,' according to *Xizang Ribao* 1989. The nine 'went up to the stage in the middle of the performance, at around 2.40 p.m. They shouted frenziedly reactionary slogans such as "Tibet Independence", openly practising splittist activities,' said the paper. A group of 21 Tibetans including seven nuns from Gari, eight nuns from Michungri and four monks from Palhalhuphug attempted to disrupt the same festival by demonstrating on 21 August the next year. They 'had the aim of fighting against the revolution and spreading separatist ideology in order to split our Motherland by shouting reactionary slogans such as "Tibet is independent" … they have thus committed the crime of inciting counter-revolutionary activities,' said the court judgement, which gave them sentences of up to seven years each (Court document, TIN ref. 1 [XN]). There were unconfirmed reports of another incident in the park during the opera festival on 18 August 1993 (see TIN 1993).

88 I have based these on interviews collected by TIN from 1987 onwards, specifically a series of 116 interviews conducted by TIN's main researcher in Dharamsala 1996–8.

in fact the nuns' accounts also describe the prisons as sites of specifically female forms of protest, in which the site of conflict and resistance becomes the prisoner's body.

Drapchi, the main prison in Tibet, has seen several kinds of organized resistance, some of them of considerable ingenuity. In one casc in 1989, for example, five male prisoners secretly formed a pro-independence group to plan an escape and tattooed, in English, the words 'Free Tibet' on the body of one prisoner, presumably because the prison guards could not read that language. That effort is little known outside the prison and was not repeated—the group was revealed by a defector and two of its members were executed shortly afterwards.[89] The initiatives in Block 3 of Drapchi, however, where the female political prisoners were housed once they had been tried and sentenced (before sentencing they were most often held at the detention centre known as Gutsa, on the eastern edge of Lhasa), seem to have been less dramatic. Like the Barkor protests, however, the nuns' prison protests were more repeatable than those carried out by their male counterparts, and in addition, reports of the incidents were more effectively disseminated by the nuns once they escaped, and thus became more widely known in the Lhasa, Tibetan, exile and global communities.

The most famous, and therefore one might say the most significant, form of protest developed by the women prisoners was remarkable in its daring and creativeness, and also in its ordinariness. In line with what again could be seen as a feminization project, it was not directly confrontational, unlike the male initiatives, which required the authorities to respond in force: the women's protest consisted of singing. There were occasions when the nuns (over eighty per cent of the female political prisoners were nuns) sang openly in front of the prison guards, notably when there were attempts to force them to recite official songs expressing loyalty to the state. The repercussions for singing the wrong songs or the wrong words were serious, and many women were badly beaten for singing Tibetan nationalist lyrics in 1990 and during new year celebrations in the prison in 1993 and 1997; one nun later died, allegedly as a result of those beatings.[90] But in June 1993 the women political prisoners found a

[89] See TIN 1990a. The relevant court documents can be found at TIN refs. 23(YY) part 2, 2(XN), 3(XN), 6(ZQ), 7(ZQ) and 23(YY)) and eyewitness statements are at TIN refs. 28(YS), 19(VN)/24(JW) and 31(JW).

[90] Phuntsok Yangkyi, 20, from Medrogungkar, died on 5 June 1994 while serving a five-year sentence for taking part in a brief pro-independence demonstration on 3 February 1992 (TIN 1994b); she was beaten after singing in Drapchi in February 1993. In August 1990 six nuns who sang a song including the words 'If all the Tibetans are united, the clouds will clear' were beaten and transferred to a 'small cell' for a year (TIN 1991b). On 10 February 1997 two other nuns at Drapchi were reportedly beaten and put in solitary confinement for

way of making their act of singing repeatable, symbolically charged, and at the same time highly public: they recorded their songs within the prison cells onto an audio cassette. How a tape recorder was smuggled into the prison, how the tape was smuggled out, or how the women managed to sing the songs without being discovered, we do not know. But they did it, and the single tape, with its sixteen songs (plus some others which were not audible), once it reached the world outside the prison, spawned several copies, one of which reached London. They thus attracted many listeners to a story of political resistance and determination told entirely by the nuns themselves.

The songs, some of which consist of nationalist Tibetan lyrics set to popular Chinese tunes, refer repeatedly to the nuns' strong sense of collectivity. Their sense of belonging is not only, as we shall see later, expressed in terms of their own group of activists, but also in terms of the wider community to which the women belonged and to which the songs are addressed: 'All of you outside, who have done all that you can for us in prison, we are deeply grateful to you and we will never forget you. Therefore I offer a song,' says one of the nuns on the tape.

> Looking from the window
> Seeing nothing but the sky—
> The clouds that float in the sky
> I wish were my parents.
>
> We, the captured friends in spirit,
> We might be the ones to fetch the jewel—
> No matter how hard we are beaten
> Our linked arms cannot be separated.
>
> The cloud from the east
> Is not a patch that is sewn—
> The time will come when the sun,
> From beneath the clouds shall appear.[91]

About one year later it became clear that the police had found out about the singing (though they seem never to have obtained a copy of the unedited tapes): fourteen of the nuns were identified by the prison authorities as responsible for the singing protest, and given lengthy additional sentences, doubling or tripling the time most of them would have to spend in the prison.[92] But, as with the Barkor protests, the nuns had again

---

two years for singing Tibetan freedom songs instead of obeying orders to sing pro-Chinese songs (TCHRD 2001a).

91 TIN 1994a. Another translation can be seen at www.tibetinfo.net.

92 The Chinese Ambassador in the United States wrote to Congressman Michael Capuano on 28 December 1999 that 12 of the 'singing' nuns including Phuntsok Nyidron, Gyaltsen

taken a simple resistance strategy, this time by using modern mechanical media, and turned it by repetition into an incident of enduring significance and political impact. The copy in London was later released to the public (after passages identifying singers had been removed), and the songs subsequently appeared in radio broadcasts, pop concerts and on commercial compact discs around the world. The nuns' songs had gone global.[93]

Singing as a form of popular opposition to the establishment has a history in Tibet, as Melvyn Goldstein has shown in his study of early twentieth century Lhasa street songs (Goldstein 1982).[94] As a strategy for the nun prisoners, it would have fulfilled their apparent commitment to non-violence, and perhaps it was attractive to the women also because it would have again exposed the authorities as self-evidently abusive or ridiculous, since it is so difficult for the Chinese state to argue that the practice of singing is threatening either to the state or to its personnel. In this sense the nuns' strategies both inside the prison and in the Lhasa streets appear more sophisticated than those of the male protestors, where the occasional threat of confrontation had provided a measure of justification for authoritarian responses. These female forms of protest appear to have been crafted and focused assertions of difference; they were chiefly symbolic and therefore operated on a more discursive level. This symbolism seems to have expressed, through their choice of non-violence, their difference by gender (the state was probably regarded as masculine, in view of the composition of the security forces and the élite), as well as, by their language, culture and religion, their difference from the state in nationality and belief. They also represented what was perhaps an even more fundamental difference from their opponents, especially those in the Party: the nuns had a radically different form of political organization, one which was collective, mutual and self-originating, as we shall see, rather than hierarchical, organized or imposed. The practice of singing as a

---

Drolkar, Lhundrub Sangmo, Tenzin Tubten, Ngawang Locho, Jigme Yangchen and Gyaltsen Chodzom had been released, but this turns out to have been incorrect. Ngawang Locho, 28, died in custody at Drapchi on 5 February 2001, where she had been since a demonstration on 14 May 1992. I am grateful to John Kamm of the Dui Hua Foundation for this information.

[93] The first CD version was released in London in July 1995 as *Seeing Nothing but the Sky—The Songs of Tibetan Nuns Recorded in a Chinese Prison*. A French version was released on audio cassette.

[94] Laypeople, including men, were also convicted for offences involving songs. For example, a woman schoolteacher, Dawa Drolma, was given a three year sentence in December 1989 for writing a 'reactionary' song on a classroom blackboard (see TIN 1992b). These singing incidents were not ritualized—they were one-off, spontaneous gestures by the participants rather than a planned or repeated form of symbolic action.

protest—specifically, singing in Tibetan in a group—can thus be seen as a performative encapsulation of difference.

Suicide

In Block 5 of the prison complex at Drapchi, where the male political activists were held, incidents of protest had, as with the women, also involved extraordinary initiative and avoided violence. The male protests included a widely reported march within the prison deploring the death in his cell of the student activist Lhakpa Tsering in 1991 (Palden Gyatso 1997), the handing of a petition openly to a visiting United States ambassador (he allowed the Chinese officials with him to take it from his hands) in April 1991 (TIN 1991a; TIN 1993: 81), and the disruption of two formal meetings in May 1998 (TCHRD 1998a, 1998b; TIN 1998a; Amnesty International 1998). The responses by the prison authorities were violent, and led to shootings, deaths, and long additional prison sentences for the participants. These protests were explicit statements of organized dissent rather than symbolic performances of difference. The female strategies were different: they seem to have been built round smaller actions which could not be interpreted as potentially violent or as threatening, and which embodied and reflected back to the authorities the incompatibility of the demands placed upon these women rather than simply expressing opposition to them. In many cases, the women represented these unbearable incompatibilities in their own bodies; they played out the conflict in themselves. Not surprisingly, therefore, we find that suicide has a special place among female political resistance in the prisons.

Suicides, especially among political prisoners, were extraordinarily common in Tibet, and indeed throughout China, in the Maoist era, when persecution was so severe and endemic that it is hard to define such acts as forms of resistance rather than as solutions to unbearable pain. In the modern era—since the 1980s reforms—the nature of Chinese totalitarianism has been transformed, conditions are generally tolerable or agreeable to some extent for most citizens, and suicides among political prisoners and activists in Tibet are much rarer than before.[95]

Among male prisoners, where it is not infrequent either among political or common prisoners, the significance of suicides seems to be ambiguous. Partly this may be because suicide is, canonically speaking, seen as an offence in Buddhist doctrine, but it may also be because the incidents of male suicide in Tibet in the reform era have not acquired added or

95 Suicides, however, remain extraordinarily high among the general population in China, and are estimated at around 600–800 a day. There is a high incidence of female suicide in China, often associated with forced or abusive marriages. See Lee and Kleinman 2000 and Wang Zheng 2000.

ritualized significance through their frequency or manner, and so have not been presented as heroic or meaningful statements.[96] Palden Gyatso, the famous monk political prisoner who escaped to India in 1993 after some thirty years or more in custody, discusses this issue in terms of the orthodox, perhaps masculine, perception of Buddhist ethics that forbid or devalue suicide. But he is speaking also with the weight of history and a sense of political strategy, because the main part of his experience derived from the Maoist era when suicides were frequent and when a violent death had no symbolic value as a statement of protest at all, since it was normal and discountable:

> Many prisoners committed suicide. Some said they were cowards, while others thought it required great courage to take one's own life. I dare not pass any judgement. No one can understand the extreme despair that reduces people to take their own lives. Death did not frighten the authorities, in fact a suicide was seen as a victory for the Party. The deaths of Nyima and Gednun affected me deeply. I felt sad at the waste of two good lives. I knew both of them well and regarded them as good people. While I often thought of death as a quick release from my suffering, I could not contemplate suicide as an answer for myself. As a Buddhist monk I was brought up to regard human life as most precious. I had to drag myself out of my despair and survive another day to show my tormenter that I had the courage to live.
>
> There was another reason why I could not kill myself. If I took my own life, the Party would not be seen to be responsible. Although everyone would recognize that the Party had driven me to my death still the Party would shun all responsibility. It would have been another matter if I was killed during an interrogation. The blame would then lie squarely with the Party and their hatchet men. When I was being tortured, I often yelled, 'Kill me! Kill me!' (Palden Gyatso 1997)

In this account Palden Gyatso indicates how acts of resistance need to be located in areas of semantic significance or exceptionality in order to acquire meaning, in order to become acts, or rather signs, of resistance at all. It is a poignant reminder of the number of deaths that are meant to make statements but which fail to do so, perhaps because their timing, manner or placement was unfortunate.[97] Among the male prisoners, suicides

[96] Champa Tenzin, a famous monk at the Jokhang temple in Lhasa, committed suicide on 22 February 1992, but the popular response among Tibetans at the time seems to have focused on doubt as to whether he had killed himself. When a Tibetan exile set himself on fire in April 1998 in India, where self-immolation has long been a form of political protest, his action was seen by exile Tibetans as a major heroic incident of martyrdom (see Agence France Presse 1998).

[97] When Geoffrey Banham set fire to himself outside Parliament in London in 1993 in protest at British inaction over the massacres in Bosnia, his suicide led only to a single paragraph note in the 'news in brief' section of a daily newspaper which implied that he was mentally disturbed.

seem not to have been much reported to foreign interviewers or human rights reporters in any detail, if at all, presumably because their colleagues did not see those incidents as important statements. For the women political prisoners of the 1990s, however, all of them too young to know the Maoist era, suicides seem to have been politically significant; in part this seems to have been because they understood that the modalities of the reform era made different sorts of actions acquire political resonance and meaning. Female prison suicides in Tibet again show signs of a repeated and accordingly highly charged pattern, which could be perceived as a suggestion that these deaths might be acts of protest rather than only signs of utter despair. This hypothesis rests largely on a single narrative: that of the discovery on 7 June 1998 of the bodies of five of the imprisoned nuns in their separate cells in Drapchi, reputedly with scarves placed in their mouths, an ancient Tibetan means of suffocation.[98]

No official statement or acknowledgement has ever been made public about these deaths. There are some important but unconfirmed reports that the women may have been murdered, but it seems to be widely believed that they were involved in a collective act of suicide—five women, all nuns, all on the same day, in response to a particularly brutal set of prison punishments imposed after prisoners refused to salute the Chinese flag at a ceremony the month before. For Tibetans who perceived these deaths as a ritual of suicide, we could speculate that the status of activist nuns was further enhanced by the selflessness of these acts. The details and resonances of the unexplained deaths that June remain unclear, because so far we still lack information about what happened, or about how these deaths are viewed by the wider community in Tibet. But there is one case of prison suicide where we do have a detailed account giving the point of view of a resistance nun. It concerns a young woman at Drapchi called Tseyang. She was not initially a political prisoner or a nun—she had been sentenced for what in the west would be called manslaughter or involuntary homicide—but she seems to have identified strongly with those nuns who were also by then political prisoners. This account of her death was given by the famous nun prisoner, Rigzin

98 See TIN 1998c; 1998d; and TCHRD 2000, plus numerous reports received directly from Tibet. The women who died on 7 June have been named unofficially as Ngawang Chokyi (also named as Tsultrim Sangmo), 21, from Phenpo; Lobsang Wangmo, 25, from Phenpo; Chokyi, 21, from Phenpo; Khedron Yonten, 23, from Nyemo; and Tashi Lhamo, 21, from Nyemo. The nuns were probably in solitary confinement and may have been singled out as ringleaders of the 4 May protest against a prison ceremony which had been designed to prepare prisoners for a visit later that day by a delegation of European Union diplomats; the nuns were already on hunger strike following the killing by guards of a prisoner four days before. The diplomats reported seeing no sign of anything amiss when they visited the prison, a few hours after major unrest had taken place.

Chonyi of Shugseb Nunnery, in an interview in India the day after her arrival there after completing a seven year sentence in Drapchi and fleeing the country. It deserves to be given in full:

'I left out one important thing. It is about a Tibetan girl who committed suicide in Drapchi prison in 1995. It was 6 September 1995. Her name was Tseyang. When she was arrested she was fifteen years old. At the time of her suicide she was sixteen and had been in prison for about one year then. She was not a political prisoner. She was from Dzayul county, near Kongpo, and was imprisoned because—she was born an orphan, she had no parents—at the age of fifteen, while playing, she had thrown a stone, a small stone, which hit an old woman on the head, who was over seventy years old. Because of being hit on the head by the stone she died. Then Tseyang was arrested and sentenced to six years' imprisonment in Drapchi prison.

'When she was put in Drapchi prison, there were different sections, and they would put a "normal person" [someone sentenced for a non-political crime] in the group of political prisoners, to get secret information, as a source of information about the political prisoners. They made this small girl into a spy, among the group of nuns sentenced as political prisoners, in the same unit (*ru-khag*), but in a different room. She was very kind and small, and she never gave information to the Chinese officials. She had a quarrel with them, she said: "I don't want to do this, I don't want to make this kind of report, I already killed a woman, so I don't want to do this." Then, because of this, she was often interrogated and warned, and called to the administration office (Tib. *pan kung hre*, Ch.: *bangongshi*), and she was warned, "If you don't want to do this, then your sentence will be increased, we will sentence you to more than six years' imprisonment."

'It was on Tuesday, 5 September 1995. She came back to the room, the cell, and she was crying, she said, "I can't do anything, the officials warned me, they said that they will increase my sentence." Then she cried continuously. The other nuns consoled her, and said "It's okay, we are also in prison." But the whole night she cried.

'Then the next day, the other prisoners, nuns, went to work in the morning, like weaving and cleaning the wool. Then she pretended to be sick, then she stayed alone in the cell. She removed some clothes and stayed with the upper part of the body naked. When one nun went back—her name was Nyima Tsamcho—she went to the cell to get something that had been left in the cell, then she found the girl half naked and crying. Nyima Tsamcho advised her not to stay like this. "Wear clothes, you will be sick," she told her. Then after a few moments another nun, called Ngawang Nyima, went to the cell and she found that the girl Tseyang had committed suicide. With a scarf, made from a kind of nylon (*bsang-ras*). With this round her neck she had tied the scarf to the bed, to the upper part of the bed—we have double bunks in prison.

'Then, after she passed away, the officials of the prison said that the political prisoners had made her commit suicide. When the dead body was brought to Sera sky burial ground, the vultures didn't eat the flesh of this girl. The officials notified the public, announced to the public that the girl had died because she had a severe case of jaundice....'

'When the girl had to give information about the nuns, she had to do that once or twice a week, and had to give the information to the administration office. She would just say things which were not real, like the nuns are praying, and things which were not related to politics. Actually we had talked with her about politics. She was just a very young girl. She didn't know how to read and write—she asked us to teach her to read and write Tibetan. After she would be released she had wanted to become a nun. At Gari Nunnery.'[99]

Tseyang's terrible decision should not be diminished or delimited by trying to define it either as an act of resistance, at some level, or as one of utter pain and hopelessness. Perhaps it was all of these, and certainly it was more. But it is clear, in this account, that Tseyang was involved in acts of deliberate and, for her, very dangerous resistance by giving false accounts of the nuns' political activities to the prison guards. In a larger and perhaps more important sense, which could be representative of many Tibetan women, she seems to have wanted deeply to express her different-ness. Her desire to learn to read and write Tibetan, and then to become a nun at Gari, thus appears as part of a gendered way of performing the nation—a process of cultural assertion and identification whereby, through the acquisition of culturally specific language and religious knowledge, she could become part of an inner group of Tibetan women whom she respected, instead of being made to spy on them for the state.[100] What then did the nakedness mean? How should it be read? It was, possibly, a statement of female autonomy in the prison, that place where no autonomy is allowed, or a demonstration that the final autonomy of a woman over her body could not be taken away from her. If so, perhaps her death should be read as having made the same statement, but writ large and irreversibly; but these are questions about which we can only speculate.

We can see in Rigzin Chonyi's account her perception of the deeply conflicting forces that were imposed on Tseyang as she sought to shift her allegiance and affiliation from one group of women prisoners to another—from that of the largely powerless female common prisoners, among them both Chinese and Tibetans, who are, it appears, generally unable to resist orders from the Chinese that they should act as spies on other women—to the group of Tibetan women political prisoners with

99 Rigzin Chonyi, interview with TIN researcher in Dharamsala, 26 January 1997, part 3.

100 'Living a lay life, taking part in everyday social and economic activity, involves many compromises, and by suppressing their own identity, Tibetans experience a high degree of frustration. Choosing to become nuns or monks today may represent a solution to the role-dilemmas. By so doing, young Tibetans stress their Tibetan cultural and religious identity and seek to make it relevant in social life. They choose what the Norwegian anthropologist Ingrid Rudie calls 'role-blockage', that is, they make alternative choices of roles impossible. In so doing they are creating cultural barriers that are meant to defend Tibetan identity.' (Havnevik 1994: 263)

their specific cultural attributes, their literacy and religiosity. Those political prisoners suffered from their membership of that group in terms of the long sentences, torture and abuses they received from prison guards and interrogators. But they nevertheless represented a point of aspiration to the girl from Dzayul. There is, therefore, in this account a reverse sense of significance, which is important to contemporary discussions about disempowerment and marginalization: the nuns, as political prisoners, appear to have acquired status, entitlement and an area of power within prison society, both among their peers and for themselves. This is reflected in the consolation that the nuns offered Tseyang, referring to themselves as a first person plural, a collective entity:

> 'The other nuns consoled her, and said "It's okay, we are also in prison." But the whole night she cried.' (ibid.)

This could be the normal language of solace, but in the context of this account, it can be read as the statement of a group of women who are aware that through their collectively constituted history of difference they have asserted themselves as a group and acquired an identity which includes access to special cultural goods such as literacy, and which also has brought in time certain privileges and powers, among which are freedom from being asked by the Chinese officials to act as quislings. In a small but significant sense, therefore, since there were areas of activity that the prison guards could not control, these women had found a way to be self-determining. The privileges they obtained were not merely psychological effects, such as the emotional benefits of collective solidarity: in 1990 the structure of Drapchi prison had been completely changed, after the men's secret pro-independence group had been discovered, so that political prisoners from then on were made to live in their own units, separate from the buildings housing common prisoners. The reason for this separation of political and non-political inmates was the officials' fear that laypeople would be influenced by the ideas of political prisoners, as indeed happened with Tseyang and others. This decision represented the concrete recognition by the state of political prisoners, which is to say of Tibetan political prisoners, as a category. This is a taxonomic concession of particular significance in a Chinese prison, where the state denies that it is even possible that there could be such a thing as a political prisoner, let alone one defined by ethnicity or religion. Although this definitional privilege was offset by other forms of material or physical hardship (the political prisoners were often made to stand during meetings, for example, or to carry out extremely demanding physical exercises), this separation amounted to a kind of granting of privileges to those prisoners. It forced the state to concede recognition symbolically of the larger difference, the reality of nation, to the Tibetan activists, so much so that it could be said that the state in this case was forced by these prisoners itself to perform *their* nation.

With the imprisoned nuns, it was even more so: the prison authorities at Drapchi imposed their own mark of distinctiveness on them from the early 1990s onwards—they were forbidden to cut their hair. This was certainly not a rule imposed on other women in the prison, or probably in any prison anywhere in the world. It thus created a unique and, to Tibetans, immediately recognisable group of long-haired women political prisoners. Again, the body is the site of the performance, this time used by the state to represent its ability to impose authority. This was presumably intended as a late twentieth century form of public humiliation, since it forced the nuns to break one of their most visible vows, in a way not unlike the more gruesome and violent forms of public humiliation of nuns recorded during the Cultural Revolution; but it must also have served to define and recognise this group of women that, according to state dogma, did not exist. In a sense therefore, the consolation offered to Tseyang in her final hours, 'we are also in prison', can be read as a statement of a group that perhaps saw itself as free from total despair and oppression because it had defined itself in its own terms and forced the state to confirm and act out that definition.

There is a further implication within this offer of collective consolation, which underlies the description of nuns' political activities throughout this period: the notion of purity of motivation. What I mean here is not a purely religious notion of spirituality, but the aspect of spiritual activity that is most relevant to the prison condition, namely trust between prisoners. It was this that Tseyang was being asked or forced by officials to breach. The implication of the fact that the officials sought out a common prisoner for this task, even at the risk of her being influenced by the political prisoners with whom she would come into contact, is that among the nuns themselves no one could be found to break that bond of trust. Thus, although there has been a debate among scholars about whether Tibetan nuns are commonly regarded as 'less pure' or 'more pure' in their motivations, among activist Tibetans, there seems to have been a perception of great purity of motivation and commitment, at least to the rest of the group. Rigzin Chonyi, in her turn, imputes a pure motivation to Tseyang in her description of that death: that death represents to her the expression of something of value and significance.

In this sense, the most significant part of Rigzin Chonyi's account of the death of Tseyang is her act of remembering—the fact that she chose at all to give this account of this incident, unsolicited, to the interviewer, and in detail. In other words, her opening statement—'I left out one important thing'—is the essential comment about her view of this event, which was that it was important, and, in particular, important within a narrative that she wished to see presented to an international audience. She reinforces this by repeating twice the date of Tseyang's death, and even the day of the week. Foreign interviewers of Tibetan escapees generally find that most have little sense of the western calendar, especially those who have been in prison where every day seems similar. Tibetans in general, apart from the highly educated, do not use dates as aids to recollection; something special is being signalled by these words.

On the primary level, the narrative asserts that Tseyang died as an expression of irreconcilable demands placed on her by the Chinese state, which contested her allegiance to her cultural roots; we shall see later that this is a recurrent theme in women's accounts of politics. But on a secondary level, the narrative implies that the resistance nuns acquired marginal areas of power through their strategies of political defiance which made it harder, it seems, for the authorities to break their will or to humiliate them, and which gave them a kind of élite status in the prison. We cannot, therefore, speak strictly of these women as powerless, at least within the prison. The action of taking part in political protest or of becoming a nun in itself, this narrative suggests, imparts a certain power and resilience.

In the Norbulingka
Many different flowers have bloomed
Neither hailstorm nor winter frost
Will untie our unity.[101]

The street song, which circulated in Lhasa after the nuns' demonstration in the Norbulingka park in 1989, indicated popular awareness among Tibetans that the nuns' primary source of strength lay in their commitment to collective loyalty.

Commitment to collectivity

At the simplest level, this sense of strength and solidarity among the women political prisoners may have been a consequence of their shared involvement in political protest, and the collective decisions which they undertook. Rigzin Chonyi's narrative, and those of other women also, emphasizes the existence of a group commitment, and suggests that that

[101] Translation by Tsering Shakya. The song is also among those sung by the Drapchi nuns in their 1993 tape, parts of which were later published in London as *Seeing Nothing but the Sky* 1995.

they had articulated principles within their group, even to the extent that it seemed preferable to be in prison rather than out of it:

'Among the political prisoners there is a strong feeling of unity. We feel for each other and we feel one. If one refuses we all refuse. If one shouts we all shout. If one says something against a guard we all join in. When one of the political prisoners leave, we all cry, and the woman who leaves feels sad to leave. Even back home her name will be with us in the prison. Out of the prison one feels strongly and actually you want to be back with your friends in the prison.'

From other texts it is clear that the nuns worked strategically to generate this form of mutuality. In particular, although it is not clear how this idea spread from one nunnery to another, they had a principle that seems to have been shared among them: everyone would take personal responsibility for their own involvement in the demonstration. This constituted a specific, pre-emptive agreement not to admit that anyone else was an initiator in the process of planning unrest; it was this that gave their protests the sense of being self-originating, and their prison groups the sense of being non-hierarchic. This practice was geared solely towards the exigencies of interrogation in Tibet. Since Chinese penology is based on the premise that every criminal action is performed by 'accomplices' stirred up by a 'ring-leader',[102] the main objective of questioning is almost always to identify the leader behind or within any given group. The nuns' pacts produced strong positions which confounded this presumption and which interrogators apparently found hard to break. Gyaltsen Pelsang, a nun at Gari nunnery who escaped to India in December 1996, gave a typical account of her interrogation after being arrested three years earlier, when she was twelve.

'When I was questioned they kept telling me "Somebody must have called you to come on, otherwise you wouldn't know at your age," and they said "The others have confessed that they had called you." So I told them nobody called me and I know for myself and I can see for myself that there is no freedom. I told them that I came to the Barkor and saw them demonstrating so I joined them. Because I was

102 These terms are defined in the PRC's Criminal Code: 'Article 27. An accomplice is one who plays a secondary or supplementary role in a joint crime. An accomplice shall, in comparison with a principal offender, be given a lesser punishment or a mitigated punishment or be exempted from punishment ... Article 97. The term 'ringleader' in this law refers to a criminal element who plays the role of organizing, planning or directing a criminal group or a crowd assembled to commit a crime.' In political cases, this is restated as 'whoever instigates to split the country and undermine national unification is to be sentenced to not more than five years of fixed-term imprisonment, criminal detention, control, or deprivation of political rights; ringleaders or those whose crimes are grave are to be sentenced to not less than five years of fixed-term imprisonment' (Article 103). Under a special 1993 provision, the death sentence can also be imposed in the latter case (Xinhua 1997).

young they were trying to kind of fool me… I kept on telling them that nobody had brought me there and that I had come on my own.'[103]

Reports of this kind are typical of all statements by activist nuns and were pre-arranged, forming what seems to have been a key constituent of a sub-culture of feminine resistance. It formed not only a principle of mutual non-incrimination among the women, but also must have been the root of a strategy of non-co-operation with officials. The same principle was applied by the women not only to police interrogators, but to political meetings in prison as well. There was nothing habitual or unconscious about this stance of collective dumbness—it was a deliberately designed strategy to frustrate authority:

'All of us nuns would have some kind of meeting before the official meeting, we have our own meeting, and then we plan our replies. So we generally give very frivolous replies and then after some time they get fed up, bored, and then they don't bother us, [they don't] ask more questions.'[104]

In some political meetings the prisoner nuns pretended not to be able to read the material they were given; in other cases they describe mentally blocking the material that they were being taught, so that they remembered none of it. Perhaps it was in response to this capacity for collective organization that so many nuns were kept in solitary confinement, especially in the first months of imprisonment.[105] The nuns thus seem to have been seen as a significant threat by the Chinese authorities. Like their two-minute demonstrations in the Barkor, they came, as a result of a constructed, deliberate history of repeated, strategic opposition, to embody a tradition of effective resistance to the state vastly disproportionate to their numbers and without offering the threat of violence.[106]

The crucial index of that strategy is the level of response it attracted from the security forces: the sentences, torture, abuse and violence received by the nuns and female activists cannot be accounted for by the actual level of threat posed by their actions or by their numbers. The

[103] Gyaltsen Pelsang, interview in Dharamsala, 18 December 1996.

[104] Ngawang Tseten, interview in Dharamsala, May 1997.

[105] 'At Gutsa [detention centre], they never allowed us to meet [during the interrogation period]—for two months we were separated and no one is allowed to meet, because they thought that we would talk to each other.' Rigzin Chonyi, interview with TIN researcher in India, 16 January 1997.

[106] The nuns were enough of a threat that Chen Kuiyuan, the TAR party secretary, even published a poem focusing on them as a symbol of deceptiveness and violence: 'The land of Kexi is barren, and its people have hard lives …/ Sly nuns break their religious precepts, and dance around prayer flag poles./ Pleased with themselves, these violent disciples exaggerate and boast'. Kexi is the village of Kyimshi, some 45 km south of Lhasa, where there was major unrest in May 1993 ('Disturbance at Kexi' in Chen Kuiyuan 1999: 70; see TIN 2000).

degree of violence done to them in custody, which has been described elsewhere,[107] seems, as far as those of us involved in the morbid archaeology of chronicling these events can tell, to have been gendered: prison interrogators in Tibet appear to have developed special forms of abuse for these women that were not recorded by the male prisoners. In particular, although there are few if any reports of rape in Tibetan prisons or police stations, the guards in Gutsa developed a practice during interrogation sessions between 1988 and 1990 of sexually violating the women prisoners with electric batons. As for the beatings, it is not that the ones the men received were necessarily any less vicious, but the women seem to have been subjected to them for even more trivial reasons, as if the guards were frustrated by the lack of violence or by the imaginativeness of the women's provocations. There are also some signs that women were more liable to be sent into solitary confinement, and for unusually long periods. The available figures suggest a higher death rate among the women prisoners—of the 1,219 men and the 404 women known to have been detained for political offences in the years 1989 to 1998, twenty-two men and eleven women are reported to have died in custody from what were either the result of torture and beatings, suicide or of untreated illnesses[108]—but our knowledge of these events is insufficient to justify reliance on statistics. But it is clear that although there is no record of any violence or threat of violence of any kind by female political prisoners, the treatment meted out to them was equivalent to and probably worse than that received by their male counterparts.

How can one explain this engendering of torture and abuse? It may well be that deeper issues are involved here, such as the guards' desire to brutalize women, an ancient disregard or contempt for women or for specifically feminine disobedience, or a reflection of the low status women including nuns held in Tibetan and Chinese societies. Perhaps, more generally, as with many forms of prejudice, the expression of difference, even when supposedly allowed or celebrated by a society, is deeply repugnant when it asserts itself, and when it demands power even slightly. These acts of feminine resistance may also have recalled historical

107 Reports on prison violence against Tibetan women, including the violation of women with electric batons, have been published by AsiaWatch 1990; Barnett and Spiegel 1992; TIN (Barnett 1989; TIN 1991; TIN 1992); Physicians for Human Rights (Kerr and Ackerley 1989); Amnesty International 1990a, 1990b; International Campaign for Tibet 1996; *Philadelphia Inquirer* 1996; International Committee of Lawyers for Tibet 1998); UN Commission on Human Rights 1990; and other organizations.

108 Marshall 1999: 3, 94. In 2001 an exile report said that there had been 72 'untimely' deaths among Tibetan political prisoners since 1987, including 13 nuns who were reported to have died in custody or shortly after leaving custody (TCHRD 2001b).

threats posed by earlier women rebels in Tibet and elsewhere. From the Chinese point of view, the most dangerous revolt in Tibet since 1959, and the most recent major incident preceding the 1987 protests, was the Nyemo uprising of 1969, which had been led by the famous nun Tinley Chodron. As a charismatic rural leader, she had been able to mobilize large numbers of armed male followers, who had swept across northern Tibet killing many officials and soldiers in isolated garrisons before being themselves wiped out and executed.[109] Nyemo Ani, as she was known, was not a political activist in the modern, rationalist sense: she was considered by her followers to have been possessed by a powerful deity, a minister of the legendary Tibetan hero King Gesar. She therefore recalled a much older tradition of threats posed to the state by millenarian and similar religious movements, familiar to the Chinese from the Taiping rebellion. In Tibetan history that threat is associated specifically with female oracles, who have existed in great numbers, primarily at the rural, grassroots level, their abilities often manifesting without prior indication or training; they are thus quite unlike monks and nuns and operate outside the state religion, and indeed can often challenge it, or even, in Tinley Chodron's case, contest the sustainability of the state itself. The idea of the feminine as a threat to civilization or to the state has deep roots, and the most popular of origination myths for the Tibetan nation-state, when it first emerged in its most expanded form as an imperial dynasty in the mid-seventh century, describes Tibet as covered by a prostrate female demoness (*srin-mo*) who had to be tied down or nailed to the soil by the ruler Songtsen Gampo before the country could be administered and pacified (Gyatso 1989; Kapstein 1992). Female spirituality, at least when it is outside the confines of Buddhism, is seen as a force that must be tamed or suppressed if the state is to survive.

There had in fact been cases before the Nyemo Uprising of women fighters and rebels in Tibetan history.[110] During the resistance war in Tibet (largely in Kham) of 1956–9 some of the fighting against the Chinese

[109] Those executed in summer 1969 for fighting with Tinley Chodron included at least one woman, named Rindron (see Barnett 1994: 71 for a photograph of her at the execution ground). See also Havnevik 1994: 265, and Shakya 1999: 344–7.

[110] Migyur Dorje Madrong, in a survey of leading Tibetan women in Tibetan history, notes few women political leaders at the national level. 'To this day I have not come across any text mentioning great women holding political power and manoeuvring the state governance. But it is true that all great women have made efforts and contributed greatly in the political, economic and social spheres.' Twelve are listed in the survey as county or regional leaders of historic note (Madrong 1992). Havnevik notes reports of a nun chieftain who ruled in Narok until 1959 and who 'administered the whole area… helped by two male subjects, one dealing with the local law and order and the other with the Central Government' (Havnevik 1989: 82–3).

military had been led by women, although these stories seem to be emerging only now in written accounts of that war.[111] In Lhasa in 1959 a major demonstration had been staged by women under the leadership of several women, most famously Kundeling Kunsang and Galingshar Ani.[112] Communist China has its own legends of militant women, notably Mulan, now heroized by the Party as an exemplar of uprisings against invaders and of female commitment to defending the nation. The traditional versions of Mulan, however, praise her because she turned down the offer of high political and military office in order to return to domestic womanhood:

> On her return [from war] she sees the Son of Heaven,
> The Son of Heaven sits in the Splendid Hall.
> He gives out promotions in twelve ranks
> And prizes of a hundred thousand and more.
> The Khan asks her what she desires.
> 'Mulan has no use for a minister's post.

[111] Dorje Yudron, wife of the Nyarong chieftain Gyari Nyima led a major revolt against the Chinese forces in the area in March 1956; a brief description is given by Jamyang Norbu in Norbu 1994: 192–3. McGranahan quotes Dorje Yudron as telling her: "At that time Gyari Nyima [my husband] and Nordzin Lhamo [my sister and his elder wife] were not there, and it fell to me to take up the leadership of the people. I was young, around 25, and was drawn into it by the circumstances. It was the first time that I had to make such decisions. I was not a heroine, but it was something that I had to do." She went on to tell me that there were other women who had similar experiences, but she did not know their names' (McGranahan 2001). See also the accounts of Ani Pachen (2000) and Ama Adhe (2000).

[112] According to Russell and Singeri, 'an *ad hoc* meeting of Lhasa women on 11 March 1959 listed five demands for the demonstration the next day. These focused on who should run Tibet, not on the question of independence: (1) The Chinese must leave Tibet. (2) Tibet belongs to the Tibetans. (3) Tibetans were and are capable of running the administration of Tibet efficiently. (4) The Chinese have no right and authority whatsoever to involve themselves in the administration of Tibet. (5) The Chinese have no right to interfere in the internal affairs of Tibet. At the demonstration Kunsang in her speech insisted on non-violence and called on women to organise themselves: "Holding to the principle of non-violence, as a last resort we will go down on our knees to the Chinese and beg them to return to their own country...Since we are all aware of what is happening in Tibet, we women of Tibet cannot stand by and tolerate these evil events. We cannot stay at home and do nothing. We must regain our freedom through non-violence and beg the Chinese to leave our country. This must be only the first meeting of Tibetan women—it must not be the last. From now we must gather often for this is just the beginning of our work." She was reportedly executed about ten years later; Galingshar Ani, a nun from Michungri nunnery, is said to died in prison, along with Pekong Penpa Dolma and other leaders.' (Russell and Singeri 1992). See also Dauncey 1993: 24–8. Havnevik also names Tsamgung Ani Yonten as a leader of the demonstration (Havnevik 1989: 84). Schwartz contrasts the 'prominent role' played by individual nuns in resistance to the Chinese occupation such as the 1959 demonstration and the Nyemo Ani uprising, with the organised political activity by nuns in the late 1980s, which has 'little or no precedent' (Schwartz 1994: 99).

I wish to ride a swift mount
To take me back to my home.'[113]

The Mulan legend could therefore be interpreted as a moral guide to the proper limits of female activism, and as an implicit reminder of the potential political, rather than military, threat posed by females to the state: it suggests that their power is discursive rather than material.[114] That view can also be seen in Tibetan sayings that refer to the dangers of female involvement in politics—for example, in warnings against the tendency of women to undermine male decision-making, particularly among leaders. Tsering Chotso, blaming Chinese or Nepali misogynist influences, cites a seventh century Tibetan law as saying 'a man should keep to his views and must not pave the way for women's voices'[115] and I know of at least one case in which a leading Tibetan cadre said of the Chinese: 'The Tibetans lost power to the Chinese, but the Chinese lost power to women.'[116] That remark has been variously explained to me as meaning that Chinese leaders are weak in that they are dominated by their wives, or that they are driven by insatiable sexual appetites to depend on women or prostitutes for sexual satisfaction. Indeed, there are occasional accounts of Chinese leaders surrounding themselves with women used to provide sexual services,[117] and the surge of Chinese-led prostitution since 1990 around the Chinese and military areas of Lhasa, which local Chinese leaders have notoriously failed to contain, fuels Tibetan perceptions of this kind (not that Tibetan men do not also frequent the brothels). Perhaps, also, the phrase recalls the Cultural Revolution era, when Mao can

113 Mulan is supposed to have joined the army dressed as a man in place of her father, who was ill or absent. She became a respected soldier and was then offered political office, with no one realizing till then that she was a woman. The translation of this anonymous poem, dated by some to the fifth century, is taken from Frankel 1976. Disney released a feature cartoon based on this story, which was also shown in China, in June 1999.

114 A modern Chinese version of the Mulan saying is used by the CCP, as in this popular rallying song: *Xiang qian jin, xiang qian jin / zhan shi de ze ren zhong / fu niu de yuan chou sheng / gu you Hua mu lan / jin you niang zi jun* ('Forge ahead, forge ahead, / The soldiers' responsibility is heavy, / The women's hatred is deep, / There was Hua Mulan in ancient times, / [She] joined the army to replace her father, / There are women soldiers today').

115 One of the Fifth Dalai Lama's writings (Ngawang Lobsang Gyatso 1995: 20) is given as a source for this law; Chotso also cites an undated proverb 'Count not on horses for your riches, / Partake not the meat for your meal, / And rely not on woman for decisive matters' (Chotso 1991).

116 '*Bod mi rgya la dbang shor ba red / yin nas rgya mi skyes dman la dbang shor ba red*' Anonymous interview, September 1999.

117 Li Zhisui 1992 describes Mao's use of women. Craig 1992 gives a detailed if unconfirmed account, based on an interview with a young Tibetan woman escapee in India, of forced sexual services demanded by a PLA leader in contemporary Tibet. For discussion of prostitution in Tibet see TIN 1999a.

be seen, in one interpretation, as having ceded power to his wife Jiang Qing; or it may be an example of generalized misogyny among some Tibetan men. In either case, among both Chinese and Tibetans there are mythical and historical reasons for recollecting female challenges to political power and consensus.

Even within more recent history in Tibet, resistance is associated with women. The most important protest between the time of the Nyemo uprising in 1969 and the Lhasa demonstrations in 1987 was the mass response received by the Dalai Lama's 'Fact-Finding Delegation' when it visited Lhasa in October 1979: according to popular accounts, it was a laywoman, the late Ama Rangtsen (Tsering Lhamo), who began to chant slogans calling for the independence of Tibet, and by so doing nearly turned the event into an anti-Chinese riot (Wangyal 1982: 150–1). But there were also factors specific to the nuns' protests after 1987 which suggest that the women participants were perceived by the authorities as disproportionately threatening to state legitimacy, even though they posed no immediate threat to safety or to property. This perception of the women's movement was achieved by the nun demonstrators—it was a narrative they constructed through their actions—in a remarkably short period of time, so that the patterns of feminine protest and the patterns of gendered state brutalization in response to those protests were already clear in reports given by nuns detained in early 1988.

In summary, three points can be made about the nuns' construction of this narrative: first, it seems to have been the product of strategic thinking, a persistent ability to make their actions of protest charged or imbued with added meaning, as if they were rituals, by repeating them in significant locations or at significant times. Second, the women were able to design modes of action, such as the avoidance of any form of violence and the refusal to answer questions or to incriminate others, which were particularly frustrating for the authorities, and which particularly exposed the contradictions of official claims to legitimacy, or of claims to tolerate difference. Third, the women developed forms of collectivity in action and strategy which made their protests more potent, and which made them into a group with a single motivation and method, rather than an assembly of individuals with varying objectives and approaches. In addition, that motivation acquired the reputation of being 'pure' and unadulterated, and thus acquired for them certain forms of social privilege and respect.

The bed-tidying protest: failed and successful strategies

To emphasize the agency of the women in this achievement is a project which risks over-simplification, because it encourages one to understate the brutality of the response they endured, and to overlook the question as to whether their resistance was in fact effective in changing political conditions. It may therefore be instructive to cite an account of a women's protest in Drapchi prison, although the brutality with which the authorities responded is mild compared to numerous other accounts of prison punishment. The central issue in this case revolved around the question of tidying one's bedclothes, a form of protest that seems to have been developed by the main nun protestors in 1996 in response to efforts to force them to condemn the Dalai Lama. It arose out of a prison re-education session on 24 April at which prisoners refused to condemn the child recognized by their exile leader as the new Panchen Lama:

> 'After that incident, the Chinese restricted everything and every morning they came to check the beds and quilts of the [women] political prisoners and they punished us by beating us severely on the excuse that the quilts and beds were untidy. They warned us that they were going to call in soldiers to teach us how to make our beds properly and tidily. It was on this day that the unit leader (Tib. *tud-krang*, Ch. *dui zhang*) called out all the group leaders of the political prisoners including Ani Phuntsok Pelmo and Ani Ngawang Sangdrol and told them off for being careless in managing the prisoners and in [ensuring] that their cells were tidy. And at that time, while telling them off, the unit leader kicked Ani Sangdrol and beat the rest of the group leaders on the grounds that they had been careless in performing their duty of making the prisoners keep their bedding tidy in the cells.
>
> 'So every political prisoner came out from their working cells in support of Ani Sangdrol and the other group leaders who were being beaten by the unit leader. We, the political prisoners, requested the unit leader to forgive the group leaders and accepted that everything was our own fault and not any mistake committed by the group leaders. Our requests and our begging for forgiveness irritated the unit leader and his companions and they started beating the two or three nuns mercilessly. Their relentless beating and torture was intolerable for us and we, the political prisoners, started to shout out slogans against their torture. So they called in the soldiers and the police to control us. Immediately many soldiers carrying weapons and with helmets on came in to control us. And the soldiers seized Ani Sangdrol-la, Phuntsok Pelmo and Norzin from Shugseb Nunnery and placed them in solitary confinement for two months.'[118]

The account here shows both failed and successful strategies. The failure to tidy the bedclothes (other accounts depict this as a deliberate form of protest by Ngawang Sangdrol and others) might be called successful in that it drove the officials to disproportionate violence and invalidated any claims to legitimacy that they or the state might have had. But the price the protest leaders paid was clearly high, and Ngawang Sangdrol was

[118] Interview by TIN researcher with a former fellow prisoner in Dharamsala, 8 July 1997. The interviewee asked to remain anonymous.

later sentenced for this and other similar prison protests, so that by 1999 her original sentence of three years for demonstrating in the Barkor had been increased to twenty-one years in all for acts of insubordination in the prison; by the year 2000 she was reported to be seriously ill, and showing signs of psychological collapse.[119] The women's strategy of pleading with the unit leader to stop the beating reinforced their solidarity as a group; but the results were counter-productive and it was clearly a disastrous tactic for them to have chosen. For each of the next several days the authorities responded by removing from the women the slight space of self-determination they had found—the freedom to obey or disobey the bed-making regulations—by removing the possibility that their beds could be satisfactorily prepared. The result was both kafkaesque and brutal and led to a new strategy:

'The soldiers had bamboo sticks and belts in their hands and they started checking our beds, which were quite tidy. The unit leader pointed out the beds and the soldiers checked everything and started beating the female prisoners with their belts and bamboo sticks. Many of us female political prisoners were mercilessly beaten. I remember Ani Dekyi-la, who was in the same cell as me and who was in the bunk below mine. The soldiers beat her so brutally after checking her bed that she started bleeding from her mouth, her nose and from her ears… Even if we made our beds properly and tidily the soldiers would still come and beat us mercilessly. It was unbearable to be tortured by the soldiers every time.

'So, on 30 April 1996, we, the political prisoners, told the unit leader that we would better die than live with unsound and invalid health. So from that day we had started a hunger strike. We continued for four days and on the fourth day of the hunger strike some higher officials of the Chinese authorities came to Drapchi to our unit and advised us not to continue the hunger strike. They said that we political prisoners were trying to harm the nation's reputation by holding a hunger strike. They said that they had the medical facilities to stop it and told us to stop rather than to continue, and they promised that they wouldn't send the soldiers to torture us if we stopped the hunger strike. We had about eighty-seven

119 The 21 year cumulative sentence is reported in Amnesty International 1999. See also TCHRD 1999. According to these reports the three year sentence imposed for a demonstration in Lhasa in 1992 was extended three times—once in October 1993 for singing songs in the prison (six years), second in July 1996 for insubordination relating to bed-tidying and disrupting meetings (eight years) and again in October 1998 for taking part in or leading the May 1998 protests in the prison just before a visit by European Union diplomats (four years). Since 1999 official Chinese statements have confirmed these additional sentences but said that they add up to 15 years. However, a Chinese Government letter to a US Congressman called Capuano of December 1999 noted that Ngawang Sangdrol was not due for release until May 2013, indicating a 21 year sentence. She was eventually released in 2002 due to international pressure, but forced to leave Tibet for the United States. She gave a detailed account of her prison experience to a US-based advocacy group called the International Campaign for Tibet in 2002, but it still not been released by that organization at the beginning of 2005.

political prisoners carrying out that hunger strike, just from our unit… They promised us that they wouldn't send the soldiers to torture us. So we started to end the hunger strike.'

The hunger strike described here was like the other strategies we have encountered: repetitive, non-violent, almost ritualized forms of protest carried out on or within the women's bodies. It was clearly a successful strategy, if, as claimed, the authorities themselves defined it as threatening the reputation of the state. In the incident described here, it persuaded senior officials to end the beatings over bed inspections. But the ability of the women to devise effective forms of non-compliance seems to have produced a progressive increase in the punishment inflicted on them in response. In 1998, following the protest at the prison flag-raising ceremony on 1 May, another hunger strike by the women produced much more aggressive responses from the prison guards; descriptions of the punishment inflicted on the women show signs of extreme frustration by the authorities with the failure of their attempts to curb the women's refusal to comply.[120] It was these events that led to the deaths a month later of the five nuns in Drapchi.

WOMEN AND THE DEEP EMBODIMENT OF CONFLICT WITH THE STATE

This focus on the role of nuns in contemporary Tibetan politics is in part a consequence of the availability of information: the nuns, in another important example of strategic self-assertion, have been active participants in the practice of testifying that has become so central to the

120 'That same night (1 May 1998), we launched a hunger strike and gave in our food bowls to protest the prison officials' treatment of all of us. By that time, all of the nuns in the 3rd Unit, about 100 in total, had sustained serious injuries and many were bleeding. On 4 May, twenty nuns were taken out for another flag-raising ceremony. That time the monks initiated pro-independence slogans, and nuns in the other female unit (the old 3rd Unit) who could view the protest from their cells joined in. From their cells, they started to shout and break windowpanes. The protest was harshly repressed again. During this time, the hunger strike was still going on. On the sixth day, some of us were so weak we were falling unconscious and vomiting blood. High-ranking prison officials and other officers from outside prison came and forced the more critical nuns to receive intravenous fluid. On the seventh day, we were called for the third time and made to learn eulogy songs. We refused to cooperate, resulting in further punishment. … The next day … we were made to stand in the sun starting at seven in the morning until eight in the night. We had to put newspaper between our legs and under our armpits and had to balance a bowl filled with water on our head. We were falling unconscious but none of us were allowed to help each other. The moment we made a movement, we received beatings. We had approximately ten minutes break in between when we could either eat or go to the toilet. After eight in the night, we were given a tiny steamed dumpling, which was not sufficient at all. In between we were called in for interrogation. This went on for seven days' (Statement by Choying Kunsang, in TCHRD 2000).

Tibetan political project since 1987—the act of creating an internationally distributed narrative of their political experience by providing first-person testimonies to western and exile researchers, sympathizers and journalists.[121] In using that material, we risk losing focus on the other groups of women involved in political activities, and other forms of political activities besides open dissent and protest, such as we saw with the teacher Nyima Drolma.

The role of lay Tibetan women in contemporary politics is immensely complicated, and a concise description of that activity has yet to be produced. By grouping themselves together as a unit of activity, with its specific ethics and modes, the nuns created a taxonomic entity which automatically acquired by that same action a recognizable identity, history and culture of self-representation; in fact, one could speculate that a central function of becoming a nun in contemporary Tibet has been to create for these women a recognizable place and role in history. The laywomen have not, so far as I know, yet constructed a narrative of themselves as political agents, or makers of history, or not in ways that can yet be recognised by outsiders. There are autobiographies in English by two women (Ama Adhe, a laywoman and Ani Pachen, a nun)[122] that describe their role in the Tibetan resistance, but these deal mostly with the 1950s period and are individualized. As far as I know, these accounts, co-written with westerners, have not appeared in Tibetan: they appear to be part of a mainly western discourse.

It is not that laywomen have not been active in the politics of resistance since the 1980s: although as a proportion of political prisoners their numbers were small compared to nuns, videos and eyewitness reports leave no doubt about the significant involvement of women in street protests, as we have seen with the account of stone-gatherers in the protest of October 1987. One small but nevertheless prominent example, in a rather literal sense, can be found in the notorious 'police video' of the March 1988 protest, which at one point shows a young woman running into the middle of a Lhasa street between the police lines and the demonstrators and baring her buttocks in the direction of the Chinese troops.[123] But to attempt a unified description of political activity among lay women from these limited examples would be, as Charlene Makley has pointed out, to group 'women' or 'Tibetan women' or 'laywomen' as a single entity and

121 See McLagan (1996: ch. 7) on the use of public testimony by exile Tibetan activists in attempts to raise the profile of the Tibet issue. The use of the media by women politicians in Tibet has not been studied yet, as far as I know.

122 See Adhe 2000 and Pachen 2000. Ama Adhe's story is also told in Patt 1992.

123 *Police Video*, official film of the March 1988 Lhasa demonstration, obtained and distributed by TIN, London.

thus to essentialize them, and to gloss over the wide range of contextual, personal and historical variations which exist (Makley 1997).[124] The group of activist nuns which I have discussed here, although it involves women from different religious schools, is itself a specific, geographically located sub-group, identified primarily with four main nunneries within a hundred miles of Lhasa (Gari, Chubsang, Shugseb and Michungri); although there are important overlaps, we do not yet know whether nun-activists in other areas of central, let alone eastern Tibet, would share the principles and characteristics of the Lhasa group.

In the case of contemporary laywomen activists, therefore, it may be more appropriate to look at an individual account rather than to attempt a description of a notional group. First, however, the history of lay female activism should be acknowledged: women played a prominent role in Tibetan resistance to the Chinese before the 1980s, as we have seen already from the biographies and cases referred to above.[125] But it is not only that there is a continuing history of lay female opposition in Tibet: there is also a history of specific persecution of Tibetan women, by the Chinese officials or by Tibetans acting in their name. There was nothing about Chinese persecution in those years which was limited to men, in part because the new Chinese state conceived of the issue of control as more an educational or ideological process than a military operation. Since enemies of the state were defined by their thinking or class status rather than by their access to power or training in bearing arms, women were among those targeted, and thousands went to prison or were killed, as far as we can tell from survivors.

Thus women activists in Tibet have personal histories that tell of abuse specifically directed at women. This can be seen in the following account, which comes from a laywoman activist whom I shall call 'P'. P was brought up in a village in Nyemo, the site of the 1969 uprising, some 100 kilometres west of Lhasa, where her grandparents had been minor tax collection officials before the Chinese arrived; the family was therefore classified as 'class enemy' (*gral-rim dgra-bo*). In an interview after her escape to India in 1997, P's account focussed on what was in theory the final moment of the Maoist era: the day of Mao's death in 1976.

'The Chinese called a meeting for all people of the so-called class struggle group on the day of Mao's death and my mother, uncle and a nun who is my mother's elder sister attended the meeting with the three of us children. During the meeting

[124] Daniella Gandolfo has discussed in some of her unpublished work on Latin America the frequent use of nakedness by women protestors in street demonstrations (personal communication).

[125] See in particular McGranahan's (2001) work on this issue in Kham.

my mother, uncle and aunt [the nun] were forced to stand before the audience and my aunt was class-struggled against so terribly. I was with my elder sister and our brother among the audience watching the unbearable class struggle against my aunt, who was accused of having expressed joy and happiness over the death of Mao. It was true that my aunt had had a talk with some other villagers on the street and because of that they had said that she was happy about the death of Mao. When we came back home after the meeting my aunt was so horribly sick from the pain in different parts of her body that it was unbearable to see. This is what I can remember now.'[126]

The situation did not end with that incident. The beating of the aunt led the grandmother to become seriously ill, and so, to help cure her from the illness, the mother began to make religious offerings on a small altar hidden in a cupboard.

'One day when everyone had gone to work in the fields so that only my invalid grandmother and my aunt were at home, unfortunately the township leader (Tib. *shang-drang*, Ch. *xiangzhang*) came suddenly to check our house and found the seven cups of water hidden in the cupboard. When he found them he started to interrogate my aunt: "Were these to celebrate the death of Mao? Who were you offering them to?" She was beaten severely and then thrown down the hillside. He also broke down the door of her room and checked every corner of it until he found some tsampa (*rtsam-pa*, roasted barley flour) on a plate. She had got the tsampa secretly from other people and had left it on the plate as an offering. He pulled her by her hair and dragged her out to the field where my mother was working and called for a meeting that evening. They were beaten very terribly. Afterwards my uncle carried the younger sister of my mother on his back and brought her back to the home. Because of our case that day they also tortured and held class struggle against many other Tibetans of our class in the village, and during that meeting my aunt confessed that she was responsible for everything in order to save my mother. Many people faced the same problem, like that of my family.'

At about the age of fifteen the narrator became seriously ill herself. Because all her family's belongings had been confiscated and they had little food, she left her village to seek work and food in Lhasa. She worked in the capital as a domestic servant until she was twenty, when she took a job on a construction site for 2.5 yuan a day (about USD 0.33) building, in an irony that could itself be considered symbolic of the Tibetan condition, the new court in which she would later decide she had no hope of receiving justice. After some three years of this work, she became in 1991 a street trader selling clothes in the southern Barkor. By that time she had already served eight months in prison for taking part in a demonstration. In 1993 she was arrested again, this time for distributing pamphlets opposing population control policies.

126 Interview by TIN researcher in Dharamsala, July 1997.

Although pamphlet and poster distributors engaged in protest appropriate far less public space than demonstrators—just a few square inches of unsigned presence on a city wall or on a piece of paper passed from hand to hand—in the current Chinese context these people seem to be considered guilty of a more serious offence than demonstrators, and they receive much longer sentences if caught. Presumably this is a tribute both to the power of discourse and to the basic strength of ritualized protest, namely that it can be endlessly repeated, a pamphlet much more easily than a personal demonstration. And in fact the authorities were right to treat P as a person with a serious potential to change political opinions in Tibet, because she was, like most writers and printers, part of a group. It was a minute operation, consisting initially only of four monks and herself, but it had a major distribution network. It also had a potential to attract quite wide support, because, unlike almost all other underground cells in Tibet, its immediate rallying was based not on calling for utopian political change, but on opposing birth control policies, which must have seemed to many a more immediate threat:

> 'The main thing was to protest against the population control policy of China over Tibet. It was a small organization formed by the four monks and me and slowly it increased in number. We spread the organization through the pamphlets. We had sent the pamphlets to many parts of Tibet including Tsongon [Qinghai], Shigatse, Lhokha and so on. The main thing in the text that I can remember was about the population of Tibet… We protested against their population control policy and our text was in support of His Holiness's wish for a free Tibet through peaceful and not through violent means.'

The account she gave in India after her release focused mainly on other prisoners still in custody about whose welfare she was concerned. But when asked, she finally gave a description of her situation in detention before the trial—many Tibetans are reluctant to give first person accounts, except when, like the nuns, they feel it is in the interests of a wider community. She described Drapchi as 'slightly better' than the detention centre where she had been held, because Drapchi prisoners, having been already tried and sentenced, are not subjected to such frequent interrogation. She had a particular explanation for why interrogation was so stressful: 'The frequent interrogation makes us mentally sick because they often threaten us to get us to confess the names of other people. It is very difficult to tell them honestly because we don't want to let others suffer in the prison, even if we are already suffering.'

This recalls the notion of a principled commitment to mutual non-incrimination among the women activists, as we have already seen among the nuns; in fact P's group had been destroyed because a monk arrested earlier had given their names during interrogation, although she does not indicate any sense of recrimination towards him, and he had been almost certainly tortured to extract the information. But it is her description of the first twenty-four hours of interrogation, given only reluctantly to the western interviewer and in response to many questions which I have edited out of this version, which I wish to point out here:

'When I had confessed that I had distributed the pamphlets alone they were not satisfied with my confession and warned me to confess honestly. I denied having had others to work with me, but that made them irritated and they forced me to stand upright from six that evening to eight-thirty the next morning. During that night there were three or four people continuously watching and interrogating me. They were changed frequently during that night. Most of them were Tibetan or half-Tibetan.

'I don't remember clearly now how often they changed. I was completely exhausted in the middle of the night and they threatened me that they had so many other methods to torture prisoners who didn't confess honestly. I can't tell everything about what they did that night. They threatened me that they were going to imprison me for fourteen years if I didn't confess honestly and they also told me that they were going to arrest everyone in my family. They lied to me that they had caught the rest of my friends who had worked with me distributing the pamphlets.

'Those people who were watching me had mobile phones in their pockets, they tried to frighten me by calling on the phones during the night. Everything they said on the phone was in Chinese. I wasn't so afraid of them even when they used the phones because I was already in their hands and in my mind my only thought was that I was going to be executed. But the only thing I was scared of was that the Chinese might arrest those of my friends and colleagues by telling lies that I had given their names to the Gong An Ju (Public Security Bureau) to get them arrested. In fact, the Chinese policy is hard to trust, they impose their laws violently against the public and it changes frequently.

'The biggest problem was that I was not even allowed to rest a second to lean on the bench and I was frequently falling asleep and I fell down onto the front of the wall, where I hit my face and my forehead very painfully. And the next morning my body had become stiff, and it seemed that the blood circulation had stopped working in the veins of my body. I could not even bend over.

'And a lady came to the room where I had been tortured and told them to go for breakfast. When every one of them left she told me to go and relax on the sofa. Once I fell down on the sofa she gave me a cup of hot water, and this flushed away the stiffness of my body. She was a Tibetan policewoman. Before they went to breakfast they had warned me seriously to confess everything about having many other companions working with me. And I couldn't say anything against them… I was only afraid that they would arrest other people whom I knew were innocent, because I know many people who didn't have any relation with the case, for distributing the pamphlets.'

P spent a year and ten months in solitary confinement at a detention centre undergoing further questioning; she never revealed other names and eventually she was given a trial and sent to Drapchi. Because she had cleaned out her house before the police arrived, knowing that her uncle had already been arrested a week earlier, little had been found to incriminate her and so at the trial she received only a three-year sentence. She turned down the formal option of appealing to the higher court that she had helped to construct some ten years earlier. Her testimony is dominated by her commitment not to incriminate others. The same concern was central to her account of her aunt's false confession in the 1976 struggle session (*'thab-'dzing*); it is central to her relief at being admitted to Drapchi, where the questioning stopped. It was central to her contract with the western interviewer, which depended on him agreeing not to publicize her name. In a way it is central, by contrast, to her remark about Chinese policy as unsafe and untrustworthy—it is a policy, she implies, which can elicit information about a person's social group in the name of helping them at one moment only to use it against them in another. This is, in terms of the participant's experience, the phenomenon described by academics as a difference/universalizing discourse: the state at one point encourages the definition of distinct social groups as a celebration of its inclusiveness and breadth of consensus, only to declare subsequently a universalizing ethos in which these distinctions are defined as threats to the state. This cycle of definitional entrapment is fundamental to the historic, lived experience of those who are 'different' in the modern Chinese state. Chinese and western writers often describe this phenomenon in terms of the 1957 Anti-Rightist Campaign, or the 1966 Cultural Revolution, but for members of nationalities—and perhaps for women too—this is a contemporary experience, not merely a recollected one.

There is a further dimension to this account. P, as she indicates, told only part of her experience to the interviewer. Although she never mentioned this in the interview, we know from other reports received from Lhasa while she was in custody, and the police interrogators surely knew it too, that P was at the mid-stage of pregnancy at the time of her arrest. Her references to the abuses of that first night, the stopping of blood circulation, the stiffening of her body and the inability to bend over, were in fact a veiled reference to a miscarriage: during that night she suffered severe bleeding and lost her child. It can be said literally that in this case, as we have seen with so many of the nuns, the body of this woman, who had been arrested for criticizing birth control, was the specific site of political conflict between the person and the state. The interrogators wrote their story of abuse on her body by making her stand all night, presumably as a statement that if they could not extract other suspects' names from her they could at least destroy her unborn child. In her narrative, however, this story does not appear, partly because, as she says herself, she did not want to aggrandize her personal experience. Her account is permeated and shaped by the deep interconnectedness of the body and the political that can be found in the histories and experience of women involved in politics in Tibet.

CONCLUSION: WOMEN AND THE BODY POLITIC

The connection of women's bodies with their political experience does not reside in specific incidents, or even in the alleged practices of forced abortion and sterilization that are sporadically reported from Tibet and China and which P's pamphlets had used as an issue for rallying national support. It manifests as an endemic condition of somatic connectedness that is implicit in P's description of her grandmother's illness, and of her own sickness at the fear of incriminating others: for these women, certain negative political experiences, such as betraying compatriots or witnessing the abuse of others, express themselves as bodily or mental illness.[127] As Vincanne Adams has indicated in her work, this phenomenon can be found with women from Lhasa as well as from the countryside, with women in the party as well as those who are uneducated, and in current times as well as earlier ones (Adams 1999). It seems, therefore, that the notion of collectivity and of mutuality has a deep-rooted psycho-social character—we might say, based on these accounts, that it is a form of political consciousness—in the case of certain women in Tibet. These women perform the nation within their bodies, just as their interrogators and prison guards perform the state upon them.

Where access to public space becomes increasingly restricted, so that cultural, political and physical opportunities for expression or performance diminish acutely, it seems that the bodies of these women become a principal site of political contestation between themselves and the state, the Party, or Chinese control over Tibet. It is to their bodies, finally, that they turn to find symbols of their cultural distinctiveness and of their identity as a group or nation. The aetiology of ritual in these situations seems to be this: that, as space is restricted, the availability of those symbols is reduced, and the symbolic acts necessarily become condensed. These acts are thus transformed into rituals—compact, repeatable, brief and often sparse but highly charged performances of certain values. Using a principle of interiorization not wholly dissimilar to that found in Tibetan Buddhist practices, in the final resort, the rituals are performed with or within the body.

127 In one interview in 2000 a nun describing the destruction of her nunnery near Lhasa said: 'I have a heart sickness. The reason why I got this sickness is that the Chinese Communist Party destroyed my monastery.' She asked for her name to be withheld.

Just as deputy party secretary Pasang conveys, some say, a counter-discourse by reciting speeches in a flat tone or by maintaining an apartment without furnishings, so P's mother seeks to cure the grandmother's illness by making covert religious offerings: both appear to be using barely perceptible actions to communicate meanings of great importance. P's survival of the twenty months she spent in solitary confinement, the most concrete example of restricted space, was attributed by her to another inward ritual, that of praying secretly to the Dalai Lama. For the women in P's family, it thus seems that political opposition, or survival during periods of acute contraction of permitted space, is closely related to the performing of rites, often in secret, that are expressions of Tibetan culture or identity. These hidden acts, these expressions of quintessential difference from the state and its hegemony, serve as cures or remedies of an almost medical kind to a political condition that manifests bodily within them.

In periods when the state allows difference to be asserted, the acts can be visible and public: the action of being a Buddhist, wearing Tibetan clothes, learning Tibetan, or starting a rural school, for example, can be ways of linking oneself to a collective culture or history. As with the girl prisoner Tseyang's unrealizable dream of becoming a nun, these options, in themselves a kind of ritual of a larger sort, seem to be experienced as a remedy for the experience of contraction. In more restrictive periods and situations, displays of certain kinds of difference might be limited to a few minutes of ritualized protest in the Barkor, or the small patches of wall where an illicit poster is put up at night, or the singing of Tibetan lyrics to Chinese tunes. In the most rigid phases, that space is reduced to hidden or would-be unnoticed spaces, like a cupboard where an offering bowl is kept, or the plate on which tsampa is left lying for the gods. In the descriptions we have seen of times and places where there is not even any hidden space, and when the forces of the state beat directly on the bodies of the women, even violating their inner space with batons, the repository of culture and of difference becomes the bodies themselves, or the spaces of memory and aspiration within them: P praying in prison, the women's prison songs, Tseyang's nakedness and death, and the refusal of the nuns on hunger strike to eat.

Such internalization of strife and opposition is familiar to us from accounts of the Cultural Revolution.[128] The accounts given by women

128 The continuous requirement on citizens during the Cultural Revolution to declare support for the state and for its policies produced a deep split between the external and the internal. As one former Tibetan cadre described it, 'all the time I praised [them], hatred burned inside my belly like a fire' (anonymous interview, 1995).

involved in resistance in the 1980s and 1990s, however, are from a period which saw an increase in the accessibility of public space both globally and within China, so that by the mid-1990s the free market, domestic travel, tourism, TV, and the internet were almost as available in Lhasa as in other modern cities. The experiences described by P and scores of other Tibetans show that highly restrictive space can exist within open space. Our models of generalization and our notions of authoritarianism are inept and insufficient: viewed in certain ways and for certain kinds of people, the open door leads to a walled up cell. These accounts—as might be the case with minorities in many societies—describe a world where oppression can be localized to certain moments of interrogation, to a particular social group, to an allocated room or office, to forms of social exclusion, or to a specialized cadre of officials: the state can mobilize its instrumentality of violence to specialized sites of operation in the midst of opposite displays of tolerance and difference.

The stories that we know of from this period are largely those of the nuns, whose strategies of protest in prison and elsewhere repeatedly provoked the state to demonstrate its inclinations to violence and abuse. In this sense, these women have been extraordinarily successful, positioning the mainly male security establishment in Tibet in the minds of the international as well as the domestic community as unpunished perpetrators of oppression. They have feminized protest by associating it with the female and with their chosen tactics of non-violence while reinforcing the perception of the state as stereotypically masculine, brutal and inherently contradictory. The Chinese state has been unable to respond effectively to this attack; recently it seems to be indicating that it wants these women out of prison and out of nunneries as fast as possible, apparently confident that they will have no recourse but to emigrate to India and beyond. Unlike the nuns, laywomen activists have not in general constructed narratives describing their forms of resistance, and detailed accounts such as P's are rarely given. There are, however, known to be a great number of such women involved in highly organized and effective resistance strategies of inconspicuous kinds; of these little is known or, where it still continues, little can be safely said. The Chinese authorities have, however, indicated by their sentencing policies that they consider the organizing of groups and the distribution of literature much more threatening than the holding of demonstrations: visibility and public testimony are not the only measure of political impact.[129]

129 This is clear from the Criminal Code; see chapter I of Part II, articles 102–113 (Xinhua 1997) and note 102 above. The story that P tells of her underground activities exactly falls within the state's definition of the dangerous, because it involves passing information rather than merely demonstrating; hence the particularly brutal treatment she

The greater achievement of the nuns, and of the laywomen activists, may therefore lie elsewhere: the ritualization of protest that they did so much to create or sustain in the late 1980s seems to have been one of the factors that led to that culture of popular re-interpretation by Tibetans, whereby the actions and histories of some Tibetan leaders in the formal leadership, including women, have come to be read as if they were mirror images or partners in some way of the nuns and other activists. This process of re-interpretation has led to the circulation of narratives of cultural assertion and identity that provide a much larger scope for the possibility of a specifically Tibetan form of politics, a politics of difference. These more nuanced narratives link the pro-independence efforts of the nuns, the laywomen's critique of birth control policies, the efforts of rural teachers to rejuvenate their classes, and the gestures of politicians towards Tibetan dress or customs in their private lives—even the emigration of the street trader with her memories to America.

The space between the women leaders and the activists with which we began has, therefore, contracted almost to the point where the distinction disappears. For the main achievement of the resistance women, whether they are street demonstrators, distributors of pamphlets, village teachers, or monastery re-builders, can now be seen to be that they have contributed to the emergence or re-emergence amongst a broader group of women, and perhaps men too, of a widely shared ideal of asserting identity and community, exemplified by their commitment not to incriminate each other. Indeed, it is clear that the nature of this shared ideal is not commensurate with classic nationalism, although it may include it, but with a larger notion of collective self-enhancement and expression. In other words, these women have demonstrated a code of political ethics based on a commitment to the welfare of the Tibetan community, and it is by this code that public politicians are now popularly assessed. These ethics are more coherent, vivid and idealist than the notions of state loyalty and national development asserted by the Party leaders in Beijing, or even by the irredentism of the exiles: that is the real source of the political threat the women activists represent. Their success can be measured by

---

received. This reflects the distributive character of many forms of women's resistance in contemporary Tibet: women distribute knowledge. P was involved in spreading political literature across Tibet, and it seems that many underground networks in Lhasa and other cities from 1987 onwards were run or operated by laywomen (see, for example, the case of Tashi Drolma in TIN 1990b). Many of the networks distributing news of arrests and abuses to the outside world, or supplying food or communications to political prisoners inside the jails seem often to have been run by women. These women present themselves as merely background figures in facilitating other forms of protest, and decline to portray themselves as leaders and initiators, which they most often are.

the extent to which the Chinese authorities now suspect current Tibetan leaders of harbouring secret sympathies for these new ethics, so that for the state too the distinction between supporters and opponents has become increasingly unclear. As for Tibetan leaders, they are no doubt well aware that they are now being judged on the one hand by China's demands for loyalty and on the other by these popular ethics of community.

By performing repeatedly and physically actions embodying internal purity of motive, female activists have shown the official body politic in Tibet to be diseased: unlike the communities created by these activists, its physical and spiritual components are at war with one another. The ethical issues provoked and dramatized by women have thus created an extraordinary moral pressure on the rising class of younger, élite Tibetan politicians, among them many women, to seek ways of accommodating the demands of the state with the interests articulated by the resistance women: the politicians are challenged to reshape the body politic and to harmonize its parts. If they were to do so, it would perhaps bring a close to the long decade of dangerous, brutalized and deeply embodied performances of nationhood and gender staged by this generation of women political activists in Tibet.

Oral sources

Gyaltsen Pelsang, interview in Dharamsala, 18 December 1996, TIN ref. 12(JW).
Interview with two participants, anonymous, November 1988, TIN ref. T2(K).
Interview in Dharamsala, anonymous, 29 September 1990, TIN ref. T6(NH).
Interview in Kathmandu, anonymous, 25 September 1991, TIN ref. T11(SM)-GR.
Interview with 'P', Kathmandu, 9/10 June, 1993, TIN ref. T3(YP).
Interview in Dharamsala, anonymous, 25 April 1997, TIN ref. 36(JW).
Interview in Dharamsala, anonymous, 8 July 1997, TIN ref. 52(JW) and 52(JW)A.
Interview in Lhasa, anonymous, 2000.
Ngawang Tseten, interview in Dharamsala, May 1997, TIN ref. 42(JW).
Rigzin Chonyi, interview in Dharamsala, 26 January 1997, TIN ref. 13(JW) parts 1–3.

BIBLIOGRAPHY

TIBETAN SOURCES

NGMPP refers to manuscripts in the Nepal-German Manuscript Preservation Project in Kathmandu, Nepal; letters and numbers specify microfilm reel location for that collection.

'Ba'-ra-ba 1970

'Ba'-ra-ba sPrul-sku Rin-chen bsTan-pa'i gSal-byed, *Grub thob dkon mchog rgyal mtshan rnam thar ngo mtshar bdud rtsi'i chu rgyun* in *Bka' brgyud gser phreng chen mo: Biographies of Eminent Gurus in the Transmission Lineage of Teachings of the 'Ba'-ra dKar-brgyud-pa Sect*, vol. 3. Dehra Dun: Ngawang Gyaltsen and Ngawang Lungtok, 90–2.

bDe-chen 1985

bDe-chen Chos-kyi dBang-mo, *mKha' 'gro rgya mtsho'i rnam thar gsang ba'i mdzod* (title from f. 278b) in *Bon po bka' 'gyur*, vol. 189, Ling-shan (Lixian) edition, *c.* 1985, ff. 1–281.

bDe mchog 1973

bDe mchog mkha' 'gro snyan rgyud (*Ras chung snyan rgyud*), n.p.: Delhi, 2 vols.

bDe mchog 1983

bDe mchog Snyan brgyud Biographies, Darjeeling: Kargyud Sungrab Nyamso Khang.

bDe-smon 1987

bDe-smon bDe-chen sGrol-dkar, 'Bod rigs kyi bud med' in *sPang rgyan me tog*, 4, 2.

bKra-shis 1991.

bKra-shis dBang-phyug, 'Ral pa'i sgyu rtsal gyi gsung rgyun spyi bshad' in *Krung go'i bod kyi shes rig*, 15.3, 44–51.

bKra-shis dPal-ldan 1991–2

bKra-shis dPal-ldan, 'Gar stegs khong gi yod tshad' in *Bod kyi rtsom rig sgyu rtsal* 1991.5, 38–55; 1991.6, 74–82; 1992.1, 75–84; 1992.2, 60–7; 1992.3, 101–104; 1992.5, 44–9.

bKra-shis Tshe-ring 1994b

bKra-shis Tshe-ring, 'Bod du grags can mi sna'i gras bud med kyi bod lugs sman pa'i lo rgyus rags tsam gleng ba yid gdung sel ba'i sman mchog' in *g.Yu-mtsho* 2. 1, 48–84.

Blo-gros n.d.

Blo-gros dBang-phyug, *rGyas 'bring 'dus gsum gyi rnam par phye pa mol gtam zab mo lo rgyus gter gyi kha byang*, NGMPP L731/3. 22 ff. n.p.: n.d.

Bod kyi 2000
'Bod kyi bud med glu dbyangs mkhas pa dbyangs can lha mo lags su bcar 'dri zhus pa' in *sGrol ma: The Voice of Tibetan Women*, 32–4.

Bod-ljongs 1980
Bod-ljongs lHa-mo Tshogs-pa, *Bod kyi lha mo'i lugs khag ngo sprod byed pa* , Lhasa, uncirculated book.

Bod rgya 1987
Bod rgya shan sbyar gyi shes bya'i rnam grangs kun btus tshig mdzod, Xining: mTsho-sngon Mi -rig dPe-skrun-khang.

bShes-gnyen 1995
bShes-gnyen Tshul-khrims, 'Sangs rgyas kyi bstan pa dang kha ba ri pa'i bud med kyi skor rags tsam gleng ba' in *Krung go'i bod kyi shes rig* , 30.2, 15–34.

bSod-nams Blo-gros 1985
bSod-nams Blo-gros, *mKhas grub chen po rnam grol bzang po'i rnam thar dad pa'i dpu long g.yo byed ngo mtshar can* , Dalhousie: Damchoe Sangpo.

bSod-nams dPal-dren n.d.
bSod-nams dPal-dren (and Rin-chen dPal), *Ye shes mkha' 'gro bsod nams dpal 'dren gyis sprul pa'i sku'i mdzad pa spyod kyi rnam par thar pa* (?) (Part *Ka*); *Ye shes kyi mkha' 'gro bsod nams dpal 'dren gyis thugs rgyud gshis kyi gnas lugs nang gi rnam thar pa mngon shes kyis bskor* (Part *Kha*); *Ye shes kyi mkha' 'gro bsod nam dpal 'dren gyis gsang ba'i rnam thar pa* (Part *Ga*), manuscript photocopy kept in the Tibetan Buddhist Resource Center, New York, n.p., n.d.

bsTan-'dzin 1971a.
bsTan-'dzin Ras-pa (1646–1723), *The Autobiography and Selected Works of Bstan-'dzin ras-pa*, n.p.

bsTan-'dzin 1971b
———, *bsTan 'dzin ras pa'i zhal gdams nor bu'i bang mdzod* in bsTan-'dzin 1971a, Section *Ga*, ff. 16.

bsTan-'dzin 1971c
———, *gZhi lam 'bras bu'i ngo sprod dris lan sems kyi me long* in bsTan-'dzin 1971a, Section *Ja*, ff. 12.

bsTan-'dzin 1971d
———, *Nyams rtogs 'byed pa'i lde mig* in bsTan-'dzin 1971a, Section *Nya*, ff. 11.

bsTan-'dzin 1971e
———, *rJe btsun bstan 'dzin ras pa de nyid kyi gsang ba'i rnam thar sa khyis phan gyis / mgur ma'i kha 'gros gnas ngo zung tshul mya ngan 'das tshul dkar chag dang bcas mchos mtshan lnga* in bsTan-'dzin 1971a, Section *Da*, ff. 36, also NGMPP L410/10.

bsTan-'dzin 1971f
———, *rJe btsun rnal 'byor gyi dbang phyug bstan 'dzin ras chen gyi rnam thar gsol 'debs byin rlabs char 'bebs* in bsTan-'dzin 1971a, Section *Ka*, ff. 2, also NGMPP L409/8.

bsTan-'dzin 1971g
———, *rNal 'byor bzhi'i zhal gdams* in bsTan-'dzin 1971a, Section *Ta*, ff. 9.

bsTan-'dzin 1971h

———, *rNal 'byor gyi dbang phyug bstan 'dzin ras pa'i zhal gdams mgur du gsungs pa rnams* in bsTan-'dzin 1971a, Section *Kha*, ff. 67.

bsTan-'dzin 1971i

———, *rNal 'byor gyi dbang phyug rje btsun bstan 'dzin ras pa'i rnam thar mdzad pa nyung ngu gcig* in bsTan-'dzin 1971a, Section *Ka*, ff. 17, also NGMPP L409/8.

bsTan-'dzin 1971j

———, *rNam rtog lam khyer gyi lhan thabs dang dris lan ma rig mun sel* in bsTan-'dzin 1971a, Section *Ca*, ff. 13.

bsTan-'dzin 1971k

———, *sKu bstod smon lam gyi rim pa* in bsTan-'dzin 1971a, Section *Cha*, ff. 2.

bTsan-lha 1997

bTsan-lha Ngag-dbang Tshul-khrims, *brDa dkrol gser gyi me long*, Beijing: Mi-rigs Dpe-skrun-khang.

Bu-ston 1965

Bu-ston Rin-chen-grub, *rGyud sde'i zab don sgo 'byed rin chen gces pa'i lde mig*, in *The Collected Works of Bu-ston*, Delhi: International Academy of Indian Culture, vol. 4, 1–92.

Byams-bzang 1985

Byams-bzang, 'dPa' bo'i lo rgyus mtshon byed kyi snyan ngag ge sar rgyal po'i rnam thar dang de min rang yul ge sar rgyal po'i rnam thar myur skyob byed pa'i las don mdor bsdus' in *Byang thang* 1985.8, 109–15.

Byams-pa 1990

Byams-pa 'Phrin-las, *Gangs ljongs gso rig bstan pa'i nyin byed rim byon gyi rnam thar phyogs bsgrigs*, Beijing: Mi-rigs dPe-skrun-khang.

Chab-'gag 1993

Chab-'gag rTa-mgrin, 'Babs sgrung mkhas pa'i khyad 'phags yon tan la dpyad pa' in *Bod ljongs sgyu rtsal zhib 'jug* 1993.2, 129–37.

Changngopa 2002

Changngopa, Tseyang, 'Grags can bud med bstan ma'i sku rten blo bzang tshe sgron dang khong gi skor mdo tsam gleng ba' in Henk Blezer (ed.), *Religion and Gender Culture in Tibet*, Tibetan Studies II, Proceedings of the Ninth Seminar of the International Association of Tibetan Studies, Leiden 2000, Leiden: E. J. Brill, 2/2, 245–59.

Changngopa forthcoming

Changngopa, Tseyang, 'Lo rgyus thog bod rigs bud med kyi 'bod srol dang lag shes thad mdo tsam dpyad pa' in Sperling (ed.), *Tibetan Studies*.

'Chi-med n.d.

'Chi-med 'Od-zer, *dPal de kho na nyid dus pa las bo dong chos 'byung gsal byed sgron me zhes bya ba*, manuscript of 35 folios kept at Bodong E monastery.

Chos-'phel 1997

Chos-'phel, *rGyal khab rim pa dang po'i 'khrab ston pa bod kyi lha mo mkhas sku gshegs a ma lhag pa lags kyi mdzad rjes rob tsam bkod pa*, Lhasa: Bod-ljongs lHa-mo Tshogs-pa manuscript.

Chos-kyi 1992
Chos-kyi Seng-ge, *Grub pa'i dbang phyug chen po rje btsun dam pa sangs rgyas kyi rnam par thar pa dngos grub 'od stong 'bar ba'i nyi ma* in *Pha dam pa dang ma cig lab sgron gyi rnam thar*, Lanzhou: mTsho-sngon Mi-rigs Dpe-skrun Khang, 1–242.

Dalai 1983
Dalai Lama VII, *The Collected Works (Gsung-'bum) of the Seventh Dalai Lama Blo-bzang-bskal-bzang-rgya-mtsho*, 13 vols, Gangtok: Sherab Gyaltsen, Palace Monastery.

Dam-pa 1985
Dam-pa Sangs-rgyas, Pha, *Phyag rgya chen po brda'i skor gsum and Zhal chems ding ri'i skor*, Thimphu: National Library of Bhutan.

Dar-mo 1982
Dar-mo sMan-ram-pa Blo-bzang Chos-grags, *Dus gsum gyi rgyal ba sras bcas kyi mkhyen brtse'i spyi gzugs mkhas pa dang grub pa'i pha rol tu son pa rigs brgya'i khyab bdag g.yu thog gsar ma yon tan mgon po'i rnam par thar pa*, Beijing: Mi-rigs dPe-skrun-khang.

dBang-'dus 1992
dBang-'dus and Zha'o ha'o, 'brTan ma gzims khang gi sku rtan pa blo bzang tshe sgron gyi lo rgyus' in *Krung go'i bod ljongs* 1992.3, 28–31.

Dil-dmar 1993
Dil-dmar dGe-bshes bsTan-'dzin Phun-tshogs, *gSo ba rig pa'i chos 'byung rnam thar rgya mtsho'i rba rlabs drang srong dgyes pa'i 'dzum phreng* in *gSo rig gces btus rin chen phreng ba*, Lanzhou: mTsho-sngon Mi-rigs dPe-skrun-khang, 683–92.

Don-grub 1985
Don-grub rGyal-mtshan (ed.), *Legs par bshad pa bka' gdams rin po che'i gsung gi gces btus nor bu'i bang mdzod*, Bir: D. Tsondu Senghe.

rDo-rje 1995
rDo-rje Phag-mo and Thub-bstan rNam-rgyal, 'bSam sdings rdo rje phag mo'i 'khrungs rabs dang sku phreng rim byon gyi mdzad rnam yar 'brog bsam sdings dgon gyi dkar chag rags tsam bko's pa', in *Krung go'i bod kyi shes rig* 2, 31–58.

dPa'-bo 1962
dPa'-bo gTsug-lag Phreng-ba, *mKhas pa'i dga' ston*, vol. *ja*. (Lokesh Chandra ed.), Delhi: International Academy of Indian Culture.

dPa'-bo 1980
dPa'-bo gTsug-lag Phreng-ba, *Dam pa'i chos kyi 'khor lo bsgyur ba rnams kyi byung ba gsal bar byed pa mkhas pa'i dga' ston*, Beijing: Mi-rigs dPe-skrun-khang.

dPal-ldan 1988
dPal-ldan Tshul-khrims, *Grwa khang kar ba'i sman pa mi thog brgyad kyi lo rgyus phun sum tshogs pa ma*, manuscript dated 19 January.

Dran shang cun 1983
Dran shang cun, 'Tshe brtan sgrol ma'i glu dbyangs sgyu rtsal gyi skor rags bsdus' in *Bod ljongs glu gar* 1983.2, 33–9.
Dung-dkar 1990
Dung-dkar Blo-bzang 'Phrin-las, 'Dzam gling thog dkon pa'i babs sgrung mkhas can rnams kyi ngo mtshar che ba'i khyad chos la dpyad pa' in *Bod ljongs sgyu rtsal zhib 'jug* 1990.2, 80–6.
Gangs dkar 1994
'Gangs dkar ti si'i glu gzhas' (1–2) in *Bod kyi rtsom rig sgyu rtsal* 1994.1, 89–90; 1994.2, 92–3.
Gang-pa 1992
Gang-pa, *Dus gsum rgyal ba kun gyi yum gcig 'phags ma lab kyi sgron ma'i rnam par thar pa phung po gzan bsgyur gyi rnam par bshad pa mkha' 'gro bye ba'i gsang lam* in *Pha dam pa dang ma cig lab sgron gyi rnam thar*, Lanzhou: mTsho-sngon Mi-rigs dPe-skrun Khang, 243–649.
gCod tshogs 1985
Gcod tshogs kyi lag len sogs, Bir: D. Tsondu Senghe.
gCod-pa 1992
gCod-pa Don-grub, 'Ngo mtshar ldan pa'i sgrung mkhan long ba'i sgrung pa klu rgyal dang bud med sgrung ba mna' ma rdo rje' in *Bod ljongs sgyu rtsal zhib 'jug* 1992.2, 89–93.
gCod-pa 2000
gCod-pa Don-grub, 'sGrung mkhan grags can grags pa dang g.yu sman gnyis kyi lo rgyus ngo sprod mdor bsdus' in *Bod ljongs sgyu rtsal zhib 'jug* 2000.1, 111–22.
Gling-za 1977
Gling-za Chos-skyid, *Three 'Das-log Stories*, Delhi: lHa-khang sPrul-sku.
gNas mchog 1992
gNas mchog glu dbyangs (1–3), Lhasa: Bod-ljongs mi-dMangs dPe-skrun-khang.
gNas mchog 1993a
'gNas mchog glu dbyangs' (1–2) in *Bod kyi rtsom-rig sgyu rtsal* 1993, 1, 66–71; 1993.2, 74–8.
gNas mchog 1993b
'gNas mchog glu dbyangs' (3) in *Bod kyi rtsom rig sgyu rtsal* 1993.3, 59–63.
'Gos 1974
'Gos Lo-tsâ-ba gZhon-nu dPal, *The Blue Annals* (*Deb gter sngon po*), Delhi: International Academy of Indian Culture.
Grags-pa 1968a
Grags-pa rGyal-mtshan, *Bla ma brgyud pa bod kyi lo rgyu* in *Sa skya pa'i bka' 'bum*, vol. 3, Tokyo: The Toyo Bunko, 173–4.
Grags-pa 1968b.
Grags-pa rGyal-mtshan, *Bod kyi rgyal rabs* in *Sa skya pa'i bka' 'bum*, vol. 3, Tokyo: The Toyo Bunko, 295.1.6–296.4.2.
Grong khyer 1994
'Grong khyer lha sa'i bu mo' in *Bod kyi rtsom rig sgyu rtsal* 1994.3, 65–6.

Grong-khyer 1995
Grong-khyer lHa-sa'i U-yon lHan-khang (ed.), 'lHa mo mkhas can a lce dwangs bzang' in *Grong khyer lha sa'i lo rgyus rig gnas, deb gsum pa: sTod lung bde chen rdzong*, Lhasa: Grong-khyer lHa-sa Srid-gros Lo-rgyus Rig-gnas dPyad-yig rGyu-cha rTsom-'bri, 92–3.

Grong-khyer 1996
Grong-khyer lHa-sa'i U-yon lHan-khang (ed.), 'lHa-mo mkhas can a ma tshe ring' in *Grong khyer lha sa'i lo rgyus rig gnas, deb lnga pa: Mal gro gung dkar rdzong*, Lhasa: Grong-khyer lHa-sa Srid-gros Lo-rgyus Rig-gnas dPyad-yig rGyu-cha rTsom-'bri.

g.Yu-thog 1984
g.Yu-thog Yon-tan mGon-po, *bDud rtsi snying po yan lag brgyad pa gsang ba man ngag gi rgyud*, Dharamsala: Tibetan Astro-medical Institute.

'Jig-rten 1969–71
'Jig-rten mGon-po, *The Collected Writings (Gsung-'bum) of 'Bri-gung Chos-rje 'Jig-rten-mgon-po Rin-chen-dpal*, Delhi: Khangsar Tulku, 5 vols.

Jo-gdan n.d.
Jo-gdan bSod-nams bZang-po, *sMyung gnas bla ma brgyud pa'i rnam thar*, block print, Lhasa: Par-pa dPal-ldan, n.d. (late twentieth century).

Jo-bo 1982
Jo-bo Lhun-grub bKra-shis and Dar-mo sMan-ram-pa Blo-bzang Chos-grags, *rJe btsun g.yu thog yon tan mgon po rnying ma'i rnam par thar pa bka' rgya ma gzi brjid rin po che'i gter mdzod*, Beijing: Mi-rigs dPe-skrun-khang.

Kaḥ-thog 1979
Kaḥ-thog Rig-'dzin Tshe-dbang Nor-bu, *dPal mchog dang po'i sangs rgyas kyi man ngag zab lam rdo rje'i rnal 'byor byin rlabs bka' brgyud bla mar gsol ba 'debs pa brgyud 'dzin mchog rgyas* (*brgyud 'debs*) in Kong-sprul 1978, vol. 15, 327–9.

Khyung-po 1984
Khyung-po Ras-pa Grub-dbang 'Gyur-med 'Od-gsal, *rJe btsun mi 'gyur dpal gyi sgron ma'i rnam thar dad pa'i gdung sel*, Thimphu: National Library of Bhutan.

Klong-chen 1977
Klong-chen-pa Dri-med 'Od-zer, *sNga 'gyur rnying ma la rgol ngan log rtog bzlog pa'i bstan bcos*, Leh: 'Khor-gdong Gter-sprul.

Kong-sprul 1978
Kong-sprul Blo-gros mTha'-yas (ed.), *Gdams ngag mdzod: A Treasury of Precious Methods and Instructions of the Major and Minor Buddhist Traditions of Tibet, Brought Together and Structured into a Coherent System by 'Jam-mgon Kong-sprul*, Paro: Lama Ngodrup and Sherab Drimey, 18 vols.

Kong-sprul 1985
Kong-sprul Blo-gros mTha'-yas, *Shes bya kun khyab*, Beijing: Mi-rigs Dpe-skrun-khang, 3 vols.

Kun-dga' 1979
Kun-dga' *et al.*, *The Tradition of Pha Dampa Sangyas: A Treasured Collection*

of His Teachings Transmitted by Tug (sic)-sras Kun-dga, Thimphu: Kunsang Tobgey, 5 vols.

Le'u kre jun 1998

Le'u kre jun (Liu Zhiqun), 'Bod kyi lha mo'i 'khrab ston sgyu rtsal pa grags can a ma lhag par dran gso shu ba', trans. sGrol-g.yang in *Bod ljongs sgyu rtsal zhib 'jug* 1998.2, 115–20.

lHag-pa 1990

lHag-pa Phun-tshogs, 'Bud med rtsom pa po zhig gi snying dbus 'bod sgra: bKras sgron lags kyi brtsams sgrung 'a shel bde chen mtsho mo' shes par rags tsam dpyad pa' in *Bod kyi rtsom rig sgyu rtsal* 3, 1–16.

Lho-kha 1987

Lho-kha Rig-gnas brNyan-'phrin Cud Rig-gnas Kho'o, 'Blo mthun mtshams gcod sgrol ma'i sgyu rtsal lo rgyus' in *Lho kha'i rtsom rig sgyu rtsal* 1987.2, 106–107.

Li'o tung phan 1995

Li'o tung phan (Liao Dongfan), 'Tshe brtan sgrol ma pha yul du bzhugs pa'i dus' in *Krung go'i bod ljongs* 1995.4, 8–13.

Mang-thos 1988

Mang-thos Klu-sgrub rGya-mtsho, *bsTan rtsis gsal ba'i nyin byed lhag bsam rab dkar* in *bsTan rtsis gsal ba'i nyin byed; Tha snyad rig gnas lnga'i byung tshul*, Lhasa: Bod-ljongs Mi-dmangs dPe-skrun-khang.

mGon-po 1998

mGon-po rGyal-mtshan, *Gangs can ral pa*, Beijing: Mi-rigs dPe-skrun-khang.

Mi nyag 1987

Mi nyag mkhas dbang lnga'i rnam thar, Si-khron Mi-rigs dPe-skrun-khang.

mKhas-pa 1987

mKhas-pa lDe'u, Chab-spel Tshe-brtan Phun-tshogs (ed.), *rGya bod kyi chos 'byung rgyas pa*, Lhasa: Bod-ljongs Mi-dmangs dPe-skrun-khang.

Ngag-dbang 1983

Ngag-dbang Blo-gro Grags-pa, 'Dzam-thang-pa, *dPal ldan jo nang pa chos 'byung rgyal ba'i chos tshul gsal byed zla ba'i sgron me* , New Delhi: D. Tsandu Senghe, 1983.

Ngag-dbang 1988–9

Ngag-dbang mKhas-btsun, 'Gangs ljongs shar khul gyi ral pa'i rgyu rtsal skor gleng ba' in *Bod-ljongs sgyu-rtsal zhib-'jug* 1988–9, 48–62.

Niu xin fang 1983

Niu xin fang, *lHa 'dre dang bkas bkod rgyud 'dzin gyi rmongs dad*, mTsho-sngon: mTsho-sngon Mi-rigs dPe-skrun-khang (trans. from the Chinese: *Gui shen yu feng jian mi xin*, Heibei: Heibei Publishing House, 1981).

Nyang-ral 1979/80.

Nyang-ral Nyi-ma 'Od-zer, *bKa' brgyad bde gshegs 'dus pa'i gter ston myang sprul sku nyi ma 'od zer gyi rnam thar gsal ba'i me long* in *bKa' brgyad bde gsegs 'dus pa'i chos skor*, Paro: Lama Ngodrup, vol. 2, 191–381.

Nyang-ral 1985

Nyang-ral Nyi-ma 'Od-zer, *Chos 'byung me tog snying po'i sbrang rtsi'i bcud* in R. O. Meisezahl (ed.), *Die grosse Geschichte des tibetischen buddhismus nach alter Tradition*, St Augustin, Germany: Wissenschaftsverlag.

Nyang-ral 1988
Nyang-ral Nyi-ma 'Od-zer., *Chos 'byung me tog snying po sbrang rtsi'i bcud*, Lhasa: Bod-ljongs Mi-dmangs dPe-skrun-khang.
O-rgyan bsTan-'dzin 1984
O-rgyan bsTan-'dzin, *rNal 'byor gyi dbang phyug o rgyan bstan 'dzin zhes bya ba'i ri khrod kyi nyams dbyangs*, Dalhousie: Damchoe Sangpo.
O-rgyan bsTan-'dzin 1985
O-rgyan bsTan-'dzin, *sPrang rgan o rgyan bstan 'dzin pas rnam thar bsdus pa*, Dalhousie: Damchoe Sangpo.
O-rgyan Chos-skyid n.d.a
O-rgyan Chos-skyid, *mKha' 'gro ma o rgyan chos skyid kyi rnam thar*, NGMPP E2825/7 (= E2933/4), ff. 86; NGMPP L122/5 (= L667/3), ff. 57.
O-rgyan Chos-skyid n.d.b
O-rgyan Chos-skyid, *mKha' 'gro ma o rgyan chos skyid kyi rnams thar bsdus pa*, NGMPP L401/3. ff. 51 (incomplete).
O-rgyan Rig-'dzin 1983
O-rgyan Rig-'dzin, *sPrang po o rgyan rig 'dzin pas zog tshig 'chal gtam 'ga' yod*, Delhi: Damcho Sangpo.
O-rgyan-pa 1972
O-rgyan-pa (misattributed in the publication to O-rgyan-pa Rin-chen-dpal), *Bka' brgyud yid bzhin nor bu yi 'phreng ba*, Leh: S. W. Tashigangpa.
Padma 'Bum 1994
Padma 'Bum, 'Don grub rgyal gyi mi tshe / sKar mda' / mTshan mo'i nam mkha' 'od kyis gshegs nas yal' in Don-grub rGyal, *Lang tsho'i rbab chu dang ljags rtsom bdams sgrigs*, Dharamsala: Amnye Machen Institute, 9–46.
Padma dBang-'dus 1979
Padma dBang-'dus, *mKha' mnyam 'gro ba'i rtsug brgyan padma dbang 'dus kyi rnam par thar pa gsal bar bkod pa la rmongs mun thib po sal ba'i sgron me* in *Autobiographies of Three Spiritual Masters of Kutang*, Thimphu: Kunsang Topgay and Mani Dorji, 145–495.
Padma Don-grub 1979
Padma Don-grub, *bDag bya btang ras pa padma don grub kyi chos byas 'tshul dang thob 'tshul dang bka' ba spyad tshul rnams* in *Autobiographies of Three Spiritual Masters of Kutang*, Thimphu: Kunsang Topgay and Mani Dorji, 1–143.
Padma Lhun-grub 1979
Padma Lhun-grub bsTan-'dzin rGya-mtsho, *rNal 'byor ras pa padma lhun grub bstan 'dzin rgya mtsho'i gsung ba'i rnams thar kun bsal me long* in *Autobiographies of Three Spiritual Masters of Kutang*, Thimphu: Kunsang Topgay and Mani Dorji, 591–757.
Padma dKar-po 1968
Padma dKar-po, 'Brug-chen IV, *Chos 'byung bstan pa'i padma rgyas pa'i nyin byed*, Delhi: International Academy of Indian Culture.
Pa-sangs 1988
Pa-sangs Yon-tan, *Bod kyi gso ba rig pa'i lo rgyus kyi bang mdzod g.yu thog bla ma dran pa'i pho nya*, Leh: Yuthok Institute of Tibetan Medicine.

'Phags-pa 1968

'Phags-pa, Chos-rgyal, *Lung dang brgyud pa sna tshogs thob pa'i gsan yig* in *Sa skya pa'i bka' 'bum* , Tokyo: The Toyo Bunko, vol. 7, 286–97.

'Phrin-las 1989

'Phrin-las Chos-grags (ed.), *Bod kyi lha mo'i zlos gar gyi 'khrab gzhung phyogs bsgrigs kun phan bdud rtsi'i char 'bebs*, Lhasa: Bod-ljongs Mi-dmangs dPe-skrun-khang, Lhasa.

rGod-tshang 1992

rGod-tshang Ras-pa, sNa-tshogs Rang-grol (1494–1570), *rJe btsun ras chung ba'i rnam thar*, Xining: mTsho-sngon Mi-rigs dPe-skrun-khang.

brGyud pa'i 1982

brGyud pa'i lo rgyus (spelled *rGyud pa'i lo rgyud*) in Dwags-po bKra-shis rNam-rgyal, *Shar dwags po bkra shis rnam rgyal gyi dmyal ba'i bskal chags rin chen phreng ba cha lag dgos 'dod kun 'byung mthong ba don ldan yid bzhin nor bu bde legs chen po 'dra ba*, Bir: Tulku Pema Lodoe, 507–21.

Rig-'dzin 1999

Rig-'dzin, 'dMangs gtso'i bcos sgyur byas nas lo bzhi bcu'i ring bod kyi gling sgrung myur skyob byed pa'i las don la thob pa'i grub 'bras skor' in *Bod ljongs zhib 'jug* 1999.1, 35–49.

Rig-'dzin Chos-nyid 1997

Rig-'dzin Chos-nyid bZang-mo, *Gangs shug ma'i lo chen rig 'dzin chos nyid bzang mo'i rnam par thar pa rnam mkhyen bde ster*, Lhasa: Bod-ljongs Mi-dmangs dPe-skrun-khang.

rJe-drung 1974–5

rJe-drung Byams-pa'i 'Byung-gnas, *The Collected Works of Ri-bo-che rje-drung byams-pa'i 'byung-gnas* , Dharamsala: Khetsun Sangpo, vols I–VI.

rJe-drung 1985

rJe-drung Byams-pa'i 'Byung-gnas, *Collected Writings of Jedrung Trinley Jampa Jungnay*, Darjeeling: Taklung Tsetrul Rinpoche Pema Wangyal, vols. I–VI.

rTa-tshag 1994

rTa-tshag Tshe-dbang rGyal, *Lho rong chos 'byung*, Lhasa: Bod-ljongs Bod-yig dPe-rnying dPe-skrun-khang.

rTse-le 1979

rTse-le rGod-tshang-pa sNa-tshogs Rang-grol, *rTse le gong 'og grwa tshang dgon gsum po rnams kyi bstan pa ji ltar btsugs pa'i lo rgyus* in *The Complete Works of Rtse-le Rgod-tshang-pa Padma-legs-grub*, Gangtok: Mgon-po-tshe-brtan, Palace Monastery, vol. 1, 313–83.

Rwa lung 1975

Rwa lung dkar brgyud gser 'phreng, Palampur: Sungrab Nyamso Gyunphel Parkhang.

Sangs-rgyas n.d.

Sangs-rgyas Dar-po, *bDe gshegs bka' brgyud chos kyi 'byung gnas ... mun sel 'od stong 'khyil ba*, photocopy of woodblock print from Gung-thang, 16th century.

sDe-srid n.d.
sDe-srid Sangs-rgyas rGya-mtsho, *dPal ldan gso ba rig pa'i khog 'bugs legs bshad vaidurya me long drang srong dgyes pa'i dga' ston*, blockprint, Lhasa: Zhol, n.d.

Shangs n.d.
Shangs Rin-po-che, *gNas chen shel gyi ri bo 'brug gi dkar chag mthong ba don ldan dad pa'i skya rengs*, NGMPP E2878/5. n.p., n.d. ff. 18.

Shes sgon n.d.
Shes sgon pa'i bcad yig mthong ba'i yid phrog, NGMPP L550/2. n.p., n.d. ff. 14.

sMan-grong 1991
sMan-grong Tshe-ring Phun-tshogs, 'Bod gzhas gsar pa'i skor las 'phros pa'i bsam tshul 'ga' zhig' in *bDag po* 1991.1, 79–85.

sMan-pa 2000
sMan-pa Chos Lo-thar, *'Gro phan sman rtsis khang gi gdan rabs dri med shel gyi me long*, Dharamsala: Men-Tsee Khang.

Sog-po 1980
Sog-po dGe-shes Chos-grags, *brDa dag ming tshig gsal ba, A Comprehensive Dictionary of the Tibetan Language*, Dharamsala: Damchoe Sangpo, 2 vols.

sTag-rtse 1971a
sTag-rtse sKu-skye Mi-pham Phun-tshogs Shes-rab, *Bya btang stag rtse sku skye'i mgur ma'i 'phros gu yangs rig pa'i rtsed 'dzo* in *The Collected Works of sTag-rtse sKu-skye Mi-pham Phun-tshogs Shes-rab*, blockprint, Lo Mustang.

sTag-rtse 1971b
sTag-rtse sKu-skye Mi-pham Phun-tshogs Shes-rab, *mNgon dga'i zhing du bzod par gzhan rgyud bskul phyir rang tshul gleng ba'i zhu 'phri* in *The Collected Works of sTag-rtse sKu-skye Mi-pham Phun-tshogs Shes-rab*, blockprint, Lo Mustang (Glo sMon-thang).

Tāranātha 1983
Tāranātha, *dPal dus kyi 'khor lo'i chos bskor gyi byung khungs nyer mkho* in *The Collected Works of Jo-nang Tāranātha*, Leh: Smanrtsis Shesrig Dpemdzod, vol. 2, 1–43.

Thub-bstan 1993
Thub-bstan, 'Rang nyid kyi mi tshe'i shul lam thog bod mi rigs kyi rig rtsal bya bzhag ched du 'bad pa cung zad bgyis pa'i gnas tshul rags rim' in Bod Rang-skyong-ljongs Srid-gros Lo-rgyus Rig-gnas dPyad-gzhi'i rGyu-cha U-yon lHan-khang, *Bod kyi lo rgyus rig gnas dpyad gzhi'i rgyu cha bdams bsgrigs*, Beijing: Mi-rigs dPe-skrun-khang, 669–94.

Tshe-rdor 1995
Tshe-rdor, 'Bud med kyi gzi brjid' in *Bod kyi rtsom rig sgyu rtsal* 1995.5, 6–19.

Ye shes n.d.
Ye shes mkha' 'gro bsod nams 'dren gyi sku skyes gsum pa rje btsun ma chos kyi sgron ma'i rnam thar, photocopy of manuscript, 144 ff.

Yu-mo 1983
Yu-mo (mistakenly attributed by the publisher to both Bu-ston Rin-chen Grub

and A-wa-dhû-ti-pa bSod-nams), *Gsal sgron skor bzhi: Khrid Material to the Practice of the Sadangayoga of the Kālacakra*, Gangtok: Sherab Gyaltsen and Lama Dawa.

Zhol-khang 1991
Zhol-khang bSod-nams Dar-rgyas, 'Kho bo dang kho bo'i sgyu rtsal 'gro lam' in *Bod ljongs sgyu rtsal zhib 'jug* 1991.1, 154–9.

Zhol-khang 1992
Zhol-khang bSod-nams Dar-rgyas, *Glu gar tshangs pa'i chabs rgyun*, Lhasa: Bod-ljongs Mi-dmangs dPe-skrun-khang.

Zla-ba'i 1999
Zla-ba'i Shes-rab, *sGor ra nang pa phun tshogs dbang rgyal (phun dbang) gyi mdzad rnam mtor bsdus*, manuscript, *c.* 1999.

Zla gzhon 1993
'Zla gzhon snyan dbyangs' (1–3) in *Bod kyi rtsom rig sgyu rtsal* 1993.4, 82–5; 1993.5, 104–108; 1993.6, 77–81.

CHINESE SOURCES

Chen Kuiyuan 1999, *Lantian baixue* (*Blue Sky, White Snow*), Beijing: Beijing Chubanshe.

Gannan 1993, *Gannan Zangchuan Fojiao Siyuan Gaikuang* (*Introduction to Tibetan Buddhist Monasteries in Gannan*) (Gannan Wenshi Ziliao 10), Hezuo: Gannan Zhou Zhengxie.

Ge-lai, Liu Yi-min, Zhang Jian-shi and An Cai-dan 1993, *Zang bei mu min—Xi zang na qudi qu she hui diao cha* (*Nomads of Northern Tibet—Investigations on the Social History of Nagchu Prefecture in Tibet*), Beijing: Zhong guo zang xue chu ban she (Chinese Tibetology Publishing House).

Geng Fu 1993, 'Xiahe Luyou Ziyuan Jianjie' ('A Brief Introduction to Xiahe's Tourism Resources') in *Xiahe Wenshi Ziliao* 1. Xiahe: Zhongguo Renmin Zhengxie Shanghuiyi Xiahe Xian Weiyuanhui Wenshi Ziliao Weiyuanhui.

Hu Xiangze and Cheng Ping 1995, *Caidan Zhuoma* (*Tseten Drolma*), Lhasa: Xizang renmin chubanshe (Tibet People's Publishing House).

Li Anzhai 1946/1992, 'Xikang Dege zhi Lishi yu Renkou' ('The History and Population of Derge in Xikang') in *Li Anzhai Zangxue Wenlun Xuan*, Beijing: Zhongguo zangxue chubanshe.

Pu Wencheng 1990, *Gan Qing Zangchuan Fojiao Siyuan* (*Tibetan Buddhist Monasteries of Gansu and Qinghai*), Xining: Qinghai renmin chubanshe.

TAR Statistical Bureau 1990, *Xizang shehui jingji tongji nianjian* (*Social and Economic Statistical Yearbook*), Beijing: Zhongguo tongji chubanshe (Chinese Tibetology Publishing House).

Tian Liantao 1996, 'Bianji de hua' (editor's preface) in Tian Liantao (ed.), *Xizang chuantong yinyue huicui* (*The Essence of Tibetan Traditional Music*), Lhasa: Xizang renmin chubanshe (Tibet People's Publishing House), 1–14.

Yang Enhong 1995, *Minjian shi shen: Ge sa'er yiren yanjiu* (*Popular Divine Poets: Study of the Singing Tradition of King Gesar*), Beijing: Zhongguo zangxue chubanshe.

WESTERN LANGUAGE SOURCES

Adams, Vincanne 1996, 'Karaoke as Modern Lhasa, Tibet: Western Encounters with Cultural Politics', *Cultural Anthropology*, 11, 4, 510–46.

——— 1999, 'Globalization and Immobility, Selling Shoes, Sexuality and the Sacred in Lhasa, Tibet, China', paper presented at the Department of Anthropology, New York University.

Adams, Vincanne and Dashima Dovchin 2000, 'Women's Health in Tibetan Medicine and Tibet's "First" Female Doctor' in Ellison Banks Findly (ed.), *Women's Buddhism, Buddhism's Women: Tradition, Revision, Renewal* , Boston: Wisdom Publications, 443–50.

Adhe, Ama 2000, *Ama Adhe: The Voice that Remembers*, Boston: Wisdom Publications.

Allione, Tsultrim 1984, *Women of Wisdom*, London: Routledge & Kegan Paul.

Amnesty International 1990a, *People's Republic of China: Torture and Ill-treatment*, London: Amnesty International, ref. ASA 17/18/90, April.

——— 1990b, *PRC (TAR): One Year under Martial Law*, London: Amnesty International.

Ardussi, John and Lawrence Epstein 1978, 'The Saintly Madman in Tibet' in James F. Fisher (ed.), *Himalayan Anthropology: The Indo-Tibetan Interface*, The Hague: Mouton, 327–38.

Aris, Michael 1979, 'Introduction' to *Autobiographies of Three Spiritual Masters of Kutang*, Thimphu: Kunsang Topgay and Mani Dorji.

——— 1987, 'The Boneless Tongue: Alternative Voices from Bhutan in the Context of Lamaist Societies', *Past and Present*, 115 (May), 131 ff., also available in *High Asia* at www.amnyemachen.org.

Asia Watch 1990, *Merciless Repression*, London: AsiaWatch.

Aziz, Barbara N. 1976, 'Views from the Monastery Kitchen', *Kailash*, 4, 2, 155–68.

——— 1978, *Tibetan Frontier Families: Reflections of Three Generations from D'ing-ri* , Delhi: Vikas Publishing House.

——— 1985, 'On Translating from Oral Traditions: Ceremonial Wedding Poetry from Dingri' in B. N. Aziz and M. Kapstein (eds), *Soundings in Tibetan Civilisation*, Delhi: Manohar, 115–32.

——— 1987, 'Toward a Sociology of Tibet', *The Tibet Journal*, 12, 4 (winter), 72–86.

——— 1988, 'Women in Tibetan Society and Tibetology' in Helga Uebach and Jampa L. Panglung (eds), *Tibetan Studies: Proceedings of the Fourth Seminar of the International Association for Tibetan Studies*, Munich: Kommission für Zentralasiatische Studien, Bayerische Akademie der Wissenschaften, 25–34.

Bacot, Jacques 1935, 'Le mariage chinois du roi tibétain Srong-btsan sGam-po', *Mélanges chinois et bouddhiques*, 3, 1–60.

——— 1936, *Three Tibetan Mysteries*, trans. by H. I. Woolf, London: George Routledge.

Bacot, Jacques, Frederick William Thomas and Charles Toussaint 1940, *Documents de Touenhouang relatifs à l'histoire du Tibet* , Paris: Annales du Musée Guimet, Bibliothèque d'Études, t. 51 (Librairie Orientaliste Paul Geuthner).

Barlow, Tani 1994, 'Politics and Protocols of Funu: (Un)making National Woman' in Angela Zito (ed.), *Body, Subject and Power in China*, University of Chicago Press.

Barnett, Robert 1989, *The Role of Nuns in Tibetan Protest: Preliminary Notes*, London: Tibet Information Network (TIN), 17 October.

——— 1992, 'Chairman's Briefing on Security, November 1990', *Background Papers on Tibet—September 1992*, London: TIN, 12–19.

——— 2000, 'Beyond the Collaborator-Martyr Model: Strategies of Compliance, Opportunism and Opposition within Tibet', paper presented at the World Congress of the International Political Scientists' Association, Quebec, August 2000.

——— forthcoming, 'The Babas are Dead: Street Talk and Contemporary Views of Leaders in Tibet' in Sperling (ed.) *Tibetan Studies*.

——— and Mickey Spiegel 1992, *Political Prisoners in Tibet*, London: TIN and New York: AsiaWatch.

——— and Shirin Akiner (eds) 1994, *Resistance and Reform in Tibet*, London: Hurst.

——— and Mickey Spiegel 1996, *Cutting Off the Serpent's Head: Tightening Policy in Tibet 1994–5*, London: TIN and New York: Human Rights Watch.

——— and Victoria Conner 1997, *Leaders in Tibet: A Directory*, London: TIN.

Bartholomeusz, Tessa 1994, *Women Under the Bo Tree: Buddhist Nuns in Sri Lanka*, Cambridge University Press.

Bass, Catriona 1998, *Education in Tibet: Policy and Practice Since 1950*, London and New York: Zed Press and St Martin's Press.

Bell, Charles 1992, *The People of Tibet*, Delhi: Motilal Banarsidass.

Bellezza, J. 1997, *Divine Dyads: Ancient Civilization in Tibet*, Dharamsala: Library of Tibetan Works and Archives.

Berglie, Per-Arne 1976, 'Preliminary Remarks on some Tibetan Spirit-Mediums in Nepal', *Kailash*, 4, 1, 85–108.

——— 1980, 'Mount Targo and Lake Dangra: A Contribution to the Religious Geography of Tibet' in Michael Aris and Aung San Suu Kyi (eds), *Tibetan Studies in Honour of Hugh Richardson*, Warminster: Aris and Phillips, 39–45.

——— 1983, 'Gudarna stiger ned: Rituell besatthet hos sherpas och tibetaner', PhD thesis, Stockholm University.

——— 1992, 'Tibetan Spirit-Mediumship: Change and Continuity' in Ihara and Yamaguchi (eds), *Tibetan Studies*, 361–69.

Bhum, Pema 1995, 'The Life of Dhondup Gyal: A Shooting Star that Cleaved the Night Sky and Vanished', trans. by Lauran Hartley, *Lungta*, 9 (winter), 17–29.

Bhushan, Ravi (ed.) 1986, *Asia's Who's Who of Men and Women of Achievements and Distinctions*, Reference Asia, vol. 2, Delhi: Rifacemento Organisation.

Børresen, Kari E. (ed.) 1995, *The Image of God. Gender Models in Judaeo-Christian Tradition*, Minneapolis: Fortress Press.

Boyer, Pascal 1994, *The Naturalness of Religious Ideas: A Cognitive Theory of Religion*, Berkeley and Los Angeles: University of California Press.

Buffetrille, Katia 1998, 'Pèlerinage et inceste. Le cas de mChod rten nyi ma' in Anne-Marie Blondeau (ed.), *Tibetan Mountain Deities: Their Cults and*

Representations, Vienna: Verlag der Österreichischen Akademie der Wissenschaften, 19–43.

Bulag, Uradyn E. 2000a, 'From Inequality to Difference: Colonial Contradictions of Class and Ethnicity in "Socialist" China' in Allen Chun (ed.), *Postcolonialism and Its Discontents, Cultural Studies*, special issue, 14, 3, July.

——— 2000b, 'Ethnic Resistance with Socialist Characteristics' in Perry and Selden (eds), *Chinese Society*, 178–97.

Butler, Judith 1990a, 'Gender Trouble, Feminist Theory and Psychoanalysis' in Linda Nicholson (ed.), *Feminism/Postmodernism*, New York: Routledge, 79–93.

——— 1990b, *Gender Trouble: Feminism and the Subversion of Identity*, New York: Routledge.

——— 1993, *Bodies that Matter: On the Discursive Limitations of 'Sex'*, New York: Routledge.

Bynum, Caroline Walker 1992, *Fragmentation and Redemption: Essays on Gender and the Human Body in Medieval Religion*, New York: Zone Books.

Cabézon, José 1997, 'The Regulations of a Monastery' in Donald S. Lopez, Jr (ed.), *Religions of Tibet in Practice*, Princeton University Press, 335–51.

Caidan Zhuoma (Tseten Drolma) 1989, 'From Serf to Songstress', *China Reconstructs* (April), 14–15.

Calkowski, Marcia 1997, 'The Tibetan Diaspora and the Politics of Performance' in Korom (ed.), *Tibetan Culture in the Diaspora*, 51–9.

Campbell, June 1996, *Traveller in Space: In Search of Female Identity in Tibetan Buddhism*, London: Athlone Press.

Cannata, Patrizia 1990, 'La profezia dell'Arhat della terra di Li riguardante il declino della feda nella vera legge' in P. Daffinà (ed.), *Indo-Sino-Tibetica. Studi in onore di Luciano Petech*, Rome: Studi Orientali IX (Bardi), 43–79.

Carnhan, Sumner, with Lama Kunga Rimpoche 1998, *In the Presence of My Enemies: Memoirs of Tibetan Nobleman Tsipon Shuguba*, Santa Fe: Heartsfire.

Chang, Garma C.C. 1977, *The Hundred Thousand Songs of Milarepa*, Boulder and London: Shambhala.

Chaoul, Marco Alejandro 1999, 'Tracing the Origins of Chö (gcod) in the Bön Tradition: A Dialogical Approach Cutting through Sectarian Boundaries', MA thesis, University of Virginia (Charlottesville).

Chavannes, Edouard 1969, *Documents sur les Tou-Kiue (Turcs) occidentaux*, Taipei, repr. Ch'eng Wen Publishing Co.

Chayet, Anne 1985, *Les Temples de Jehol et leurs Modeles Tibetains*, Paris: Éditions Recherche sur les Civilisations.

——— 1993, *La femme au temps des Dalaï-Lamas*, Paris: Stock-L. Pernoud.

——— and Fernand Meyer 1983, 'La chapelle de Srong-btsan sgam-po au Potala', *Arts Asiatiques*, 37, 82–5.

Chimpa, Lama and Alaka Chattopadhyaya, trans. 1990, *Tāranātha's History of Buddhism in India*, Delhi: Motilal Banarsidass.

Chopathar Wayemache (Ma, Jiao Ba Ta) 1998, *Musical Arts in Tibet: Selected Essays (trans. from the Chinese by Shih Pu Wang and Kristina Dy-Liacco)*, vol. prepared by Kristina Dy-Liacco and Lauran Hartley on the occasion of the Tibetan Music Festival held in Bloomington, Indiana, April 2–5 1997.

Chotso, Tsering 1991/1997, 'A Drop from an Ocean: The Status of Women in Tibetan Society', *The Tibet Journal*, 22, 2, 1997, 63 (the article first appeared as 'Bod rigs bud med skor gyi zhib 'jug rgya mtsho'i chu thigs', *Bod ljongs zhib 'jug* 1991, 3, 79–88).

Cixous, Hélène 1981, 'The Laugh of the Medusa', trans. Keith Cohen and Paula Cohen, repr. in Elaine Marks and Isabelle de Courtivron (eds), *New French Feminisms*, New York: Schocken Books, 245–64.

Craig, Mary 1992, *Tears of Blood: A Cry for Tibet*, London: HarperCollins.

Crook, John and James Low 1997, *The Yogins of Ladakh: A Pilgrimage Among the Hermits of the Buddhist Himalayas*, Delhi: Motilal Banarsidass.

Crossley-Holland, Peter 1986, 'The State of Research in Tibetan Folk Music' in Norbu, 105–24.

Cunningham, Robert 1940, 'Nangsal Obum', *Journal of the West China Border Research Society*, 12, 35–75.

Daixan (Don-grub rDo-rje) 1995, *Gangs ljong kyi bud med: Women in the Land of Snow*, Beijing: Minzu Chu Banshe.

Dalai Lama 1990/1999, *Freedom in Exile*, London: Abacus.

Das, Sarat Chandra *et al.* 1973, *A Tibetan-English Dictionary*, repr. Delhi: Motilal Banarsidass.

Das, Surya 1992, *The Snow Lion's Turquoise Mane: Wisdom Tales from Tibet*, San Francisco: HarperCollins.

Dauncey, Sarah 1993, 'Women in Tibet', MA thesis, Durham University.

Day, Sophie 1989, 'Embdodying Spirits: Village Oracles and Possession Ritual in Ladakh, North India', PhD thesis, London School of Economics and Political Science.

del Valle, Teresa 1993, 'Introduction' in T. del Valle (ed.), *Gendered Anthropology*, London: Routledge, 1–16.

Delog Dawa Drolma 1995, *Delog: Journey to Realms Beyond Death*, trans. by Richard Barron and H. E. Chagdud Tulku Rinpoche, Junction City: Padma Publishing.

Demiéville, Paul 1952, *Le concile de Lhasa*, Paris: Bibl. de l'Institut des Hautes Études Chinoises, VII (Presses Universitaires de France).

Devine, Carol 1993, *Determination: Tibetan Women and the Struggle for an Independent Tibet*, Ithaca, NY: Snow Lion Publications.

Diehl, Kiela 1996, 'The Wedding Hostesses (Khrung zhu ma) of Central Tibet', *Chö Yang: The Voice of Tibetan Religion and Culture*, 7, 102–05.

——— 1997, 'When Tibetan Refugees Rock, Paradigms Roll: Echoes from Dharamsala's Musical Soundscape' in Korom (ed.), *Constructing Tibetan Culture*, 122–59.

——— 1998, 'Echoes from Dharamsala: Music in the Lives of Tibetan Refugees in Northern India', PhD thesis, University of Texas, Austin.

Diemberger, Hildegard 1993, 'Blood, Sperm, Soul and the Mountain: Gender Relations, Kinship and Cosmovision among the Khumbo (N. E. Nepal)' in del Valle (ed.), *Gendered Anthropology*, 88–127.

——— 1998, 'The Horseman in Red: On Sacred Mountains of La stod Lho (Southern Tibet)' in A. M. Blondeau (ed.), *Tibetan Mountain Deities, Their*

Cults and Representations, Vienna: Verlag der Österreichischen Akademie der Wissenschaften, vol. VI, 43–55.

Diemberger, Hildegard and Pasang Wangdu 1997, *Feast of Miracles: The Life and Tradition of Bodong Chole Namgyal*, Clusone: Porong Pema, Chöling Editions.

——— and Guntram Hazod 1999, 'Machig Zhama's Recovery: Traces of Ancient History and Myth in the South Tibetan Landscape of Kharta and Phadrug' in Toni Huber (ed.), *Sacred Spaces and Powerful Places in Tibetan Culture*, Dharmasala: The Library of Tibetan Works and Archives, 34–51, also in *The Tibet Journal*, 19, 4 (winter), 23–45.

——— and Guntram Hazod 1997, 'Animal Sacrifices and Mountain Deities in Southern Tibet: Mythology, Rituals and Politics' in Karmay and Sagant (eds), *Les habitants du Toit du monde*, 261–82.

——— and Pasang Wangdu 2000, *dBa' bzhed: The Royal Narrative of Bringing Buddha's Doctrine to Tibet*. Vienna: Verlag der Österreichischen Akademie der Wissenschaften.

Dowman, Keith 1984, *Sky Dancer: The Secret Life and Songs of the Lady Yeshe Tsogyel*, London: Routledge & Kegan Paul.

Drikung Kyabgon Chetsang, Head of the Drikung Kagyu Order, 1998, Dehra Dun: Drikung Kagyu Institute.

Duan Zhipu 1995, 'Emphasis Now on Education for Girls', *Window* (10 February), 26–7.

Duchesne, Isabelle 1994, 'The Chinese Opera Star: Roles and Identity' in John Hay (ed.), *Boundaries in China*, London: Reaktion Books, 217–42.

Dunham, Carroll and Ian Baker 1993, *Tibet. Reflections from the Wheel of Life*, New York: Abbeville Press.

Edou, Jérôme 1996, *Machig Labdrön and the Foundations of Chöd*, Ithaca, NY: Snow Lion.

Ehrhard, Franz-Karl 1994, 'Tibetan Sources on Muktināth: Individual Reports and Normative Guides', *Ancient Nepal: Journal of the Department of Archaeology*, 134, 23–41.

——— 1996, 'Two Further Lamas of Dolpo: Ngag-dbang-rnam-rgyal (born 1628) and rNam-grol-bzang-po (born 1504)', *Journal of the Nepal Research Centre*, 10, 55–76.

——— 1998, 'Sa-'dul dgon-pa: A Temple at the Crossroads of Jumla, Dolpo and Mustang', *Ancient Nepal: Journal of the Department of Archaeology*, 140, 3–21.

Eimer, Helmut 1983, 'Die Auffindung des Bka'-chems Ka-khol-ma' in Steinkellner and Tauscher (eds), *Contributions on Tibetan Language, History and Culture*, 45–51.

Ellingson, Ter 1990, 'Tibetan Monastic Constitutions: the Bca'-yig' in Epstein (ed.), *Reflections on Tibetan Culture*.

Epstein, Julia and Kristina Straub (eds) 1991, *Body Guards: The Cultural Politics of Gender Ambiguity*, London: Routledge.

Epstein, Lawrence 1982, 'On the History and Psychology of the *'Das-log'*, *The Tibet Journal*, 7, 4, 20–85.

——— and Richard F. Sherburne (eds) 1990, *Reflections on Tibetan Culture: Essays in Memory of Turrell V. Wylie*, Lewiston: Edwin Mellen Press.

Evans-Wentz, W. Y. (ed.) 1969, *Tibet's Greatest Yogi Milarepa*; (1929) 2nd edn repr., London: Oxford University Press.

Feuchtwang, S. 1992, *The Imperial Metaphor*, London, New York: Routledge.

Five Thousand Personalities of the World, 1986, North Carolina: American Biographical Institute.

Frankel, Han H. 1976, *The Flowering Plum and the Palace Lady: Interpretations of Chinese Poetry*, Yale University Press.

Gellner, David 1994, 'Priests, Healers, Mediums and Witches: The Context of Possession in the Kathmandu Valley, Nepal', *Man*, 29, 1 (March), 27–48.

Germano, David 1994, 'Architecture and Absence in the Secret Tantric History of the Great Perfection (*rdzogs chen*)', *Journal of the International Association of Buddhist Studies*, 17, 2, 203–335.

Germano, David and Janet Gyatso 2000, 'Longchenpa and the Possession of the *ḍākinīs*', in David White (ed.), *Tantra in Practice*, Princeton University Press, 239–65.

Gethin, Rupert 1998, *The Foundations of Buddhism*, New York: Oxford University Press.

Gilmartin, Christina 1990, 'Violence Against Women in Contemporary China' in Jonathan Lipman and Stevan Harrell (eds), *Violence in China: Essays in Culture and Counterculture*, Albany: State University of New York Press.

Giraudon, Liliane 1999, 'Carnet tibétain (Pièces détachées) juillet-août 1998', *Action Poétique*, 157, 78–83.

Gladney, Dru C. 1994, 'Representing Nationality in China: Refiguring Majority/ Minority Identities', *Journal of Asian Studies*, 53,1, 92–123.

Godelier, Maurice 1982, *La production des grands hommes*, Paris: Fayard.

——— 1990, 'Inceste, parente, pouvoir', *Psychanalistes*, 213 (September), 1141–55.

Golan, Daphna 1997, 'Between Universalism and Particularism: The "Border" in Israel Discourse' in V. Y. Mudimbe (ed.), *Nations, Identities, Cultures*, Durham, NC: Duke University Press.

Goldstein, Melvyn C. 1964, 'A Study of the Ldap Ldop', *Central Asiatic Journal*, 9, 123–41.

——— 1982, 'Lhasa Street Songs: Political and Social Satire in Traditional Tibet', *The Tibet Journal*, 7, 1–2, 56–66.

——— 1986, 'Re-examining Choice, Dependency and Command in the Tibetan Social System: Tax Appendages and Other Landless Serfs', *The Tibet Journal*, 9, 4, 79–112.

——— 1989, *A History of Modern Tibet, 1913–1951: The Demise of the Lamaist State*, Berkeley: University of California Press.

——— 1990, 'Religious Conflict in the Traditional Tibetan State' in Epstein and Sherburne (eds), *Body Guards*, 231–47.

——— 1995, *Tibet, China and the United States: Reflections on the Tibet Question*, The Atlantic Council of The United States, Occasional Paper (also developed in a similar form in *Foreign Affairs*, January 1998, and in *The Snow Lion and the Dragon: China, Tibet and the Dalai Lama*, Berkeley: University of California Press, 1997).

Goldstein, Melvyn C., William R. Siebenschuh, and Tashi Tsering 1997, *The Struggle for Modern Tibet: The Autobiography of Tashi Tsering*, Armonk, N.Y.: M. E. Sharpe.

Gross, Rita M. 1989, 'Yeshe Tsogyel: Enlightened Consort, Great Teacher, Female Role Model' in J. Willis (ed.), *Feminine Ground*, 11–32.

——— 1993, *Buddhism after Patriarchy: A Feminist History, Analysis and Reconstruction of Buddhism*, Albany: State University of New York Press.

Gutschow, Kim 1997, 'Unfocused Merit-making in Zangskar: A Socio-economic Account of Karsha Nunnery', *The Tibet Journal*, 22, 2 (summer), 30–58.

——— 2004, *Being a Buddhist Nun: The Struggle for Enlightenment in the Himalayas*, Cambridge, MA: Harvard University Press.

Gyaco, Jambal 1988, 'Un Homère tibétain: Zaba Ngawang Gyatso', *Les Tibétains à propos du Tibet*, Beijing: La Chine en construction, 101–106.

Gyatso, Janet 1985, 'The Development of the Gcod Tradition' in Aziz and Kapstein (eds), *Soundings in Tibetan Civilisation*, 320–41.

——— 1989, 'Down with the Demoness: Reflections on a Feminine Ground in Tibet' in Willis (ed.), *Feminine Ground*, 33–51.

——— 1992, 'Autobiography in Tibetan Religious Literature: Reflections on its Modes of Self-presentation' in Ihara and Yamaguchi (eds) *Tibetan Studies*, 465–78.

——— 1998a, *Apparitions of the Self: The Secret Autobiographies of a Tibetan Visionary*, Princeton University Press.

——— 1998b, Introduction to Lama Chonam and Sangye Khandro, trans., *The Lives and Liberation of Princess Mandarava*, Boston: Wisdom Publications, 1–14.

——— 1999, 'Female Sex and/or Gender: Glimmers from the Tibetan Medical Tradition', paper delivered at the University of Chicago (12 April).

——— 2003, 'One Plus One Makes Three: Buddhist Gender Conception and the Law of the Non-Excluded Middle', *History of Religions*, 43, 2, 89–115.

——— forthcoming, 'A Partial Genealogy of the Lifestory of Yeshe Tsogyal', *Journal of the International Association of Tibetan Studies*.

Gyatso, Ngawang Lobsang (Fifth Dalai Lama), *A History of Tibet* (*rGyal rabs rdzogs ldan gzhon nu dga' ston*), trans. Zahiruddin Ahmad, Bloomington: Indiana University Press, 1995.

Gyatso, Palden 1997, *Fire under the Snow: The Testimony of a Tibetan Prisoner* (with Tsering Shakya), London: Harvill.

Hamayon, Roberte 1990, *La chasse à l'ame*, Paris: Société d'éthnologie.

——— 2000, 'Reconstuction identitaire autour d'une figure imaginaire chez les Bouriates post-sovietiques' in J. C. Attias, P. Gisel and L. Kaennel (eds), *Messianismes: Relgions et perspectives*, 10, 229–52.

Haarh, Erik 1969, *The Yar-lung Dynasty*, Copenhagen: G. E. C. Gads Forlag.

Hartley, Lauran 1999, 'Contemporary Tibetan Literature', *Lungta*, 12, Dharamsala: Amnye Machen Institute (summer), 31–2.

——— 2003, 'Con*text*ually Speaking: Tibetan Literary Discourse and Social Change in the People's Republic of China (1980–2000)', PhD thesis, Indiana University.

Harrell, Stevan 1995, 'Civilizing Projects and the Reaction to Them' in Stevan Harrell (ed.), *Cultural Encounters on China's Ethnic Frontiers*, Seattle: University of Washington Press, 3–36.

Harrer, Heinrich 1955, *Seven Years in Tibet*, London: Hart-Davis.

——— 1997, *Lhassa. Le Tibet disparu*, Paris: Editions de la Martinière.

Harris, Clare 1997, 'Struggling with Shangri-La: a Tibetan Artist in Exile' in Korom (ed.), *Constructing Tibetan Culture*, 160–77.

Harris, Elizabeth J. 1999, 'The Female in Buddhism' in Tsomo (ed.), *Buddhist Women Across Cultures*, 49–66.

Havnevik, Hanna 1989, *Tibetan Buddhist Nuns: History, Cultural Norms and Social Reality*, Oslo: Norwegian University Press.

——— 1994, 'The Role of Nuns in Contemporary Tibet' in Barnett and Akiner (eds), *Resistance and Reform in Tibet*, 259–66.

——— 1995, *Combats des nonnes tibétaines, Religieuses bouddhistes du Pays des neiges*, St Michel en l'Herm: Editions Dharma.

——— 1997, 'The Autobiography of Jetsun Lochen Rinpoche: A Preliminary Research Report' in Ernst Steinkellner *et al.* (eds), *Tibetan Studies: Proceedings of the 7th Seminar of the International Association for Tibetan Studies, Graz 1995*, Vienna: Verlag der Österreichischen Akademie der Wissenschaften, vol. I, 355–68.

——— 1998, 'On Pilgrimage for Forty Years in the Himalayas: The Female Lama Jetsun Lochen Rinpoche's (1865–1951) Quest for Sacred Sites' in Alex McKay (ed.), *Pilgrimage in Tibet*, Richmond, Surrey: Curzon Press, 85–107.

——— 1999, 'The Life of Jetsun Lochen Rinpoche (1865–1951) as Told in Her Autobiography,' *Acta Humaniora*, 50, PhD thesis, 2 vols, Faculty of Arts, University of Oslo.

——— 2002, 'A Tibetan Female State Oracle' in Henk Blezer (ed.), *Religion and Secular Culture in Tibet* (Tibetan Studies II: Proceedings of the Ninth Seminar of the International Association for Tibetan Studies), Leiden: E. J. Brill, 2/2, pp. 259–89.

Hazod, Guntram forthcoming, 'Ancient Places in Yar stod' in Sperling (ed.), *Tibetan Studies*.

Heissig, Walter 1953, 'A Mongolian Source to the Lamaist Suppression of Shamanism in the 17th Century', *Anthropos*, 48, 1–29 and 493–536.

——— 1970, 'Die Religionen der Mongolei' in Tucci and Heissig, *Die Religionen Tibets und der Mongolei*, Stuttgart: Kohlhammer.

Helffer, Mireille 2000, 'Musiche dal tetto del mondo' in M. Helffer (ed.), *Musiche dal tetto del mondo*, Turin: Testo & Immagine, 2–130.

Henrion-Dourcy, Isabelle and Tsereng Dhondup 2001, 'Tibet (III.1 Folk song and dance; III.6 Instruments, III.3 Nangma; III.5 Lhamo)' in Sadie (ed.), *The New Grove Dictionary of Music and Musicians*, 49–60.

——— 2004, 'Ache Lhamo. Jeux et Enjeux d'une Tradition Théâtrale Tibétaine' (Ache Lhamo: Playing and Tradition in Tibetan Theatre), PhD thesis, Free University of Brussels.

Herrmann-Pfandt, Adelheid 1998, review article, *The Tibet Journal*, 23, 3 (autumn), 92–102.

——— 2001, *Ḍākinīs. Zur Stellung und Symbolik des Weiblichen im tantrischen Buddhismus*. rev. edn 2. erweiterte Auflag Indica und Tibetica Band 20. Bonn: Indica und Tibetica Verlag.

Hilary, John 1992, 'Note on Chinese Policies towards Sects in the 1980s', *Background Papers on Tibet: September 1992*. London: TIN.

Hitchcock, J. T. and R. L. Jones 1976, *Spirit Possession in the Nepal Himalayas*, London: Aris and Phillips.

Hobsbawm, Eric and Terence Ranger 1983, *The Invention of Tradition*, Cambridge University Press.

Hopkins, Jeffrey (trans.) 1998, *Buddhist Advice for Living and Liberation: Nāgārjuna's Precious Garland*, Ithaca, NY: Snow Lion Publications.

Huber, Toni 1994, 'Why Can't Women Climb Pure Crystal Mountain? Remarks on Gender, Ritual and Space at Tsa-ri' in Kvaerne (ed.), *Tibetan Studies*, vol. 1, 350–71.

Humphrey, Caroline 1994, 'Shamanic Practices and the State in Northern Asia: Views from the Centre and Periphery' in N. Thomas and C. Humphrey (eds), *Shamanism, History and the State*, Ann Arbor: University of Michigan Press, 191–228.

——— 1995, 'Chiefly and Shamanist Landscapes' in E. Hirsch and M. O'Hanlon (eds), *The Anthropology of Landscape: Perspectives on Place and Space*, Oxford University Press, 135–62.

——— 1996, *Shaman and Elders*, Oxford University Press.

Haarh, Erik 1969, *The Yar-lung Dynasty*, Copenhagen: G. E. C. Gad.

Ihara, Shoren and ZuihoYamaguchi (eds) 1992, *Tibetan Studies: Proceedings of the 5th Seminar of the International Association for Tibetan Studies, Narita 1998*, Narita: Naritasan Shinsoji, 2 vols.

International Campaign for Tibet 1996, *A Season to Purge: Religious Repression in Tibet*, Washington, DC.

The International Who's Who of Intellectuals 1985, Cambridge: International Biographical Centre, vol. 6.

Irigaray, Luce 1991, 'Sexual Difference' in Margaret Whitford (ed.), *The Irigaray Reader*, Oxford: Blackwell, 165–77.

Jackson, David P. 1984, *The Mollas of Mustang: Historical, Religious and Oratorical Traditions of the Nepalese-Tibetan Borderland*, Dharamsala: Library of Tibetan Works and Archives.

——— 1990, *Two Biographies of Śākyaśrībhadra*, Stuttgart: Franz Steiner Verlag.

Jackson, Roger 1997, 'A Fasting Ritual' in Donald S. Lopez, Jr (ed.), *Religions of Tibet in Practice*, Princeton University Press, 271–93.

Jäschke, H. 1882/1991, *A Tibetan-English Dictionary*, Delhi: Motlilal Banarsidass.

Jest, Corneille 1975, *Dolpo: Communautés de Langue Tibétaine du Népal*, Paris: Centre National de la Recherche Scientifique.

——— 1981, *Monuments of Northern Nepal*, Paris: Unesco.

Josayma, Tashi Tsering and K. Dhondup 1990, *Dolma and Dolkar: Mother and Daughter of Tibetan Medicine*, Delhi: Yarlung Publications.

Kapstein, Matthew 1992, 'Remarks on the Mani bKa'-'bum and the Cult of Avalokiteśvara in Tibet' in S. D. Goodman and R. M. Davidson (eds), *Tibetan Buddhism: Reason and Revelation*, Albany: State University of New York Press, 79–93.

Karmay, Heather 1977, 'Tibetan Costume, Seventh to Eleventh Centuries' in A. Macdonald and Y. Imaeda (eds), *Essais sur l'art du Tibet*, Paris: J. Maisonneuve, 65–81.

Karmay, Samten G. 1987, 'L'âme et la turquoise', *L'Ethnographie* LXXXIII, 97–130.

——— 1988, *The Great Perfection: A Philosophical and Meditative Teaching of Tibetan Buddhism*, Leiden: E. J. Brill.

——— 1994, 'Mountain Cults and National Identity in Tibet' in Barnett and Akiner (eds), *Resistance and Reform in Tibet*, 112–20.

——— 1995, 'Gesar. The Epic Tradition of the Tibetans', *Lungta*, 9 (*Two Thousand Years and More of Tibetan Poetry*), 3–7.

——— 1998, 'A General Introduction to the History and Doctrines of Bon' in Samten G. Karmay (ed.), *The Arrow and the Spindle. Studies in History, Myths, Rituals and Beliefs in Tibet*, Kathmandu: Mandala Book Point, 104–57.

——— and Philippe Sagant (eds) 1997, *Les habitants du Toit du monde. Volume in Honour of Alexander Macdonald*, Paris: Société d'Ethnologie, Nanterre.

Karsten, Joachim 1983, 'A Note on Ya Sor and the Secular Festivals following the sMon lam chen mo' in Steinkellner and Tauscher (eds), *Contributions on Tibetan Language, History and Culture*, 117–49.

Kay, Ernest (ed.) 1982, *The World Who's Who of Women*, Cambridge: International Biographical Center, 6th edition.

Kerr, Blake 1991, 'Tibetans Under the Knife' in Petra Kelly, Gert Bastian and Pat Aiello (eds), *The Anguish of Tibet*, Berkeley: Parallax Press, 100 ff.

——— and John Ackerley 1989, *The Suppression of a People: Accounts of Torture and Imprisonment in Tibet*, Massachusetts: Physicians for Human Rights.

Keesing, Roger M. 1976, *Cultural Anthropology: A Contemporary Perspective*, New York: Holt, Rinehart and Winston.

Keyes, Charles 1986, 'Ambiguous Gender: Male Initiation in a Northern Thai Buddhist Society' in Caroline W. Bynum, Stevan Harrell and Paula Richman (eds), *Gender and Religion: On the Complexity of Symbols*, Boston: Beacon Press, 66–96.

Khangkar, Tsewang Dolkar 1990, *Health and Harmony through the Balance in Pulse Reading: The Diagnostic Art My Mother Taught Me*, Delhi: Yarlung Publications.

——— 1998, *Tibetan Medicine: The Buddhist Way of Healing*, Delhi: Lustre Press, Roli Books.

Khangkar, Docteur Dolkar and Marie-José Lamothe 1997, *Médecin du toit du monde.* Monaco: Editions du Rocher.

King, Ursula 1995, 'Introduction' in Ursula King (ed.), *Religion and Gender*, Oxford: Blackwell.

Klein, Anne Carolyn 1985, 'Primordial Purity and Everyday Life: Exalted Female Symbols and the Women of Tibet' in Clarissa W. Atkinson, Constance H. Buchanan and Margaret Ruth Miles (eds), *Immaculate and Powerful: The Female in Sacred Image and Social Reality*, Boston: Beacon Press.

——— 1995, *Meeting the Great Bliss Queen: Buddhists, Feminists, and the Art of the Self*, Boston: Beacon Press.

Kollmar-Paulenz, Karénina 1993, *'Der Schmuck der Befreiung'. Die Geshichte der Źi byed-und gCod-Schule des tibetischen Buddhismus*, Wiesbaden: Otto Harrassowitz.

——— 1998, 'Ma gcig Lab sgron ma: The Life of a Tibetan Woman Mystic between Adaptation and Rebellion' In *The Tibet Journal*, 23, 2 (summer), 1–32.

Korom, Frank J. (ed.) 1997a, *Tibetan Culture in the Diaspora*, papers presented at the panel of the 7th Seminar of the International Association for Tibetan Studies. Vienna: Verlag der Österreichischen Akademie der Wissenschaften, vol. 4.

——— 1997b, *Constructing Tibetan Culture: Contemporary Perspectives*, Québec: World Heritage Press.

Koskoff, Ellen (ed.) 1989, *Women and Music in Cross-cultural Perspective*, Urbana and Chicago: University of Illinois Press.

Kvaerne, Per (ed.) 1994a, *Tibetan Studies: Proceedings of the 6th Seminar of the International Association for Tibetan Studies, Fagernes 1992*, Oslo: Institute for Comparative Research in Human Culture, 2 vols.

——— 1994b, 'The Ideological Impact on Tibetan Art' in Barnett and Akiner (eds), *Resistance and Reform in Tibet*, 166–85.

Larsen, Kjersti 1995, 'Where Humans and Spirits Meet: Incorporating Difference and Experiencing Otherness in Zanzibar Town', PhD thesis, University of Oslo.

Laufer, Berthold 1911, *Der Roman einer tibetischen Königin*, Leipzig: Otto Harrassowitz.

Lee, Sing and Arthur Kleinman 2000, 'Suicide as Resistance in Chinese Society' in Perry and Selden (eds), *Chinese Society*, 221–41.

Levine, Nancy 1988, *The Dynamics of Polyandry: Kinship, Domesticity and Population on the Tibetan Border*, University of Chicago Press.

Lewis, I. M. 1971, *Ecstatic Religion: An Anthropological Study of Spirit Possession and Shamanism*, Harmondsworth: Penguin Books.

——— 1989, *Ecstatic Religion*, repr. London: Routledge.

Lhalungpa, Lobsang P. 1972, 'Tibetan Music: Sacred and Secular', *Tibetan Review*, 7, 9–10, 11–15.

——— 1977, *The Life of Milarepa* (trans.), New York: E. P. Dutton.

Lhamo, Rinchen 1926/1985, *We Tibetans*, New York: Potala.

Liao Dongfan 1995, 'An Adobe House Named Xaqen', *China's Tibet*, 37–8, 40.

Lichter, David and Lawrence Epstein 1983, 'Irony in Tibetan Notions of the Good Life' in Charles F. Keyes and E. Valentine Daniel (eds), *Karma: An Anthropological Inquiry*, Berkeley: University of California Press.

Li, Fang Kuei and W. South Coblin 1987, *A Study of the Old Tibetan Inscriptions*, Taipei: Institute of History and Philology, Academia Sinica, Special publ. no. 91, Nankang, Taiwan.

Li Xiaojiang 1999, 'Where Have We Got to in the Last Fifty Years? A Review of the Process of Chinese Women's Liberation and Growth', *Asian Women*, 9 (December), Seoul: Sookyung Women's University Press, 45–68.

Li Zhisui 1994, *The Private Life of Chairman Mao: The Memoirs of Mao's Personal Physician*, New York: Random House.

Liu Qizhong and Chen Gengtao (eds) 1991, *Profiles of 50 Tibetans*, Beijing: Xinhua.

Liu Suinian and Wu Qungan (eds) 1986, *China's Socialist Economy: An Outline History (1949–1984)*, Beijing Review Press.

Liu Zhonglu 1994, *Women of Tibet*, Beijing: Wuzhou Bochu Banshe.

Lo Bue, Erberto 1994, 'A Case of Mistaken Identity: Ma-gcig Labs-sgron and Ma-gcig Zha- ma' in P. Kvaerne (ed.), *Tibetan Studies*, 481–90.

Luzi, Laetitia 1999, 'La musique contemporaine tibétaine. Quand l'épopée de Gesar se chante en rap', *Action poétique*, 157, 75–77.

——— 2001, 'Tibet (II.7. Contemporary popular music)' in Sadie (ed.), *The New Grove Dictionary of Music and Musicians*.

Macdonald, Ariane 1971, 'Une lecture des Pelliot tibétain 1286, 1287, 1038, 1047, et 1290. Essai sur la formation et l'emploi des mythes politiques dans la religion royale de Srong-btsan sGam-po' in *Études tibétaines dédiées à la mémoire de Marcelle Lalou*, Paris: Adrien-Maisonneuve, 190–391.

Madrong, Migyur Dorje 1997, 'A Discussion on Some Great Women in Tibetan History', trans. by Sonam Tsering, *The Tibet Journal*, 22, 2 (summer), 69–90 (The article originally appeared as 'Gangs ljongs bud med lo rgyus mi sna'i skor gleng ba', *Bod ljongs zhib 'jug* 1, 1992, 118–45).

Makley, Charlene 1997, 'The Meaning of Liberation: Representations of Tibetan Women', *The Tibet Journal*, 22, 2 (summer), 4–29.

——— 1999, 'Embodying the Sacred: Gender and Monastic Revitalization in China's Tibet', PhD thesis, Department of Anthropology, University of Michigan.

Makley, Charlene, Keith Dede, Hua Kan and Wang Qingshan 2000, 'Labrang Amdo Dialect: a Phonology', *Linguistics of the Tibeto-Burman Area* 22 (spring).

Marshall, Steve 1999, *Hostile Elements*, London: TIN.

Martin, Dan 1984, review of Gtsan-smyon He-ru-ka, *The Life of Marpa the Translator*, trans. by Nalanda Translation Committee, *The Journal of the Tibet Society*, 4, 83–92, with addenda in *The Journal of the Tibet Society* 5, 1985, 112–7.

——— 1992, 'A Twelfth-Century Tibetan Classic of Mahāmudrā, "The Path of Ultimate Profundity: The Great Seal Instructions of Zhang"', *Journal of the International Association of Buddhist Studies*, 15, 2, 243–319.

——— 1996a, 'Lay Religious Movements in 11th- and 12th-Century Tibet: A Survey of Sources', *Kailash*, 18, 3–4, 23–56.

——— 1996b, 'The Star King and the Four Children of Pehar: Popular Religious Movements of 11th- to 12th-Century Tibet', *Acta Orientalia Hungarica*, 49, 171–95.

——— 1996c, 'Wrapping Your Own Head: Problems of Context and Individuality as Pre- and Post-Considerations for Translating 'The Path of Ultimate

Profundity, The Great Seal Instructions of Zhang,' a Twelfth-Century Tibetan Verse Compendium of Oral Instructions on Mahāmudrā' in Enrica Garzilli (ed.), *Translating, Translations, Translators: From India to the West*, Cambridge: Harvard Oriental Series, 59–73.

——— 1997, *Tibetan Histories: A Bibliography of Tibetan-Language Historical Works*, London: Serindia Publications.

——— 2001, 'Meditation is Action Taken: On Zhang Rinpoche, a Meditation-based Activist in Twelfth-century Tibet', *Lungta*, a publication of the Amnye Machen Institute, McLeod Ganj, India, 14 (spring), 45–56.

Mathes, Klaus-Dieter 1999, 'The Sacred Crystal Mountain in Dolpo: Beliefs and Pure Visions of Himalayan Pilgrims and Yogis', *Journal of the Nepal Research Centre*, 11, 61–90.

Ma Yin (ed.) 1989, *China's Minority Nationalities*, Beijing: Foreign Languages Press.

McGranahan, Carole 1996, 'Miss Tibet, or Tibet Misinterpreted? The Trope of Woman-as-nation in the Struggle for Tibet' in Colleen Ballerino Cohen, Richard Wilk and Beverly Stoeltje (eds), *Beauty Queens on the Global Stage: Gender, Contests and Power*, London and New York: Routledge, 161–84.

——— 2001, 'Between Empire and Exile: A Khampa History of Twentieth Century Tibet', PhD thesis, University of Michigan.

McLagan, Meg 1996, 'Mobilizing for Tibet: Transnational Politics and Diaspora Culture in the Post-cold War Era', PhD thesis, Dept. of Anthropology, New York University.

——— 1997, 'Mystical Visions in Manhattan: Deploying Culture in the Year of Tibet' in Korom (ed.), *Tibetan Culture in the Diaspora*, 69–89.

Meserve, Walter J. and Ruth I. Meserve 1979, 'Theatre for Assimilation: China's National Minorities', *Journal of Asian History*, 13, 2, 95–120.

Moon, Adrian A. 1991, 'The Yaso Generals', *Chö Yang: The Voice of Tibetan Religion and Culture*, 4, 207–13.

Moss, Martin 1995, *Children of Despair*, London: Independent Tibet Network.

Mullin, Glenn H 1978, 'Lobsang Dolma: Tibet's Foremost Lady Doctor', *Tibetan Review* (May), 9–15.

Myers, Kathleen A. and Amanda Powell 1999, *A Wild Country out in the Garden: The Spiritual Journals of a Colonial Mexican Nun*, Bloomington: Indiana University Press.

Nahachewsky, Andriy 1995, 'Participatory and Presentational Dance as Ethnochoreological Categories,' *Dance Research Journal*, 27, 1 (spring).

Nag-dban-blo-bzan-rgya-mtsho, Dalai Lama V 1995, *A History of Tibet*, trans. by Zahiruddin Ahmad, Bloomington: Indiana University Press.

Nam-mkha'i-snying-po 1983, *Mother of Knowledge: The Enlightenment of Yeshes mTsho-rgyal*, trans. by Tarthang Tulku with Jane Wilhelms. Berkeley: Dharma Publishing.

Nebesky-Wojkowitz, René de 1975, *Oracles and Demons of Tibet: The Cult and Iconography of the Tibetan Protective Deities*, repr. Graz: Akademische Druck- und Verlagsanstalt.

Norbu, Jamyang 1986, 'Introduction: The Role of the Performing Arts in Old Tibetan Society' in Jamyang Norbu (ed.), *Zlos-Gar. Performing Traditions of Tibet*, Dharamsala: Library of Tibetan Works and Archives, 1–6.

——— 1992, 'Blowing the Sounds of Emptiness', *Tibetan Bulletin* (May-June), 36–8.

——— 1993, 'Interdiction, perversion et sauvegarde. Questions culturelles et intellectuelles posées aux tibétains d'aujourd'hui' in Oliver Moulin (ed.), *Tibet, l'envers du décor*, Geneva: Olizane, 151–66.

——— 1994, 'The Tibetan Resistance Movement and the Role of the C.I.A.' in Barnett and Akiner (eds), *Resistance and Reform in Tibet*, 186–96.

Orofino, Giacomella 1987, 'Contributo allo studio dell'insegnamento di Ma gcig Lab sgron', *Annali, Istituto Orientale di Napoli*, 47, 4, supplement no. 53, 1–87.

——— 1994, 'Divination with Mirrors: Observations on a Simile Found in the Kālacakra Literature' in Kvaerne (ed.), *Tibetan Studies*, 612–28.

Ortner, Sherry B. 1978, *Sherpas through their Rituals*, Cambridge University Press.

——— 1983, 'The Founding of the First Sherpa Nunnery and the Problem of "Women" as an Analytic Category' in Vivian Patraka and Louise A. Tilly (eds), *Feminist Revisions: What Has Been and Might Be*, Ann Arbor: University of Michigan Women's Studies Program, 98–134.

——— 1989, *High Religion: A Cultural and Political History of Sherpa Buddhism*, Princeton University Press.

——— 1996, *Making Gender: The Politics and Erotics of Culture*, Boston: Beacon Press.

Pachen, Ani, with Adelaide Donnelley 2000, *Sorrow Mountain: The Journey of a Tibetan Warrior Nun*, Kodansha International.

Patt, David 1992, *A Strange Liberation: Tibetan Lives in Chinese Hands*, Ithaca, NY: Snow Lion Publications.

Paul, Diana 1985, *Women in Buddhism*, repr. Berkeley: Asian Humanities Press (first edition 1979).

Paul, Robert A. 1982, *The Tibetan Symbolic World. Psychoanalytic Explorations*, University of Chicago Press.

Pelliot, Paul 1961, *Histoire ancienne du Tibet*, Paris: Adrien-Maisonneuve.

Perry, Elizabeth J. and Mark Selden (eds) 2000, *Chinese Society: Change, Conflict and Resistance*, New York: Routledge.

Petech, Luciano 1967, 'Glosse agli Annali di Tun-huang', *Rivista degli Studi Orientali*, 42, 241–79.

Pinto, Sarah 1999, 'Pregnancy and Childbirth in Tibetan Culture' in Tsomo 1999, pp. 159–68.

Pommaret, Françoise 1989, *Les revenants de l'au-delà dans le monde tibétain. Sources littéraires et tradition vivante*, Paris: Editions du Centre national de la recherche scientifique (CNRS).

Rabgay, Losang 2004, 'En-gendering Tibet: Nation, Narration and the Woman's Body in Diaspora', PhD thesis, London University (School of African and Oriental Studies).

Ramble, Charles (forthcoming), *In Search of Zhang Zhung: The Mirror Illuminating the Royal Genealogies*.

Richardson, Hugh 1974, *Ch'ing Dynasty Inscriptions at Lhasa* , Roma: IsMEO.

——— 1985, *A Corpus of Early Tibetan Inscriptions*, Hertford: James G. Forlong series, no. 29 (Stephen Austin and Sons).

Rinchen Lhamo 1926/1997, *We Tibetans*, Delhi: Srishti.

Riskin, Carl 1997, *China Human Development Report: Human Development and Poverty Alleviation 1997*, Beijing: United Nations Development Programme.

Robertson, Carol E. 1989, 'Power and Gender in the Musical Experiences of Women' in Koskoff (ed.), *Women and Music in Cross-cultural Perspective*, 225–44.

Robertson, Jennifer 1992, 'The Politics of Androgyny in Japan: Sexuality and Subversion in the Theater and Beyond', *American Ethnologist* 19, 3.

Robin, Françoise 1998, 'Don grub rgyal (1953–85), l'enfant terrible de la nouvelle littérature tibétaine', MA thesis, INALCO, Paris.

Roerich, George N. (trans. with Gendun Chomphel) 1988, *The Blue Annals*, repr., Delhi: Motilal Banarsidass.

Rosalind C. Morris 1995, 'All Made Up: Performance Theory and the New Anthropology of Sex and Gender,' *Annual Review of Anthropology*, 24, 567–92.

Ross, Joanna 1995, *Lhamo: Opera from the Roof of the World*, Delhi: Paljor Publications.

Rossi, Donatella, forthcoming, 'Sacred Female Biographies in the Bon Religion: A 20th Century gTer-ma', in Sperling (ed.), *Tibetan Studies*.

Russell, Philippa and Sonam Lhamo Singeri 1992, 'The Tibetan Women's Uprising', *Chö Yang: The Voice of Tibetan Religion and Culture*, 5, 51–61.

Sadie, Stanley (ed.) 2001, *The New Grove Dictionary of Music and Musicians*, London: Macmillan. 20 vols.

Sagant, Philippe 1996, *The Dozing Shaman*, Delhi: Oxford University Press.

Sakya, Jamyang and Julie Emery 1990, *Princess in the Land of Snow: The Life of Jamyang Sakya in Tibet*, Boston: Shambhala.

Samdup, Tseten 1994, 'Tibetan Women in Europe', *Tibetan Bulletin* (March–April), 20.

Samuel, Geoffrey B. 1976, 'Songs of Lhasa', *Ethnomusicology*, 20, 3, 407–49.

——— 1993, *Civilized Shamans: Buddhism in Tibetan Societies*, Washington D.C.: Smithsonian Institution Press.

——— 2002, 'The Epic and Nationalism in Tibet,' in Benjamin Penny (ed.), *Religion and Biography in China and Tibet*, Richmond: Curzon Press, 178–89.

Samuels, Jeffrey 1999, 'Views of Householders and Lay Disciples in the Sutta Pitaka: A Reconsideration of the Lay / Monastic Opposition', *Religion*, 29, 231–41.

Sautman, Barry 1997, 'Myths of Descent, Racial Nationalism and Ethnic Minorities in the People's Republic of China' in Frank Dikötter (ed.), *The Construction of Racial Identities in China and Japan*, London: Hurst, 75–95.

Savvas, Carol D. 1990, 'A Study of the Profound Path of Gcod: The Mahayana Buddhist Meditation Tradition of Tibet's Great Woman Saint Machig Labdron,' PhD thesis, University of Wisconsin, Madison.

Schaeffer, Kurtis R. 2000, 'The Religious Career of Vairocanavajra: A Twelfth-Century Indian Buddhist Master from Dakṣina Kosala', *Journal of Indian Philosophy* 28, 4 (August), 361–84.

——— 2004, *Himalayan Hermitess: The Life of a Tibetan Buddhist Nun*, Oxford University Press.

Schenk, Amelie 1993, 'Inducing Trance: on the Training of Ladakhi Oracle Healers' in Charles Ramble and Martin Brauen (eds), *Anthropology of Tibet and the Himalaya*, Zurich: Ethnological Museum of the University of Zurich, 331–42.

——— 1994, *Schamanen auf dem Dach der Welt. Trance, Heilung und Initiation in Kleintibet*, Graz: Akademische Druck- und Verlagsanstalt.

Schicklgruber, Christian 1992, '*Grib*: On the Significance of the Term in a Socio-religious Context' in Ihara and Yamaguchi (eds), *Tibetan Studies*, 723–35.

Schuh, Dieter 1976, 'Der Schauspieler des Tibetischen Lha-mo Theaters', *Zentralasiatische Studien*, 10, 339–84.

——— 1993–95, 'Investigations in the History of the Muktināth Valley and Adjacent Areas', *Ancient Nepal: Journal of the Department of Archaeology* 137–38, pt 1: 137, 9–91. pt 2: 138, 5–54.

Schwartz, Ronald 1994, *Circle of Protest. Political Ritual in the Tibetan Uprising*, London: Hurst.

Scott, James 1985, *Weapons of the Weak: Everyday Forms of Peasant Resistance*, New Haven: Yale University Press.

Scott, Joan Wallach 1988, 'Gender: A Useful Category of Historical Analysis', in *Gender and the Politics of History*, New York: Columbia University Press, 28–50.

Seele-Nyima, Claudia 2001, 'Tibetische Frauen zwischen Tradition und Innovation. Eine Untersuchung zum soziokulturellen Wandel im indischen Exil', *Interethnische Beziehungen und Kulturwandel*, Band 45, Hamburg: Lit Verlag.

Shakya, Tsering 1998, 'Historical Introduction' in Barnett and Conner (eds), *Leaders in Tibet*, 1–14.

——— 1999, *The Dragon in the Land of Snow*, London: Pimlico.

——— 2000, 'The Waterfall and Fragrant Flowers: The Development of Tibetan Literature since 1950' in Frank Stewart, Herbert J. Batt and Tsering Shakya (eds), *Song of the Snow Lion: New Writing from Tibet*, Manoa 12, 2. Honolulu: University of Hawaii Press, 28–40.

Shapiro, Judith 1991, 'Transsexualism: Reflections on the Persistence of Gender and the Mutability of Sex' in Epstein and Straub (eds), *Body Guards*.

Sharlho, Tseten Wangchuk 1993, 'China's Reforms in Tibet: Issues and Dilemmas', *Journal of Contemporary China*, 1, 1 (autumn), 34–43, 55–60.

Shaw, Miranda 1994, *Passionate Enlightenment: Women in Tantric Buddhism*, Princeton University Press.

Silver, Joan 1987, 'The Madman and Fool in Buddhism', *The Pacific World*, 3 (autumn), 46–52.

Simmer-Brown, Judith 2001, *Dakini's Warm Breath: The Feminine Principle in Tibetan Buddhism*, Boston: Shambhala.

Siu, Helen F. 1993, 'Cultural Identity and the Politics of Difference in South China', *Daedalus*, 122, 2 (spring), 19–43.

Skinner, Debra and Dorothy Holland 1997, 'An Introduction' in D. Skinner and D. Holland (eds), *Selves in Time and Place. Identities, Experience and History in Nepal*, Boston: Rowman & Littlefield, 3–16.

Snellgrove, David L. 1967, *Four Lamas of Dolpo: Autobiographies of Four Tibetan Lamas (15th–18th Centuries)*, London: Bruno Cassirer (2 vols).

——— 1979, 'Places of Pilgrimage in Thag (Thakkhola)', *Kailash*, 7, 2, 75–170.

——— 1987, *Indo-Tibetan Buddhism: Indian Buddhists and Their Tibetan Successors*, Boston: Shambhala.

——— 1989, *Himalayan Pilgrimage: A Study of Tibetan Religion by a Traveller through Western Nepal*, repr., Boston: Shambala.

——— and Hugh Richardson 1968, *A Cultural History of Tibet*, London: Weidenfeld & Nicolson.

Spanien, Ariane and Yoshiro Imaeda 1979, *Choix de documents Tibétains conservés à la Bibliothèque Nationale complété par quelques manuscrits de l'India Office et du British Museum*, vol. 2, Paris: Bibliothèque Nationale.

Sperling, Elliot (ed.), forthcoming, *Tibetan Studies: Proceedings of the Eighth Seminar of the International Association for Tibetan Studies*. Bloomington: Uralic and Inner Asian Series of the Research Institute for Inner Asian Studies.

Sponberg, Alan 1992, 'Attitudes toward Women and the Feminine in Early Buddhism' in José Cabezón (ed.), *Buddhism, Sexuality, and Gender*, Albany: State University of New York Press, 3–36.

Stary, G. 1977, *Viaggio nell'oltretomba di una sciamana mancese*, Florence: Sansoni.

Stearns, Cyrus 1996, 'The Life and Tibetan Legacy of the Indian Mahāpandita Vibhūticandra', *Journal of the International Association of Buddhist Studies*, 19, 1, 127–71.

——— 1999, *The Buddha from Dolpo: A Study of the Life and Thought of the Tibetan Master Dolpopa Sherab Gyaltsen*, Albany: State University of New York Press.

——— 2001, *Luminous Lives: The Story of the Early Masters of the Lam 'Bras Tradition in Tibet*, Boston: Wisdom Publications.

Stein, Rolf Alfred 1959, *Recherches sur l'épopée et le barde au Tibet*, Paris: Bibliothèque de l'Institut des Hautes Etudes Chinoises.

——— 1961, *Une chronique ancienne de bSam-yas: Ba-byed*, Paris: Publications de l'Institut des Hautes Études Chinoises, Textes et Documents, I.

——— 1972, *Tibetan Civilization*, trans. by J. E. Stapleton Driver, London: Faber and Faber.

——— 1986, *La civilization Tibétaine*, repr. Paris: L'Asiathèque.

Steinkellner, Ernst and Helmut Tauscher (eds) 1983, *Contributions on Tibetan Language, History and Culture*, Proceedings of the Csoma de Körös Symposium held at Velm-Vienna, Austria, 13–19 September 1981, vol. 1, Universität Wien: Arbeitskreis für Tibetische und Buddhistische Studien.

Stoddard, Heather 1994, 'Don Grub Rgyal (1953–85), Suicide of a Modern Tibetan Writer and Scholar' in Kvaerne (ed.), *Tibetan Studies*, 825–36.

Strickman, M. 1982, 'India in the Chinese Looking-Glass' in Deborah Klimburg-Salter (ed.), *The Silk Route and the Diamond Path*, Los Angeles: UCLA Art Council, 52–63.

Sunim, Hae-ju (Ho-Ryeon Jeon) 1999, 'Can Women Achieve Enlightenment? A Critique of Sexual Transformation for Enlightenment' in Tsomo (ed.), *Buddhist Women Across Cultures*, 123–41.

Sørensen, Per 1994, *The Lamp Illuminating the Royal Genealogies*, Wiesbaden: Otto Harrasowitz.

——— 1999, 'The Prolific Ascetic Lce-sgom Śes-rab rdo-rje Alias Lce-sgom Źig-po: Allusive, but Elusive', *Journal of the Nepal Research Center*, 11, 175–200.

Taklha, Namgyal Lhamo 1996, 'Women in Tibetan Community: A Tibetan Woman from Aristocratic Background Offers her Perspective', *Tibetan Review* (January), 12–14.

Taring, Rinchen Dolma. 1978 *Daughter of Tibet*, repr., Delhi: Allied Publishers.

Tethong, Rakra 1979, 'Conversations on Tibetan Musical Traditions', *Asian Music*, 10, 2, 5–22.

TIN (Tibet Information Network) 1991, *Defying the Dragon: China and Human Rights in Tibet*, London: TIN and Sydney: LawAsia.

——— 1999a, *Social Evils: Prostitution and Pornography in Lhasa*, London: TIN.

——— and Asia Watch 1992, *Political Prisoners in Tibet*, London: TIN and New York: AsiaWatch.

Thomas, Frederick William 1935, *Tibetan Literary Texts and Documents Concerning Chinese Turkestan*, vol. I: Hertford, Oriental Translation Fund, New Series, vol. XXXII, Royal Asiatic Society (Stephen Austin and Sons); vol. II: Hertford 1951.

——— 1936, 'Law of Theft in Chinese Kansu: A IXth to Xth Century Fragment from Tun-huang', *Zeitschrift für vergleichende Rechtswissenschaft*, 50, 275–87.

Thondup, Tulku 1986, *Hidden Teachings of Tibet: An Explanation of the Terma Tradition of the Nyingma School of Buddhism*, London: Wisdom Publications.

——— 1990, *Enlightened Living: Teachings of Tibetan Buddhist Masters*, Boston: Shambhala.

Thubten Zopa Rinpoche, Lama and George Churinoff 1995, *Nyung Nä: The Means of Achievement of the Eleven-Faced Great Compassionate One, Avalokiteshvara*, Boston: Wisdom Publications.

Tong Zhan 1995, 'The United Front Work System and the Nonparty Élite' in Carol Lee Hamrin and Suisheng Zhao (eds), *Decision-making in Deng's China: Perspectives from Insiders*, Armonk: M. E. Sharpe, 66–75.

Trébinjac, Sabine 1997, 'Comprendre un état en écoutant les gens chanter' in Marc Abélès and Henri-Pierre Jeudy (eds), *Anthropologie du politique*, Paris: Armand Colin, Collection U, 59–66.

——— 2000, *Le pouvoir en chantant, vol. 1: L'Art de fabriquer une musique chinoise*, Nanterre: Société d'Ethnologie.

Tsarong, Namgyal Dundul 1995, *Le Tibet tel qu'il était*, Nancy: Anako / Mémoires de l'Humanité.

Tsarong, Dundul Namgyal 2003, *In the Service of His Country: The Biography of Dasang Damdul Tsarong Commpander General of Tibet*, Ithaca: Snow Lion Publications, 2000.

Tsering, Norbu 1999, *Ache Lhamo is my Life*, Turin: Legenda.

Tsering, Tashi 1985, 'An Introductory Survey of the Writings of Tibetan Women', paper presented at the fourth seminar of the International Association of Tibetan Studies at Schloss Hohenkammer, Munich.

——— 1993, 'A Preliminary Reconstruction of the Successive Reincarnations of Bsam sding rdo rje Phag mo: The Foremost Woman Incarnation of Tibet', *g. Yu mtsho* 1. 1, 20–54.

——— 2000, 'Introductory Notes on the Dakini Bsod Nams Dpal 'Dren', paper presented at the ninth seminar of the International Association of Tibetan Studies in Leiden.

Tsering, Tobden 1997, 'To the Voiceless She Gives Voice: Yungchen Brings the Melody of Tibet to the World's Attention', *Tibetan Bulletin* (September–October), 26–7.

——— 1999, 'The Opera Power', *Tibetan Bulletin* (May–June), 12–14.

Tsomo, Karma Lekshe 1989, 'Tibetan Nuns and Nunneries' in Willis (ed.), *Feminine Ground*, 118–34.

——— 1996, *Sisters in Solitude: Two Traditions of Buddhist Monastic Ethics for Women*, Albany: State University of New York Press.

——— (ed.) 1999, *Buddhist Women Across Cultures: Realizations*, Albany: State University of New York Press.

Tsomo, Tsering 1994, 'Women in Tibetan Society', *Tibetan Bulletin* (May–June), 3.1.

Tsonawa, Lobsang N. (trans.) 1985, *Indian Buddhist Pandits from 'The Jewel Garland of Buddhist History'*, Dharamsala: Library of Tibetan Works and Archives.

Tucci, Giuseppe 1950, *The Tombs of the Tibetan Kings*, Roma: Serie Orientale Roma I (Is.M.E.O.).

——— 1956, *Preliminary Report on Two Scientific Expeditions in Nepal*, Istituto Italiano per il Medio ed Estremo Oriente, Roma, Serie Orientale Roma X.

——— 1971, *Deb t'er dmar po gsar ma*, Roma: Serie Orientale Roma XXIV (Is.M.E.O.).

———, 1988, *The Religions of Tibet*, Berkeley: University of California Press.

Tumursukh, Undarya 2000, 'Nationalism and Women in Post-Socialist Mongolia', paper presented at the fifth annual world convention of the Association for the Study of Nationalities, Columbia University, New York (April).

Tung, Constantine 1987, 'Introduction. Tradition and Experience of the Drama of the People's Republic of China' in Constantine Tung and Colin Mackerras (eds), *Drama in the People's Republic of China*, New York: State University of New York, 1–27.

Tung, Rosemary Jones 1980, *A Portrait of Lost Tibet* (photographs by Ilya Tolstoy and Brooke Dolan), New York: Holt, Rinehart and Winston.

Uebach, Helga 1987, *Nel-pa Paṇḍitas Chronik Me-tog phreng-ba*, Munich: Studia Tibetica I (Kommission für zentralasiatische Studien).

——— 1990, ‘On Dharma-Colleges and Their Teachers in the Ninth Century Tibetan Empire’ in Paolo Daffinà (ed.), *Indo-Sino-Tibetica. Studi in onore di Luciano Petech*, Rome: Bardi Editore, 393–417.

——— 1997, ‘Eminent Ladies of the Tibetan Empire according to Old Tibetan Texts’ in Karmay and Sagant (eds), *Les habitants du Toit du monde*, 53–74.

Upton, Janet 1996, ‘Home on the Grasslands? Tradition, Modernity, and the Negotiation of Identity by Tibetan Intellectuals in the PRC’ in Melissa Brown (ed.), *Negotiating Ethnicities in China and Taiwan*, China Research Monograph 46, Institute of East Asian Studies, Center for Chinese Studies. Berkeley: University of California, 98–124.

——— 2002, ‘The Poetics and Politics of Sister Drum: “Tibetan” Music in the Global Marketplace’ in Timothy J. Craig and Richard King (eds), *Global Goes Local: Popular Culture in Asia*, Hong Kong University Press.

Uray Géza 1972, ‘Queen Sad-mar-kar’s Songs in the Old Tibetan Chronicle’, *Acta Orientalia Hungarica*, 25, 5–38.

——— 1975, ‘L’annalistique et la pratique bureaucratique au Tibet ancien’, *Journal Asiatique*, 263, 157–70.

van der Kuijp, Leonard W. J. 1994, ‘On the Lives of Śākyaśrībhadra (?–?1225), *Journal of the American Oriental Society*, 114, 4, 599–616.

van Ede, Yolanda 1999, ‘House of Birds: A Historical Ethnography of a Tibetan Buddhist Nunnery’, PhD thesis, School of Social Science Research, University of Amsterdam.

Vashishta, B. K. (ed.) 1976, *Encyclopaedia of Women in India*, Delhi: Praveen Encyclopaedia Publications.

Virtanen, Riika J. 2000, *A Blighted Flower and Other Stories*, Dharamsala: Library of Tibetan Works and Archives.

Vitali, Roberto 1996, *The Kingdoms of Gu.ge Pu.hrang: According to Mnga’.ris rgyal.rabs by Gu.ge mkhan.chen Ngag.dbang grags.pa*, Dharamsala: Tho.ling Gtsug.lag.khang lo.gcig.stong ’khor.ba’i rjes.dran.mdzad sgo’i go.sgrig tshogs.chung.

Volf, Pavel 1994, *Seger åt gudarna. Rituell besatthet hos ladakhier*, Stockholm Studies in Comparative Religion 31, Stockholm: Almquist & Wiksell.

von Fürer-Haimendorf, Chistoph 1976, ‘A Nunnery in Nepal’, *Kailash*, 4, 2, 121–54.

Waddell, L. Austine 1895/1972, *Tibetan Buddhism with its Mystic Cults, Symbolism and Mythology, and in its Relation to Indian Buddhism*, New York: Dover Publications.

Wang Xiaoqiang 1994, ‘The Dispute between the Tibetans and the Han: When will it be Solved?’ in Barnett and Akiner (eds), *Resistance and Reform in Tibet*, 290–5.

Wangyal, Phuntsog 1982, ‘The Report from Tibet’ in *From Liberation to Liberalisation: Views on ‘Liberated’ Tibet*, Dharamsala: Information Office of HH the Dalai Lama.

Wang Yao 1994, ‘Hu Yaobang’s visit to Tibet, 22–31 May 1980: An Important Development in the Chinese Government’s Tibet Policy’ in Barnett and Akiner (eds), *Resistance and Reform in Tibet*, 285–89.

Wang Zheng 2000, 'Gender, Employment and Women's Resistance' in Perry and Selden (eds), *Chinese Society*, 62–83.

Watkins, Joanne C. 1996, *Spirited Women: Gender, Religion, and Cultural Identity in the Nepal Himalaya*, New York: Columbia University Press.

Willis, Janice D. 1984, 'Tibetan Ani-s: The Nun's Life in Tibet', *The Tibet Journal*, 9, 4 (winter), 14–32.

——— (ed.) 1989a, *Feminine Ground: Essays on Women and Tibet*, Ithaca: Snow Lion Publications.

——— 1989b, 'Ḍākinīs: Some Comments on Its Nature and Meaning' in Willis (ed.), *Feminine Ground*, 57–75.

——— 1999, 'Tibetan Buddhist Women Practitioners, Past and Present: A Garland to Delight Those Wishing Inspiration' in Tsomo (ed.), *Buddhist Women Across Cultures*, 45–58.

Wilson, Liz 1996, *Charming Cadavers: Horrific Figurations of the Feminine in Indian Buddhist Hagiographic Literature*, University of Chicago Press.

Yang, Enhong 1999, 'The Study of Singing Tradition of the Tibetan Epic 'King Gesar', *IIAS Newsletter*, 18 (February).

Ye, Xiaowen 1996, 'China's Current Religious Question: Once Again an Inquiry into the Five Characteristics of Religion' in M. Spiegel, *China: State Control of Religion*, New York: Human Rights Watch, 1998, 116–44.

Yuthok, Dorje Yudon 1990, *House of the Turquoise Roof*, Ithaca, NY: Snow Lion Publications.

Zito, Angela 1994, 'Silk and Skin: Significant Boundaries' in Angela Zito and Tani E. Barlow (eds), *Body, Subject and Power in China*, University of Chicago Press, 103–31.

Zwilling, Leonard 1992, 'Homosexuality as Seen in Indian Buddhist Texts' in José Cabézon (ed.), *Buddhism, Gender and Sexuality*, Albany: State University of New York Press, 203–14.

SHORT NGO PUBLICATIONS AND PRESS ARTICLES

Agence France Presse 1998, 'Tibetan protester cremated amid anti-Chinese rallies in India', Delhi, 1 May.

Amnesty International 1998, 'Torture and ill-treatment/Fear for safety', London, 24 July.

——— 1999a, 'Torture and ill-treatment/Fear for safety—People's Republic of China: Ngawang Sangdrol, age 22 (female); 11 other named Tibetans', 2 August.

Associated Press 1999a, 'China Approves Anti-Cult Law' by C. Hutzler, 30 October.

——— 1999b, 'Tibetan Protesters Said Fired Upon', Beijing, 4 November.

Human Rights Watch 1999, 'Arrests in Xinjiang', New York, 13 August.

——— 2000, 'China: Eight Year Sentence for Uighur Businesswoman: State Secrets Conviction Ahead of U.N. Meeting in Geneva', New York, 10 March.

International Committee of Lawyers for Tibet (Tibet Justice Center) *et al.* 1998, *Violence and Discrimination Against Tibetan Women: A Report submitted to the United Nations Committee on the Elimination of Discrimination Against Women*, [San Francisco], December.

Kuensel (Bhutan National Paper) 1993, vol. VIII, no. 32, 14 August.

Medical Institute 1973, *The Annual Report of the Medical Institute for the Year 1972*. Dharamsala. 25 January.

——— 1978, *Annual Report*. Dharamsala.

New York Times 1987, 'China Denounces Tibetan Leader as Responsible for Violent Protest' by Edward A. Gargan, 4 October.

October Review 1995, 'An alternative view of the status of women in China today' by Zhang Kai, Hong Kong, 30 July; see or@iohk.com.

Philadelphia Inquirer 1996, 'Bodies Scarred, Spirits Unbroken' by Loretta Tofani, 11 June.

Reuters 1991, 'Officials in Tibet "lose faith in Marx"', *South China Morning Post*, Hong Kong, 17 October, citing *Xizang Ribao* (Tibet Daily, Chinese language edn).

TCHRD (Tibetan Centre for Human Rights and Democracy) 1998a, 'Firing at 150 Tibetan Political Prisoners', Dharamsala, 15 May.

——— 1998b, 'More Firing at Tibetan Prisoners—Severe Repression Continues in Drapchi Prison', Dharamsala, 18 May.

——— 1998c, 'Closing the Doors: Religious Repression in Tibet', Dharamsala, 22 May.

——— 1998d, 'Over 3,993 monks and nuns expelled—religious repression continues in Tibet', Dharamsala, May.

——— 1999, 'A nun's prison sentence extended to 21 years—Ngawang Sangdrol's prison sentence extended for the third time', Dharamsala, 30 July.

——— 2000, 'New Information on the 2nd Anniversary of the Drapchi Protests', Dharamsala, 1 May.

——— 2001a, 'January 2001 Human Rights Update', Dharamsala, 15 January.

——— 2001b, 'February 2001 Human Rights Update', Dharamsala, 4 March.

Tibet People's Broadcasting Station 1997, 'Tibet party leader justifies religious policies, denies "rumours"' of personnel changes', Tibet People's Broadcasting Station, Lhasa, 9 November, published in translation in the *BBC Summary of World Broadcasts*, FE/D3078/CNS 171197, 17 November.

Tibet Press Watch 1993a, 'Tibet's most prominent defector performs at event with Dalai Lama: Pop star known throughout Tibet and China defected to fight for Tibetan independence', 4–5 May.

——— 1993b, 'A magical evening in honour of Tibet. Benefit brings attention to the plight of the Tibetan people', 3 May.

Tibetan Bulletin 2001, 'Playing for peace: A self-taught musician travels across the globe to spread the message of peace and Tibet', 5,1 (January–February), 24–26.

Tibet Human Rights Update 1994, 'Dolma Tsamchoe, Tibetan Lady Oracle, Gets Eight Years in Prison', Dharamsala, Department of Information and International Affairs, Central Tibetan Administration, 31 May.

Tibetan Review 1978, 'Dr Dolma Sacked from her Post', 8–9 October.

TIN (Tibet Information Network) 1990a, 'Two Tibetans Sentenced to Immediate Death in Lhasa', *TIN News Update*, London, 24 May.

——— 1990b, 'Topgyal Arrest: Video Crime in Tibet' in *Reports from Tibet June/July*, London, August.

——— 1991a, 'US Ambassador "Deceived", Political Prisoners Beaten, says report', *TIN News Update*, London, 17 July.

——— 1991b, 'Reports of Prison Maltreatment: aerial suspension; beaten for singing; blood extraction', *TIN News Report*, London, 11 December.

———1992a, '"Counter-Revolutionary" Plan to Wear Tibetan Clothes', *TIN News Update*, London, 20 February.

——— 1992b, 'Teacher Sentenced to 5 Years for Song: Women in Prison', *TIN News Update*, London, 21 February.

——— 1993, 'UN Rejects Tibet Resolution as Lhasa Protests Continue; China Accused of "Threats" in UN', *TIN News Update*, London, 22 August.

——— 1994a, 'Nuns' Sentence Increased to 17 years for Singing Songs', *TIN News Update*, TIN, London, 21 February.

——— 1994b, 'Death of Nun in Lhasa Prison', *TIN News Update*, London, 8 June.

——— 1998a, 'New Protests at Drapchi Prison', *TIN News Update*, 21 May.

——— 1998b, 'Demolition of Important Religious Sites: monks and nuns expelled', *TIN News Update*, London, 11 June.

——— 1998c, 'Ten Deaths at Drapchi Prison Following May Protests', *TIN News Update*, London, 4 August.

——— 1998d, 'Officials Confirm Drapchi Protest; Fears for the Safety of Prisoners', *TIN News Update*, London, 21 October.

——— 1999b, 'Closure of Religious Sites Following 'Patriotic Education'', *TIN News Update*, 27 January.

——— 1999c, 'Demonstration in Sichuan Follows Arrest of Religious Leader', *TIN News Update*, London, 17 November.

——— 2000, 'Handover of Power Reflects Party Line', *TIN News Update*, London, 8 December.

UN Commission on Human Rights 1990, 'Report to the UN Commission on Human Rights by the Special Rapporteur on Torture and Other Forms of Cruel, Inhuman or Degrading Treatment', by P. Kooijmans. Ref: E/CN.4/1990/17, paras. 41–5, February.

UPI (United Press International) 1996, 'China's women have little to celebrate' by Ruth Youngblood, Beijing, 8 March.

Xinhua 1997, 'Text of (Revised) Criminal Law', Beijing, 17 March 1997 (republished by *Foreign Broadcast Information Service* as FBIS-CHI-97–056).

Xinhua 1999, 'Chinese agency on improvement in Tibetans' personal freedoms, rights', Lhasa, 21 January (republished by *BBC Summary of World Broadcasts* on the same day; title as given in BBC version).

Xinhua 2000, Beidahe, 6 August (republished in translation in *BBC Summary of World Broadcasts*, 7 August.

Xizang Ribao (*Tibet Daily*, Chinese language edn) 1989, 'In Order to Enforce the Laws and Discipline and to Attack the Criminals, Nine Nuns Who Did Splittist Activities were Punished with Re-education of Delinquents through Labour', 14 September.

Xizang Ribao 1991, 'On the Regional Characteristics of Party Construction in Tibet', by Zhang Shuring and Gao Wutian, 7 January.

Xizang Ribao 2000, 'Dinggye County sternly rectifies feudal superstitions activities', by Yang Zhengjian, 21 July.

Zasgiin Gazryn Medee (Government News) 1996, 'The Shadow of Democracy is Wandering Across Mongolia' by Ochirbatyn Dashbalbar. Ulaanbaatar, 79, no. 519, 30 April.

GOVERNMENTAL AND OTHER DOCUMENTS

Administrative Detention Order, TIN (Tibet Information Network) ref. Doc 9(ZQ) (Lhasa [Municipal Committee of] Re-education Through Labour Document No: 910085), 26 September 1991.

Court document, TIN ref. 2(XN) (Court statement in the case of Dondrub Tsering and others; (Lhasa Intermediate Court Document No. 13 (1990), 14 May 1990, handwritten copy).

Court document, TIN ref. 23(YY) part two (Court statement in the case of Dondrub Tsering and others, 17 May 1990, handwritten copy).

Court document, TIN ref. 1(XN) (Lhasa Intermediate Court Sentencing Document No 34 (1990), 30 November, 1990).

Handwritten account, TIN ref. 1(XN).

———, TIN ref. 19(VN)/24(JW).

———, TIN ref. 28(YS).

———, TIN ref. 31(JW).

———, RB ref. 92rb3, before August 1998.

———, RB ref. 54rb3(TB), September 1998.

PRC Government 1994, 'A Submission by the Chinese Government', UN Working Group on Arbitrary Detentions, Doc. 94–18128 [G/So 218/2 22/5/94], paragraphs 11–16, 22 May.

PRC Government 1997, Letter from the Chinese Ambassador to the United Nations Commission on Human Rights, Geneva, addressed to the UN Rapporteur on Summary and Arbitrary Executions, 11 March.

PRC Government 1998, Letter to United Nations Rapporteur, 15 April.

Procuracy document, TIN ref. 3(XN) (Lhasa Prison Procuracy Document No. 2 [1989], 11 March 1989 [?], handwritten copy).

Procuracy document, TIN ref. 6(ZQ) (Lhasa Prison Procuracy Document No. 2 [1989], 11 March 1989 [?], handwritten copy).

Procuracy document, TIN ref. 7(ZQ) (Lhasa Legal Document No. 13 [1990]—Criminal Investigation Report of the Lhasa Municipality Intermediate Procuracy, 14 May 1990, handwritten copy).

Publicity materials for the UN Women's Conference, TAR Government, 1995, TIN ref. 10(VG).

Zhongguo gongchangdang Xizang zizhiqu zuzhishi ziliao 1950–1987 ('Materials on the History of the CCP in the TAR 1950–1987'), TAR Party Committee on Party History, internal publication, Lhasa: TAR Publishing House, 1993.

DISCOGRAPHY

Choying Drolma and Steve Tibbetts, *Chö*, Hannibal Rykodisc, HNCD 1404, 1997.

Choying Drolma and Sina Vodgani, *Dancing Dakini*, International Music Company, 2000.

Choying Drolma, *Choying*, Vinapa, 2000.

Collection of Songs by Caidan Zhuoma (Tseten Drolma), Pacific Audio and Video Co., PCD-5096, ISRC CN-F12–95–362–00/A.J6, 1995.

Dadon, *Cuckoo, Gyi ma gyi*, …, Superdups, Wilmington, USA, 1997.

Dechen Shak-Dagsay, *Dewa Che*, Polyglobe/Ethic 19920, 2000.

Gang Chenpa, *Voices from Tibet*, MW Records, MWCD5005, The Netherlands, 2000.

HMV (Dum Dum) 1944–56. Recordings made in Lhasa between 1943–1945 by the British mission under the direction of Basil Gould (lhamo: *Zukki* [sic] *Nyima, Norsang, Drowa Zangmo, Thimed Kunden, Gyasa, Patma Hyotma* [= *Padma 'od-'bar*?]; nangma and toshe: *Rechungma, Shagyatso ri, Hrukchala, Talashiba, Dzongpa Namsum, Sonam Yungchen, Sungla Miang, Kamsum Wangdu*).

Koch, Ulrike, *12 Treasures: Gesar Songs and Prayers from 'The Saltmen of Tibet'*, Terton 007, CL 5565, 1998 (with Gesar epic bard Yumen).

Seeing Nothing But the Sky… The Songs of Tibetan Nuns Recorded in a Chinese Prison, FREEFTCIDC, Free Tibet Campaign, London, 1995.

The Treasurable Version of Hundred Anthologies of Vocal Music Performed by Famous Chinese Musicians—Caidan Zhuoma (Tseten Drolma) / *20° shiji zhonghua getan mingren baiji zhencangban—Caidan Zhuoma*, Zhongguo changpian zong gongsi, ISRC CN-A01–96–386, 1996.

Yang Du Tso, *Tibet: My Homeland* (private recording), Belgium, 2000.

Yungchen Lhamo, *Tibetan Prayer*, Natural Symphonies (Australia), 1995.

Yungchen Lhamo, *Tibet, Tibet*, Real World Records, CDRW59, 1996.

Yungchen Lhamo, *Coming Home*. Real World Records, LC 3098 / Narada Productions CDRW72, 1998.

CASSETTE TAPE ALBUMS PRODUCED IN TIBET

Bod kyi gna' bo'i dbyangs snyan: stod gzhas (*Beautiful Melodies of the Past: Toshe*). Lhasa: Bod-ljongs sGra-brnyan dPe-skrun-khang, 1996 (recordings made at the beginning of the 1980's, including songs by Anan on side A, by Chung Putri on side B, and a sample of Chushur Yeshe Drolma playing the lute on side A).

Zla-sgron (Dadon), Five cassette albums: (1) *Zla gzhon snyan dbyangs* (The Beautiful Melodies of the Young Dadon); (2) *gCes pa'i pha yul* (My Beloved Country); (3) *Gangs ljongs dang nga* (Tibet and Myself); (4) *Zla gzhon snyan dbyangs legs 'dems* (Compilation Album of the Beautiful Melodies of the Young Dadon); (5) *Ibidem*, translated into Chinese. Lhasa: Bod-ljongs sGra-brnyan dPe-skrun-khang, 1987–92.

TRANSLITERATION OF PHONETICIZED TIBETAN TERMS

Phonetic spellings have been assigned as consistently as possible in this book, but they are by no means fully systematic or scientific. We endeavoured to maintain the spelling of names of Tibetans who have phoneticized their own names in publications, documents and other written materials. There is considerable regional variation in the pronounciation of names and words, and such variations are sometimes reflected in the choice of phonetic renderings.

Some names whose phonetic spellings are the same as their roman transliteration have not been included in this list. In addition, some names or terms were learned by the contributors to this volume only through oral sources, and their spelling in Tibetan is not certain; these names too are not included in this list. A number of other transliterations provided here are based upon oral or written sources that may not necessarily represent standard or 'correct' spellings.

Aba Lhagyal	A-ba lHa-rgyal
Abopo Gangtsen	A-bo-pho Gang-btsan
Acha Shilog	A-lcag Shi-log
Acha Tashi-la	A-lcag bKra-shis-lags
Acha Yitsa	A-lcag Ye-tsha
Ache Dangsang	A-che Dwangs-bzangs
akhu	*a-khu*
Akong Rinpoche	A-kong Rin-po-che
Alak Zenkar Rinpoche	A-lags gZan-dkar Rin-po-che
Ama Trasil	A-ma Phra-sil
Ama Adhe	A-ma A-dhe
Ama Dachung	A-ma Zla-chung
Ama Lhagpa	A-ma lHag-pa
Ama Lobsang Dolma	A-ma Blo-bzang sGrol-ma
Ama Pujungma	A-ma Bu-byung-ma
Ama Rangtsen	A-ma Rang-btsan
Ama Seril	A-ma Ser-ril
Ama Tsering	A-ma Tshe-ring
Amala	A-ma-lags
Amdo Chabcha	A-mdo Chab-cha
Amdowa	A-mdo-ba
Anan	A-nan
Angu Lambar	'Ang-gu Lam-'bar
ani	*a-ne*

Ani Chosangmo	A-ne Chos-bzang-mo
Ani Dekyi-la	A-ne bDe-skyid-lags
Ani Drubamo Pelden Drolma	A-ne sGrub-pa-mo dPal-ldan sGrol-ma
Ani Drubchenma Sonam Drolma	A-ne sGrub-chen-ma bSod-nams sGrol-ma
Ani Dzompa Kyi	A-ne 'Dzom-pa sKyid
Ani Kunga Chokyi	A-ne Kun-dga' Chos-skyid
Ani Kunga Drolma	A-ne Kun-dga' sGrol-ma
Ani Ngawang Sangdrol	A-ne Ngag-dbang Sangs-sgrol
Ani Nyishar	A-ne Nyi-shar
Ani Pachen	A-ne dPa'-chen
Ani Peldzom	A-ne dPal-'dzom
Ani Phuntsok Pelmo	A-ne Phun-tshogs dPal-mo
Ani Sangmo	A-ne bZang-mo
Ani Sonam Drolma	A-ne bSod-nams sGrol-ma
Ani Thubten Chokyi	A-ne Thub-brtan Chos-dkyid
Ani Tsering Kyebma	A-ne Tshe-ring sKyabs-ma
Ani Tsuga	A-ne Tsu-ga
Arya Wati Sangpo	Arya Wa-ti bZang-po
Azha	'A-zha
Ba Serkhang	'Ba' gSer-khang
Baba	'Ba'-pa
Bamen	sBa-sman
Baraba Kagyu	'Ba'-ra-pa bKa'-brgyud
Baraba Namkha Dorje	'Ba'-ra-pa Nam-mkha' rDo-rje
Bardo Tulku	'Bar-rdo sPrul-sku
Bare Lhaje	sBa-red lHa-rje
Barkhor	'Bar-skor
Batang	'Ba'-thang
Batsab Gompa	Ba-tshab sGom-pa
Batsab Ton Bumdrak	Ba-tshab sTon 'Bum-grags
Bayu Nyadrong Tsang	Ba-yu gNya'-grong gTsang
Bhedu	'Be-dha
Beji	Be-ji
Bentser	Ban-'tsher
Beyul Khenpa Lung	sBas-yul mKhan-pa Lung
Bharima	Bha-ri-ma
Bichi Gache	Bi-byi dGa'-byed
Bila Gadze	Bi-lha dGa'-mdzes
Bilhama Gadze	Bi-lha-ma dGa'-mdzes
Bo Rangkyong Jongkyi Lingdrung Nyurkyob Zhung Lekhung	Bod Rang-skyong lJongs-kyi Gling- sgrung Myur-skyobs gZhung Las-khang
Bodong	Bo-dong
Bodong Chokle Namgyal	Bo-dong Phyogs-las rNam-rgyal

Bojong Chinyer Lobdra	Bod-ljongs sPyi-gnyer sLob-grwa
Bojong Dogar Tuntsok Tsandzin Truzhi	Bod-ljongs Zlos-gar mThun-tshogs mTshan-'dzin Kru'u-zhi
Bojong Dranyen Pardrun Khang	Bod-ljongs sGra-brnyan Par-skrun Khang
Bojong Gyalche Zhonui Rigne Nyamdrel Tsokpa	Bod-ljongs rGyal-gces gZhon-nu'i Rig-gnas mNyam-'brel Tshogs-pa
Bojong Lhamo Tsokpa	Bod-ljongs lHa-mo Tshogs-pa
Bojong Lobdra Chenmoi Gesar Zhung Lekhung	Bod-ljongs sLob-grwa Chen-mo'i Gesar gZhung Las-khung
Bojong Mirig Lobdra	Bod-ljongs Mi-rigs sLob-grwa
Bokyi Rigzhung Menchin Lobkhang	Bod-kyi Rig-gzhung sMan-sbyin sLob-khang
Bonpo	Bon-po
Bruzha	'Bru-zha
Buchung	Bu-chung
Bumseng	'Bum-seng
Bumtang	'Bum-thang
Burto	sBur-stod
Buton Rinchen Drub	Bu-ston Rin-chen Grub
Chadab Gen Ngawang Tabke	Bya-'dab rGan Ngag-dbang Thabs-mkhas
Chag Lotsawa	Chag Lo-tsā-ba
Chakpori Dropen Rigcheling Dratsang	lCag-po-ri 'Gro-phan Rig-byed-gling Grwa-tshang
Chagtra Ani	Phyag-gra A-ni
Chaksampa	lCags-zam-pa
Chalmo Tseten Drolma	'Chal-mo Tshe-brtan sGrol-ma
cham	*lcam*
Chamdo	Chab-mdo
Chamdo Labrang	Chab-mdo Bla-brang
Chamo Beta	lCam-mo Be-ta
Chamo Jetsunma Konchok Tsomo	lCam-mo rJe-btsun-ma dKon-mchog mTsho-mo
Chamo Ladu	lCam-mo La-'dus
Champa Tenzin	Byams-pa bsTan-'dzin
Chang	Byang
Chang Targo	Byang rTa-sgo
Changchub	Byang-chub
Changlung Budtra	lCang-lung sBud-tra
changma	*chang-ma*
Changpa Dingpon	lCang-pa lDing-dpon
Changpa Namgyal Draksang	Byang-pa rNam-rgyal Grags-bzang
Changseb Shar	lCang-gseb Shar

Changtang	Byang-thang
Changtsen Takyong	Byang-btsan rTa-skyong
Changtsen Targo Dablha	Byang-btsan rTa-sgo dGra-lha
Chatral Rinpoche	Bya-bral Rin-po-che
Chedeshol	lCe-lde Zhol
Chegom Dzongpa	lCe-sgom rDzong-pa
Chegom Dzongpa Sherab Dorje	lCe-sgom rDzong-pa Shes-rab rDo-rje
Cheje	Che-rje
Cheje Tri-o Menlungba	Che-rje Khri-'od sMan-lung-pa
Chemen Jodor	lCe-sman Jo-rdor
Chemo Namkhamo	'Chad-mo/'Phyad-mo Nam-mkha'-mo
Cheton Gyanag	lCe-ston rGya-nag
chi	*phyi*
Chigmen Gawo	mChig-sman dGa'-bo
Chim	mChims
Chime Dorje	'Chi-med rDo-rje
Chime Ozer	'Chi-med 'Od-zer
Chimgyal	mChims-rgyal
Chingphu	mChing-phung
Cho	gCod
Chodrag	Chos-grags
Chogro	Cog-ro
Chogyal Norsang	Chos-rgyal Nor-bzang
Chogyen	Chos-rgyan
Chokor	Chos-'khor
Chokyab Pelsang	Chos-skyabs dPal-bzang
Chokyi	Chos-skyid
Chokyi Drolma	Chos-kyi sGrol-ma
Chokyi Dronma	Chos-kyi sGron-ma
Chokyi Gyaltsen	Chos-kyi rGyal-mtshan
Chokyi Wangchuk	Chos-kyi dBang-phyug
Chokyong Sangmo	Chos-skyong bZang-mo
Choying Dolma	Chos-dbyings sGrol-ma
Choying Drolma	Chos-dbyings sGrol-ma
Choying Kunsang	Chos-dbyings Kun-bzang
chuba	*phyu-pa*
Chubsang	Chub-bzang
Chung	Cung
Chung Putri	Chung Bu-khrid
Chushur Yeshe Drolma	Chu-shur Ye-shes sGrol-ma
Chuzhi Gangdrug	Chu-bzhi Gang-drug
Dadon	Zla-[ba] sGron-[ma]
Dag	Dwags
Dagmo Nordzin	bDag-mo Nor-'dzin

Dagmo Peldzin Pangmo	bDag-mo dPal-'dzin dPang-mo
Dagpo	Dwags-po
Damema	bDag-med-ma
Dangra Yumtso	Dang-ra g.Yu-mtsho
Dangseng Lhamo	Dwangs-bzang Lha-mo
Darding	Dar-ldings
Darso	Dar-bsod
Darton Gendun	Dar-ston dGe-'dun
Dasel Wangmo	Zla-gsal dBang-mo
Dawa	Zla-ba
Dawa Buti	Zla-ba Bu-'khrid
Dawa Chodon	Zla-ba Chos-sgron
Dawa Dolma	Zla-ba sGrol-ma
Dawa Drolma	Zla-ba sGrol-ma
Dawa Norbu	Zla-ba Nor-bu
Dawa Ozer	Zla-ba 'Od-zer
Dawa Samten	Zla-ba bSam-gtan
Dechen Chodon	bDe-chen Chos-sgron
Dechen Wangmo	bDe-chen dBang-mo
Dekyi/Deji	bDe-skyid
Dekyi Drolkar/Deji Zhuogar	bDe-skyid sGrol-dkar
Dekyi Khangkar	bDe-skyid Khang-dkar
Dekyi Metok	bDe-skyid Me-tog
Dekyi Pedron	bDe-skyid Pad-sgron
Dekyi Tsomo/Deji Cuomu	bDe-skyid mTsho-mo
delog	*'das-log*
Demon Dechen Drolkar	bDe-smon bDe-chen sGrol-dkar
Denma	lDan-ma
Denza Lhasang	lDan-za lHa-bzang
Derge	sDe-dge
Derge Gonchen	sDe-dge dGon-chen
Desi Sangye Gyatso	sDe-srid Sangs-rgyas rGya-mtsho
Desong Tsen	lDe-srong bTsan
Determa	bDe-gter-ma
Dilgo Khyentse Rinpoche	Dil-mgo mKhyen-brtse Rin-po-che
Dingpon Tsering Wangdu	lDing-dpon Tshe-ring dBang-'dus
Dingri	Ding-ri
Dingri Gangmar	Ding-ri sGang dmar
Dingri Langkhor	Ding-ri Glang-'khor
Dokar Zurpa	mDo-mkhar Zur-pa
Dondam Mawe Senge	Don-dam sMra-ba'i Seng-ge
Dondrub Gyal	Don-grub rGyal
Dondrub Tsering	Don-grub Tshe-ring
Dongna	gDong-sna
Dorje Gyaltsen	rDo-rje rGyal-mtshan

Dorje Phagmo	rDo-rje Phag-mo
Dorje Phagmo Chokyi Drolma	rDo-rje Phag-mo Chos-kyi sGrol-ma
Dorje Phagmo Dechen Chodron/ Ch: Doje Pamo Deqing Quzhen	rDo-rje Phag-mo bDe-chen Chos-sgron
Dorje Rabjom	rDo-rje Rab-'joms
Dorje Tsomo	rDo-rje mTsho-mo
Dorje Yudron	rDo-rje g.Yu-sgron
Dowa	Zlo-ba
Dowa Drubchen	rDo-ba Grub-chen
Dozur	mDo-zur
Dozur Tsering Wangyal	mDo-zur Tshe-ring dBang-rgyal
Dra	Grwa
Dra Khangkar	Grwa Khang-dkar
Dragkar	Brag-dkar
Dragkha Tegchen Ling	Brag-kha Theg-chen Gling
Dragmar	Brag-dmar
Drago Kaṇi	Brag-sgo Kaṇi
Dragri Dorje Chang	Brag-ri rDo-rje 'Chang
Dragton Champa Gyaltsen	Brag-thon Byams-pa rGyal-mtshan
Dragtonpa	Brag-mthon-pa
Dragyab Rinpoche	Brag-g.yab Rin-po-che
Drakpa	Grags-pa
Drakpa Dorje	Grags-pa rDo-rje
Dram	'Gram
Drangsong Phuntsok	Drang-srong Phun-tshogs
Drangti	Brang-ti
Drangti Gyalnye Kharphug	Brang-ti rGyal-mnyes mKhar-phug
Dranyedo	Gra-snye-mdo
dranyen	*sgra-snyan*
Drapa	Grwa-pa
Drapa Ngonshe	Grwa-pa mNgon-shes
Drapchi	Grwa-bzhi
Drapchi Yangdzom	Grwa-bzhi gYang-'dzoms
Dreje Gyagar Vajra	'Dre-rje rGya-gar Vajra
Dremo	bGres-mo
Drenka Pelkyi Yonten	Bran-ka dPal-gyi Yon-tan
Drepung	'Bras-spungs
Drepung Loseling	'Bras-spungs Blo-gsal Gling
Drepung Tenma	'Bras-spungs brTan-ma
Drichamma	'Gri-lcam-ma
Drigung	'Bri-gung
Drigungpa	'Bri-gung-pa
Dringma Togo	'Bring-ma Thog-dgos
Dro	'Bro

Drogmi	'Brog-mi
Drogmi Lotsawa Shakya Yeshe	'Brog-mi Lo-tsā-ba Sākya Ye-shes
Drolkar	sGrol-dkar
Drolma	sGrol-ma
Drolma Lhamtso	sGrol-ma lHa-mTsho
Drolma Tsamcho/e	sGrol-ma mTshams-gcod
Drolma Tsering	sGrol-ma Tshe-ring
Dromto	'Brom-stod
Dromton	'Brom-ston
Dromton Lhariwa	'Brom-ston lHa-ri-ba
Drongnyen De-u	'Brong-snyan lDe'u
Drongpa	'Brong-pa
Dronla	sGron-lags
Dronmalo	'Dron-ma-lod
Dropen U Mentsikhang	'Gro-phan dBus sMan-rtsis-khang
Drowa Sangmo	'Gro-ba bZang-mo
Dru Jamyang Dragpa	'Bru 'Jam-dbyangs Grags-pa
Drupai Gyalmo	Grub-pa'i rGyal-mo
Drubchungma	Grub-chung-ma
Drubtop Namkha O	Grub-thob Nam-mkha' 'Od
Drugchen	'Brug-chen
Drugpa	'Brug-pa
Drugpa Kagyupa	'Brug-pa bKa'-brgyud-pa
Drugyal Tsangdrub	'Brug-rgyal Tshangs-grub
drung	*sgrung*
Drungdo	Drung-rdo
Drungtso Tsering Peldren	Drung-tsho Tshe-ring dPal-'dren
Dumra	lDum-ra
Dungi Torchogchen	Dung-gi Thor-cog-can
Dusong Mangpoje Lungnam Trulgyi Gyalpo	'Dus-srong Mang-po-rje rLung-gnam 'Phrul-gyi rGyal-po
Dzayul	'Dza-yul
Dzema	mDdzes-ma
Dzeng	'Dzeng
Dzeng Dharmabodhi	'Dzeng Dharma-bo-dhi
Dzeng Jo-se	'Dzeng Jo-sras
Dze-se	mDzes-se
Dzomyang Drolma	'Dzoms-g.yang sGrol-ma
Dzong	rDzong
Dzongdol	rDzong-dol
E	dBye
Emnyal	E-mnyal
E-yul	dBye-yul
Ga Kyongma	dGa' sKyong-ma
Gadong	dGa'-gdong

Gaga	dGa'-dga'
Galingshar Ani	dGa'-gling-shar A-ne
Gami	dGa'-mi
Gampopa	sGam-po-pa
Ganden	dGa'-ldan
Ganden Tripa	dGa'-ldan Khri-pa
Gangchenpa	Gangs-can-pa
Gao	dGa'-'od
gar	*gar*
Gar	mGar
Gari	sGa-ri/Ga-ri
Garpa	Gar-pa
Garu	dGa-ru(?)
Gatun	Ga-tun
Gawa Pelde	dGa'-ba dPal-lde
Gedingpa	dGe-sdings-pa
Gegye	dGe-rgyas
gelong	*dge-slong*
gelongma	*dge-slong-ma*
Gelongma Pelmo	dGe-slong-ma dPal-mo
Gelug[pa]	dGe-lugs[-pa]
Gen Rigzin	rGan Rig-'dzin
Gendun	dGe-'dun
Gengya	rGan-gya
genyen	*dge-bsnyen*
Gesar	Ge-sar
Geshe Lharampa	dGe-bshes lHa-rams-pa
Geshe Rabgyal	dGe-bshes Rab-rgyal
Gewa	dGe-ba
Gewa Bum	dGe-ba 'Bum
Gewe Lodro	dGe-ba'i Blo-gros
Ge-ye	dGe-ye
Golog	mGo-log
Gomchung Dragtsen	sGom-chung Drag-btsan
Gonkar	Gung-dkar
Gongkar Gyatso	Gong-dkar rGya-mtsho
Gontang Pakshi	dGon-thang Pakshi
Goranangba Phuntsok Wangyal	sGo-ra-nang-pa Phun-tshogs dBang-rgyal
Goshri Gyaltsab	Go-shri rGyal-tshab
Gowo Lobsang Tenzin	Go-bo Blo-bzang bsTan-'dzin
Goyang	sGo-byang
Gungru Yeshe Khandro	Gung-ru Ye-shes mKha'-'gro
Gungsong Gungtsen	Gung-srong Gung-btsan
Gungtang	Gung-thang
Gutsa	dGu-rtsa

Gutsig Lambar	dGu-tshig Lam-'bar
Gyagar Lhamo	rGya-gar lHa-mo
Gyagoma	rGya-sgom-ma
Gyalche Zhonui Tundrok Tsokpa	rGyal-gces gZhon-nu'i mThun-grogs Tshogs-pa
Gyalmo Tridze	rGyal-mo Khri-mdzes
Gyalmotsen	rGyal-mo-brtsan
Gyalmotsun	rGyal-mo-btsun
Gyaltang Pombor Gang	rGyal-thang sPom-'bor sGang
Gyaltsa Rinchen Gonpo	rGyal-tsha Rin-chen mGon-po
Gyaltsen Chonden	rGyal-mtshan Chos-ldan
Gyaltsen Chotso	rGyal-mtshan Chos-mTsho
Gyaltsen Chodzom	rGyal-mtshan Chos-'dzom
Gyaltsen Dekyi	rGyal-mtshan bDe-skyid
Gyaltsen Kalsang	rGyal-mtshan sKal-bzang
Gyaltsen Norbu	rGyal-mtshan Nor-bu
Gyaltsen Pelsang	rGyal-mtshan dPal-bzang
Gyaltsen Shakya Rinpoche	rGyal-mtshan Shakya Rin-po-che
Gyaltsen Tsondru	rGyal-mtshan brTson-'grus
Gyaltsen Wangchuk	rGyal-mtshan dBang-phyug
Gyaltsugru	rGyal-gtsug-ru
Gyalwa	rGyal-ba
Gyamo	rGya-mo
Gyanema	rGyan-ne-ma
Gyangkar Minyak Sakyong	rGyang-mkhar Mi-nyag Sa-skyong
Gyankar	rGyang-mkhar
Gyantse	rGyal-rtse
Gyari Nyima	rGya-ri Nyi-ma
Gyasa Chokyi Dronme	Gya-sa Chos-kyi sGron-me
Gyasa	rGya-sa
Gyaton Jozung	rGya-ston Jo-gzungs
Gyatsa	rGya-tsha
Gyatso Chagdor	rGya-tsha Phyag-rdor
Gye Laga	Gyad lHa-dga'
Gye Luga	Gyad Klu-dga'
gyencha	*rgyan-cha*
Gyenlog	Gyen-log
Gyere	Gye-re
Gyina	Gyi-na
Gyudrul[ma]	sGyu-'phrul[-ma]
gyurkhug	*'gyur-khug*
Gyuto	rGyud-stod
Gyuto Dratsang	rGyud-stod Grwa-tshang
Horpa	Hor-pa
Hum Barwa	Hūṁ 'Bar-ba

Jampa Tinley	Byams-pa 'Phrin-las
Jampa Tsering	Byams-pa Tshe-ring
Jampel Kunkhyab	'Jam-dpal Kun-khyab
Jamsar Sherab Ozer	'Jam-sar Shes-rab 'Od-zer
Jamyang Kyi	'Jam-dbyangs sKyid
Jamyang Shepa	'Jam-dByangs bZhad-pa
Jangmen Lewe	lJangs-sman Le-bas
Je	'Jad
Je Mikyo Zhab	rJe Mi-skyod Zhabs
Jedrung Jampa Jungne	rJe-drung Byams-pa'i 'Byung-gnas
Jetsun Lochen Rinpoche	rJe-btsun Lo-chen Rin-po-che
Jetsun Pema	rJe-btsun Pad-ma
Jetsunma Phuntsok Lodro Tsomo	rJe-btsun-ma Phun-tshogs Blo-gros mTsho-mo
jewa	*je-ba*
Jigme Lingpa	'Jigs-med Gling-pa
Jigme Ngapo	'Jigs-med Nga-phod
Jigme Wangchuk	'Jigs-med dBang-phyug
Jigten Drak	'Jig-rten Grags
Jigten Gonpo	'Jig-rten mGon-po
Jim	'Jim
Jobum	Jo-'bum
Jobumma	Jo-'bum-ma
Jocham Phurmo	Jo-lcam Phur-mo
Joden Sonam Sangpo	Jo-gdan bSod-nams bZang-po
Jojam Norbu Sangmo	Jo-'jam Nor-bu bZang-mo
Jokhang	Jo-khang
jomo	*jo-me*
Jomo Ba-u-ma/or A-u-ma	Jo-mo Ba'u-ma/Jo-mo 'A-'u-ma
Jomo Changchub	Jo-mo Byang-chub
Jomo Dremo	Jo-mo bGres-mo
Jomo Dron-ne	Jo-mo sGron-ne
Jomo Gyalmotsen	Jo-mo rGyal-mo-brtsan
Jomo Legmotsen	Jo-mo Legs-mo-brtsan
Jomo Mangchungma	Jo-mo Mang-chung-ma
Jomo Mangkhama	Jo-mo rMang Kha-ma
Jomo Namo	Jo-mo sNa-mo
Jomo Nyangmo	Jo-mo Myang-mo
Jomo Sangye	Jo-mo Sangs-rgyas
Jomo Tsengyal	Jo-mo brTsan-rgyal
Jomo Tsunma	Jo-mo bTsun-ma
Jomo Wangmo	Jo-mo dBang-mo
Jomo Yango	Jo-mo g.Yang-'gos
Jomolangma	Jo-mo Glang-ma
Jonang	Jo-nang

Jong Mangtro Gyutsal Tsokpa	lJongs dMangs-khrod sGyu-rtsal Tshogs-pa
Jo-se Jigten Drak	Jo-sras 'Jig-rten Grags
Joton Wangchuk Drak	Jo-ston dBang-phyug Grags
Jumla	'Dzum-lang
Kadam[pa]	bKa'-gdams-[pa]
Kagyu[pa]	bKa'-brgyud-[pa]
Kalden Tso	sKal-ldan mTsho
Kalsang Gyatso	sKal-bzang rGya-mtsho
Kangyur	bKa'-'gyur
Karchung	sKar-chung
Kardze/Ganzi	dGar-mdzes
Kareg Tsangmen Dorje	mKha'-reg gTsang-sman rDo-rje
Karma Drakpa	Karma Grags-pa
Karma Tenzin	Karma bsTan-'dzin
Karma Tsultrim Namgyal	Karma Tshul-khrims rNam-rgyal
Karmapa	Karma-pa
kashag	*kha-shags*
Ke'u Tsangma	Ke'u Tshang-ma
Khakyong	mKha'-skyong
Khakyong Dragpa	mKha'-skyong Brag-pa
Kham	Khams
Kham Aro	Khams A-ro
Kham Riwoche	Khams Ri-bo-che
Khando Yang-ga	mKha'-'gro dByangs-dga'
Khandro Tsering Chodron	mKha'-'gro Tshe-ring Chos-sgron
Khangkar	Khang-dkar
Khangkar Dingpon	Khang-dkar lDing-dpon
Khangpa Gongma	Khang-pa Gong-ma
Khangpa Karpo	Khang-pa dKar-po
Kharta	Kha-rta/mKhar-rta
Kharchen	mKhar-chen
Khata	Kha-btags
Khata Lambar	Kha-btags Lam-'bar
Khatse Trapa Ngawang Gyatso	Kha-tshe Pra-pa Ngag-dbang rGya-mtsho
Khedron Yonten	mKhas-sgron Yon-tan
Khon Konchok Gyalpo	'Khon dKon-mchog rGyal-po
Khonphuwa Chokyi Gyaltsen	'Khon-phu-ba Chos-kyi rGyal-mtshan
Khulung Gochen Mentsun	Khu-lung Go-chen sMan-btsun
Khumbo	Khum-bo
Khyenrab Norbu	mKhyen-rab Nor-bu
Khyung Tsangpa	Khyung Tshang-pa
Khyunglung Ngulkar	Khyung-lung dNgul-mkhar

Khyunglung Thogme Thinley Dorje	Khyung-lung Thogs-med 'Phrin-las rDo-rje
Khyungpo Dorje	Khyung-po rDo-rje
Khyungpo Repa	Khyung-po Ras-pa
Kimcheng Kungchu	Kim-cheng Kung-cu
Kimshang Kongcho	Kim-shang Kong-co
Kimsheng Ongcho	Gyim-shing Kong-jo
Kongcho	Kong-co
Konchok Gyaltsen	dKon-mchog rGyal-mtshan
Konchok Kyab	dKon-mchog sKyabs
Konchok Sangmo	dKon-cog bZang-mo
Kongpo	Kong-po
Kongpo Giamda	Kong-po rGya-mda'
Kugtsal	lKugs-tshal
Kundeling Kunsang	Kun-bde-gling Kun-bzang
Kundeling	Kun-bde-gling
Kunden Rema	Kun-ldan Ras-ma
Kunden Repa	Kun-ldan Ras-pa
Kunga	Kun-dga'
Kunga Bar	Kun-dga' 'Bar
Kunga Dondrub	Kun-dga' Don-grub
Kunga Pelsang	Kun-dga' dPal-bzang
Kunga Pendar	Kun-dga' Phan-dar
Kunga Sangmo	Kun-dga' bZang-mo
Kungo Juchen Tubten Namgyal	sKu-ngo 'Ju-chen Thub-bstan rNam-rgyal
Kungo Trekhang Khenchung Tubten Tsephel	sKu-ngo bKras-khang mKhan-chung Thub-bstan Tshe-'phel
Kungyur Nyarong Shag	Kun-'gyur Nyag-rong Shag
Kunpang Chenpo	Kun-spangs Chen-po
Kunsang	Kun-bzang
Kurung Peltsewa Norlha Phuntsok Dradul	Ku-rung dPal-rtse-ba Nor-lha Phun-tshok dGra-'dul
Kutang	sKu-thang
kuten	*sku-rten*
Kyabje Ling Rinpoche	sKyabs-rje Gling Rin-po-che
Kyabje Triyang Rinpoche	sKyabs-rje Khri-byang Rin-po-che
Kyebu Melha	sKyes-bu Me-lha
Kyebu Melha Chagdum	sKyes-bu Me-lha Phyag-ldum
Kyepa	sKyed-pa
Kyichu	sKyid-chu
Kyidrong	sKyid-grong
Kyidrong Dzongshar	sKyid-grong rDzong-shar
Kyidrong Jowo	sKyi-grong Jo-bo
Kyidrong Samten Ling	sKyid-grong bSam-gtan Gling

Kyidrong Zhol	sKyid-grong Zhol
Kyikhang Damcho	sKyid-khang Dam-chos
Kyi-kya/Ji jia	sKyi-skyag
Kyilog	sKyid-log
Kyimshi	Khyim-gzhis
Kyo Shakya Yeshe	sKyo Shākya Ye-shes
Kyomolung	sKyor-mo-lung
Labja Gongmo	Bla-bya Gong-mo
Lablung Drotsa Gyen	Lab-lung 'Bro-tsha rGyan
Labrang Tashi Khyil	bLa-Brang bKra-Shis 'Khyil
Ladu	La-'dus
Lama Karta	Bla-ma Kar-bkra
Lama Zhang	Bla-ma Zhang
Lambar	Lam-'bar
Lamdre	Lam-'bras
Langdro Jemen	Lang-gro rJe-sman
Lantogma	Lan-thog-ma/Lan-to-ma
Lapa-la	La-pa-lags
Lapchi	La-phyi
Lato	La-stod
Lato Jomo Namo	La-stod Jo-mo sNa-mo
La-u	sLa'u
Legmotsen	Legs-mo-brtsan
Legse [Bum]	Legs-se ['Bum]
Lha Totori Nyanshe	lHa Tho-tho-ri sNyan-shal
Lha Totori Nyantsen	lHa Tho-tho-ri'i sNyan-btsan
lhabon/lhaven	*lha-bon*
Lhabumen	lHa-bu-sman
Lhacham Deva Peldren	lHa-lcam De-va dPal-'dren
Lhachig Dembu	lHa-gcig lDem-bu
Lhadron	lHa-sgron
Lhagdron	lHag-sgron
Lhagyal Mangmoje	lHa-rgyal Mang-mo-rje
Lhai Metok	lHa'i Me-tog
Lhaje Dawa Ozer	lHa-rje Zla-ba'i 'Od-zer
Lhaje Jobum	lHa-rje Jo-'bum
Lhajema	lHa-rje-ma
lhaka	*lha-bka'*
lhakama	*lha-bka'-ma*
Lhakdron (Ch. Nazhen)	lHag-sgron
Lhakhang Rashag Terton	lHa-khang Rag-shag gTer-ston
Lhakpa Tsering	lHag-pa Tshe-ring
lhamo	*lha-mo*
Lhamo Chokyong	La-mo Chos-skyong
Lhamo Lhatso	lHa-mo lHa-mtsho
Lhamo Peldren	lHa-mo dPal-'dren

Lhamotsen	lHa-mo-btsan
lhapa	*lha-pa*
Lhapang	lHa-pangs
Lhatse	lHa-rtse
Lhawon	lHa-dbon
Lhodrag	lHo-brag
Lhokha	lHo-kha
Lhopa	lHo-pa
Lhundrub Lodro	lHun-grub Blo-gros
Ligmyihya	Lig-myi-rhya
Ling	Gling
Ling Gesar	Gling Ge-sar
Ling Rinpoche	Gling Rin-po-che
Lingkawa	Gling-ka-ba
Lingsa Chokyi	Gling-bza' Chos-skyid
Lo	Glo/Blo
Lobsang	Blo-bzang
Lobsang Chodron	Blo-bzang Chos-sgron
Lobsang Dechen	Blo-bzang bDe-chen
Lobsang Dolma Khangkar	Blo-bzang sGrol-ma Khang-dkar
Lobsang Drolma	Blo-bzang sGrol-ma
Lobsang Ngodrub	Blo-bzang dNgos-grub
Lobsang Rabgye	Blo-bzang Rab-rgyas
Lobsang Samten	Blo-bzang bSam-gtan
Lobsang Tsedron	Blo-bzang Tshe-sgron
Lobsang Wangmo	Blo-bzang dBang-mo
Lodar	Blo-dar
Lodro Chenpo	Blo-gros Chen-po
Lodro Gyaldzo	Blo-gros rGyal-mdzod
Lodro Gyatso	Blo-gros rGya-mtso
Lodro Rabsel	Blo-gros Rab-gsal
Lodro Sangmo	Blo-gros bZang-mo
Lodro Shenyen	Blo-gros bShes-gnyen
Lodro Tsungme	Blo-gros mTshungs-med
Longchen Rapchampa	Klong-chen Rab-'byams-pa
Longchenpa	Klong-chen-pa
Loro	Lo-ro
Loten	Blo-bstan
Loton Yontan	Lo-ston Yon-tan
Lotsawa Rinchen Sangpo	Lo-tswa-ba Rin-chen bZang-po
Lotsawa Senge Gyalpo	Lo-tswa-ba Seng-ge rGyal-po
Lotsawa Zhazer Chen	Lo-tswa-ba Zhwa-ser-can
Lubug Chime Drolkar	Klu-sbug 'Chi-med sGrol-dKar
Lugo Lambar	Lug-mgo Lam-'bar
Lugtrug Lambar	Lug-phrug Lam-'bar
Lukye	Lug-skyes

Lungnag Shelkar	Lung-nag Shel-dkar
Lung sho	Klung-shod
Lutsa	Klu-rtsa
Ma	rMa
Machig Angcho	Ma-gcig Ang-co
Machig Kongcho	Ma-gcig Kong-'byo
Machig Labdron	Ma-gcig Lab-sgron
Machig Ongjo	Ma-gcig Ong-jo
Machig Rebma Darma Changchub	Ma-gcig Reb-ma Dar-ma Byang-chub
Machig Rema	Ma-gcig Re-ma
Machig Zhama	Ma-gcig Zha-ma
Magyal Dongkar	rMa-rgyal lDong-skar
Majo Chonema	Ma-jo mChod-gnas-ma
Majo Darma	Ma-jo Dar-ma
Majo Dron-ne	Ma-jo sGron-ne
Majo Gyale Cham	Ma-jo rGyal-le lCam
Majo Rama	Ma-jo Ra-ma
Majo Sangye Kyi	Ma-jo Sangs-rgyas sKyid
Majo Yagma	Ma-jo Yag-ma
Majo Yangmo	Ma-jo g.Yang-mo
Makye Chopa Tar	Ma-khye gCod-pa Thar
Mal Tsondru Lama	Mal brTson-'grus Bla-ma
Maldro	Mal-gro
Mande Sangmo	Mande bZang-mo
Mangkhar	Mang-mkhar
Mangkhar Chelung	Mang-mkhar Che-lung
Manglon Mangtsen	Mang-slon Mang-rtsan
Mangmoje	Mang-mo-rje
Mangmoje Shiteng	Mang-mo-rje bZhi-steng
Mangmoje Trikar	Mang-mo-rje Khri-skar
Mangpang	Mang-pangs
Mangsong Mangtsen	Mang-srong Mang-btsan
Mangyul	Mang-yul
Mangyul Kyidrong	Mang-yul sKyid-grong
Mapham	Ma-pham
Marpa	Mar-pa
Me-agtsom	Mes-ag-tshom
Mebar	Me-'bar
Medrogungkar	Mal-gro Gung-dkar
Mekhab	sMan-khab
Mempa Chewa	Mam-pa Che-ba
Mempa Chungwa	Mam-pa Chung-ba
Menag	sMan-nag
Menjor Khang	Man-sbyor Khang
Menkar	sMan-dkar

Menlungpa	sMan-lung-pa
Menpa Kachupa	sMan-pa dKa'-bcu-pa
Menram Chungwa	sMan-rams Chung-ba
Menram Dringwa	sMan-rams 'Bring-ba
Mentsikhang	sMan-rtsis-khang
Metok	Me-tog
Mi Gyalpo	Mi rGyal-po
Michungri	Mi-chung-ri
Migmar	Mig-dmar
Migmar Gyaltsen	Mig-dmar rGyal-mtshan
Migyur Dorje Madrong	Mi-'gyur rDo-rje Ma-grong
Mikyo Dorje	Mi-bskyod rDo-rje
Milarepa	Mi-la Ras-pa
Mindrol Ling	sMin-grol gLing
Mingyur Peldron	Mi-'gyur dPal-sgron
Minyak	Mi-nyag
Minyak Dotsang	Mi-nyag mDo-Tshang
Mon	Mon
Monkha Zermo	Mon-kha Zer-mo
Monlam Dorje	sMon-lam rDo-rje
Monpa	Mon-pa
Mowo Tagcho	rMo-bo Thag-gcod
Munchang Kongcho	Mun-chang Kong-co; Ch. Wen-ch'eng kung-chu
Mu-ne Tsen	Mu-ne bTsan/brTsan
Mutig Tsenpo	Mu-tig bTsan-po
Mutri Tsenpo	Mu-khri bTsan-po
Nagchu	Nag-chu
Nagi Gompa	Nagi dGon-pa
Nama Dorje	mNa'-ma rDo-rje
Namdrol Sangpo	rNam-sgrol bZang-po
Namdrol	rNam-sgrol
Namgyal	rNam-rgyal
Namgyal Dorje	rNam-rgyal rDo-rje
Namkha Drolma	Nam-mkha' sGrol-ma
Namkha Gonpo	Nam-mkha' mGon-po
Namkha Gyen	Nam-mkha' rGyan
Namkhai Norbu	rNam-kha'i Nor-bu
Namlha Taklha	rNam-lha sTag-lha
Namri Songtsen	gNam-ri Srong-btsan
Namtso	gNam-mtsho
Namtsowa Mikyo Dorje	gNam-mtsho-ba Mi-bskyod rDo-rje
Nanam	sNa-nam
Nang	sNang
nangma	*nang-ma*

Nangme Kyidug	Nang-ma'i sKyid-sdug
Nangsa	sNang-sa
Nangsa Obum	sNang-sa/sNang-gsal 'Od-'bum
Nangsa Odebum	sNang-sa 'Od-de-'bum
Naro Chodrug	Na-ro Chos-drug
natug	*snab-stug*
Natug Lambar	sNab-stug Lam-'bar
Nawa	Na-ba
Ne'udong	sNe'u-gdong
Nechung	gNas-chung
Nedo Karma Chagme	gNas-mdo Karma Chags-med
Nedong	sNe-gdong
Ngamring	Ngam-ring
Ngapo Ngawang Jigme	Nga-phod Ngag-dbang 'Jigs-med
Ngapo Tseten Drolkar	Nga-phod Tshe-brtan sGrol-dkar
Ngari	mNga'-ris
Ngawang Champa	Ngag-dbang dByams-pa
Ngawang Chokyi	Ngag-dbang Chos-skyid
Ngawang Drakpa Tinley Jampa Jungne	Ngag-dbang Grags-pa 'Phrin-las Byams-pa'i 'Byung-gnas
Ngawang Drolma	Ngag-dbang sGrol-ma
Ngawang Khetsun	Ngag-dbang mKhas-btsun
Ngawang Lobsang Gyatso	Nga-dbang Blo-bzang rGya-mtsho
Ngawang Locho	Nga-dbang Blo-chos
Ngawang Namgyal	Ngag-dbang rNam-rgyal
Ngawang Nyima	Ngag-dbang Nyi-ma
Ngawang Peltso	Ngag-dbang dPal-mtsho
Ngawang Phuntsok	Ngag-dbang Phun-tshogs
Ngawang Sangdrol	Ngag-dbang Sangs-sgrol
Ngawang Tseten	Ngag-dbang Tshe-brtan
Ngendzong Tonpa	Ngan-rdzong sTon-pa
Ngogmen Gyongpo	rNgog-sman Gyong-po
Ngok Do-de	rNgog mDo-sde
Ngom Sagang Depa	Ngom Sa-sgang sDe-pa
Ngulmo Gyale Cham	dNgul-mo rGyal-le lCam
Niguma	Ni-gu-ma
Norbu Chophel	Nor-bu Chos-'phel
Norbu Tsering	Nor-bu Tshe-ring
Norbulingkha	Nor-bu Gling-kha
Norzin Seldron	Nor-'dzin gSal-sgron
Norzin/Nordzin	Nor-'dzin
Nub	sNubs
Nya	gNya'
Nyal	gNyal
Nyalmen	gNyal-sman

Nyamdrel	mNyam-sbrel
Nyamoteng	sNya-mo-stengs
Nyanang	sNya-nang
Nyanang Phelgyay Ling	gNya'-nang 'Phel-rgyal Gling
Nyanchen Tanglha	gNyan-chen Thang-lha
Nyang Tingngedzin	Myang Ting-nge-'dzin
Nyangdren	Nyang-bran
Nyangmen Lotsa	Nyang-sman Lo-tsā
Nyangrel Nyima Ozer	Nyang-ral Nyi-ma 'Od-zer
Nyangri	Nyang-ri
Nyangto	Nyang-stod
Nyantob Jobum	gNyan-thob Jo-'bum
Nyarong	Nyag-rong
Nyarong Shag	Nyag-rong Shag
Nyashur Pungyegyug	Nya-shur sPungs-rye-rgyug
Nyemo	sNye-mo
Nyemo Ani	sNye-mo A-ne
Nyenpa Tashi Dorje	gNyan-pa bKra-shis rDo-rje
Nyima	Nyi-ma
Nyima Drolma	Nyi-ma sGrol-ma
Nyima Phug	Nyi-ma'i Phug
Nyima Tsamcho	Nyi-ma mTshams-gcod
Nyingma[pa]	rNying-ma-[pa]
nyungne	*smyung-gnas*
Ochen Tulku	'Od-chen sPrul-sku
Odrung	'Od-srung
Olkha	Ol-kha
Ombu	Om-bu
On	'On
Onchangdo	'On-cang-do
Onpo Lode	dBon-po Blo-bde
Orgyan Chokyi	O-rgyan Chos-skyid
Orgyan Tenzin	O-rgyan bTan-'dzin
Ozer Phen	'Od-zer 'Phen
Padma Dondrub	Padma Don-grub
Padma Wangdu	Padma dBang-'dus
Palhalhuphug	Brag-lha Klu-sgug/phug
Panchen Rinpoche	Paṇ-chen Rin-po-che
panden	*pang-gdan*
Pangchen	sPang-chen
Pasang	sPa-bzang
Pasang/Basang	Pa-sangs
Pasang Gyalmo	Pa-sangs rGyal-mo
Pasang Pentok	Pa-bsangs Phan-thog
Patsab	Pa-tshab

Patsab Tsultrim Bar	Pa-tshab Tshul-khrims 'Bar
Pawo Tsuglag Trengwa	dPa'-bo gTsug-lag Phreng-ba
Pehar	Pe-har
Pekong Penpa Drolma	Pad-khang sPen-pa sGrol-ma
Pelbar Geshe Lungtok Nyima	dPal-'bar dGe-bshes Lung-rtogs Nyi-ma
Pelbar Geshe Rinpoche	dPal-'bar dGe-bshes Rin-po-che
Pelbum	dPal-'bum
Peldar Bum	dPal-dar 'Bum
Pelden	dPal-ldan
Pelden Gyatso	dPal-ldan rGya-mtsho
Pelden Tsomo	dPal-ldan mTsho-mo
Peljor	dPal-'byor
Pelkhortsen	dPal-'khor-btsan
Pelkyi	dPal-skyid
Pelkyi Ngangchul	dPal-gyi Ngang-chul
Pelkyi Zijima	dPal-gyi gZi-brjid-ma
Pema	Padma
Pema Chogyal	Pad-ma Chos-rgyal
Pema Karpo	Padma dKar-po
Pema O	Padma 'Od
Pema Tenzin	Padma bstan-'dzin
Pema Yangjien	Padma dByangs-can
Pemako	Padma bKod
Penor	sPen-nor
Penpa Drolma	sPen-pa sGrol-ma
Peson	Phe-sron
Peta	Pe-ta
Petsel Ritro	dPa'-tshal Ri-khrod
Pewar Rinpoche	dPe-war
Phadampa Sangye	Pha Dam-pa Sangs-rgyas
Phadrug	Pha-drug
Phagmo Drupa	Phag-mo Gru-pa
Phagpa Wati Sangpo	'Phags-pa Wa-ti bZang-po
Phenpo	'Phen-po
Phenyul	'Phan-yul
Phorok Lambar	Pho-rog Lam-'bar
Phoyong	Pho-yong
Phuntsok Norbu	Phun-tshogs Nor-bu
Phuntsok Nyidron	Phun-tshogs Nyi-sgron
Phuntsok Wangmo	Phun-tshogs dBang-mo
Phuntsok Yangkyi	Phun-tsogs Yang-skyid
Phuntsoling	Phun-tshogs-gling
Phurbu Dolma	Phur-bu sGrol-ma
Phurbu Drolma	Phur-bu sGrol-ma
Pomen Chape	sPo-sman Bya-dpe

Pomra Geshe Bayu Lobsang Gyaltsen	sPom-ra dGe-bshes Ba-yu Blo-bzang rGyal-mtshan
Ponmo Shertsul	dPon-mo Sher-tshul
Porong	sPo-rong
Porong Pemo Choding	sPo-rong dPal-mo Chos-sdings
Purang	sPu-rangs
Purang Tsewang Namgyal	Pu-hrang Tshe-dbang rNam-rgyal
Rabgyal Tse	Rab-rgyal rTse
Rabnga Riwo Pelbar Samten Phug	Rabs-lnga Ri-bo dPal-'bar bSam-gtan Phug
Rabten	Rab-brtan
Rabten Gompa	Rab-brtan dGon-pa
Raidi/Redi	Rag-sdig
Rakhor	Ra-'khor
Rakra Tethong	Rak-ra bKras-mthong
ralpa	*ral-pa*
Ralpachen	Ral-pa-can
Ramoche	Ra-mo-che
Rangchung Dorje	Rang-byung rDo-rje
Rangtsen Shonu	Rang-btsan gZhon-nu
Ratso Ruri	Ra-tsho Ru-ri
Rechungma	Ras-chung-ma
Rechungpa	Ras-chung-pa
Reting	Rwa-sgreng
Reting Rinpoche	Rwa-sgreng Rin-po-che
Rigtsal Rukhag	Rig-rtsal Ru-khag
Rigzin Chonyi	Rigs-'dzin Chos-nyid
Rinzin Dhondup	Rig-'dzin Don-grub
Rinzin Lhundrub Paljor	Rig-'dzin Lhun-grub dPal-'byor
Rinzin Wangmo	Rig-'dzin dBang-mo
Rikha Tsetay	Ri-kha Tshe-bkra
Rima	Ri-ma
Rinchen Pel	Rin-chen dPal
Rinchen Sangpo	Rin-chen bZang-po
Rinchen Drak	Rin-chen Grags
Rindron	Rin-sgron
Riwoche	Ri-bo-che
Rogchung Nyangto	Rog-chung Myang-stod
Rok Sherab O	Rog Shes-rab 'Od
Rong Chutsen	Rong Chu-tshan
Rongpo	Rong-po
Rongton Chosang	Rong-ston Chos-bzang
Rozenma	Ro-zan-ma
Ru Emchi Tsang of Nyemo	Ru Em-chi Tshang of sNye-mo
rukhak	*ru-khag*
Rutok	Ru-thog

Rutsam	Ru-mtshams
Sachen Kunga Nyingpo	Sa-chen Kun-dga' sNying-po
Sadul Gonpa	Sa-'dul dGon-pa
Sadul	Sa-'dul
Sakya	Sa-skya
Sakya Trizin Rinpoche	Sa-skya Khri-'dzin Rin-po-che
Sa-le O	Sa-le 'Od
Samding	bSam-lding
Samding Dorje Phagmo	bSam-sdings rDo-rje Phag-mo
Samdrub	bSam-grub
Sampho	bSam-pho
Samten Ling	bSam-gtan Gling
Samye	bSam-yas
Sangmo Kon-ne	bZang-mo dKon-ne
Sangye Balampa	Sangs-rgyas Ba-lam-pa
Sangye Darpo	Sangs-rgyas Dar-po
Sangye Dulwa	Sangs-rgyas 'Dul-ba
Saspol	Sa-spol
Semarkar	Sad-mar-kar
Semo Chewa Namkha Gyaltsen	Se-mo Che-ba Nam-mkha' rGyal-mtshan
Semo Dingo Tsang Chime Wangmo	Sras-mo Dil-mgo Tshang Chi-med dBang-mo
Semo Ko-ne	Srad-mo Ko-ne
Semodo	Se-mo-do
Senge Zhangro	Seng-ge Zhang-ro
Sepa	Se-pa
Sera	Se-ra
Sera Khandro	Se-ra mKha'-'gro
Sera Khandro Dekyong Wangmo	Se-ra mKha'-'gro Kun-bzang bDe-skyong dBang-mo
Sera Mey	Se-ra sMad
Serchung	gSer-chung
Sertang	gSer-thang
Serwa Me-me	Ser-ba sMed-me
Seton Kunrig	Se-ston Kun-rig
Sha Pa-le Shapalep	Sha-bag-leb
Shabamo Chamchig	Shab-pa-mo lCam-gcig
Shabru	Shab-ru
Shagrampa Nyima Pel	Shag-rams-pa Nyi-ma dPal
Shambu	Sham-bu
Shang	Shangs
Shapale	Sha-bag-lebs
Shapku	Shab-ku
Shar Nyanchen Tanglha	Shar gNyan-chen Thang-lha
Shekar	Shel-dkar

Shelgyi Riwo Drugdra	Shel-gyi Ri-bo 'Brug-sgra
Shelmo Gyacham	Shel-mo rGya-lcam
Shen Dormo	gShen rDor-mo
Shenton Yeshe Lodro	gShen-ston Ye-shes Blo-gros
Sherab Tsomo/Xirao Cuomu	Shes-rab mTsho-mo
Sherpa	Shar-pa
Shershag	Sher-shag
Shey	Shes/Shel
Shigatse	gZhis-ka-rtse
Shingmo Sa Lhamo	Zhing-mo bZa' lHa-mo
Sholkhang Sonam Dargye	Zhol-khang bSod-nams Dar-rgyas
Shoton	Zho-ston
Shugden	Shugs-ldan
Shugseb	Shug-gseb
Shumoza Mangkyi	Shud-mo-za Mang-skyid
sinmo	*srin-mo*
Sinpori	Srin-po-ri
Sog	Sog
Sogpo Geshe Chodrak	Sog-po dGe-bshes Chos-grags
Sonam	bSod-nams
Sonam Kyidzom	bSod-nams sKyid-'dzoms
Sonam Peldren	bSod-nams dPal-'dren
Sonam Tsering	bSod-nams Tshe-ring
Songtsen Gampo	Srong-btsan sGam-po
Suki Nyima	gZugs-kyi Nyi-ma
Summen Joso	Sum-sman Jo-bsod
Taglung	sTag-lung
Taglung Tangpa	sTag-lung Thang-pa
Takri Nyansig	sTag-ri sNan-gzigs
Takring	sTag-ring
Taktse Kukye Mipham Phuntsok Sherab	rTag-rtse sKu-skye Mi-pham Phun-tshogs Shes-rab
Taktse	rTag-rtse/sTag-rtse
Takyong	rTa-skyong
Tanag	rTa-nag
Tandru	rTa-gru
Tandrug	Khra-'brug
Tangchung	Thang-chung
Tangkya	Thang-skya
Tanglha	Thang-lha
Tangmey Konchok Pelmo	Thang-smad dKon-mchog dPal-mo
Tangtong Gyalpo	Thang-stong rGyal-po
Tarap	rTa-rab
Tare Lhamo	Ta-re Lhamo
Targo	rTa-sgo

Targo Gungtang Ringmo	sTa-sgo Gung-thang Ring-mo
Tashi	bKra-shis
Tashi Dondrub	bKra-shis Don-grub
Tashi Drolma	bKra-shis sGrol-ma
Tashi Lhamo	bKra-shis lHa-mo
Tashilhunpo	bKra-shis lHun-po
Tashi Paldon	bKra-shis dPal-sgron
tashi sholpa	*bkra-shis zhol-pa*
Tashi Tsering	bKra-shis Tshe-ring
Taton Jobum	rTa-ston Jo-'bum
Tawo Lobsang Pelden	rTa-bo Blo-bzang dPal-ldan
Taykhang Jampa Tubwang	bKras-khang Byams-pa Thub-dbang
Taykhang Jetsunma Jampel Chodron	bKras-khang rJe-btsun-ma 'Jam-dpal Chos-sgron
Tazhi	mTha'-bzhi
Tazhi Shakya Dar	mTha'-bzhi Shakya-dar
Tengyaling	bsTan-rgyas-gling
Tengyur	bsTan-'gyur
Tenma	rTan-ma
Tenma Lobsang Tsedron	rTan-ma Blo-bzang Tshe-sgron
Ten-ne	rTen-ne
Tenzin Chodak	bsTan-'dzin Chos-grags
Tenzin Chodon	bsTan-'dzin Chos-sgron
Tenzin Gompo	bsTan-'dzin dGon-po
Tenzin Gyatso	bsTan-'dzin rGya-mtsho
Tenzin Repa	bsTan-'dzin Ras-pa
Tenzin Tubten	bsTan-'dzin Thub-bstan
Terchen Barwe Dorje	gTer-chen 'Bar-ba'i rDo-rje
Terdag Lingpa	gTer-bdag Gling-pa
Terong	gTer-rong
Tinley Chodron	'Phrin-las Chos-sgron
Tinley Dolkar	'Phrin-las sGrol-dkar
Tinley Paldon Nyarong Shag	'Phrin-las dPal-sgron Nyag-rong Shag
To Drogpa	sTod 'Brog-pa
Tobten Tseriag	sTobs-ldan Tsering
Toepa Kyidug	sTod-pa sKyid-sdug
Togme Tinley Dorje	Thogs-med 'Phrin-las rDo-rje
Tognyi	rTog-nyi
Tolung	sTod-lung
Tolung Dechen	sTod-lung bDe-chen
Tomo Dorje Tso	sTod-mo rDo-rje mTsho
Tong	sTong
Tongmen Sengdrak	sTong-sman Seng-grags
Tongmen Tagchung	sTong-sman sTag-chung

Tongmun	mThong-smon
Tonyon Samdrub	Thod-smyon bSam-grub
toshe	*stod-gzhas*
Tramdrug	Khra-'brug
Tramo Lampa	Phra-mo Lam-pa
trapa	*grwa-pa*
Tratsang Druglha	Khra-tshang 'Brug-lha
Tre Goma Kon-ne	dBrad sGom-ma dKon-ne
Trehor Kyorpon Rinpoche	Tre-hor sKyor-dpon Rin-po-che
Trengge Dragtsen	Phreng-ge Brag-btsan
Trensang	'Gran-bzang
Trewel	Kre-wel
Tri Darma	Khri Dar-ma
Trichang Rinpoche	Khri-byang Rin-po-che
trichen	*khri-chen*
Tride Songtsen	Khri-lde Srong-brtsan/btsan
Tride Tsugtsen	Khri-lde gTsug-rtsan
Tridusong	Khri 'Dus-srong
Trigyal Mangmotsen	Khri-rgyal Mang-mo-btsan
Trijang Rinpoche	Khri-byang Rin-po-che
Trimalo	Khri-ma-lod
Trimalo Triteng	Khri-ma-lod Khri-steng
Trimoleg	Khri-mo-legs
Trimonyen Dongteng	Khri-mo-mnyen lDong-steng
Trimoteng	Khri-mo-stengs
Trinyen Sugtsen	Khri-snyan gZugs-btsan
Trisong Detsen	Khri-srong lDe-brtsan/btsan
Tritsug Detsen	Khri-gtsug lDe-brtsan/btsan
Tritsun	Khri-btsun
Triwang	Khri-bangs
Tro Gawo Gyurme Ngawang Samphel Rinpoche	Khro dGa'-bo 'Gyur-med Ngag-dbang bSam-'phel Rin-po-che
Tronag	Khro-nag
Trophu	Khro-phu
Trophu Lotsawa	Khro-phu Lo-tsā-ba
Trulshig	'Khrul-zhig
Trulshig Darma Senge	'Khrul-zhig Dar-ma Seng-ge
Trungo Dogar Khechan Bojong Yanlag Tuntsok	Krung-go'i Zlos-gar mKhas-can Bod-ljongs Yan-lag mThun-tshogs
trungshuma	*'khrung(s)-zhu-ma*
Trungyang Mirig Lugar Tsokpa	Krung-dbyang Mi-rigs Glu-gar Tshogs-pa
Tsalpa	Tshal-pa
Tsamgung Ani Yonten	mTshams-gur A-ne Yon-tan
tsampa	*rtsam-pa*

Tsamten	mTshams-brten
Tsang	gTsang
Tsangmo Gyau	gTsang-mo rGya'u
Tsangnyon Heruka	gTsang-smyon He-ru-ka
Tsangpa Jo-se	gTsang-pa Jo-sras
Tsangpay Lulenma	Tshangs pa'i Glu-len-ma
Tsangpa Sumpa	gTsang-pa Sum-pa
Tsangpo	gTsang po
Tsangtsa Jotsul	gTsang-tsha Jo-tshul
Tsarguza Kyi-de	'Tshar-dgu-gza' sKyid-de
Tsari	Tsa-ri
Tsarma	rTsar-ma
Tsarong Se	Tsha-rong Sras
Tsarong Tsewang Jigme	Tsha-rong Tshe-dbang 'Jig-med
Tse Rigne Lobdra	rTse Rig-gnas sLob-grwa
Tse-de	rTse-lde
Tsechogling	Tshe-mchog-gling.
Tsele	rTse-le
Tsele Gotsangpa	rTse-le rGod-tshang-pa
Tsemonling	Tshe-smon-gling
Tsengyal	brTsan-rgyal
Tsenmatok	bTsan-ma-thog
Tsenmatok Togteng	bTsan-ma-thog Thog-steng
tsenmo	*btsan-mo*
tsenpo	*btsan-po*
Tsenyi Lhamo	mTshan-nyid Lha-mo
Tsepong	Tses-spong
Tsering Chenga	Tshe-ring mChed-lnga
Tsering Chotso	Tshe-ring Chos-mtsho
Tsering Dorje	Tshe-ring rDo-rje
Tsering Drolkar/Cering Zhuoga	Tshe-ring sGrol-dkar
Tsering Lhamo/Ciren Lamu	Tshe-ring lHa-mo
Tsering Wangdu	Tshe-ring dBang-'dus
Tsering Wangyal	Tshe-ring dBang-rgyal
Tsering Yudron/Ciren Yuzhen	Tshe-ring g.Yu-sgron
Tseseng	rTse-seng
Tsetang	rTses-thang
Tseten Drolma	Tshe-brtan sGrol-ma
Tseten Drolmai Gyustal Tebtsa	Tshe-brtan sGrol-ma'i sGyu-rtsal Thebs-rtsa
Tsetrul Ngawang Pelden	rTse-sprul Ngag-dbang dPal-ldan
Tsewang Dolkar Khangkar	Tshe-dbang sGrol-dkar Khang-dkar
Tsewang Gyurme	Tshe-dbang 'Gyur-med
Tsewang Jigme Tsarong	Tshe-dbang 'Jig-med Tsha-rong
Tsewang Norbu	Tshe-dbang Nor-bu

Tsewang Sangmo	Tshe-dbang bZang-mo
Tseyang	Tshe-g.yang
Tsibri	rTsib-ri
Tsikhang Phuntsok Kopa	rTsis-khang Phun-tshogs bKod-pa
Tsipon Shuguba	rTsis-dpon Shu-bkod-pa
Tsodag Lhamo	mTsho-bdag lHa-mo
Tsogyal	mTsho-rgyal
Tsomrig Lhantsok	rTsom-rig lHan-tshogs
Tsona Gontse Jamyang Tashi	mTsho-sna dGon-rtse 'Jam-dbyangs bKra-shis
Tsonga	mTsho-lnga
Tsongon	Tshon-dgon
Tsongton Gompa	Tshong-ston sGom-pa
Tsonseng	brTson-seng
Tsonyi Dencho	Tsho-gnyis gDan-gcod
Tsultrim	Tshul-khrims
Tsultrim Sangmo	Tshul-khrims bZang-mo
Tsun Chungma	bTsun Chung-ma
Tsungla	gChung-lags
tsunma	*btsun-ma*
Tsurphu	mTshur-phu
Tubten Gyatso	Thub-bstan rGya-mtsho
Tubten Samdrub	Thub-bstan bSam-grub
Tubten Tsering	Thub-bstan Tshe-ring
Tudao Dorje	Thu-stobs rDo-rje
Tugje Ling	Thugs-rje Gling
Tugse Namkha Peljor	Thugs-sras Nam-mkha' dPal-'byor
tulku	*sprul-sku*
Tulku Jobum	sPrul-sku Jo-'bum
Tulku Orgyen Rinpoche	sPrul-sku O-rgyan Rin-po-che
Tulku Se Jo-se	sPrul-sku Se Jo-sras
U	dBus
Ugpa	'Ug-pa
Uidumtsen	'U'i-dum-brtsan
Urto	dBur-stod
Urto Pelseng	dBur-stod dPal-seng
Uru	dBu-ru
Uyug	'U-yug
Wang Chungma	dBang Chung-ma
Wangmo	dBang-mo
won	*dbon*
Won Dagyal	dBon Da-rgyal
Yabshi Sonam Drolma	Yab-gzhis bSod-nams sGrol-ma

Yabshi Tsering Drolma	Yab-gzhis Tshe-ring sGrol-ma
Yacho	Ya-gcod (?)
Yadong	Yar-dung
Yalung	g.Ya'-lung
Yamdrok	Yar-'brog
Yanga	dByangs-dga'
Yangchen Lhamo	dByangs-can lHa-mo
Yangchen	dByang-can
Yangden Pao	Yang-gdan-pa'o/Len-dan-pa'o
Yangdu Tso	gYang-sgron 'Tsho
Yangdzom/Yangzong	g.Yang-'dzoms
Yangjin lamu	dByang-can lHa-mo
Yangon Labrang	Yangs-dgon Bla-brang
Yangonpa	Yang-dgon-pa
Yarlung	Yar-klungs
Yarnga	Yar-mnga
Yarto Gyewo	Yar-stod sGye-bo
Yartrok	Yar-'brog
Yasor	Ya-sor
Yemo Peldren	g.Yas-mo dPal-'dren
Yerpawa	Yer-pa-ba
Yeshe Donden	Ye-shes Don-ldan
Yeshe Drolma	Ye-shes sGrol-ma
Yeshe Khando	Ye-shes mKha'-'gro
Yeshe Khandro Sonam Drenma	Ye-shes mKha'-'gro bSod-nams 'Gren-ma
Yeshe Kunden	Ye-shes Kun-ldan
Yeshe O	Ye-shes 'Od
Yeshe Tsogyal	Ye-shes mTsho-rgyal
Yeshe Wangmo	Ye-shes dBang-mo
Yikyi Rolcha	Yid-kyi Rol-cha
Yindrok Lhamo	Yid-'phrog lHa-mo
Yo	g.Yo
Yogmen Tashi	g.Yog-sman bKra-shis
Yolmo	Yol-mo
Yolmo Gegye	Yol-mo dGe-rgyas
Yonggon Tulku	Yongs-mgon sPrul-sku
Yongzin Ling Rinpoche	Yongs-'dzin Gling Rin-po-che
Yumbu Lakhar	Yum-bu Bla-mkhar
Yumen	g.Yu-sman
Yumi	g.Yu-sman
Yumig	g.Yu-mig
Yumo	Yu-mo
Yungchen Lhamo	dByangs-can lHa-mo
Yutok	g.Yu-thog
Yutok Champa Deleg	g.Yu-thog Byams-pa bDe-legs

Yutok Deter	g.Yu-thog bDe-ster
Yutok Drogon	g.Yu-thog 'Gro-mgon
Yutok Jampa Tugje	g.Yu-thog Byams-pa Thugs-rje
Yutok Jose Pel	g.Yu-thog Jo-sras dPal
Yutok Nyima	g.Yu-thog rNying-ma
Yutok Yonten Gonpo	Yu-thog Yon-tan mGon-po
za	*za'/bza'*
Zangri	Zangs-ri
Zangri Machig Lamdron	Zangs-ri'i Ma-cig Lam-sgron
Zemen	gZe-sman
Zhalu	Zhwa-lu
Zhama	Zhwa/Zha-ma
Zhama Chungma	Zha-ma Chung-ma
Zhama Dorje Gyaltsen	Zha-ma rDo-rje rGyal-mtshan
Zhama Lotsawa	Zha-ma Lo-tsā-ba
Zhama Lotsawa Senge Gyalpo	Zha-ma Lo-tsā-ba Seng-ge rGyal-po
Zhang Chungma	Zhang Chung-ma
Zhang Lotsawa	Zhang Lo-tsā-ba
Zhang Mazham	Zhang Ma-zham
Zhang Yudragpa	Zhang g.Yu-brag-pa
Zhangmo Gyating	Zhang-mo rGya-'thing.
Zhangton Ziji Bar	Zhang-ston gZi-brjid-'bar
Zhangzhung	Zhang-zhung
Zhetong Mon	bZhad-mthong sMon
Zhiche	Zhi-byed
Zhigpo Dutsi	Zhig-po bDud-rtsi
Zhigpo Rinchen Sherab	Zhig-po Rin-chen Shes-rab
Zhimi Lambar	Zhi-mi Lam-'bar
Zholkhang Sonam Dargye	Zhol-khang bSod-nams Dar-rgyas
Zhongkha	Zhong-kha
Zhungpa Lhatsun Rinpoche	gZhung-pa lHa-btsun Rin-po-che
Zolung	Zo-lung
Zopa Sangmo	bZod-pa bZang-mo
Zur	Zur
Zurkar Nyamnyi Dorje	Zur-mkhar mNyam-nyid rDo-rje
Zurra	Zur-ra

INDEX